Textual Criticism of the Hebrew Bible

Textual Criticism of the Hebrew Bible

SECOND REVISED EDITION

EMANUEL TOV

Fortress Press, Minneapolis
Royal Van Gorcum, Assen

Dedicated with love to
Juda Koekoek ז״ל and Elisabeth Koekoek-Toff

TEXTUAL CRITICISM OF THE HEBREW BIBLE
Second Revised Edition

Translation by the author of *Biqqoret Nusah ha-Miqra'—Pirqê Mabo'*, *The Textual Criticism of the Hebrew Bible: An Introduction* (The Biblical Encyclopaedia Library IV; Mosad Bialik: Jerusalem, 1989; Heb.).

Cover design: Lika Tov
Cover art: Lika Tov

Library of Congress catalogued the First English Edition as:

Tov, Emanuel
[Bikoret nusah ha-Mikra. English]
Textual criticism of the Hebrew Bible / Emanuel Tov.
Includes bibliographical references and indexes.
ISBN 0-8006-2687-7 (alk. paper)
1. Bible. O.T.-Criticism, Textual. I. Title

BS1136.T6813 1992 92-22889
221.4'4-dc20 CIP
p. cm.
Includes bibliographical references and indexes.

ISBN 0-8006-3429-2 (Fortress)
ISBN 90-232-3715-3 (Van Gorcum)

Printed in the Netherlands by Koninklijke Van Gorcum bv, Assen
AF 1-3429

06 05 04 03 02 01 1 2 3 4 5 6 7

CONTENTS

TABLES

Chapter 2

Chapter 4

Chapter 7

Chapter 8

Chapter 9

PLATES

(pp. 379-410)

1*. One of the two minute silver rolls, II, found in Ketef Hinnom (Num 6:24-26). By permission of the Israel Museum, Jerusalem, Israel. Drawing and transliteration of ll. 5-12 according to G. Barkay, "The Priestly Benediction on the Ketef Hinnom Plaques," *Cathedra* 52 (1989) 37-76 (Heb.).

2*. A large Exodus scroll from cave 4 in Qumran in the paleo-Hebrew script, 4QpaleoExod^{m}, col. I (Exod 6:25–7:16). By permission of the Israel Antiquities Authority, Jerusalem, Israel.

3*. The large Isaiah scroll from cave 1 in Qumran, 1QIsa^{a}, col. XXVIII (Isa 34:1–36:2). By permission of the Israel Museum and the Shrine of the Book, Jerusalem, Israel.

4*. The large Isaiah scroll from cave 1 in Qumran, 1QIsa^{a}, col. XXXIII (Isa 40:2–28). By permission of the Israel Museum and the Shrine of the Book, Jerusalem, Israel.

5*. The large Isaiah scroll from cave 1 in Qumran, 1QIsa^{a}, a transcription of col. XXXIII (Isa 40:2-28) from: M. Burrows, *The Dead Sea Scrolls of St. Mark's Monastery, I, The Isaiah Manuscript and the Habakkuk Commentary* (New Haven 1950).

6*. The short Isaiah scroll from cave 1 in Qumran, 1QIsa^{b}, p. 6 = plate 8 (Isa 48:17–49:15), according to the edition by E.L. Sukenik, *ʾwṣr hmgylwt hgnwzwt šbydy hʾwnybrsyṭh hʿbryt* (Jerusalem 1954).

7*. A fragment of the book of Psalms from cave 4 in Qumran, 4QPs^{b} (Ps 102:10–103:11). By permission of the Israel Antiquities Authority, Jerusalem, Israel.

8*. The so-called Psalms Scroll from cave 11 in Qumran, 11QPs^{a}, cols. X and XI (Ps 119:82–96, 105-120), from: J.A. Sanders, *The Psalms Scroll of Qumrân Cave 11 (11QPs^{a})* (DJD IV; Oxford 1965). By permission of the Israel Museum and the Shrine of the Book, Jerusalem, Israel.

8a*. A Jeremiah text from cave 4 in Qumran, 4QJer^{c}, col. XXI (Jer 30:17–31:4). By permission of the Israel Antiquities Authority, Jerusalem, Israel.

9*. *Tefillin*, 4QPhyl J verso, from Qumran (Deut 5:24–32; 6:2–3), from J.T. Milik, *Qumrân grotte 4, II* (DJD VI; Oxford 1977). By permission of the Israel Antiquities Authority, Jerusalem, Israel.

10*. The Aleppo codex, p. 7 (Deut 31:28–32:14). By permission of the Hebrew University Bible Project, Jerusalem, Israel.

11*. The Aleppo codex, p. 48 (Judg 5:25–6:10). By permission of the Hebrew University Bible Project, Jerusalem, Israel.

12*. The codex Leningrad B19^{A} (Exod 14:28–15:14).

13*. A manuscript with Palestinian vocalization from the Cairo Genizah (Ps 71:5–72:4): Cambridge University Library T-S 12, 196. By permission of the University Library, Cambridge.

14*. A manuscript with "simple" Babylonian vocalization from the Cairo Genizah, EC 11, with notes from the *Masorah* (1 Chr 3:15–4:9): Cambridge University Library T-S Box A38,5. By permission of the University Library, Cambridge.

15*. Table of the biblical accents, from K. Elliger and W. Rudolph, *Biblia Hebraica Stuttgartensia* (Stuttgart 1967–1977).

16*. A manuscript of the Samaritan Pentateuch (Num 34:26–35:8) written by the scribe Abi-Berakhatah in the year 1215/6 (Jewish and National University Library, Jerusalem, Sam. 2° 6). By permission of the Jewish and National University Library, Jerusalem.

17*. The Kennicott edition of Gen 49:6–14: B. Kennicott, *Vetus Testamentum hebraicum, cum variis lectionibus*, vols. I-II (Oxford 1776–80). See p. 37.

18*. A. and R. Sadaqa, *Jewish and Samaritan Version of the Pentateuch* (Tel Aviv 1961–1965). By permission of A. and R. Sadaqa, Holon, Israel.

19*. Codex Vaticanus (Cod. Vat. Gr. 1209 *or* B) of the Septuagint (1 Sam 17:44–18:22) from *Bibliorum SS. graecorum codex Vaticanus 1209 (cod. B) denovo phototypice expressus iussa et cura praesidium bybliothecae Vaticanae, pars prima, Testamentum Vetus*, vol. I (Mediolani 1905) 333.

20*. The Göttingen edition of the Septuagint (Jer 1:1-5): J. Ziegler, *Ieremias, Baruch, Threni, Epistula Ieremiae, Septuaginta, Vetus Testamentum graecum auctoritate societatis litterarum gottingensis editum*, vol. XV (2d ed.; Göttingen 1976).

21*. The Greek Minor Prophets Scroll from Naḥal Ḥever (Zech 8:19–9:5) from E. Tov, *The Greek Minor Prophets Scroll from Naḥal Ḥever, (8ḤevXIIgr) (The Seiyal Collection I)* (DJD VIII; Oxford 1990). By permission of the Israel Antiquities Authority, Jerusalem, Israel.

22*. Manuscript Berlin Or. Fol. 1-4 of the Prophets, number 150 in the collection of Kennicott (see plate 17*) (Isa 1:1-4). By permission of the Staatsbibliothek Preussischer Kulturbesitz, Berlin, Orientabteilung.

23*. Manuscript Vatican Neophyti 1 of the Palestinian Targum to the Torah (Lev 15:31–16:11), from: *The Palestinian Targum to the Pentateuch Codex Vatican (Neofiti 1)* (Jerusalem 1970). By permission of the Bibliotheca Apostolica Vaticana, Rome.

24*. Manuscript Ambrosianus (Milan, Ambrosian Library, B. 21 Inf.) of the Peshitta (Lam 3:41–5:22), from: *Translatio Syra-Pescitto, Veteris Testamenti ex codice Ambrosiano* (Milan 1876-1883).

25*. Second Rabbinic Bible (*Miqraʾot Gᵉdolot*), Venice, 1524–1525 (Gen 42:3–20).

26*. R. Kittel and P. Kahle, *Biblia Hebraica* (3d [7th] edition; Stuttgart 1951): Gen 22:18–23:13.

27*. K. Elliger and W. Rudolph, *Biblia Hebraica Stuttgartensia* (Stuttgart 1967–1977): Isa 1:10-21.

28*. Hebrew University Bible (Isa 1:7-12), from: M.H. Goshen-Gottstein, *The Hebrew University Bible, The Book of Isaiah, Vols. I-II* (Jerusalem 1975, 1981).

29*. The development of the "early" Hebrew script, from: J. Naveh, *Early History of the Alphabet—An Introduction to West Semitic Epigraphy and Palaeography* (2d ed.; Jerusalem 1987), fig. 70. By permission of the Magnes Press, Hebrew University, Jerusalem.

30*. The development of the Aramaic and Assyrian ("Jewish") script, from: F.M. Cross, Jr., "The Development of the Jewish Scripts," in: G.E. Wright, ed., *The Bible and the Ancient Near East, Essays in Honor of W.F. Albright* (Garden City, NY 1965) 137, figure 1. By permission of F.M. Cross, Jr., Cambridge, MA.

ABBREVIATIONS AND NOTATIONS

General Abbreviations

α′	Aquila
B.M.	British Museum
𝔊	Septuagint translation (LXX)
𝔊*	The "original" text of the LXX presented in the editions of the Göttingen series (see p. 140) or the edition of Rahlfs (ibid.) as opposed to later revisions correcting the translation towards MT.
𝔊^{Luc}	The Lucianic tradition (mainly MSS b,o,c_2,e_2) of 𝔊
K	*Ketib* (see p. 58)
𝔐	The Masoretic Text
𝔐^{K}	*Ketib* (see p. 58)
𝔐$^{MS(S)}$	Individual manuscript(s) of 𝔐 according to the editions of Kennicott and de Rossi (see p. 37)
𝔐^{Q}	*Qere* (see p. 58)
Mm	*Masorah magna* (see p. 73)
Mp	*Masorah parva* (see p. 73)
P.	Papyrus
p.m.	*Prima manu* (the original scribe)
Q	*Qere* (see p. 58)
R.	Rabbi
RaDaK	Rabbi David Kimḥi
σ′	Symmachus
𝔖	Peshitta translation, in Syriac (see p. 151)
s.m.	*Secunda manu* (a second "hand" in a manuscript)
θ′	Theodotion
𝔗^{F}	Fragmentary Targum(im) (see p. 150)
𝔗^{J}	Targum Jonathan (see p. 151)
𝔗^{N}	MS Vatican Neophyti 1 of the Targum (see p. 150)
𝔗^{O}	Targum Onqelos (see p. 150)
𝔙	Vulgate translation (see p. 153)
ɯɯ	The Samaritan Pentateuch (see p. 80)
vid.	*(ut) videtur*, "apparently"
[ ]	Reconstruction, especially in fragmentary texts
//	A parallel text
<. . .>	The author's additions

Manuscripts of the Hebrew Bible

A	The Aleppo codex (see p. 46)
C	The codex of the Prophets from the Cairo Genizah (see p. 47)
C 3	Pentateuch codex 3 from the Karaite synagogue in Cairo (see p. 47)
L	Codex Leningrad B19A (see p. 47)
N	MS 232, Jewish Theological Seminary, New York
S1	MS Sassoon 1053 (see p. 47)

Rabbinic Texts

b. Babylonian Talmud

m. Mishna

t. Tosepta

y. Jerusalem Talmud

The abbreviations of the tractates in the Mishna, Tosepta, Babylonian Talmud, Jerusalem Talmud, and other rabbinic works follow the conventions of *JBL* 107 (1988) 579-596. *Massekhet Soferim* (abbreviated: *Sof.*) is quoted according to M. Higger, *mskt swprym wnlww ʿlyh mdrš mskt swprym b'* (New York 1937; repr. Jerusalem 1970).

Editions of the Hebrew Bible

Adi

A. Dotan, תורה נביאים וכתובים מדויקים היטב על פי הניקוד הטעמים והמסורה של אהרן בן משה בן אשר בכתב יד לנינגרד (Tel Aviv 1976)

BH

Biblia Hebraica (see chapter 9B)

BHS

Biblia Hebraica Stuttgartensia (see chapter 9B)

Breuer

M. Breuer, תורה נביאים כתובים, מוגהים על פי הנוסח והמסורה של כתר ארם צוֹבה וכתבי יד הקרובים לו, vols. 1-3 (Jerusalem 1977–1982)

Cassuto

U. Cassuto, תורה נביאים וכתובים הוצאת ירושלים, מוגהים לפי המסורה עפ"י בן-אשר בידי משה דוד קאסוטו (Jerusalem 1952–1953)

Ginsburg
C.D. Ginsburg, תורה נביאים כתובים, מדויק היטב על-פי המסרה ועל פי דפוסים ראשונים עם חלופים והגהות מן כתבי יד עתיקים ותרגומים ישנים (London 1926; repr. Jerusalem 1970)

HUB
Hebrew University Bible (see chapter 9C)

Koren
M. Koren, תורה נביאים כתובים (Jerusalem 1966)

Letteris
M.H. Letteris, תורה נביאים וכתובים (London 1852)

Miqra'ot G^e^dolot
Rabbinic Bible (see p. 78)

Sinai
תורה נביאים כתובים (Tel Aviv 1983)

Snaith
N.H. Snaith, ספר תורה נביאים וכתובים מדויק היטיב על פי המסורה (London 1958)

Biblical Books

Gen	Genesis
Exod	Exodus
Lev	Leviticus
Num	Numbers
Deut	Deuteronomy
Josh	Joshua
Judg	Judges
1-2 Sam	1-2 Samuel
1-2 Kgs	1-2 Kings
Isa	Isaiah
Jer	Jeremiah
Ezek	Ezekiel
Hos	Hosea
Joel	Joel
Amos	Amos
Obad	Obadiah
Jonah	Jonah
Mic	Micah
Nah	Nahum

Hab	Habakkuk
Zeph	Zephaniah
Hag	Haggai
Zech	Zechariah
Mal	Malachi
Ps	Psalms
Job	Job
Prov	Proverbs
Ruth	Ruth
Cant	Canticles
Qoh	Qoheleth
Lam	Lamentations
Esth	Esther
Dan	Daniel
Ezra	Ezra
Neh	Nehemiah
1-2 Chr	1-2 Chronicles

Texts from the Judean Desert

In quotations from the Judean Desert scrolls the following *diacritical marks* are used:

אׄ	a letter which has not been fully preserved, but which can be identified with a reasonable degree of certainty.
א̊	a letter of which only a fraction has been preserved.
[א]	a reconstructed letter (not preserved on the leather).
<א>	erased letter.

The texts from the Judean Desert are indicated as follows:

number of the cave (for Qumran: 1-11)
identification of the site (Q = Qumran, Mas = Masada, Ḥev = Ḥever)
name of the biblical book (e.g., Gen = Genesis)
number of the copy (the first copy found in the excavations is called "a", the second copy "b", etc.)

Papyrus fragments are denoted "pap," and fragments written in the paleo-Hebrew script (see pp. 217–220) are indicated "paleo" (e.g., 4QpaleoExod^{m}).

The numbers listed after the cave numbers (1-11) of the Q(umran) scrolls refer to their sequential number in the official publications. The great majority of the texts mentioned in this monograph have now been published, such as 4QTest(imonia), presented as 4Q175 in vol. IV of the official publication of the texts from the Judean Desert: *Discoveries in the Judaean Desert (of Jordan)* = *DJD,* vols. I– (Oxford 1955–). Full bibliographical details until 1999 concerning the published and unpublished texts are found in: E. Tov, "Texts from the Judean Desert," in: P. H. Alexander and others (eds.), *The SBL Handbook of Style* (Peabody, MA 1999) 176–233 (= Appendix F). The final details are to be included in E. Tov (ed.), *The Texts from the Judaean Desert: Introduction and Indexes* (DJD XXXIX; Oxford, in press).

Some abbreviations follow.

1QapGen	The Genesis Apocryphon from Qumran, cave 1
1QH[a]	The Thanksgiving Scroll from Qumran, cave 1
1QIsa[a]	The first, long, Isaiah scroll from Qumran, cave 1
1QIsa[b]	The second, short, Isaiah scroll from cave 1
1QM	The War Scroll, *Milḥamah,* from Qumran, cave 1
1QpHab	The *pesher* on Habakkuk from Qumran, cave 1
1QpMic	The *pesher* on Micah from Qumran, cave 1
1QpZeph	The *pesher* on Zephaniah from Qumran, cave 1
1QS	The Manual of Discipline, *Serekh ha-Yaḥad,* from Qumran, cave 1
1QSa	Appendix A to 1QS
4QMMT	*Miqṣat Maʿaśê ha-Torah,* "Some of the Torah Observations," from Qumran, cave 4
4QpIsa[c]	The *pesher* on Isaiah (third copy) from Qumran, cave 4
4QpPs37	The *pesher* on Psalm 37 from Qumran, cave 4
4QRP	The "Reworked Pentateuch" from Qumran, cave 4 (= 4Q158, 4Q364-367)
4QTanḥ	4QTanḥumim (= 4Q176) from Qumran, cave 4
4QTest	4QTestimonia (= 4Q175) from Qumran, cave 4
5/6ḤevPs	The Psalms scroll from Naḥal Ḥever, cave "5/6"
8ḤevXIIgr	The Greek Minor Prophets Scroll from Naḥal Ḥever, cave 8
11QT[a]	The Temple Scroll from Qumran, cave 11 (11Q19)
MasPs[a, b]	The Psalms manuscripts from Masada
MasSir	The Ben Sira manuscript from Masada

Editions of Textual Sources Quoted in this Book

𝔊	The individual volumes in the Göttingen Septuagint series (see p. 140), when extant; otherwise the text of 𝔊 is quoted from the edition of Rahlfs (p. 141).
𝔊$^{MS(S)}$	The individual volumes in the Göttingen Septuagint series (see p. 140), when extant; otherwise the text of the manuscripts is quoted from the editions of the Cambridge series (see p. 140).
𝔊*	The "original" text of 𝔊 reconstructed in the Göttingen editions (see p. 140) or the edition of Rahlfs (p. 141) as opposed to later revisions correcting the translation towards 𝔐)
𝔊^{Luc}	The Lucianic tradition (mainly MSS b,o,c_2,e_2 according to the sigla used in the "Cambridge Septuagint") of 𝔊, quoted according to the Göttingen and Cambridge editions (p. 140).
𝔐	BHS (see pp. 374-377)
𝔐$^{MS(S)}$	Individual manuscript(s) of 𝔐 according to the editions of Kennicott and de Rossi (see p. 37)
𝔖	The Leiden edition (see p. 152, n. 110), when extant, or otherwise the edition of Lee (see p. 153)
𝔗^{F}	The edition of Klein (see p. 149, n. 104)
𝔗^{J}	The edition of Rieder (see p. 149, n. 104)
𝔗^{N}	The edition of Díez Macho (see p. 150, n. 106)
𝔗^{O}	The edition of Sperber (see p. 149, n. 104)
𝔙	The edition of Weber (see p. 153, n. 112)
𝔙$^{MS(S)}$	The edition of Weber (see p. 153, n. 112)
𝔪	The edition of Sadaqa (see p. 84)
𝔪$^{MS(S)}$	The edition of von Gall (see p. 83)

PERIODICALS, REFERENCE WORKS, AND SERIALS

AASF	Annales Academiae Scientiarum Fennicae
AB	Anchor Bible
AbrN	*Abr-Nahrain*
AnBib	Analecta biblica
ANRW	*Aufstieg und Niedergang der römischen Welt*
AOAT	Alter Orient und Altes Testament
AOS	American Oriental Series
ASTI	*Annual of the Swedish Theological Institute*
ATAbh	Alttestamentliche Abhandlungen
BA	*Biblical Archaeologist*
BASOR	*Bulletin of the American Schools of Oriental Research*
BETL	Bibliotheca ephemeridum theologicarum lovaniensium
Bib	*Biblica*
BibOr	Biblica et orientalia
BIOSCS	*Bulletin of the International Organization for Septuagint and Cognate Studies*
BJPES	*Bulletin of the Jewish Palestine Exploration Society*
BJRL	*Bulletin of the John Rylands University Library of Manchester*
BK	Biblischer Kommentar
BSac	*Bibliotheca Sacra*
BT	*The Bible Translator*
BWANT	Beiträge zur Wissenschaft vom Alten und Neuen Testament
BZ	*Biblische Zeitschrift*
BZAW	Beihefte zur Zeitschrift für die alttestamentliche Wissenschaft
CATSS	Computer Assisted Tools for Septuagint Studies
CB	Cambridge Bible for Schools and Colleges
CBQ	*Catholic Biblical Quarterly*
ConB	Coniectanea biblica
DB	*Dictionnaire de la Bible*
DBSup	*Dictionnaire de la Bible, Supplément*
EBib	*Etudes bibliques*
EncBib	*Encyclopaedia biblica* (Heb.)

EncBrit	*Encyclopaedia Britannica*
EncJud	*Encyclopaedia judaica*
ErIsr	*Eretz Israel*
EstBib	*Estudios bíblicos*
ETL	*Ephemerides theologicae lovanienses*
FRLANT	Forschungen zur Religion und Literatur des Alten und Neuen Testaments
HAR	*Hebrew Annual Review*
HAT	Handbuch zum Alten Testament
HSM	Harvard Semitic Monographs
HSS	Harvard Semitic Studies
HTR	*Harvard Theological Review*
HUCA	*Hebrew Union College Annual*
ICC	International Critical Commentary
IDBSup	*The Interpreter's Dictionary of the Bible, Supplementary Volume*
IEJ	*Israel Exploration Journal*
IOMS	The International Organization for Masoretic Studies
JANESCU	*Journal of the Ancient Near Eastern Society of Columbia University*
JAOS	*Journal of the American Oriental Society*
JBL	*Journal of Biblical Literature*
JBR	*Journal of Bible and Religion*
JCS	*Journal of Cuneiform Studies*
JJS	*Journal of Jewish Studies*
JNES	*Journal of Near Eastern Studies*
JNSL	*Journal of Northwest Semitic Languages*
JQR	*Jewish Quarterly Review*
JQRSup	Jewish Quarterly Review Supplement
JSJ	*Journal for the Study of Judaism in the Persian, Hellenistic and Roman Period*
JSOT	*Journal for the Study of the Old Testament*
JSOTSup	Journal for the Study of the Old Testament—Supplement Series
JSS	*Journal of Semitic Studies*
JTS	*Journal of Theological Studies*
KeH	Kurzgefasstes exegetisches Handbuch zum Alten Testament
MGWJ	*Monatsschrift für Geschichte und Wissenschaft des Judentums*

MSU	Mitteilungen des Septuaginta-Unternehmens
NAWG	Nachrichten der Akademie der Wissenschaften in Göttingen
NCB	New Century Bible
NKZ	*Neue kirchliche Zeitschrift*
NTT	Nederlands Theologisch Tijdschrift
OBO	Orbis biblicus et orientalis
OCD	*Oxford Classical Dictionary*
OLZ	*Orientalische Literaturzeitung*
OTS	*Oudtestamentische Studiën*
PAAJR	*Proceedings of the American Academy of Jewish Research*
PSBA	*Proceedings of the Society of Biblical Archaeology*
RB	*Revue biblique*
REJ	*Revue des études juives*
RHR	*Revue de l'histoire des religions*
RQ	*Revue de Qumran*
SBL	Society of Biblical Literature
SBLDS	Society of Biblical Literature Dissertation Series
SBLMasS	Society of Biblical Literature Masoretic Series
SBT	Studies in Biblical Theology
SCS	Septuagint and Cognate Studies
ScrHier	*Scripta hierosolymitana*
TLZ	*Theologische Literaturzeitung*
TRE	*Theologische Realenzyklopädie*
TRu	*Theologische Rundschau*
TSK	*Theologische Studien und Kritiken*
TU	Texte und Untersuchungen
TynBul	*Tyndale Bulletin*
UF	*Ugarit-Forschungen*
VT	*Vetus Testamentum*
VTSup	Vetus Testamentum, Supplements
WTJ	*Westminster Theological Journal*
ZAW	*Zeitschrift für die alttestamentliche Wissenschaft*
ZDMG	*Zeitschrift der deutschen morgenländischen Gesellschaft*

SHORT TITLES AND ABBREVIATIONS OF WORKS FREQUENTLY CITED

The following list contains short titles and abbreviations. Much additional literature is mentioned in the course of the discussion, especially in the headings of the various sections.

Barr, *Comparative Philology*

J. Barr, *Comparative Philology and the Text of the OT* (Oxford 1968; Winona Lake, IN 1987, "with additions and corrections")

Barr, *Variable Spellings*

J. Barr, *The Variable Spellings of the Hebrew Bible* (The Schweich Lectures of the British Academy; Oxford 1989)

Barthélemy, *Etudes*

D. Barthélemy, *Etudes d'histoire du texte de l'Ancien Testament* (OBO 21; Fribourg/Göttingen 1978)

Barthélemy, *Report*

D. Barthélemy et al., *Preliminary and Interim Report on the Hebrew OT Text Project,* vols. 1-5 (2d ed.; New York 1979–1980)

Barthélemy, *Critique textuelle 1992*

D. Barthélemy, *Critique textuelle de l'AT* (OBO 50/3; Fribourg/Göttingen 1992) esp. vii-cxvi ("Les diverses formes du texte hébreu")

BDB

F. Brown, S.R. Driver, and Ch.A. Briggs, *A Hebrew and English Lexicon of the OT* (Oxford 1907)

Bentzen, *Introduction*

A. Bentzen, *Introduction to the OT,* vols. I–II (Copenhagen 1948–1949)

Cohen, *Miqraʾot Gedolot*

M. Cohen, *Miqraʾot Gedolot 'Haketer'—A Revised and Augmented Scientific Edition of 'Miqraʾot Gedolot' Based on the Aleppo Codex and Early Medieval MSS,* vols. 1–5 (Heb.; Ramat Gan 1992–1997)

Cross, *ALQ*

F.M. Cross, Jr., *The Ancient Library of Qumran and Modern Biblical Studies* (2d ed.; New York 1961; repr. Grand Rapids 1980)

Cross, "Some Notes"

F.M. Cross, Jr., "Some Notes on a Generation of Qumran Studies," in: L. Trebolle Barrera and L. Vegas Montaner, eds., *The Madrid*

Qumran Congress. Proceedings of the International Congress on the Dead Sea Scrolls, Madrid 18-21 March, 1991 (Studies on the Texts of the Desert of Judah 11; Madrid/Leiden 1992) 1-14

Cross–Talmon, *QHBT*

F.M. Cross and S. Talmon, eds., *Qumran and the History of the Biblical Text* (Cambridge, MA/London 1976)

Crown, *The Samaritans*

A.D. Crown, ed., *The Samaritans* (Tübingen 1989)

Deist, *Text*

F.E. Deist, *Towards the Text of the OT* (Pretoria 1978; 2d ed.: 1981)

Deist, *Witnesses*

F.E. Deist, *Witnesses to the OT—Introducing OT Textual Criticism* (The Literature of the OT, vol. 5; Pretoria 1988)

Delitzsch, *Lese- und Schreibfehler*

F. Delitzsch, *Die Lese- und Schreibfehler im AT nebst den dem Schrifttexte einverleibten Randnoten Klassifiziert* (Berlin/Leipzig 1920)

DJD

Discoveries in the Judaean Desert (of Jordan), vols. I– (Oxford 1955–)

Driver, *Samuel*

S.R. Driver, *Notes on the Hebrew Text and the Topography of the Books of Samuel, with an Introduction on Hebrew Palaeography and the Ancient Versions* (2d ed.; Oxford 1913)

Eichhorn, *Einleitung*

J.G. Eichhorn, *Einleitung ins AT* (Leipzig 1780-1783; 2d ed.: Leipzig 1787 and Reutlingen 1790; 3rd ed.: Leipzig 1803; 4th ed.: Göttingen 1823)

Eissfeldt, *Introduction*

O. Eissfeldt, *The OT, An Introduction, Including the Apocrypha and Pseudepigrapha, and also the Works of Similar Type from Qumran. The History of the Formation of the OT* (trans. P.R. Ackroyd; Oxford 1965)

Fitzmyer, *Dead Sea Scrolls*

J.A. Fitzmyer, *The Dead Sea Scrolls, Major Publications and Tools for Study, Revised Edition* (SBL Resources for Biblical Study 20; Atlanta, GA 1990)

Flint–VanderKam, *DSS*
P.W. Flint and J.C. VanderKam (eds.), *The Dead Sea Scrolls after Fifty Years—A Comprehensive Assessment* 1–2 (Leiden/Boston/Köln 1998, 1999)

Freedman–Mathews, *Leviticus*
D.N. Freedman and K.A. Mathews, *The Paleo-Hebrew Leviticus Scroll (11QpaleoLev)* (Winona Lake, IN 1985)

Geiger, *Urschrift*
A. Geiger, *Urschrift und Übersetzungen der Bibel in ihrer Abhängigkeit von der innern Entwickelung des Judentums* (2d ed.; Frankfurt a. Main 1928)

Gesenius, *Pent. Sam.*
W. Gesenius, *De Pentateuchi Samaritani origine indole et auctoritate commentatio philologico-critica* (Halle 1815)

Gesenius–Kautzsch
E. Kautzsch, *Gesenius' Hebrew Grammar* (2d ed.; Oxford 1910)

Ginsburg, *Introduction*
C.D. Ginsburg, *Introduction to the Massoretico-Critical Edition of the Hebrew Bible* (London 1897; repr. New York 1966)

Habermann, *Ketav*
A.M. Habermann, *Ketav, Lashon Wa-Sefer, Reflections on Books, Dead Sea Scrolls, Language and Folklore* (Heb.; Jerusalem 1973)

Hendel, *Genesis 1-11*
R.S. Hendel, *The Text of Genesis 1-11—Textual Studies and Critical Edition* (New York/Oxford 1998)

IDBSup
The Interpreter's Dictionary of the Bible, Supplementary Volume (Nashville 1976)

Kahle, *Cairo Geniza*
P. Kahle, *The Cairo Geniza* (2d ed.; Oxford 1959)

Klein, *Textual Criticism*
R.W. Klein, *Textual Criticism of the OT—The Septuagint after Qumran* (Guides to Biblical Scholarship, OT Series 4; Philadelphia 1974)

van der Kooij, *Textzeugen*
A. van der Kooij, *Die alten Textzeugen des Jesajabuches, Ein Beitrag zur Textgeschichte des ATs* (OBO 35; Freiburg/Göttingen 1981)

Kutscher, *Language*
E.Y. Kutscher, *The Language and Linguistic Background of the Isaiah Scroll (1 Q Is[a])* (Studies on the Texts of the Desert of Judah VI; Leiden 1974)

Lieberman, *Hellenism*
S. Lieberman, *Hellenism in Jewish Palestine* (2d ed.; New York 1962)

Martin, *Scribal Character*
M. Martin, *The Scribal Character of the Dead Sea Scrolls*, vols. I–II (Louvain 1958)

McCarter, *Textual Criticism*
P.K. McCarter, *Textual Criticism, Recovering the Text of the Hebrew Bible* (Guides to Biblical Scholarship, OT Series 11; Philadelphia 1986)

Mulder, *Mikra*
M.J. Mulder, ed., *Mikra, Text, Translation, Reading and Interpretation of the Hebrew Bible in Ancient Judaism and Early Christianity* (Compendia Rerum Iudaicarum ad Novum Testamentum, Section Two, Vol. 1; Assen–Maastricht/Philadelphia 1988)

NEB
The New English Bible with the Apocrypha (Oxford/Cambridge 1970)

NJPST
Tanakh, The Holy Scriptures, The New JPS Translation according to the Traditional Hebrew Text (The Jewish Publication Society; Philadelphia/New York/Jerusalem 1988)

Noth, *OT World*
M. Noth, *The OT World* (trans. V.I. Gruhn; Philadelphia 1966)

NRSV
The Holy Bible Containing the Old and New Testaments with the Apocryphal/Deuterocanonical Books, New Revised Standard Version (Glasgow/London 1989)

Oesch, *Petucha*
J.M. Oesch, *Petucha und Setuma, Untersuchungen zu einer überlieferten Gliederung im hebräischen Text des AT* (OBO 27; Freiburg/Göttingen 1979)

Payne, "OT Textual Criticism"
D.F. Payne, "OT Textual Criticism: Its Principles and Practice Apropos of Recent English Versions," *TynBul* 25 (1974) 99-112

Perles, *Analekten*
F. Perles, *Analekten zur Textkritik des ATs*, vol. I (München 1895); vol. II (Leipzig 1922)

REB
The Revised English Bible with the Apocrypha (Oxford/ Cambridge 1989)

Roberts, *OTTV*
B.J. Roberts, *The OT Text and Versions—The Hebrew Text in Transmission and the History of the Ancient Versions* (Cardiff 1951)

RSV
The Bible, Containing the Old and New Testaments, Revised Standard Version (The British and Foreign Bible Society 1971)

Sanderson, *Exodus Scroll*
J. Sanderson, *An Exodus Scroll from Qumran: 4QpaleoExod^{m} and the Samaritan Tradition* (HSS 30; Atlanta, GA 1986)

Schiffman, *DSS*
L.H. Schiffman and others (eds.), *The Dead Sea Scrolls: Fifty Years After Their Discovery—Proceedings of the Jerusalem Congress, July 20–25, 1997* (Jerusalem 2000)

Sperber, *Grammar*
A. Sperber, *A Historical Grammar of Biblical Hebrew—A Presentation of Problems with Suggestions to Their Solution* (Leiden 1966)

Steuernagel, *Einleitung*
C. Steuernagel, *Lehrbuch der Einleitung in das AT mit einem Anhang über die Apokryphen und Pseudepigraphen* (Tübingen 1912)

Talmon, "OT Text"
S. Talmon, "The OT Text," in: R.P. Ackroyd and C.F. Evans, eds., *The Cambridge History of the Bible,* vol. I (Cambridge 1970) 159–199; repr. in Cross–Talmon, *QHBT* (1976), 1-41

Talmon, *Masada VI*
S. Talmon in: S. Talmon and Y. Yadin, *Masada VI, The Yigael Yadin Excavations 1963–1965, Final Reports, Hebrew Fragments from Masada* (Jerusalem 1999) 1–149

Tigay, *Models*
J.H. Tigay, ed., *Empirical Models for Biblical Criticism* (Philadelphia 1985)

Tov, *TCU*

E. Tov, *The Text-Critical Use of the Septuagint in Biblical Research* (Second Edition, Revised and Enlarged; Jerusalem Biblical Studies 8; Jerusalem: Simor, 1997)

Trebolle, *Biblia*

J. Trebolle Barrera, *La Biblia judía y la Biblia cristiana* (Madrid 1993)

Würthwein, *Text*

E. Würthwein, *Der Text des ATs—Eine Einführung in die Biblia Hebraica von Rudolf Kittel* (5th ed.; Stuttgart 1988)

Yeivin, *Introduction*

I. Yeivin, *Introduction to the Tiberian Masorah* (trans. and ed. E.J. Revell; SBLMasS 5; Missoula, MT 1980)

PREFACE

This volume presents the reader with a much revised and updated version of my Hebrew book, ביקורת נוסח המקרא – פרקי מבוא, published in 1989 by Mosad Bialik, Jerusalem.

The revision and updating turned out to be much more pervasive than was originally planned. Almost every paragraph was revised, including the adding, omitting, or changing of examples. Further insights were introduced and some views were changed. The present formulation of the *Urtext*, for example, is more refined. Special attention was paid to the exegetical aspects of the textual transmission which were treated too briefly in the Hebrew edition (pp. 262-275 in the present edition). Chapter 6C (preferable readings) is new, and in chapter 4 the section "Additions to the body of the text" (pp. 275-285) is almost completely new. Chapter 7, dealing with textual and literary criticism, has been expanded and refined. From the outset literary issues are so far removed from the topics usually treated by textual critics that the relevance of textual data to literary criticism would seem to be remote. Chapter 7, however, demonstrates that this is not the case. The delicate relation between the problems of the original shape of the biblical text, discussed in chapter 3B and chapter 7, has been defined better. Finally, with the publication of many new texts from the Judean Desert, and with new insights on previously published texts, the description and analysis in this edition are even more indebted to the discoveries from the Judean Desert than the Hebrew edition.

In the previous edition several examples have been presented as part of the running text of the discussion. Now almost all of them are presented in a graphically clear fashion. The differences between the readings are graphically highlighted by the use of bold characters and italics.

Most of the examples are translated into English, and the very translation has helped me to better understand the examples themselves. As for the translation itself, while I am responsible for the English translations of the biblical verses, most of them follow the lead of the NJPST (see p. xxxi). The NRSV (see p. xxxii) has guided my translations as a second choice. The NJPST is preferable for our purpose as it follows 𝔐 without exception and its exegesis is reliable. It is one of the few translations which breaks away from the chain of translations into modern languages, most of which influence each other; the NJPST reflects thorough and fresh thinking about the meaning of words in their contexts. Our own translations deviate from time to time from existing ones when the literal translation is necessary in order to highlight a certain textual variation.

Textual criticism is a dynamic area, and many views change with new studies carried out and with the discovery of new texts. Therefore some data and views expressed in this book may need to be updated or corrected in the years to come. Furthermore, the book may even contain an occasional error. The stages of editorial and textual transmission, even of a book devoted to textual criticism, are not flawless.

The English version of this book has benefited from the remarks by several colleagues. I am grateful to Professors A. van der Kooij of Leiden University and M. Vervenne of the University of Leuven for their critical observations on the complete manuscript. Prof. Y. Maori of Haifa University made many helpful remarks on chapter 2. Prof. I. Yeivin of the Hebrew University read the first section of chapter 2. Prof. M. Haran of the Hebrew University and Dr. J. Biemans, curator of manuscripts of the University Library of Amsterdam, remarked on the first fifteen pages of chapter 4. Prof. J. W. van Henten of the University of Utrecht and Dr. F. Polak of the University of Tel Aviv sent me many helpful remarks on chapters 3 and 4 respectively. Prof. L. Schiffman of NYU and Dr. M. Zippor of Bar-Ilan University shared with me some criticisms of the Hebrew book which I was able to incorporate in the present version. To all these scholars I express my sincere gratitude.

I am also grateful to several graduate students at the Hebrew University who helped me in various ways. Ms. Nehamah Leiter made many valuable remarks on matters of content and style in most of the chapters. At an earlier stage Ms. Ruth Henderson stylized sections translated by myself and translated other sections. Mr. Chang Shih-hsien and my son Amitai checked the biblical references, Mr. C. Hutt verified the bibliographical references, Mr. T. van der Louw checked several cross-references, and Mr. G. Hartman stylized several chapters and checked other references. Mr. Hartman and Ms. Miriam Berg helped me in compiling the indexes.

Mr. O. Joffe, Ms. Ronit Shamgar, Ms. Sandra Rovin, and Mr. G. Marquis assisted me very ably with all questions relating to the computer files and the preparation of the camera-ready manuscript.

My son Ariel typed in many of the corrections and he also manipulated some of the computer files.

A special word of thanks is extended to Fortress Press, which has accompanied my work on this edition for the past two years. Mr.

Marshall Johnson, Th.D. was a source of constant encouragement and he guided the work from the first stage of my contact with the press onwards. The copy editor of the press, Ms. Lenore Franzen, carefully read the manuscript and found many an inconsistency.

The first stage of the translation was prepared during my research stay at the Institute for Advanced Studies at the Hebrew University of Jerusalem in 1989-90. At the end of that year I was in possession of a rough draft of the book. At that point I thought that the book was more or less ready. However, as remarked above, the material was extensively rewritten in the next year, during my research stay in 1990-1991 at NIAS, the Netherlands Institute for Advanced Studies in Wassenaar. The various facilities provided by NIAS enabled me to complete the manuscript of the book. To both of these fine institutions I would like to express my gratitude.

In the course of my sabbatical year in Holland in 1990-91, I gave many lectures at universities and learned societies in Holland, England, and Germany on sections of this book. Many of the revisions carried out derived from insights gained in the course of preparations for these lectures, response to them, and in some cases my own insights jotted down while lecturing.

This book is dedicated to Elisabeth Koekoek-Toff and Juda Koekoek, who raised me with much love and affection.

Jerusalem, Pesach 5752, April 1992.

PREFACE TO THE SECOND REVISED EDITION

After almost a decade of continuing research on the textual criticism of the Hebrew Bible and its versions by others and myself, a revised edition of the present textbook became mandatory. The urgency of this revision became apparent not only because of the new publications of biblical texts from the Judean Desert, all of which have now been released, but also because in some areas I changed my views in light of these new publications, the research of others, and clearer insights gained. Larger revisions are visible in pp. 97–100 (Pre-Samaritan Texts), 100–117 (The Biblical Texts Found in Qumran), 171–172, 177–181 (The Original Shape of the Biblical Text [change in my position]), and 201–219 (The Copying of the Biblical Text). Two sections were added on pp. 345–346: A Different Recension of Joshua Reflected in 4QJosh^{a}, and Rearranged and Shorter Texts (?).

Many small details in the wording and bibliography have been changed or added in this edition, especially in the wake of recent studies and new details which have become known through the texts from the Judean Desert. The bibliographical abbreviations on pp. xxix–xxxiv have been updated and expanded. Indexes 1 and 2 have been changed accordingly.

Concrete suggestions by scores of reviewers have been taken into consideration (thanks are due especially to the suggestions by N. Stratham in many small details). It should be admitted, however, that this second revised edition was limited by the boundaries of the individual camera-ready pages which were submitted to the publisher. Had we not been bound by these technical limitations, many additional small changes would have been inserted. These small changes have found their way into the German (trans. H.-J. Fabry; Stuttgart/Berlin/Köln: Kohlhammer, 1997) and Russian (trans. C. Burmistrov and G. Jastrebov; Moscow, St. Andrews Theological Seminary, 2001) editions of this handbook, although in other, often more important, details (changes made in 1998–2000) the present version is more up-to-date.

Thanks are due to Fortress Press of Minneapolis for their fine work on the initial edition and their consent to publish a revised version and to the Van Gorcum publishing company of Assen/Maastricht for their careful work in the production of this revised edition and their constant encouragement. I am especially grateful to Mr. T. Joppe, and at an earlier stage to Mr. A. Pilot, of Van Gorcum who piloted this work through the press.

Jerusalem, 1 January 2001

SYSTEM OF TRANSLITERATION

א	ʾ
בּ	*b*
ב	*b*
ג	*g*
ד	*d*
ה	*h*
ו	*w*
ז	*z*
ח	*ḥ*
ט	*ṭ*
י	*y*
כּ	*k*
כ	*k*
ל	*l*
מ	*m*
נ	*n*
ס	*s*
ע	ʿ
פּ	*p*
פ	*p*
צ	*ṣ*
ק	*q*
ר	*r*
שׁ	*š*
שׂ	*ś*
ת	*t*

Note, however, that traditional spelling is used for some proper nouns, e.g., "Moses," rather than Moshe, and for a few other words, e.g., *soferim*, rather than *soph*^{e}*rim* or *sof*^{e}*rim*.

1

INTRODUCTION

"A man who possesses common sense and the use of reason must not expect to learn from treatises or lectures on textual criticism anything that he could not, with leisure and industry, find out for himself. What the lectures and treatises can do for him is to save him time and trouble by presenting to him immediately considerations which would in any case occur to him sooner or later." (A.E. Housman, "The Application of Thought to Textual Criticism," *Proceedings of the Classical Association* 18 [1922] 67).

General Bibliography

D.R. Ap-Thomas, *A Primer of OT Text Criticism* (2d ed.; Oxford 1964); D. Barthélemy, "Text, Hebrew, History of," *IDBSup*, 878–884 = *Etudes*, 341–364; idem, *Critique textuelle de l'AT* (OBO 50/1,2,3; Fribourg/Göttingen 1982, 1986, 1992); Deist, *Text*; idem, *Witnesses*; Eichhorn, *Einleitung*; Eissfeldt, *Introduction*, 669–719; Y. Grintz, *Mbwʾy mqrʾ* (Tel Aviv 1972); Hendel, *Genesis 1-11*; Klein, *Textual Criticism*; A. van der Kooij, *Die alten Textzeugen des Jesajabuches, Ein Beitrag zur Textgeschichte des ATs* (OBO 35; Freiburg/Göttingen 1981); McCarter, *Textual Criticism*; Noth, *OT World*, 301–363; Roberts, *OTTV*; M.Z. Segal, *Mbwʾ hmqrʾ*, vol. IV (Jerusalem 1960) 842–977; Steuernagel, *Einleitung*, 19–85; Talmon, "OT Text"; J.A. Thompson, "Textual Criticism, OT," *IDBSup*, 886–891; J. Weingreen, *Introduction to the Critical Study of the Text of the Hebrew Bible* (Oxford/New York 1982); Würthwein, *Text*.

Textual criticism deals with the origin and nature of all forms of a text, in our case the biblical text. This involves a discussion of its putative original form(s) and an analysis of the various representatives of the changing biblical text. The analysis includes a discussion of the relation between these texts, and attempts are made to describe the external conditions of the copying and the procedure of textual transmission. Scholars involved in textual criticism not only collect data on differences between the textual witnesses, but they also try to evaluate them. Textual criticism deals only with data deriving from the textual transmission—in other words, readings included in textual witnesses which have been created at an earlier stage, that of the literary growth of the biblical books, are not subjected to textual evaluation (see chapter

7). One of the practical results of textual analysis is that it creates tools for exegesis.

The nature and procedures of the textual criticism of the Hebrew Bible are further defined in chapter 5A, while this chapter deals with other introductory issues. Furthermore, in section D of this chapter several basic concepts in textual criticism are defined. Section A attempts to demonstrate that involvement in textual criticism is imperative, not only in a comparative analysis of all the textual sources of the Bible (A1,2), but also when we consult the so-called Masoretic Text (A3,4).

A. The Need for the Textual Criticism of the Hebrew Bible

Our first task within the present framework is to clarify the nature of the textual criticism of the Hebrew Bible. Even before we deal with definitions and examples we ought to express our views on some basic issues which require the involvement of textual criticism.

1. Differences between the Many Textual Witnesses of the Bible

The biblical text has been transmitted in many ancient and medieval sources which are known to us from modern editions in different languages: We now have manuscripts (MSS) in Hebrew and other languages from the Middle Ages and ancient times as well as fragments of leather and papyrus scrolls two thousand years old or more. These sources shed light on and witness to the biblical text, hence their name: "textual witnesses." All of these textual witnesses differ from each other to a greater or lesser extent. Since no textual source contains what could be called "the" biblical text, a serious involvement in biblical studies clearly necessitates the study of all sources, including the differences between them. The comparison and analysis of these textual differences hold a central place within textual criticism.

Textual differences are also reflected in modern editions of the traditional text of the Hebrew Bible, the so-called Masoretic Text (MT = 𝔐), since these editions are based on different manuscripts. We shall first turn to these *printed editions*, as they are easily accessible. (Bibliographic references to the printed editions are found on pp. xx–xxi). Similar discrepancies between the various ancient witnesses are even reflected in the modern translations.[1]

---

1 See the following sample of renderings of עד כי יבא שִׁילֹה in Gen 49:10:
1. "Until Shiloh come" (King James Version) = 𝔐 שִׁילֹה
2. "So long as tribute is brought to him" (NEB; similarly NJPST and NRSV) = שַׁי לוֹ.

One would not have expected differences between the printed editions of the Hebrew Bible, for if a fully unified textual tradition would have been possible at any one given period, it would certainly seem to be so after the invention of printing. Such is not the case, however, since all the editions of the Hebrew Bible, which actually are editions of 𝔐, go back to different medieval manuscripts of that tradition, or combinations of such manuscripts (cf. pp. 77–79), so that the editions also necessarily differ from each other. Moreover, these editions reflect not only the various medieval manuscripts, but also the personal views of the different editors. Furthermore, each edition contains a certain number of printing errors. Therefore, there does not exist any one edition which agrees in all of its details with another, except for photographically reproduced editions or editions based on the same electronic (computer encoded) text. Some editions even differ from each other in their subsequent printings (which sometimes amount to different editions), without even informing the readers. Note, for example, the differences between the various printings of the editions of Letteris and Snaith concerning the printing errors to be mentioned below, and note the Adi and Koren editions regarding some editorial decisions.[2] The edition of *Biblia Hebraica Stuttgartensia* (BHS) originally appeared in fascicles which were corrected in the final printing which carried the date 1967–1977. It was corrected again in the 1984 printing, yet even this printing contains mistakes, on which see below.

It should be remembered that the number of differences between the various editions is very small. Moreover, all of them concern minimal, even minute details of the text, and most affect the meaning of the text in only a very limited way.

The differences between the most frequently used editions of 𝔐 are exemplified below.

a. Sequence of Books

The sequence of the books differs in the various editions regarding the position or internal sequence of the following books: Chronicles, the

---

3. "Until he receives what is his due" (REB), "until he comes to whom it belongs" (RSV and similarly The Jerusalem Bible), all based on a reading שֶׁ(י)לֹּה—thus already 𝔊 𝔖 $𝔗^{ON}$; for a detailed discussion, see L. Prijs, *Jüdische Tradition in der Septuaginta* (Leiden 1948; repr. Hildesheim 1987) 67-70.

2 Thus the Hebrew Koren edition differs from the Hebrew-English edition concerning the numbering of the verses in the transitions between Genesis 31 and 32 and Ezekiel 13 and 14. See below concerning other differences between the various printings of the Adi and Koren editions.

אמ"ת books (acronymic for Job, Proverbs, and Psalms), and the Five Scrolls.[3] In most editions (*Miqra᾿ot Gᵉdolot*, Letteris, Ginsburg, Cassuto, Snaith, Koren, Adi, Sinai, BH, BHS) Chronicles appears as the last book of the Hagiographa, while in the edition of Breuer it occurs as the first book of that collection, because of its position in various codices (among them A and L). The internal sequence of the אמ"ת books differs in Breuer, BH, BHS (Psalms, Job, Proverbs [thus *b. B. Bat.* 14b]) from that of *Miqra᾿ot Gᵉdolot*, Letteris, Ginsburg, Cassuto, Snaith, Koren, Adi, Sinai (Psalms, Proverbs, Job). For the Five Scrolls one finds the following arrangements: Ruth, Canticles, Qoheleth, Lamentations, Esther (Breuer, BH, BHS); Canticles, Ruth, Lamentations, Qoheleth, Esther (some printings of *Miqra᾿ot Gᵉdolot*, Letteris, Ginsburg, Cassuto, Snaith, Adi, Sinai). Again a different sequence is found in some printings of the *Miqra᾿ot Gᵉdolot*, where individual books of the Five Scrolls follow individual books of the Torah.

b. Chapter Division

The exact content of chapters sometimes differs among the various editions because of a divergent concept of one particular verse which then causes a difference in numbering. For example, the verse starting with the words "At that time, declares the LORD, I will be . . . " sometimes appears as the last verse of Jeremiah 30, 30:25 (e.g., the editions of Letteris, Breuer, Koren, Adi 1976, and Sinai), and sometimes as the first verse of chapter 31 (e.g., the editions of Cassuto, Snaith, Adi 1988, BH, and BHS). These two representations of the biblical text are based on a different way of understanding the verse in its context.

"Certain elders of Israel came to me" forms the first verse of Ezekiel 14 in the editions of Letteris, Snaith, Koren, Adi, Breuer, Sinai, BH, and BHS, but in the editions of Cassuto and Ginsburg it appears as the last verse of chapter 13—in accordance with the notation of the "closed section" (see p. 51) indicated after this verse, 13:24.

Likewise, the verse starting with the words "Early in the morning Laban arose . . . " appears as the last verse of Genesis 31 (31:55) in the edition of Koren, but as the first verse of chapter 32 in the editions of Letteris, Snaith, Adi, Breuer, Sinai, BH, and BHS.

---

3 On the differences between the manuscripts and editions in this regard, see especially N.M. Sarna, *EncJud* 4 (Jerusalem 1971) 827–830.

c. The Layout of the Text

Since the layout of the text as either poetry or prose depends on the editor's views, in this detail, too, differences exist between the various editions. For example, BH, more than the other editions—including BHS—tends to present texts as poetry. See, for example, the song of Lamech (Gen 4:23-24) and the words of God to Rebekah (Gen 25:23).

Most editions present the majority of the biblical books as continuous passages, with only a few texts as poetry. The editions of Letteris (in most of their printings) and Cassuto, however, also present the אמ"ת books (Job, Proverbs, and Psalms) as poetry. Several of the printings of the Letteris edition represent only the book of Psalms as poetry.

d. Verse Division

The scope of the verses sometimes differs from one edition to another. For example, in Exodus 20 and Deuteronomy 5, the sixth, seventh, eighth, and ninth commandments are recorded in some editions as one verse (Exod 20:12 or 13; Deut 5:17), but in other editions as four different verses (Exod 20:13-16; Deut 5:17-20). These discrepancies account for the differences in verse numbering in these chapters among the various editions. The editions of Letteris, Snaith, Sinai, BH, and BHS record these four commandments in Exodus 20 as separate verses, while the editions of Cassuto, Adi, Koren, and Breuer list them as one verse. Not every edition treats the Ten Commandments in Deuteronomy 5 in the same way, but the picture is similar. In the editions of Letteris, Sinai, Adi, Koren, and Breuer the sixth through ninth commandments are treated as one verse, but in the editions of Cassuto, Snaith, BH, and BHS they are treated as four different verses because of their special (upper) cantillation. In Deuteronomy the situation is even more complicated, since the second commandment ("Thou shalt not . . . ") sometimes starts a new verse, viz., 5:7 (in the editions of Cassuto, Snaith, Koren, Breuer, Sinai, BH, and BHS), but in the Adi edition it starts in the middle of 5:6, after the *ʾetnaḥ*.[4]

---

[4] On other aspects of the different traditions of the writing of the Decalogue see M. Breuer, "The Division of the Decalogue into Verses and Commandments," in: B.-Z. Segal, ed., *The Ten Commandments as Reflected in Tradition and Literature throughout the Ages* (Heb.; Jerusalem 1985) 223–254. For a complete list of the differences between the editions, see J. Penkower, "Verse Divisions in the Hebrew Bible," *VT* 50 (2000) 378-393.

e. Single Letters and Words

The number of differences in single letters is relatively small, and most of them concern small details, such as *matres lectionis* (see pp. 220–229). For example:

Deut 23:2	דַּכָּא	Cassuto, Snaith, Adi, Breuer, BH, BHS
	דַּכָּה	Koren

There are, however, a few differences in complete words, such as:

Prov 8:16	שפטי ארץ	judges of *the earth* editions of Sinai and Koren 1977
	שפטי צדק	*righteous* judges editions of Letteris, Cassuto, Adi, Koren 1983, Breuer, BH, and BHS
1 Sam 30:30	בְּבוֹר-עָשָׁן	Cassuto, Snaith, Adi, Breuer, BHS
	בְּכוֹר-עָשָׁן	Letteris and Koren

A full list of such differences relating to the text printed by Koren is appended to that edition.

f. Vocalization and Accentuation

The relatively numerous differences in vocalization (vowel signs) and accents (cf. pp. 67–71) usually do not affect the meaning of the text, but they are illustrated here with an example which is relevant to matters of meaning.

Jer 11:2	ודברתֶּם	and you (plural) shall say Letteris, Snaith, Adi 1965, Koren, Sinai, and Breuer
	ודברתָּם	and you (singular) shall recite them Adi (most of its printings), BH, and BHS

Most of the differences in this group pertain to the *gaʿyah* (secondary stress)—cf. p. 68.

g. The Notes of the Masorah

The modern editions include from the Masorah (see p. 72) mainly the *Qere* and *Sebirin* notes (see pp. 58, 64) and the notation of sections in the text (cf. pp. 50–53) as either "open" or "closed." In all these details the editions differ from each other. E.g., Ginsburg, *Introduction*, 9–24 criticizes the earlier edition of Baer (see p. 79, n. 55) regarding its imprecise notations of the sections.

Since in one way or another editions are based on manuscripts, it should be stressed that these manuscripts are interpreted in different ways. It is therefore not surprising that the editors of three different editions (which actually represent only two editions), claim that their edition faithfully presents the important codex Leningrad B19^{A} (L): BH and its revised version, BHS (cf. pp. 374-377), as well as the Adi edition. These editions nevertheless differ from each other in many details, partly because of the difficulties in deciphering details (especially vowels and accents) and partly because of different editorial conceptions. In addition, all three editions also contain printing errors.

Printing errors are found in the older as well as in the modern editions.[5] For example, in the first printings of the Letteris edition (from 1852) one finds

Num 11:30 מֹשֶׁת, *Mošet* (nonexistent word)
which should be read
מֹשֶׁה, *Mošeh* ("Moses").

In the Snaith edition (London 1958) one finds

Exod 10:3 אד מתי which should be read:
עד מתי
Esth 7:7 עַל
should be אַל
Esth 7:8 ובני
should be ופני
Esth 8:5 ככל
should be בכל

Many of the printing errors found in BH were corrected in BHS—for example, Isa 35:1 בחבצלת (which should be read כחבצלת)[6]—but there remain some misprints and inaccuracies even in the 1984 printing of BHS.[7] For example,

Gen 35:27 הֶברון
should be חֶברון
2 Sam 14:30 Q יהציתוה
should be והציתוה

---

5 See J.G. Bidermannus, *Programma de mendis librorum et nominatim bibliorum hebraicorum diligentius cavendis* (Freiburg 1752); Ginsburg, *Introduction*, 790; M.B. Cohen and D.B. Freedman, "The Snaith Bible—A Critical Examination of the Hebrew Bible Published in 1958 by the British and Foreign Bible Society," *HUCA* 45 (1974) 97–132.

6 See I. Yeivin, "The New Edition of the Biblia Hebraica—Its Text and Massorah," *Textus* 7 (1969) 114-123.

7 Cf. R. Wonneberger, *Understanding BHS—A Manual for the Users of Biblia Hebraica Stuttgartensia (BHS)* (Subsidia Biblica 8; Rome 1984) 74-75.

Dan 11:8 חַצָּפוֹן
should be הַצָּפוֹן

These small, but material differences between the editions as well as the various printing errors and many additional factors necessitate our involvement in textual criticism. When examining the source of the differences between the various editions, we soon discover that most of them go back to differences between the medieval manuscripts on which they are based. Indeed, the analysis in chapter 2 demonstrates that medieval manuscripts and texts from the Second Temple period differ in numerous details, ranging from single letters and whole words to entire verses and section divisions. Medieval Masoretic manuscripts differ in these details as well as in vocalization, accentuation, and details of the Masorah.

The differences between the various texts, some of which involve differences in content, are exemplified in chapter 4C.

2. *Mistakes, Corrections, and Changes in the Textual Witnesses, Including 𝔐*

Most of the texts—ancient and modern—which have been transmitted from one generation to the next have been *corrupted* in one way or another. For modern compositions the process of textual transmission from the writing of the autograph until its final printing is relatively short, so that the possibilities of its corruption are limited.[8] In ancient texts, however, such as the Hebrew Bible, these corruptions (the technical term for various forms of "mistakes") are found more frequently because of the difficult physical conditions of the copying and the length of the process of transmission, usually extending until the period of printing in recent centuries. The number of factors which could have created corruptions is large: the transition from the "early" Hebrew to Assyrian ("square") script (see pp. 217–220), unclear handwriting, unevenness in the surface of the material (leather or papyrus) on which the text was written, graphically similar letters which were often confused (pp. 243–251), the lack of vocalization (pp. 41–42, 255), and unclear boundaries between words in early texts (pp. 252–253), etc.

8 See, for example, the many mistakes that have entered into all the editions of *Ulysses* by James Joyce as a result of misunderstandings of the author's corrections in the proof sheets of his book. Only recently have these mistakes been corrected in a critical edition: H.W. Gabler et al., eds., *James Joyce, Ulysses—Student's Edition, The Corrected Text* (Harmondsworth: Penguin, 1986).

A second phenomenon pertains to *corrections* and *changes* inserted in the biblical text. In contradistinction to mistakes, which are not controllable, the insertion of corrections and changes derives from a conscious effort to change the text in minor and major details, including the insertion of novel ideas. Such tampering with the text is evidenced in all textual witnesses (see the discussion in chapter 4C3), including 𝔐. Tradition ascribes to the *soferim*, "scribes," 8, 11, or 18 such "corrections" in 𝔐 itself (see pp. 64–67), but even if these transmitted corrections are questionable, many other similar ones are evidenced elsewhere (see pp. 264–275).

Corruptions as well as various forms of scribal intervention (changes, corrections, etc.) are thus evidenced in all textual witnesses of the Hebrew Bible, including the group of texts now called the (medieval) Masoretic Text as well as in its predecessors, the proto-Masoretic texts. Those who are unaware of the details of textual criticism may think that one should not expect any corruptions in 𝔐 or any other sacred text, since these texts were meticulously written and transmitted. Indeed, the scrupulous approach of the *soferim* and Masoretes is manifest in their counting of all the letters and words of 𝔐 (see pp. 22–23, 73–74). Therefore, it is seemingly unlikely that they would have corrupted the text or even corrected it. Yet, in spite of their precision, even the manuscripts which were written and vocalized by the Masoretes contain corruptions, changes, and erasures. More importantly, the Masoretes, and before them the *soferim*, acted in a relatively late stage of the development of the biblical text, and before they had put their meticulous principles into practice, the text already contained corruptions and had been tampered with during that earlier period when scribes did not as yet treat the text with such reverence. Therefore, paradoxically, the *soferim* and Masoretes carefully preserved a text that was already corrupted. The discussion in the following chapters will expand on the subject of these corruptions which occurred in the manuscripts of the Hebrew Bible, including the manuscripts of 𝔐.

The preceding analysis has surmised that 𝔐, too, contains occasional errors. In our analysis of the witnesses of the biblical text no exception is made in this regard for 𝔐, because that text, like all other texts, may have been corrupted in the course of the scribal transmission. It is not easy to provide convincing proof of such errors in 𝔐 at this early stage of the discussion in this monograph, but it nevertheless is necessary to provide some examples. We believe that the examples in section 4 below ("Differences between Inner-Biblical Parallel Texts") provide partial proof of such errors. As was already recognized in the Middle

Ages by R. David Kimḥi (RaDaK), to be quoted on p. 13, several similar letters (*daleth/resh* and *waw/yod)* were interchanged by mistake. As a result, in such situations there is no escape from the view that one of the two similar readings, occurring in parallel texts, is "correct" or "original" (for the concept, see p. 19) and the other a corruption, and in this regard it does not matter which one is designated as "correct" or "original" and which as "corrupt." This pertains, for example, to such pairs of readings as ורודנים/ ודדנים and עיבל/ עובל, quoted on pp. 12-13. The evidence forces us to surmise that there is such a concept as a "correct" or (probably) "original" reading and a "corrupt" one.

The assumption of corruptions in the biblical text pervades many of the examples in this book. Such corruptions are recognized in the Qumran scrolls (e.g., 1QIsa^{a} in Isa 13:19 [p. 251]; 26:3-4 [pp. 237–238]; 30:30 [p. 240]; 40:7-8 [pp. 239–240]) on the basis of their comparison with 𝔐 and other texts, and, by the same token, in 𝔐 itself, when compared with other texts. See, for instance, the following texts in 𝔐 as analyzed below: 1 Sam 1:24 (p. 254); 4:21-22 (pp. 242–243); 2 Sam 23:31 (p. 250); 2 Kgs 11:13 (p. 242); Jer 23:33 (p. 303); 29:26 (p. 256); 41:9 (p. 304). In all these cases the assumption of a corruption is based on the comparison of 𝔐 and the other texts. Such a comparison is based on objective textual data and recognized scribal phenomena. However, the final decision, at the level of the evaluation of these readings is necessarily subjective (see below p. 19 and chapter 6). In other, less frequent, instances, the recognition of a mistake is *not* based on comparative textual evidence but on content analysis. For example,

1 Sam 13:1 𝔐 בן *שנה* שאול במלכו ושתי *שנים* מלך על ישראל (= 𝔙; ≈ 𝔗)
literally: Saul was *one year* old when he began to reign; and he reigned *two years* over Israel.
NRSV Saul was . . . years old when he began to reign; and he reigned . . . *and two* years over Israel.

The problematical aspects of this unusual text are indicated in the NRSV[9] by dots to which the following footnotes are added for the first and the second instance respectively: "the number is lacking in the Heb text"; "*Two* is not the entire number; something has dropped out." These explanations are acceptable (cf. p. 235 below), but at the same time it should be remembered that a literal translation of the received Hebrew text (that is, 𝔐) yields a very difficult meaning. We are thus left with the assumption that the received text contains a textual error and

9 This applies also to the NJPST and P.K. McCarter, *I Samuel* (AB 8; Garden City, NY 1980) 222.

that the earlier ("correct") text probably mentioned realistic numbers for Saul's age at the beginning of his reign, such as 30 years in 𝔊Luc(*b*goe2) (accepted by the REB), 21 years in 𝔖, or 50 years suggested by the NEB.

Jer 27:1 𝔐 בראשית ממלכת *יהויקם* בן יאושיהו מלך יהודה היה הדבר הזה אל ירמיה מאת ה׳ לאמר (= 𝔗 𝔙)

At the beginning of the reign of king *Jehoiakim* son of Josiah of Judah, this word came to Jeremiah from the LORD.

This verse serves as the heading of chapter 27, which speaks of actions taking place in the time of Zedekiah (see vv. 3,12; 28:1). Therefore, the mentioning of Jehoiakim in the heading does not suit the contents of the chapter and it probably erroneously repeats the first verse of the previous chapter, 26. The heading of chapter 27 was probably added in the forerunner of most textual witnesses at a later stage in the development of the book, while the earlier stage, in which it was lacking, is represented by 𝔊 (cf. pp. 322–324).

3. In Many Details 𝔐 Does Not Reflect the "Original Text" of the Biblical Books

It has become clear from the preceding paragraphs that one of the postulates of biblical research is that the text preserved in the various representatives (manuscripts, editions) of what is commonly called the Masoretic Text, does *not* reflect the "original text" of the biblical books in many details. Even though the concept of an "original text" necessarily remains vague (see chapter 3B), differences between the Masoretic Text and earlier or different stages of the biblical text will continue to be recognized. Moreover, even were we to surmise that 𝔐 reflects the "original" form of the Bible, we would still have to decide *which* Masoretic Text reflects this "original text," since the Masoretic Text is not a uniform textual unit, but is itself represented by many witnesses (cf. pp. 21–25).

Similar problems arise when one compares 𝔐 with the other textual witnesses, such as the Qumran scrolls and the putative Hebrew source of the individual ancient translations. We do not know which of all these texts reflects the biblical text faithfully. Thus, it should not be postulated in advance that 𝔐 reflects the original text of the biblical books better than the other texts. For a detailed analysis of this subject see chapter 3B.

The decision regarding details in 𝔐 and the other textual witnesses pertains to elements that developed in the course of the textual transmission of the biblical books, for which 𝔐 represents one of several witnesses. On the other hand, the literary composition reflected by 𝔐—and not earlier or later literary forms or stages—serves as the focus of our interest when thinking of the original shape of the biblical text as defined in chapter 3B.

4. Differences between Inner-Biblical Parallel Texts

In various places all textual witnesses of the biblical books contain parallel versions of the same literary unit. Some of these reflect different formulations of the same psalm (Psalm 18 // 2 Samuel 22; Psalm 14 // Psalm 53), the same genealogical list (Ezra 2 // Neh 7: 6-72), segments of books (Jeremiah 52 // 2 Kgs 24:18–25:30; Isa 36:1–38:8 // 2 Kgs 18:13–20:11), and even large segments of a complete book, viz., Chronicles, large sections of which run parallel to the books of Samuel and Kings. These parallel sources are based on ancient texts which already differed from each other before they were incorporated into the biblical books, and which underwent changes after they were transmitted from one generation to the next as part of the biblical books. Hence, within the scope of the present analysis, these parallel texts, which are found in all biblical witnesses, including 𝔐, are of particular interest. The differences between these parallel texts in 𝔐, as well as in other texts, *could* reflect very ancient differences created in the course of the copying of the biblical text, similar to the differences known from a comparison of ancient scrolls and manuscripts.

Even though there is no direct, archeological, evidence for the earliest stage of the transmission of the biblical books, there thus exists indirect evidence for this stage in the parallel texts within 𝔐 itself. Differences between the parallel texts attest readings developed in one of the first stages of the textual transmission, as, for example, between the two parallel versions of the "Table of the nations" (Genesis 10 and 1 Chronicles 1):

Gen 10:4 𝔐 ובני יון אלישה ותרשיש כתים ודדנים (= $\mathfrak{T}^{OJ}$)
The descendants of Javan: Elishah and Tarshish, the Kittim and *D*odanim.[10]

---

10 In ancient manuscripts, in several modern translations, and in certain editions (Letteris, Sinai) these differences have been removed by harmonizing the text in Chronicles with that of Genesis. Note that a similar interchange is known for Ezek 27:15 𝔐 דדן—𝔊 'Ροδίων.

1 Chr 1:7 𝔐 ובני יון אלישה ותרשישה כתים ורודנים (= 𝔖𝔪 𝔊 ʽΡόδιοι in Genesis)
The descendants of Javan: Elishah and Tarshish***ah,*** the Kittim and ***R***odanim.

Gen 10:28 𝔐 ואת עובל ואת אבימאל
Obal and Abimael

1 Chr 1:22 𝔐 ואת עיבל ואת אבימאל (= 𝔖𝔪 $𝔊^{MSS}$ in Genesis; idem Gen 36:23)
Ebal and Abimael

This applies also to the two versions of the list of David's mighty men:

2 Sam 23:28-29 מהרי הנטפתי 29חֵלֶב בן בענה הנטפתי
Maharai the Netophathite, 29Ḥele***b*** son of Baʿanah the Netophathite

1 Chr 11:30 מהרי הנטפתי חֵלֶד בן בענה הנטופתי
Maharai the Netophathite, Ḥele***d*** son of Baʿanah the Netophathite

The scribal background of these differences was already recognized by R. David Kimḥi's (RaDaK) commentary on "and ***R***odanim" in 1 Chr 1:7:

> This word is written with a *resh* at the beginning. And in the book of Genesis it is written with two *daleths*: "and **D**o**d**anim." Since the *daleth* and *resh* are similar in appearance, and among the readers of the genealogies which were written in ancient times, some read a *daleth* and some read a *resh*, some names were preserved for posterity in two forms with either a *daleth* or a *resh*. Thus it <the word ***D*/*R***odanim> is written in the book of Genesis with one of the readings and in this book <that is, 1 Chronicles> with the other one. This goes to show that both forms represent one name whether read with a *daleth* or with a *resh*. This applies also to "**R**iblatah" (2 Kgs 25:6,20; Jer 39:5; 52:9,10,26) written with a *resh* and "**D**iblatah" (Ezek 6:14) with a *daleth* . . . Likewise, words with *waw* and *yod* are interchanged as they are similar in appearance.

In chapter 4C many similar differences between parallel texts are presented.[11] See also p. 173. The differences between Psalm 18 and 2 Samuel 22 and Isa 36:1–38:8 // 2 Kgs 18:13–20:11 are listed in *Sof.* 8.1-2.

---

11 It is exactly these parallel biblical passages that have prompted the development of the textual criticism of the Hebrew Bible, because they necessitated the comparison of texts. See especially H. Owen, *Critica Sacra, Or a Short Introduction to Hebrew Criticism*

B. A Modern Approach to the Textual Criticism of the Bible

Since the discovery in 1947 of Hebrew texts in the Judean Desert dating from approximately 250 BCE until 135 CE , our knowledge on the text of the Bible has increased enormously (see pp. 29–35, 100–117). It should be remembered that until that time no earlier texts of the Hebrew Bible were known, except for the Nash papyrus (see p. 118) of the Decalogue,[12] so that the manuscripts of 𝔐 from the Middle Ages served as the earliest Hebrew sources. Therefore the research before 1947 was based on texts of the Bible that had been copied 1200 years or more after the composition of the biblical books. At the same time, one should remember that scholars did not use only Hebrew sources. They also relied on manuscripts and early papyrus fragments of the ancient translations, especially of the Septuagint (𝔊) and the Vulgate (𝔙)—see chapter 2II—which brought them much closer to the time of the composition of the original biblical books. All these, however, are translations, whose Hebrew source will always remain uncertain. It therefore goes without saying that the discovery of the many Hebrew texts from the Judean Desert dating from ancient times has considerably advanced our knowledge of the early witnesses and the procedure of the copying and transmitting of texts in antiquity.

This new knowledge has necessarily changed our understanding of the text of the Bible and, accordingly, our approach to writing a new introduction to the textual criticism of the Hebrew Bible. Such a new approach is *not* reflected in previously written introductions. The most extensive modern introduction, Roberts, *OTTV*, was written in 1951, after the discovery of the first texts in the Judean Desert, but its author was not able to incorporate the new discoveries in his description. In our view the introductions of Klein, *Textual Criticism* (1974), Deist, *Text* (1978), idem, *Witnesses* (1988), and McCarter, *Textual Criticism* (1986), although written at a time when the main facts were known, in many aspects still reflect the approach of the period before the discovery of the new data.

(London 1774). Further studies on this topic are listed by I. Kalimi, *Chronicles, The Books of Chronicles—A Classified Bibliography* (Simor Bible Bibliographies, Jerusalem 1990) 52–66.

12 However, this papyrus does not reflect a witness for the biblical text in the generally accepted sense of the word because it presumably contains a liturgical text.

In our opinion,[13] the new discoveries have not only added new data which are of major importance, but have also necessitated a new approach to the texts that were known before 1947.

Ever since the seventeenth century, equal attention has been given to all texts. Scholars regarded the ancient translations, especially the Greek and Latin versions, with esteem, because their manuscripts preceded those of 𝔐 by many centuries, and also because Greek and Latin sources were highly valued in the Church and in the centers of learning in Europe. Therefore in all scholarly descriptions of the ancient texts much attention has been given not only to 𝔐, but also to the Greek, Latin, and Aramaic versions, including the Peshitta (𝔖), and even to the "daughter" (or secondary) versions made from 𝔊, such as the Latin, Armenian, Coptic, and Ethiopic translations (cf. p. 134). After some time scholars realized that most of these translations were only of limited value for the textual criticism of the Hebrew Bible, their importance being confined mainly to biblical exegesis. Nevertheless, these primary and secondary translations were still given extensive treatment in textual descriptions. In our view this approach is no longer relevant within the framework of modern textual criticism. Therefore, this introduction devotes but little attention to the description of texts, including most of the ancient versions, whose importance for textual criticism—as opposed to exegesis—is limited.[14] On the other hand, much attention is devoted to texts whose relevance has been proven, that is, 𝔐, the Qumran texts, the Samaritan Pentateuch (𝔐𝔰𝔥), and 𝔊.

The study of the biblical text was initiated as an auxiliary science to biblical exegesis. Therefore, the results of textual investigation have always been taken into consideration in exegesis, and that practice continues to be followed today. Textual criticism thus has a distinctly practical aspect, but as a rule this feature has not been reflected sufficiently in the extant handbooks on textual criticism. In contradistinction to them, chapters 6–9 of this book deal extensively with those practical aspects. Within this framework, the relation between textual and literary criticism, a topic which is usually not treated in handbooks such as this, is treated separately (see chapter 7).

---

13 See E. Tov, "A Modern Textual Outlook Based on the Qumran Scrolls," *HUCA* 53 (1982) 11-27 and likewise more recent articles mentioned on pp. 100, 164.

14 It is noteworthy that BH and BHS contain almost no notes referring solely to the Aramaic or Latin translations of 𝔐, or one of the "daughter" translations of 𝔊. Such evidence is mainly referred to in conjunction with additional sources.

C. The Beginnings of the Critical Inquiry of the Biblical Text

D. Barthélemy, *Critique textuelle de l'AT* (OBO 50/1 Fribourg/Göttingen 1982) 1*-63*; B. Chiesa, "Appunti di storia della critica del testo dell'Antico Testamento ebraico," *Henoch* 12 (1990) 3–14; L. Diestel, *Geschichte des AT in der christlichen Kirche* (Jena 1869); Eichhorn, *Einleitung;* M.H. Goshen-Gottstein, "Hebrew Biblical Manuscripts: Their History and Their Place in the HUBP Edition," *Bib* 48 (1967) 243-290; repr. in Cross–Talmon, *QHBT*, 42-89; K.F. Keil, *Manual of Historico-Critical Introduction to the Canonical Scriptures of the OT*, vol. II (Edinburgh 1892); E. König, *Einleitung in das AT mit Einschluss der Apokryphen und der Pseudepigraphen ATs* (Bonn 1893); H.J. Kraus, *Geschichte der historisch-kritischen Erforschung des ATs* (3d ed.; Neukirchen 1982); F. Laplanche, *L'Ecriture, le sacré et l'histoire—Erudits et politiques protestants devant la Bible en France au XVIIe siècle* (Amsterdam/Maarssen 1988); E.F.C. Rosenmüller, *Handbuch für die Literatur der biblischen Kritik und Exegese*, vol. I (Göttingen 1797); Steuernagel, *Einleitung*, § 22.

Interest in the text of the Bible began in the first centuries of the common era when learned church fathers compared the text of the Hebrew Bible and different Greek versions. In the third century Origen prepared a six-column edition (hence its name: Hexapla) of the Hebrew Bible, which contained the Hebrew text, its transliteration into Greek characters, and four different Greek versions (see pp. 146–148). Likewise, Jerome included in his commentaries various notes comparing words in the Hebrew text and their renderings in Greek and Latin translations (see pp. 48, 153).

The critical investigation of the relation between the various textual witnesses did not begin before the seventeenth century, when the scholarly knowledge then available was expanded by the appearance of the Polyglot editions (see pp. 77–78) which, through their printing in parallel columns of the various witnesses, enabled and almost required their comparison. The first extensive textual treatises are those by Morinus, Cappellus, and Richard Simon: J. Morinus, *Exercitationum biblicarum de hebraei graecique textus sinceritate libri duo* (Paris 1633; 2d ed. 1660); L. Cappellus, *Critica Sacra* (Paris 1650; 2d ed. Halle, 1775–1786); Richard Simon, *Histoire critique du VT* (Paris 1680 and Rotterdam 1685; repr. Frankfurt 1969); idem, *A Critical History of the OT* (London 1682).

After the middle of the seventeenth century there appeared a great many treatises on the text of the Bible, though it should be recognized that in this and the following century the borderline between genuine philological analysis and theological discussion was often vague. The three aforementioned works, as well as many works by Bauer, Buxtorf, Glassius, Hottinger, Houbigant, Kennicott, Rosenmüller, and de Rossi, contributed much to the development of the critical view of the biblical text. The *Einleitung* of Eichhorn* also stands out as a work of immense learning and major influence. The works of the mentioned scholars have been described in detail by Rosenmüller*, Keil*, and Barthélemy*. Of the many names that may be mentioned from the nineteenth century, see especially de Lagarde, Perles, Cornill, and Wellhausen because of their remarkable insight into textual criticism. In many areas of the textual criticism of the Bible it is often best to start with these older works, since in textual criticism (called an art by some and a science by others), an intuitive grasp of the issues underlying divergent texts is just as important as recently discovered data (e.g., the Qumran texts). Particularly Wellhausen in his commentary on Samuel (Göttingen 1881) and König* and Steuernagel* in their introductions exhibited that kind of intuition. At the same time, the modern description of the textual criticism of the Bible differs significantly from earlier discussions because of the relevance of the newly discovered Qumran texts to almost every aspect of textual criticism. On many other aspects of the history of the investigation of the biblical text see chapter 3A (pp. 155-163).

D. Definitions and Concepts

In the course of our analysis, basic concepts will be defined precisely, but from the outset there is a need for short, practical definitions.

Textual criticism. For a brief definition, see p. 1, and for a more detailed one, see chapter 5A.

Lower criticism is an expression used widely in previous generations (probably starting with Eichhorn*, *Einleitung*) to refer to textual criticism. This term has to be understood as referring to the lowest stratum of one's treatment of the biblical books, and it serves as the antithesis of another term, **higher** (or literary) **criticism**. Higher criticism deals with various issues relating to the composition in its entirety, such as origin, date, structure, authorship, and, in particular, authenticity and uniformity, topics which indeed refer to the highest level of the study of the biblical books. Emphasis on the antithesis between the higher and lower criticism is, however, misleading, for textual criticism is not the only discipline on which higher criticism is based. Linguistic, historical, and geographical analysis, as well as the exegesis of the text, also provide material for higher criticism.

Urtext is the putative original form of the text of the Bible as defined on p. 177. According to the description in this book, the *Urtext* aimed at by textual critics is the completed literary composition which had already passed through several written stages and which stood at the beginning of the process of textual transmission. At the same time, the consecutive formulations of some biblical books, each of which was accepted as authoritative by its own generation, may be considered as consecutive 'original texts' (see pp. 178–180).

Textual witnesses (sources) represent tangibly different forms of the biblical text. These include 𝔐, the Sam. Pent. (𝔪𝔪), the texts from the Judean Desert, biblical quotations—especially in Hebrew compositions from the Second Temple period—and, indirectly, the reconstructed Hebrew source of each of the ancient translations. The text of the Bible forms an abstract entity known from its textual witnesses.

(Variant) readings. The details of which texts are composed (letters, words) are "readings," and, accordingly, all readings which differ from a text accepted as central are usually called "variant readings" or "variants." Some scholars use the term *variants* in the same neutral way as the term *readings* is used in this book and in most text-critical discussions. In the critical edition of any text, all the readings which are quoted in the "critical apparatus" as deviating from the central text are thus considered variants. The distinction between the central reading and a variant therefore is not evaluative. It merely follows a separation between the central text and deviating textual traditions.[15] Variants can thus be superior to the printed text, but for the sake of convenience they are presented as details deviating from the central text. In the case of the biblical text, 𝔐 serves as such a central text to which all other texts are compared in the critical editions and discussions. Therefore, all the details in the textual witnesses of the Bible differing from 𝔐 are variant readings of one type or another, viz., (1) omissions or (2) additions of details and (3) differences in details or (4) in sequence. At the same time, in the critical editions of the non-Masoretic textual witnesses (such as the editions of Qumran texts), the text of 𝔐 is often presented as a variant text.

Ancient translations. In antiquity several translations (versions) were made of the Bible from different Hebrew texts, which modern scholars attempt to reconstruct. Among the ancient translations LXX (𝔊) is especially important. See pp. 134–148.

---

[15] On the other hand, when the central text has been composed by a selective process and thus represents a critically reconstructed "original text" (or a textual form approaching that original text), the notion of variants is evaluative. In that case all variants listed in the critical apparatus are by definition, in the editor's mind, inferior to the main text. Such "eclectic" editions (for the concept see p. 20) do not exist for the complete Hebrew Bible (for some experiments in this area, see p. 372, n. 2).

The Masoretic Text (𝔐), sometimes called the "received text," is strictly speaking a medieval representative of a group of ancient texts of the Bible which already at an early stage was accepted as the sole text by a central stream in Judaism. As a result, the slightly different forms of this text (often named the 𝔐 group) were copied and circulated more than other texts. The final form of this text was determined in the Middle Ages, and it is that form which is usually called the Masoretic Text, while earlier forms found in the Judean Desert, lacking the later vocalization and accentuation, are named **proto-Masoretic.** In the first century CE the central position of the proto-Masoretic texts was strengthened because of the weakening or cessation of the other streams in Judaism. Because of its place in Judaism as the central text of the Hebrew Bible, 𝔐 also became the determinative text for the Hebrew Bible of Christianity and of the scholarly world. All printed editions of the Bible contain 𝔐. Nevertheless, 𝔐 reflects merely one textual tradition out of many that existed in the period of the First and Second Temple. This text has been preserved meticulously and apparatuses of vocalization, accentuation, and Masorah have been added to it. See pp. 22–79.

The Samaritan Pentateuch (𝔪) is an ancient text of the Torah written in a special form of the "early" Hebrew script and preserved by the Samaritan community. Its basis was a Jewish text, very much like the so-called **pre-Samaritan** texts from Qumran (see pp. 97–100). One of these texts was used as the basis for the Samaritan Pentateuch, and to this text the Samaritans added a thin layer of ideological and phonological changes. See pp. 94–95.

Texts from the Judean Desert are Hebrew, Aramaic, and Greek texts (both biblical and non-biblical) which were probably copied between the mid-third century BCE and 135 CE and were found in the Judean Desert, especially at Qumran, between 1947 and 1956.

Conjectural emendation is an attempt to reconstruct the original form of a detail in the biblical text by suggesting a new reading when, according to a scholar, the original reading has not been preserved in the extant textual witnesses. See chapter 8.

Evaluation of readings is the comparison of readings (variants), created in the course of the textual transmission (excluding the details added during the stage of the literary growth of the books), regarding their comparative merits. Most scholars agree that this evaluation involves a decision regarding the question of which particular reading would have preceded the other ones in the textual transmission or from which the other ones developed (for examples, see the readings denoted in chapter 4 as "<preferable>"). Some scholars would phrase this procedure as the wish to locate or reconstruct the one reading which was presumably contained in the original text. See chapter 6 and the above definition of *Urtext*.

A critical edition of the Hebrew Bible or of any other composition presents a carefully transmitted form of that text, or a reconstructed original text, together with tools for the comparison of the details in the text with other (all, most) witnesses of the same text. Usually a distinction is made between diplomatic and eclectic editions. Most of the critical editions of the Hebrew Bible are diplomatic, that is, they reproduce without any changes a particular form of 𝔐 as the base text, while recording divergent readings (variants) from Hebrew and non-Hebrew texts in an accompanying critical apparatus. Eclectic editions present the reconstructed original text which is selected from elements found in all known sources; in addition, they provide a critical apparatus of variants, often together with their evaluation.

2

TEXTUAL WITNESSES OF THE BIBLE

I. HEBREW WITNESSES

The text of the Bible is known to us from many textual witnesses (sources), in Hebrew and in translation. The discussion of the Hebrew sources in this chapter is central for this introductory monograph as a whole, since all other chapters are somehow based upon this description and constantly refer to it. It is thus natural that the description of the procedure of textual criticism (chapter 5), of the transmission of the biblical text (chapter 4), and of the evaluation of individual readings (chapter 6) be based on these textual witnesses, especially those in Hebrew. In our discussion it is also important to take into consideration the relation between all these textual witnesses (chapter 3), since all of them relate differently to the abstract concept of "the biblical text," a concept which is important for our understanding of the textual procedure.

The sequence of the analysis follows a certain logic. In the description that follows, Hebrew witnesses (part I of this chapter) are separated from the ancient translations (part II of this chapter). Part I contains direct evidence, while the data described in part II are indirect because of the uncertainty regarding the reconstruction of the Hebrew source of these translations. Within each group the sources are described in chronological order, although precision is impossible. The first two sections in part I (A,B) discuss texts which are well known from medieval sources (𝔐 and 𝔪), and each of them is discussed here together with less known early texts, from which they developed (proto-Masoretic and pre-Samaritan texts). In our terminology a distinction is made between the *proto*-Masoretic texts which are the actual forerunners of the Masoretic Text, belonging to the same family, and the *pre*-Samaritan texts on one of which the Samaritan Pentateuch presumably was based. In other words, the proto-Masoretic texts were basically Masoretic, so to speak, while the pre-Samaritan texts were not Samaritan.

A. Proto-Masoretic Texts and the Masoretic Text

D. Barthélemy, *Critique textuelle de l'AT* (OBO 50/3; Fribourg/Göttingen 1992) vii-cxvi; M. Beit-Arié, "Some Technical Practices Employed in Hebrew Dated Medieval Manuscripts," *Litterae textuales* (Codicologica 2, Eléments pour une codicologie comparée; Leiden 1978) 72–92; M. Breuer, *The Aleppo Codex and the Accepted Text of the Bible* (Heb. with Eng. summ.; Jerusalem 1976); M. Cohen, "The 'Masoretic Text' and the Extent of Its Influence on the Transmission of the Biblical Text in the Middle Ages," *Studies in Bible and Exegesis* 2 (Heb.; Ramat Gan 1986) 229-256; A. Díez Macho, *Manuscritos hebreos y arameos de la Biblia* (Studia Ephemerides "Augustinianum" 5; Rome 1971); A. Dotan, "Masorah," *EncJud* 16 (1971) 1401–1482; Ginsburg, *Introduction*; M. Glatzer, "The Aleppo Codex—Codicological and Paleographical Aspects," *Sefunot* 4 (Heb. with Eng. summ.; Jerusalem 1989) 167–276; M.H. Goshen-Gottstein, *Biblia Rabbinica, A Reprint of the 1525 Venice Edition* (Heb.; Jerusalem 1972) 5–16; A.M. Habermann, "Bible and Concordance," in: S.E. Loewenstamm and J. Blau, *Thesaurus of the Language of the Bible*, vol. 1 (Jerusalem 1957) xix–xxxviii; M.J. Mulder, "The Transmission of the Biblical Text," in: idem, *Mikra*, 87-135; H. Rabin, *Mḥqrym bktr ʾrm ṣwbh* (Publications of the HUBP 1; Jerusalem 1960); A. Sperber, "Problems of the Masora," *HUCA* 17 (1942–1943) 293-394; idem, *Grammar*; I. Yeivin, "Mqrʾ, ktby yd šl hmqrʾ," *EncBib* 5 (Jerusalem 1968) 418-438; idem, "Mswrh," ibid., 130–159; idem, *Mbḥr ktby-yd bšyṭwt nyqwd ṭbrny wʾrṣ-yśrʾly* (Akademon, Jerusalem 1973); idem, *Introduction*.

The name *Masoretic Text* (also referred to as the 𝔐 group) refers to a group of manuscripts which are closely related to each other. Many of the elements of these manuscripts including their final form were determined in the early Middle Ages, but they continue a much earlier tradition. The name *Masoretic Text* was given to this group because of the apparatus of the Masorah attached to it (see below, pp. 72–76). This apparatus, which was added to the consonantal base, developed from earlier traditions in the seventh to the eleventh centuries—the main developments occurring in the beginning of the tenth century with the activity of the Ben Asher family in Tiberias.

As a rule the term *Masoretic Text* is limited to a mere segment of the representatives of the textual tradition of 𝔐, namely, that textual tradition which was given its final form by Aaron Ben Asher of the Tiberian group of the Masoretes. Since all the printed editions and most manuscripts reflect this Ben Asher tradition, the term *Masoretic Text* is imprecise, since it is actually used only for part of the Masoretic tradition, viz., that of Ben Asher. In order to remove this imprecision, Goshen-Gottstein* distinguishes between MT in general and the Tiberian MT. When using the term MT, most scholars actually refer to the Tiberian MT.

The term *Masoretic Text* is imprecise for another reason, too, for 𝔐 is not attested in any one single source. Rather, 𝔐 is an abstract unit reflected in various sources which differ from each other in many details. Moreover, it is difficult to know whether there ever existed a single text which served as the archetype of 𝔐. Another aspect pointing to the inadequacy of the term *Masoretic Text* is, as Cohen* has demonstrated, the fact that the Masoretic notes (below, pp. 72–76) are not relevant to all of the manuscripts belonging to the group of 𝔐. Therefore, a term like *Masoretic Texts* or the *group/family* of 𝔐 would reflect the evidence more precisely. In this book, however, we shall continue to use the conventional term *Masoretic Text* or 𝔐.

The principal component of 𝔐 is that of the consonants (letters), evidenced in Second Temple sources, and to this text all other elements were added during the early Middle Ages. Therefore, although the medieval form of 𝔐 is relatively late, its consonantal framework reflects an ancient tradition that was in existence more than a thousand years earlier in many sources, among them, many texts from the Judean Desert. Accordingly, scholars often designate the consonantal base of 𝔐 (deriving from the Second Temple period) as *proto-Masoretic* although sometimes, anachronistically, also as the Masoretic Text. 𝔐 contains

1. The consonantal framework already attested in proto-Masoretic texts of the Second Temple period, as well as the Masorah (see below, pp. 72–76), prepared by generations of Masoretes. The Masorah consists of several elements, viz.,
2. Vocalization
3. Para-textual elements
4. Accentuation
5. The apparatus of the Masorah

For many centuries 𝔐 has served as the most commonly used form of the Hebrew Bible, since it came to be accepted as authoritative by all Jewish communities from the second century CE onwards, at first in its consonantal form only, and after some centuries, in conjunction with its vocalization, accentuation, and the apparatus of Masoretic notes. Because of this acceptance, first of the proto-Masoretic text by a central stream in Judaism and later, of 𝔐 by all sections of the Jewish people, 𝔐 is attested in a very large number of sources. More than six thousand manuscripts belonging to the group of 𝔐 are known; in addition, all printed editions of the Hebrew Bible are based on 𝔐. ". . . of some 2700 extant *dated* Hebrew manuscripts prior to 1540, six dated codices from the tenth century, eight from the eleventh century, and 22 from the twelfth century are known to us, most of them Oriental. In addition, there are about sixty small fragments of Oriental codices dated before 1200 among the geniza fragments" (Beit-Arié*, 72).

The Masoretic codices, consisting of single pages bound like books (see examples in plates 10*-12*, 14*), were written by scribes in accordance with the *halakhot,* "religious instructions," relating to the external aspects of copying, such as materials, measurements, and corrections. This topic is treated in chapter 4B.

The various components of the text were inserted by different people. *Soferim,* "scribes," wrote down the consonantal text, *naqdanim,* "vocalization experts," added the vowels and accents, and the Masoretes (*ba'alê ha-masorah,* "masters of the Masorah") wrote the notes of the Masorah. However, the Masoretes were often involved with more than one layer of the text (vocalization, accentuation, and Masoretic notes and occasionally even all of these components of the text). Therefore, in the discussion below they are called by the same name: the Masoretes.

1. *The Consonantal Framework: Proto-Masoretic Texts and* 𝔐

F.I. Andersen and D.N. Freedman, "Another Look at 4QSam[b]," *RQ* 14 (1989) 7–29; M. Cohen, "Some Basic Features of the Consonantal Text in Medieval Manuscripts of the Hebrew Bible," in: U. Simon and M.H. Goshen-Gottstein, eds., *Studies in Bible and Exegesis, Arie Toeg in Memoriam* (Heb.; Ramat Gan 1980) 123–182; idem, "The 'Masoretic Text' . . . " (see p. 22); M.H. Goshen-Gottstein, "Hebrew Biblical Manuscripts: Their History and Their Place in the HUBP Edition," *Bib* 48 (1967) 243–290 = Cross–Talmon, *QHBT*, 42–89; Y. Maori, "mwbʾwt mqrʾywt bsprwt ḥz"l," *Maḥanayim* 70 (1962) 90-99; J.S. Penkower, "A Tenth-Century Pentateuchal MS from Jerusalem (MS C3), Corrected by Mishael Ben Uzziel," *Tarbiz* 58 (1988) 49–74 (Heb. with Eng. summ.); see further the literature on **p. 233.**

The representatives of 𝔐 form a tight group which differs from other texts. Nevertheless, no special characteristics of 𝔐 can be identified on a textual level, except for the accuracy and quality of its text for most of the biblical books. On the other hand, on a socio-religious level this text has a unique character, since at a certain stage it was preferred to the others by a central stream in Judaism (the Pharisees?). However, when evaluating the different texts one should disregard this situation, for the preference of 𝔐 by a central stream in Judaism does not necessarily imply that it contains the best text of the Bible. Both the Hebrew parent text of 𝔊 (below IIB) and certain of the Qumran texts (below C) reflect excellent texts, often better than that of 𝔐.

When 𝔐 became the central text, at first of a central stream in Judaism and later of the whole Jewish people, no further changes were inserted into it and no additions or omissions were allowed (below *c*), not even in small details such as the use of *matres lectionis* (see pp. 220–230). Therefore 𝔐 came to preserve the biblical text in the exact form in which it was current at a particular time in a particular circle; it preserved such minutiae as scribal points above or below letters and other para-textual elements (below 3).

After the proto-Masoretic text had become the accepted text in Judaism, it was copied many times and as a result of its central status most of the ancient translations were based upon one of the representatives of the group of 𝔐: the Targumim, the Peshitta (𝔖), the revisions (recensions) of 𝔊 (among them *kaige*-Theodotion, Aquila, Symmachus, and the fifth column of the Hexapla) and the Vulgate (𝔙)—on all these, see part II of this chapter. Likewise, 𝔐 is often quoted in both early and late rabbinic literature, and the great majority of the texts from the Judean Desert also reflect this text (below *d*).

a. Internal Differences in the Group of 𝔐

The group of Hebrew and translated texts which reflects the consonantal framework of 𝔐 is the largest among the textual witnesses of the Bible. As remarked above, this fact should not be taken as a qualitative evaluation of this text, since the size of this group of textual witnesses is determined by socio-religious rather than qualitative factors, that is, when the proto-Masoretic text became determinative for a central stream of Judaism, it was copied, translated, and quoted many times.

It is difficult to know whether there ever existed a single archetype of 𝔐, and, even if such a text had existed, it cannot be identified or reconstructed. The only evidence in favor of such a hypothesis could be the possibly distinctive textual character of all the books of 𝔐 or of one particular book, and such distinctiveness is only recognizable in the slightly corrupt character of 𝔐 in Samuel, as contrasted with the other textual witnesses. In any event, at an early stage there already existed a relatively large number of differences between the various texts belonging to the group of 𝔐. Moreover, as the number of the texts of the group of 𝔐 increased, the internal differences between the members of this group were multiplied as a result of the process of copying. Differences of this type are recorded in the modern scholarly literature as discrepancies between 𝔐 on the one hand and the rabbinic literature, the Hebrew source of certain translations, and the texts from the Judean Desert on the other, and naturally much attention was devoted to them by scholars (see Table 3 on p. 34 and the discussion there). However, such lists of differences create an optical illusion, since the agreements between the members of the group of 𝔐 are more numerous and idiosyncratic than the differences between them. Therefore, one should stress the internal unity of this group rather than the differences between its representatives.

These internal differences within the group of 𝔐 are illustrated below (*d*) according to the attestation of 𝔐 in the different periods. At this point in the discussion, we will describe three groups of differences which have become institutionalized in the tradition of the copying of 𝔐 itself. Other differences are discussed later (pp. 33–39).

a. Mᵉdinḥāʾê—Maʿarbāʾê

Ginsburg, *Introduction*, 197-240; idem, "On the Relationship of the So-called Codex Babylonicus of A.D. 916 to the Eastern Recension of the Hebrew Text," *Receuil des travaux . . M.D. Chwolson* (Berlin 1899) 149–188; Yeivin, *Introduction*, 139–141.

A special group of internal variants within the group of 𝔐 has been preserved in the notes of the Masorah (below pp. 72–76) as מְדִינְחָאֵי, *Mᵉdinḥāʾê*, that is, the Masoretes of the East and מַעַרְבָאֵי, *Maʿarbāʾê*, the Masoretes of the West.

Even though the scribes of 𝔐 meticulously preserved a uniform text, breaches in this unity are nevertheless visible. Between the early sources of 𝔐 there existed differences in consonants between texts from the West (Palestine) and the texts from the East (Babylon). Some 250 such differences are mentioned in the Masoretic notes as *Mᵉdinḥāʾê* and *Maʿarbāʾê*. For example,

2 Kgs 8:16 יהורם (Je**h**oram)—*Mᵉdinḥāʾê*: יורם (Joram); that is, for "Je**h**oram" a variant "Joram" is known to the Masoretes of the East

Notes of this type referred especially to differences between *Ketib* and *Qere* (see pp. 58–63). For example,

Job 17:10 (BH, not BHS) *Maʿarbāʾê*: ובאו ("and come!")
Mᵉdinḥāʾê: 𝔐ᴷ יבאו ("they will come")
𝔐ᵠ ובאו ("and come!")

Most of the manuscripts of 𝔐 that have been preserved are Tiberian (see p. 43), that is, Western, and therefore the majority of the Masoretic notations comparing different traditions refer to readings of the *Mᵉdinḥāʾê,* when the Tiberian manuscripts differed from Eastern sources. These differences were collected in the Middle Ages in separate lists which preserved evidence of this type even if in the manuscripts themselves such evidence was lacking or was not denoted consistently. The lists refer only to discrepancies in consonants, which may mean that their origin must have been early, before vowels and accents were inserted.

β. Variants in Manuscripts Reflecting Different Systems of Vocalization

When the Masoretes added the vocalization to the consonants, that consonantal text was already fixed and therefore one would not expect to find many differences in consonants between the manuscripts written in different systems of vocalization. Nevertheless, manuscripts vocalized in the Palestinian and Babylonian tradition (see pp. 43–44) sometimes also differ from Tiberian manuscripts in consonants.[1]

γ. Masoretic Notes

In the notation of the Masorah several variants have been preserved which pertain to the notation of *Ketib–Qere* (see pp. 58-63) and *Sebirin* (p. 64).

All these internal differences within the 𝔐 group point to a certain amount of textual variation at an early stage of the development of 𝔐, in contrast with its later unity. The above-mentioned differences were institutionalized in the notation of the Masorah, but a still larger number of internal differences (see below *d*) has not been recorded.

b. The Early Origin of the Consonantal Framework of 𝔐

The many sources which constitute the group of 𝔐 are attested in early texts from the Judean Desert, in manuscripts from the Middle Ages, in quotations from the Bible in the rabbinic literature, and in several ancient translations. Only from the early medieval period, when the apparatuses of vocalization, accentuation, and Masoretic notes were added to the consonants, can one speak of a real Masoretic Text. Nevertheless, the main constituent of 𝔐, its consonantal framework, already existed many centuries beforehand, as it is attested in various texts from the Judean Desert, which date from the third pre-Christian century until the second century CE. As remarked above, the consonantal framework of the proto-Masoretic texts is more or less identical with that of the medieval manuscripts, even though they also differ in small details. The differences between the early texts are greater than those between the late sources, as the desire to transmit the texts with precision increased in the course of the years. In other words, the scope of the differences between the medieval manuscripts is much smaller than that between the early scrolls.

1 See B. Chiesa, *L'antico Testamento ebraico secondo la tradizione palestinese* (Torino 1978). Differences of this type are included in L. Díez Merino, *La Biblia babilónica* (Madrid 1975) as well as in the HUB (see p. 378). On the other hand, the internal unity of the Hebrew tradition is emphasized by E.J. Revell, *Biblical Texts with Palestinian Pointing and Their Accents* (SBLMasS 4; Missoula, MT 1977).

The early origins of 𝔐 can also be inferred indirectly from the Qumran texts written in the paleo-Hebrew script (see pp. 104–105). Since almost all paleo-Hebrew texts found in Qumran (see p. 220) reflect 𝔐, they provide information about 𝔐 from a period preceding its attestation in masoretic manuscripts. The texts written in this script were probably copied from other texts also written in the paleo-Hebrew script rather than from texts written in the Assyrian ("square") script (see pp. 218–220), so that with the aid of these texts we can now obtain information concerning an earlier period. The antiquity of this tradition is also indicated by the use of scribal dots as word dividers in the paleo-Hebrew texts from Qumran (see pp. 208–209).

c. The Origin and Nature of 𝔐

One can only conjecture on the origin of 𝔐 since there is no evidence which points clearly in any one direction. An elucidation of the origin of 𝔐 must involve an analysis of its nature. As a rule, the scribes treated 𝔐 with reverence, and they did not alter its orthography and morphology as did the scribes of ɯɯ (pp. 89–91) and of many of the Qumran scrolls (see pp. 108–110). Since 𝔐 contains a carefully transmitted text, which is well-documented in a large number of copies, and since it is reflected in the rabbinic literature as well as in the Targumim and many of the Jewish-Greek revisions of 𝔊, it may be surmised that it originated in the spiritual and authoritative center of Judaism (later to be known as that of the Pharisees), possibly in the temple circles. It was probably the temple scribes who were entrusted with the copying and preserving of 𝔐. Though this assumption cannot be proven, it is supported by the fact that the temple employed correctors (מגיהים, *maggihim*) who scrutinized certain scrolls on its behalf (see p. 32). The fact that all the texts left by the Zealots at Masada (dating until 73 CE) reflect 𝔐 is also important.

But there is a snag in this description. While on the one hand it was claimed above that those involved in the transmission of 𝔐 did not insert any change in 𝔐 and as a result its inconsistency in spelling as well as its mistakes have been preserved for posterity, on the other hand, there never existed any one single text that could be named *the* Masoretic Text. In fact at a certain stage there was a *group* of Masoretic texts and naturally this situation requires a more precise formulation. Although at one time an attempt was made not to insert any changes in 𝔐, at that time the texts within the group of Masoretic texts already differed internally one from another. In other words, although there indeed existed the express wish not to insert any changes in the

Masoretic texts, the reality was in fact paradoxically different, since the texts of the 𝔐 group themselves already differed one from the other. There thus existed a strong desire for textual standardization, but this desire could not erase the differences already existing between the texts. The wish to preserve a unified textual tradition thus remained an abstract ideal which could not be accomplished in reality.[2] Moreover, despite the scribes' meticulous care, changes, corrections, and mistakes were added to the internal differences already existing between the members of the 𝔐 group. The various texts from the Second Temple period thus differed from each other, but in the course of the centuries, the number of these differences decreased rather than increased, not only because of the activities of the temple scribes (see p. 32), but also because of the addition of the vocalization and accentuation, which added an element of precision and prevented changes in consonants. Also, the addition of the apparatus of the Masorah (see pp. 72–77) was intended to decrease the number of the differences between the manuscripts, especially in regard to consonants.

d. The Evolution of the Early Consonantal Text of 𝔐

α. Background

The different attestations of the early consonantal text of 𝔐 allow us to discern three main periods which reflect a growing measure of consistency and agreement between texts. The borders of these periods are determined in accordance with the textual evidence. The description that follows refers only to 𝔐, and must be integrated into the description of the development of the biblical text as a whole, provided in chapter 3C (pp. 180-197).

i. The *first* period, characterized by internal differences in the textual transmission, extends over a long span of time. While its beginning is not clear, since it is not known when 𝔐 came into being, its end coincides with the destruction of the Second Temple.

The witnesses for this period are Hebrew texts from Qumran (copied between 250 BCE and 68 CE), Masada (copied before 73 CE), Wadi Murabbaʿat, Wadi Sdeir, Nahal Ḥever, and Naḥal Ṣeʾelim in the Judean Desert (copied before 135 CE),[3] and early witnesses of several

2 Thus especially M. Cohen, "hʾydyʾh bdbr qdwšt hnwsḥ lʾwtywtyw wbyqwrt hṭksṭ," *Deoth* 47 (1978) 83-101 = U. Simon, ed., *The Bible and Us* (Heb.; Tel Aviv 1979) 42–69.

3 For the texts from Qumran, see pp. 100–117; for Masada, see Talmon, *Masada VI*; and for the other texts, see *DJD* II (1961), XXXVIII (2000).

ancient translations. Although there is no evidence pertaining to the internal differences within the 𝔐 group before the time of these texts, it would appear from a comparison of parallel texts within 𝔐 itself (see pp. 12–13) that such differences already existed between the various textual witnesses at an early stage.

In this first period of the development of 𝔐, that is, until the destruction of the Second Temple, in the texts from Qumran there existed a relatively large number of small differences between the members of the 𝔐 group in matters of content and orthography, while the differences in content were usually limited to single words and phrases.

Such differences should be studied through an internal comparison of ancient sources. However, because of the scarcity of complete sources from antiquity, scholars usually describe these differences within the 𝔐 group by comparing them with a later source. At an earlier stage of research, a central witness in this group, namely, the second Rabbinic Bible (see pp. 78–79) served this purpose and, in recent generations, the codex Leningrad B19A (abbreviated as L) likewise served as a source for comparisons.[4] When the early Qumran texts of the 𝔐 group are compared with the consonantal framework of L (dating from 1009), one realizes how close they are to medieval sources. This applies to all the Qumran texts and the reconstructed Hebrew source of several Targumim and of an early revision (recension) of 𝔊, *kaige*-Theodotion (see pp. 144–145). The combined evidence shows that the consonantal framework of 𝔐 changed very little, if at all, in the course of more than one thousand years. Even more striking is the fact that the texts from the other sites in the Judean Desert are virtually identical with the medieval texts, probably because they derived from similar cicles.

When comparing the Qumran text 1QIsa^b (see plate 6*), dating from the first century BCE, with codex L (see plate 12*), which is one thousand years younger, one easily recognizes the close relation, sometimes almost identity, between these two texts. Thus, on p. 7 = plate 9 (Isa 50:7–51:10 [13 verses]) of the preserved part of this scroll, one finds only four differences in minor details and two differences in orthography (our reading differs slightly from that of Sukenik [see n. 5]). On p. 6 = plate 8 (Isa 48:17–49:15, likewise 13 verses), one finds 16 differences all of which concern only minutiae: 7 differences in orthography and 9 minor, mainly linguistic, differences.

4 Codex L is more appropriate for this purpose than the printed editions, since it reflects an extant source, whereas the editions combine details from various manuscripts (see pp. 77–79 and chapter 9).

Table 1

Differences between L and 1QIsa^b^ in Isa 48:17–49:15 (p. 6 = plate 8)[5]

	*1QIsa^b^*	*Codex L*
48:17	מדרכיך	מַדְרִיכֲךָ
18	ולא	לוּא
	שלמך	שְׁלוֹמֶךָ
21	צר	צוּר
49 : 3	הת[פאר]	אתפאר
4	כלתי	כִלֵּיתִי
	אך	אָכֵן
5	כה	—
	יוצרי	יֹצְרִי
6	הנקל	נָקֵל
	ארץ	הָאָרֶץ
7	אדני יהוה	יהוה
	גואל	גֹּאֵל
	יקומו	וָקָמוּ
	קדוש	קְדֹשׁ
8	[ש]ממת	שֹׁמֵמוֹת

Table 1 refers to one column only in 1QIsa^b^. When examining all the fragments of 1QIsa^b^, which comprises segments of 46 chapters, we find the following types of differences between the scroll and codex L, all of which concern minutiae.

Table 2

Types of Differences between 1QIsa^b^ and Codex L[6]

Orthography	107
Addition of conjunctive *waw*	16
Lack of conjunctive *waw*	13
Article (addition/omission)	4
Differences in consonants	10
Missing letters	5
Differences in number	14
Differences in pronouns	6
Different grammatical forms	24
Different prepositions	9

5 According to E.L. Sukenik, *ʾwṣr hmgylwt hgnwzwt šbydy hʾwnybrsyṭh hʿbryt* (Jerusalem 1954). A reproduction of this column is adduced in plate 6* of the present book.

6 According to M. Cohen, *op. cit.* (n. 2) 86, n. 4.

Different words	11
Omission of words	5
Addition of words	6
Different sequence	4

A similar analysis is suggested by Andersen–Freedman*, 22, in their analysis of 4QSam^b, one of the earliest Qumran texts: " . . . insofar as there is nothing un-Massoretic about the spellings in *4QSam^b*, we can infer that the Massoretic system and set of spelling rules were firmly in place in all principles and particulars by the third century BCE."

Because of the meticulous care of those who were involved in the copying of 𝔐, the range of the differences between the members of the 𝔐 group was from the outset very small. One should remember that the temple employed professional *maggihim*, "correctors" or "revisers," whose task it was to safeguard precision in the writing and transmission of the text: "*Maggihim* of books in Jerusalem received their fees from the temple funds" (*b. Ketub.* 106a). The Talmud also uses the term *sefer muggah*, "a corrected/revised scroll": "and when you teach your son, teach him from a corrected scroll" (*b. Pesaḥ.* 112a). Likewise one finds the term *sefer šeʾêno muggah*, "a book that is not corrected" (*b. Ketub.* 19b). Furthermore, it is not impossible that an effort was made to limit the range of differences between early texts, for a Talmudic tradition reports on the limiting of the differences between three specific texts by comparing their readings in each individual instance of disagreement. Apparently this was done in order to compose from them one single copy which would reflect the majority readings (the agreement of two sources against the third one). Although such a procedure seems to be the implication of the *baraita* to be quoted below, the procedures followed are not sufficiently clear.

> Three scrolls of the Law were found in the temple court. These were the *maʿon* ("dwelling") scroll, the *zaʿ^{a}ṭuṭê* ("little ones") scroll, and the *hyʾ* scroll. In one of the scrolls they found written, "The eternal God is (your) dwelling place (מעון *maʿon*)" (Deut 33:27). And in two of the scrolls it was written, "The eternal God is (your) dwelling place (*m^{e}ʿonah* מענה = 𝔐)." They adopted the reading found in the two and discarded the other. In one of them they found written, "He sent the little ones (*zaʿ^{a}ṭuṭê*) of the sons of Israel" (Exod 24:5). And in two it was written, "He sent young men (*naʿ^{a}rê* = 𝔐) of the sons of Israel." They adopted the reading of the two and discarded the other. In one of them they found written הִוא, *hwʾ*, nine times, and in two, they found it

written היא, *hy*ʾ, eleven times. They adopted the reading found in the two and discarded the other (*y. Taʿan.* 4.68a).[7]

Scribal activity involving the correction of the base manuscript of 𝔐 according to another source seems also to be at the base of the omission of some words in 𝔐 indicated in the Masorah with the so-called "extra-ordinary points" (see pp. 55–57).

The precision in the transmission of 𝔐 is also reflected in the words of R. Ishmael: "My son, be careful, because your work is the work of heaven; should you omit (even) one letter or add (even) one letter, the whole world would be destroyed" (*b. Soṭ.* 20a). This precision even pertained to matters of orthography, since various *halakhot*, "religious instructions," were, as it were, fixed on the basis of the exact spelling of words. For example, the number of the walls of the *sukkah* (four) is determined according to the spelling סֻכֹּת (*b. Sukk.* 6b), rather than a spelling סוכות (five letters, cf. Isa 1:8 on p. 113).[8] Some of the examples of this type actually were formulated in a later period.

ii. The *second* period of transmission, characterized by a relatively large degree of textual consistency (except for the Severus Scroll, whose text frequently differs from 𝔐 [see pp. 119–120]), extends from the destruction of the Second Temple until the eighth century CE. Most of the witnesses for this period pertain either to its beginning or its end, while for the intervening time there exists but little evidence. From the beginning of this period there have been preserved the documents from the Judean Desert (Naḥal Ḥever, Wadi Murabbaʿat) written before the revolt of Bar-Kochba (132-135 CE). More precisely, fragments of the Torah, Isaiah, and the Twelve Minor Prophets were found in Wadi Murabbaʿat (see *DJD* II [Oxford 1961] 1-3, 88) and fragments of Genesis, Numbers, and Psalms were found in Naḥal Ḥever (for references see Fitzmyer, *Dead Sea Scrolls*, 85-88). From the end of this period date the earliest texts from the Cairo Genizah (a *genizah*, "storage area," contains documents and writings of religious importance which are damaged or no longer in use). In the 1890s more than 200,000 fragments of manuscripts, from the ninth century onward, among them tens of thousands of biblical fragments, were found in the Cairo Genizah, the genizah of the synagogue of Fusṭat, "Old Cairo." However, most of these fragments have not yet been published.[9]

---

7 For a thorough analysis, see S. Talmon, "The Three Scrolls of the Law That Were Found in the Temple Court," *Textus* 2 (1962) 14-27. See also n. 42.

8 See also Y.Y. Yelin, *Hdqdwq kyswd bhlkh* (Jerusalem 1973) 336-356.

9 See M.C. Davis, *Hebrew Bible Manuscripts in the Cambridge Genizah Collections*, vols. 1-2 (Cambridge 1978, 1980); I. Yeivin, *Geniza Bible Fragments with Babylonian Massorah and*

The destruction of the Second Temple and the subsequent demographic and socio-religious changes accelerated the already existing trend of diminishing textual variation. Thus, the texts of 𝔐 from this second period are characterized by a very small range of differences between them. This is evident from a comparison of codex L with the texts found in Naḥal Ḥever and Wadi Murabbaʿat and with the ancient translations made in that period: several of the Targumim, 𝔖, revisions (recensions) of 𝔊 (Aquila, Symmachus, the fifth column of the Hexapla), and 𝔙. Also in the rabbinic literature[10] and the *piyyuṭim*, "liturgical hymns,"[11] the great majority of the biblical quotations agree with 𝔐. The following examples of differences (cf. n. 10) point to the exceptions rather than the rule.

Table 3

Differences between Codex L and Biblical Quotations in Rabbinic Literature

Isa 1:1	𝔐	ישעיה**ו**
	Gen. Rab. 13.1	ישעיה
Isa 1:3	𝔐	עמי לא התבונן
	Sifre Deut 309 MS ר (p. 349)[12]	**ו**עמי

Vocalization (Heb.; Jerusalem 1973). Plates 13* and 14* in this book include two texts from the Cairo Genizah. For an evaluation of these fragments, see Kahle, *Cairo Geniza*, 3-13; J. Hempel, "Der textkritische Wert des Konsonantentextes von Kairener Genizafragmenten in Cambridge und Oxford zum Deuteronomium nach Kollationen von H.P. Rüger untersucht," *NAWG* I., Phil.-hist. Kl. 1959, 10, pp. 207-237; M.H. Goshen-Gottstein, "Biblical Manuscripts in the United States," *Textus* 2 (1962) 28-59.

10 At the same time, the biblical quotations in the rabbinic literature also differ from time to time from 𝔐, both in direct quotations and in variants underlying the *derashah*, "sermon." For an analysis and for the history of research, see Y. Maori, "The Text of the Hebrew Bible in Rabbinic Writings in the Light of the Qumran Evidence," in D. Dimant and U. Rappaport, eds., *The Dead Sea Scrolls—Forty Years of Research* (Leiden/Jerusalem 1992) 283–289, and idem, "Rabbinic Midrash as a Witness of Textual Variants of the Hebrew Bible: The History of the Issue and Its Practical Application in the Hebrew University Bible Project," in: M. Bar-Asher and others, eds., *Studies in Bible and Exegesis III, Moshe Goshen-Gottstein—in Memoriam* (Heb.; Ramat Gan 1993) 267–286. These differences have been collected in the following treatises: S. Rosenfeld, *Spr mšpḥt swprym* (Wilna 1883); V. Aptowitzer, *Das Schriftwort in der rabbinischen Literatur*, vols. I–IV (Vienna 1906–1915; repr. New York 1970). The most complete collection is found in the HUB, but so far this edition covers only a few biblical books (see p. 378). The importance of these variants was stressed much by Kahle (see p. 184), but they are nevertheless negligible in light of the large amount of agreement with 𝔐 of the biblical quotations in the rabbinic literature.

11 Cf. M. Wallenstein, "The Piyyut, with Special Reference to the Textual Study of the OT," *BJRL* 34 (1952) 469-476.

12 *Sifre* is quoted according to the edition of Finkelstein (Berlin 1940).

Isa 1:18	𝔐	(אם יהיו חטאיכם) כשני**ם** (כשלג ילבינו)
	Sifre Deut 6 MS ד (p. 15); 28 MS ד (p. 45)	כשני (= 1QIsa^{a})
Jer 30:4	𝔐	ואלה הדברים אשר דבר ה'
	Sifre Deut 1 MSS ד, ט,ל	ואלה הדברים אשר דבר ירמיה
Hab 1:13	𝔐	מראות רע
	Pesiq. Rab Kah. 4.10; 25.1	מראות **ב**רע (= 1QpHab)

Table 3[13] does not include cases of *ʾal tiqrê* (see n. 40) or of rabbinic *midrashim* based on presumably different readings, as these do not necessarily reflect readings that would have been known to the rabbis. Rather, these instances reflect an exegetical play with readings that would have been possible in the context.

All textual evidence preserved from the second period reflects 𝔐, but this fact does not necessarily imply the superiority of that textual tradition. The communities which fostered other textual traditions either ceased to exist (the Qumran covenanters) or dissociated themselves from Judaism (the Samaritans and Christians). See further p. 195.

iii. The *third* period of transmission, characterized by almost complete textual unity, extends from the eighth century until the end of the Middle Ages. The main sources for this period are Masoretic manuscripts containing the complete apparatus of the Masorah and biblical quotations in the writings of the medieval commentators.[14] The earliest dated Masoretic manuscripts are from the ninth century.[15] During this period 𝔐 became almost completely standardized, due largely to the addition of the apparatuses of vocalization, accentuation, and Masorah necessitating the fixation of the consonants which formed their base.

The sources from this period are subdivided into manuscripts from the early Middle Ages (until about 1100) and later manuscripts. In all aspects the early manuscripts are more reliable.

---

13 See the extensive discussion of the relevant evidence by D. Rosenthal, "The Sages' Methodical Approach to Textual Variants within the Hebrew Bible," in: A. Rofé and Y. Zakovitch, eds., *Isac L. Seeligmann Volume, Essays on the Bible and the Ancient World* (Heb. with Eng. summ.; Jerusalem 1983) 395-417; Y.Y. Yelin, *op. cit.* (n. 8) 183-185.

14 See, for example, S. Esh, "Variant Readings in Mediaeval Hebrew Commentaries; R. Samuel Ben Meir (Rashbam)," *Textus* 5 (1966) 84-92.

15 According to Birnbaum, a manuscript found at Jews College, London, was written somewhat earlier: S.A. Birnbaum, "A Sheet of an Eighth Century Synagogue Scroll," *VT* 9 (1959) 122-129.

Table 4

Internal Differences between Medieval Masoretic Manuscripts

a. According to the Collections of Kennicott and de Rossi (see below)

Gen 1:14	all MSS	ויאמר אלהים יהי מארת ברקיע השמים
	MS 776 of Kennicott adds להאיר על הארץ (= 𝔪; cf. 𝔊) (this addition is influenced by v. 15 והיו למאורת ברקיע השמים להאיר על הארץ ויהי כן and v. 17)	
Lev 10:1	all MSS	ויקחו בני אהרן נדב ואביהוא
	MSS 5,181 of Kennicott	ויקחו *שני* בני וגו' (= 𝔊*)
1 Kgs 11:20	all MSS	ותגמלהו תחפנס בתוך *בית* פרעה
	MSS 23,154,182,271A,283A of Kennicott בני (= 𝔊; cf. the end of the verse: בתוך בני פרעה)	
1 Kgs 12:12	all MSS	רחבעם
	MS 202 of Kennicott	*המלך* רחבעם (= 𝔊)

b. According to Early Manuscripts (following Breuer)*

Josh 3:3	MS L	כראותכם
	MSS A,C,S1, Rabb. Bible	כראתכם
Josh 3:4 K	MS L, Rabb. Bible	ובינו
	MSS A,C,S1	ובניו
Josh 6:6	MS S1	ארון *ברית* ה'
	MSS A,L,C, Rabb. Bible	ארון ה'
Josh 6:9	MS C	השופרת
	MSS A,L,S1, Rabb. Bible	השופרות

The differences in group *b* in Table 4 characterize the type of differences between medieval manuscripts; all the differences pertain to minutiae. Group *a* records greater differences which are less characteristic of this period.

β. Sources

The number of medieval manuscripts is very large and the differences between them have been recorded in several collections of variants. The first five collections mentioned below pertain only to manuscripts written after 1100, while the more recent collections also include variants in early manuscripts.[16]

16 Apart from the editions mentioned in this section, see also the first printed editions (below pp. 77–79) which contain readings that are not known from other sources. It appears that the editors of these editions had access to manuscripts which were subsequently lost.

Minḥat Shay, written in the seventeenth century by Yedidyah Sh^{e}lomo from Norzi, was printed in various editions of the Bible (starting with the edition of Mantua, 1742-1744), among them the Rabbinic Bibles (see pp. 78–79), and subsequently also in a separate edition (Vienna 1813–1815).

B. Kennicott, *Vetus Testamentum hebraicum cum variis lectionibus*, vols. I-II (Oxford 1776–1780)—see plate 17*.

J.B. de Rossi, *Variae lectiones Veteris Testamenti*, vols. I-IV (Parma 1784–1788; repr. Amsterdam 1969). This edition was meant as a supplement to the Kennicott edition.

J.C. Döderlein and J.H. Meisner, *Biblia Hebraica* (Halle/Berlin 1818). This edition selects variants from the earlier editions of Kennicott and de Rossi.

C.D. Ginsburg—see p. 79.

The Hebrew University Bible, The Book of Isaiah (Jerusalem 1995), *The Book of Jeremiah* (Jerusalem 1997). At the present time this edition contains the fullest collection of variants, since it contains sources that were not known to previous compilers. See the third and fourth apparatuses in plate 28* and see p. 378.

BH and BHS quote from the collections of Kennicott and de Rossi, but without detailed information; e.g., "20 MSS" (see Table 5). BHS also quotes, without details, from the fragments from the Cairo Genizah.

γ. The Value of the Differences between Medieval Manuscripts

The differences between the medieval manuscripts of 𝔐 and their value need not be discussed at greater length than any other group of variants within the family of 𝔐, but since scholars have made an exception for them, we must also do so.

The opinions of scholars concerning the value of the differences between the medieval manuscripts are divided. Many scholars, among them the editors of BH and BHS, attach considerable significance to the readings attested to in the above-mentioned collections by quoting them, while other scholars are more reserved with regard to their value for biblical criticism.

The scholars who value the readings contained in medieval manuscripts are essentially influenced by procedures developed in biblical criticism in the previous centuries rather than by content considerations relating to the readings themselves. For when critical biblical scholarship began to develop, manuscripts from the Middle

Ages formed the major and almost exclusive source of information for the study of the Hebrew Bible text, so that every detail in those manuscripts received attention exceeding their real significance. Thus, in BH and BHS the *number* of manuscripts (according to Kennicott) containing a certain reading is mentioned specifically. For details, see plates 26* and 27* and Table 5.

Table 5

Quotations in BH from Medieval MSS (according to Kennicott)

Isa 1:3	עמי	ca 30 MSS 𝔊 𝔖 𝔙	ועמי
Jer 14:14	לכם	𝔅 et nonn MSS	להם
Ezek 7:5	אחת	ca 30 MSS Edd 𝔗	אחר

Explanation of the first item: Some thirty Hebrew manuscripts of 𝔐 (according to the edition of Kennicott) as well as 𝔊, 𝔖, and 𝔙 read ועמי, "and my people," instead of עמי, "my people," in the printed ("received") text of 𝔐 (= codex L).

In recent times the tendency of attaching significance to the differences between the medieval manuscripts has been strengthened by Cohen* (p. 24), who, by stressing the independence of the Ashkenazi and Sephardic manuscripts from the Middle Ages, attempted to prove that each group of manuscripts had a different background in the period preceding the Middle Ages. In his view the Sephardic manuscripts are close to the accurate Tiberian manuscripts (see pp. 43-47), while Ashkenazi manuscripts, such as the manuscripts denoted as N and L18, reflect other ancient traditions, including traditions of pronunciation. For example, the *plene* spelling of לוא, *lw*ʾ, as against לא, *l*ʾ, possibly reflects a different tradition of pronunciation which has also been preserved by the Samaritans. In his article mentioned on p. 22, Cohen* distinguishes between "the authorized text of the Masoretic type" and "the extraneous authorized traditions within the framework of the Masoretic type." The latter group does not accurately reflect the Masorah lists, but rather ancient traditions which the Masorah notations did not succeed in eradicating. These Masoretic notes are best reflected in the Sephardic manuscripts.

Much criticism has been voiced against the approach which attaches significance to the differences between the medieval manuscripts. Goshen-Gottstein* claims:

(1) The majority of the readings in manuscripts written in the Middle Ages were created in that period and only a few of them reflect earlier traditions.

(2) The broad basis of the textual attestation of some readings as against the narrow basis of other readings is immaterial. Since a large number of manuscripts could have been copied from a single source, well-attested readings do not necessarily have more weight than singly attested readings. Therefore one should take into consideration the intrinsic value of each reading rather than the number of manuscripts in which it is attested. In this context scholars usually quote the methodological rule formulated as *manuscripta ponderantur, non numerantur*, "manuscripts are to be considered for their worth and not reckoned according to their number."

(3) Most of the agreements between medieval manuscripts and ancient sources do not necessarily point to the ancient origin of the readings. Usually the agreement is coincidental, since in the Middle Ages, as in antiquity, the same processes were in operation which created secondary Hebrew variants and caused contextual adaptations within the translations. For some examples, see Table 5. For another example, see:

Prov 15:20 — בן חכם ישמח אב וכסיל אדם בוזה אמו
A wise son makes a glad father, but *a foolish man* despises his mother.

8 MSS of Kenn. — בן חכם ישמח אב ובן כסיל בוזה אמו (= 𝔊 𝔗 𝔖)
A wise son makes a glad father, but *a foolish son* despises his mother.

This secondary reading, however, could also have developed independently under the influence of the parallel stich and 10:1. For further examples of harmonizing changes, see p. 261.

2. *Vocalization*

Kahle, *Cairo Geniza;* S. Morag, "nyqwd," *EncBib* 5 (Jerusalem 1968) 837-857.

a. Tiberian Vocalization

A. Dotan, "Masorah," *EncJud* 16 (1971) 1401-1482; idem, "Deviation in Gemination in the Tiberian Vocalization," *Estudios Masoréticos* (Textos y Estudios "Cardenal Cisneros" 33; Madrid 1983) 63-77; M.H. Goshen-Gottstein, "The Rise of the Tiberian Bible Text," in: A. Altmann, ed., *Biblical and Other Studies* (Cambridge, MA 1963) 79-122; Gesenius–Kautzsch, 24-98; S. Morag, "The Tiberian Tradition of Biblical Hebrew: Homogeneous and Heterogeneous Features," *P'raqim* 2 (Heb.; Jerusalem 1969–1974) 105-144; M.J. Mulder, "The Transmission of the Biblical Text," in: idem, *Mikra*, 87-135; J.S. Penkower, "A Pentateuch Fragment from the Tenth Century Attributed to Moses Ben-Asher (Ms Firkowicz B 188)," *Tarbiz* 60 (1991) 355-369 (Heb. with Eng. summ.); H. Rabin, ed., *Mḥqrym bktr ᵓrm ṣwbh* (Publications of the HUBP 1; Heb.; Jerusalem 1960).

b. Palestinian Vocalization

M. Dietrich, *Neue palästinisch punktierte Bibelfragmente veröffentlicht und auf Text und Punktuation hin untersucht* (Leiden 1968); P. Kahle, *Masoreten des Westens*, vols. I–II (Stuttgart 1927, 1930); E.J. Revell, *Hebrew Texts with Palestinian Vocalization* (Toronto 1970); idem, *Biblical Texts with Palestinian Pointing and Their Accents* (SBLMasS 4; Missoula, MT 1977).

c. Babylonian Vocalization

L. Díez Merino, *La Biblia babilónica* (Madrid 1975); P. Kahle, *Der Masoretische Text des ATs nach der Überlieferung der Babylonischen Juden* (Leipzig 1902; repr. Hildesheim 1966); idem, *Masoreten des Ostens* (Leipzig 1913; repr. Hildesheim 1966); S. Morag, "The Yemenite Tradition of the Bible—The Transition Period," in: E. Fernández Tejero, ed., *Estudios Masoréticos (V Congreso de la IOMS)* (Madrid 1983) 137-149; I. Yeivin, *The Hebrew Language Tradition as Reflected in the Babylonian Vocalization* (Heb.; Jerusalem 1985). See also the series *Biblia babilónica* (Madrid 1976–1982) in which several of the prophetic books and the Hagiographa have appeared.

a. Background

Diacritical signs, which were added to the consonantal framework of 𝔐, determined—at a rather late point of time—the vocalization of the text in a final form. In this regard the example and pattern of the older Syriac vocalization was followed (see Gesenius-Kautzsch § 7h). This system has no parallel in the other textual traditions of the Hebrew Bible; that is, although during the Middle Ages the Samaritans developed a similar system for some texts, most manuscripts of 𝔖𝔐 remained without systematic vocalization (see p. 81). At the same time, a comparison with the other textual traditions of the Hebrew Bible regarding the use of vocalization is irrelevant since after the first century CE most of the other texts were no longer in active use as the communities which fostered the other texts ceased to exist. Had such communities continued to use their texts, it is possible that they, too, would have developed systems of vocalization.

The late origin of the vocalization is evident from its absence in the texts from the Judean Desert. Nevertheless, Jewish and Christian tradition both believed in the divine origin of the vocalization, and only in the sixteenth century was a serious attempt made to refute this supposition; see Elias Levita, *Massoreth ha-Massoreth* (Venice 1538; ed. C.D. Ginsburg, London 1867; repr. New York 1968). The discussion which Elias Levita's book aroused has been described by Steuernagel, *Einleitung*, 84ff. and Roberts, *OTTV*, 68-69.

The main function of the vocalization was to remove doubts regarding the reading of the text when this allowed for more than one interpretation. It was also a necessary component of 𝔐, since this text was sparing in its use of *matres lectionis* (see pp. 220–229) which facilitate the reading of the consonants. On the other hand, in such texts as some of the Qumran scrolls, which make abundant use of *matres lectionis* (see pp. 108-109), vocalization was required less.

The authors of the biblical texts intended a certain reading of the consonantal framework, but since this reading was not recorded, traditions of reading the biblical texts developed which were not necessarily identical with the "original intention" of the texts. It is not clear whether one or more different reading traditions were in vogue from the very beginning. In principle, the existence in antiquity of multiple consonantal texts differing from each other would preclude a unified reading tradition, and would allow for the assumption of different reading traditions (on the textual variety see pp. 191–192). On the other hand, since the biblical texts probably developed in a linear way, one from the other (cf. p. 172), it is not impossible that some form of a unified reading tradition nevertheless existed, which was adapted time and again to the various attestations of the biblical text. At the same time, the various reading traditions from antiquity (see next paragraph) differ from each other to a limited extent only (see below), and it is not clear whether these differences are large enough to allow for more than one tradition.

These reading traditions are reflected in antiquity in the ancient versions, the second column of the Hexapla (see p. 147), transliterated words in 𝔊 and in the writings of Jerome (see p. 153), and in the Middle Ages in the vocalized manuscripts of 𝔐. The traditions are rather uniform with regard to the understanding of the consonants, but nevertheless contain internal differences regarding some words (cf. p. 255). Since the consonantal framework of many words allowed for different explanations, different readings of those consonants sometimes developed. See, for example, the differences in reading between 𝔐 𝔗 𝔖 on the one hand and 𝔊 on the other in Exod 22:12 (pp. 70–71) and further in the following examples.

Isa 9:7 — 𝔐 דָּבָר (שלח אדני ביעקב) *dabar* (= 𝔗 𝔖)
𝔊 θάνατον = דֶּבֶר *deber*

Isa 24:23 — 𝔐 (וחפרה) הַלְּבָנָה (ובושה) הַחַמָּה *hall*ᵉ*banah . . . haḥammah* (≈ 𝔗 𝔖)
𝔊 ἡ πλίνθος . . . τὸ τεῖχος
= הַלְּבֵנָה . . . הַחֹמָה = *hall*ᵉ*benah . . . haḥomah*

Accordingly, beyond the general agreement with regard to the understanding of the consonants, differences are recognizable in details which derive from different exegetical traditions in each of the sources in which the vocalization is expressed, including the medieval manuscripts of 𝔐. Nevertheless, the group of 𝔐 (that is, Hebrew medieval manuscripts and such versions as the Targumim, Aquila, and Theodotion) is rather uniform, even though one should note such instances as Jer 7:3,7 recorded on p. 274. A single reading tradition for 𝔐 is also reflected in the practices of *Qere* and *ʾal tiqrê*, for which see pp. 58–59.

The vocalization in the manuscripts of 𝔐 reflects not only ancient exegetical traditions but also the views of the Masoretes themselves. For example, in Joshua 21 מִגְרָשֶׁהָ (*migrašeha*, "its fields") was written 49 times without a *yod*—which usually appears for a noun in the plural with the third person feminine singular pronominal suffix. The *yod* appears in this word (see, e.g., vv. 11,13,14) in the Aleppo codex (see p. 46) as well as the other manuscripts, though with less consistency. On the basis of this evidence it has been suggested by Barr[17] that the "original" text of Joshua actually intended a form מִגְרָשָׁה, *migrašah*, a noun in the singular with the third person singular pronominal suffix which had been altered by the Masoretes. In his view this word was vocalized in 𝔐 as a plural form since the precise meaning of *migraš* as a collective concept ("a common area near the walls") had already been forgotten by the time of the writing of 1 Chr 6:40ff., in which it was conceived of as a "single field"; this development may have necessitated the vocalization of the word as a plural form.

In Deut 12:5 the Masoretes also expressed their exegesis in the vocalization and accentuation: לשום את שמו שם ^ לְשִׁכְנוֹ תדרשו ("to establish His name there, ^ you shall seek *His habitation*"). The vocalization and accents in this verse reflect the exegesis of the Masoretes who connected לשכנו, *lšknw*, with the following words and took it as a noun שֵׁכֶן* (*šēken**, "habitation," cf. 𝔪 לשכינו) which is elsewhere not attested in biblical literature and which is also grammatically problematic.[18] However, probably originally לְשַׁכְּנוֹ, *lešakkeno*, was intended[19] and this vocalization was changed because the word was difficult in its context.

---

17 J. Barr, "*Migraš* in the OT," *JSS* 29 (1984) 15-31.

18 In biblical language one seeks "*to* a place" or "*to* God," but not to "His habitation" (שִׁכְנוֹ). The word is further evidenced in Ben Sira 14:25.

19 In its presumably original vocalization לְשַׁכְּנוֹ reflects a doublet of לשום, "to put"; cf. the interchangeable formulae לשום שמו שם, "to establish His name there" (Deut 12:21; 14:24; 1 Kgs 9:3, etc.) and לשכן שמו שם, "to make His name dwell there" (Deut 12:11; 14:23; 16:2, etc.). Note further the variant of 𝔪 לשכן for 𝔐 לשום in 12:21. The double reading (cf. p. 241) was adapted to its context by means of a change in vocalization. See Geiger, *Urschrift*, 321-324 and below pp. 274–275.

These examples show that the Masoretes added their vowels to a consonantal framework which they did not allow themselves to alter. This is also shown by the constant spelling of יְרוּשָׁלִַם (in the printed editions: יְרוּשָׁלַיִם, e.g., Josh 10:1), reflecting as it were *y^e^rušālaim*. This vocalization indicates that in their manuscripts the Masoretes found the ancient form ירושלם (= יְרוּשָׁלֵם, *y^e^rušālēm*) and that they added the *hireq* between the *lamed* and the final *mem* because they could not change the consonantal text by adding a *yod*. The addition was meant to accomodate the pronunciation *y^e^rušālayim* which had become standard in the Second Temple period.

Since a large number of words could be read in different ways, the vocalization served the very practical purpose of indicating precisely the way in which the consonants should be read. This pertains also to the designation of the letter ש as either *sin* or *shin*.

Finally, the vocalization had a function within a system of denoting phonemes which is not usually connected with the meaning of the words, namely the indication of the letters *b, g, d, k, p, t* as either with or without the *dagesh lene*.

Among the various sources there are many differences in vocalization, some of which affect the meaning of the word such as the above-mentioned differences between 𝔐 and 𝔊, and others which concern details in the representation of words according to the different systems of vocalization (see below). Textual critics record some of these differences (see BH(S) and the fourth apparatus of HUB [plates 26*–28*]), but do not deal with a description of the linguistic background of the vocalization, a subject which is usually treated by linguists. For examples of different vocalizations, see pp. 41–42, 71, and 274.

b. Systems of Vocalization

The signs for Hebrew vocalization, although created at a relatively early stage—apparently between the years 500 and 700 CE—were only much later developed into a full-fledged system. Three systems have been developed for 𝔐.

(1) Tiberian (also named North-Palestinian) vocalization—see plates 10*-12*;

(2) Palestinian (also named South-Palestinian) vocalization—see plate 13* (the vowel signs are placed above the consonants);

(3) Babylonian vocalization, subdivided into "simple" and "compound"—see plate 14*. In this system the vowel signs are placed above the consonants.[20]

In addition to these systems there also exists a Tiberian-Palestinian system (the "extended" Tiberian system), which is used for example in codex Reuchlin. The opinions of scholars are divided concerning the nature of this vocalization.[21]

While from the outset there existed different systems of vocalization, in due course the Tiberian system was gradually accepted as authoritative in most Jewish communities and thus slowly replaced the other systems. As a consequence, these other systems were unknown in the European centers of learning until the nineteenth century, when manuscripts from Yemen and the Cairo Genizah were discovered. Only the Yemenites continued to maintain the Babylonian tradition, though not in its original form (see Morag*).

c. Differences between the Systems of Vocalization

The various vocalization systems differ from each other with regard to the *graphic* form of the vowel markers which were usually written either below the consonants (the Tiberian system) or above them (the Palestinian and Babylonian systems).

Beyond these graphic differences, the various systems also differ in certain linguistic features, such as the letters ʾ, *w*, *y*, the *sheva*, and the phonetic content of the vowels. For example, the two Tiberian signs *pataḥ* and *segol* are represented in the Babylonian system by the same sign; in most of the manuscripts in Palestinian vocalization there are interchanges between *qameṣ* and *pataḥ* as well as between *ṣere* and *segol*. For details, see the comparative table *apud* Morag*.

The differences between the manuscripts in matters of vocalization have been recorded in various sources, particularly in the editions listed on p. 79. They refer particularly to differences within the same system, e.g., between the Tiberian manuscripts, but also the differences between the systems. Table 6 exemplifies the differences between the Tiberian and the Babylonian-Yemenite system. The latter is represented here with the Tiberian signs.

---

20 The Palestinian and Babylonian systems of vocalization have become known in particular from the documents from the Cairo Genizah (see p. 33) from the ninth to the eleventh centuries.

21 See Morag*, 842.

Table 6

Differences in Vocalization between Codex L and a Babylonian-Yemenite Manuscript (Sample)[22]

		L	*MS Bodl. 2333*
Qoh	2:7	מקנֶה בקר וצאן	מקנֵה בקר וצאן
	10	מִכָּל שמחה	מִכֹּל שמחה
	13	אָני	אֲני
	22	וברעְיון	וברעֲיון
	3:16	השָּׁמש	השֶּׁמש
	18	שְׁהם	שֶׁהם
	4:4	ואֵת	ואֶת

All the printed editions of the Bible present a system of vocalization which was accepted by most of the Jewish communities, viz., the Tiberian vocalization or, more precisely, the vocalization according to the system of Aaron (son of Moses) Ben Asher. His vocalization system—a major branch of the Tiberian system—is faithfully represented in the Aleppo codex (see below). Some scholars claim that the Ben Asher system actually consists of various subsystems of vocalization (for differences within the Ben Asher system, see especially Dotan*, 1971 and 1983). Alongside the Ben Asher system the system of the Ben Naftali family was also used, but to a lesser extent, and therefore it is not well attested.[23] Actually, these two systems were closely related to each other,[24] and the differences between them (in 867 specific passages as well as in a few general issues) have been recorded in the *Sefer ha-Ḥillufim*, "The Book of the Differences," composed by Mishael ben Uzziel, as exemplified in Table 7.

22 According to Y. Ratzabi, "Massoretic Variants to the Five Scrolls from a Babylonian Yemenitic MS," *Textus* 5 (1966) 93-113.

23 It was suggested by Kahle among others that this system has been preserved in codex Reuchlin, mentioned on p. 44, but this suggestion has been rejected by many scholars. According to Penkower* (p. 24), the original text of codex C 3, before its correction (see p. 47), reflects the Ben Naftali text well.

24 On the difficulties inherent in this description, see M. Cohen, "The Victory of the Ben-Asher Text—Theory and Reality," *Tarbiz* 53 (1984) 255-272 (Heb. with Eng. summ.). See also A. Dotan, *Ben Asher's Creed—A Study of the History of the Controversy* (SBLMasS 3; Missoula, MT 1977); D. Barthélemy, *Critique textuelle de l'AT* (OBO 50/3; Fribourg/Göttingen 1992) vii-xviii.

Table 7

Differences between the Systems of Ben Asher and Ben Naftali (Sample)[25]

	Ben Asher	*Ben Naftali*
passim	בְּיִשְׂרָאֵל	בִּישְׂרָאֵל
passim	יִשָּׂשכָר	יִשְּׂשָכָר
Gen 48:19	יהיה לְֽעם	יהיה לְעם
Exod 15:13	עם זו גָּֽאלת	עם זו גָאלת

For a long period scholars were of the opinion that the Ben Asher text was represented faithfully in the second Rabbinic Bible (see pp. 78–79), upon which most of the subsequent editions of the Bible were based. It has been demonstrated, however, that this edition does not reflect any specific manuscript and that the following sources better reflect the vocalization of the Ben Asher tradition (see Yeivin, *Introduction*, 16-32).

(1) The Aleppo codex, indicated as א or A (see plates 10*, 11*), written by Shᵉlomo ben Buyaʿa (the consonants only) and vocalized and accented by Aaron Ben Asher himself in approximately 925 CE.[26] The latter also added the Masoretic notes. Three quarters of this manuscript have been preserved, and it has been published in a facsimile edition by M.H. Goshen-Gottstein, *The Aleppo Codex* (Jerusalem 1976). The HUB (see chapter 9) is based on this manuscript. Already in the Middle Ages this manuscript was recognized as a model codex by Maimonides, among others; see the latter's *Mishneh Torah, II, Hilkhot Sefer Torah* 8,4: "In these matters we relied upon the codex, now in Egypt, which contains the twenty-four books of Scripture and which had been in

25 According to L. Lipschütz, *Kitāb al-Khilaf, The Book of the Hillufim—Mishael Ben Uzziel's Treatise on the Differences between Ben Asher and Ben Naphtali* (Publications of the HUBP, Monograph Series 2; Jerusalem 1965) and idem, *Textus* 4 (1964) 1-29. See also A. Ben David, "The Differences between Ben Asher and Ben Naftali," *Tarbiz* 26 (1957) 384-409 (Heb. with Eng. summ.).

26 The literature on the Aleppo codex is very extensive. See A. Shamosh, *Ha-Keter—The Story of the Aleppo Codex* (Heb.; Jerusalem 1987), which includes, inter alia, a thorough discussion on the question of whether its vocalization, accentuation, and Masorah were really inserted by Aaron Ben Asher himself. See especially the articles in *Textus* 1 (1960) and H. Rabin, ed., *op. cit.* (p. 39). See also: A. Dotan, "Was the Aleppo Codex Actually Vocalized by Aharon ben Asher?" *Tarbiz* 34 (1965) 136-155 (Heb. with Eng. summ.); I. Yeivin, *The Aleppo Codex of the Bible, A Study of Its Vocalization and Accentuation* (Publications of the HUBP, Monograph Series 3; Heb. with Eng. summ.; Jerusalem 1968); Breuer*; M.H. Goshen-Gottstein, "ktr ʾrm ṣwbh whlkwt spr twrh l-RMB"M," *Spr hywbl l-r' y"d Soloveichik* (Jerusalem/New York 1984), vol. II, 871-888; M. Glatzer, "The Aleppo Codex—Codicological and Paleographical Aspects," *Sefunot* 4 (Jerusalem 1989) 167-276 (Heb. with Eng. summ.); J. Offer, "M.D. Cassuto's Notes on the Aleppo Codex," ibid., 277-344 (Heb. with Eng. summ.).

Jerusalem for several years. It was used as the standard text in the correction of books. Everyone relied on it, because it had been corrected by Ben Asher himself who worked on its details closely for many years and corrected it many times whenever it was being copied."[27] Kept for centuries by the Jewish community of Aleppo, in Syria, this manuscript was thought to have been lost in a fire in 1948; however, most of the books had been saved, while the Torah and several other books were lost.

(2) A tenth-century codex from the Karaite synagogue in Cairo (indicated as C 3) containing the Pentateuch. According to Penkower* (see p. 24), this codex agrees in most cases with the Ben Naftali tradition, but was systematically corrected by Mishael ben Uzziel towards the vocalization and accentuation of the Ben Asher tradition as reflected in Mishael ben Uzziel's *Sefer ha-Ḥillufim* (see p. 45). In Penkower's view, this codex is the closest to the Ben Asher tradition from amongst the known "accurate Tiberian manuscripts."

(3) Codex Leningrad B19^{A}, abbreviated as L, from 1009 (see plate 12*). This manuscript, now in Leningrad, is known to have been corrected according to a Ben Asher manuscript, and its vocalization is indeed very close to that of the Aleppo codex. Codex L comprises the single most complete source of all of the Bible books which is closest to the Ben Asher tradition, and therefore it has been made the base of two editions: BH/BHS and Adi (see plates 26*, 27*). Facsimile edition: D.S. Loewinger, *Twrh nbyʾym wktwbym, ktb yd lnyngrd B19^{A}* (Jerusalem 1970).

(4) Codex B.M. Or. 4445, indicated as B, containing significant sections of the Torah (from the first half of the tenth century).

(5) The Cairo codex of the Prophets, abbreviated as C (896 CE). Published by: F. Pérez Castro, *El codice de Profetas de el Cairo* (Madrid 1979–). Facsimile edition by D.S. Loewinger (Jerusalem 1971). For doubts regarding the attribution of C to Moses Ben Asher, see Penkower*.

(6) Codex Sassoon 507 of the Torah (tenth century), indicated as S.

(7) Codex Sassoon 1053 of the Bible (tenth century), indicated as S^{1}.

d. The Character of the Tiberian Vocalization

Barr, *Comparative Philology,* 188-222; G. Khan, "Vowel Length and Syllable Structure in the Tiberian Tradition of Biblical Hebrew," *JSS* 32 (1987) 23-82; S. Morag, "On the Historical Validity of the Vocalization of the Hebrew Bible," *JAOS* 94 (1974) 307-315; idem, "'Latent Masorah' in Oral Language Traditions," *Sefarad* 46 (1986) 333-344.

---

27 See J.S. Penkower, "Maimonides and the Aleppo Codex," *Textus* 9 (1981) 39-128.

The opinions of the scholars are divided over the nature of the Tiberian vocalization, especially with regard to its authenticity.[28] Such questions arose especially in the wake of the recognition of differences between the vocalization of 𝔐 and the traditions embedded in the transliterations of Hebrew words in the second column of the Hexapla (see p. 146), in 𝔊, and in Jerome's commentaries (see p. 153), as exemplified in Table 8.

Table 8

Differences between the Tiberian Vocalization and Transliterations in Greek and Latin Sources[29]

	𝔐		*transliteration*	
Jer 3:12	(וְ)קָרָאתָ	[(*w*^{e})*qārāʾtā*]	carath	
Jer 32:7	דֹּדְךָ	[*dod*^{e}*ka*]	dodach	
Ps 18:34	רַגְלַי	[*raglay*]	ρεγλαι	[*reglai*]
Ps 31:3	אָזְנְךָ	[*ʾozn*^{e}*ka*]	οζναχ	[*oznach*]
ibid.	הַצִּילֵנִי	[*haṣṣilēni*]	εσιληνι	[*esileni*]
Ps 36:1	לְעֶבֶד	[*l*^{e}*ʿebed*]	λααβδ	[*laabd*]
Ps 89:39	הִתְעַבַּרְתָּ	[*hitʿabbartā*]	εθαββαρθ	[*ethabbarth*]
ibid.	זָנַחְתָּ	[*zānaḥtā*]	ζαναθ	[*zanath*]
1 Chr 1:53	מִבְצָר	[*mibṣār*]	μαβσαρ 𝔊^{AN}	[*mabsar*]

On the basis of differences of this type various scholars, especially P. Kahle,[30] claimed that the Tiberian vocalization does not reflect the tradition of reading the Bible current in the time of the Second Temple, but rather an artificial reconstruction devised at a later period by the Masoretes in order to represent what seemed to them to be the original pronunciation. This view was based especially on the double representation of the letters *b, g, d, k, p, t* and the ending of the second person masculine singular pronoun as ךָ- (-^{e}*ka*) in 𝔐 as against ךְ- (*-ak*) represented in the various transliterations (see examples in Table 8), in the *piyyuṭim*, "liturgical hymns," and the early prayers.

However, it has become clear that Kahle's position is questionable and needs to be revised. It now seems that some of the Tiberian

---

28 See the survey by L.L. Grabbe, *Comparative Philology and the Text of Job—A Study in Methodology* (SBLDS 34; Missoula, MT 1977) 179-197 ("Survey of Literature on the Authenticity of Masoretic Vocalization").

29 Collected by Sperber, *Grammar*, 105-229. The Latin words are taken from the commentaries of Jerome, whereas the Greek words (except for the last example) are taken from the second column of the Hexapla.

30 Kahle, *Cairo Geniza*, 171-179 ("The Final Vowels in the Masoretic Text"). Contra Kahle see: E.Y. Kutscher, *A History of the Hebrew Language* (Jerusalem/Leiden 1982) 32-35 and the bibliography there.

vocalizations are not artificial, but rather dialectical or late. In the case of the second person masculine singular pronouns the Tiberian tradition probably superimposed alternative forms on the earlier writing tradition. Indeed, there is sufficient ancient evidence (see especially many Qumran texts [below, pp. 108–109]) in favor of *-ᵉka* as an ending for the pronominal suffix of the second person masculine singular. See the full orthography כה– [*-kah*] in words such as in חסדכה, עבדכה, *ḥsdkh*, *ʿbdkh*, in 11QPs[a], col. X, ll. 2, 3 (see plate 8*). The longer and shorter forms probably coexisted in early times (for a full analysis, see Barr, *Variable Spellings*, 114-127, and Cross, "Some Notes") and the long forms were superimposed on the shorter ones (note the anomalous *qameṣ* under the final *kaph*). While external evidence from antiquity strengthens the Masoretic pronunciation against other traditions, the Tiberian vocalization also reflects traditions different from those known from early sources. For example, the Tiberian forms אַתֶּם, *ʾattem*, and אַתֵּן/אַתֶּן, *ʾatten/ʾattēn*, were pronounced as *attima* and *attina* in the Samaritan tradition, although written as אתם and אתן,[31] and they were even written as אתמה, *ʾtmh*, and אתנה, *ʾtnh*, in many of the Qumran texts (see p. 109). Furthermore, it seems that the Tiberian tradition reflects in many details a Tiberian pronunciation of the eighth and ninth centuries, while the above-mentioned Samaritan tradition, as well as the transliterations in 𝔊, the second column of the Hexapla, and the writings of Jerome sometimes reflect earlier or dialectical forms. For example, in Table 8, αβδ, *abd*, represented in 𝔐 as עֶבֶד, *ʿebed*, is transliterated without an auxiliary vowel; ρεγλαι, *reglai*, represented in 𝔐 as רַגְלַי, *raglay*, is recorded in this transliteration with an *e* (as in the Babylonian vocalization); and *mabsar*, represented in 𝔐 as מִבְצָר, *mibṣār*, is recorded in the transliteration with an *a* sound as in the Babylonian vocalization. In all these details the Tiberian vocalization reflects forms which are late or dialectical, but not artificial.

3. *Para-Textual Elements*

L. Blau, *Masoretische Untersuchungen* (Strassburg 1891); J. Fraenkel, *Drky hʾgdh whmdrš*, I (Tel Aviv 1991) 45-65 (Heb.); Ginsburg, *Introduction*; M.M. Kasher, *The Script of the Torah and Its Characters, II: Irregular Letters in the Torah* (Torah Shelemah 29; Heb.; Jerusalem 1978); Y.Z. Moshkowitz and H. Ḥamiel, *Introduction to the Study of the Bible*, I (Heb.; Ramat Gan 1987).

Having decided to insert no further changes into 𝔐, the *soferim* actually perpetuated that text in all its details, including its special

---

31 R. Macuch, *Grammatik des samaritanischen Hebräisch* (Berlin 1969) 240; S. Morag, "On the Historical Validity of the Vocalization of the Hebrew Bible," *JAOS* 94 (1974) 307–315.

characteristics, its inconsistent orthography (see pp. 223–229), and even its errors. Their insistence upon retaining the exact form of 𝔐 included attention to the smallest details such as various para-textual elements which are exponents of scribal activity.

These para-textual elements, such as the division of the text into sections, are not unique to 𝔐. We now know that they belong to the textual transmission of the biblical text as a whole. Thanks to the precision of those who fostered 𝔐, the para-textual elements have been preserved in this text, but with the exception of the *Ketib–Qere*, all of them are known from other sources, especially from the Qumran texts, both biblical and nonbiblical, as well as from Hellenistic Greek texts.

The para-textual elements discussed below refer to textual division (*a,b*) and to various details within the text (*c,d,e,f*) and around it (*g,h,i,j*).

a. The Division of the Text into Sections (Parashiyyot *or* Pisqa'ot), *Verses, and Chapters*

L. Blau, "Massoretic Studies, III.–IV.: The Division into Verses," *JQR* 9 (1897) 122-144, 471-490; J. Conrad, "Die Entstehung und Motivierung alttestamentlicher Paraschen im Licht der Qumranfunde," in: *Bibel und Qumran* (Berlin 1968) 47-56; Ginsburg, *Introduction*, 9-108, 977-982; F. Langlamet, "'Le Seigneur dit à Moïse . . . '—Une clé de lecture des divisions massorétiques," *Mélanges bibliques et orientaux en l'honneur de M. Mathias Delcor* (AOAT 215; 1985) 255-274; Y. Maori, "The Tradition of Pisqa'ōt in Ancient Hebrew MSS—The Isaiah Texts and Commentaries from Qumran," *Textus* 10 (1982) א-נ; Martin, *Scribal Character*, vol. I, 122, 5*-6*; G.F. Moore, "The Vulgate Chapters and Numbered Verses in the Hebrew Bible," *JBL* 12 (1893) 73-78; Oesch, *Petucha*; Ch. Perrot, "Petuhot et setumot. Etude sur les alinéas du Pentateuque," *RB* 76 (1969) 50-91; idem, "The Reading of the Bible in the Ancient Synagogue," in: Mulder, *Mikra*, 137-159; Sperber, *Grammar*, 511-514.

Before the text of the Masoretic tradition was divided into verses, and in the Middle Ages also into chapters (cf. p. 52), the division of the text into textual units was indicated by different types of paragraphing, named *parashiyyot* or *pisqa'ot*. The division of the text into units in 𝔐, which is described here, is more or less in agreement with the tradition of the proto-Masoretic texts found in Qumran (see below).

A unit in 𝔐 beginning a new topic (a main subdivision) started on a new line. Thus, the last line had to be left blank after the last word of the preceding unit. For this practice the Masoretes used the term פרשה פתוחה, *parašah p^etuḥah*, "open section (or: paragraph)"—see plate 11* for an example.

The main textual unit could itself be subdivided into smaller units separated by a space–amounting to nine letters according to the later tradition–within the line. For the spacing in the middle of the line the

Masoretes used the term פרשה סתומה, *paraš̌ah s^{e}tumah*, "closed section (or: paragraph)"—see plate 14* for examples.

This scribal custom, practiced by the scribes of the medieval texts of 𝔐, continues earlier habits, known in antiquity from various sources, both Hebrew and non-Hebrew: biblical texts in Hebrew, written in the Hebrew and Assyrian ("square") script (see plates 2*-8*), and in Greek (see plate 21*) from various places in the Judean Desert, Hebrew non-biblical texts from Qumran as well as Greek and Aramaic documents from the Hellenistic period. In the late-medieval Masoretic manuscripts the sections were indicated according to the terminology of the Masoretes by the letters פ(תוחה) or ס(תומה) written in the spaces themselves.

The subdivision itself into open and closed sections reflects exegesis on the extent of the content units; in the Torah the paragraph system often coincides with the beginning of divine speech (thus Langlamet*), but this is merely one aspect of a developed system which reflects content exegesis in other details as well. It is possible that the subjectivity of this exegesis created the extant differences between the various sources. What in one Masoretic manuscript is indicated as an open section may appear in another as a closed section, while the indication of a section may be altogether absent from yet a third source. Nevertheless, a certain uniformity is visible in the witnesses of 𝔐. In the modern editions the division into sections in the Torah usually reflects the system outlined by Maimonides, *Mishneh Torah, II, Hilkhot Sefer Torah*, 8 (see n. 27 and Ginsburg*, 977-982).

Although the medieval manuscripts continue the tradition of the proto-Masoretic texts from Qumran in general, they often differ with regard to the indication of individual section breaks. The studies by Oesch* and Maori* concerning 1QIsa^a show that in 80 percent of the cases that scroll agrees with the medieval manuscripts of 𝔐 (MSS A,C). This also applies, though to a lesser extent, to the Minor Prophets Scroll from Wadi Murabbaʿat, MurXII. 4QJer^a and 4QJer^c, otherwise very close to the medieval text of 𝔐, contain more section divisions than the medieval texts (cf. Table 7 on p. 231). See further pp. 210–211. It is, however, difficult to evaluate the relation of the medieval manuscripts of 𝔐 to the proto-Masoretic and other texts in this regard: An agreement between any two sources in the use of an open or closed section does not necessarily imply dependence, since sometimes the context simply requires such a section break.

The Masoretes also indicated a division into *verses*, since every unit ending with a *silluq* accent (see p. 69), by definition, forms a verse. Note, however, that there are differences between parallel passages within 𝔐 (see Sperber*), since sometimes one-and-a-half verses in one book form one verse in another one. For example, Gen 25:14-15a form only one verse in 1 Chr 1:30 and Ps 96:8-9a likewise form only one verse in 1 Chr 16:29. The concept of a verse, *pasuq*, as a subdivision of a section is known from the Talmud (*m. Meg.* 4.4 "He that reads in the Torah may not read less than three verses"; see further *b. Meg.* 3a; *b. Ned.* 37b; *Gen. Rab.* 36.8), and according to Blau* the rabbis were used to a fixed division of the biblical text into verses. A similar division into verses was indicated in other sources, for which see p. 211. As a result, the lists of the Masoretes (see p. 74) include notes on the number of verses in the book, on the middle of the book according to the number of verses, etc.

The *numbering* of the verses and the division of the books into chapters does not stem from a Jewish source, but from the manuscript tradition of 𝔙.

The division into *chapters* was established in the thirteenth century by Archbishop Stephen Langton from Canterbury, England, who also worked in Paris. The earliest manuscript containing the division of Bishop Langton is the Paris manuscript of 𝔙 from the thirteenth century. From 𝔙, this division was transferred to the manuscripts and editions of the Hebrew Bible.[32]

Since the division into chapters was prepared a very long time after the writing of the text, it reflects late exegesis, and is not always precise. For example, the second discourse of Moses, which begins towards the end of chapter 4 of Deuteronomy (4:44), would have begun more appropriately at the beginning of the next chapter (thus 𝔪). Likewise, the last verses of Deuteronomy 11 (11:31-32) actually belong to the subject matter of the next chapter. Further, the last verse of Exodus 21 (21:37) and the first ones of chapter 22 (22:1-3) actually constitute one unit (thus the division into sections) now divided into two segments by the division into chapters. This pertains also to the last verses of Deuteronomy 16 (16:21-22) together with 17:1, as well as to Gen 1:1–2:3 (thus the division into sections), Isa 9:1–10:4, and Psalms 42–43. It

32 Details are discussed by Moore*; Ginsburg, *Introduction*, 25-31; A. Landgraf, "Die Schriftzitate in der Scholastik um die Wende des 12. zum 13. Jahrhundert," *Bib* 18 (1937) 74-94; B. Smalley, *The Study of the Bible in the Middle Ages* (2d ed.; Notre Dame, IN 1964) 221-224.

should further be noted that the various editions of 𝔐 differ from each other slightly with regard to the chapter division, the verse division, and the numbering of the verses (see examples on pp. 4–5).[33]

The Torah has also been subdivided into larger units according to the tradition of reading in the synagogue: 54 (or 53) *parashot* (sections for the Sabbath readings) according to the annual Babylonian cycle and 154 or 167 sections (named *sedarim*) according to the triennial Palestinian cycle (see Perrot* in Mulder, *Mikra*). Differences in *parashot* and *sedarim* between the manuscripts have been reviewed by Ginsburg, *Introduction*, 32-65.

b. Pisqah b^{e}ʾemṣaʿ pasuq

R. Kasher, "The Relation between the *Pisqah Beʾemṣaʿ Pasuq* and the Division into Verses in the Light of the Hebrew MSS of Samuel," *Textus* 12 (Heb. with Eng. summ.; 1985) לב–נה; P. Sandler, "lḥqr hpysqʾ bʾmṣʿ hpswq," *Sefer Neiger* (Jerusalem 1959) 222-249; S. Talmon, "Pisqah Beʾemṣaʿ Pasuq and 11QPs^{a}," *Textus* 5 (1966) 11-21.

The great majority of section divisions of 𝔐 appear after the ends of what are now known as verses, but in addition, the *Mp* (see p. 73) to Gen 4:8 notes 28 instances of a *pisqah b^{e}ʾemṣaʿ pasuq*, "a section division in the *middle* of a verse." According to the *Mp* to Gen 35:22 there are 35 such instances, indicated in some or all of the manuscripts and editions by a space of the size of either an open or a closed section (see paragraph *a* above). For example,

Gen 4:8	Cain said to his brother Abel. And when they were in the field . . . (cf. p. 236; this *pisqah b^{e}ʾemṣaʿ pasuq* is not found in all manuscripts.)
Gen 35:22	While Israel stayed in that land, Reuben went and lay with Bilhah, his father's concubine; and Israel found out. Now the sons of Jacob were twelve in number.
1 Sam 16:2	Samuel replied: "How can I go? If Saul hears of it, he will kill me." The LORD answered: "Take a heifer with you, and say: 'I have come to sacrifice to the LORD.'"

The indication of a *pisqah b^{e}ʾemṣaʿ pasuq* signifies a break in content similar to the one indicated at the ends of verses as described in

33 For an extensive analysis of these issues, see P. Finfer, *Mswrt htwrh whnbyʾym* (Wilna 1906; repr. [no place] 1970) 45-83.

paragraph *a* above. That such a break is intended is also evident from the writing of the *silluq* accent, subsequently erased, in the spaces indicating a *pisqah bᵉʾemṣaʿ pasuq* in the Aleppo codex. Since in most cases the *pisqah bᵉʾemṣaʿ pasuq* refers to a real break in content, their notation probably preceded that of the *silluq* accent. This scribal practice probably reflects an exegetical tradition which is unevenly distributed in the Bible, since 65 percent of all instances of *pisqah bᵉʾemṣaʿ pasuq* in the Bible, according to the Aleppo codex, occur in one book only, viz., 1-2 Samuel.

According to Talmon* the *pisqah bᵉʾemṣaʿ pasuq* reflects a scribal-exegetical system of cross-references to content expansions based on the verse in question at some other place in Scripture. For example, according to him, the mentioned occurrence of the *pisqah bᵉʾemṣaʿ pasuq* in Gen 35:22 refers to 1 Chr 5:1, that in 2 Sam 7:4 refers to Psalm 132, and the one in 1 Sam 16:2 refers to the apocryphal Psalm 151.

c. Inverted Nunim

L. Blau, *Masoretische Untersuchungen* (Strassburg 1891) 40-45; Freedman–Mathews, *Leviticus*, 12; Ginsburg, *Introduction*, 341-345; S.Z. Leiman, "The Inverted *Nuns* at Numbers 10:35-36 and the Book of Eldad and Medad," *JBL* 93 (1974) 348-355; Lieberman, *Hellenism*, 38-43; Yeivin, *Introduction*, 46-47.

In the printed editions one finds inverted *nunim* (also named *nunim mᵉnuzarot*, "separated" or "isolated" *nunim*) before and after Num 10:35-36, as well as in Ps 107:23-28 (in codex L before vv. 21-26 and 40).[34] The sign found in the manuscripts resembles an inverted *nun*, though tradition also describes it as a *kaph*. Actually it does not represent a letter, but a misunderstood scribal sign that was also used by other scribes in antiquity. In Greek sources, especially Alexandrian, that sign is known as περιγραφή, παραγραφή, or ἀντίσιγμα, that is, the reversed letter *sigma* (see the extensive discussion by Lieberman*). Indeed, in *b. Shabb.* 115b the *nunim* are called סימניות, "signs."

The original meaning of these signs in Greek sources was that the section enclosed by the *sigma* and *antisigma* did not suit its present place in the text. In other words, these signs represented a subtle means of removing an element or section from the text. For this and other means

---

34 An additional case, not attested in the manuscripts, is mentioned in *Minḥat Shay* (see p. 75) and the *Mp* of the second Rabbinic Bible on Gen 11:32 בְּחָרָן "in Haran," with Rashi as the earliest source for this detail. It is possible that the inverted *nun* in this place showed that the verse did not occur in its correct place, for a chronological calculation reveals that the death of Terah mentioned here ought to have occurred after what is recorded in the following sections (cf. Rashi). Cf. Ginsburg, *Introduction*, 345.

of removing details from early manuscripts, see p. 215. The function of these scribal signs is discussed in the rabbinic literature on Num 10:35-36, verses which are indicated in the Masorah with inverted *nunim*:[35]

> "When the Ark was to set out . . . " There are dots above and below it <this pericope> to indicate that this was not its correct place. Rabbi says, "It is because the pericope at hand constitutes a scroll unto itself." . . . R. Simeon says, "In the written version there are dots above and below it <this pericope> to indicate that this was not its correct place." And what ought to have been written instead of this pericope? "And the people complained in the hearing of the LORD" (Num 11:1 ff.) (*Sifre* 84 [p. 80] to Num 10:35; cf. *b. Shabb.* 115a-116a).

In *Sifre* this explanation clarifies the addition of dots to our passage (not known from the manuscripts *ad loc.*) and not the writing of inverted *nunim* as in the Masorah. However, the two scribal conventions denoted a similar situation, that is, uncertainty concerning the elements thus indicated (see below *d*).

Likewise, in 11QpaleoLev^{a} the notation of a *sigma* and *antisigma* serves to indicate verses which had been written in the wrong place (Lev 20:23-24 written in the middle of 18:27). Similar notations are found in 1QM, col. III, l. 1 and 1QS, col. VII, l. 8. Examples of the use of these signs in Greek sources are mentioned by Turner.[36] Hebrew scribes employed these signs as well, but when their meaning was no longer understood, they came to be denoted by the Masoretes as inverted *nunim*. The modern parenthesis has developed from the use of the Greek *sigma* and *antisigma*, and this pair of signs likewise may indicate that the enclosed segment is not an integral part of the text.

d. The Extraordinary Points (Puncta Extraordinaria)

L. Blau, *Masoretische Untersuchungen* (Strassburg 1891) 6-40; R. Butin, *The Ten Nequdoth of the Torah* (Baltimore 1906; repr. New York 1969); Ginsburg, *Introduction*, 318-334; Lieberman, *Hellenism*, 43-46; Sperber, *Grammar*, 516-518; Yeivin, *Introduction*, 44-46.

In fifteen places 𝔐 has points (dots) above certain letters and in one place (Ps 27:13) also below them. Ten of these instances are found in the Torah, four in the Prophets, and one in the Hagiographa. The earliest list of these instances is found in *Sifre* 69 (p. 64) to Num 9:10 (the ten instances in the Torah); the full list is in the *Mm* on Num 3:39. In this list the high percentage of instances in the Torah is remarkable. The

---

35 On the deviating order of these verses in 𝔊 see p. 339 below.

36 E.G. Turner, *Greek Manuscripts of the Ancient World* (Oxford 1971), plates 15, 25.

following instances are included in the full list: Gen 16:5, 18:9, 19:33, 33:4, 37:12; Num 3:39, 9:10, 21:30, 29:15; Deut 29:28; 2 Sam 19:20; Isa 44:9; Ezek 41:20, 46:22; Ps 27:13. For example:

Gen 16:5	ובינֿיך (*wbnẏk*)
Gen 19:33	ובקוֿמה (*wbqẇmh*)
Gen 33:4	וֿיֿשֿקֿהֿוֿ (*ẇẏšq̇ḣẇ*)

In all the places in which these dots appear the scribes of the original manuscripts, which later became 𝔐, intended to *erase* the letters. This scribal habit was employed in various ancient sources, both in the Qumran fragments (see the analysis and references to plates on p. 214) and in Greek and Latin texts. Indeed, there is reason to believe that in most of the biblical verses listed above the letters or words indicated in this way were meant to be omitted by scribes, and in several instances their omission is attested in ancient sources, e.g.:

Num 3:39	ואהרן (*ẇ'ḣṙṅ*)—the word is lacking in 𝔐MSS 𝔐 𝔖
Num 21:30	אשר (*'šṙ*)—𝔐 (= 𝔊 and *b. B. Bat.* 79a) reads אש, *'š*

One of the dotted words (הֿמֿהֿ, *ḣṁḣ*, in Isa 44:9) occurs in 1QIsa[a] as a supralinear addition without dots (ועדיהמה המה). Possibly in the forerunner of 𝔐 this word was considered inappropriate, superfluous, or incorrect and was therefore omitted. However, although these dots originally denoted the erasure of letters, they were explained in the tradition as indicating doubtful letters (see the detailed discussion by Butin* and Ginsburg*, quoting rabbinic sources). At the same time, the wording in *'Abot R. Nat.* shows that the habit of canceling letters and words by means of dots was known to some rabbinic sources:

> The words "unto us and to our children" (Deut 29:28) are dotted. Why is that? . . . This is what Ezra said: If Elijah comes and says to me, "Why did you write in this fashion?" I shall say to him: "That is why I dotted these passages." And if he says to me, "You have written well," I shall remove the dots from them. (*'Abot R. Nat.* A, 34; p. 51 in Schechter's edition; cf. *y. Pesaḥ.* 9.36d).

The fact that the manuscripts of 𝔐 agree among themselves regarding such small details as the writing of dots above certain letters points to the internal unity of the 𝔐 group. Within the history of biblical research these dots are of particular importance; de Lagarde considered them so significant that he made them the basis of his assumption that all the manuscripts of 𝔐 had been copied from a single source (see p. 183).

It is not clear why scribes wanted to omit the afore-mentioned elements included in the traditional list of extraordinary points. It stands to reason that in some cases simple errors are involved. In other cases, however, certainly in the case of dots above the single letters of complete words, it is not impossible that scribes of an early source of 𝔐 omitted elements on the basis of another source in which these elements were lacking.

*e. Suspended Letters (*Litterae Suspensae*)*

C. McCarthy, *The Tiqqune Sopherim and Other Theological Corrections in the Masoretic Text of the OT* (OBO 36; Freiburg/Göttingen 1981) 225-229.

In four words in 𝔐 a letter has been added as a "hanging," superscribed, suspended, letter with the intention of correcting the earlier text with the added letter. In Judg 18:30 מנשה (*M^{e}našeh*, Manasseh), a suspended *nun* corrected an original משה (*Mošeh*, Moses) to מְנַשֶּׁה—as indicated by the vocalization of 𝔐.[37] This addition was apparently meant to correct an earlier reading which ascribed the erecting of the idol in Dan to one of the descendants of Moses (see *b. B. Bat.* 109b). The addition can therefore be understood as a deliberate change of content (cf. pp. 262–275).

In three other verses guttural letters that were possibly wrongly omitted by the original scribes (see p. 215) have been added in the same way: Ps 80:14 מיער; Job 38:13 רשעים; ibid., v. 15 מרשעים). In many Qumran texts laryngeals and pharyngeals were also added supralinearly as corrections (see pp. 112-113 and plates 3*-6*, 9*). A different explanation of one of the three verses can be found in *b. Qidd.* 30a where it is said that the letter *ʿayin* in Ps 80:14 מיער "marks the middle of the Psalms."

f. Special Letters

M.M. Kasher (see p. 49) 183-227; Roberts, *OTTV*, 31; S. Schnitzer, "ʾwtywt gdwlwt wzʿyrwt bmqrʾ," *Beth Mikra* 89-90 (1982) 249-266 (Heb.); Sperber, *Grammar*, 518-520; Yeivin, *Introduction*, 47-48.

Large or uppercase letters have been indicated in most manuscripts of 𝔐 and many editions in order to emphasize a certain detail. So, for example, the first letter of a book (Genesis [בראשית], Proverbs, Canticles, Chronicles) or section (סוף Qoh 12:13), the middle letter in the Torah

---

37 The two forms are also reflected in the Greek tradition: MS A of 𝔊 reads Μωυσῆ, "Moses" as against MS B which reads Μανασση, "Manasseh." Many manuscripts and editions of 𝔐 (as well as 𝔗) read "Moses" without any added letter.

(גחון Lev 11:42), and the middle verse in the Torah (והתגלח Lev 13:33) have been emphasized.[38]

B. Qidd. 66b, *Sof.* 9.1-7, and the Masorah also indicated a few imperfectly written letters, such as Num 25:12 שלום, written with a "broken *waw*," that is, a *waw* with a crack in the middle. It is not clear from which period the scribal practices described here derive. The occurrence of some of these special letters (e.g., Gen 30:42 ובהעטיף; Num 27:5 משפטן; Deut 29:27 וישלכם) is probably random, that is, the special letters may have differed coincidentally from the surrounding ones, and hence they carry no particular message. Similarly insignificant are a few lowercase letters such as the *he* in בהבראם in Gen 2:4.

At least some of the special letters go back to ancient texts and are mentioned in the Talmud. Thus in *b. Menaḥ.* 29b בהבראם ("when they <the heaven and earth> were created," Gen 2:4) is explained as two words, בה, "with the letter *he*," and בראם, "He created them"—see further pp. 252–253.

g. Ketib–Qere

J. Barr, "A New Look at Kethibh-Qere," *OTS* 21 (1981) 19-37; M. Breuer, "ʾmwnh wmdʿ bnwsḥ hmqrʾ," *Deoth* 47 (1978) 102-113; P. Cassuto, "Qeré-Ketiv et Massora Magna dans le manuscrit B 19a," *Textus* 15 (1990) 84-119; R. Gordis, *The Biblical Text in the Making—A Study of the Kethib–Qere* (Philadelphia 1937; repr. New York 1971); Y.M. Grintz, *Mbwʾy mqrʾ* (Tel Aviv 1972) 60-82; S. Levin, "The קרי as the Primary Text of the תנ"ך," *Hagut Ivrit be'Amerika* I (Heb.; Yavneh 1972) 61-86; Y.Z. Moshkowitz and H. Ḥamiel, *Introduction to the Study of the Bible*, vol. I (Heb.; Ramat Gan 1987) 72-86; H.M. Orlinsky, "The Origin of the Kethib-Qere System—A New Approach," *VTSup* 7 (1960) 184-192; Sperber, *Grammar*, 493-510; J. Simonis, *Analysis et explicatio lectionum masorethicarum, Kethiban et Krijan vulgo dictarum, Ea forma, qua illae in textu S. exstant, Ordine alphabetico digesta* (Amsterdam 1753); G.E. Weil, "Qere-Kethib," *IDBSup*, 716-723; Yeivin, *Introduction*, 52-62.

In a large number of instances—ranging from 848 to 1566 in the different traditions—the *Mp* notes that one should disregard the written form of the text (in the Aramaic language of the Masorah: כְּתִיב, *k^{e}tib*, "what is written") and read instead a different word or words (in Aramaic: קְרֵי, *q^{e}rê*, or קְרִי, *q^{e}ri*, "what is read"). In some modern editions (such as the editions of Koren and Adi) the *Ketib* forms are recorded without vowel points, since the vocalization, hypothetically provided by Simonis*, has not been transmitted. In most manuscripts and editions, however, the *Qere* is included in the *Mp* without vocalization, while the *Ketib*, written in the text itself, is vocalized with the vowels of the *Qere*:

---

38 Cf. *b. Qidd.* 30a: "The ancients were called *soferim* because they counted every letter in the Torah. They said that the *waw* in גחון (Lev 11:42) is the middle consonant in the Torah, דרש דרש (Lev 10:16) the middle word and והתגלח (Lev 13:33) the middle verse."

Josh 6:13	𝔐^{K}	הָולֵךְ
	𝔐^{Q}	הלוך
2 Sam 22:51	𝔐^{K}	מִגְדִּיל (the consonants equal Ps 18:51)
	𝔐^{Q}	מגדול

The notation of the *Ketib* and *Qere* in the manuscripts of 𝔐 derives from a relatively late period, but the practice was already mentioned in the rabbinic literature (the opinions of the medieval commentators are quoted in Sperber* and Moshkowitz–Ḥamiel*). For example, *b. ʿErub.* 26a notes that in 2 Kgs 20:4 "It is written 'the city,' but we read 'court'." Manuscripts and editions likewise indicate: *Ketib* **העיר**, "the city," *Qere* **חצר**, "court."[39]

The rabbinic literature also mentions *ʾal tiqrê* formulae phrased as "do not read (*ʾal tiqrê*) X, but Y," but their nature differs from that of the *Qere* system. These formulae do not necessarily reflect readings that would have been known to the rabbis. Rather, they reflect an exegetical play on words, especially on words with an addition or omission of a *mater lectionis* that would have been possible in the context.[40]

The "constant *Qere*" (*Qere perpetuum*) is not indicated explicitly with a Masoretic note, but in these cases the *Ketib* is vocalized with the vowels of the *Qere*. Thus 𝔐^{K} יהוה, *YHWH*, is vocalized as יְהוָה on the basis of its *Qere* אדני, *ʾadonay* (or, when appearing next to אדני, as יֱהוִה on the basis of אלהים, *ʾelohim*).

In early manuscripts the *Qere* was sometimes denoted by a vertical sign similar to a final *nun* or possibly *zayin* (see Yeivin*). A few of the *Qere* words have been indicated in some manuscripts of the Masorah as *yatir*, "superfluous" (usually: *yatir yod*, or *yatir waw*), i.e., when reading, the *yod* or *waw* must be disregarded. For an example, see Josh 10:24 on p. 227.

---

39 For further examples see *b. Yoma* 21b (on Hag 1:8); *b. Ned.* 37b; *Gen. Rab.* 34.8; *Sof.* 7. See also *Midrash Qere we-la Ketib* included in the collection of A. Jellinek, *Bet ha-Midrasch* 5 (Vienna 1873; repr. Jerusalem 1967) 27-30.

40 The evidence on the *ʾal tiqrê* formulae has been collected by N.H. Torczyner, "ʾl tqrʾ," *ʾEshkol, ʾnṣyqlwpdyh yśrʾlyt*, vol. II (Berlin 1932) 376-386 (Heb.). The items have been classified by A. Rosenzweig, "Die Al-tikri-Deutungen," in: M. Brann and J. Elbogen, eds., *Festschrift zu Israel Lewy's siebzigstem Geburtstag* (Breslau 1911) 204-253. By way of example, see *b. Ber.* 64a: "R. Eleazar said in the name of R. Hanina: The disciples of the wise increase peace in the world, as it says, 'And all thy children shall be taught of the LORD, and great shall be the peace of thy children.' Read not (*ʾal tiqrê*) *b**a**nayik*, "thy children," but *b**o**nayikh*, "thy builders," or "those of you who understand" (Isa 54:13). It appears that this statement, as several others, is based on a variant reading known from the supralinear addition of a *waw* in 1QIsa^{a}. See the discussion and further examples in S. Talmon, "Aspects of the Textual Transmission of the Bible in the Light of Qumran Manuscripts," *Textus* 4 (1964) 95-132 (esp. p. 126) = idem, *The World of Qumran from Within* (Jerusalem 1989) 71-116.

In some instances the *Mp* directs the reader to read a word which is not included in the text. *Qere wela᾽ ketib* indicates a word which is "read but not written." In such cases only the vocalization is included in the text.

2 Sam 8:3	𝔐K	להשיב ידו בנהר ‏ ַ ְ to restore his power at the river (P)*e*(r)*a*(t)
	𝔐Q	פרת . . . *Perat* (= 𝔊 𝔗 𝔖 𝔙 and 1 Chr 18:3)
Judg 20:13	𝔐K	ולא אבו ‏ ְ ֵ בנימין לשמע and the (s)*o*(ns) of Benjamin would not listen
	𝔐Q	בני sons (= 𝔊 𝔖 𝔙)

Further examples of *qere wela᾽ ketib* are mentioned in *b. Ned.* 37b-38a and *Sof.* 6.8. A full list of such cases can be found in *Okhlah we-Okhlah* (see p. 74), list 97.

In other instances the *Mp* instructs the reader to disregard a word included in the text. *Ketib wela᾽ qere* indicates a word which is "written but not read." In these cases the word is not vocalized.

2 Sam 13:33 כִּי אם אַמְנוֹן לְבַדּוֹ
Mp: "אם is written and not read"

The full list is found in *Sof.* 6.9 and *Okhlah we-Okhlah*, list 98.

In addition to the examples of *Ketib–Qere* given in this section, many instances are mentioned elsewhere, especially in chapter 4C. All these examples are referred to in index 3, *Ketib–Qere*. The *Ketib–Qere* instances have been subdivided into different categories in *Okhlah we-Okhlah*, in *Massoreth ha-Massoreth* (see p. 74), and also in the studies by Gordis* and Cassuto*. Opinions vary regarding the *original* meaning of the *Qere* readings. Four main views have been suggested.

a. The Qere Corrects the Ketib, As Indicated by the Masorah

According to this assumption the *Qere* words were originally added to the written text as *corrections*. Words, not previously known from other manuscripts, were thus meant to replace the existing text. Some aspects of this assumption are problematical.

(1) Exactly the same words—with identical meaning—sometimes form the *Qere* word in one verse, and the *Ketib* word in another one. For example,

Gen 39:20	𝔐K	אסורי (= 𝔐𝔖𝔪)
	𝔐Q	אסירי

Judg 16:21, 25	𝔐K	האסירים
	𝔐Q	האסורים

There are also many *Ketib-Qere* interchanges in both directions for the pairs עניים/ענוים, שבית/שבות.

(2) In addition to several instances of *Ketib* words presumably corrected by a *Qere* there are identical words which have not been corrected in other places. For example,

Gen 24:33	𝔐K	ויישם (לפניו לאכול)
	𝔐Q	ויושם (= 𝔪)
Gen 50:26		ויישם בארון במצרים (ויושם 𝔪)

(3) The *Qere* words include several forms that are less plausible than the *Ketib* with regard to either context or grammar. For example,

Gen 8:17	𝔐K	הוֹצֵא
	𝔐Q	הַיְצֵא
2 Sam 3:25	𝔐K	(את מוצאך ואת) מְבוֹאֶךָ
	𝔐Q	מוֹבָאֶךָ

(4) The consonants of the *Qere* word are almost always similar to those of the *Ketib* word, and it is unlikely that the presumed correctional activity would have been limited to similar consonants.

β. The Qere Word Was Written alongside the Ketib as a Variant

According to Orlinsky*, the *Qere* words were originally written in the margins of the manuscripts as *variants* culled from one or more other sources. As a variation on this view, Sperber* refers to the *Ketib* text of Samuel and the text of Chronicles, usually agreeing with the *Qere* words of Samuel, as two "parallel historic narratives." In favor of this view one may argue that most of the differences between *Ketib* and *Qere* pertain to small details, especially interchanges of similar letters, which are also known as variations between manuscripts (cf. pp. 243–249). For example,[41]

Josh 3:16	𝔐K	באדם	(*at* Adam)
	𝔐Q	מאדם	(*from* Adam) (= 𝔗 𝔖 𝔙)
Josh 4:18	𝔐K	בעלות	
	𝔐Q	כעלות	
Josh 15:47	𝔐K	הגבול	(the boundary)
	𝔐Q	הגדול	(the great) (= 𝔐MSS 𝔊 𝔗 𝔖 𝔙)

41 See also the examples mentioned below in this section.

2 Kgs 16:6	𝔐^{K}	וארמים	(and the Arameans) (= 𝔗^{MSS} 𝔖 𝔙^{MSS})
	𝔐^{Q}	ואד(ו)מים	(and the Edomites) (= 𝔊 𝔗 𝔙)
Prov 20:21	𝔐^{K}	מבחלת	
	𝔐^{Q}	מבהלת	

According to this explanation one need not look for a logical explanation for each of the *Qere* words, since these are mere variants which are not necessarily better in the context than the *Ketib* words.

The *Qere* readings, originally written in the margins of manuscripts as optional variants, were later taken as corrections of the body of the text. This assumption may be strengthened by evidence from ancient sources, in which certain of the *Qere* words indeed appear as readings in ancient witnesses (see Gordis*, 55-56). For example,

Lev 11:21	𝔐^{K}	לא	(not)
	𝔐^{Q}	לו	(has; literally: for him) = 𝔊 𝔗^{OJN} 𝔖 𝔙
2 Sam 23:13	𝔐^{K}	שלשים	(thirty)
	𝔐^{Q}	שלשה	(three) = 𝔐^{MSS} 𝔊 𝔗 𝔖 𝔙 and 1 Chr 11:15

For further examples, see Josh 3:16, 15:47; 2 Kgs 16:6, all mentioned above, and many of the instances on pp. 236–253.

Against the view that the *Qere* readings are variants one may claim that it is not logical that in each case there would have existed only one variant. By way of compromise it may therefore be surmised that the manuscript containing the *Ketib* readings was collated against another source, or against the majority reading of more sources, and that the details culled from these sources later became the *Qere* readings.[42]

γ. *Intermediate Positions*

Three intermediate views have been suggested. According to one of them, that of Gordis*, scribes at first wrote marginal corrections, but later this type of notation was also used for denoting optional variants, which in due course became obligatory.

---

42 This assumption may be supported by the story of the three scrolls of the Law found in the temple court (see above p. 32). When composing a new text on the basis of these three scrolls, the rabbis supposedly followed the majority reading. It is not impossible that the *Qere* reading would reflect that majority text, and the *Ketib* the minority reading. It remains, however, problematical in this description that the rabbis did not include the majority reading in the text itself. See the discussion in chapter 3C and p. 210, n. 8 .

As examples of real corrections one should regard the *Qere* words which avoid profanation such as the perpetual *Qere* of *YHWH* as *ʾadonay* (p. 59), as well as the replacement of possibly offensive words with euphemistic expressions. See *b. Meg.* 25b: "Our rabbis taught: wherever an indelicate expression is written in the Torah, we substitute a more polite one in reading. <Thus for> ישגלנה, 'he shall enjoy (?) her,' <we read> ישכבנה, 'he shall lie with her'."[43] The main examples of euphemisms are:

Deut 28:27	$\mathfrak{M}^K$	ובעפלים	(and with *hemorrhoids* [?])
	$\mathfrak{M}^Q$	ובטחרים	(and with *tumors* [?])

The same *Ketib–Qere* is found in 1 Sam 5:6,9,12; 6:4,5.

Deut 28:30	$\mathfrak{M}^K$	ישגלנה	(he shall enjoy [?] her)
	$\mathfrak{M}^Q$	ישכבנה	(he shall lie with her)

The same *Ketib–Qere* is found in Isa 13:16; Jer 3:2; Zech 14:2.

For further instances, see *Sof.* 9.8. For other euphemisms used in biblical manuscripts, see pp. 271–272.

According to another intermediate view all the *Qere* words were initially optional variants which were subsequently taken as corrections on the basis of their location in the margins of the manuscripts.

Another assumption is that all the *Qere* words were collected as corrections from an obligatory text such as an exemplary manuscript. Such a source could also have contained inferior readings, so that not all the corrections of this type were necessarily consistent or logical.

δ. The Qere *as the Reading Tradition*

According to Levin*, Breuer*, and Barr* the *Qere* tradition did not originate in written sources but rather in the reading tradition. In Barr's opinion, the fact that one never finds more than one *Qere* word in the manuscripts points to a reading tradition, which is naturally limited to one word.

Most scholars now adhere to the first intermediate view described in paragraph γ. If that view is correct, most of the *Ketib-Qere* interchanges should be understood as an ancient collection of variants. Indeed, for many categories of *Ketib-Qere* interchanges similar differences are known between ancient witnesses (cf. chapter 4C).

---

[43] See list 2 *apud* Gordis*.

h. *Sebirin*

Ginsburg, *Introduction*, 187-196; Yeivin, *Introduction*, 62-64.

Between 70 and 200 cases of *Sebirin* notes are found in the various manuscripts. For example,

Gen 49:13	וירכתו על צדון	
	and his border shall be *at* Sidon	
Sebirin	עד	

These notes resemble the *Qere* (several *Qere* words have indeed been transmitted in some sources as *Sebirin* and vice versa), but the *Sebirin* notes have no binding force.

A *Sebirin* note refers to a word or form that is difficult in the context, and indicates that one could "suggest" (*sbr*) that another word should be read in its stead, even though such an assumption would be incorrect. The Masoretic terminology is therefore: סבירין ומטעין, "it has been suggested wrongly."

As a matter of fact, the *Sebirin* note strengthens 𝔐 and serves exclusively as a *caveat* to the reader. For example,

Jer 48:45	אש יָצָא	
	fire went forth (masculine form of the verb)	
Sebirin	יצאה	(feminine form)

The implication of the *Sebirin* note is that although אש usually appears as a feminine noun (including in the parallel text Num 21:28), the masculine form of the verb is nevertheless correct.

It is possible that the origin of the *Sebirin* words, like that of many of the *Qere* words, is to be found in ancient variants, but this assumption cannot be verified. In any event, on a practical level, *Sebirin* words are approached differently from *Qere* words, since, unlike *Qere* words, *Sebirin* words are not part of the reading tradition.

i. *Corrections of the Scribes*

W.E. Barnes, "Ancient Corrections in the Text of the OT (Tikkun Sopherim)," *JTS* 1 (1899-1900) 387-414; D. Barthélemy, "Les tiqquné sopherim et la critique textuelle de l'AT," *VTSup* 9 (1963) 285-304 = *Etudes*, 91-110; R. Fuller, "Early Emendations of the Scribes—The Tiqqun Sopherim in Zechariah 2:12," in: H.W. Attridge et al., eds., *Of Scribes and Scrolls, Studies on the Hebrew Bible, Intertestamental Judaism, and Christian Origins Presented to J. Strugnell* (College Theology Society Resources in Religion 5; Lanham, MD 1990) 21–28; Geiger, *Urschrift*, 308-345; Ginsburg, *Introduction*, 347-367; Lieberman, *Hellenism*, 28-37; C. McCarthy, *The Tiqqune Sopherim and Other Theological Corrections in the Masoretic Text of the OT* (OBO 36; Freiburg/ Göttingen 1981); W. McKane, "Observations on the Tikkûnê Sôpᵉrim," in: M. Black, ed., *On Language, Culture and Religion — In Honor of Eugene A. Nida*

(The Hague 1974) 53-77; E.Z. Melamed, *Bible Commentators*, vol. I (Heb.; Jerusalem 1975) 56-61; Yeivin, *Introduction*, 49-51.

The *tiqqunê soferim*, "corrections of the scribes," recorded in the *Mm*, are words in 𝔐 referred to in the Masorah as representing early corrections by the *soferim*. The *Mm* records for these "corrected words" the specific words representing the presumed uncorrected, original text.

According to various sources, the scribes corrected the text in several places—8 (7) according to *Sifre* 84 (pp. 81–82) to Num 10:35, and 11 (9) according to *Mek. Shirata* 6 to Exod 15:7 (the various manuscripts of these compositions contain different items), and 18 according to additional sources.[44] The list in the *Mekhilta* to Exod 15:7 contains the following eleven instances (in this sequence in the edition of Horowitz): Zech 2:12; Mal 1:13; 1 Sam 3:13; Job 7:20; Hab 1:12; Jer 2:11; Ps 106:20; Num 11:15; 1 Kgs 12:16; Ezek 8:17; Num 12:12.

For these verses the rabbis use two main terms, viz., כינה הכתוב, "the verse uses a euphemism," in the early sources (*Sifre* 84 [p. 80] to Num 10:35; *Mekhilta* to Exod 15:7) and *tiqqun*, "correction," in the later lists. The two terms may reflect ancient conflicting views of the phenomenon, that is, either euphemisms or ancient textual corrections (thus Lieberman*, 31). However, since the terms are used in lists of different dates, it is more likely that the differences in terminology reflect a development in conception (thus McCarthy*). Probably the tradition originally referred to mere "euphemisms" (substitutions) and only afterwards were they taken as corrections (for a similar development see the discussion in paragraph *g* on the practice of the *Qere*).

Even though many scholars accept the tradition about the corrections made by the *soferim* as basically correct, in all probability these corrections were not carried out in reality, and the tradition actually reflects an exegetical *Spielelement* (thus McCarthy*) and "a midrashic fancy" (Barnes*, 387). However, this view which regards the corrections of the scribes as exegetical cannot be proven in detail. It is based on the assumed development of the terminology as described above which implies that the "corrections" alter exegetically earlier readings which were considered irreverent. E.g., *Exod. Rab.* 13.1:

> "Whoever touches you touches the pupil of *his* own eye, עינו" (𝔐 and other witnesses to Zech 2:12); R. Joshua son of Levi said: "This is a correction of the scribes, for it was written as עיני, *My* eye <that is, the eye of God>."

44 *Midrash Tanḥuma Bešallaḥ*, 16 to Exod 15:7, *Okhlah we-Okhlah*, list 168, C.D. Ginsburg, *The Massorah . . .* (p. 76) vol. II, 710.

The latter word is reflected in 𝔊^{MS} 𝔙^{MSS}.

In one instance the correction refers to an element which was considered irreverent towards Moses, viz., in Num 12:12:

> "([11]Aaron said to Moses . . .) [12]. . . as one dead, who emerges from the womb of *his* mother, אמו, . . . with half *his* flesh, בשרו, eaten away" (𝔐 = 𝔗^{JN} 𝔖 𝔙).

This verse was corrected, according to the Masorah, from earlier readings, אמנו, "*our* mother," . . . and בשרנו, "*our* flesh."

Another common characteristic of the corrections of the scribes is that most of them correct merely one or two letters, principalxly the pronominal suffix. If the corrections had represented changes in the text, it is hard to believe that the correctors would have limited themselves to such small details. Moreover, for some corrections it is improbable that the original text would indeed have read as the Masorah claims. For example, *Gen. Rab.* 49.7, also included in the list of the Masorah:

> "The men went on from there to Sodom, while *Abraham* remained standing before the LORD" (Gen 18:22 𝔐 and the other witnesses). R. Simon said: "This is a correction of the scribes for the *Shekhinah* was actually waiting for Abraham."

It is unlikely that the original text would have read "while *the* LORD remained standing before Abraham," as claimed by the Masorah.

Even though the practice of correcting a text out of respect for a god or gods is also known in the Hellenistic world,[45] and although corrections such as these were certainly inserted into the biblical text (see pp. 264–275), the corrections of the scribes do not necessarily prove the existence of such a practice. It should be noted, however, that a few of the alleged original, uncorrected readings mentioned by the Masorah are known as variants from other sources—see Zech 2:12 mentioned above and further

1 Sam 3:13 𝔐 כי מקללים *להם* בניו
that his sons committed sacrilege (cursed?) *at will* (?)
Mm כי מקללים *אלהים* בניו
that his sons cursed *God* (= 𝔊 θεόν)

---

45 The Alexandrian grammarians sometimes marked a word or phrase in the Homeric writings as "inappropriate" (ἀπρεπές) and corrected it accordingly. These corrections include simple changes such as ἡμῖν, "to us," which was corrected to ὑμῖν, "to you." For example, according to the grammarian Zenodotus it was not befitting for Aphrodite to carry a chair for Helen and thus he deliberately altered the text of Iliad III 423-426 (see Lieberman*).

Job 7:20 𝔐 ואהיה עלי למשא
. . . and I shall be a burden for *myself*
Mm ואהיה עליך למשא (= 𝔐^MSS 𝔊 ἐπὶ σοι)
. . . and I shall be a burden for *You*

Assuming that the corrections of the scribes represent a firmly established practice in the development of the Hebrew text, scholars usually assume that a large number of additional instances in 𝔐 had been corrected by the scribes. These additional instances are not mentioned by the Masorah and textual evidence is usually lacking for them (see pp. 264–275).

j. Omission of the Scribes

b. Ned. 37b mentions five words as עיטור סופרים, *ʿiṭṭur soferim*, "omission of the scribes," in which, according to tradition, the scribes omitted a *waw* conjunctive.[46] For example,

Gen 18:5 𝔐 אחר תעברו then go on
b. Ned. ואחר תעברו *and* then go on

In this case 𝔐^MSS 𝔖 𝔊 𝔗^J reflect a *waw*.

4. Accentuation

M. Breuer, *Pyswq ṭʿmym šbmqrʾ* (Jerusalem 1957); idem, *Ṭʿmy hmqrʾ b-k"ʾ sprym wbspry ʾm"t* (Jerusalem 1982); M. Cohen, "Subsystems of Tiberian 'Extramasoretic' Accentuation and the Extent of Their Distribution in Mediaeval Biblical Manuscripts," *Leshonenu* 51 (1987) 188-206 (Heb. with Eng. summ.); M.B. Cohen, "Masoretic Accents as a Biblical Commentary," *JANESCU* 4 (1972) 2-11; idem, *The System of Accentuation in the Hebrew Bible* (Minneapolis 1969); A. Dotan, "The Relative Chronology of Hebrew Vocalization and Accentuation," *PAAJR* 48 (1981) 87-99; idem, "The Relative Chronology of the Accentuation System," *Language Studies*, 2-3 (Jerusalem 1987) 355-365 (Heb. with Eng. summ.); D.B. Freedman and M.B. Cohen, "The Massoretes as Exegetes: Selected Examples," *1972 and 1973 Proceedings IOMS* (Masoretic Studies 1; Missoula, MT 1974) 35-46; T. Jansma, "Vijf teksten in de Tora met een dubieuze constructie," *NTT* 12 (1957-1958) 161–179; S. Kogut, "The Authority of Masoretic Accents in Traditional Biblical Exegesis," in: M. Fishbane and E. Tov, eds., *"Shaʿarei Talmon"—Studies in the Bible, Qumran, and the Ancient Near East Presented to Shemaryahu Talmon* (Winona Lake, IN 1992) 153*-165* (Heb. with Eng. summ.); M. Medan, "Ṭʿmym," *EncBib* 3 (Jerusalem 1958) 394-406; G.E. Weil et al., *Concordance de la cantilation du Pentateuque et des cinq Megillot* (Editions du C.N.R.S.; [Paris] 1978); idem, *Concordance de la cantilation des Prémiers Prophètes, Josue, Juges, Samuel et Rois* (Editions du C.N.R.S.; Paris 1982); W. Wickes, *A Treatise on the Accentuation of the Three So-called Poetical Books of the OT, Psalms, Proverbs and Job* (Oxford 1881); idem, *A Treatise on the Accentuation of the Twenty-One So-called Prose Books of the OT* (Oxford 1887); Yeivin, *Introduction*, 157-296.

---

46 The scribes probably corrected the text in these places, as distinct from the *Qere* readings which were merely written in the margin (cf. Yeivin, *Introduction*, 56).

The accents, also named cantillation signs (טעמים, *ṭeʿamim*), which add an exegetical layer and musical dimension to the consonants and vowels, have three different functions:

(1) to direct the biblical reading in the synagogue with musical guidelines;

(2) to denote the stress in the word;

(3) to denote the syntactical relation between the words as either disjunctive or conjunctive.

The system of accentuation also includes three signs that are actually not accents, since they do not have a musical function: *maqqeph*, a conjunctive sign, *paseq* or *peśiq*, a sign denoting a slight pause, and *gaʿyah* (literally: "raising" of the voice), also named *metheg*, a sign indicating a secondary stress.

At the outset, the accentuation was probably intended to indicate the melodic pattern of the reading, although according to some scholars, its primary function was exegetical-syntactic. The tradition of the accents is ancient, as is apparent from *y. Meg.* 4.74d (with differences also *b. Meg.* 3a mentioning פסקי טעמים; *b. Ned.* 37b; *Gen. Rab.* 36.8):

> "They read from the book, from the law of God, translating it and giving the sense; so they understood the reading" (Neh 8:8) . . . "And giving the sense"—this refers to the accents, טעמים.

Exegetical traditions implying a syntactic understanding such as reflected in the accentuation are mentioned elsewhere in the Talmudic literature. Thus *b. Yoma* 52a-b (cf. *Gen. Rab.* 80.6; *y. ʿAbod. Zar.* 3.41c) mentions five verses in the Torah "for which doubt exists" (אין להן הכרע) concerning the type of relation between a word and the one preceding or following (cf. Jansma*). For example, in Exod 17:9 מחר, "tomorrow," can be linked with either the preceding or the following part of the verse. The verse reads as following:

. . . בחר לנו אנשים וצא הלחם בעמלק *מחר* אנכי נצב על ראש הגבעה . . .

The two different options are:

> Pick some men for us, and go out and do battle with Amalek *tomorrow*. (= 𝔐𝔖MSS ; cf. 𝔊 𝔖)

and

> *Tomorrow* I will station myself on the top of the hill . . . (𝔐 [according to the *etnaḥ* on the preceding word, בעמלק], 𝔐𝔖MS, and *Mek. Amalek* 1).

From these cases, which are in the nature of exceptions, one may infer that as a rule the rabbis (or some rabbis) did have an opinion as to how to understand the syntactical relation between words. This understanding, as reflected in the Talmudic literature either as the sole view or as one of several possibilities, is usually, though not necessarily, reflected in the system of accents as perpetuated in the later tradition.

As with the vocalization, there are three systems of accentuation: Tiberian, Palestinian, and Babylonian. In addition, in the Tiberian system the אמ"ת books (acronymic for Job, Proverbs, and Psalms) are accented with a separate system. Within the Tiberian system itself, signs pointing to the existence of different traditions can be recognized (see Cohen*). The names and forms of the accents are illustrated in plate 15*.

The accents are subdivided into two classes, disjunctive and conjunctive. The disjunctive accents are again subdivided into four groups in accordance with the duration of the pause:

"emperors" (*silluq*, *ʾetnaḥ*),
"kings" (*seḡolta*ʾ, *shalshelet*, *zakeph*, *ṭipḥa*),
"dukes," and "counts."

Some of the conjunctive accents ("servants") are: *munaḥ*, *mehuppakh* or *mahpakh*, *merkha*ʾ, *darga*ʾ, and ʾ*azla*ʾ. In the main, the disjunctive and conjunctive accents have a genuine meaning of connection or separation, although frequently the notation of the accents is a mere formality since they appear in every verse in a somewhat fixed sequence (cf. the concordances of Weil*).

Ancient exegesis is often reflected in the indication of the type of relationship between the words. For example:

Exod 24:5 𝔐 ויעלו עלת ^ ויזבחו זבחים שלמים ליהוה פרים
And they offered burnt offerings ^ and sacrificed offerings of well-being to the LORD, bulls.

A priori פרים, "bulls," could be explained as referring either to the verse as a whole, or to the preceding words זבחים שלמים ליהוה, "offerings of well-being to the LORD." The accents on עלת (ʾ*etnaḥ*) and ליהוה (*ṭipḥa*) show, however, that the Masoretes had the second explanation in mind–for both explanations, see *b. Ḥag.* 6b. Had they intended the first one, the accent on עלות would have been a *r^e^bia^ʿ^*, a disjunctive accent of a slighter pause.[47]

Isa 1:9 — 𝔐 — לולי ה׳ צבאות הותיר לנו שריד כמעט ∧ כסדם היינו לעמרה דמינו
Had not the LORD of hosts left us *some* survivors, ∧ we would have been like Sodom, and become like Gomorrah.

In this verse the Masoretes divided the sentence as indicated, but various sources prefer to have the break after שריד (that is, " . . . a remnant, ∧ we would *almost* be like Sodom"): *b. Ber.* 19a, 60a; 𝔗; Rashi and Luzzatto *ad loc.*

Exegesis of a similar type is reflected in the accentuation of Deut 12:5 (see p. 42).[48]

Several medieval commentators and more recent commentators such as Luzzatto (as in the example quoted from Isa 1:9) use the accents in their commentaries as a basis for their interpretations.[49]

The exegetical dimension of the accentuation can also be recognized through a comparison of differences between 𝔐 and several ancient sources, especially 𝔊:

Exod 1:19 — 𝔐 — כי חיות הנה ∧ בטרם תבוא אלהן המילדת וילדו (= 𝔗^{OF} 𝔖 𝔙)
For they <the Hebrew women> are lively; ∧ before the midwife comes to them they give birth.

𝔊 — τίκτουσιν γὰρ πρὶν ἢ εἰσελθεῖν πρὸς αὐτὰς τὰς μαίας ∧ καὶ ἔτικτον.
For they give birth before the midwives come to them. ∧ And they gave birth.
= כי חיות הנה בטרם תבוא אלהן המילדת ∧ וילדו

The translator's understanding of חיות ("lively" or "vigorous") coincided with the different view of the syntax of the sentence in 𝔊.

Exod 22:12 — 𝔐 — אם טרף יטרף יבאהו עֵד ∧ הטרפה לא ישלם (≈ 𝔗^{ON} 𝔖)

---

[47] See also the interpretations of Ibn Ezra and Nachmanides on the biblical text and Rashi on *b. Ḥag.* 6b. See further Kogut*, 156*.

[48] Additional examples *apud* Freedman–Cohen*.

[49] For examples, see Yeivin, *Introduction*, 218-221, as well as the detailed discussion by Kogut*.

If it was torn, he shall bring it *as evidence.* ^
He need not make restitution for the prey.

𝔊 ἄξει αὐτὸν ἐπὶ τὴν θήραν καὶ οὐκ ἀποτείσει
(If it was torn,) he shall bring him <the owner> *to* the prey. ^ He need not make restitution.

= אם טרף יטרף יבאהו עַד הטרפה ^ לא ישלם
(cf. 𝔗ᴶ [doublet] 𝔙)
Mek. Nezikin 12 knows both possibilities.

The different understanding of the relation between the words in this verse is connected with the difference in vocalization (עֵד / עַד). See further L. Prijs, *Jüdische Tradition in der Septuaginta* (Leiden 1948; repr. Hildesheim 1987) 6-8.

Isa 3:11 𝔐 ... אוי לרשע רע ^ כי גמול ידיו יעשה לו (cf. 𝔗 𝔖 𝔙)
Woe unto the wicked! It shall be ill with him.
^ For what his hands have done shall be done to him.

𝔊 οὐαὶ τῷ ἀνομῷ, ^ πονηρὰ κατὰ τὰ ἔργα τῶν χειρῶν αὐτοῦ συμβήσεται αὐτῷ.

= ... אוי לרשע ^ רע כגמול ידיו יעשה לו
Woe to the transgressor! ^ Bad things shall happen to him according to the works of his hands.

Likewise, the *pesharim* from caves 1 and 4 in Qumran occasionally differ from the Masoretic tradition regarding the connection between the words. Thus, the lemmas quoting the biblical text in 1QpHab usually conform with what is now a verse in the Masoretic tradition of Habakkuk (e.g., 2:14; 3:4, 5), or a half-verse (2:12b, 13a, 13b). Sometimes, however, the quotations deviate from the Masoretic tradition. One of the lemmas comprises 3:1a,bα and the next one 3:1bβ, 2, 3. Another lemma contains 3:6 together with v. 7a. Similar differences from 𝔐 are found in 4QpPs^{a}. Differences of this type are found also in parallel verses within 𝔐 itself (cf. p. 52).

Exegesis is also reflected in *pausal* forms, that is, words whose vocalization has been altered because of their accentuation with a disjunctive accent.[50]

---

50 See E.J. Revell, "Pausal Forms in Biblical Hebrew, Their Function, Origin and Significance," *JSS* 25 (1980) 165-179.

5. The Apparatus of the Masorah

D. Barthélemy, *Critique textuelle de l'AT* (OBO 50/3; Fribourg/Göttingen 1992) lxix-xcvii; M. Breuer, *The Aleppo Codex and the Accepted Text of the Bible* (Heb. with Eng. summ.; Jerusalem 1976) 193-283; A. Dotan, "Masorah," *EncJud* 16 (Jerusalem 1971) 1401-1482; A. Rubinstein, "Singularities in the Massorah of the Leningrad Codex (B19a)," *JJS* 12 (1961) 123-131; idem, "The Problem of Errors in the Massorah Parva of Codex B19a," *Sefarad* 25 (1965) 16-26; P.H. Kelley and others, *The Masorah of Biblia Hebraica Stuttgartensia, Introduction and Annotated Glossary* (Grand Rapids, MI 1998); M. Serfaty, *De la Massorah à l'ordinateur—Les concordances de la Bible: Etude historique et philologique—Un nouveau modèle: la concordance automatique*, vols. 1–4, unpubl. diss., Paris 1987–1988; Sperber, *Grammar*, 520-553; G.E. Weil, "La Massorah," *REJ* 131 (1972) 5-104; idem, "Les décomptes de versets, mots et lettres du Pentateuque selon le manuscrit B 19a de Léningrad," *Mélanges D. Barthélemy* (OBO 38; Fribourg/Göttingen 1981) 651-703; R. Wonneberger, *Understanding BHS* (Subsidia Biblica 8; Rome 1984) 61-68; I. Yeivin, "Mswrh," *EncBib* 5 (Jerusalem 1968) 130-159; idem, *Introduction*, 33-155.

a. Content

The Masorah (or *masoret*) in the narrow and technical sense of the word[51] refers to an apparatus of instructions for the writing of the biblical text and its reading. This apparatus was prepared by generations of Masoretes and was written around the text (see plates 10*-12*, 14*). The purpose of this apparatus was to ensure that special care would be exercised in the transmission of the text.

According to tradition, the Masorah stemmed from the time of Ezra, called a סופר מהיר, "an expert scribe," in Ezra 7:6, and the time of the *soferim* in the generations after him. See *b. Qidd.* 30a: "The ancients were called *soferim* because they counted every letter in the Torah." The early origin of their activity is clear from the fact that several of the notes in the *Mm* are paralleled by notes in rabbinic literature, for example:

> All *tol^edot*, "generations," found in Scripture are defective, except two, viz., "These are the תולדות, *twldwt*, of Pereṣ" (Ruth 4:18) and the present instance (*Gen. Rab.* 12.6 on Gen 2:4).

The activity of the *soferim* was continued by the Masoretes. The identity of the men of both groups is not generally known to us.

---

51 There is no consensus concerning the vocalization of the term מסורה and its exact meaning. See W. Bacher, "A Contribution to the History of the Term 'Massorah'," *JQR* 3 (1891) 785-790; Roberts, *OTTV*, 42-43. Most scholars explain the word as מָסוֹרָה (others: מַסּוֹרָה), designating the apparatus of instructions accompanying the transmission of the biblical text from one generation to the next. On the other hand Z. Ben-Ḥayyim, "mswrh wmswrt," *Leshonenu* 21 (1957) 283-292, explains the word according to Aramaic as "counting" or "enumerating" and in his opinion it is related to the tradition that the scribes counted all the words and verses in the Bible. The vowel pattern of the word and its etymology are discussed by Hendel, *Genesis 1-11*, 103–105.

Since the purpose of the Masorah was to ensure the precise transmission of the biblical text, it focused on the aspect most problematic for scribes, that is, orthography. The Masoretes and their followers described in various treatises the rules of the biblical orthography and they wrote marginal notes—in Aramaic—on the *exceptions* to these rules. Their main attention was directed toward the question of how many times a certain orthography occurred in a given biblical book or in the Bible as a whole. For example, Elias Levita remarked in his treatise *Massoreth ha-Massoreth* (see p. 74) that words belonging to the pattern קָטוֹל, *qṭwl* = *qaṭol* (such as שָׁלוֹם, *šlwm*; קָרוֹב, *qrwb*) and the pattern קִטָּלוֹן, *qṭlwn* (such as זִכָּרוֹן, *zkrwn*) are usually written *plene*, with a *waw*.[52] Consequently, the Masorah focused on the exceptions to this rule, indicating the words belonging to these patterns which were written defectively. Thus on זִכָּרֹן, *zkrn* in Exod 28:12 (twice), 29 the Masorah notes ג̊ חס̊, that is, זִכָּרֹן occurs *three* times in the Bible in its defective, *ḥs(r)*, orthography. On Amos 9:9 the Masorah notes יִפּוֹל: ז̊ מל̊ , that is, *ypwl* occurs seven times *plene (mlʾ)*.

The apparatus of the Masorah, which guided many generations of scribes, consists of two main parts:

a. The *main* apparatus of the Masorah, written in an extended set of notes in the side margins of the text. This apparatus is named מסורה קטנה, *Masorah q^{e}ṭannah* (*Masorah parva* = *Mp*;) and contains notes on the following matters:

(1) The number of specific occurrences of spellings or vocalizations, e.g., on Deut 32:39 וַאֲחַיֶּה it notes: ל̊ וחד אני אֲחַיֶּה, that is, this particular form occurs only here in the Bible (ל̊ = לית, "not extant <elsewhere>") and recurs once without a conjunctive *waw*: אני אֲחַיֶּה (Jer 49:11).

(2) The *Qere* forms, *Sebirin,* and all para-textual elements described in section 3.

(3) Special details such as the shortest verse or the middle verse in the Torah as a whole or in a specific book (see pp. 57–58), verses that contain all the letters of the alphabet, etc.

b. The מסורה גדולה, *Masorah g^{e}dolah* (*Masorah magna* = *Mm*), written in the upper or lower margins. This apparatus is closely connected with the *Mp* as its function is to list in detail the particulars mentioned by way of allusion in the *Mp*, especially the verses referred to by that apparatus. For example, if the *Mp* states that a certain word occurs eight

---

52 *Massoreth ha-Massoreth,* p. 57 in Ginsburg's edition.

times in the Bible, the *Mm* lists the verses in detail. It does not note chapter and verse, but rather quotes a key word or phrase from the verse, or a part thereof in which the word under discussion is found. This apparatus also contains the "collative Masorah" (מסורה מצרפת, *Masorah m^e^ṣarepet*), that is, the Masorah which contains lists of certain phenomena, e.g., different types of *hapax* forms.

In addition, many manuscripts contain at the beginning and/or end of the biblical books various Masoretic lists, such as lists of "open" and "closed" sections and lists of the differences between Ben Asher and Ben Naftali. More extensive than the lists in biblical manuscripts are the lists at the ends of books in the second Rabbinic Bible (see pp. 78–79), which were culled from various sources by the editor of that edition. This collection, named מערכת, *Maʿarekhet*, became known later as *Masorah finalis*. In addition to the lists of phenomena such as mentioned above, this final Masorah of the second Rabbinic Bible counts the number of letters, words, and verses in the different books of the Bible. For example, at the end of the book of Genesis the final Masorah reads: "the total number of verses in the book is one thousand, five hundred and thirty four."

b. Masoretic Handbooks

The Masoretic apparatuses were developed far beyond the activity of the first generations of Masoretes into collections of notes written, not only alongside the text, but also in separate volumes or handbooks of detailed observations on the biblical text. These included, above all, observations about orthography.

The orthographical practices of 𝔐 were described by Elias Levita, *Massoreth ha-Massoreth* (Venice 1538); see in particular the edition of C.D. Ginsburg (London 1867; repr. New York 1968).

The most extensive Masoretic handbook is *Okhlah we-Okhlah* containing lists of various types such as the list of *hapax* words occurring once with and once without a *waw* (see the example from Deut 32:39 quoted on p. 73). The book is named after this list starting with the pair אָכְלָה (1 Sam 1:9) and וְאָכְלָה (Gen 27:19). See the edition of S. Frensdorff based on the Paris manuscript (*Das Buch Ochlah W'ochlah*, Hannover 1864; repr. Tel Aviv 1969) and the edition by F. Díaz Esteban prepared on the basis of the Halle manuscript: *Sefer Oklah we-Oklah* (Madrid 1975). *Okhlah we-Okhlah* contains 374 lists together with 24 additional items, altogether 398 lists. For a representative sample, see Table 9.

Table 9

Representative Sample of the Lists in Frensdorff's Edition of Okhlah we-Okhlah

List 117	12 cases of a *waw* lacking in the beginning of the *Ketib* word, but added in the *Qere*, e.g., 2 Kgs 4:7 𝔪^{K} בניכי, 𝔪^{Q} ובניך.
List 118	11 cases of a *waw* written in the beginning of the *Ketib* word, but omitted in the *Qere*, e.g., 2 Sam 16:10 𝔪^{K} וכי, 𝔪^{Q} כי.
List 338	10 verses in which the second word is שמה, e.g., Gen 29:3.
List 339	5 verses containing הנה and afterwards והנה, e.g., Gen 31:51.
List 341	8 verses containing והוא and afterwards הוא, e.g., Judg 3:24.
List 356	12 verses in which גם occurs three times, e.g., Gen 24:25.

Additional Masoretic works, early and late:

Diqduqqê ha-Ṭeʿamim by Aaron Ben Asher (see p. 46).

Masoret Siyag la-Torah by Meir ben Ṭodros ha-Levi Abulafia (1180-1244).

ʿEyn ha-Qoreʾ by Yequtiʾel ben Yehuda ha-Naqdan (probably from the last half of the twelfth century).

Minḥat Shay by Yedidyah Sheʾlomo from Norzi (see p. 37).

On all these see Yeivin, *Introduction*, 128-155.

The details of the *Mp* and *Mm* differ from one manuscript to the next, but even within a single manuscript the notes are not always consistent or precise (see examples in Sperber* as well as in Rubinstein*, 1961, 1965). This imprecision reveals itself in incorrect listings of the number of occurrences of words in the text and in the incongruity between the notes of the *Mp* and the biblical text itself. Examples of inconsistency include the following: one occurrence of a word may be accompanied by a note of the Masorah, while another occurrence of the same word will not be remarked upon. For example, the note on Gen 1:1 בראשית, "in the beginning," indicates that this word occurs 5 times in the Bible, of which 3 times at the beginning of verses. The five verses referred to are Gen 1:1; Jer 26:1; 27:1; 28:1; 49:34. However, the formulation of the *Mp* in codex L appears in 3 different forms in Jer 27:1, 28:1, and 49:34, while there is no remark at all in Jer 26:1 (see the facsimile edition of L by Loewinger mentioned on p. 47 and not the printed form of the Masorah in BHS).

A note may state that a specific word occurs a certain number of times in the Bible either *plene* or defectively, while the actual spelling of the word as it appears in that manuscript may not always be consistent with the note itself. This inconsistency derives from the complicated development of the Masorah. Originally, it was transmitted on the manuscript to which it belonged and for which it was composed, but at a later stage the Masorah was transmitted separately and was even copied in the margins of other manuscripts. The situation was not improved with the invention of the printing, since the notes of the *Mp* in the second Rabbinic Bible (see pp. 78–79) were collected from different manuscripts.

The Masorah continued to develop from the sixth to the tenth centuries, until it reached its present form. Like the vocalization and accents, it was transmitted in three main systems: Tiberian, Palestinian, and Babylonian. Of these, the best known is the Tiberian Masorah which together with the Tiberian system of vocalization and accentuation has been accepted in all Jewish communities.

The Aramaic terms of the Masorah are listed and explained in BH and BHS, in Frensdorff's edition of *Okhlah we-Okhlah* (see p. 74), in Yeivin, *Introduction*, 80-120, and Wonneberger*.

c. Editions of the Masorah

The Masorah of the second Rabbinic Bible (see pp. 78–79), together with various Masoretic treatises, was published with a translation and notes by C.D. Ginsburg, *The Massorah Compiled from Manuscripts, Alphabetically and Lexically Arranged*, vols. I–IV (London/Vienna 1880-1905; repr. Jerusalem 1971). An index of the same Masorah was prepared by S. Frensdorff, *Die Massora Magna* (Leipzig 1876; repr. New York 1968).

Since the Masorah of the second Rabbinic Bible, culled from different manuscripts, was imprecise, scholars often prefer to consult the Masorah of a specific manuscript, especially as contained in the following two editions:

G.E. Weil, *Massorah Gedolah manuscrit B.19a de Léningrad*, vol. I (Rome 1971).

D.S. Loewinger, *Massorah Magna of the Aleppo Codex* (Jerusalem 1977).

6. *Editions of 𝔐*

M. Cohen, "The Consonantal Character of First Biblical Printings: The *Editio Princeps* of the Entire Bible Soncino 1488," *Bar-Ilan* XVIII–XIX (Ramat Gan 1981) 47-67 (Heb. with Eng. summ.); Ginsburg, *Introduction*, 779-976; idem, *Jacob Ben Chajim Ibn Adonijah's Introduction to the Rabbinic Bible* (London 1867; repr. New York 1968); M.H. Goshen-Gottstein, *Biblia Rabbinica, A Reprint of the 1525 Venice Edition* (Heb.; Jerusalem 1972) 5-16; Habermann, *Ketav*; M.J. Mulder, "The Transmission of the Biblical Text," in: idem, *Mikra*, 87-135; H.M. Orlinsky, "Prolegomenon" to Ginsburg, *Introduction*, x-xx; J.S. Penkower, *Jacob Ben Ḥayyim and the Rise of the Biblia Rabbinica*, unpubl. diss., Hebrew University, Jerusalem 1982 (Heb. with Eng. summ.); idem, "Bomberg's First Bible Edition and the Beginning of His Printing Press," *Kiryat Sefer* 58 (1983) 586-604 (Heb.); H. Rabin, "Mqrʾ, dpwsy hmqrʾ," *EncBib* 5 (Jerusalem 1968) 368-386; B.J. Roberts, "The Hebrew Bible since 1937," *JTS* 15 (1964) 253-264.

𝔐 has been printed many times from various sources, usually without critical principles such as applied in the edition of other texts.[53] Only in recent times have editions been prepared which faithfully reflect a certain manuscript.

Since the Tiberian branch of the Ben Asher system of 𝔐 became the determinative text in Jewish tradition, it was followed in all editions. Of these editions, the second Rabbinic Bible (see below) was very influential and served almost as the "received text" of the Bible (see Goshen-Gottstein*). As a consequence, most of the subsequent editions are based on this edition. In recent times, however, several editions appeared which are based on a single manuscript. The history of the printing of the Bible is described by Ginsburg*, Rabin*, and Mulder*, 133-134. Only the major facts are mentioned here.

The first printed edition[54] of the complete biblical text appeared in 1488 in Soncino, a small town in the vicinity of Milan.

Particularly important for the advance of biblical research have been the so-called Polyglots, multilingual editions. With the development of biblical criticism, scholars have increasingly based their work on these editions because of their rich content. The Polyglot editions present in parallel columns the biblical text in Hebrew (𝔐 and 𝔐𝔰), Greek, Aramaic, Syriac, Latin, and Arabic, accompanied by Latin versions of these translations and introduced by grammars and lexicons. The first

---

53 See, for example, the introductory words (at the end of the book) in the Koren edition explaining its textual basis: " . . . on the basis of the opinions of the Masoretes, the grammarians, and the interpreters and according to what was found in the majority of the manuscripts and printed editions accepted as authoritative, *and not as a slavish copy of a specific edition or manuscript*" (italics mine).

54 Cohen* maintains that the consonantal base of the early editions reflects ancient traditions and not a mixture of manuscripts.

B. Pre-Samaritan Texts and the Samaritan Pentateuch

L.A. Mayer, *Bibliography of the Samaritans* (Supplements to AbrN 1; Leiden 1964); R. Weiss, *Studies in the Text and Language of the Bible* (Heb.; Jerusalem 1981) 283-318 ("Literature on the Samaritans").

M. Baillet, "Les divers états du Pentateuque Samaritain," *RQ* 13 (1988) 531-545; idem, "Samaritains," *DBSup,* vol. XI (Paris 1990) 773-1047; Z. Ben-Ḥayyim, "The Samaritan Vowel-System and Its Graphic Representation," *Archiv Orientalni* 22 (1954) 515-530; idem, *The Literary and Oral Tradition of Hebrew and Aramaic amongst the Samaritans,* vols.1-5 (Heb.; Jerusalem 1957–1977); I. Ben-Zvi, *The Book of the Samaritans* (Heb.; Jerusalem 1976) R.J. Coggins, *Samaritans and Jews. The Origins of Samaritanism Reconsidered* (Atlanta, GA/Oxford 1975); M. Cohen, "The Orthography of the Samaritan Pentateuch, Its Place in the History of Orthography and Its Relation with the MT Orthography," *Beth Mikra* 64 (1976) 54-70; ibid., 66 (1976) 361-391 (Heb.); A.D. Crown, "Studies in Samaritan Scribal Practices and Manuscript History: III. Columnar Writing and the Samaritan Massorah," *BJRL* 67 (1984) 349-381; idem, ed., *The Samaritans* (Tübingen 1989); idem, *The Form and Codicology of Samaritan Biblical, Historical and Liturgical Manuscripts,* in press; F. Dexinger, "Das Garizimgebot im Dekalog der Samaritaner," in: G. Braulik, ed., *Studien zum Pentateuch Walter Kornfeld zum 60 Geburtstag* (Vienna/Freiburg/Basel 1977) 111-133; E. Eshel, "4QDeut^{n}—A Text That Has Undergone Harmonistic Editing," *HUCA* 62 (1991) 117–154; Gesenius, *Pent. Sam.*; R. Macuch, *Grammatik des samaritanischen Hebräisch* (Berlin 1969); J. Margain, "Samaritain (Pentateuque)," *DBSup,* vol. XI (Paris 1990) 762-773; J.D. Purvis, *The Samaritan Pentateuch and the Origin of the Samaritan Sect* (HSM 2; Cambridge, MA 1968); J.-P. Rothschild, "Samaritan Manuscripts," in: Crown, *The Samaritans,* 771-794; Sanderson, *Exodus Scroll*; Sperber, *Grammar,* 234-297; S. Schorsch, "Die (sogenannten) anti-polytheistischen Korrekturen im samaritanischen Pentateuch," *Mitteilungen und Beiträge, Forschungsstelle Judentum, Theologische Fakultät Leipzig* 15/16 (Leipzig 1999) 4–21; A. Tal, "Samaritan Literature," in: Crown, *The Samaritans,* 413-467; S. Talmon, "Observations on the Samaritan Pentateuch Version," *Tarbiz* 22 (1951) 124-128 (Heb.); B.K. Waltke, "The Samaritan Pentateuch and the Text of the OT," in: J.B. Payne, ed., *New Perspectives on the OT* (Waco, TX 1970) 212-239; R. Weiss, *Mšwṭ bmqr'* (Jerusalem 1976) 317-337.

The Samaritan Pentateuch (𝔪) contains the text of the Torah, written in a special version of the "early" Hebrew script (see plate 16*) as preserved for centuries by the Samaritan community (see below *1*). This text contains a few ideological elements which form only a thin layer added to the text (see below *4b*). Scholars are divided in their opinion on the date of this version (below *2*), but it was probably based upon an early text, similar to those found in Qumran, which, because of the lack of a better name, is usually called pre-Samaritan (below *5*). This text was changed by the Samaritans as described in section *4b*. The pre-Samaritan texts are typologically older than 𝔪, but they have been fragmentarily preserved. Therefore, 𝔪 is discussed first. In any event, the differences between 𝔪 and the pre-Samaritan texts are minor, so that the characterization of the former essentially pertains also to the latter.

1. *Background*

⅏ is the Samaritan text of the Torah[56] written in a special version of the "early" Hebrew script as preserved by the Samaritan community in many copies. This text is consonantal only, and the reading tradition which was developed alongside the text remained at the oral stage. The Samaritans developed vowel signs, but only rarely were some of these inserted—in an inconsistent manner—into late manuscripts. Only in recent generations have the Samaritans written a few manuscripts—only for use outside their own community—with full vocalization. The reading tradition has also been recorded in scholarly transliteration by several scholars, most recently by Ben-Ḥayyim*. This reading tradition is also reflected in translations that were made from ⅏ into Aramaic and Arabic. See A. Tal, *The Samaritan Targum of the Pentateuch: A Critical Edition*, vols. I-III (Tel Aviv 1980–1983) and H. Shehadeh, *The Arabic Translation of the Samaritan Pentateuch, Prolegomena to a Critical Edition*, unpubl. diss., Hebrew University (Jerusalem 1977); idem, "The Arabic Translation of the Samaritan Pentateuch," in Crown*, 1989, 481-516; idem, *The Arabic Translation of the Samaritan Pentateuch, Volume One: Genesis-Exodus* (Jerusalem 1989). The scribal tradition of ⅏ reflects several features which are similar to those of many of the Qumran scrolls (see many of the items discussed in chapter 4B) and, at a different level, to the Masorah of the Jewish Bible. The Samaritan Masorah pertains to the *parashiyyot* (see p. 50) and their number, the fixed written form of certain sections (see Crown*, 1984, and p. 213), and also, at an earlier stage, to musical directions similar to the Masoretic accentuation.

Because ⅏ was largely based on a textual tradition that was extant in ancient Israel, the descriptive name "Samaritan" is almost irrelevant. The content and typological characteristics of this text were already found in the pre-Samaritan texts found in Qumran (below 5), that is, in the ancient nonsectarian texts upon one of which ⅏ was based. These texts are also named proto-Samaritan, but since that term is often mistakenly interpreted to mean that these early texts contained the beginnings of Samaritan features, the term pre-Samaritan is preferable.

---

[56] The Samaritans also possess a revised version of the book of Joshua which, among other things, contains several readings agreeing with 𝔊 as against 𝔐. This text was published by M. Gaster, "Das Buch Josua in hebräisch-samaritanischer Rezension, Entdeckt und zum ersten Male Herausgegeben," *ZDMG* 62 (1906) 209-279, 494-549. See also Ben-Zvi*, 292-322. The Samaritans likewise possess a historical work containing material parallel to the biblical books of Joshua, Judges, Samuel, Kings, and 2 Chronicles. In modern research this is called "Chronicle II" (see P. Stenhouse, "Samaritan Chronicles," in: Crown, *The Samaritans*, 222-223). For further details see Baillet*.

text any internal contradiction or irregularity which could be taken as harmful to the sanctity of the text. This feature, which is characteristic of 𝔪, was already found in all the pre-Samaritan texts which preceded it (below 5). The harmonizing changes described below are neither thorough nor consistent. They reflect a mere tendency. The approach behind many of the harmonizations is very formalistic, sometimes even thoughtless. Thus 𝔪 preferred to use the same name for one person, and even when mentioning the change of הושע to יהושע, 𝔪 uses that name twice (Num 13:15 ויקרא משה ליהושע בן נון יהושע, "and Moses named *Joshua* son of Nun *Joshua*"!). Moreover, in 𝔪 (against all other witnesses, including the pre-Samaritan text 4QNum^b), Hosea is already called Joshua in Exod 17:9 in all witnesses and in Num 13:8 𝔪, even before the actual change of names.

Some of the alterations reflect editorial techniques which are not usually in evidence at such a relatively late stage of the transmission of the biblical text, but are rather to be found in the stage of the literary development of the biblical books (for the distinction between the two stages, see chapter 7; see further Tigay*).

(1) Changes on the Basis of Parallel Texts, Remote or Close

Some of the harmonizations pertain to differences between parallel texts in the Torah. These mainly include additions made to one verse on the basis of another. Indeed, the Torah provides many opportunities for comparing parallel texts, especially in the narrative sections of Deuteronomy compared with its parallels in the earlier books. Apparently, some readers and scribes of the Torah were more sensitive to internal "inconsistencies" within stories and to divergencies between narratives in the books of the Torah than to differences between parallel laws, since the latter were conceived of as completely different texts. Similarly, outside the Torah, the differences between parallel sections in Joshua // Judges and in Samuel-Kings // Chronicles were not harmonized very much in the course of the textual transmission of these books. Thus, with some exceptions, textual developments such as those known for the Torah in 𝔪 and the pre-Samaritan texts are not in evidence for the other biblical books.

The changes due to harmonization in 𝔪 are numerous, especially in Moses's discourses in the first nine chapters of Deuteronomy which are often paralleled by sections in Exodus and Numbers (esp. ch. 1-3). This is probably due to the fact that Deuteronomy (*mišneh torah*, the "repetition of the Law," in Jewish tradition) is expected to "repeat" the content of the earlier books. E.g., the two versions of the story on the appointment of the judges by Moses differ from each other in 𝔐, inter alia in the description of the characteristics of the judges: in 𝔐 of Exod 18:21 (as well as in the ancient versions) they are described as אנשי חיל יראי אלהים אנשי אמת שנאי בצע, "capable men who fear God, trustworthy men who hate a bribe," but in Deut 1:13 as אנשים חכמים ונבנים וידֻעים, "men who are wise, understanding and experienced." In 4QpaleoExod^{m} and 𝔖𝔪, on the other hand, the account of Deut 1:9-18 has been repeated as an integral part of the story of Exodus being inserted after 18:24 and in v. 25. Thus the differences between the two books have been minimized, and, as a result, in the formulation of 4QpaleoExod^{m} and 𝔖𝔪, Deuteronomy "repeats" details already mentioned in Exodus. See further the addition in 4QpaleoExod^{m} and 𝔖𝔪 in Exod 32:10 from Deut 9:20 (below p. 98). Other additions which are made in 𝔖𝔪 in Numbers in accordance with Deuteronomy 1 are: an addition after Num 10:10 in accord with Deut 1:6-8; after Num 12:16 in accord with Deut 1:20-23; and after Num 13:33 in accord with Deut 1:27-33. For similar additions in 4QpaleoExod^{m}, 4QNum^{b}, 4QDeut^{n}, and 4Q364*, see section *5*.

Other harmonizing additions in Exodus in 4QpaleoExod^{m} and 𝔖𝔪 "improve" on the structure of the first chapters of this book, the story of the building of the Tabernacle, and other units.

𝔖𝔪 and the pre-Samaritan texts also include *small* harmonizing changes made on the basis of the immediate context or a nearby verse. These are exemplified in Table 10.

Table 10

Small Harmonizing Changes in 𝔖𝔪

Gen 7:2	𝔐	איש ואשתו a male (literally: *a man*) and its mate (literally: *his wife*)
	𝔖𝔪	זכר ונקבה (= 𝔊 𝔗^{OJN} 𝔖 𝔙; cf. 1:27; 6:19; 7:3, 9 𝔐 and 𝔖𝔪) male and female
Exod 8:20	𝔐	ערב כבד (= 𝔗^{N}) heavy swarms of insects
	𝔖𝔪	4QpaleoExod^{m} ערב כבד *מאד* (= 𝔗^{OJ} 𝔙 [vid.] and cf. 9:3, 18, 24 𝔐 and 𝔖𝔪) *very* heavy swarms of insects
Exod 18:26	𝔐	את הדבר *הקשה* יביאון אל משה (≈ 𝔗^{OJN} 𝔖 𝔙) the *difficult* matter they would bring to Moses
	𝔖𝔪	את הדבר *הגדול* יביאון אל משה (≈ 𝔊; cf. v. 22 𝔐 and 𝔖𝔪)

		the *major* matter they would bring to Moses
Num 27:8	𝔐	*והעברתם* את נחלתו לבתו (≈ 𝔊 𝔗^{OJN} 𝔙)
		you shall *transfer* his property to his daughter
	ɯɯ	*ונתתם* את נחלתו לבתו (= 𝔖; cf. vv. 9, 10, 11 𝔐 and ɯɯ)
		you shall *assign* his property to his daughter
Num 35:25	𝔐	והצילו העדה את *הרצח* מיד גאל הדם (≈ 𝔊 𝔗^{OJN})
		the assembly shall protect the *manslayer* from the blood-avenger
	ɯɯ	והצילו העדה את *המכה* מיד גאל הדם (= 𝔖; cf. v. 24 𝔐 ɯɯ)
		the assembly shall protect *the slayer* from the blood-avenger

(2) The Addition of a "Source" for a Quotation

Since Deuteronomy is expected to "repeat" the content of the preceding four books, the technique of inserting verses from Deuteronomy in the earlier books can also be described as the providing of a "source" for a quotation, especially in the divine speech in Deuteronomy chapters 1–3. This technique was also applied to relatively small details, in sections that are not parallel.

For example, in the story of the assembly at Sinai in Exodus 20 a section is added to ɯɯ, as well as to 4Q158 (= 4QRP^{a}) and 4QTest (see below 5) which is seemingly unrelated to this event, viz., Deut 18:18-22: "I will raise up a prophet for them from among their own people, like yourself . . . " This section was added because of the content of Deut 18:16 𝔐 ɯɯ: "This is just what you asked of the LORD your God at Horeb <i.e., Sinai>, on the day of the assembly, saying . . ." However, in the story of Sinai in 𝔐 and in the other sources there is no express mention of the pericope of the "raising of the prophet," and therefore it was deemed necessary to add it at this point to the text lying at the base of 4Q158 (= 4QRP^{a}), 4QTest (= 4Q175), and ɯɯ.

Similar phenomena are recognizable in discourse. In Exod 14:12 the Israelites murmur against Moses after he led them through the Red Sea: "Is this not the very thing we told you in Egypt, saying, 'Let us alone, and let us serve the Egyptians, for it is better for us to serve the Egyptians than to die in the wilderness'?" The exact wording of this complaint is not found earlier in the text, and therefore the source of this quotation is inserted in ɯɯ as an addition to an earlier verse (Exod 6:9). Another illustration is in Gen 31:11-13, where Jacob tells his wives of a dream that he has had. However, there is no mention of such a dream in the preceding verses. In 𝔪 and 4Q364 (= 4QRP[b]), therefore, the content of the dream is added at an earlier stage in the story, after 30:36. A similar addition is found in 𝔪 after Gen 42:16 on the basis of Gen 44:22.

(3) Commands and Their Fulfillment

It is characteristic of the style of the biblical narrative to relate commands in great detail, while their fulfillment is mentioned only briefly, with the words ". . . and he (etc.) did as . . ." Often in 𝔪 the execution of such commands is also elaborated on with a repetition of the details of the command. These additions reflect the editorial desire to stress that the command had indeed been carried out. This pertains, for example, to some of the divine commands in the first chapters of Exodus, namely, the commands telling Moses and Aaron to warn Pharaoh before each plague. In these instances the description of the execution was added in 4QpaleoExod[m] and 𝔪 according to the formulation of the command. For example, after Exod 8:19, 4Qpaleo-Exod[m] and 𝔪, following the formulation of vv. 16ff., add: "And Moses and Aaron went to Pharaoh and said to him: 'Thus says the LORD: Let My people go that they may worship Me. For if you do not let My people go, I will let loose . . .'" Similar additions are found in 4QpaleoExod[m] and/or 𝔪 after 7:18,29; 9:5,19—cf. plate 18* recording such an addition in 𝔪 after 7:29 and see p. 98 below, in 4Q158 (= 4QRP[a])— see below *5* (pp. 97-100), and in 𝔊[Luc] and 𝔖 in 1 Sam 9:3.

β. Linguistic Corrections

It appears that most of the linguistic corrections of 𝔪 were already found in its pre-Samaritan substratum, since they resemble the harmonizing changes described above, and some of them are indeed found in the pre-Samaritan text 4QpaleoExod[m].

(1) Orthographical Peculiarities

Unusual spellings are often corrected in the texts under consideration. Thus pronominal suffixes of the third person masculine singular of the type הֹ– were almost always corrected to וֹ–, as exemplified in Table 11. Likewise, the writing of הוא (= הִוא) is always corrected to היא in 4QpaleoExod[m] (e.g., 22:26, 31:13), 4QDeut[n] (5:5), and in 𝔪 (e.g., Gen 3:12,20; 7:2). A similar reading is evidenced in an early proto-Masoretic manuscript, 4QLev[c] in Lev 5:12.

Table 11
Correction of Unusual Spellings in 𝔖

Gen 9:21	𝔐	אהלה
	𝔖	אהלו; likewise: 12:8; 13:3; contrast 35:21
Gen 49:11	𝔐	עירה
	𝔖	עירו
Gen 49:11	𝔐	סותה
	𝔖	כסותו; likewise Exod 22:26 𝔐 כסותה; 𝔖 כסותו
Exod 22:4	𝔐	בעירה
	𝔖	4QpaleoExod^m, 4Q366 (= 4QRP^d) בעירו

(2) Unusual Forms

Just as the contents of the narratives are smoothed out in 𝔖 (see Table 10), unusual forms in the text are often replaced in 𝔖 with regular ones. This applies especially to archaic forms, as exemplified in Table 12. In this regard 𝔖 resembles the author of Chronicles and the scribe of 1QIsa[a].

Table 12
Replacement of Unusual Forms with Regular Ones in 𝔖

Gen 1:24	𝔐	וְחַיְתוֹ אֶרֶץ
	𝔖	וחית הארץ
Gen 10:8	𝔐	יָלַד
	𝔖	הוליד
Gen 31:39	𝔐	גְנֻבְתי יום וגְנֻבְתי לילה
	𝔖	גנובת יום וגנובת לילה
Gen 42:11	𝔐	נחנו
	𝔖	אנחנו
Gen 46:3	𝔐	אל תירא מֵרְדָה
	𝔖	אל תירא מרדת
Exod 4:9	𝔐	ישמעון
	𝔖	ישמעו
Exod 8:14	𝔐	הכנם
	𝔖	4QpaleoExod^m, 4Q365 (= 4QRP^c) הכנים
Exod 15:16	𝔐	אימתה ופחד
	𝔖	אימה ופחד

Exod 22:6	𝔐		וגֻנב מבית האיש
	⅏	4QpaleoExod[m]	ו**נ**גנב מבית האיש (thus also Gen 40:15 ⅏)
Deut 19:11	𝔐		הערים האל
	⅏	4QDeut[k2]	הערים האל**ה**
Deut 33:16	𝔐	שֹׁכְ**נִי** סנה	
	⅏	שכן סנה	

(3) Grammatical Adaptations

Many forms are adapted in ⅏ to a more formal conception of the grammar, as if with the intention of correcting incorrect forms, for example, the non-agreement of the predicate with the subject in number and gender. A similar phenomenon in 1QIsa[a] is exemplified in Table 20 on p. 111.

Table 13

Adaptation in ⅏ of Unusual Grammatical Forms and Constructions to a Formal Conception of the Grammar

	𝔐	⅏
Gen 13:6	נשא . . . הארץ	נשא**ה** . . . הארץ
Gen 30:42	והי**ה** העטפים ללבן	והי**ו** העטופים ללבן
Gen 49:15	וירא מנחה כי טוב	וירא מנוחה כי טוב**ה**
Gen 49:20	מאשר שמ**נה** לחמו	מאשר שמן לחמו
Exod 17:12	ויהי ידיו	ויהי**ו** ידיו = 4QpaleoExod[m]
Exod 18:20	הדרך ילכו בה	הדרך אשר ילכו בה = 4QpaleoExod[m]
Num 9:6	ויהי אנשים	ויהי**ו** אנשים

γ. Content Differences

Many of the readings of ⅏ differ from 𝔐 with regard to their content. These are interchanges of single consonants and different words, as exemplified in Table 14. Although several such content differences were undoubtedly inserted in the Samaritan stratum of ⅏, it appears from a comparison with the pre-Samaritan texts that most of these differences are ancient. Some of these differences may be the result of scribal errors that crept into either 𝔐 or ⅏. See also Schorsch*.

Table 14

Differences in Content between ⅏ and 𝔐 (and Other Sources)[65]

Gen 2:2	𝔐	ויכל אלהים ביום *השביעי* (= 𝔗^{OJN} 𝔙) <preferable>
		On the *seventh* day God finished . . .
	⅏	ויכל אלהים ביום *הששי* (= 𝔊 𝔖)
		On the *sixth* day God finished . . .
Gen 14:14	𝔐	וירק את חניכיו
		he *armed* (?) his followers
	⅏	וידק את חניכיו
		he *crushed* (?) his followers
Gen 47:21	𝔐	ואת העם העביר אתו לערים (= 𝔗^{OJN} ; ≈ 𝔖)
		And as for the population, he *transferred* them *to the cities* (?).
	⅏	ואת העם העביד אתו לעבדים (= 𝔊)
		And as for the population, he *enslaved* them to *servitude.*
Gen 49:7	𝔐	ארור אפם (= 𝔊 𝔗^{OJFN} 𝔖 𝔙) <preferable>
		cursed be their anger
	⅏	אדיר אפם
		mighty was their anger
Exod 15:3	𝔐	*איש* מלחמה (≈ 𝔗^{OJN} 𝔙)
		a warrior (literally: a *man* of war)
	⅏	*גבור* במלחמה (≈ 𝔖)
		a war *hero*
		cf. 𝔊 συντρίβων πολέμους, possibly reflecting *שובר* מלחמה , "someone who breaks war"
Num 24:17	𝔐	וקרקר כל בני שת
		. . . the *foundation* (?) of all the children of Seth
	⅏	וקדקד כל בני שת (≈ Jer 48:45)
		. . . the *pate* of all the children of Seth

Note also the many chronological differences between 𝔐 and ⅏ concerning the patriarchal period. Comparative tables between 𝔐, ⅏,

65 According to our definition, within the framework of the present discussion every difference which did not arise from a scribe's orthographic or linguistic inclinations is defined as a difference of *content*. Such differences are visible even in very minute details, such as between consonants.

and 𝔊 are provided by J. Skinner, *Genesis* (ICC; 2d ed.; Edinburgh 1930) 134, 167, 233—see p. 337 below.

δ. Linguistic Differences

It is difficult to know which linguistic variants in 𝔪 are pre-Samaritan and which were inserted by the Samaritans. Most variants, it seems, should be assigned to the early pre-Samaritan layer since similar differences in vocabulary and morphology are found in the pre-Samaritan texts, though not necessarily in the same details. The phonological variants of 𝔪, however, appear to be Samaritan, and are therefore discussed below in paragraph *b*. An extensive linguistic description of 𝔪 is found *apud* Ben-Ḥayyim*, Macuch*, and Sperber*.

(1) Morphology

Like the pre-Samaritan and other texts from Qumran, 𝔪 reflects morphological variants in many details, as exemplified in Table 15.

Table 15

Morphological Differences between 𝔐 and 𝔪

Gen 6:17	𝔐	לשחת
	𝔪	להשחית (cf. also 7:3; Lev 23:32)
Gen 49:4	𝔐	אל תּוֹתַר
	𝔪	אל תותיר
Gen 49:15	𝔐	לְמַס עבד
	𝔪	למוס עבד (different pattern)
Exod 8:14	𝔐	בלטיהם
	𝔪	בלהטיהם (≈ בלהטיהמה 4Q365 [= 4QPP] and 7:11 𝔐 𝔪)

(2) Vocabulary

R. Weiss, *Studies in the Text and Language of the Bible* (Heb.; Jerusalem 1981) 63-189 ("Synonymous Variants in Divergences between the Samaritan and Massoretic Texts of the Pentateuch").

Many readings in 𝔪 are synonymous with words in 𝔐, as exemplified in Table 16. See an extensive discussion by Weiss*. For similar phenomena in the other textual witnesses, see pp. 260–261.

Table 16

Synonymous Words in 𝔐 and 𝔖𝔪

Gen 24:42	𝔐	אנכי I
	𝔖𝔪	אני I (another form more frequent in the Second Temple period)
Exod 2:10	𝔐	הילד the *child*
	𝔖𝔪	הנער the *lad*
Exod 7:14	𝔐	ויאמר יהוה אל משה The LORD said to Moses
	𝔖𝔪	4QpaleoExod^{m} וידבר יהוה אל משה (similarly in other verses; see Weiss*, 77)
Lev 5:5	𝔐	והיה כי יאשם when he *is guilty*
	𝔖𝔪	והיה כי יחטא when he *sins*
Num 21:5	𝔐	למה העליתנו ממצרים Why did you *bring us up* from Egypt?
	𝔖𝔪	למה הוצאתנו ממצרים Why did you *take us out* of Egypt?

b. Samaritan Elements

α. Ideological Changes

The main ideological change in 𝔖𝔪 concerns the central place of worship. In every verse in the Hebrew Bible in which Jerusalem is alluded to as the central place of worship, the Samaritans have inserted in its stead, sometimes by way of allusion, their own center, Mount Gerizim, הרגריזים (one word in their orthography). This change is particularly evident in both versions of the Decalogue in the addition[66] of a tenth commandment (see Dexinger* [p. 80]) referring to the sanctity of Mount Gerizim. The commandment is made up entirely of verses occurring elsewhere in the Torah: Deut 11:29a, Deut 27:2b-3a, Deut 27:4a, Deut 27:5-7, Deut 11:30—in that sequence in 𝔖𝔪 (Exodus and Deuteronomy). The addition includes the reading of 𝔖𝔪 in Deut 27:4 "Mount Gerizim" instead of "Mount Ebal" in most other texts as the name of the place

---

66 The Samaritans consider the first commandment of the Jewish tradition as an introduction to the Decalogue, so that in their tradition there is room for an additional commandment.

where the Israelites were commanded to erect their altar after the crossing of the Jordan.[67]

Another change based on the Samaritan ideology pertains to the frequent Deuteronomic formulation המקום אשר יבחר יהוה, "the site which the LORD *will* choose." This reference to an anonymous site in Palestine actually envisioned Jerusalem, but its name could not be mentioned in Deuteronomy since that city had not yet been conquered at the time of Moses' discourse. From the Samaritan perspective, however, Shechem had already been chosen at the time of the patriarchs (Gen 12:6; Gen 33:18-20), so that from their point of view the future form "*will* choose" needed to be changed to a past form בחר, "*has* chosen." See, e.g., Deut 12:5, 14. Possibly also the following reading in 𝔖𝔐 reflects the same ideological change:

Exod 20:21 (24)	𝔐	In *every* place where I *will* cause my name to be mentioned I will come to you and bless you.
	𝔖𝔐	In *the* place where I *have* caused my name to be mentioned I will come to you and bless you.

Further possible ideological changes in 𝔖𝔐 are mentioned by Margain* (p. 80), 767-768.

β. Phonological Changes

Many of the phonological features of 𝔖𝔐, exemplified in Table 17, are also known from other Samaritan writings. Interchanges of gutturals in general are also found in the non-Samaritan Qumran scrolls, but interchanges of *ʿayin/ḥeth* are particularly frequent in Samaritan sources as they are in Galilean Aramaic. For a full discussion see Macuch*, 32 and Ben-Ḥayyim*, vol. 5 (Jerusalem 1977) 25-29.

Table 17

Differences in Gutturals between 𝔐 and 𝔖𝔐

Gen 2:14	𝔐	חִדֶּקֶל
	𝔖𝔐	הדקל

[67] The reading הרגריזים in 𝔖𝔐 is usually taken by scholars as tendentious, but since it is also found in the Vetus Latina (see p. 139) it should probably be taken as an ancient non-sectarian reading. See also R. Pummer, "ΑΡΓΑΡΙΖΙΝ: A Criterion for Samaritan Provenance?" *JSJ* 18 (1987) 18-25. The "Samaritan" reading, without space between the words, occurs also in a Masada fragment written in the "early" Hebrew script. See S. Talmon, "Fragments of Scrolls from Masada," *ErIsr* 20 (1989) 286-287 (Heb. with Eng. summ.). However, the Samaritan nature of that fragment is contested by H. Eshel, "The Prayer of Joseph, a Papyrus from Masada and the Samaritan Temple on ΑΡΓΑΡΙΖΙΝ," *Zion* 56 (1991) 125-136 (Heb. with Eng. summ.).

Gen 19:29	𝔐	הַהֲפֵכָה
	𝔖𝔪	האפכה
Gen 25:9	𝔐	צֹחַר
	𝔖𝔪	צהר
Gen 49:7	𝔐	ועברתם
	𝔖𝔪	וחברתם
Exod 28:26	𝔐	עֵבֶר
	𝔖𝔪	חבר
Num 24:6	𝔐	באהלים נָטַע יהוה
	𝔖𝔪	באהלים נטה יהוה
Deut 32:21	𝔐	בְּהַבְלֵיהֶם
	𝔖𝔪	באבליהם

c. Orthography

Since the pre-Samaritan sources are not consistent in their orthography, it is difficult to know whether the main features of the orthography of 𝔖𝔪 were determined in the early textual layer which preceded 𝔖𝔪, or whether these features were inserted by the Samaritans themselves. The orthography of some of the pre-Samaritan texts is more defective than that of 𝔖𝔪, while 4QpaleoExod^{m} and 4QDeut^{n} reflect a fuller orthography.

Although the orthography of 𝔖𝔪 is usually fuller than that of 𝔐 (see Table 18 and see also the discussions in Purvis*, 52-69 and Macuch*, 3-9), Cohen* showed that in certain grammatical categories 𝔐 is fuller.

Table 18

Differences in Orthography between 𝔐 and 𝔖𝔪 in Genesis 49

	𝔐 (according to BHS)	𝔖𝔪 (according to the edition of Sadaqa)
3	בכרי	בכורי
	כחי	כוחי
6	בסדם	בסודם
	תבא	תבוא
	כבדי	כבודי
	וברצנם	וברצונם
10	ומחקק	ומחוקק
	יבא	יבוא
	שִׁילֹה	שלה
11	לְבֻשׁו	לבושו
13	צידן	צידון

14	חמֹר	חמור
	מִנְחָה	מנוחה
17	שְׁפִיפֹן	שפפון
21	שְׁלֻחָה	שלוחה
	הנֹתן	הנותן

Table 18 shows that in Genesis 49 ɯɯ is written with a fuller orthography than that of 𝔐 in 14 words, and that only in שלֹה in v. 10 the situation is reversed. That word in ɯɯ, however, may reflect a different vocalization (cf. p. 2, n. 1). See further v. 17 𝔐 שְׁפִיפֹן / ɯɯ שפפון, in which 𝔐 and ɯɯ have a different *mater lectionis.*

Only rarely ɯɯ and the pre-Samaritan texts contain full spellings of the type occurring in some of the Qumran scrolls (see pp. 108-109).[68]

Gen 24:41b	𝔐	נקי
	ɯɯ	נקיא cf. v. 41a 𝔐 תנקה, ɯɯ תנקיא
Deut 10:3	𝔐	כראשנים
	ɯɯ	כראישונים = 4Q364 (= 4QRP^{b}) כראיש]ונים; idem v. 1 ɯɯ

5. *The Pre-Samaritan Texts*

Before the Qumran discoveries ɯɯ was thought to be an ancient text, whose nature could not be determined more precisely beyond its popular character. However, since the discovery in Qumran of texts which are exceedingly close to ɯɯ, this situation has changed. These texts are now called pre-Samaritan on the assumption that one of them was adapted to form the special text of the Samaritans. The use of the term *pre-Samaritan* (others: harmonistic [see below] or Palestinian) is thus based on the assumption that the connections between ɯɯ and the pre-Samaritan texts are exclusive. The so-called pre-Samaritan texts are thus no Samaritan documents,[69] as they lack the specifically Samaritan readings: the tenth commandment of ɯɯ (see above p. 94) is found neither in 4QpaleoExod^{m} (see Sanderson, *Exodus Scroll*, 13, 235 and *DJD* IX [1992] 101–102), in 4Q158 (4QRP^{a}; see p. 99), nor in 4QDeut^{n}.

---

68 See Cohen* (p. 80). Various scholars also refer to a certain similarity between the Qumran scrolls and ɯɯ with regard to specific linguistic and orthographical characteristics. See below, p. 110 and see Kutscher, *Language*, 566-567; Z. Ben-Ḥayyim, "mswrt hšwmrwnym wzyqth lmswrt hlšwn šl mgylwt ym hmlḥ wlšwn ḥz"l," *Leshonenu* 22 (1958) 223-245; M. Mansoor, "Some Linguistic Aspects of the Qumran Texts," *JSS* 3 (1958) 46-49.

69 On the other hand, M. Baillet claims that several Qumran texts actually are witness to ɯɯ itself: "Le texte samaritain de l'Exode dans les manuscrits de Qumrân," in: A. Caquot and M. Philonenko, eds., *Hommages à André Dupont-Sommer* (Paris 1971) 363-381.

The best preserved pre-Samaritan text is 4QpaleoExod^{m} of which large sections of 44 columns from Exodus 6 to 37 have been preserved (see plate 2*).[70] Significant sections of several additional texts have been found as well (see below).

The main feature characterizing these texts is the appearance of harmonizing additions within Exodus and of harmonizing additions in Exodus and Numbers taken from Deuteronomy (see above pp. 86-87), or in one case, vice versa (as a result, the group as a whole is named "harmonistic" by Eshel* [p. 80]). This feature links these texts exclusively with 𝔐. In addition, the pre-Samaritan texts usually also agree with regard to the details themselves as described in *4* above.

Most of the evidence on harmonizing readings pertains to 4QpaleoExod^{m}. For example, after Exod 32:10 in this text, as well as in 𝔐, a verse is added which is based on the parallel description in Deut 9:20:

> (או[תך] לגוי גדול) [ובאהרון התאנף יה]וה מאד להשמידו ו[י]תׄפלל משה בעד א[הרון]
>
> (. . . of [you] a great nation.) [And the LO]RD[was angry with Aaron,] so much that He was ready to destroy him; and Moses interce[de]d for A[aron]—thus also $\mathfrak{G}^{MS\ 58}$.

Likewise, in this scroll, as well as in 𝔐, an addition from Deut 1:9-18 concerning the appointing of the judges has been inserted after Exod 18:24 and in v. 25 (see p. 87).

4QpaleoExod^{m}, like 𝔐, also contains harmonizing additions mentioning the fulfillment of a command given beforehand (see p. 89). The following *additions* report the explicit fulfillment of the divine command to Moses and Aaron to warn Pharaoh before each plague.

After	7:18	(based upon 7:15-18)	(col. II, ll. 5-11)
	7:29	(based upon 7:26-29 [reconstr.])	(col. III, ll. 2-4)
	8:19	(based upon 8:16-19 [reconstr.])	(col. IV, ll. 4-9)
	9:5	(based upon 9:1-5 [reconstr.])	(col. V, ll. 1-3)
	9:19	(based upon 9:13-19)	(col. V, ll. 28-31)
	10:2	(based upon 10:3)	(col. VI, ll. 27-29)

In 4QpaleoExod^{m} col. XXX, as in 𝔐, the verses in which the construction of the altar of incense is commanded follow 26:35 rather

70 See *DJD* IX for its publication. Col. XXXVIII has been published preliminarily by P.W. Skehan, "Exodus in the Samaritan Recension from Qumran," *JBL* 74 (1955) 182-187 and cols. I-II in idem, "Qumran IV, Littérature de Qumran, A, Textes bibliques," *DBSup*, vol. IX (Paris 1979) 887. For an extensive description of the whole scroll, see Sanderson, *Exodus Scroll*, as well as idem, "The Contribution of 4QpaleoExod^{m} to Textual Criticism," *RQ* 13 (1988) 547-560.

than in chapter 30, as in 𝔐. Harmonizations in small details in this scroll are mentioned in Tables 10-16.

In 4QNum^{b},[71] as in 𝔪𝔪, similar harmonizations have been added.

After 20:13 (based upon Deut 3:24-28; 2:2-6) (col. XI, ll. 25-30)
21:12 (based upon Deut 2:9, 17-19) (col. XIII, ll. 15-17)
21:21 (based upon Deut 2:24-25) (col. XIII, ll. 27-30)
27:23 (based upon Deut 3:21-22) (col. XXI, ll. 30ff.)

4QDeut^{n} adds the text of Exod 20:11 after Deut 5:15.

These features are also shared by other sources: 4Q158 (= 4QRP^{a}), like 𝔪𝔪, interweaves sections from the parallel account in Deut 5:25-26 (28-29) into the description of the Mount Sinai theophany after Exodus 20:21; cf. 4QpaleoExod^{m} col. XXI, ll. 21-28 and 𝔪𝔪 which add Deut 5:21-24 (25-28) after Exod 20:19. 4Q158 integrates the divine command (Deut 18:18-22) to establish a prophet like Moses into this pericope (see p. 88). This text, against all other textual witnesses, adds an account of the fulfillment of the divine word of Deut 5:30. In this verse, 𝔐 and the other texts read "Return to your tents," to which 4Q158 adds: "And the people returned to their tents . . ." 4Q364 (= 4QRP^{b}) adds, like 𝔪𝔪, an account of Jacob's dream after Gen 30:36 (equaling 31:11-13 [see p. 88]) and, like 𝔪𝔪, it has an addition based on Num 20:17-18 before Deut 2:8. Finally, the sequence of the anthology of verses in 4QTest follows that of 𝔪𝔪: Deut 5:28-29, 18:18-19 (both appearing in 𝔪𝔪 [and partially also in 4Q158 = 4QRP^{a}] in Exod 20:18 as well as in Deuteronomy), Num 24:15-17, Deut 33:8-11.

All these sources comprise a group reflecting a uniform textual character with regard to their readings and their approach to the text of the Bible. The main characteristic of this group is the insertion of harmonizing additions. The pre-Samaritan texts lack the distinguishing Samaritan characteristics, that is, the ideological and phonological changes (above *4b*). But they share with 𝔪𝔪 linguistic corrections, harmonizations in minutiae, and various readings.

Even though the pre-Samaritan texts and 𝔪𝔪 share distinctive typological traits and agree with each other in many details, they also diverge from time to time. The number of harmonizations differs somewhat in the various sources: 4QpaleoExod^{m} has less than 𝔪𝔪, while 4QNum^{b} has more. In addition, individual texts of this group also display unique readings. In spite of these variations, however, the harmonizing readings common to the above-mentioned texts distinguish

71 See N. Jastram in: E. Ulrich and F.M. Cross, eds., *Qumran Cave 4.VII: Genesis to Numbers* (DJD XII; Oxford 1994) 205–267.

them to such a degree that they clearly belong to one distinct group bearing a recognizably unique character. ⅏ relates to them in the same way as the pre-Samaritan texts relate to each other, even though ⅏ is somewhat removed from them on account of the ideological corrections and phonological variants inserted at a later stage.

Little can be said with certainty on the supposed relation between the various pre-Samaritan texts. Their agreement in important and idiosyncratic features would indicate one common text which was subsequently developed in various ways in the different manuscripts. An alternative model would necessitate the assumption that there was no common pre-Samaritan text, and that various scribes independently produced copies of the biblical text reflecting certain editorial-scribal tendencies. The large degree of agreement between the various pre-Samaritan texts, however, does not support such an assumption.

It is difficult to know why the community which in due course became known as the Samaritans chose a text now called pre-Samaritan as the basis for its Holy Writings. In all probability there was no special reason for this choice, since texts such as these must have been current in ancient Israel. However, it should be noted that the proto-Masoretic text, usually associated with the temple circles, was not chosen for this purpose. It is also noteworthy that all five books of the Samaritan Pentateuch bear the same character.

C. The Biblical Texts Found in Qumran

C. Burchard, *Bibliographie zu den Handschriften vom Toten Meer* (BZAW 76, 89; Berlin 1957; 2d ed. 1959; 1965); Fitzmyer, *Dead Sea Scrolls*; F. García Martínez, "Estudios Qumránicos 1975-1985—Panorama crítico (VI)," *EstBib* 47 (1989) 225-266; B. Jongeling, *A Classified Bibliography of the Finds in the Desert of Judah, 1958-1969* (Leiden 1971); A.S. van der Woude, "Fünfzehn Jahre Qumran-forschung (1974-1988)," *TRu* 55 (1990) 274-307; 57 (1992) 1–57.

Cross, *ALQ*; Cross–Talmon, *QHBT*; P.W. Skehan, "The Biblical Scrolls from Qumran and the Text of the OT," *BA* 28 (1965) 87-100; idem, "The Scrolls and the OT Text," in: D.N. Freedman and J.C. Greenfield, eds., *New Directions in Biblical Archaeology* (New York 1971) 99-112; idem, "Qumran, Littérature de Qumran, A. Textes bibliques," *DBSup*, vol. IX (Paris 1979) 805-822; Y. Sussmann, "The History of *Halakha* and the Dead Sea Scrolls—Preliminary Observations on *Miqṣat Maʿase Ha-Torah* (4QMMT)," *Tarbiz* 59 (1989-1990) 11-76; E. Tov, ed., *The Hebrew and Greek Texts of Samuel* (Jerusalem 1980); id., "A Modern Textual Outlook Based on the Qumran Scrolls," *HUCA* 53 (1982) 11-27; id., "The Orthography and Language of the Hebrew Scrolls Found at Qumran and the Origin of These Scrolls," *Textus* 13 (1986) 31–57; id., "Hebrew Biblical Manuscripts from the Judaean Desert: Their Contribution to Textual Criticism," *JJS* 39 (1988) 5-37; idem, "Groups of Hebrew Biblical Texts Found at Qumran," in: D. Dimant and L.H. Schiffman (eds.), *A Time to Prepare the Way in the Wilderness* (Studies on the Texts of the Desert of Judah 16; Leiden 1995) 85-102; id., "The Socio-Religious Background of the Paleo-Hebrew Biblical Texts Found at Qumran," H. Cancik and others (eds.), *Geschichte – Tradition – Reflexion, Festschrift für Martin Hengel zum*

70. Geburtstag (Tübingen 1996) vol. I, 353–374; id., "Further Evidence for the Existence of a Qumran Scribal School," in: Schiffman, *DSS* (2000), 199–216; id., "Die biblischen Handschriften aus der Wüste Juda – Eine neue Synthese," in: U. Dahmen and others (eds.), *Die Textfunde vom Toten Meer und der Text der Hebräischen Bibel* (Neukirchen-Vluyn 2000) 1–34; E.C. Ulrich, "The Dead Sea Scrolls and the Biblical Text," in: Flint–VanderKam, *DSS* 1:1:79–100; id., "The Qumran Scrolls and the Biblical Text", in: Schiffman, *DSS*, 51–59; G. Vermes, *The Dead Sea Scrolls—Qumran in Perspective* (rev. ed.; London 1994).

1. Background

Some of the Qumran texts have already been discussed above in the sections dealing with the proto-Masoretic and pre-Samaritan texts (A and B above). Those sections treated important textual witnesses (𝔐, ⅏) attested not only in medieval sources but also in early texts now found in Qumran. In this section the complete evidence that has been discovered in Qumran is presented, and, for this reason, there is a certain disproportion in the description of the Hebrew witnesses. While in the preceding sections, relatively late textual traditions were presented together with their earliest representatives found in Qumran, in the present section the latter texts will be discussed again, though briefly, together with all the other evidence from Qumran. These texts provide an overview of the evidence relating to the biblical text in the Second Temple period, as seen from the Qumran finds, including texts from which 𝔐 and ⅏ developed at a later period.

The thousands of fragments found near Ḥirbet-Qumran, some 15 km south of Jericho near the Dead Sea, were deposited there, as it seems, by the group of people who dwelled there. Even though this assumption appears to be the most plausible of various options, it remains problematic (see p. 102). Any explanation of the Qumran finds will have to account for two types of data: the enormous quantity of texts found at the spot (fragments of approximately 900 biblical and nonbiblical scrolls once complete) and the wide textual variety reflected in the biblical texts (see pp. 112–117). Supposedly the original scrolls comprised a collection of texts, possibly a library, deposited by the Qumranites, but we possess no information regarding the role of these texts, or their use, if at all, in the daily life of the community over a period of more than two hundred years. The term *library* is applicable to this collection, mainly in regard to the texts found in cave 4, only if defined in the limited sense of a collection of books maintained by a certain community and if it is not assumed that all the books contained in this library received the same amount of credence, authority, and use. In this connection it is relevant to note that the individual caves contain different collections of texts, but these collections cannot be characterized in any special way.

In the caves of Qumran, which are numbered from 1 until 11 according to the order of their discovery from 1947 onwards, many thousands of fragments of leather scrolls and several hundred papyrus fragments have been found; among these are biblical scrolls and compositions in which the biblical text was quoted. Although the identification of the community is relevant to an understanding of its writings, for the present discussion of the text of the Bible it is of limited importance, since many of the biblical scrolls found in Qumran were apparently brought from other places in ancient Israel. Besides, the biblical scrolls copied in Qumran or elsewhere in ancient Israel do not show evidence of any sectarian views of Essenes or other groups (cf. n. 37 on p. 266). In any event, it appears that Qumran was inhabited by Essenes (possibly identical with the Boethusians mentioned in rabbinic literature), whose halakhic practice may have derived from that of the Sadducees, as suggested by an analysis of 4QMMT (see Sussmann*).

The number of the texts found in Qumran is extremely large (approximately 900, of which many represent multiple copies of the same composition). The covenanters were actively involved in the writing of new compositions, and possibly also in the copying of existing texts, and possibly the room in which this activity took place, the so-called scriptorium, can be identified.[72]

The biblical texts found in Qumran not only contribute to our understanding of the copying of the biblical text. They also provide extensive information on the text of the Bible and the relation between the textual witnesses. It is therefore very important to clarify the place of origin of the texts found in Qumran. Some were apparently written in Qumran, while others were brought there from outside. Tov*, 1986, 1988, 2000a suggested different criteria for distinguishing between

---

72 Many scholars believe that the room in Ḥirbet Qumran now named scriptorium (scribes' room) was indeed the room where the copying of the scrolls took place. In this room archeologists found a 5 meter long table, small tables, and two inkwells. However, several scholars have raised doubts with regard to this identification: Golb has claimed that the height of the table, 40 cm, was too low for writing and, according to him, the fact that no remnants of scrolls were found in the room also indicates that it was not used for the purposes of writing. See See N. Golb, *Who Wrote the Dead Sea Scrolls—The Search for the Secret of Qumran* (New York 1994), with references to his earlier writings. Similar doubts, though in less detail, had been voiced earlier by H.E. del Medico, *L'énigme des manuscrits de la Mer Morte* (Paris 1957); K.H. Rengstorf, *Hirbet Qumrân und die Bibliothek vom Toten Meer* (Studia Delitzschiana 5; Stuttgart 1960). The theory of Golb has been refuted in detail by F. García Martínez and A.S. van der Woude, "A 'Groningen' Hypothesis of Qumran Origins and Early History," *RQ* 14 (1990) 521-541.

these two groups referring to orthography, morphology, and scribal practice. All the special writings of the Qumran covenanters were probably written according to the same system of orthography, morphology, and scribal practice which is named here the Qumran practice or Qumran scribal school (below 5). It is assumed that all the biblical and non-biblical texts written according to this practice derived from the same scribal school, whereas the texts lacking these characteristics came from elsewhere. According to this assumption, the texts found in Qumran thus reflect the textual situation of the Bible not only in Qumran, but also elsewhere in ancient Israel.

2. *The Evidence*

Between 1947 and 1956 fragments of more than 200 biblical scrolls were found in the eleven caves of Qumran.[73] Most of the fragments are small, containing no more than one-tenth of a biblical book (for the system of notation, see n. 74). However, the complete text of a long book, viz., Isaiah in 1QIsa[a], has also been found. The script of the texts serves as the main criterion for distinguishing between the supposedly different copies even when only tiny fragments have been preserved. Therefore, one has to be cautious when making an estimate of the number of the scrolls on the basis of small fragments. If a particular scroll was written by more than one scribe, any two fragments of a biblical book written in different scripts could have belonged to that scroll.

Fragments[74] have been found of all the biblical books except Esther[75] and Nehemiah (however, Ezra–Nehemiah formed one book represented in Qumran by a fragment of Ezra), as well as of many of the so-called Apocrypha and Pseudepigrapha, of previously unknown books, and of the special writings of the Qumran covenanters (see Tov 1999 [p. xxiii]).[76] Although most of the scrolls contain only one biblical

73 See the data on pp. 104-105.

74 The sigla indicating the texts from the Judean Desert are composed of the following elements: Number of the cave (1-11 for Qumran), identification of the site (Q = Qumran, Mas = Masada, Mur = Murabbaʿat, Ḥev = Ḥever), name of the biblical book (e.g., Gen = Genesis) and number of the copy (the first copy found in the excavations is called "a", the second copy "b", etc.). Papyrus fragments are indicated "pap," and fragments written in the paleo-Hebrew script are indicated "paleo" (e.g., 4QpaleoExod[m]).

75 It seems probable that it was only by chance that fragments of this relatively small book were not preserved. For example, only a tiny fragment was preserved from the lengthy book of Chronicles (4QChr).

76 It is difficult to know whether the finds from the caves at Qumran reflect any canonical conception of the Qumranites, since there is little evidence concerning the position of these writings in the Qumran community.

book, 5 Torah scrolls contain two consecutive books (see Table 19). Likewise, the individual books of the Minor Prophets were considered as one book contained in one scroll (thus the Minor Prophets Scroll from Wadi Murabbaʿat, MurXII). At the same time, some scrolls contained mere sections of books. Thus 4QDeut^{q} probably contained only the poem in Deuteronomy 32 and some of the Psalms scrolls only contained selections of the book of Psalms (see pp. 203–205).

One should take special note of the books of which many copies were found (see Table 19). These were apparently the books that were especially popular among the Qumranites, that is, Deuteronomy, Isaiah, and Psalms, and secondarily also Genesis and Exodus. A close affinity with the first three books is also manifest in the writings of the Qumran covenanters.[77]

Table 19

The Number of Copies of the Biblical Manuscripts from Qumran as Summarized in 2000[78]

Book	Square Assyrian Script	Paleo-Hebrew Script	Notes
Genesis	16–17	3	4QGen-Exod^{a} and 4QpaleoGen-Exod^{l} include Exodus
Exodus	14	1	4QExod^{b} includes Genesis; 4QExod-Lev^{f} includes Leviticus
Leviticus	8	4	4QLev-Num^{a} includes Numbers
Numbers	5	1	see Leviticus
Deuteronomy	28	2	
Joshua	2		
Judges	3		

77 The Qumranites wrote several prose compositions in the style of Deuteronomy as well as poetical works influenced by the biblical book of Psalms. Likewise the writings of the community often quote from Isaiah, which held a unique place in their thinking. All three books are often quoted in the sectarian Qumran writings. For 1QH^{a}, see P. Wernberg-Møller, "The Contribution of the *Hodayot* to Biblical Textual Criticism," *Textus* 4 (1964) 133-175.

78 The numbers are based on E. Tov, "A Categorized List of All the 'Biblical Texts' Found in the Judaean Desert," *DSD* 8 (2001), in press; idem, 1999 (see p. xxiii).

Samuel	4	
Kings	3	
Isaiah	21	
Jeremiah	6	
Ezekiel	6	
Minor Prophets	8	
Psalms	36	
Job	3	1
Proverbs	2	
Ruth	4	
Canticles	4	
Lamentations	4	
Qoheleth	2	
Daniel	8	
Ezra-Nehemiah	1	
Chronicles	1	

The background and nature of the texts written in the paleo-Hebrew script need to be clarified further. Fragments of 12 biblical scrolls in the paleo-Hebrew script have been found at Qumran.[79] These fragments contain only texts of the Torah and Job, both of which are traditionally ascribed to Moses (cf. manuscripts and editions of 𝔖 in which Job follows the Torah). The longest preserved texts written in the paleo-Hebrew script are 11QpaleoLev^{a} (see Freedman–Mathews, *Leviticus*) and the pre-Samaritan 4Qpaleo-Exod^{m} (see p. 97).

3. *Chronological Background*

G. Bonani, M. Broshi, I. Carmi, S. Ivy, J. Strugnell, W. Wölfli, "Radiocarbon Dating of the Dead Sea Scrolls," *Atiqot* 20 (1991) 27-32; A.J.T. Jull, D.J. Donahue, M. Broshi, E. Tov, "Radiocarbon Dating of Scrolls and Linen Fragments from the Judean Desert," *Radiocarbon* 37 (1995) 11–19

The texts are dated in various ways. The radiocarbon (carbon 14) dating (see Bonani* and Jull*) examining the radioactivity of minute segments of material has determined that the fragments are approximately two

[79] 1QpaleoLev, 1QpaleoNum (?); 2QpaleoLev; 4QpaleoGen-Exod^{l}, 4QpaleoGen^{m}, 4QpaleoExod^{m}, 4QpaleoDeut^{r,s}, 4QpaleoJob^{c}; 6QpaleoGen, 6QpaleoLev; 11QpaleoLev^{a}. Note also three nonbiblical texts (4Q124–125; 11Q22). The texts from cave 4 are included in P.W. Skehan, E. Ulrich, J.E. Sanderson, *Qumran Cave 4, IV—Palaeo-Hebrew and Greek Biblical Manuscripts* (DJD IX; Oxford 1992). The paleo-Hebrew texts are copied more carefully and with less scribal intervention than the other Qumran texts; for their possible background (Sadducean?), see Tov* 1996. See further: M.D. McLean, *The Use and Development of Palaeo-Hebrew in the Hellenistic and Roman Periods*, unpubl. diss., Harvard University, Cambridge, MA 1982, 41-47 (University Microfilms).

thousand years old, and that the presumed dates of the individual texts are close to the dates previously assigned to them on the basis of their paleographical analysis. For example, with the aid of the carbon 14 test, 1QIsa[a] is now dated between 202 and 107 BCE (paleographical date: 125-100 BCE) and 11QT[a] between 97 BCE and 1 CE (paleographical date: late first century BCE to early first century CE).

The mentioned paleographical method, which has been improved in recent years, and which allows for absolute dating on the basis of a comparison of the shape and stance of the letters with external sources such as dated coins and inscriptions, has established itself as a relatively reliable method. Dates have been suggested for individual texts, and the earliest ones have been ascribed to the middle of the third century BCE.[80]

Less valuable for the dating of the individual texts than the carbon 14 test and the paleographical analysis are the archeological data. They merely point to the upper and lower limits of the period of residence in Ḥirbet-Qumran: beginning from the middle of the second century BCE, or a little later, until 68 CE.[81] However, some of the texts found in the caves are older. Apparently they were brought there from other places by the residents of Qumran.

Paleographical analysis suggests that the texts written in the paleo-Hebrew script do not belong to the earliest group of the Qumran scrolls (cf. n. 79 and R.S. Hanson *apud* Freedman–Mathews, *Leviticus*, 20-23 who suggests "a date around 100 B.C.E."—ibid., 23). Nevertheless, these scrolls reflect ancient traditions, since they were probably copied from texts which were also written in that script, rather than from scrolls written in the later Assyrian ("square") script.

Two manuscripts of Daniel, 4QDan[c,e], containing portions of the second part of the book, were probably copied between 125 and 100 BCE, not more than sixty years after the completion of the final stage of the editing of that book.

---

80 According to this analysis, the oldest biblical scrolls, starting with the most ancient one, are: 4QSam[b], 4QExod-Lev[f], 4QQoh[a], 4QXII[a], and 4QJer[a], as described in the following articles: F.M. Cross, Jr., "The Oldest Manuscripts from Qumran," *JBL* 74 (1955) 147-172; D.N. Freedman, "The Masoretic Text and the Qumran Scrolls—A Study in Orthography," *Textus* 2 (1962) 87-102; A. Yardeni, "The Palaeography of 4QJer[a]—A Comparative Study," *Textus* 15 (1990) 233-268.

81 See R. de Vaux, *Archaeology and the Dead Sea Scrolls* (London 1973); E.M. Laperrousaz, *Qumrân, L'établissement essénien des bords de la Mer Morte. Histoire et archéologie du site* (Paris 1976).

4. Publication of the Texts

All texts are published in the official publication of these finds: *DJD* = *Discoveries in the Judaean Desert (of Jordan)*, I– (Oxford 1955–) and often also, preliminarily, elsewhere. Full bibliographical details concerning the published texts are provided in Tov, 1999 (p. xxiii) and *DJD* XXXIX (in press).

The publication of a text contains photographic plates, sometimes based on infrared photographs, a transcription which also denotes doubtful letters (see examples in Table 7 on p. 231; Tables 2 and 5 on pp. 325 and 342; and plates 5* and 8a*), an external description of the text (referring to the material on which the text is written, the script, measurements of the scroll, columns, lines, and margins), sometimes a full reconstruction of the text beyond the fragments actually preserved, and critical apparatuses containing paleographical and textual notes (for an example, see Table 7 on p. 231).

5. Characterization of the Texts Written in the Qumran Practice

The fragments of the more than 200 biblical texts found in Qumran do not share any major textual, linguistic, or scribal characteristics. Since they were written in different periods and at different places, they reflect a textual variety to be described below. For this reason a comprehensive description of the character of all of the Qumran texts cannot be given. The Qumran texts are therefore subdivided into different groups which are briefly described on pp. 114–117. Two main groups of texts found at Qumran, the proto-Masoretic and pre-Samaritan texts have been described in detail on pp. 29–33 and 97–100 respectively. This section refers only to the one group of Qumran texts which ought to be described here, viz., group (1) on p. 114. The texts belonging to this group bear a unique character among the biblical texts found at Qumran. They display a scribal practice which is described here as the Qumran practice. It appears that the texts belonging to this group were copied by the Qumran covenanters themselves.

The special characteristics recognizable in the biblical scrolls written according to the Qumran practice are visible in virtually *all* the texts written and copied by the Qumran covenanters (non-biblical, especially sectarian, and biblical texts), and it seems that all these scrolls were copied by the same school of scribes who wrote in their distinctive orthography and morphology, while utilizing scribal practices different from those reflected in the other Qumran texts (see below *d* on p. 111 and see Tov*, 1986, 1988, 2000a). From the great liberties which these scribes took it is evident that they do not reflect a tradition of precise copying, but rather a popular or vulgar one (see pp. 193–195).

It must be conceded that the term *Qumran practice,* used here, is somewhat misleading, but no better term suggests itself. In many ways this was *a* Palestinian scribal system, but it would be equally, if not more, misleading, to call these texts Palestinian, since the use of such terminology would imply that there are no other Palestinian texts. The name *Qumran practice* merely indicates that as a scribal system it is known mainly from a number of Qumran scrolls, without implying that this practice was not used elsewhere in ancient Israel.

a. Orthography

Cross, "Some Notes"; Kutscher, *Language;* E. Qimron, *The Hebrew of the Dead Sea Scrolls* (HSS 29; Atlanta, GA 1986); Freedman–Mathews, *Leviticus,* 51-82; Martin, *Scribal Character.*

Many Qumran texts are characterized by a distinctive orthography which has no equal among the known documents from other places and which, for want of a better name, has been called the Qumran practice (Tov*, 1986, 2000a). This Qumran orthography is very full, but in addition, it has some special features, which occur in conjunction with a series of morphological and scribal features (see below). Cross, "Some Notes" describes the orthography of these texts as a "baroque style" and he includes the morphological features described below under the heading of orthography.

The orthography of the Qumran practice has been described in various studies, especially in the detailed description of 1QIsa[a] by Kutscher*, in an analysis of all the Qumran texts by Qimron*, and in Tov*, 1986, 2000a.

It is characterized by the addition of many *matres lectionis* whose purpose it is to facilitate the reading (cf. pp. 220–230). Below are several examples which should be viewed in conjunction with plates 3*-5* and Table 21 on pp. 112-113.

In the orthography of the Qumran practice /o/ and /u/ are almost always represented by a *waw*. The *waw* is also used to indicate the short *ḥolem* (e.g., מושה, פוה, חושך), the *qameṣ ḥatuf* (אצורכה, חוכמה, כול), and the *ḥatef qameṣ* (אוניה). Because of the inconsistency of scribes, many words appear in the same text with different spellings, e.g., זאות/זות/זואת and רוש/רואש/ראוש in 1QIsa[a]. *Yod* represents not only /i/ (usually: not short i), but also *ṣere*: אבילים (1QIsa[a] 61:2), מית (38:1). Unique for certain lexemes is the representation of /i/ in final position by -יא, especially in כיא, and sometimes also in מיא (less frequent: נקיא,

49:7; פיא, 40:5), apparently by analogy to הביא, היא *et sim.* in which the *ʾaleph* belongs to the root. *He* as a *mater lectionis* for /a/ is very frequent at the end of words, such as in *qṭlth* (e.g., שמרתה) and the pronominal suffix of the second person singular, e.g., מלככה, *mlkkh*, etc. On the other hand, if the parallel form of such words originally was *malkak*, rather than *malk^{e}kah* as in 𝔐 (see pp. 48–49), the difference between the two forms should be considered morphological rather than orthographical, on which see p. 110. *He* as a *mater lectionis* in final position for /e/ occurs in an unusual fashion also in חוטה in 1QIsa^{a} 1:4 (𝔐 חוטא) and קורה in 6:4 (𝔐 קורא). *ʾAleph* as a *mater lectionis* denotes /a/ in final position: עליהא (34:11), בניהא (66:8), and even in medial position: יאתום (1:17), יאכה (30:31).

The orthography of a complete section is exemplified in Table 21.

The scribes working within this scribal school wrote according to certain rules, but at the same time, each scribe also maintained a certain amount of independence. Sound evidence for the Qumran practice exists with regard to the following biblical texts: 1QDeut^{a}, 1QIsa^{a}, 2QExod^{a,b} (?), 2QNum^{b} (?), 2QDeut^{c}, 2QJer, 4QExod$^{b,j(?)}$, 4QNum^{b}, 4QDeut^{j,k1,k2,m}, 4QSam^{c}, 4QIsa^{c*}, 4QXII^{c,e,g}, 4QPs^{o}, 4QLam, 4QQoh^{a}, 11QLev^{b}; 4QPhyl A,B,G-I,J-K,L-N,O,P,Q. To this group also belong virtually *all* the sectarian compositions written by the Qumran covenanters (such as 1QH^{a}, 1QM, 1QS, and the *pesharim*) and the following biblical paraphrases and collections of Psalms: 4Q158, 4Q364, 4Q365 (all three containing 4QRP), 11QPs$^{a,b,c,d(?)}$. Although there is no characteristic representative of this group, 1QIsa^{a}, [82] which contains the longest Qumran text of a biblical book and whose practice is described by Kutscher*, is often referred to (incorrectly) as if it were the main text written in the Qumran practice.

b. Morphology

See the bibliography in the preceding section on p. 108 and also:

M.H. Goshen-Gottstein, *Text and Language in Bible and Qumran* (Jerusalem/Tel Aviv 1960); S. Morag, "Qumran Hebrew—Some Typological Observations," *VT* 38 (1988) 148-164.

The biblical and non-biblical texts written in the orthography of the Qumran practice also reflect distinctive morphological features whose most striking characteristics are:

---

[82] In this scroll, more than in other texts, Aramaic influence and the weakening of the gutterals is recognizable. See Kutscher, *Language*, 91-95 and 505-511 and see Table 21 on p. 113 (under "Language").

(1) Lengthened independent pronouns: ***huʾah***, ***hiʾah***, ***ʾatemah***, ***ʾatenah***, ***hemah*** and ***henah*** (the latter two forms are also found elsewhere);

(2) lengthened pronominal suffixes for the second and third persons plural, e.g., *bmh*, *bhmh*, *mlkmh*;

(3) words which serve in 𝔐 as pausal forms, such as *(w)tqṭwlw*, *(w)yqṭwlw*, occurring in these texts as free forms;

(4) lengthened future forms: *(wᵉ)ʾeqṭolah*;

(5) verbal forms with pronominal suffixes construed as *yᵉquṭlenu*;[83]

(6) the form *qᵉṭaltemah* for the second person plural;

(7) מואדה, מאודה, מודה containing an adverbial ending *-ah*;[84]

(8) the long Qumran forms of the second person singular pronominal suffix (e.g., מלככה, *mlkkh*) differing from the short ones in 𝔐 (*mlkk*) possibly reflect morphological rather than orthographical differences (cf. p. 109).

The distinctive morphological features reflected in these scrolls have been described in detail by Kutscher* and Qimron*. Some of these features may be based on analogy with other forms in the language, while others may be dialectical. Certain forms are described as archaic by Kutscher*, 52, 434-440; Qimron*, 57; and Cross*. Although the evidence known to date does not provide a good parallel to the combined morphological and orthographical features of the Qumran practice, certain of these features are also known from the Samaritan reading tradition.[85]

c. Contextual Adaptations

More than other scribes, the scribes of the texts written in the Qumran practice adapted seemingly irregular forms to the context. These changes reflect a free approach to the biblical text, as exemplified in Table 20 below (a similar phenomenon in 𝔐 is exemplified in Table 13 on p. 91).

---

83 See I. Yeivin, "The Verbal Forms יקוטלנו, יקטולנו in DSS in Comparison to the Babylonian Vocalization," in: B. Uffenheimer, ed., *Bible and Jewish History* (Tel Aviv 1971) 256-276 (Heb. with Eng. summ.).

84 Cf. P. Wernberg-Møller, "Two Biblical Hebrew Adverbs in the Dialect of the Dead Sea Scrolls," in: P.R. Davies and R.T. White, eds., *A Tribute to Geza Vermes, Essays on Jewish and Christian Literature and History* (JSOTSup 100; Sheffield 1990) 21-35.

85 See n. 68 above.

Table 20

Contextual Changes in 1QIsa[a]

Isa 1:23	𝔐	(שריך סוררים וחברי גנבים) כלו אהב שחד ורדף . . .
	1QIsa[a]	כולם אוהבי שוחד רודפי . . . (cf. 𝔊)
Isa 14:30	𝔐	(והמתי ברעב שרשך ושאריתך) יהרג (I will kill your stock by famine) and *it* shall slay (the very last of you).
	1QIsa[a]	אהרוג *I* shall slay
Isa 46:11	𝔐	(דברתי אף אביאנה) יצרתי אף אעשנה (I have spoken, so I will bring it to pass;) I have designed <it>, so I will complete it.
	1QIsa[a]	יצרתיה אף אעשנה I have designed *it*, so I will complete it.
Isa 51:19	𝔐	מי אנחמך
	1QIsa[a]	מי ינחמך (cf. 𝔊)

d. Scribal Practices

The texts written in the Qumran practice also reflect several scribal practices which set them apart from the other Qumran texts, while at the same time they are rather unique among the known textual witnesses of the Bible in the frequency of their characteristic phenomena (see p. 107 and Tov*, 2000a). These features are: (1) The occurrence of scribal marks, such as described on pp. 213–216, in large frequency, especially cancellation dots; (2) the use of initial-medial letters in final position (cf. p. 210); and (3) the writing of the divine names יהוה, אלה(ים), and אל, sometimes in conjunction with another divine appellation and together with their prefixes, in paleo-Hebrew characters in texts written in the Assyrian ("square") script (cf. pp. 216, 220). In addition, the content of the phylacteries written in the Qumran scribal system can be connected with the Qumran covenanters.

6. Variants in the Qumran Texts

There are many differences in readings between the individual Qumran texts, or, phrased differently, these texts reflect many variants vis-à-vis 𝔐. Many such variants are quoted in this book (see the index of ancient sources). The more significant deviations from 𝔐 in the Qumran texts are described in chapter 7B, sections 1, 10, 11 as well as in the next pages. Phrased again differently, the Qumran texts, as well as differing from one another, relate to 𝔐, 𝔊, ⅏, and the other texts in a ramified system of agreements and disagreements. Therefore, one should describe the relation of the Qumran texts to the combined evidence of all the other texts, although on a formal level they are often compared only with 𝔐, 𝔊, or 𝔖.

On the basis of several types of variants in the Qumran texts, different groups of Qumran texts are recognized. These groups are briefly described on pp. 114–116. The two main groups of texts found at Qumran, the proto-Masoretic and pre-Samaritan texts have been described in detail on pp. 29–33 and 97–100. The tables adduced in this section exemplify some of the more characteristic types of variants found in the Qumran texts, without exhausting the evidence. The Tables exemplify, among other things, the readings found in texts written in the Qumran practice (section *5* above), represented in Table 21 by 1QIsa[a] and elsewhere by 4QJer[c] (Table 7 on p. 231). Two of the five groups of texts listed on pp. 115–116, viz., groups *4* and *5*, are exemplified in Table 22 by 4QSam[a].

The texts exemplified in Table 21 display a much greater number of differences in orthography and morphology than in other types of differences, whereas in the texts exemplified in Table 22 the relation is reversed: differences in morphology and orthography are few, if any, in contrast with a large number of other types of differences; some of these are in minor details, others in major ones. Most of the variants listed for 4QSam[a] in Table 22 are substantial.

Table 21

Classified Differences between 𝔐 and 1QIsa[a] in Isa 1:1-8

1. *Orthography* (cf. pp. 108–109)

	𝔐	*1QIsa[a]*	
2	כי	כי**א**	
3	קֹנֵהוּ	קונ֗הו	(supralinear letter)
	לא	לוא (2x)	
4	חט**א**	חוט**ה**	
	עָוֹן	עוון	
5	כל	כול	
	ראש	רואש	
	לָחֳלִי	לחולי	
	וכל	[ו]כול	
6	ראש	רואש	
	לא	לוא	
	חֻבְּשׁוּ	חובשו	

	ולא	ולוא (2x)	
7	שרֻפות	שרופות	
	אֹכלים	אוכלים	
	אֹתה	אותה	
8	כסֻכה	כסוכה	

2. *Language, Including Phonology* (cf. pp. 109–110)

1	ישעיהו	ישעיהו	Supralinear letter; omission of *ʿayin* indicates the weakening of laryngeals and pharyngeals.
	וירושלם	וירושלים	Supralinear letter.
	בימי	ביומי	Supralinear letter; addition of *waw* is probably due to Aramaic influence.
	עוזיהו	עוזיה	Short theophoric names are more frequent in the Second Temple period.
	חזקיהו	חזקיה	Supralinear letter; see further the previous item.
2	והם	והמה	See p. 109.
7	כמהפכת	כמאפכת	Supralinear letter; the addition of *ʾaleph* is probably influenced by the parallel Aramaic root.
8	ונותרה	ונתרת	The variant probably reflects an Aramaic verbal form for the third person feminine singular.

Notes 1. The supralinear letters (cf. p. 215) concern details that were not included in the first writing.

2. The linguistic variants listed above are typical of the scrolls written in the Qumran practice, while the linguistic variants included in the next category are not.

3. *Other Differences*

2	ארץ	הארץ	
3	עמי	ועמי	
5	דַּוָּי	דוה	(different patterns)
7	וּשְׁמָמָה	ושממו עליה	(cf. Lev 26:32)
8	כמלונה	וכמלונה	

Table 22

Differences between 𝔐 and 4QSam^a in 1 Sam 1:22-28

There are no differences in language and orthography. All the differences relate to matters of content (see p. 112). Square brackets indicate reconstructions.

	𝔐	*4QSam^a*	*Notes*
22	עד	עד אשר	(cf. 𝔊)
	שם	לפני [יהוה ? שם]	(cf. 𝔊)
	עולם	adds [ונת]תׄיהו נזיר עד עולם כול ימי [חייו]	
23	את דברו	היוצׄא מפׄיך	(= 𝔊; cf. p. 176)
24	ותעלהו עמה	ותעל אותו	(cf. 𝔊; see p. 305)
	—	שילה	(= 𝔊)
	בְּפָרִים שְׁלֹשָׁה	[בפר בן] בקר משלש	(cf. 𝔊; see p. 254)
	—	ולחם	(= 𝔊)
	וְהַנַּעַר נָעַר	**והנער** [עמם ויבאו לפני יהוה וישחט אביו את] הׄזב[ח כ]אׄשר [יעשה מימים ימימה ליהוה ותבא את **הנער**]	(= 𝔊; cf. p. 240)
25	וישחטו	[וי]שחט	(cf. 𝔊)
28	וישתחו שם ליהוה	[ותעזב]הׄו שם ותשתחוׄ [ליהוה]	

7. The Textual Status of the Qumran Texts

From the point of view of their textual status the Qumran texts belong to five different groups, four of which were unknown before the Qumran discoveries (1, 3, 4, 5)—see especially Tov*, 2000b. These groups are recognized mainly on the basis of the content of the variants, and in one case a different criterion is used, as required by the evidence, viz., the recognition of orthographical, morphological, and scribal idiosyncracies in group *1*, but its textual profile is characterized as well.

(1) Texts Written in the Qumran Practice

Texts written in the Qumran practice of orthography, morphology, and scribal practice (see pp. 108–110) reflect a free approach to the biblical text which is reflected in adaptations of unusual forms to the context, in frequent errors, and in numerous corrections. These texts were probably written by one scribal school, probably in Qumran (see p. 111). Some of these texts may have been copied from proto-Masoretic texts, while the majority are textually independent (group *5* below). The documents written in the Qumran practice, often described as typical Qumran texts, comprise some *20* percent of the Qumran biblical texts.

(2) Proto-Masoretic (or: Proto-Rabbinic) Texts

In accordance with the description on pp. 22-39 these texts contain the consonantal framework of 𝔐, one thousand years or more before the time of the Masorah codices. These texts are exemplified by 1QIsa^{b} in Tables 1 and 2 (pp. 31-32) and by 4QJer^{c} in Table 7 (p. 231). They have no special textual characteristics beyond their basic agreement with 𝔐. These texts comprise some *35* percent of the Qumran biblical texts.

(3) Pre-Samaritan (or: Harmonizing) Texts

Pre-Samaritan texts, such as 4QpaleoExod^{m} and 4QNum^{b} (also close to 𝔊), are described in detail on pp. 97–100. These texts reflect the characteristic features of 𝔖 with the exception of the latter's ideological readings, but they occasionally deviate from 𝔖. It appears that one of the texts of this group formed the basis of 𝔖, and the Samaritan ideological changes and phonological features were inserted into that text. The group comprises non-Samaritan texts which bear a common and exclusive textual character. Their main characteristic is the preponderance of harmonizing readings, and hence they are named "harmonistic" by Eshel* (p. 80). This group comprises no more than *5* percent of the Qumran biblical texts of the Torah (for all of the Bible this group would have comprised some 15 percent).

(4) Texts Close to the Presumed Hebrew Source of 𝔊

Although no text has been found in Qumran that is identical or almost identical with the presumed Hebrew source of 𝔊, a few texts are very close to 𝔊: 4QJer^{b,d} bear a strong resemblance to 𝔊 in characteristic details, with regard both to the arrangement of the verses and to their shorter text.[86] Similarly close to 𝔊, though not to the same extent, are 4QLev^{d} (also close to 𝔖), 4QExod^{b} (thus F.M. Cross in *DJD* XII) and 4QDeut^{q} (see p. 159), and secondarily also 4QSam^{a} (close to 𝔊 and 𝔊^{Luc}; see further below, group *5*).[87] Agreements with 𝔊 are also found in 4QDeut^{c,h,j}, but these texts actually belong to group *5*. Texts containing a relatively small number of individual readings that are identical with the Hebrew parent text of 𝔊 are not included in this group.

---

86 See the discussion in chapter 7B on pp. 319-327.

87 For some details, see Table 22 above. See especially: F.M. Cross, "A New Qumran Biblical Fragment Related to the Original Hebrew Underlying the Septuagint," *BASOR* 132 (1953) 15-26; E. Ulrich, *The Qumran Text of Samuel and Josephus* (HSM 19; Missoula, MT 1978); Cross, "Some Notes"; E. Tov, "The Contribution of the Qumran Scrolls to the Understanding of the LXX," in: G.J. Brooke and B. Lindars, eds., *Septuagint, Scrolls and Cognate Writings (Manchester, 1990)* (SCS 33; Atlanta, GA 1992) 11-47.

There is not enough evidence for speculating on the internal relation between the texts which are close to 𝔊. They do not form a closely-knit textual family like the 𝔐 group or the 𝔖 group, nor were they produced by a scribal school, like group *1*. They represent individual copies that in the putative stemma of the biblical texts happened to be close to the Hebrew text from which 𝔊 was translated. Since the *Vorlage* of 𝔊 was a single biblical text, and not a family or recension, the recognition of Hebrew scrolls that were close to the *Vorlage* of 𝔊 is of limited importance for our understanding of the textual procedure. The texts which are close to 𝔊 comprise some *5* percent of the Qumran biblical texts.

(5) Non-Aligned Texts

Many texts are not exclusively close to any one of the texts mentioned above and are therefore considered non-aligned. They agree, sometimes significantly, with 𝔐 against the other texts, or they agree with 𝔖 and/or 𝔊 against the other texts, but the non-aligned texts also disagree with the other texts to the same extent. They furthermore contain readings not known from one of the other texts, so that they are not exclusively close to one of the other texts or groups.[88] This characterization is important when one tries to determine the full range of texts current in the Second Temple period as described in chapter 3C. Usually the employment of the term *non-aligned* merely implies that the texts under consideration follow an inconsistent pattern of agreements and disagreements with 𝔐, 𝔖, and 𝔊, as in the case of 2QExod[a,b], 4QExod-Lev[f], 11QpaleoLev[a], 4QDeut[b,c,h,k1,k2,m], 5QDeut, 6QpapKings, 1QIsa[a], 4QIsa[c], 2QJer, 4QEzek[a], 4QXII[a,c,e,g], 4QDan[a], 6QpapDan, 4QQoh[a], 4QLam, and 6QCant. But the texts which are most manifestly non-aligned, and actually independent, are texts which contain readings that diverge significantly from the other texts, such as 4QJosh[a], 4QJudg[a] as well as excerpted and liturgical texts. 4QSam[a] holds a special position in this regard, since it is closely related to the *Vorlage* of 𝔊, while reflecting independent features as well. These texts comprise some *35* percent of the Qumran evidence (including the liturgical texts [Exodus, Deuteronomy, Psalms]). See the discussion in Tov*, 2000b and see also below p. 162 and chapter 7B14.

Whether we assume that all aforementioned texts have been written at Qumran, or that only some were written there while others were brought from elsewhere (thus Tov*, 2000b), the coexistence of all these different categories of texts in the Qumran caves is noteworthy.

---

88 See Tov*, 1982, 1995, 2000b.

The fact that all these different texts were found in the same Qumran caves probably reflects a certain textual reality in the period between the third century BCE and the first century CE. In our reconstruction of the history of the biblical text in that period in pp. 187-197 this situation is described as textual plurality and variety. At the same time, the great number of the proto-Masoretic texts probably reflects their authoritative status (cf. p. 191). Since there is no evidence concerning the circumstances of the depositing of the scrolls in the caves or concerning their possibly different status in the Qumran sect, no solid conclusions can be drawn about the approach of the Qumranites towards textual variety. It stands to reason that they did not pay any special attention to differences of the types described here.

8. The Contribution of the Qumran Texts to Biblical Research

The Qumran texts contribute much to our knowledge of the biblical text at the time of the Second Temple—a period for which there was hardly any Hebrew evidence before 1947. Until that year, scholars based their analyses mainly on manuscripts from the Middle Ages. The Qumran evidence enriches our knowledge in the following areas.

(1) Readings not known previously help us to better understand many details in the biblical text, sometimes pertaining to matters of substance (for examples, see chapters 4, 6, 7). The Qumran texts, though early, are still removed much from the original texts as defined in 3B.

(2) The textual variety reflected in the five groups of texts described above provides a good overview of the condition of the biblical text in the Second Temple period (see the discussion in chapter 3C).

(3) The scrolls provide much background information on the technical aspects of the copying of biblical texts and their transmission in the Second Temple period (see chapter 4).

(4) The reliability of the ancient translations, especially 𝔊, is strengthened by the Qumran texts. 𝔊 is one of the important texts for biblical research (below, pp. 141–142), but since it is written in Greek, its Hebrew source has to be reconstructed from that language. The reconstruction of many such details is now supported by the discovery of identical Hebrew readings in Qumran scrolls. See, for example, the reconstruction of 𝔊 in Deut 31:1 (p. 129), 1 Sam 1:23 (p. 176), 1 Sam 1:24 (p. 254), 2 Sam 8:7 (p. 131), and also the examples on pp. 113–114. This evidence provides support for the procedure of reconstructing the Hebrew parent text of the translations.[89]

---

89 This claim was already made by G.R. Driver, "Hebrew Scrolls," *JTS* n.s. 2 (1951) 17-30, esp. 25-27.

D. Additional Witnesses

During the First and Second Temple periods many texts were in existence in ancient Israel beyond those known today. Such information is available from the textual sources to be discussed below, including documents which are not biblical texts in the usual sense of the word (thus *1,2,3* below).

1. Minute Silver Rolls from Ketef Hinnom

G. Barkay, "The Priestly Benediction on the Ketef Hinnom Plaques," *Cathedra* 52 (1989) 37-76 (Heb.).

Two minute silver rolls (amulets?), whose presumed date is the seventh or sixth century BCE, were discovered in 1979 in the excavations at Ketef Hinnom in Jerusalem (see plate 1*). The rolls contain the priestly blessing (Num 6:24-26) in a formulation that differs in certain details from 𝔐. Roll II lacks the words ויחנך, "He will deal graciously with you" (v. 25) and ישא ה׳ פניו אליך, "The LORD will bestow his favor upon you" (v. 26). Since these documents contain no running biblical texts, their contribution to textual criticism is limited.

2. The Nash Papyrus

W.F. Albright, "A Biblical Fragment from the Maccabaean Age: The Nash Papyrus," *JBL* 56 (1937) 145-176; S.A. Cook, "A Pre-Massoretic Biblical Papyrus," *Proceedings of the Society of Biblical Archaeology* 25 (1903) 34-56; E. Eshel, *ʿrykh hrmwnysṭyt bḥmyšh ḥwmšy twrh btqwpt byt šny*, unpubl. M.A. thesis, Hebrew University, Jerusalem 1990; N. Peters, *Die älteste Abschrift der zehn Gebote, der Papyrus Nash* (Freiburg im Breisgau 1905).

The so-called Nash papyrus, dating from the first or second century BCE, was discovered in Egypt in 1902. This text contains the Decalogue according to a mixed formulation of Exodus 20 and Deuteronomy 5 as well as the *shemaʿ* pericope (Deut 6:4-5). The orthography is fuller than that of 𝔐. Apparently this composite text reflects a liturgical rather than a biblical text (for its content cf. several *tefillin* and *mezuzot* from Qumran), so that its relevance for textual criticism is limited. The Nash papyrus probably reflects mainly the text of Deuteronomy rather than that of Exodus, even though part of the Sabbath commandment gives the text of Exodus (20:11). Details in the text of that commandment, however, are close to other Deuteronomy texts such as 4QDeut^{n}, 4QMez A, 4QPhyl G, and 8QPhyl (see Eshel*), in all of which the Exodus pericope replaces that of Deuteronomy or is added to it.

3. **Tefillin** *and* **Mezuzot** *from the Judean Desert*

S. Goren, "htpylyn mmdbr yhwdh lʾwr hhlkh," *Mḥnym* 62 (1962) 5-14; K.G. Kuhn, "Phylakterien aus Höhle 4 von Qumran," *Abhandl. der Heidelberger Akademie der Wissenschaften*, Phil.-Hist. Kl. 1957, 5-31; J.T. Milik, *Qumrân grotte 4, II* (DJD VI; Oxford 1977); J.H. Tigay, "Tpylyn," *EncBib* 8 (Jerusalem 1982) 883-895; Y. Yadin, *Tefillin (Phylacteries) from Qumran (XQ Phyl1-4)* (Jerusalem 1969).

Many fragments of biblical texts contained in *mezuzot*, head-*tefillin*, and arm-*tefillin* from the second and first centuries BCE until the first and second centuries CE were discovered in the Judean Desert, mainly in Qumran (see plate 9*), but also in Wadi Murabbaʿat and Naḥal Ṣeelim and were published by Yadin*, Kuhn*, and Milik*. They include parts of Exodus 12-13 and Deuteronomy 5-6, 10-11, 32.

The biblical texts reflected in these *tefillin* and *mezuzot* often differ from 𝔐, possibly because they were written from memory, as stated by *b. Meg.* 18b: תפלין ומזוזות נכתבות שלא מן הכתב, "*Tefillin* and *mezuzot* may be written out without a written source <that is, from memory>." At the same time many readings in the *tefillin* and *mezuzot* which differ from 𝔐 are identical with other ancient witnesses, among them several Qumran texts, so that nevertheless some *tefillin* and *mezuzot* probably preserve ancient textual traditions.

Some *tefillin* and *mezuzot* from Qumran are written in the Qumran practice (see pp. 108–110).

4. The Severus Scroll and R. Meir's Torah

Habermann, *Ketav*, 166-175; D.S. Loewinger, "spr twrh šhyh gnwz bbyt knst swyrws brwmʾ—yḥsw ʾl mgylt yšʿyhw mmdbr yhwdh wʾl 'twrtw šl rby mʾyr'," *Beth Mikra* 42 (1970) 237-263; J.P. Siegel, *The Severus Scroll and 1QIs^a* (SBLMasS 2; Missoula, MT 1975).

The rabbinic literature preserves various pieces of information on biblical scrolls whose text differed from 𝔐. The largest number of such testimonies refers to a Torah scroll which Titus brought to Rome as booty after the destruction of the temple. In a later period this scroll was given as a present by Severus (reigned 222-235 CE) to a synagogue that was being built with his permission. In rabbinic literature various words are quoted as having been derived from this Torah scroll, while other quotations, apparently from the same source, are attributed to "R. Meir's Torah," since the Torah scroll from the synagogue of Severus was apparently known to R. Meir. The main sources quoting from the Severus Scroll are *Gen. Rab.*, *Gen. Rabbati* of Moses ha-Darshan (a collection of *midrashim* from the eleventh century), the Farḥi Bible (14th century), and the MS Hebr. 31, Fol. 399, Bibl. Nat., Paris, all of which are described by Siegel* and Loewinger*. Although the exact quotations from the Severus Scroll have often been corrupted, they can usually be reconstructed with some degree of probability (see Siegel*).

From the scant information known about the contents of the Severus Scroll, it appears that its characteristic features are the weakening of the gutturals (cf. p. 95 concerning ⅏ and pp. 112–113 concerning some Qumran texts), the writing of non-final letters in final position (cf. p. 210 regarding some Qumran texts), and the interchange of similar letters (cf. pp. 243–249), as exemplified in Table 23. Thirty-three different readings from the scroll are known, but from the evidence preserved in the quotations, it is sometimes difficult to determine the precise difference between this Torah text and the other texts. Loewinger* and Siegel* emphasize the typological resemblance between the readings of this scroll and 1QIsa^{a}, both of which are characterized by an imprecise (*vulgar*) textual transmission—see pp. 193–195.

Table 23

Select Differences between 𝔐 and the Severus Scroll
(according to Siegel)*

Gen 1:31	𝔐	טוב מאד
		very good
	Sev.	טוב מות (sources: MS Paris, Farḥi Bible)
		death is good
Gen 3:21	𝔐	כתנות עור (= all other ancient texts)
		garments of *skins*
	Sev.	כתנות אור (source: *Gen. Rabbati*)
		garments of *light*
Gen 25:33	𝔐	וימכר את בכרתו (= all other ancient texts)
		he sold his *birthright*
	Sev.	וימכר את מכרתו (sources: *Gen. Rabbati*, MS Paris, Farḥi Bible)
		he sold his *sword* (?)
Gen 27:2	𝔐	יום מותי
		the day of my death
	Sev.	יוממותי (sources: MS Paris, Farḥi Bible)
		the day-of my death
Gen 27:27	𝔐	שדה
		field
	Sev.	סדה (sources: MS Paris, Farḥi Bible)
		field

Gen 36:10	𝔐	בן-עדה the son of Adah
	Sev.	בנעדה (sources: MS Paris, Farḥi Bible) the son-of Adah

E. Texts That Have Been Lost

Ginsburg, *Introduction*, 430-437; H.L. Strack, *Prolegomena critica in VT hebraicum* (Leipzig 1873) 14-29.

Additional texts that have been lost and about which very little is known from medieval works are reviewed by Ginsburg*. The main texts of this type are *Sefer* ("codex") *Hilleli, Sefer Zanbuqi, Sefer Yerushalmi, Sefer Yeriḥo, Sefer Sinai,* and *Sefer Babli.*

II. THE ANCIENT TRANSLATIONS

A. The Use of the Ancient Translations in Textual Criticism

A. Aejmelaeus, "What Can We Know about the Hebrew *Vorlage* of the Septuagint," *ZAW* 99 (1987) 58-89; Barr, *Comparative Philology*, 238-272; idem, "The Typology of Literalism in Ancient Biblical Translations," MSU 15 (NAWG I, Phil.-Hist. Kl. 1979) 279-325; S.P. Brock, "Bibelübersetzungen, I," *Theologische Realenzyklopädie*, vol. VI (Berlin/New York 1980) 161ff.; idem, "Translating the OT," in: D.A. Carson and H.G.M. Williamson, eds., *It Is Written: Scripture Citing Scripture—Essays in Honour of B. Lindars, SFF* (Cambridge 1988) 87-98; S.R. Driver, *Notes on the Hebrew Text and the Topography of the Books of Samuel, with an Introduction on Hebrew Palaeography and the Ancient Versions* (2d ed.; Oxford 1913) xxxiii-xxxix; N. Fernández Marcos, "The Use of the Septuagint in the Criticism of the Hebrew Bible," *Sefarad* 47 (1987) 59-72; M.H. Goshen-Gottstein, "Theory and Practice of Textual Criticism—The Text-Critical Use of the Septuagint," *Textus* 3 (1963) 130-158; M.L. Margolis, "Complete Induction for the Identification of the Vocabulary in the Greek Versions of the OT with Its Semitic Equivalents—Its Necessity and the Means of Obtaining It," *JAOS* 30 (1910) 301-312; Mulder, *Mikra;* E. Tov, "The Use of Concordances in the Reconstruction of the *Vorlage* of the LXX," *CBQ* 40 (1978) 29-36; idem, *TCU*; J. Ziegler, *Untersuchungen zur Septuaginta des Buches Isaias* 3 (ATAbh XII, 1934).

1. Background

In the ancient world and in the Middle Ages the Bible was translated into different languages, the most important of which are: Greek, Aramaic, Syriac, Latin, and Arabic. These translations are very significant for the textual criticism of the Hebrew Bible, since this discipline collects all the relevant material that is available from antiquity and the Middle Ages, including material derived from translated works. It goes without saying that these texts cannot be used in their own languages, since the textual discussion can only take into consideration *Hebrew* data. Therefore, elements of the Hebrew texts underlying the various ancient translations need to be reconstructed. This reconstructed text from which a translation was made is called the *Vorlage* of a translation, that is, the text that *lay before* the translator.

The importance of the ancient translations for the textual criticism of the Bible was more evident before 1947 than in recent times, since before the discovery of the Qumran scrolls, manuscripts of the ancient translations were the earliest sources for our knowledge of the biblical text. In the absence of ancient Hebrew material, scholars attached much importance to the ancient translations, since their early attestations (in the case of 𝔊: papyrus fragments from the second and first centuries BCE and manuscripts from the fourth century CE) preceded the medieval manuscripts of 𝔐 by many centuries.

The Qumran discoveries thus seemingly decreased the value of the ancient translations, since reliance on Hebrew texts is preferable to the use of ancient translations whose Hebrew source is not known. The Qumran scrolls are, however, very fragmentary, and even if they were complete, some ancient translations, especially 𝔊, would remain highly significant, since they reflect important textual traditions differing from both 𝔐 and the Qumran texts. Several important readings are also reflected in the other translations.

The views of scholars are divided concerning the feasibility of the *reconstruction* of the Hebrew *Vorlage* of the ancient translations. Some stress the ability of scholars to reconstruct words or sentences, while others emphasize the difficulties involved. Some general rules for reconstruction have been formulated, but they are of limited value. For even if scholars were to agree concerning abstract rules, the very use of one particular rule or another is based on subjective opinion.

Most of the rules formulated for the reconstruction of the Hebrew source of the ancient translations were made in reference to 𝔊, since that translation yields more information relevant to the study of the Bible than all the other translations together; it was therefore studied most extensively. At the same time, most of the rules for the reconstruction from 𝔊 also apply to the other translations.

In reconstructing the Hebrew source of ancient translations one can take several points of departure. Every reconstruction is made with 𝔐 in mind because of the large degree of congruence between 𝔐 and the presumed *Vorlage* of the ancient translations and because of the centrality of 𝔐 in the textual procedure. Indeed, a first rule in our approach to the ancient translations is that when the content of an ancient translation is identical with 𝔐, in all probability its Hebrew *Vorlage* was also identical with 𝔐. At the same time, this information does not make the task of the reconstruction easier: since identity in content is not easily definable, all the words in the translation must be analyzed in detail.

In the case of the Targumim, 𝔙, and 𝔖 there is an almost complete identity between their Hebrew source and the consonantal framework of 𝔐, so that reconstruction is limited to a small number of words. This identity is less extensive in the case of 𝔊, and in some of its chapters identity with 𝔐 is very limited. These data should be kept in mind in order not to lose one's sense of proportion when referring to the differences between 𝔐 and the ancient translations. We are confronted with only a relatively small number of differences between 𝔐 and the Hebrew *Vorlage* of the ancient translations. Nevertheless, since these details are often very significant, the analysis of the ancient translations is a necessary part of textual criticism.

As remarked above, when the meaning of a given word in an ancient translation is identical with 𝔐 or close to it, there is no reason to assume a difference between 𝔐 and the Hebrew *Vorlage* of the translations. Textual criticism is especially interested in those cases in which a critical analysis yields a difference in meaning in which the Hebrew *Vorlage* of the ancient translations presumably deviated from 𝔐. But here lies the difficulty: how can we know in which cases this *Vorlage* was indeed different from 𝔐? Although there are thousands of differences between 𝔐 and the translations, only a fraction of them was created by a divergence between 𝔐 and the *Vorlage* of the translation. Most of the differences were created by other factors that are not related to the Hebrew *Vorlage*. These are inner-translational factors, especially in the area of exegesis (below 2), which created many renderings that are now described as differences between the translation and 𝔐. From the text-critical point of view, such differences are not very significant, since they were created by the translator, and do not indicate a Hebrew source which deviated from 𝔐. (At another level, that of the exegesis of the biblical text, these instances are very significant). Another category of inner-translational factors includes corruptions in the textual transmission of the translation which caused apparent differences between it and 𝔐 (see 4).

The implication of all this is that before one makes use of a translation within the framework of textual criticism, one has to know all the intricacies of the exegetical system and translation technique of the translator. Information of this type does not relate directly to the Hebrew source of the translation, but one needs to have a thorough knowledge of the character of each translation unit in order to reconstruct its source.

Tools have been developed for reconstructing the Hebrew source of a translation which has been made faithfully (literally), since such a translation usually employed the same equivalent for a particular Hebrew word or grammatical structure in most of its occurrences. On the other hand, if the translation was made freely or even paraphrastically, it is difficult, and often impossible, to reconstruct the Hebrew *Vorlage*. Hence an overall knowledge of the exegesis (below 2) and representation of Hebrew constructions in specific translation units (below 3) is essential in order to be able to attempt a reconstruction.

2. *Exegesis*

Within the present framework there is only room for the most essential information about the exegesis of the translators. This topic encompasses many secondary areas, and the reader will have to peruse the bibliography relevant to the various translations to be discussed below.

a. Linguistic Exegesis

Every translation reflects linguistic exegesis which is essential to any translation. This exegesis consists of the following three levels.

α. Linguistic identifications which identify all forms in the source language and the connection between the words. Without this identification the words of the source text cannot be translated. Among other things, an analysis of all the morphemes of the nouns and verbs is essential. For example, a homograph such as יראו requires the translator to decide whether it is derived from a root *rʾh*, "to see," or from *yrʾ*, "to fear," that is, in the Tiberian vocalization either יִרְאוּ, "they will see" (passim in the Bible), or יְראוּ, "fear!" (plural), e.g., Ps 34:10. The same decision had to be made regarding וירא which may be derived from either *rʾh* (וַיַּרְא, "and he saw") or from *yrʾ* (וַיִּרָא = וַיִּירָא, "and he feared").

β. Semantic exegesis of all the words in the source language. Before turning to equivalents, the translator has to determine the meaning of each Hebrew word. For example, any form of the verb נשא can be taken in at least four entirely different ways, even though there is no doubt about the identity of the root. Brock*, 1988, 87 shows how the different textual traditions of Gen 4:7 reflect four different ways of understanding that verb in the phrase הלוא אם תיטיב שאת.

γ. Determining the equivalents of words of the source language in the target language on the basis of the knowledge and sensitivity of the translator in the language of the translation.

All translations reflect these three levels of linguistic exegesis. Nevertheless, only a few translation units (such as Aquila [p. 145]) are confined to such exegesis. As a rule, translations also reflect the first two types of exegesis that are described below. The more a translation unit uses fixed equivalents, the more it is considered literal, and the less that such equivalents are found in it, the freer it is considered. This also applies to exegetical elements, though in a reversed order: the more (the less) exegetical elements that are found in a translation unit, the freer (the less free) it is considered.

Among the exegetical elements reflected in the translations it is thus possible to distinguish between linguistic exegesis which follows the text closely, and other forms of exegesis which are further removed from it. Some exegetical elements form a necessary part of the translation process, while others infuse the text with elements of the personal taste, understanding, and personality of the translator, sometimes to such a point that the plain meaning of the text is completely concealed. In such a way certain translators allowed themselves the freedom of alluding to other verses in the Bible in their translation, or of inserting their own reflections into the translation. One should, however, keep in mind that with all types of exegesis the translators had one prevailing intention, namely, to transmit the message of the Bible to their readers, and even if, according to our understanding, the translators seem to be a long way from the simple meaning of the Bible, they were, nevertheless, reflecting what the translators considered to be the basic message of the Bible. The three types of non-linguistic exegesis which are found in most of the translations are exemplified below.

b. Contextual Exegesis

The translator sometimes explains a detail according to another detail in the context or he may add or omit a detail from the context. For example,

Num 20:19 𝔐 (רק אין) דבר (ברגלי אעברה)
(It is but a small) matter, (on my feet I would pass through.)

	𝔗^O	פתגם ביש a bad thing (i.e., a matter of offense)
Exod 32:26	𝔐	מי לה' אלי Who is on the LORD's side? To me!
	𝔊	τίς πρὸς κύριον ἴτω πρός με (cf. 𝔗^O NRSV) Who is on the LORD's side? *Let him come* to me!

In this verse a verb is added.

Stylistic shortening is exemplified in the next example.

Josh 4:14	𝔐	ויראו אתו כאשר יראו את משה . . . and they revered him as *they had revered* Moses.
	𝔊*	. . . καὶ ἐφοβοῦντο αὐτὸν ὥσπερ Μωυσῆν . . . and they revered him *like* Moses.

The linguistic exegesis mentioned in paragraph *aγ* describes the determining of equivalents on the basis of linguistic-semantic identification alone. Like linguistic exegesis, contextual exegesis also has linguistic aspects, but often the overall meaning of the context is more influential for determining equivalents. For example,

Exod 6:12	𝔐	ערל שפתים of uncircumcised lips
	𝔊	ἄλογος lacking verbal fluency
Exod 6:30	𝔐	ערל שפתים
	𝔊	ἰσχνόφωνος having an impediment in one's speech
Exod 18:7	𝔐	וישאלו איש לרעהו לשלום . . . and they asked each other of their welfare.
	𝔊	καὶ ἠσπάσαντο ἀλλήλους . . . and they greeted each other.
Deut 23:13	𝔐	ויד (תהיה לך מחוץ למחנה) (You shall have) an area (outside the camp.)
	𝔗^O	אתר מתקן an arranged place / a set area
Isa 9:13	𝔐	כפה ואגמון palm branch and reed
	𝔊	μέγαν καὶ μικρόν (cf. 𝔗^J) great and small

The translator of this verse thus gave up the exact rendering of the Hebrew words and translated them according to their context.

Beyond the types of exegesis described above various translations also reflect the following *exegetical tendencies*:

c. Theological Exegesis

Theological exegesis may relate to the description of God and His acts, the Messiah, Zion, the exile, as well as various ideas, such as that of repentance. Such exegesis may be expressed through theologically motivated choices of translation equivalents, in changes in words and verses (either slight or great) or in expansions or omissions of ideas considered offensive.

The theological world of the Greek translator of Isaiah is clearly recognizable in his exegesis.

Thus the idea that God brings σωτήριον, "salvation," referring particularly to salvation from the exile, has often been added to 𝔊 in places where it is not found in 𝔐. For example,

Isa 38:11	𝔐	I shall never see the LORD, the LORD in the land of the living.
	𝔊	I shall never see *the salvation* of God on earth (cf. v. 11b).
Isa 40:5	𝔐	(And the glory of the LORD shall appear) and all flesh shall see <it> together.
	𝔊	. . . and all flesh shall see *the salvation of God.*

As a rule the translators did not flinch from rendering literally verses or words which may be considered to be anthropomorphic or anthropopathic, that is, portraying God's appearance and feelings according to those of human beings. Sometimes, however, they avoided literal renderings. For example,

Isa 6:1	𝔐	. . . and *the skirts of His robe* filled the temple.
	𝔗J	. . . and the temple was filled with the *brightness of His glory.*

Cf. 𝔊 τῆς δόξης αὐτοῦ, "of His glory"; for a prominence of δόξα in 𝔊 (against 𝔐) see Exod 15:1-18; Isa 11:3; 30:27; 33:17; 40:6; 52:14; 53:2.

The Targumim of the Torah vary in their renderings of the divine names, especially מימרא דיוי, "the word of the LORD"—e.g., in 𝔗O to Gen 28:20 (𝔐 אלהים); and יקרא דיוי, "the glory of the LORD"—e.g., in 𝔗O to Gen 28:13 (𝔐 יהוה).

Exod 4:24	𝔐	ויפגשהו ה׳ the LORD met him
	𝔊	the *angel of the* LORD met him (= $\mathfrak{T}^{O}$)
Exod 19:3	𝔐	and Moses went up to God
	𝔊	and Moses went up to *the mountain of* God
Exod 24:10	𝔐	and they saw the God of Israel
	𝔊	and they saw the *place* where the God of Israel stood
Num 12:8	𝔐	(פה אל פה אדבר בו ומראה ולא חידת) וּתְמֻנַת ה׳ יביט . . . and he beholds the *likeness* of the LORD
	𝔊	. . . and he beholds the *glory*, δόξα, of the LORD (cf. $\mathfrak{T}^{O}$ and Ps 17:15 𝔊).

d. Midrashic Tendencies

The ancient translations of several biblical books include midrashic elements similar to or identical with midrashic exegesis known from rabbinic literature. By definition such midrashic elements add a dimension to the plain meaning of Scripture. Such exegesis is particularly frequent in the Targumim, but it is also found in 𝔊 and 𝔙.

3. Systems for the Representation of Hebrew Constructions in the Translation

The translators found ways of representing in their own languages the grammatical categories of the Hebrew, even when these did not exist in the target language. Thus the translators had to locate ways of representing the intricacies of the Hebrew verbal system, the construct formation, conjunctions, and particles as well as constructions unique to Hebrew, such as אשר . . . בו (literally: "which/that . . . upon which"). In all these instances the translators sometimes deviated from the exact wording of their source in accordance with the needs of the target language.

4. Inner-Translational Phenomena

The ancient translations reflect many types of *inner*-translational corruptions, such as the omission or addition of a letter or a word or the interchange of similar letters (in the text of the translation). Likewise, many scribes copying the manuscripts of the translations added short explanatory notes (glosses and interpolations), and even adapted the sometimes slavish language of the translation to the style of the target language. For examples pertaining to 𝔊, see Tov, *TCU*, 88-95.

5. The Reconstruction of the Hebrew Source of the Translation

Almost all translations reflect a certain amount of content exegesis and inner-translational corruption which have to be taken into consideration when the differences between 𝔐 and the Hebrew source of the ancient translations are being analyzed.

If the deviation of a translation from 𝔐 did not result from such exegesis or inner-translational corruption, one may assume that the translation is based on a different Hebrew reading.

The rules for the reconstruction of such readings have not been finalized, but important aspects have been discussed in methodological discussions by Margolis*, Ziegler*, Goshen-Gottstein*, Barr*, Tov*, and Aejmelaeus*, mainly in relation to 𝔊. Reconstruction is based on the assumption that the Hebrew *Vorlage* of the translation can be determined more accurately the more consistently the translator used fixed equivalents for individual words and grammatical categories. If a certain translation unit is freely rendered, it is much more difficult to reconstruct the elements of its Hebrew source, and often it is impossible to do so.

Details in the Hebrew *Vorlage* of the translations can be reconstructed primarily on the basis of intuition in conjunction with the use of various tools, especially the concordances to the translations which record all the equivalents of the translation and 𝔐. For example,

Deut 31:1	𝔐	וילך משה וידבר (= 𝔗^{OJ} 𝔖 𝔙)
		And Moses *went* and spoke.
	𝔊	καὶ συνετέλεσεν Μωυσῆς λαλῶν
		And Moses *finished* speaking.
	=	ויכל משה לדבר

The Hatch-Redpath concordance of 𝔊 (see p. 141) shows that the verb συντελέω, "to finish," usually reflects the root כל״ה, "to finish," and since the deviation in 𝔊 cannot be explained in terms of exegesis on the part of the translator, it would appear that 𝔊 reflects a variant reading ויכל, "and he finished." Either וילך, "and he went," of 𝔐 or ויכל of the Greek *Vorlage* developed by way of metathesis of the last two consonants (see p. 250). In this case the reconstructed reading also appears in a Hebrew source, viz., 1QDeut^{b} (frag. 13 ii, l. 4) and in 𝔐 of Deut 32:45: ויכל משה לדבר, "And Moses *finished* speaking." Furthermore, the reverse interchange is known from Josh 19:49, 51 𝔐 𝔗 𝔖 ויכלו as compared with 𝔊 καὶ ἐπορεύθησαν (= וילכו).

When a rendering is encountered in one of the ancient translations which is problematic when considering its equivalent in 𝔐, various factors have to be taken into consideration.

a. The aspect of the translation: an examination of equivalents elsewhere in the translation, after a prior analysis of possible exegetical elements in that version.

b. The aspect of the scholar: reliance on intuition when a reconstruction is suggested.

c. The aspect of the Hebrew text: textual probability, that is, the choice of retroverted readings that appear reasonable with regard to what is known about the textual transmission of 𝔐, involving, e.g., known interchanges, such as ר/ד and ו/י.

d. The aspect of the Hebrew composition: linguistic plausibility, that is, the degree of the conformity of the reconstructed reading to the grammar, vocabulary, and style of biblical Hebrew, especially in the book in which the reconstructed reading is found.

e. Possible support from other Hebrew texts (see below β).

As a rule, the criteria for the reconstruction of Hebrew readings are considered subjective. Some types of retroversions, however, can be considered objective.

α. If the reconstructed reading was developed by way of corruption from the reading of 𝔐 or vice versa—especially in the case of interchanges of consonants, cf. pp. 243-252—and if the Hebrew words are remote from each other with regard to content, the reconstruction is plausible. For example,

Jer 23:9	𝔐	שכור (= שִׁכּוֹר, "drunk")—see Table 24
	𝔊	συντετριμμένος ("broken")
	=	שבור (= שָׁבוּר)

The variant itself may have been influenced by נשבר לבי, "my heart is broken," at the beginning of the verse. The distance in subject matter between the two words compared with the graphic similarity of the *beth* and *kaph* leads to the assumption that the translator indeed read שבור.

The degree of certainty in the reconstruction of proper nouns is greater than in the reconstruction of common nouns, since no exegetical factors are involved in the transliteration of proper nouns; e.g., in Gen 10:4 𝔊 Ῥόδιοι reflects רודנים, *R*odanim (cf. רוֹדָנִים in 𝔰𝔪 in Genesis and in 𝔐 in 1 Chr 1:7) instead of דֹּדָנִים, *D*odanim, in 𝔐 𝔗[OJ]. Cf. pp. 12-13.

β. Some reconstructions are *supported* by other (usually: extra-Masoretic) Hebrew evidence. For example,

Isa 36:11	𝔐	העם	(the people)	(= 𝔗 𝔖 𝔙)
	𝔊	τῶν ἀνθρώπων	(the men)	
	=	האנשים	(the men)	= 1QIsa[a]

This retroversion of 𝔊 is supported by the identical reading of 1QIsa[a].

1 Sam 2:20	𝔐	יָשֵׂם	(he will give)	(= 𝔖)
	𝔊	ἀποτείσαι	(he will repay)	(= 𝔙)
	=	ישלם	(he will repay)	= 4QSam[a]

This retroversion of 𝔊 is supported by the identical reading of 4QSam[a].

In fact, the discovery of the Qumran scrolls has provided much support to the procedure of retroverting (cf. p. 117). Before the Qumran discoveries many readings had been retroverted from the versions, but only when such readings actually turned up in Hebrew manuscripts in Qumran could there be greater certainty regarding the correctness of the *procedure*, although doubts still remain in matters of detail. In the following example the long addition to 𝔐 in 𝔊 in 2 Sam 8:7 appears also in 4QSam[a] and can therefore be retroverted easily.

> καὶ ἔλαβεν αὐτὰ Σουσακειμ βασιλεὺς Αἰγύπτου ἐν τῷ ἀναβῆναι αὐτὸν εἰς Ιερουσαλημ ἐν ἡμέραις Ροβοαμ υἱοῦ Σολομωντος
>
> And Sousakeim, king of Egypt, took them when he went up to Jerusalem in the days of Roboam son of Solomon.
>
> 4QSam[a], in the reconstruction of E. Ulrich (n. 87) 45: גם [ ]אֹותם [לקח אחר שושק מלך מצרים ב]עֹלותו אל ירֹ[ושלים] בימי רחבעם בן שלו[מה]

See further the agreements between 4QSam[a] and 𝔊 listed on pp. 114 and 254. Table 24 exemplifies variant readings reconstructed from the ancient translations. For further possible examples, see Table 22 on p. 114.

Table 24

Variant Readings Reconstructed from the Ancient Versions

Exod 1:12	𝔐	ויקֻצו מפני בני ישראל (= 𝔖)
		And they felt a loathing for the Israelites
	𝔊	καὶ ἐβδελύσσοντο οἱ Αἰγύπτιοι ἀπὸ τῶν υἱῶν Ισραηλ
		And *the Egyptians* felt a loathing for the Israelites.
	𝔗[O]	ועקת למצראי מן קדם בני ישראל (= 𝔗[J] 𝔙)

	=	ויקֻצו מצרים מפני בני ישראל (thus apparently also 2QExod[a] according to letter count)
Isa 24:3	𝔐	כי ה׳ דבר (= 𝔗 𝔖 𝔙) for the LORD spoke
	𝔊	τὸ γὰρ στόμα κυρίου ἐλάλησε for *the mouth of* the LORD spoke
	=	כי פי ה׳ דבר
Jer 23:9	𝔐	הייתי כאיש שִׁכּוֹר וכגבר עֲבָרוֹ יין (= 𝔗) I was like a *drunken* man, and like a man overcome by wine.
	𝔊	ἐγενήθην ὡς ἀνὴρ συντετριμμένος καὶ ὡς ἄνθρωπος συνεχόμενος ἀπὸ οἴνου I was like a *broken* man, and like a man overcome by wine.
	=	הייתי כאיש שָׁבוּר וכגבר עֲבָרוֹ יין
Ps 104:17	𝔐	חסידה בְּרוֹשִׁים בֵּיתָהּ (cf. 𝔖 𝔙) The stork has her home in *the junipers.*
(103:17)	𝔊	τοῦ ἐρωδιοῦ ἡ οἰκία ἡγεῖται αὐτῶν The house of the stork *leads them.*
	=	חסידה בְּרוֹשָׁם בֵּיתָהּ (note the Qumran orthography [cf. p. 108])
	cf. Mic 2:13	וה׳ בראשם—ὁ δὲ κύριος ἡγήσεται αὐτῶν . . . and the LORD shall lead them.

For examples of similar reconstructions, see pp. 236–286.

In spite of what has been said above it should be stressed that only some deviations from 𝔐 can be reconstructed in Hebrew. Often one does not know whether the deviation derived from a different Hebrew reading or from some other factor, such as a free translation. Moreover, even if the assumption of a different Hebrew reading seems well founded, it is possible that the reading itself actually never existed, since the translator may have misread the source (1) or may have interpreted it etymologically (2).

First an example for category (1): A possible misreading may be found in 𝔊 in 1 Sam 21:8; 22:9,18. This version wrongly calls Doeg—always an Edomite in 𝔐 and the other texts—a Syrian, ὁ Σύρος, as against, הָאֲדֹמִי, "the Edomite" in 𝔐. It is nevertheless impossible to determine whether the source of 𝔊 actually read הארמי, "the Aramean," or whether the translator mistakenly read הארמי for האדמי. In either case, it could be said that 𝔊 reflects a *reading* הארמי, even though this reading may not have existed in any Hebrew source whatsoever. Thus the concept of a reconstructed reading must necessarily remain imprecise.

As for category (2), a translator's *etymological exegesis* also makes it difficult to recognize variants underlying the translation. Translators often turned to etymology in their attempt to understand their Hebrew *Vorlage* (see p. 124), and when doing so they played, as it were, with the letters of the Hebrew (for some examples and bibliography, see Tov, *TCU*, 241-250). While many examples are not relevant to textual criticism, some are. Consider the following case.

Exod 3:18	𝔐	יהוה אלהי העבריים נקרה עלינו
	𝔊	ὁ θεὸς τῶν Ἑβραίων προσκέκληται ἡμᾶς (= 𝔖 𝔗)

It is not clear whether the three translators derived this rendering from a Hebrew text like 𝔐 by way of etymology or from a variant נקרא as in 𝔐𝔖 *ad loc.* and in 𝔐 in the parallel 5:3.

The reconstruction of readings in the Hebrew *Vorlage* of the ancient translations pertains to all the elements of the text found before the translator, that is, additions, omissions, differences in letters or words, and differences in sequence. However, it also includes elements that are not expressed in the manuscripts, but which form an integral part of the exegetical tradition accompanying the biblical text, that is, the vocalization and the syntactical relationship between words and verses.

The process of reconstruction is necessarily limited to words that can be reconstructed with some degree of probability. Besides these, there are not a few differences between 𝔐 and the translations concerning which one cannot easily decide whether they reflect a different Hebrew *Vorlage* or translational changes. In many cases the analysis of the translation technique and the translator's exegesis does not provide sufficient information in order to determine whether deviations in certain grammatical categories derived from the translator or from his Hebrew *Vorlage*. Thus, generally speaking, one often gropes in the dark when encountering differences in number (singular/plural), the tenses of the verb, pronominal suffixes, prepositions, the article, etc.

Since there is disagreement among scholars concerning the reconstruction of the Hebrew *Vorlage* of the ancient translations, many of the deviations from 𝔐 in the translations which have been reconstructed by some scholars as variant Hebrew readings have been described by others as inner-translational differences. Moreover, in certain cases where a deviation is recognized as reflecting a reading, the possible reconstructions appear to be endless.

B. The Evidence

The following ancient translations are relevant to textual criticism

1. The Septuagint (𝔊, Greek)
2. The revisions (recensions) of the Septuagint (Greek)
3. The Targumim (Aramaic)
4. The Peshitta (𝔖, Syriac)
5. The Vulgate (𝔙, Latin)
6. The translation of Saadia (Arabic)

Note: Other introductions to textual criticism also discuss secondary translations ("daughter translations") made from 𝔊 into the following languages: Latin (the Vetus Latina), Syriac (the Syro-Palestinian translations), Armenian, Coptic (Sahidic, Bohairic, Akhmimic), Georgian, Old Slavic, Ethiopic, Gothic, and Arabic. Only one of these versions, Vetus Latina (see p. 139), has any bearing on the Hebrew text of the Bible through its Greek source which, however, is not extant. All the other secondary translations have relevance mainly for the transmission of 𝔊.

1. The Septuagint (𝔊)

S.P. Brock et al., *A Classified Bibliography of the Septuagint* (Leiden 1973).

E. Bickerman, "Some Notes on the Transmission of the Septuagint," in: *A. Marx Jubilee Volume* (New York 1950) 149-178 = idem, *Studies in Jewish and Christian History, Part One* (Leiden 1976) 137–166; P.-M. Bogaert, "Les études sur la Septante—Bilan et perspectives," *Revue théologique de Louvain* 16 (1985) 174-200; idem, "Septante et versions grecques," *DBSup*, vol. XII (Paris 1993) 536-692; S.P. Brock, "The Phenomenon of the Septuagint—The Witness of Tradition," *OTS* 17 (1972) 11-36; G. Dorival, M. Harl, O. Munnich, *La Bible grecque des Septante—Du judaïsme hellénistique au christianisme ancien* (Paris 1988); S. Jellicoe, *The Septuagint and Modern Study* (Oxford 1968); S. Olofsson, *The LXX Version—A Guide to the Translation Technique of the Septuagint* (ConB, OT Series 30; Lund 1990); I.L. Seeligmann, "Problems and Perspectives in Modern Septuagint Research," *Textus* 15 (1990) 169-232 (previously published in Dutch in 1940); H.B. Swete, *An Introduction to the OT in Greek* (2d ed.; Cambridge 1914); Tov, *TCU*; idem, "Die griechischen Bibelübersetzungen," in: *ANRW* II, 20.1 (Berlin/New York 1987) 121-189; idem, "The Septuagint," in: Mulder, *Mikra*, 161-188; idem, "The Contribution of the Qumran Scrolls to the Understanding of the LXX," in: G.J. Brooke and B. Lindars, eds., *Septuagint, Scrolls and Cognate Writings—Papers Presented to the International Symposium on the Septuagint and Its Relations to the Dead Sea Scrolls . . . (Manchester, 1990)* (SCS 33; Atlanta, GA 1992) 11-47.

𝔊 is a Jewish translation which was made mainly in Alexandria. Its Hebrew source differed greatly from the other textual witnesses (𝔐 𝔗 𝔖 𝔙 and many of the Qumran texts), and this accounts for its great significance in biblical studies. Moreover, 𝔊 is important as a source for early exegesis, and this translation also forms the basis for many elements in the NT.

a. Name

𝔊 is known in various languages as the translation of the seventy (two elders). Its traditional name reflects the tradition that seventy two elders translated the Torah into Greek (see especially the Epistle of Aristeas, an apocryphal composition describing the origin of 𝔊). In the first centuries CE this tradition was expanded to include all of the translated biblical books, and finally it encompassed all of the Jewish-Greek Scriptures, including compositions originally written in Greek.

Today, the name Septuagint(a) denotes both the original translation of the Bible into Greek and the collection of sacred Greek Writings in their present form. The former use is imprecise, since the name Septuaginta is not suitable for a collection which contains, in addition to the original translation, late revisions (recensions) of that translation as well as compositions written in Greek. Because of this, scholars usually distinguish between the collection of sacred Greek writings named the Septuagint and the original translation, called the Old Greek (OG) translation. The presumed original translation is known from two sources: the greater part is included in the collection of sacred Greek writings (𝔊) and a smaller segment is reconstructed by modern scholars from various later sources. In places where it is necessary to stress the diverse nature of the collection of books included in 𝔊, its name is placed in quotation marks ("𝔊").

b. Scope

"𝔊" contains two types of books:

(a) The Greek translation of the twenty-four canonical books. These books contribute significantly to biblical studies, in particular to textual criticism.

(b) Books not included in the collection of the Holy Scriptures of the Jews of Palestine and therefore named *Apocrypha* (the "hidden" books) in Greek and *ḥiṣoniyyim* (the "outside" books) in Hebrew. These books are subdivided into two groups:

(1) the Greek translation of certain books, whose Hebrew source has either been lost, or preserved only in part;

(2) compositions composed from the outset in Greek, such as the Wisdom of Solomon.

c. Sequence of the Books

The twenty-four books of the Hebrew canon included in 𝔊 are arranged in a different sequence from that of the Hebrew Bible. Whereas the books of the Hebrew canon are arranged in three sections reflecting different stages of their acceptance into the canon, the Greek tripartite arrangement of the books is made in accordance with their literary genre:

(1) legal and historical books (starting with the Torah),

(2) poetic and sapiential books,

(3) prophetic books—in some manuscript traditions the latter two sections appear in a reverse order.

Within each section the Greek books are arranged in a sequence different from that of the twenty-four books of the Hebrew Bible. The apocryphal books are integrated into the three sections in accordance with their literary genre.

d. The Original Form of 𝔊 and Its Date

Most scholars are of the opinion that there once existed only one original translation of each of the books of the Hebrew Bible—see the opinion of de Lagarde described on p. 183—and accordingly, various attempts have been made to reconstruct their original translation—see p. 140. At the same time, a minority of scholars accept the opinion of Kahle (p. 183), who claimed that initially there were various attempts at translation as was the case with the Targumim. The discussion below of the dates of the Greek translations takes both possibilities into account.

The books of the Bible were translated at different times and there are various attestations of the date of composition of the books of 𝔊. Some of the evidence is external, e.g., quotations from 𝔊 in ancient sources, and some internal, e.g., reflections of historical situations or events found in the translation.

According to the generally accepted explanation of the testimony of the Epistle of Aristeas, the translation of the Torah was carried out in Egypt in the third century BCE. This assumption is compatible with the early date of several papyrus and leather fragments of the Torah from Qumran and Egypt, some of which have been ascribed to the middle or end of the second century BCE (4QLXXLev^{a}, 4QLXXNum, Pap. Fouad 266, Pap. Rylands Gk. 458).

The translations of the books of the Prophets, Hagiographa, and the apocryphal books came after that of the Torah, for most of these translations use its vocabulary, and quotations from the translation of the Torah appear in the Greek translations of the Latter Prophets, Psalms, Ben Sira, etc. Since the Prophets and several of the books of the Hagiographa were known in their Greek version to the grandson of Ben Sira at the end of the second century BCE, we may infer that most of the books of the Prophets and Hagiographa were translated in the beginning of that century or somewhat earlier. There is only limited explicit evidence concerning individual books: Chronicles is quoted by Eupolemos in the middle of the second century BCE, and Job is quoted by Pseudo-Aristeas in the beginning of the first century BCE (see Swete*, 25-26). The translation of Isaiah contains allusions to historical situations and events which point to the years 170-150 BCE.[90]

The corpus of "𝔊" also contains revisions (recensions) of original translations (below 2). These revisions were made from the first century BCE onwards (parts of Samuel-Kings [below, pp. 144–145]) until the beginning of the second century CE (Qoheleth, if indeed translated by Aquila). Therefore, some four hundred years separate the translation of the Torah from the latest translation contained in "𝔊."

e. Evidence

There are many witnesses of 𝔊, some direct, such as papyrus fragments and manuscripts, and others indirect, such as the translations made from 𝔊, and quotations by early authors.

a. Direct Witnesses[91]

The sources which contain 𝔊, either completely or in part, are numerous. Some of them have been published in separate editions, while others are known to scholars from the critical editions of 𝔊. The date of these witnesses varies from the second century BCE until the late Middle Ages.

---

[90] See I.L. Seeligmann, *The Septuagint Version of Isaiah—A Discussion of Its Problems* (Leiden 1948) 76-94.

[91] For an updated description of all the direct witnesses, see Jellicoe*. A more extensive description including all the details on the sources known until 1914 is found in A. Rahlfs, *Verzeichnis der griechischen Handschriften des ATs für das Septuaginta Unternehmen* (Berlin 1914). All the papyrus fragments known until 1975–1976 are listed by J. O'Callaghan, "Lista de los papiros de los LXX," *Bib* 56 (1975) 74-93; K. Aland, *Repertorium der griechischen christlichen Papyri, I. Biblische Papyri—AT, NT, Varia, Apokryphen* (Patristische Texte und Studien 18; Berlin 1976). Fragments discovered subsequently are listed by Bogaert* 1993, 666-672.

In the description of the witnesses of 𝔊 one usually distinguishes between

1. early texts written on papyrus and leather including both scrolls and codices;

2. uncial (*uncialis*) or majuscule (*majusculus*) manuscripts from the fourth century onwards, written with "capital" letters;

3. minuscule (*minusculus*) or cursive manuscripts, written with small letters, from medieval times.

(1) Early texts dating from the second century BCE onwards, mainly fragments of the Torah, were discovered in Palestine and Egypt. With the aid of these fragments one now gains insights about the period before the Hexapla (see p. 147). The textual tradition of that composition supplanted most of the early traditions from the third century CE onwards.

Of the many papyrus fragments, particular significance is attached to those belonging to the Chester Beatty/Scheide collection, discovered in Egypt in 1931. This collection contains large sections of most of the biblical books; especially significant are the papyri containing Daniel (numbered 967-8) which serve as the sole witness (except for the late Hexaplaric manuscripts) of the 𝔊 of this book, since all other manuscripts and, in their wake, the early editions do not contain the Old Greek version of Daniel, but contains instead the revision of Theodotion which had replaced the original translation in the corpus of "𝔊."

Among the leather fragments of 𝔊 found in Qumran, 4QLXXLev^{a}, published in *DJD* IX, is especially significant. This text contains a freer translation of Leviticus than that found in the other manuscripts. According to Skehan,[92] this fragment contains the original text of 𝔊, while all the other texts reflect a tradition corrected according to 𝔐.

(2) *Uncial* manuscripts of 𝔊 dating from the fourth to the tenth century CE (see an example on plate 19*) are the main source for our knowledge of 𝔊. The three most important manuscripts containing all or almost all books of 𝔊 are B, A, and S.

B (Cod. Vat. Gr. 1209, indicated as "Vaticanus") dates from the fourth century. Codex B is the best complete manuscript of 𝔊 (see plate 19*), and therefore several editions are based on it. It is relatively free of corruptions and influences from the revisions of 𝔊. At the same time, its text of Isaiah is Hexaplaric and in Judges it contains another type of revision.

---

92 P.W. Skehan, "The Qumran Manuscripts and Textual Criticism," *VTSup* 4 (1957) 159-160.

S also named א (B.M. Add. 43725, indicated as "Sinaiticus") dates from the fourth century. Codex S usually agrees with the text of B, when the two reflect the Old Greek translation, but it also is influenced by the later revisions of 𝔊. This manuscript was brought by C. von Tischendorf to Russia in the middle of the nineteenth century from St. Catherine's monastery in Sinai, from which it derives its name.

A (B.M. Royal MS 1 D V-VIII, indicated as "Alexandrinus") dates from the fifth century. Codex A is greatly influenced by the Hexaplaric tradition and in several books represents it faithfully. The scribe of A often adapted the text to similar verses and added harmonizing details.

(3) *Minuscules*—Many minuscule manuscripts from the ninth to the sixteenth centuries are known. Some of them are recorded in the Göttingen and Cambridge editions (below pp. 140-141), while others are known from the edition of Holmes-Parsons (ibid.). Even though minuscules are relatively late, they often preserve ancient traditions, as, for example, in the Lucianic tradition known mainly from the four minuscules denoted as b,o,c_2,e_2 in the Cambridge editions.

β. Indirect Witnesses: Daughter Translations of 𝔊

In the first centuries CE 𝔊 served as the official source of the Bible for the Christian Church and therefore many translations were made from it in accordance with the needs of the churches in the East and West. Several of these translations are important for our knowledge of 𝔊 and its revisions in the first centuries CE. The testimony of the daughter versions is adduced in the editions of Cambridge and Göttingen.

Particularly important among these is the Vetus Latina, "The Old Latin" <translation>. This translation preserved many important Greek readings sometimes as their only witness, but more frequently in conjunction with the Lucianic manuscripts (see p. 148).[93] The Vetus Latina translation derived directly from the Greek, but some of its "Hebraizing" elements may have entered the Latin translation directly from a Hebrew source, possibly during the oral citation of the text in the synagogue service in North Africa, as surmised by Quispel.[94]

---

93 See J. Trebolle Barrera, "From the 'Old Latin' through the 'Old Greek' to the 'Old Hebrew' (2 Kings 10:23-25)," *Textus* 11 (1984) 17-36, as well as his earlier studies quoted there. For an example, see 2 Sam 23:8 (p. 268 below).

94 G. Quispel, "African Christianity before Minucius Felix and Tertullian," in: J. den Boeft and A.H.M. Kessels, eds., *Actus—Studies in Honour of H.L.W. Nelson* (Utrecht 1982) 257-335, esp. 260-265. These elements could also have derived from Greek manuscripts which have been lost or from revisional activity on the Vetus Latina. For a discussion of these possibilities, see D.S. Blondheim, *Les Parlers Judéo-Romans et la Vetus Latina* (Paris 1925) xlvii-xlviii.

f. Editions

Almost all the uncial manuscripts of 𝔊 have been published in *diplomatic editions* (editions which present the text of a particular manuscript without any changes and with or without an accompanying critical apparatus of variants). The two major diplomatic editions are:

(1) R. Holmes and J. Parsons, *Vetus Testamentum graecum cum variis lectionibus,* vols. I-V (Oxford 1798-1827). This edition records variants from 164 manuscripts, the daughter translations of 𝔊, and the first editions of 𝔊. The text of this extensive edition itself is based on the editio Sixtina of 1587. This edition, although often imprecise, is nevertheless very significant since it contains the largest collection of the variants of 𝔊.

(2) A.E. Brooke, N. McLean, and H.St.J. Thackeray, *The Old Testament in Greek according to the Text of Codex Vaticanus* (Cambridge 1906-1940), also known as "The Cambridge Septuagint." This series contains the books Genesis until Nehemiah, as well as Esther, Judith, and Tobit in four volumes, according to codex B, and where that manuscript is lacking, it has been supplemented by A or S. Together with the editions of the Göttingen series, this edition is used by scholars for precise research.

Another type of edition is called *critical* or *eclectic.* Such editions present the reconstructed "original" text which is selected from elements found in all known sources; in addition these editions provide a critical apparatus of variants. The idea of publishing such a reconstructed text derives from the assumption that there once existed an original text of 𝔊 (see p. 136). Obviously, any attempt to reconstruct such a text is based on all the data known prior to the preparation of the edition, and any new data may bring about changes in the reconstructed text and even in the evaluation of the known data. For example, some of the papyrus fragments belonging to the Chester Beatty/Scheide collection (p. 138), which were published after the publication of the critical editions, have brought about changes in the evaluation of the data included in these editions.

The Göttingen Septuagint series, named *Septuaginta, Vetus Testamentum graecum auctoritate societatis litterarum gottingensis editum,* comprises the most precise and thorough critical editions of 𝔊. Each volume contains a detailed critical apparatus in which the witnesses are divided into groups and subgroups, so that readers can find their way through the maze of manifold variants—see plate 20* for an example. In Jeremiah, for example, the witnesses of the Lucianic tradition are subdivided into a main group (*L*) and a secondary group (*l*), and when a reading occurs in both it is recorded as *L'*. Each book commences with an introduction containing a detailed evaluation of all the textual witnesses of that book, a description of orthographical variants, and a bibliography.

An abridged critical edition according to the Göttingen system was published by A. Rahlfs, *Septuaginta, id est Vetus Testamentum graece iuxta LXX interpretes* (Stuttgart 1935).

The great problems surrounding the transmission of the text of 𝔊 make the reconstruction of its presumed original text difficult. Nevertheless, with regard to the evaluation of at least three categories of readings relatively stable criteria can be used:

1. grammatical variants;
2. readings which have been corrupted from other readings;
3. readings known as belonging to one of the revisions of the presumably original text of 𝔊.

g. Auxiliary Tools for the Study of 𝔊

The main auxiliary tool is the bilingual concordance by E. Hatch and H.A. Redpath, *A Concordance to the Septuagint and the Other Greek Versions of the OT* (Oxford 1897–1906; repr. Graz 1954; 2d ed.: Grand Rapids, MI 1998). This work lists the Hebrew and Aramaic equivalents for most of the words of 𝔊—for the Apocrypha the Greek words are listed without equivalents. This work does not take a stand regarding the presumed *Vorlage* of the Greek words contained in 𝔊 but only lists the "formal" equivalents of 𝔊 and 𝔐. The Hebrew/Aramaic-Greek index of Hatch–Redpath refers to the numbers of the pages where the reverse equivalents are mentioned, that is, Greek-Hebrew/Aramaic. These equivalents are recorded explicitly (with data concerning frequency) in the index to Hatch-Redpath by Camilo dos Santos[95] and in the reverse index by T. Muraoka in the second edition of Hatch-Redpath (1998).

Precise electronic concordances of all the equivalents of 𝔐 and 𝔊 have been prepared on the basis of a computer-assisted comparison of 𝔐 and 𝔊. See J.R. Abercrombie and others, *Computer Assisted Tools for Septuagint Studies (CATSS), Vol. 1, Ruth* (SCS 20; Atlanta, GA 1986);

---

95 E. Camilo dos Santos, *An Expanded Hebrew Index for the Hatch-Redpath Concordance to the Septuagint* (Jerusalem [1973]). The concordance of A. Tromm (Amsterdam/Utrecht 1718) also lists these equivalents explicitly. This concordance remains of importance for the study of 𝔊, even though the equivalents included are not always precise.

E. Tov, *A Computerized Data Base for Septuagint Studies, The Parallel Aligned Text of the Greek and Hebrew Bible, CATSS Vol. 2* (*JNSL*, Supplementary Series 1; Stellenbosch 1986); E. Tov, *The Parallel Database of the MT and LXX*, Accordance computer program, version 4, Gramcord 1999 (division of the CATSS database, directed by R. A. Kraft and E. Tov). This database allows detailed bilingual searches.

h. The Importance of 𝔊 for Biblical Studies

Among the witnesses of the Bible special importance is attached to 𝔐, some of the Qumran scrolls, 𝔐𝔰𝔞𝔪, and 𝔊. The importance of 𝔊 is based on the fact that it reflects a greater variety of important variants than all the other translations put together (see Tov*, 1991). Many details in the Hebrew source of the translation can be reconstructed, since large sections have been translated with a high degree of literalness. Examples of such retroversions are listed in Table 24 on pp. 131-132 as well as in chapters 4 and 7. Although one should not generalize, the importance of 𝔊 should be stressed especially for the study of the following books. See especially Bogaert*, 1993, 576-608.

Genesis: genealogies, chronological data (see chapter 7B, section 6).

Exodus: the second account of the building of the Tabernacle in chapters 35-40.

Numbers: sequence differences, pluses and minuses of verses.

Joshua: significant transpositions, pluses, and minuses (see chapter 7B, section 2).

Samuel-Kings: many major and minor differences, including pluses, minuses, and transpositions, involving different chronological and editorial structures (see chapter 7B, sections 4, 7, 9, 10).

Jeremiah: differences in sequence, much shorter text (see chapter 7B, section 1).

Ezekiel: slightly shorter text (see chapter 7B, section 3).

Proverbs: differences in sequence, different text (see chapter 7B, section 5).

Daniel and Esther: completely different text, including the addition of large sections, treated as "apocryphal."

Chronicles: "synoptic" variants, that is, readings in the Greek translation of Chronicles agreeing with 𝔐 in the parallel texts.

Some of these data bear on the literary development of the Hebrew book (see chapter 7A).

2. *The Revisions of the Septuagint*

a. General

A given textual tradition is considered a revision (recension) of 𝔊 if two conditions are met:

(1) 𝔊 and the revision share a common textual basis. If such a common basis cannot be recognized, the two sources comprise separate translations rather than a source and its revision. The existence of a common basis is based upon the assumption of distinctive agreements in vocabulary between the two texts which set them apart from the remainder of the books of 𝔊.

(2) The revision corrects 𝔊 in a certain direction, generally towards a more precise reflection of its Hebrew source.

b. The Background of the Revisions

Various factors were instrumental in the creation of the revisions:

(1) *Differences between 𝔊 and the Hebrew text.* The Greek-speaking Jews required a Greek translation that would faithfully reflect the Hebrew Bible, for their religious needs and, at a later stage, also for the purpose of their polemics with the Christians. Since the Hebrew text had changed in the course of the years, the need was felt to adapt 𝔊 to the Hebrew text that was current in Judaism from the first century BCE until the second century CE.

(2) *The abandonment of 𝔊.* The first Christians quite naturally chose 𝔊 as their Holy Writ and as the source for additional writings since Greek was their language. As a result, 𝔊 influenced them not only by the content of the translation in general, but also by its terminology. The frequent use of 𝔊 by the Christians caused the Jews to dissociate themselves from it and to initiate new translations. In light of this, one should view the criticisms against 𝔊 in *Sof.* 1.7: "It happened once that five elders wrote the Torah for King Ptolemy in Greek, and that day was as ominous for Israel as the day on which the golden calf was made, since the Torah could not be accurately translated."

(3) *Jewish exegesis.* The need was felt for new Jewish-Greek versions that would reflect Jewish exegesis.

c. The Nature of the Revisions

The revisions corrected 𝔊 in different and sometimes opposing directions. What is common to most of them is the desire to present the Bible more precisely and consistently than the original translation, the "Old Greek." The general development is from slight and unsystematic corrections in the early revisions to the extensive and consistent changes in the later ones, but this does not necessarily apply in all cases.

The revisions are known from various and sometimes unusual sources: early papyrus fragments, vellum fragments from the Middle Ages, quotations from "𝔊," the substratum of certain textual traditions, and even several of the books contained in the corpus of "𝔊."

Several of the revisions, like that of Aquila, contained the entire Scriptures of the Jews living in Palestine. In most cases, however, it is not known how many of the biblical books the revision encompassed. Some may have contained merely one book. The *kaige*-Theodotion revision (see p. 145) contained at least Baruch and the expanded version of Daniel in addition to the canonical books of the Bible, while the revisions of Origen and Lucian included most of the Apocrypha.

Some of the revisions were widely circulated, as can be seen from (1) the numerous quotations from *kaige*-Theodotion; (2) the inclusion of the *kaige*-Theodotion revision of Daniel in the corpus of "𝔊"; (3) the continued use of the revision of Aquila in synagogues until the sixth century CE.

The following early revisions were probably of Jewish origin: *kaige*-Theodotion, Aquila, Pap. Oxy. 1007, and Pap. Rylands Gk. 458.

Because of its paramount importance for the textual history of 𝔊, the Hexapla occupies a central position in the classification of the revisions, which are thus subdivided into the following three groups: pre-Hexaplaric revisions, the Hexapla, and post-Hexaplaric revisions.

d. Pre-Hexaplaric Revisions

The revisions of Aquila, Symmachus, and Theodotion—in that order—are referred to in both ancient sources and modern research as the "Three" (οἱ γ'). Relatively numerous parts from these three revisions have been preserved among the remnants of the Hexapla (see below), in various papyrus fragments, in marginal notes in Hexaplaric manuscripts, and in quotations by the church fathers.

The surviving fragments of the "Three" have been recorded in the Cambridge and Göttingen editions as part of the Hexaplaric evidence.

The concordance to 𝔊 of Hatch–Redpath (see p. 141) also contains the vocabulary of the "Three" known up to 1900—without Hebrew equivalents. Fragments of Aquila have also been entered in a separate bilingual index.[96]

α. Kaige-*Theodotion*

D. Barthélemy, *Les devanciers d'Aquila* (VTSup 10; Leiden 1963); van der Kooij, *Textzeugen*, 127-150; R.A. Kraft, "Septuagint, Earliest Greek Versions," *IDBSup*, 811-815; A. Schmitt, *Stammt der sogenannte "θ"-Text bei Daniel wirklich von Theodotion?* (NAWG I, Phil.-hist. Kl.; Göttingen 1966).

The Greek scroll of the Minor Prophets, found in Naḥal Ḥever (1952) and published in *DJD* VIII (see plate 21*), contains an early revision of 𝔊 named *kaige* by Barthélemy* (see below). A similar revision is reflected, among others, in the following sources: the sixth column of the Hexapla (attributed to Theodotion) and the *Quinta* (fifth Greek) column of the Hexapla (see n. 101), several segments of "𝔊" in Samuel-Kings (2 Sam 11:1 [10:1?] – 1 Kgs 2:11 and 1 Kings 22:1–2 Kings), part of the manuscript tradition of the "𝔊" of Judges, and the "𝔊" of Lamentations.

In antiquity this anonymous revision was ascribed to Theodotion, who apparently lived at the end of the second century CE. Hence the translational units which are ascribed to Theodotion also belong to this revision. Consequently, the revision is now named *kaige*-Theodotion, though it should be noted that its various attestations are not uniform in character (see Schmitt*). Its presumed early date, the middle of the first century BCE, solves the so-called proto-Theodotionic problem which has long preoccupied scholars.[97]

Barthélemy named the anonymous revision καίγε, *kaige,* because one of its distinctive features is that גם, "also," is usually translated with καίγε, "at least," apparently following the rabbinic hermeneutical rule that each *gam* in the Bible refers not only to the word(s) occurring after it, but also to one additional word (one of the 32 hermeneutical rules, *middot*, of R. Eliezer ben Yose ha-Gelili which is called "inclusion and exclusion").

---

96 J. Reider–N. Turner, *An Index to Aquila* (VTSup 12; Leiden 1966).

97 Theodotion's revision was quoted in sources which preceded the period of the historical Theodotion by two hundred years or more. Therefore scholars came to the conclusion that these quotations were cited from a previous translation ("proto-Theodotion") on which the historical Theodotion was based. We now know that the conjectured proto-Theodotion is none other than *kaige*-Theodotion tentatively ascribed to the middle of the first century BCE.

β. Aquila

Barthélemy (p. 144); L.L. Grabbe, "Aquila's Translation and Rabbinic Exegesis," *JJS* 33 (1982) 527-536; K. Hyvärinen, *Die Übersetzung von Aquila* (ConB, OT Series 10; Lund 1977).

Aquila prepared his revision in approximately 125 CE. For some biblical books he issued two different editions of his revision, but the relation between them cannot be easily assessed. The translation system of Aquila is the most literal of the biblical translators. His approach to Scripture, acquired from his teacher R. Akiba, determined that every letter and word in the Bible is meaningful. Aquila therefore made an attempt to represent accurately every word, particle, and even morpheme. For example, he translated the *nota accusativi* את separately with σύν, "with," apparently on the basis of the other meaning of את, namely "with" (–אֵת).

According to Friedmann and Silverstone,[98] "Aquila the proselyte" is identical with "Onqelos the proselyte" mentioned in the Talmud (*b. Meg.* 3a and elsewhere) as the author of the Targum of the Torah. Although the names Aquila, עקילס, and Onqelos, אונקלוס, are indeed closely related, there is no evidence that it was one and the same person who translated the Torah into Aramaic and revised 𝔊. Both translations are exact, but the precision of the Greek translation is much greater than that of the Aramaic one.

γ. Symmachus

Barthélemy (p. 144); J.R. Busto Saiz, *La traducción de Símaco en el libro de los Salmos* (Textos y Estudios "Cardenal Cisneros" 22; Madrid 1978); A. Geiger, *Gesammelte Abhandlungen* (Warchau 1910) 51-59; J. González Luis, *La versión de Símaco a los Profetas Mayores* (Madrid 1981); A. van der Kooij, "Symmachus, 'de vertaler der Joden'," *NTT* 42 (1988) 1-20; A. Salvesen, *Symmachus in the Pentateuch* (*JSS* Monograph 15; Manchester 1991).

Conflicting data have been transmitted concerning Symmachus's biographical details and religious affiliation. His revision is usually dated at the end of the second century or beginning of the third century CE. According to Epiphanius, Symmachus was a Samaritan who had become a proselyte, while Eusebius and Jerome state that he belonged to the Jewish-Christian Ebionite sect. Geiger* and Salvesen* are of the opinion that Symmachus was Jewish, while Barthélemy even identified him with Somchos, סומכוס, a disciple of R. Meir, mentioned in *b. ʿErub.* 13b.[99]

---

[98] M. Friedmann, *Onkelos und Akylas* (Vienna 1896); A.E. Silverstone, *Aquila and Onkelos* (Manchester 1931).

[99] D. Barthélemy, "Qui est Symmaque?" *CBQ* 36 (1974) 451-65.

Two diametrically opposed tendencies are visible in Symmachus's revision. On the one hand he was very precise (like Aquila, he based his revision on *kaige*-Theodotion), while on the other hand, he very often translated *ad sensum* rather than representing the Hebrew words with their stereotyped renderings.

During the twentieth century additional early revisions have been discovered.[100]

e. Hexapla

B. Johnson, *Die hexaplarische Rezension des 1. Samuelbuches der Septuaginta* (Studia Theologica Lundensia 22; Lund 1963); A. Salvesen, ed., *Origen's Hexapla and Fragments* (Tübingen 1997); I. Soisalon-Soininen, *Der Charakter der asterisierten Zusätze in der Septuaginta* (AASF B 114; Helsinki 1959).

In the middle of the third century CE, Origen arranged a comprehensive edition of the Bible in six columns (hence its name: Hexapla) which included the Hebrew text, its transliteration in Greek characters, and four Greek translations.[101] This composition was mainly intended for the internal requirements of the church. Origen invested much effort in the preparation of the fifth column, containing an edition of the 𝔊. This column included a notation of the quantitative differences between 𝔊 and the Hebrew text: Elements extant in Greek, but not in Hebrew, were denoted with an *obelos* (÷), while elements extant in Hebrew, but not in 𝔊, which were added in the fifth column

---

[100]a. MSS A, F, M of Exodus-Deuteronomy;
b. Pap. Rylands Gk. 458 of Deuteronomy;
c. Pap. Chester Beatty/Scheide 967 of Ezekiel;
d. Pap. Antinoopolis 8 of Proverbs;
e. Pap. Oxy. 1007.

[101]The principle behind the order of columns is not sufficiently clear. Possibly Origen wanted to provide the readers with an effective tool for the use and study of the Bible. The first column contained the Hebrew text (without vocalization), the reading of which was facilitated by the Greek transliteration in the second column. The literal translation in the third column (Aquila) provided the meaning of the individual words and the fourth column (Symmachus) focused on the meaning of the context as a whole. The fifth column, an "annotated" version of 𝔊, served as the basis of a comparison between the Jewish Scriptures and those of the Christians. The nature of the remaining columns has not been clarified. The sixth column ("θ′") generally contains *kaige*-Theodotion, but in the Minor Prophets it contains a translation from an unclear source, and in parts of Samuel-Kings it contains a text which is almost identical with the Lucianic tradition. For certain books there are additional columns called *Quinta* and *Sexta*, i.e., the fifth and sixth columns according to the Greek numbering of the columns. The *Quinta* apparently reflects the *kaige*-Theodotion revision (cf. p. 145), while the nature of the *Sexta* has not yet been clarified. See further H.M. Orlinsky, "The Columnar Order of the Hexapla," *JQR* n.s. 27 (1936-37) 137-149.

from one of the other columns (mainly from the sixth column, *kaige*-Theodotion), were denoted with an *asteriskos* (⊗).

The extant remnants of the Hexapla are recorded in separate critical apparatuses in the Cambridge and Göttingen editions as well as in critical editions.[102]

f. Post-Hexaplaric Revisions

Barthélemy (p. 144); N. Fernández Marcos and J.R. Busto Saiz, *El Texto Antioqueno de la Biblia Griega, II, 1-2 Reyes* (Textos y Estudios "Cardenal Cisneros" 53; Madrid 1992); E. Tov, "Lucian and Proto-Lucian—Toward a New Solution of the Problem," *RB* 79 (1972) 101-113.

The most important post-Hexaplaric revision is that of Lucian, who died in 312 CE. This revision, which was rediscovered in the nineteenth century in some minuscule manuscripts (denoted b,o,c_2,e_2 in the "Cambridge Septuagint"), is also known from Greek and Latin sources antedating the time of the historical Lucian. Especially noteworthy are the agreements between the Lucianic tradition and some Hebrew texts from Qumran (in particular 4QSam[a], cf. p. 115), but because of the fragmentary state of preservation of the textual traditions of the Bible this evidence may be misleading. In those sections of the historical books in which "𝔊" contains the *kaige*-Theodotion revision, the Lucianic tradition, $𝔊^{Luc}$, possibly reflects the original Greek translation (thus Barthélemy*). It is also possible that $𝔊^{Luc}$ is composed of a substratum containing the original translation and a second layer containing a revision by Lucian (thus Tov*). In any case, in these books the Lucianic tradition reflects important Hebrew readings (see, e.g., 2 Sam 12:9 [p. 271]; 23:8 [p. 268]; 1 Kgs 16:34 [p. 346]). For an eclectic edition of $𝔊^{Luc}$, see Fernández Marcos–Busto Saiz*.

3. *The Targumim (𝔗)*

B. Grossfeld, *A Bibliography of Targum Literature*, vols.1-2 (Cincinnati/New York 1972, 1977).

P.S. Alexander, "Jewish Aramaic Translations of Hebrew Scriptures," in: Mulder, *Mikra*, 217-253; J. Gray, "The Massoretic Text of the Book of Job, the Targum and the Septuagint Version in the Light of the Qumran Targum (11QtargJob)," *ZAW* 86 (1974) 331-350; B. Grossfeld, *The Targum Onqelos to Genesis-Deuteronomy* (The Aramaic Bible, The Targums, vols. 6-9; Edinburgh 1982–1988); M.M. Kasher, *Aramaic Versions of the Bible* (Torah Shelemah 24; Heb.; Jerusalem 1974); Y. Komlosh, *The Bible in the Light of the Aramaic Translations* (Heb.; Tel Aviv 1973); E. Levine, *The Aramaic Version of the Bible: Contents and*

---

[102]F. Field, *Origenis Hexaplorum quae supersunt sive veterum interpretum graecorum in totum Vetus Testamentum fragmenta* (Oxford 1875); G. Mercati, *Psalterii Hexapli reliquiae* (Rome 1958, 1965); A. Schenker, *Hexaplarische Psalmenbruchstücke* (OBO 8; Freiburg/Göttingen 1975); idem, *Psalmen in den Hexapla—Erste kritische und vollständige Ausgabe der Hexaplarischen Fragmente auf dem Rande der Handschrift Ottobonianus Graecus 398 zu den Ps 24-32* (Studi e Testi 295; Città del Vaticano 1982).

Context (BZAW 174; 1988); M. McNamara, "Targums," *IDBSup*, 856-861; R. Weiss, "Recensional Variations between the Aramaic Translation to Job from Qumran Cave 11 and the Massoretic Text," *Shnaton* 1 (Heb. with Eng. summ.; Jerusalem 1975) 123-127; idem, *The Aramaic Targum of Job* (Heb. with Eng. summ.; Tel Aviv 1979).

The meaning of the word *targum* is explanation, commentary, and even translation, and later, specifically, translation into Aramaic.

Among the various biblical translations, the Jewish Targumim (as opposed to the Samaritan Targum [see p. 81]) had a special status in Judaism. The medieval commentators often quoted from them, and in the Rabbinic Bible (see p. 78) their texts were printed in full alongside the Hebrew text. Different Targumim were made of almost all the books of the Bible (excluding Ezra, Nehemiah, and Daniel).

Probably some of the Jewish Targumim were originally created orally and were committed to writing only at a later stage. From the outset it seems surprising that Aramaic translations were made at all, since this language is so close to Hebrew. During the Second Temple period, however, the knowledge of Hebrew began to decrease when it was replaced by Aramaic. Therefore, the people became more fluent in this language than in Hebrew.

Although tradition ascribes the first Targum to Ezra, it is not clear when the first Targumim were produced. In any event, the Targum fragments found in Qumran (4QtgLev [4Q156], 4QtgJob [4Q157], 11QtgJob)[103] are early. Both free and literal Targumim were made, and it is generally assumed that the freer Targumim are earlier.

The Hebrew text reflected in all the Targumim is very close to 𝔐, except for the Job Targum from Qumran, which sometimes deviates from the other textual witnesses. Since the Qumran fragments are the earliest evidence of Targumim preserved, it is possible that the other Targumim also once deviated more from 𝔐, but were subsequently adapted towards its text.

Many of the Targumim have been published in critical editions.[104]

---

[103] See n. 107 and see also *DJD* VI (Oxford 1977) 86-89 (4QtgLev); J.A. Fitzmyer, "The Targum of Leviticus from Qumran Cave 4," *Maarav* 1 (1978) 5-23.

[104] Pseudo-Jonathan: D. Rieder, *Pseudo-Jonathan—Targum Jonathan ben Uzziel on the Pentateuch Copied from the London MS.* (Jerusalem 1974); Fragmentary Targumim: M.L. Klein, *The Fragment-Targums of the Pentateuch according to their Extant Sources*, vols. I-II (AnBib 76; Rome 1980); Onkelos, Targum Jonathan to the Prophets, and the Targum to the Hagiographa: A. Sperber, *The Bible in Aramaic Based on Old Manuscripts and Printed Texts*, vols. I-IVa (Leiden 1959–1968); the Targum from the Cairo Genizah: M.L. Klein, *Genizah Manuscripts of Palestinian Targum to the Pentateuch* (Cincinnati/Rome 1986). See also nn. 105, 106.

a. Targumim to the Torah

α. Targum Onqelos

Targum Onqelos ($\mathfrak{T}^{O}$) is the best known of the Targumim, and according to the Talmudic tradition (*b. Meg.* 3a) it was made by Onqelos the proselyte, "under the guidance of R. Eliezer and R. Joshua" (see also n. 98).

Scholars are divided in their opinions about the date (first, third, or fifth century CE) and origin (Babylon or Palestine) of $\mathfrak{T}^{O}$. Nevertheless, even if its final literary form is late, it was possibly preceded by a written or oral formulation similar to the one contained in the fragments of Leviticus found in Qumran.

As a rule $\mathfrak{T}^{O}$ follows the plain sense of Scripture, but in the poetical sections it contains many exegetical elements. It almost invariably reflects $\mathfrak{M}$, although sometimes its *Vorlage* cannot be recognized easily behind the extensive layer of exegesis. Sperber noted some 650 variants of $\mathfrak{T}^{O}$, all of which pertain to minor details.[105]

β. Palestinian Targumim

(1) *Jerusalem Targum I = Targum Pseudo-Jonathan*. From the fourteenth century on this translation has been incorrectly named Targum Jonathan (from the abbreviation ת"י = Targum Yerushalmi). This translation also integrates elements from $\mathfrak{T}^{O}$.

(2) *Jerusalem Targum II, III* = The "Fragment(ary) Targum(im)" (= $\mathfrak{T}^{F}$), so named because only fragments of it have been preserved in manuscripts and in printed editions (see plate 25*).

(3) *Targumim from the Cairo Genizah* (see p. 33 and Klein [n. 104]).

(4) *Vatican Neophyti 1* (see plate 23*), discovered in 1956 in a manuscript dating from 1504 (= $\mathfrak{T}^{N}$). According to its editor, the Targum contained in this manuscript originated in the first or second century CE,[106] while others ascribe the translation to the Talmudic period (fourth or fifth century CE).

---

[105] A. Sperber, "The Targum Onkelos in Its Relation to the Masoretic Hebrew Text," *PAAJR* 6 (1935) 309-351; idem, *The Bible in Aramaic, IV.B: The Targum and the Hebrew Bible* (Leiden 1973).

[106] A. Díez Macho, *Neophiti I*, vols. I–V (Madrid/Barcelona 1968–1978).

b. Targum to the Prophets

Targum Jonathan to the Prophets (see plate 22*) varies from book to book. The Babylonian tradition ascribes it to Jonathan ben ʿUzziel, a pupil of Hillel the Elder.

c. Targum to the Hagiographa

According to the story in *t. Shabb.* 13.2; *b. Shabb.* 115b; *y. Shabb.* 16.15c, the Job Targum already existed at the time of Gamaliel the Elder (first half of the first century CE), and an early source of this Targum has indeed been found in Qumran.[107] The Job Targum from Qumran contains a literal translation, sometimes reflecting a *Vorlage* different from 𝔐 (see Weiss*, 1979, 27-30 and Gray*), and it possibly lacks the last verses of the book, 42:12-17. The printed version of the Job Targum differs from the Qumran text.

For Esther two different Targumim, *Targum rishon,* "first Targum," and *Targum sheni,* "second Targum," are known, both of which are midrashic in nature.

4. Peshitta (𝔖)

P.B. Dirksen, *An Annotated Bibliography of the Peshitta of the OT* (Monographs of the Peshitta Institute 5; Leiden 1989).

P.B. Dirksen and M.J. Mulder, *The Peshitta—Its Early Text and History* (Leiden 1988); P.B. Dirksen, "The OT Peshitta," in: Mulder, *Mikra*, 255-297; A. Gelston, *The Peshitta of the Twelve Prophets* (Oxford 1987); M.H. Goshen-Gottstein, "Prolegomena to a Critical Edition of the Peshitta," *ScrHier* 8 (1961) 26-67; idem, "trgwmym swryym," *EncBib* 8 (Jerusalem 1982) 847-854; Y. Maori, *The Peshitta Version of the Pentateuch and Early Jewish Exegesis* (Jerusalem, 1995); M.J. Mulder, "The Use of the Peshitta in Textual Criticism," in: N. Fernández Marcos, ed., *La Septuaginta en la investigacion contemporanea* (Textos y Estudios "Cardenal Cisneros" 34; Madrid 1985) 37-53; A. Vööbus, "Syriac Versions," *IDBSup*, 848-854; M.P. Weitzman, "The Peshiṭta Psalter and Its Hebrew *Vorlage*," *VT* 35 (1985) 341-354; idem, "From Judaism to Christianity—The Syriac Version of the Hebrew Bible," in: J.M. Lieu et al., eds., *The Jews among Pagans in the Roman Empire* (London/New York 1994); id., *The Syriac Version of the Old Testament: An Introduction* (Cambridge 1999).

The name Peshitta, "the simple <translation>," was used for the translation of the Bible into Syriac, a dialect of Aramaic. This name was meant to distinguish the Peshitta from the Syro-Hexapla (the

---

[107] F. García Martínez, E. J. C. Tigchelaar, and A. S. van der Woude, *Qumran Cave 11.II: 11Q2–18, 11Q20–30* (DJD XXIII; Oxford 1998); A.D. York, *A Philological and Textual Analysis of the Qumran Job Targum (11Qtg)*, unpubl. diss., Cornell University, Ithaca, 1973; M. Sokoloff, *The Targum to Job from Qumran Cave XI* (Ramat Gan 1974); A.S. van der Woude, "Fünfzehn Jahre Qumran-forschung (1974-1988)," *TRu* 57 (1992) 38–41.

translation of the Greek Hexapla [see pp. 147-148] into Syriac, prepared in the sixth century by Paul from Tella), since the language of that version was often unnatural. Several scholars identified Christian elements in 𝔖 and, accordingly, believe that 𝔖 originated with the early Christians in the first or second century CE. It has been surmised that this translation was made in the second century CE at the time of the conversion by Abgar IX, King of Edessa, to Christianity. However, scholars (among them Maori*) have shown that this translation contains a distinct substratum of Jewish exegesis, especially in the Torah. The evidence is reviewed in detail by Dirksen*, *Mikra*, 295, who concludes that "no decisive arguments for either Christian or Jewish authorship have been advanced." Scholars also note distinctive agreements between 𝔖 and the Jewish Aramaic Targumim which have been explained in different ways. In several books the exegesis of 𝔖 is close to 𝔊 in exclusive common elements, but the nature of these agreements is not sufficiently clear. In Isaiah and Psalms the two translations often reflect a common exegetical tradition,[108] while in Proverbs the Syriac translator may have been based on 𝔊.[109]

The Hebrew source of 𝔖 is close to 𝔐, containing fewer variants than 𝔊, but more than the Targumim and 𝔙. Probably its greatest deviations from 𝔐 are in Chronicles (see Weitzman*), where clusters of verses are lacking in 𝔖, e.g., 1 Chr 2:47-49; 4:16-18, 34-37; 7:34-38; 8:17-22. This translation also contains several substantial additions (e.g., after 1 Chr 12:1; 29:18). In several ancient (Jacobite) manuscripts Job follows the Torah (cf. p. 105).

The oldest dated manuscript of 𝔖 is the MS London, British Library, Add. 14,512 written in 459/460. A critical edition of 𝔖 is being prepared by the Peshitta Institute of the University of Leiden on the basis of codex Ambrosianus (Milan, Ambrosian Library, B. 21 Inf., sixth to seventh century [see plate 24*]).[110] The first volumes of the Leiden edition offer a diplomatic edition of codex Ambrosianus with a critical apparatus of variants. The volumes appearing after 1976 emend the text of this codex if it is not supported by two other manuscripts from the period preceding 1000. Noncritical but complete editions of 𝔖 include

---

[108]Cf. especially L. Delekat, "Die Peschitta zu Jesaja zwischen Targum und Septuaginta," *Bib* 38 (1957) 185-199, 321-335; idem, "Ein Septuagintatargum," *VT* 8 (1958) 225-252; J.A. Lund, *The Influence of the Septuagint on the Peshitta—A Re-evaluation of Criteria in Light of Comparative Study of the Versions in Genesis and Psalms*, unpubl. diss., Hebrew University, Jerusalem 1988.

[109]For the data, see especially A.J. Baumgartner, *Etude critique sur l'état du texte du livre des Proverbes d'après les principales traductions anciennes* (Leipzig 1890).

[110]*The Old Testament in Syriac according to the Peshiṭta Version* (Leiden 1966–).

the edition of S. Lee (London 1823) and the editions published in Urmia (1852) and Mosul (1888-1892). For a modern translation, see G.M. Lamsa, *The Holy Bible from Ancient Eastern Manuscripts* (Nashville 1933).

5. The Vulgate (𝔙)

B. Kedar-Kopfstein, *The Vulgate as a Translation*, unpubl. diss., Hebrew University, Jerusalem 1968; idem, "Textual Gleanings from the Vulgate to Jeremiah," *Textus* 7 (1969) 36-58; idem, "The Latin Translations," in: Mulder, *Mikra*, 299-338; W. Nowack, *Die Bedeutung des Hieronymus für die alttestamentliche Textkritik* (Göttingen 1875); F. Stummer, *Einführung in die lateinische Bibel* (Paderborn 1928).

Between 390 and 405 CE the church father Jerome (Hieronymus) translated the Bible into Latin after having undertaken at an earlier stage the revision of the Vetus Latina (see p. 139) of Psalms, later called "Psalterium Romanum," and the revision of the book of Psalms in the Hexapla, the "Psalterium Gallicanum." After some time Jerome began to realize the importance of what he called the *hebraica veritas* (literally: "the Hebrew truth," i.e., the truth emanating from the Hebrew text), and, with the help of Jewish scholars, he translated the Bible from Hebrew into Latin. The name Vulgata, "the common one," reflects the degree of popularity of this translation.

The Hebrew source of 𝔙 was almost identical with 𝔐 and the Vulgate closely followed its Hebrew source while preserving certain literary principles.[111] Jerome also wrote commentaries on most of the biblical books.

Two critical editions are available.[112]

𝔙 is important for the history of the exegesis of the Bible, especially when compared with Jerome's commentaries on the Minor Prophets, Isaiah, and Jeremiah, written between 406 and 420 CE. These commentaries, as well as the translation, show that Jerome did not base himself exclusively on 𝔐, but often was guided by the exegesis of 𝔊, Symmachus, Aquila, and Theodotion (in this order).

[111] See the studies by Kedar-Kopfstein*.

[112] The Benedictines are involved in the preparation of a modern critical edition entitled *Biblia Sacra iuxta latinam Vulgatam versionem* (Rome 1926–). This edition contains a great many—mainly orthographic—variants. But the eclectic text does not always evidence a judicious insight, often preferring readings on account of their similarity with 𝔐 or 𝔊. Containing fewer data in its apparatus, but showing a keener insight is the *editio minor* of R. Weber, *Biblia Sacra iuxta Vulgatam versionem* (2d ed.; Stuttgart 1975), also available in machine-readable form.

6. The Arabic Translation of Saadia

The Arabic translation of Saadia (882–942 CE) is usually regarded as the last of the ancient translations, and at the same time as the first medieval translation. It contains only some biblical books.

The older editions of this translation represent in one way or another the MS Arabe I of the Bibliothèque Nationale in Paris. Recent editions are also based on other manuscripts: P. de Lagarde (Leipzig 1867; Göttingen 1876), J. Derenbourg (Paris 1893), and P. Kahle (Leipzig 1904).

3

THE HISTORY OF THE BIBLICAL TEXT

A. The Relation between the Textual Witnesses

B. Chiesa, "Appunti di storia della critica del testo dell'Antico Testamento ebraico," *Henoch* 12 (1990) 3-14; D.W. Gooding, "An Appeal for a Stricter Terminology in the Textual Criticism of the OT," *JSS* 21 (1976) 15-25; P. Kahle, "Untersuchungen zur Geschichte des Pentateuchtextes," *TSK* 88 (1915) 399-439 = idem, *Opera Minora* (Leiden 1956) 3-37; Klein, *Textual Criticism*; Talmon, "OT Text"; idem, "The Textual Study of the Bible—A New Outlook," in: Cross–Talmon, *QHBT*, 321-400.

This section deals with the relation between the textual witnesses described in the previous chapter. Over the years scholars have approached this topic in different ways which, in turn, have influenced other aspects of the study of the biblical text.

1. The Relation between the Textual Witnesses in Research until 1947

Until 1947—when the first Qumran scrolls were discovered—the biblical text was known from many texts, both Hebrew and translated, early and late, such as described in chapter 2. Some of these are more significant for the knowledge of the biblical text than others. These texts were generally described according to a certain hierarchy. From the beginning of the seventeenth century, when 𝔖𝔪 became known in Europe, scholars presupposed the central status of three textual witnesses, 𝔐, 𝔖𝔪, and the Hebrew *Vorlage* of 𝔊, with the remaining textual witnesses in a subordinate relation to one or the other of them.

When examining the research literature of the last three centuries, one sees residues of two central conceptions of the textual witnesses which supplement each other. One conception presents all the textual witnesses according to a division into the three exclusive groups mentioned above, while the other is recognizable from the terminology used for these units, which are usually named recensions or text-types. In that literature, the terms *recension* and *text-type* are generally applied to a textual tradition which contains some sort of editing of earlier texts, while the term *recension* is also used with the general meaning of textual tradition or simply text.

As a rule, the text of the Torah has been represented as an entity subdivided into three recensions or text-types: 𝔐, 𝔖𝔪, and 𝔊. Moreover, scholars regarded these three texts as central and exclusive axes around which other texts formed groups. The text of the Prophets and Hagiographa was similarly presented as consisting of two recensions (for there is no Samaritan tradition for these books), although it was sometimes nevertheless described as consisting of three sub-groups. The theories, descriptions, and terminology changed from one generation to the next, but the assumption of a tripartite division of the Torah and also, occasionally, of the rest of the biblical books remained constant throughout. Likewise, the understanding that these three texts (or two of them) constitute the central pillars of the biblical text remained constant, and upon this belief were based far-reaching theories on the development of the biblical text such as those of de Lagarde and Kahle* (below C).

Little has been written on the two conceptions described above and, since they developed as something that was self-evident, they have yet to be proven in research. From the seventeenth century until 1947 relatively few studies were written on the relation between the textual witnesses and the assumed process of the development of the biblical text. The first thorough description of its development is contained in an article by Kahle*, 1915. Before this time, scholars referred to the character of each of the textual witnesses separately, sometimes in connection with its relationship to 𝔐. Most of the descriptions, however, did not rise to the level of a comprehensive description of the development of the biblical text as a whole.

Even though few comprehensive descriptions of the history of the biblical text have been written in the period reviewed, the assumed relation between the textual witnesses has always been reflected in the terminology used for these witnesses. This terminology is subject to passing tendencies, and upon analyzing it, one may draw conclusions concerning the approach of scholars to the textual witnesses. Until the beginning of the present century the three main texts were usually called recensions—a term described above. Sometimes additional descriptions such as "the Egyptian recension" (the Hebrew *Vorlage* of 𝔊), "the Babylonian recension" (𝔐), and the "Samaritan recension" (𝔖𝔪) were used.[1]

1 See, for example, J. Olshausen, *Die Psalmen* (KeH; Leipzig 1853) 17-22; P. de Lagarde, *Anmerkungen zur griechischen Übersetzung der Proverbien* (Leipzig 1863) 4; J. Wellhausen, *Der Text der Bücher Samuelis* (Göttingen 1871) 3, 5; M. Löhr, ed., in: O. Thenius, *Die*

A change in the terminology began to occur with the appearance of the influential article by Kahle* on the text of the Torah. In this article Kahle called the three main witnesses of the Torah "drei Haupttypen des Pentateuchtextes" (p. 436). Kahle was in fact referring to three text-types which differed from each other recensionally, that is, each of them had undergone a different recension. For example, in his opinion, 𝔐 did not always exist in its present form, but was created as the result of a process of revision of earlier texts in approximately 100 CE. In fact, Kahle's innovation was in terminology only rather than in the concepts underlying it, for he simply continued ideas that were current in previous generations, given expression in the term *recension*. This new terminology slowly penetrated the scholarly literature, which now often spoke about text-types (Texttypen). The clearest exemplification of Kahle's ideas is to be found in a chart in the introduction by Sellin and Fohrer,[2] in which the development of the text of the Torah is described as a three-branched tree (𝔐, 𝔊, and ⅏), presenting three text-types. This chart illustrates the classical view of both the tripartite division and the character of the textual witnesses. It should be noted that in the past (as in the present), there existed no uniform terminology for the textual witnesses. Various scholars used, and continue to use, different terms when referring to the same entity. For example, de Lagarde (see n. 1) used the terms *recension* and *family* interchangeably, and this also applies to the mixed terminology used by those who adhere to the theory of local texts (pp. 186–188). On this terminological problem, see especially Gooding*.

The type of studies undertaken and the conclusions drawn from them are instructive with regard to the scholarly opinion on the relation between the textual witnesses. These studies and conclusions show the self-imposed limitations of the textual approach, since scholars always limited themselves to a comparison of the three so-called central texts mentioned above. Likewise, each new source upon its discovery was immediately integrated into the existing framework of a bipartite or, at an earlier stage, tripartite division. This approach can be illustrated by considering the evaluation of ⅏ at a time when scholars still adhered to the view of two central recensions (𝔐 and 𝔊): From the seventeenth century it was declared that of the assumed six thousand differences between ⅏ and 𝔐, nineteen hundred involved readings common to ⅏

Bücher Samuels erklärt (Leipzig 1898) LXX; H.S. Nyberg, "Das textkritische Problem des ATs, am Hoseabuche demonstriert," *ZAW* 52 (1934) 254.

2 E. Sellin and G. Fohrer, *Einleitung in das AT* (10th ed.; Heidelberg 1965) 567.

and 𝔊.[3] After scholars had recognized this, an endless number of theories appeared concerning the special relation between ⅏ and 𝔊. Such views derive from the restricted view that the biblical text was current in a small number of recensions and that all textual witnesses necessarily belonged to one of them. In this case, it was suggested that 𝔊 was translated from ⅏,[4] or that ⅏ was revised according to 𝔊, or, conversely, that 𝔊 was revised according to ⅏.[5] These and other theories show the limitations of an approach that was bound by the assumption of a tripartite or bipartite division of the textual witnesses of the Bible.[6]

The model of the tripartite division which was originally devised for the Torah, for which ⅏ has been preserved alongside 𝔐 and 𝔊, was later also applied to the other books of the Bible, especially by scholars who followed the local texts theory (pp. 186–188).

2. *The Relation between the Textual Witnesses in Research after 1947*

The description of the relation between the textual witnesses was not changed essentially with the discovery of the first Qumran scrolls in 1947. Scholars continually tried to determine the place of the individual texts within the given framework of the tripartite division of the textual witnesses. With regard to the Prophets and Hagiographa, some scholars thought in terms of a bipartite division of texts, while others, also here, adhered to a tripartite division. Scholars also continued the previous line of approach in their view of the characterization of the Qumran texts as recensions or text-types.

The assignation of individual Qumran texts to a particular text-type is reflected in the literature from the first volumes of the *DJD* series (see p. 107), in which most of the texts were described as belonging to the "type" of 𝔐, although there are also texts that were assigned to the "type" of 𝔊 or of ⅏.

For example, in *DJD*, vol. III, 2QDeut^{c} was described as reflecting a textual tradition close to 𝔊 and 𝔙.[7] According to Milik 5QDeut was

---

3 Cf. p. 84, n. 62.

4 Thus L. de Dieu, J. Selden(us), J.H Hottinger(us), and Hassencamp(ius); for a detailed description of their views and bibliographical references, see Gesenius, *Pent. Sam.*, 11.

5 Thus H. Grotius and Usserius; see Gesenius, ibid., 13.

6 The relation between 𝔊 and ⅏ needs to be reinvestigated, since all of the descriptions, both old and new, derive from the list referred to in chapter 2, n. 62, which is based on information from the era before the publication of the critical editions of the two texts. Furthermore, the list does not distinguish between different types of agreement between the two.

7 *DJD* III (Oxford 1962) 61.

systematically revised according to the Hebrew *Vorlage* of 𝔊.[8] Similarly, 5QKings was described as reflecting a mediating position between the recension of 𝔐 and that of 𝔊.[9] All these cases refer to short fragments which contain a small number of unconvincing agreements with 𝔊. Apart from the *DJD* series, similar claims were made, mainly concerning the textual character of the Samuel scrolls from cave 4. The approach which was soon to be accepted by scholars was already indicated by the name of an article by Cross on 4QSam^{a}: "A New Qumran Fragment Related to the Original Hebrew Underlying the Septuagint."[10] Similar claims were afterwards made concerning 4QSam^{b}.[11] Nevertheless, in the latest formulation of his theory in 1975, Cross laid less emphasis on the close relation between the Samuel scrolls and 𝔊.[12] Scholars also discussed the close relation between 𝔊 and the following texts: 4QJer^{b,d} (see pp. 325–327), 4QExod^{a*},[13] 4QDeut^{q},[14] and surprisingly, even 1QIsa^{a} [15]—on all these, see p. 115.

The argumentation was completed when additional scrolls that belonged to the "type" of 𝔪 were found in Qumran: 4QpaleoExod^{m} and 4QNum^{b}—on these and other texts resembling 𝔪, see pp. 97–100.

On the basis of these finds it was now stressed that the Qumran scrolls belonged to three textual groups, which were congruent with the three text-types known before the discovery of the scrolls: 𝔐, 𝔊, and 𝔪.[16] Although most of the texts found in Qumran actually belonged to one group, namely that of 𝔐, it could not be denied—or so it was claimed—that the three text-types were nevertheless represented at Qumran. Even if some scholars still insisted on the textual variety of the

---

8 Ibid., 170.

9 Ibid., 172.

10 *BASOR* 132 (1953) 15-26.

11 F.M. Cross, Jr., "The Oldest Manuscripts from Qumran," *JBL* 74 (1955) 147-172.

12 "The Evolution of a Theory of Local Texts," in: Cross–Talmon, *QHBT*, 306-320.

13 Cross, *ALQ*, 184.

14 The most recent and detailed statement is found in P.-M. Bogaert, "Les trois rédactions conservées et la forme originale de l'envoi du Cantique de Moïse (Dt 32,43)," in: N. Lohfink, ed., *Das Deuteronomium, Entstehung, Gestalt und Botschaft* (BETL 68; Leuven 1985) 329-340. For earlier discussions, see especially P.W. Skehan, "A Fragment of the 'Song of Moses' (Deut. 32) from Qumran," *BASOR* 136 (1954) 12-15; E.S. Artom, "Sul testo di Deuteronomio XXXII, 37-43," *Rivista degli studi orientali* 32 (1957) 285-291; R. Meyer, "Die Bedeutung von Deuteronomium 32,8f. 43 (4Q) für die Auslegung des Mosesliedes," in: A. Kuschke, ed., *Verbannung und Heimkehr, Beiträge . . . W. Rudolph zum 70. Geburtstage* (Tübingen 1961) 197-209.

15 See the material adduced by H.M. Orlinsky, "Qumran and the Present State of OT Text Studies: The Septuagint Text," *JBL* 78 (1959) 26-33.

16 See, for example, the remarks by Cross (n. 12) and also in Cross, *ALQ*. Likewise, see P.W. Skehan, "The Biblical Scrolls from Qumran and the Text of the OT," *BA* 28 (1965) 99; J.T. Milik, *Ten Years of Discovery in the Wilderness of Judea* (SBT 26; London 1959) 20-31.

Qumran scrolls, they nevertheless noted that within this variety three textual streams were visible.[17]

3. A New Approach to the Relation between the Textual Witnesses

𝔐, 𝔊, and 𝔰𝔪 have rightly been described as the main sources of our knowledge of the biblical text in the period preceding the Qumran finds, since all the other sources reflect far fewer significant variants. Therefore, before 1947, although justifiably described as the three most important textual traditions, these witnesses were erroneously presented as being the sole traditions of the biblical text. At that time scholars could not have known whether or not further texts would be discovered. It was also erroneous then, as it is today, to describe these texts as recensions or text-types. It should be noted that this is not merely a matter of terminology, since scholars indeed believed that these traditions reflected three separate recensions that had reached their present form after various stages of editing and textual manipulation.

As an alternative to the generally accepted theory of a tripartite division of the textual witnesses, it was suggested by Tov[18] that the three above-mentioned textual witnesses constitute only three of a larger number of *texts*. This suggestion thus follows an assumption of a multiplicity of texts, rather than of a tripartite division. The texts are not necessarily unrelated to each other, since one can recognize among them several groups (below C2). Nevertheless, they are primarily a collection of individual texts whose nature is that of all early texts and which relate to each other in an intricate web of agreements and differences. In each text one also notices unique readings, that is, readings found only in one source. As will be clarified below, all early texts, and not only those that have been preserved, were once connected to one another in a similar web of relations.

Since they do not usually show the distinctive features of recensional activity, the textual witnesses should not be characterized as either recensions or text-types.

We will now turn to the characterization of the textual witnesses, beginning with the use of terms such as *text-type* or *recension*. The use of these terms requires that the witnesses actually differ from each other typologically, that is, that each of them be characterized by distinctive textual features. A witness reflecting a text-type or recension by

17 For example, see Talmon*, "OT Text," 192.

18 "A Modern Textual Outlook Based on the Qumran Scrolls," *HUCA* 53 (1982) 11-27.

definition should show a conscious effort to change an earlier text systematically in a certain direction. Textual recensions bear recognizable textual characteristics, such as an expansionistic, abbreviating, harmonizing, Judaizing, or Christianizing tendency, or a combination of some of these characteristics. However, this cannot be claimed of two of the witnesses under discussion even though each of them does reflect typological features in small units. 𝔐 reflects a text like all other texts, and has no specific characteristics—the single typological feature that could be attributed to it is the slightly corrupt nature of the book of Samuel. 𝔊 reflects a text as well, and not a textual recension; it should, however, be emphasized that in certain sections it does contain a literary recension, so to speak, that is, a literary edition differing from the one contained in 𝔐 𝔖 𝔗 𝔙 (for examples, see many of the sections in chapter 7B). On the other hand, 𝔖𝔐 indeed reflects certain typological features throughout the Torah,[19] but since these features are also found in the pre-Samaritan texts which do not share the Samaritan ideological features, as described on p. 97–100, no claim can be made for a Samaritan recension; rather, one should speak of a group of texts having similar typological features.

Accordingly, the theory of the division of the biblical witnesses into three recensions cannot be maintained. It apparently resulted from a prejudice that was born out of a combination of two factors: on the one hand, the preservation of three representatives of the biblical text by important religious groups and on the other hand, the drawing of a parallel with the traditionally accepted tripartite division of the manuscripts of the NT. The preservation of the three texts was, however, coincidental on a textual level, even though it reflects a socio-religious reality: these three texts were considered authoritative in three religious communities, 𝔐 for the Jews, 𝔖𝔐 for the Samaritans, and 𝔊 for the early Christian community (see Chiesa*). This sociological approach was especially stressed by Talmon*.

If the tripartite division is merely a matter of prejudice, attention should now be directed to the actual relation between the textual witnesses. The textual reality of the Qumran texts does not attest to three groups of textual witnesses, but rather to a textual multiplicity, relating to all of Palestine to such an extent that one can almost speak in terms of an unlimited number of texts. Indeed, in the discussion of the textual status of the Qumran texts (pp. 114–116), five different groups of texts have emerged. Three of these were known—though in a different

19 See especially the harmonizing alterations and linguistic corrections (pp. 85–91).

form—to the generations preceding the discovery of the scrolls (proto-Masoretic and pre-Samaritan texts as well as texts close to 𝔊). The other two groups were not known before the Qumran discoveries, namely, texts written in the Qumran scribal practice and non-aligned texts, that is, texts that are not exclusively close to one of the other groups, and hence give a special dimension to all of the Qumran texts. The latter group, in particular, sheds a special light on the web of relations which exist between the textual witnesses. For example, although Freedman attempted to determine the place of 11QpaleoLev^{a} within the tripartite division,[20] it has since been clarified that the scroll is not particularly linked with any of the three main textual witnesses. It agrees at times with 𝔐, but sometimes also deviates from it. The same applies to its relation to ⅏ and 𝔊. In addition to this, it contains exclusive readings not found elsewhere.[21] These exclusive readings are often not very distinctive in their content, but they nevertheless differ from the other three texts. Accordingly, the Leviticus scroll from cave 11 actually forms a fourth text alongside the three sources that were known before the Qumran discoveries. This text possesses no specific characteristics, but its uniqueness consists in its independence from the other textual witnesses. The four textual witnesses relate to each other in a network of agreements, differences, and unique readings, in exactly the same manner as 𝔐, 𝔊, and ⅏, described above.

The discovery of the Leviticus scroll was quite coincidental, just as the preservation of 𝔊 and ⅏ alongside with 𝔐 was a matter of textual coincidence. Therefore, it would not be logical to assume that for the book of Leviticus there once existed merely four early texts. Rather, one has to think in terms of a larger number of such texts that related to each other in the same manner as the four known ones.

The above description of the textual situation of Leviticus is not specific to that book. In other books of the Bible one also discerns more than just two or three texts, as has been recognized from an examination of 4QJosh^{a}, 4QJudg^{a}, and 5QDeut, and the other texts mentioned on p. 116.

---

20 D.N. Freedman, "Variant Readings in the Leviticus Scroll from Qumran Cave 11," *CBQ* 36 (1974) 525-534. See also the official publication (Freedman–Mathews, *Leviticus*) as well as the following note.

21 See my article, "The Textual Character of the Leviticus Scroll from Qumran Cave 11," *Shnaton* 3 (1978/1979) 238-244 (Heb. with Eng. summ.) and also K. Mathews, "The Leviticus Scroll (11QpaleoLev) and the Text of the Hebrew Bible," *CBQ* 48 (1986) 171-207, esp. 198.

Therefore, the three texts which are generally described as the three central witnesses of the biblical text actually reflect only three of a much larger number of ancient texts. Alongside these, there once existed additional texts such as those found in Qumran which have been described here as non-aligned texts, that is, texts which are not exclusively close to any one of the other texts. In antiquity this latter group of texts probably consisted of many texts, as can now be imagined following the Qumran discoveries.

The picture portrayed here is one of textual multiplicity, but it should not be forgotten that within this variety, a few groups of closely related texts are discernible—below C2—and there is even one group which bears exclusive typological features, namely, 𝔖𝔪 together with the pre-Samaritan texts (pp. 80–100).

There is one additional aspect of the analysis of the relation between textual witnesses which is relevant to the present discussion. Relations between texts are determined on the basis of significant (dis)agreements setting off one, two, or more texts from the other ones. In this way the "family" of 𝔐 differs from other groups and individual texts, and this pertains also to 𝔊 and the group consisting of 𝔖𝔪 and the pre-Samaritan texts. In this regard agreements are as important as disagreements. At a certain level of the discussion, however, agreements may be more important than disagreements, especially when they pertain to very significant details, such as common errors. This principle has been stressed much by P. Maas, who, in a general treatise on textual criticism, stressed very much the importance of *Leitfehler* ("indicative errors").[22] The notion of these *Leitfehler* allows us to posit close connections between certain Qumran texts as well as between particular scrolls and 𝔊 (below, pp. 115–116). One should always be cautious in this regard, since the existence of *Leitfehler* only points to the proximity of the witnesses in the putative stemma of the manuscripts of the Hebrew Bible, and not necessarily to a direct derivation of one text from another. In the biblical realm this principle has been invoked, among others, by Sacchi[23] and Cross, "Some Notes," who stressed the notion of what he terms the "bad genes" of manuscripts.

22 P. Maas, *Textual Criticism* (trans. B. Flower; Oxford 1958) 42 = *Textkritik*, in: A. Gercke and E. Norden, *Einleitung in die Altertumswissenschaft*, I, VII (3d ed.; Leipzig 1957).

23 P. Sacchi, "Il rotolo A di Isaia. Problemi di storia del testo," *Atti e Memorie dell'Academia Toscana di scienze e lettere La Colombaria* 30 (Florence 1965) 31-111, esp. 47, 89, 106.

B. The Original Shape of the Biblical Text

Barthélemy, *Report*, vi-vii; P.G. Borbone, *Il libro del profeta Osea, Edizione critica del testo ebraico* (Quaderni di Henoch 2; Torino [1990]); B.S. Childs, *Introduction to the OT as Scripture* (Philadelphia 1979) 84-106; B. Chiesa, "Appunti di storia della critica del testo dell'Antico Testamento ebraico," *Henoch* 12 (1990) 3-14; R.B. Coote, "The Application of Oral Theory to Biblical Hebrew Literature," *Semeia* 5 (1976) 60-62; Eichhorn, *Einleitung*, Vol. I, Kap. II, Erster Abschnitt; M.H. Goshen-Gottstein, "The History of the Bible-Text and Comparative Semitics," *VT* 7 (1957) 195-201; M. Greenberg, "The Use of the Ancient Versions for Interpreting the Hebrew Text," *VTSup* 29 (1978) 131-148; A. Jepsen, "Von den Aufgaben der alttestamentlichen Textkritik," *VTSup* 9 (1962) 332-341; P. Kahle, *op. cit.* (p. 155); idem, *Die hebräischen Handschriften aus der Höhle* (Stuttgart 1951); R. Kittel, *Über die Notwendigkeit und Möglichkeit einer neuen Ausgabe der hebräischen Bibel* (Leipzig 1902) 32-47; J. Olshausen, *Die Psalmen* (KeH; Leipzig 1853) 17-22; S. Talmon, "Double Readings in the Massoretic Text," *Textus* 1 (1960) 144-184; idem, "The Textual Study of the Bible—A New Outlook," in: Cross–Talmon, *QHBT*, 321-400; idem, "OT Text," 162, 198-199; idem, "1QIs^{a} as a Witness to Ancient Exegesis of the Book of Isaiah," *ASTI* 1 (1962) 62-72 = idem, *The World of Qumran from Within* (Jerusalem 1989) 131-141; idem, "Between the Bible and the Mishna," ibid., 11-52; E. Tov, "The Original Shape of the Biblical Text," *Congress Volume Leuven 1989* (VTSup 43; Leiden 1991) 345-359; N.H. Tur Sinai, *Bʾylw drkym wbʾyzw mydh nwkl lhgyʿ lnwsḥm hmqwry šl ktby hqdš* (Proceedings of the Israel Academy of Sciences and Humanities, vol. 1; Jerusalem 1966); E. Ulrich, "The Canonical Process, Textual Criticism, and Latter Stages in the Composition of the Bible, in: M. Fishbane and E. Tov, eds., *"Shaʿarei Talmon"— Studies in the Bible, Qumran, and the Ancient Near East Presented to Shemaryahu Talmon* (Winona Lake, IN 1992) 267-291; S.D. Walters, "Hannah and Anna—The Greek and Hebrew Texts of I Samuel 1," *JBL* 107 (1988) 385-412.

Interest in the original shape of the biblical text is a relatively new development in the history of research. Before that interest developed, the biblical text was considered to have once existed in exactly or approximately the same form as that known from the medieval manuscripts and printed editions of 𝔐. With the development of the critical view in the seventeenth century, however, scholars began comparing 𝔐 with 𝔊 and the other textual witnesses. These comparisons produced a new approach, according to which one could somewhat improve 𝔐 by adopting certain details from 𝔊, or reversely, improve the content of 𝔊 by adopting details from 𝔐. As a result of this comparison, the concept of the originality of individual readings was recognized. This understanding was most clearly formulated by B. Walton,[24] who asserted at an early stage in research that only one of two readings found in different manuscripts could be original. At the same time, at that early stage the actual comparison of readings did not immediately create the understanding that 𝔐 and 𝔊 form only *part* of a

24 See his analysis of the rules for the "correction" of the biblical text: *Biblia Polyglotta, Prolegomena* (London 1657) vol. I, 36-37 (republished in the edition of F. Wrangham [Cambridge 1826] vol. I, 332-336, esp. 333).

larger entity of texts which could be called the text of the Bible, and that the original shape of this entity could be different from that which can be inferred from the known witnesses. Also, the assumption of the existence of recensions described in section A above did not give rise to theories on the original form of the biblical text. Nevertheless some isolated observations were made on the original form of the Bible. Thus, Eichhorn's* influential *Einleitung* (vol. I; Leipzig 1780; 2d ed.: Leipzig 1787 and Reutlingen 1790; 3d ed.: Leipzig 1803; 4th ed.: Göttingen 1823) spoke about the "original external *shape* of the books of the OT" (title of vol. I, chapter II, section 1), but his analysis did not yet involve a discussion of the *content* of the original text of the Bible as a whole.

The first reflections about an original text are visible in the work of Bauer, who spoke about the "reconstruction of the text of the OT such as existed before the time of the Masoretes, that is, such as came from the hands of the authors."[25] According to Bauer, for the reconstruction of this original text use should be made not only of inner-biblical parallels, but also of the ancient versions. Other scholars must have made similar remarks, which remained unnoticed for a long period.[26] It was the fame as well as the systematic thinking of another scholar, however—de Lagarde—which caused later generations to link this view with his name. The first lucid and systematic formulations about the original text of the Bible were formulated by de Lagarde (see pp. 183ff.). De Lagarde's discussion was brief, and more than what he actually said was ascribed to him by generations of scholars who drew inspiration from his clear and pertinent formulations. His discussions mainly touched upon the original shape of 𝔐 and 𝔊, but he also referred to the biblical text as a whole. De Lagarde was preceded by Bauer (n. 25), as well as by Eichhorn*, Rosenmüller (see p. 182), and Olshausen* (see p. 183), but the latter three scholars referred only to the original text of the Masoretic family and its antecedents, and not to that of the Bible as a whole. In any event, after de Lagarde had proposed his views, most scholars took a stand, either for or against.

After de Lagarde promulgated his theory on the existence of an original text of the biblical books, more scholars became interested in the shape of the biblical text before the time of the earliest witnesses. In particular, they raised the question whether there once existed a single copy, also called the (an) *Urtext*, from which all other texts were copied

---

25 G.L. Bauer, *Salomonis Glassii Philologia sacra his temporibus accomodata, post primum volumen Dathii opera in lucem emissum nunc continuata et in novi plane operis formam redacta, Tomus secundus, sectio prior, Critica Sacra* (Leipzig 1795) 235.

26 For an analysis of the views of Bauer, see especially Borbone*, 20-21.

or derived. This assumption is very important in the light of the many differences between the early textual witnesses which would seem to contradict it. An elucidation of the question concerning the original form of the biblical text does not only have theoretical aspects pertaining to an understanding of its history, but also very practical ones, since it determines (or should determine) the approach of scholars to all existing differences. Those who adhere to an assumption of one original text will try to reconstruct it, partially or fully, from these differences (see chapters 5, 6), while those who reject this view rarely resort to reconstructions, sometimes renouncing them altogether. In spite of the importance attached to this issue, the question of the original text of the biblical books cannot be resolved unequivocally, since there is no solid evidence to help us to decide in either direction. Yet each generation has to clarify the issues involved, especially now, in view of the evidence revealed in the Judean Desert.

The formulation of the different positions was greatly influenced by the descriptions of two scholars who expressed views supported mainly by abstract arguments which might even be called prejudices: on the one hand, de Lagarde, mentioned above, who was the first scholar to give pertinent expression to an opinion in favor of the assumption of an original text of the Bible as a whole (below, p. 183) and on the other hand, Kahle*, who expressed the opposite view. Kahle's formulations referred both to the history of individual texts and to the text of the Bible as a whole (see pp. 183-184). Apart from these scholars, others determined their positions on the basis of the evidence itself—as opposed to abstract arguments alone—but were not able to break free from the positions of de Lagarde and Kahle*.

It is difficult to describe at the very beginning of our discussion the views from which one has to choose, since these views have not been clearly defined. The presentations of the different positions by Childs* and before him by Kittel* and Jepsen* are the most detailed (the tables in Deist, *Witnesses*, 11-15, represent the various positions in a concrete manner). Beyond the mere acceptance or refutation of the assumption of one original text it would be ideal if those who adhere to the assumption of one original text should not be content with a vague statement of such a view, but should also express an opinion on its repercussions. It is particularly important to know which stage in the development of the biblical book, if any, can be identified as the original text. Likewise, it would be ideal if those who reject the assumption of one original text should actually formulate an alternative model which explains the development of the texts and the relation between the existing differences. There are no ideal discussions in scholarship, however, and many questions remain unanswered.

Even though the fundamental problems have often not even be mentioned, let alone solved, two main opinions on the original text of the Bible have been expressed and applied to the evidence. In brief, while some scholars have proposed the existence of one original text of the biblical books from which all or most of the known texts derived, others have rejected this assumption. The latter view can also be formulated positively, but so far it has not been clearly defined. According to the latter view, there existed at an early stage various pristine texts of the Bible which, rather than deriving one from another, apparently had equal status. The opposition between these two views pertains not only to the number of the pristine texts (one or more), but also to their relation to the various stages of the development of the biblical books. Those who think in terms of different pristine texts do not express themselves clearly with regard to the nature of these assumed texts and their relation to the stages of the development of the biblical books, while those who accept one original text refer to a presumed original shape of the text which was preceded by stages of literary development. There is almost no room for an intermediary position between these two views. It should, however, be noted that the presumably different development of the various biblical books may necessitate different theories in these books.

The question of the original text of the Bible may have entered research "through the back door" as part of the textual discussion, but beyond textual criticism, it also forms a central issue in our understanding of the general development of the biblical books, including their literary history. Without entering into details, whoever presupposes one original text of a biblical book assumes that the extant textual witnesses derived from one literary composition which, at a certain stage, existed as a single textual entity from which all texts of that book have derived. In research this entity is usually denoted with the German terms *Urtext* or *Urschrift*, "the original (or: early) text," since the German scholars were the first to deal with this abstract question. Sometimes the term *archetype* is used as well, but this term tends to be misleading, for in classical philology from which it derives, it leaves open the possibility of a large interval of time between the date of the archetype, reconstructed from the existing evidence, and the original composition. The term *Urtext*, on the other hand, refers to the original composition itself.

Because of the many problems inherent with it, the supposition of an original text has often been rejected by scholars. Some did not formulate an alternative view, while others thought in terms of several pristine texts which they defined in different ways. Common to these formulations is the assumption that the early texts were of equal importance: No text was considered more authoritative than the others. The most detailed descriptions of this view are found *apud* Greenberg* and Walters*.

In addition to these two basic positions, there are scholars who consciously refrain from taking any standpoint (e.g., Roberts, *OTTV*, and also the authors of various introductions to the Bible). Since the questions are very complex, it is understandable why scholars would refrain from expressing a view. For the praxis of textual criticism, however, it is almost necessary to accept some approach. Almost all scholars are involved with the evaluation of textual variants (see chapter 6). Those who claim that a certain reading is preferable to another actually presuppose one original text, since they claim that that reading better reflects the original composition from the point of view of the language, vocabulary, ideas, or meaning. The very use of such an argument is generally based on the perception of one original text, since otherwise two or more readings could have been equally "original," with each reflecting a different meaning. Note, for example, the well-known variation in Gen 2:2 between the reading of 𝔐 (= 𝔗^OJN^ 𝔙) ויכל אלהים ביום *השביעי* מלאכתו אשר עשה and ביום *הששי* in 𝔰𝔪 and likewise in 𝔊, 𝔖, and Jubilees 2:16—see pp. 270, 303. Those who claim that one of the two readings is preferable (e.g., REB: "sixth") imply that that reading reflects or could reflect the original text. In fact, they are claiming that either the reading of 𝔐 𝔗^OJ^ 𝔙 or the other reading better reflects the original composition, and thus they do not leave room for two alternative readings. Actually, the situation is more complicated, since even those who reject the assumption of an original text sometimes rightly speak about preferable readings in cases where, in their view, one reading was corrupted from another. The linear development presupposed by scribal corruptions enables them to react to such cases in a special way. For example, a scholar who rejects the reading of 𝔐 ויצטירו (meaning unclear) in Josh 9:4 in favor of ויצטידו, "and they made provisions," in 𝔐^MSS^ and all the ancient translations (cf. צידם, "their provisions," in v. 5 and הצטידנו in v. 12), thinks that in this case most witnesses have been corrupted, and that the uncorrupted ("original") reading has been preserved only in a few texts. In other details, however, such a scholar may think in terms of texts of equal status.

After these initial thoughts, we now turn to the difficulties that need to be taken into consideration in determining a position with regard to the original form of the biblical text.

(1) Even after the discovery of ancient texts in the Judean Desert, we still have no knowledge of copies of biblical books that were written in the first stage of their textual transmission, nor even of texts which are close to that time—with the exception of 4QDan^{c,e}, whose presumed date, 125-100 BCE, is close to that of the last stage of the composition of the book, approximately 165 BCE. A second exception is the LXX translation of the late biblical books—from the second century BCE—which is closer to the time of their composition than are many Hebrew texts from Qumran. However, in comparison with the great distance between these Qumran texts and 𝔊 on the one hand and the time of composition of most of the biblical books on the other, the availability of these texts does not diminish the distance significantly. Thus, the extant textual evidence brings us only close to the time of the composition of the biblical books. Since the centuries preceding the extant evidence presumably were marked by great textual fluidity, everything that is said about the pristine state of the biblical text must necessarily remain hypothetical. The textual diversity visible in the Qumran evidence from the third pre-Christian century onwards is probably not representative of the textual situation in earlier periods, at which time the text must have been much more fluid. The latter assumption is suggested by a comparison of parallel texts in the Bible (cf. pp. 12–13) and by the material presented in chapter 7B.

(2) Most of the biblical books were not written by one person nor at one particular time, but rather contain compositional layers written during many generations (see chapter 7A and the table in Deist, *Witnesses*, 11-16). This especially applies to the books that underwent literary processes such as the deuteronomistic revisions (that is, revisions made in accordance with the book of Deuteronomy) in the historical books from Joshua to Kings and in Jeremiah. Since the process of literary development was long, one needs to decide which, if any, of the final stages in the presumed literary development of the book should be considered the determinative text for textual criticism. This problem, discussed in particular by Kittel*, has now become more acute in the light of the situation that sections of the earlier formulations of the biblical books which were circulated at the time have coincidentally been preserved in textual witnesses. These witnesses are described in detail in chapter 7.

original text. Moreover, even this more modest aim cannot be realized, since it is impossible to reconstruct the various texts that were current in the fourth to third centuries BCE. For these reasons it is preferable to adhere to an abstract, albeit remote, aim. Even if this aim can be accomplished in only a few details, it would at least appear to be correct on a theoretical level, and must therefore be adhered to.

(4) The assumption of consecutive 'original editions' in some biblical books does not preclude the reconstruction of elements in the original text, but it does complicate such a procedure. By definition, such a reconstruction does not pertain to elements which the editors of consecutive literary editions would or could have changed (see chapter 7, esp. pp. 348–349), but it does pertain to readings created by the vicissitudes of textual transmission, often visible in textual corruptions. In other words, the genetic readings mentioned on p. 170 need to be located and evaluated in every possible scenario.

This discussion of the original form of the biblical text pertains not only to an understanding of a stage in the development of the text, but also to one's approach to the multiplicity of variants mentioned above. According to the aforementioned analysis, textual criticism attempts to reconstruct details from both the preserved evidence and suggested emendations (chapter 8) in a textual entity (a tradition or single witness), which stood at the beginning of the textual transmission stage. Not all the textual evidence is taken into consideration for this purpose, since part of it was created during the stage of the earlier literary growth (see chapter 7) or later midrashic development. Furthermore, even if one holds to a view of different pristine texts, at least some details in the early texts need to be reconstructed and emendations need to be made. All critical scholars recognize the existence of genetic readings created by scribal corruption (see p. 170), such as interchanges of similar letters, and in such cases one has to consider their comparative value in order to determine the relation between the readings.

C. Some Aspects of the Development of the Biblical Text

B. Albrektson, "Reflections on the Emergence of a Standard Text of the Hebrew Bible," *VTSup* 29 (1978) 49-65; W.F. Albright, "New Light on Early Recensions of the Hebrew Bible," *BASOR* 140 (1955) 27-33; B. Chiesa, "Appunti di storia della critica del testo dell'Antico Testamento ebraico," *Henoch* 12 (1990) 3-14; idem, "Textual History and Textual Criticism of the Hebrew OT—Some Reflections upon 'A Modern Textual Outlook Based on the Qumran Scrolls'," in press; F.M. Cross, "The Contribution of the Qumrân Discoveries to

Making–A Study of the Kethib–Qere (Philadelphia 1937; repr. New York 1971) xi-lvi; M.H. Goshen-Gottstein, "Hebrew Biblical Manuscripts: Their History and Their Place in the HUBP Edition," *Bib* 48 (1967) 243-290; repr. in Cross–Talmon, *QHBT*, 42-89; M. Greenberg, "The Stabilization of the Text of the Hebrew Bible Reviewed in the Light of the Biblical Materials from the Judean Desert," *JAOS* 76 (1956) 157-167; A.F.J. Klijn, "A Library of Scriptures in Jerusalem?" *Studia Codicologica* 124 = *TU* 124 (1977) 263-272; Lieberman, *Hellenism*, 20-27; J. Olshausen, *Die Psalmen* (KeH; Leipzig 1853) 17-22; M. Saebø, "From Pluriformity to Uniformity, Some Remarks on the Emergence of the Massoretic Text, with Special Reference to Its Theological Significance," *ASTI* 11 (1977–1978) 127-137; M.Z. Segal, "ltwldwt msyrt hmqrʾ," *Mnḥh ldwd, spr hzkrwn ld' ylyn* (Jerusalem 1935) 1-22, 254-255; idem, "The Promulgation of the Authoritative Text of the Hebrew Bible," *JBL* 72 (1953) 35-47; Talmon, "OT Text"; idem, "Tn"k, nwsḥ," *EncBib* 8 (Jerusalem 1982) 621-641; E. Tov, "The Textual Base of the Corrections in the Biblical Texts Found in Qumran," in: D. Dimant and U. Rappaport, eds., *The Dead Sea Scrolls—Forty Years of Research* (Leiden/Jerusalem 1992) 299-314; E. Ulrich, "Horizons of Old Testament Textual Research at the Thirtieth Anniversary of Qumran Cave 4," *CBQ* 46 (1984) 613-636; A.S. van der Woude, "Pluriformity and Uniformity—Reflections on the Transmission of the Text of the OT," in: J.N. Brenner and F. García Martínez, eds., *Sacred History and Sacred Texts in Early Judaism. A Symposium in Honour of A.S. van der Woude* (Kampen 1992) 151-169.

1. The History of Research

A description of the development of the biblical text must be based on solid evidence relating to textual witnesses (chapter 2) and the relation between them (section A above). Too often, however, scholars take as their point of departure abstract assumptions and preconceived ideas.

Such preconceived ideas find acceptance by all scholars, and certainly, this book is not free of them. Positions taken with regard to the composition of the biblical books and their copying, the issue of the *Urtext*, and the development of textual traditions have all been influenced by abstract assumptions and prejudices. When speaking of the latter type of approach, we refer to those scholars who describe the development of several texts in a similar way, even though each text probably developed according to different internal dynamics. For example, de Lagarde (see n. 1) described the development of the biblical text in general as well as that of 𝔊 and 𝔐 in particular along the same lines, while for Kahle (p. 184), the Targumim served as the model for describing the development of all other texts.

Taking the influence emanating from these preconceived ideas into consideration, we now turn to a description of the development of the biblical text. In this description, we first review the opinions expressed in the research and afterwards present our own views.

The reader will find only partial answers to the questions relating to the development of the biblical text in the following review, for, in the past, scholars usually referred only to limited aspects of the development of the text, even though they themselves often thought that their views pertained to all aspects. A posteriori, one could say that occasionally their opinions were correct for their time only, since the discoveries of texts from the Judean Desert, which completely altered the face of research, were not known at the time. Furthermore, one should note that many scholars described the history of the research schematically in terms of a thesis (usually: the views of de Lagarde), antithesis (usually: the views of Kahle), and occasionally, even synthesis. However, on closer examination of the details of this presentation, such a schematic presentation is found to be untenable.

One should remember that the following description pertains to the biblical text in its entirety and that 𝔐 is only one component within this framework. Scholars did not always make a clear distinction between these two levels, as can be seen, for example, from their approach to the view of Rosenmüller (see below (1)), which in fact pertains only to 𝔐.

Below we mention the views of scholars who dealt directly with important aspects of the development of the biblical text. What follows should be supplemented with the information given in section A on the relation between the textual witnesses, and the discussion in section B on the original form of the biblical books.

(1) The first theoretical statements about the development of the biblical text were by Eichhorn (1781 and later),[33] Bauer (1795),[34] and Rosenmüller (1797)[35]—in modern research Rosenmüller is often credited with the priority rights for this view, but Chiesa* has shown that he was actually preceded by Eichhorn and Bauer. All three dealt solely with the manuscripts of 𝔐 from the Middle Ages, and not with the biblical text as a whole. On seeing that these manuscripts agree even in the minutest details, these scholars determined that all manuscripts of 𝔐 reflect one textual recension, a recension which was different from the "recension" of 𝔊 (see the discussion of Rosenmüller's opinion *apud* Goshen-Gottstein*, Talmon*, and Chiesa*). This view remains valid even today, except that one should substitute *recension* with a term that is less definitive, such as *group* or *family* (above, pp. 161–162). Beyond Eichhorn (n. 33) and Bauer (n. 34), Rosenmüller claimed that all Hebrew manuscripts derived from "one source" (ibid.).

33 J.G. Eichhorn, *Einleitung ins AT*, vol. II (Leipzig 1781; 2d ed.: Leipzig 1787 and Reutlingen 1790; 3d ed.: Leipzig 1803; 4th ed.: Göttingen 1823) 129 in the first edition, and more clearly in the second edition, 111, 113, 203.

34 G.L. Bauer, *Salomonis Glassii Philologia sacra his temporibus accomodata . . .* (see n. 25) (Leipzig 1795) 396ff.

35 E.F.C. Rosenmüller, *Handbuch für die Literatur der biblischen Kritik und Exegese*, vol. I (Göttingen 1797) 244.

(2) In concise, abstract terms, de Lagarde proposed that all manuscripts of 𝔐 derived from one source which served as an archetype of what he called the "recension" of 𝔐.[36] The brief, pertinent formulations of de Lagarde, though having great influence, did not break completely new ground since they continued the line of thought of Eichhorn, Bauer, Rosenmüller (all these are quoted above), and Olshausen* in their research on the Hebrew Bible, and of K. Lachmann in the field of NT study.[37] De Lagarde resorted principally to abstract reasoning with regard to textual development but also added a concrete argument pertaining to 𝔐. In his opinion, the identical transmission of even small details, such as the *puncta extraordinaria,* in all manuscripts of 𝔐 (above pp. 55–57) proves that they were all copied from one source (the presumed *archetype* of 𝔐). This claim, without argumentation, was also applied to the manuscripts of 𝔊, all of which, in his opinion, also derived from one archetype. Moreover, de Lagarde claimed that it was possible to reconstruct the original form of the biblical text from the reconstructed first copies of 𝔐 and 𝔊. This original text was not described by him; later it was depicted in general terms by Buhl, who also claimed that it had authoritative status.[38]

This proposition became known in scholarly literature as the *Urtext* theory of de Lagarde (above, p. 165). One should note that de Lagarde's statements were very succinct and that more than what he actually said was attributed to him, partly due to a confusion of his views with those of Rosenmüller and others (see above *1*), who ascribed all the manuscripts of 𝔐 to one recension.

De Lagarde's intuitive views have been accepted by many scholars even though we do not possess the tools necessary for reconstructing the original biblical text from 𝔐 and 𝔊 in accordance with his opinion. Our argumentation in section B in connection with the original form of the Hebrew Bible in its entirety is also very close to the opinion of de Lagarde. Similarly, his view that the manuscripts of 𝔊 derived from one source (see p. 136) is generally accepted, although for different reasons: the translation is conceived of as a single act even if it later passed through a process of revision, especially correction towards the changing Hebrew text.

(3) In a series of studies Kahle (see p. 173) dealt with the original form of both the individual textual witnesses and the biblical text in its

36 See n. 1 and further: *Mittheilungen* I (Göttingen 1884) 19-26.

37 On the relation between the views of these scholars, see especially Goshen-Gottstein* and Chiesa*.

38 F. Buhl, *Canon and Text of the OT* (trans. J. Macpherson; Edinburgh 1892) 256.

entirety. In his opinion none of these textual witnesses were created in a single act, but rather through a process of editing and revising. Basing himself, on the one hand, on the internal differences between the medieval manuscripts of 𝔐 and, on the other hand, on the variants contained in the Cairo Genizah texts and the biblical quotations in the Talmud,[39] Kahle stressed, against de Lagarde, the difficulty in assuming one original text for 𝔐. Similarly, he claimed that 𝔊 did not originate in a single act of translation but rather, that various translations were originally attempted, which only at a later stage were revised into the form now known to us through the uncial manuscripts of this translation (see p. 136). With regard to the Hebrew Bible in its entirety, Kahle did not in fact reject the assumption of one original text, but emphasized that the textual sources known to us were created from an intermediary source which he at first (1915) named *Vulgartext* ("vulgar" text), and later (1951), in the plural *Vulgärtexte*, that is, texts created to facilitate the reading (see p. 193).[40] He described both 𝔖𝔪 and 𝔊 as such texts and also 𝔐, although, in his opinion, it passed through a stage of refinement in approximately 100 CE.

According to Kahle, these texts thus developed from a textual plurality into a unity, whereas de Lagarde had maintained that the unity preceded the textual plurality. Kahle's approach is in many aspects opposed to that of de Lagarde, but one cannot appropriately define the differences between them, since de Lagarde's exposition was very concise and also, the textual information on which Kahle based his opinions was not known in the time of de Lagarde.

The following points may be raised against Kahle: (1) Although there were undoubtedly texts which facilitated reading ("vulgar" texts in the terminology of Kahle), to be described on pp. 193–195, these did not have the central status that Kahle attributed to them, and there is also no proof of their early date as Kahle had supposed. (2) Kahle's claim that both 𝔊 and 1QIsa^b (see p. 31) were "vulgar" texts is unfounded. (3) Even in Kahle's time there was no justification for his claim that 𝔐 was a text that had been edited at a later period, how much more so at the present time, after the discoveries of Qumran when many proto-Masoretic texts from the third century BCE onward have become known, among which are those written in the "early" Hebrew script (pp. 217–220) that were apparently based on even more ancient scrolls. (4) Although 𝔐, like any other text, contains deliberate

39 See chapter 2, Table 3 and the discussion there.

40 In addition to the studies mentioned on pp. 155, 164 see also the three editions of his book *The Cairo Geniza* (Oxford 1947, 1959; Berlin 1962 [German ed.]).

changes, there is no reason to assume that it was created by textual revision. (5) The texts from the Cairo Genizah, from which Kahle drew his theory of textual multiplicity, are late and do not even pertain to the situation in the Second Temple period, much less the First Temple period. (6) Criticism of the approach which sees the ancient texts as recensions was discussed on pp. 155–158.

(4) Those who accepted the rather extreme opinions of Kahle are few in number. Among them one should mention in particular Gerleman* and A. Sperber. The latter scholar reduced the textual multiplicity to two principal traditions: northern—𝔖 and 𝔊^{B}—and southern—𝔐 and 𝔊^{A}.[41] In his book *Grammar*, Sperber collected internal differences both within the 𝔐 group (parallel texts, *Ketib–Qere,* etc.) and between certain manuscripts of 𝔊, as well as between 𝔐 on the one hand and 𝔖 and the transliterations in the Greek and Latin traditions on the other.

Various scholars accepted from Kahle's writings the concept of "vulgar" texts, albeit with certain changes. Nyberg,[42] Lieberman,[43] Gerleman*, Greenberg*, and Kutscher, *Language,* 77-89 ("vernacular and model texts") posited in their descriptions the "exact" tradition of 𝔐 alongside the "vulgar" texts. These texts are in essence what their name describes, that is, texts whose writers approached the biblical text in a free manner inserting changes of various kinds, including orthography. While accepting the plausibility of this opinion, we presuppose different proportions for the "vulgar" texts and use a different terminology and formulation (below, pp. 193–195).

(5) In the wake of a brief article by Albright* a new view developed, mainly in the United States, according to which all Hebrew textual witnesses were divided into groups, which were at first described as "recensions" and, later, "families."[44] These groups were linked to particular areas: Babylon (𝔐), Palestine (𝔖, 𝔐 of Chronicles, several Qumran texts), and Egypt (the Hebrew *Vorlage* of 𝔊). This view was developed in particular in the articles of Cross* (see the latest formulation in *QHBT*).

---

41 A. Sperber, *Septuaginta-Probleme* (Texte und Untersuchungen zur vormasoretischen Grammatik des Hebräischen; BWANT 3,13; Stuttgart 1929); idem, "New Testament and Septuagint," *JBL* 59 (1940) 193-293.

42 See n. 1.

43 Lieberman, *Hellenism,* 20-27; see also p. 192 below.

44 A similar view had been expressed previously by Wiener, but his views did not receive much attention: H.M. Wiener, "The Pentateuchal Text—A Reply to Dr. Skinner," *BSac* 71 (1914) 218-268, esp. 221.

The principal argument in favor of such an assumption is an abstract and logical one, which posits that texts developed in different ways and directions in the different locations in which they were preserved and/or copied.[45] According to this view, the lack of contact between the centers in which the three recensions/families were developed, created different textual characteristics. For example, the Palestinian recension is held to be expansionistic and full of glosses and harmonizing additions (cf. the features of ࠔ [p. 85–97]), the Egyptian recension is considered to be full, whereas the Babylonian recension is conservative and short.[46] The three families developed during the fifth to third centuries BCE.

The assumption of local textual families uses the logical argumentation that, in the absence of close contact between remote centers, each text developed its own form. Even if the characterizations mentioned above do not appear convincing (see below), other features of the textual witnesses do indeed fit the theory. Thus, it would seem that the editorial differences between 𝔐 and the Hebrew source of 𝔊 described in chapter 7 could well have been preserved (rather than created) in Egypt on account of its distance from Palestine. Apparently the Greek translation was made from ancient manuscripts, which had been replaced by a new edition (𝔐) in Palestine. This reasoning also pertains to the preservation in Qumran of a different edition of Jeremiah, contained in 4QJer^{b,d} (see pp. 325–327). Geographical (𝔊) or sociological (Qumran) distance from the influential circles in Palestine must have been determinative in the mentioned instances.

On the negative side, one should note that there is no possibility of verifying the details of this theory of local textual families as proposed by Cross, and it appears to lack plausibility in its present form: (1) The textual characterization is too general and cannot be proven; only the description of the Palestinian group can be supported with solid evidence, i.e., the typological characteristics of ࠔ (see pp. 85–97, 161). (2) The reconstructed Hebrew *Vorlage* of 𝔊 does not reflect any proven Egyptian characteristics; rather, it is more likely that 𝔊 was translated from Palestinian texts, as claimed by the Epistle of Aristeas (see p. 134). (3) The discovery of Hebrew texts in Qumran (such as 4QJer^{b,d}, see pp. 325–327), which are very close to 𝔊 contradicts the theory which

45 In addition, Albright* mentioned a few assumed Egyptian characteristics of the Hebrew *Vorlage* of 𝔊 as well as some Babylonian features found in 𝔐, but his examples are unconvincing and have not even been discussed in the literature.

46 See Cross* in *IEJ*, 86. The discussion in *QHBT* provides more details on the characterization of the individual witnesses in the various biblical books. For the most detailed analysis according to this system, see McCarter, *Textual Criticism*, 87-94.

connects them to the Egyptian local text. (4) Finally, in Qumran, located in Palestine, a mixture of texts, said to reflect all three local textual groups, has been found, and this fact actually contradicts the logic of the theory of local families.

2. A New Description

The development of the biblical text is described relatively briefly in this section since various aspects are discussed in other sections. In this section readers will find less information than they would like, since we do not (yet?) possess sufficient knowledge to be able to give this topic a full description. The theories and descriptions discussed in the preceding section clarify the subject from one angle only and are often too dogmatic. Since a textual theory which could explain the development of the biblical text in its entirety does not exist, one must be content with partial descriptions of limited phenomena.

The first question in any discussion on the development of the biblical text is that of its chronological framework. The lower limit for the period of the development of the biblical text can be fixed at the end of the first century CE, for the biblical text did not change greatly beyond this point in time. At that time, the texts had become firmly anchored in various socio-religious frameworks and did not continue to develop to a great extent. On the other hand, the upper limit of the textual development is not clearly defined. It is natural to assume that this period began at the moment the compositions contained in the biblical books had been completed since, from this point in time on, they were copied many times over. Limited copying had, however, already begun at an earlier stage. Segments of the books existed in writing even before the process of the composition was complete, i.e., at a stage prior to that reflected in 𝔐 (see also chapter 7). In other words, a description of the development of the biblical text begins with the completion of the literary compositions and, to a certain extent, even beforehand.

The Hebrew Bible itself occasionally contains explicit evidence of the writing of segments of the books prior to the writing of the biblical books as they are now known to us. Thus the Ten Commandments were inscribed on the stone tablets of the Covenant (Exod 34:1). Exod 24:4 states that "Moses then wrote down all the commands of the LORD." This statement probably refers to the "Book of the Covenant" (Exodus 21-23). Finally, Jeremiah dictated to his scribe Baruch the scroll containing "all the words that I have spoken to you—concerning Israel and Judah and all the nations—from the time I first spoke to you in the days of Josiah to this day" (Jer 36:2). Similarly, it appears that the editorial process, assumed for most biblical books, presupposes previously written texts. It is reasonable to assume that editors who inserted their words into an earlier formulation of a composition had to base themselves on written texts. We refer in particular to the revision by the deuteronomistic editor(s) of Joshua–Kings and Jeremiah (see p.169). It thus follows that the editors of the final stage in the composition of the biblical books acted as both authors and copyists, since in the course of their editing, they copied from earlier compositions. The same applies to the author of Chronicles who, in the process of rewriting, copied considerable portions of Genesis and Samuel–Kings, either as known from 𝔐 or a similar form of these books, as well as limited sections of other compositions. A comparison of Chronicles with its sources and, likewise, a comparison of the pairs of parallel psalms 2 Samuel 22 // Psalm 18, Psalm 14 // Psalm 53, and, like them, other parallel texts (cf. p. 12), points to many scribal differences (for examples see chapter 4C) which were perhaps created at a very early stage, before these units were integrated into the complete compositions now found in 𝔐.

At some stage, the literary growth was necessarily completed. It is possible that at an early stage there existed different early compositions that were parallel or overlapping, but none of these have been preserved (cf., however, p. 178). At a certain point in time the last formulations were accepted as final from the point of view of their content and were transmitted and circulated as such. But sometimes this process recurred. Occasionally a book reached what appeared at the time to be its final form, and as such was circulated. However, at a later stage another, revised, edition was prepared, which was intended to take the place of the preceding one. This new edition was also accepted as authoritative, but the evidence shows that it did not always succeed in completely eradicating the texts of the earlier edition which survived in places which were geographically or socially remote. So it came about that these earlier editions reached the hands of the Greek translators in Egypt and remained among the scrolls at Qumran. This pertains to many of the examples analyzed in chapter 7, especially the shorter text forms described there (pp. 319–336).

The aforementioned acceptance of the final form of the books can, in retrospect, also be considered as the determining of the authoritative (canonical) status of the biblical books. This process took place by degrees, and it naturally had great influence on the practice and procedures of the copying and transmission of the biblical books.

Since we describe the development of the biblical books in this section, it is important to connect our survey with the discussion in section B on the original form of the biblical text. According to that description, the biblical books in their final and canonical edition (as defined in the preceding paragraphs) are the objective of textual criticism. From this point of view it seems that the opinion of de Lagarde, who posited an *Urtext* for all the biblical books, is acceptable, even if several details of his view are not plausible. Our description corresponds, therefore, with the accepted view in research of one original text, albeit in a more moderate formulation, for it takes into account the possibility of earlier, written stages. It is an ancient text such as this, or various pristine texts, that scholars have in mind when they speak of the original form of the Hebrew Bible or, in a less abstract way, when they compare and evaluate readings, as described in chapter 6.

The period of relative textual unity reflected in the assumed pristine text(s) of the biblical books was brief at best, but in actual fact it probably never even existed, for during the same period there were also current among the people a few copies representing stages which preceded the completion of the literary composition, as described above. It is possible that parallel literary compositions were also current, as mentioned in the paragraph above, although no remnants of these have been preserved. If this situation could be described as one of relative textual unity, it certainly did not last long, for in the following generations it was soon disrupted as copyists, to a greater or lesser extent, continuously altered and corrupted the text. It is possible that there were mutual influences between the different stages of the literary composition or between parallel literary compositions, if such existed. The lack of unity was also due to changes that occurred in the transmission of the text in various areas, among them word division (see pp. 208–209), final forms of letters (see p. 210), script (pp. 217–220), and orthography (pp. 220–229).

Many scribes took the liberty of changing the text from which they copied, and in this respect continued the approach of the last authors of the books. Several scholars even posit a kind of intermediary stage between the composition and the copying of the books, a stage which one could call compositional-transmissional or editorial-scribal. This free approach taken by the scribes finds expression in their insertion of changes in minor details and of interpolations, such as those described on pp. 258–285. Although many of these changes also pertain to content, one should draw a quantitative and qualitative distinction between the intervention of the authors-editors before the text received its authoritative (canonical) status and the activity of the copyists which took place after this occurred. The latter made far fewer and smaller changes and were less free in their approach than the former—as can be seen from most of the Qumran texts (see further pp. 193–197).

At this stage many significantly different texts were circulating such as 𝔐, 𝔖𝔪, 𝔊, and some of the Qumran texts (p. 116). If the analysis in section B is correct, these texts are probably genetically related in such a way that they derive from one common ("original") text. At the same time it is now impossible to relate the surviving data to one common stemma, such as is often done with manuscripts in a medieval text tradition, partly due to a lack of information, and partly because there is no certainty that these texts indeed derived from one common text.

Given the fact that different copies of the biblical text were circulated, it is possible that a certain tendency developed to compare texts or even to revise or correct some texts according to others. It is therefore relevant to note that there is little evidence that such a process took place. For one thing, there is no evidence that non-Masoretic texts were corrected to a form of the proto-Masoretic text (which according to our knowledge was the majority text from the last centuries BCE onwards) or any other text. There is, however, some evidence of the comparison of texts within the group of 𝔐. Thus the so-called *maggihim*, "correctors, revisers" (cf. p. 32), were involved in safeguarding the precision in the writing and transmission of specific texts, within the family of proto-Masoretic texts. Furthermore, it is possible that the Talmudic sources preserve a tradition suggesting a conscious effort to limit the range of variation within the proto-Masoretic group of texts, but the evidence (cf. p. 32) is not sufficiently clear.[47]

It is possible that all scribes initially approached the text freely in the manner described above. It is also possible that even then there were those who did not adopt this free approach and refrained from changing the text. In any case, the earliest Qumran finds dating from the third pre-Christian century bear evidence, among other things, of a tradition of the exact copying of texts belonging to the Masoretic family, that is,

---

47 The texts from the Judean Desert are often taken as reflecting evidence of revisional activity because they contain many instances of corrections, additions, and omissions. However, most of these are corrections of mistakes by the first scribe or a subsequent one. For details, see pp. 213–216, 285. Some of the texts thus corrected with a high frequency are proto-Masoretic (MurXII, 4QJer^{a}, 1QIsa^{b}), that is, the corrections are within the proto-Masoretic family, so to speak, while other frequently corrected texts are written in the Qumran practice (4QSam^{c}, 1QIsa^{a}, 11QPs^{a}).

the proto-Masoretic texts. However, it is difficult to know whether such an approach was characteristic of this textual tradition from its earliest times. One should note that even these texts occasionally reflect the intervention of scribes (see pp. 213–216 and 285), although to a limited extent.

In this survey we have not yet referred to absolute chronological data. Although the evidence does not allow precision, in the wake of the discoveries of the scrolls from the Judean Desert it is now possible to express a sufficiently well-founded opinion on the textual developments in the last three centuries BCE. During this period several of the biblical books developed in different ways—if we are not misled by the evidence—and among the various groups within Judaism, the approach to the biblical text was not a unified one. The extant discoveries only allow for a discussion of 𝔐, 𝔊, 𝔰𝔪, and the Qumran scrolls. The latter give a good reflection of the period from the mid-third century BCE to the year 68 CE for Palestine in general, and not necessarily only for the Qumran sect. It appears that during the last three pre-Christian centuries many texts were current in Palestine; in other words, this period was characterized by textual plurality.

Although this textual plurality was characteristic for all of ancient Israel, it appears that in temple circles there existed a preference for one textual tradition, i.e., the texts of the Masoretic family (see pp. 28–33). In this connection it should be remembered that all the texts found in the Judean Desert, except for the ones found at Qumran, reflect 𝔐.

The Qumran discoveries bear evidence of the various texts that were current during this period. On pp. 107–110 these were described as texts produced by a school of Qumran scribes, proto-Masoretic and pre-Samaritan texts, texts close to the Hebrew *Vorlage* of 𝔊, and non-aligned texts which are not exclusively close to any one of these groups. Because of the existence of this latter group of texts, it would appear that for every biblical book one could find an almost unlimited number of texts, differing from each other, sometimes in major details.

In the past scholars regarded such textual variety as evidence of proximity to the so-called "main" texts, sometimes called recensions or text-types, that were known before the Qumran discoveries. This method of describing the Qumran scrolls is, however, a mere convention deriving from the chance situation that for several centuries no Hebrew texts earlier than the medieval manuscripts of 𝔐 and 𝔰𝔪 were known. Because of this unusual situation, the data were described inversely, and in recent generations texts from antiquity were compared to medieval ones. The new manuscript discoveries, however, now enable a correct description of the relations between the texts. This means that today one should not emphasize the proximity of the proto-Masoretic texts to the much later 𝔐, but rather, place the early texts at the center of the description. Similarly, one should not stress the proximity between the pre-Samaritan texts and the later 𝔖𝔐, but rather, the opposite. Thus, the way in which 𝔐 developed from ancient texts which are now called proto-Masoretic and the way in which 𝔖𝔐 was based on one of the so-called pre-Samaritan texts can be understood more easily (cf. pp. 29–36 and 97–100).

The textual variety which is characteristic of the entire corpus of the sacred writings did not exist to the same extent for every book. This is due in no small degree to the randomness of the textual transmission. That is to say, scribes who left their mark on the character of a specific text (book) by means of expansion, abridgement, rewriting, by modernizing the orthography, or by changing linguistic features did so in an inconsistent manner for certain biblical books only, so that it is impossible to draw an analogy between the specific textual development known from one book and the rest of the biblical books.

Within this textual plurality two principal textual approaches which gave rise to different texts are recognizable: less precise texts, usually and somewhat mistakenly named "vulgar," in general use by the people, and texts which were not "vulgar." The latter usually bore a conservative character and some of them were preserved with great caution by specific groups who also used them in the liturgy. Extant discoveries do not permit us to distinguish three types of texts as Lieberman* has claimed. This scholar distinguished between "inferior" (φαυλότερα) texts which were used by the populace, texts which were used for purposes of instruction and learning (κοινότερα, "widely circulated"), and "exact copies" (ἠκριβωμένα) which were fostered by the temple circles. Although this claim appears logical, there is not, as stated above, the evidence to support it. Therefore it seems that one should think in terms of only two approaches to the text. However, although the latter assumption is more straightforward, it is still difficult to know under which circumstances and in which social circles the various texts were created, perpetuated, and used. It stands to reason that the vulgar texts were not used for official purposes, such as the liturgy, but one cannot be sure of this with regard to the Qumran sect. Among the nonvulgar texts the 𝔐 group stands out. This group was circulated widely, but apparently not exclusively, by a central stream in Judaism.

Vulgar texts—these texts are known from various places in Palestine. Their copyists allowed themselves the freedom of inserting many changes and corrections into the text and even of introducing an idiosyncratic orthographic and morphological practice, such as found in many Qumran texts. Vulgar texts contained also many simplified readings, as was claimed at the time by Kahle (see p. 184). Typical representatives of this group are the majority of the texts written in the Qumran practice (see pp. 108–110). These texts are sometimes written with a great degree of carelessness and contain many erasures and corrections. From a textual point of view, their secondary nature is recognizable in orthographic and morphological alterations and innovations and in the insertion of changes in keeping with the context (see chapter 2, Table 20). It appears that the Severus Scroll and R. Meir's Torah (see pp. 119–120) also contained many secondary readings of this type, in particular, phonetic ones.

To this group also belong the pre-Samaritan texts and ꭑ. Although these texts are certainly not written negligently (see in particular 4QpaleoExod^{m}) and do not contain the unusual orthography and morphology of the Qumran practice, their scribes did permit themselves great freedom in intervening in the text. The harmonizing additions, the linguistic corrections, and contextual changes in these texts are very clearly non-original, and this secondary nature is also characteristic of the vulgar texts. The Nash papyrus (see p. 118), though not a biblical text in the usual sense of the word, also belongs to this group.

By definition, the vulgar texts contain many secondary variants (compare, for example, Table 21 and Table 22 in chapter 2), but they also contain original readings which may have been preserved in them just as in any other text. Thus, both the Qumran scrolls written in the special Qumran practice and ꭑ whose content is sometimes very artificial, occasionally contain ancient readings which are superior to all other texts, that is 𝔐 𝔊 𝔗 𝔖 𝔙.

Nonvulgar texts—Alongside the vulgar texts another relatively large number of texts lacking signs of secondary nature have become known. These are described here as nonvulgar texts and are usually conservative in nature, that is, they disallowed changes more than the other texts. Each one contains original elements which were altered in the other texts, but it is difficult to decide which text contains the greater number of such elements.

Among the nonvulgar texts those best known to us are the proto-Masoretic texts (see pp. 27–33), from which 𝔐 was created in the early

Middle Ages. Despite the scrupulous care taken in the transmission of these texts, changes and corrections such as the "corrections of the scribes" (pp. 64–67) and other corrections (pp. 213–216, 285) were inserted into them and they also were corrupted (see, for example, the text of Samuel extant in 𝔐 𝔗 𝔖 𝔙). This text is attested among the Hebrew scrolls from Qumran beginning from the third century BCE. The formation and development of 𝔐 is described on pp. 27–39.

Another text of this category is reflected in 𝔊. By chance a few Hebrew texts containing a text similar to that which stood before the Greek translators were preserved at Qumran (see p. 115).

Also belonging to this category are some of the non-aligned Qumran texts, defined on p. 116 as being texts which are not exclusively close to any one of the other texts.

All of the texts described here as vulgar and nonvulgar were current in ancient Israel during the last three centuries BCE and the first two centuries CE—it is not clear what the situation was in earlier periods. It is not known which texts were most widely circulated, for the archeological evidence is liable to be random. If one can regard the evidence from Qumran as providing a reliable picture for all of ancient Israel, a specific pattern emerges from it, namely, the relatively large representation of 𝔐: as indicated on p. 115, a large percentage of the Qumran manuscripts reflect this text. It is unclear whether the preponderance of the proto-Masoretic texts visible in the collection of texts found at Qumran and dating from the mid-third century BCE onwards is indeed representative for all of that period. For it is not impossible that the preponderance of the proto-Masoretic texts started only in the later part of the period covered by the Qumran finds, that is, in the first century BCE, or the first century CE, as suggested by the other finds in the Judean Desert. The preponderance of the proto-Masoretic texts should probably be traced to the influence of a central stream in Judaism which impelled the copying and circulation of these texts.

After several centuries of textual plurality, a period of uniformity and stability can be discerned at the end of the first century CE. This situation was not a consequence of the processes of textual transmission, but was rather due to political and socio-religious events and developments. By the end of the first century CE, 𝔊 had been more or less accepted by Christianity and rejected by Judaism. Copies of 𝔐𝔖 were in use within the Samaritan community, but since that community had become a separate religion, its text was no longer considered Jewish. The Qumran community, which preserved a wide variety of texts, had ceased to exist after 70 CE. Consequently, the main copies of the text of the Hebrew Bible found in that period were those which were copied and circulated by the central stream of Judaism. Thus, the texts from the Bar-Kochba period, found in Naḥal Ḥever and Wadi Murabbaʿat (see p. 33), reflect only 𝔐, although the evidence could be misleading.[48] Additional evidence from this period is mentioned on p. 33. These data relating to the post-70 CE period in the past have led to the questionable conclusion that 𝔐 had replaced the remaining texts, but such a construction is reminiscent of a modern cultural struggle and does not necessarily reflect the situation as it actually was. There probably was no stabilization (this term is mentioned frequently in the professional literature) or standardization bringing about what is often called the "victory of the proto-Masoretic family." The situation was probably an outcome of political and socio-religious factors (thus in particular Albrektson*). It is not that 𝔐 triumphed over the other texts, but rather, that those who fostered it probably constituted the only organized group which survived the destruction of the Second Temple. Thus, after the first century CE a description of the transmission of the text of the Hebrew Bible actually amounts to an account of the history of 𝔐—see pp. 33–36. The Torah scroll from the synagogue of Severus and R. Meir's Torah (see pp. 119–121) probably are an exception to this situation.

We do not possess evidence on whether during this period some sort of official meeting took place during which a decision was reached on the authoritative status of the twenty-four books of the Hebrew Bible according to 𝔐. Various scholars have mentioned in this context a meeting or council that was held at *Jabneh*, Jamnia, between the years 75 and 117 CE.[49] In the ancient texts, however, we find only references to a *beth din*, "law court," a *metibta*ʾ, "academy," a *yeshivah*, and a *beth midrash* ("school" or "college") at Jabneh. There is no reference to any convention or council. In addition to this, according to Leiman,[50] the only decision reached at Jabneh was that "the Song of Songs and Ecclesiastes render the hands unclean" (*m. Yad.* 3.5). No decision was

---

48 Possibly the evidence does not give a correct representation of the situation in all of Palestine at the time of the Bar Kochba revolt. The documents found at Naḥal Ḥever and Wadi Murabbaʿat were left there by Bar Kochba's warriors, and since the revolt was supported by various rabbis, the scrolls probably were representative only for the mainstream in Judaism.

49 See J.P. Lewis, "What Do We Mean by Jabneh?" *JBR* 32 (1964) 125-132.

50 See S. Leiman, *The Canonization of Hebrew Scripture—The Talmudic and Midrashic Evidence* (Transactions of the Connecticut Academy of Arts and Sciences 47; Hamden, CO 1976) 120-124.

taken on the authoritative (canonical) status of all of the biblical books and it is hard to know whether the activities of the rabbis at Jabneh had any influence on the position of the text during that period.

The above survey has dealt with the Hebrew Bible as an entity, but one should remember that each of the biblical books had a separate history—each one developed in a different way and received canonical status at a different time. The number of variant readings that one might expect to find in a particular book is a direct result of the complexity of its literary development and textual transmission.

Within this framework, one should pay attention to the Torah, which had a history of development as complex as the rest of the biblical books, but which also had a distinctive status and on account of this, might be expected to have a special position from a textual point of view. The evidence does not, however, support such an assumption. While on the one hand, the orthography of the Torah in 𝔐 is usually more conservative than that of the rest of the biblical books (see p. 229), on the other hand, the quantity of variant readings that it contains was not less than that of the other books. 𝔊 also reflects in the Torah as wide a range of variant readings as in the other books and the pre-Samaritan texts and 𝔖𝔪 also exhibit extensive editorial intervention in the Torah. At the same time, there is one area in which a special approach to the Torah may be detected. As mentioned on p. 86, some readers and scribes of the Torah were more sensitive to divergencies in narratives between the books of the Torah and to "inconsistencies" within stories than to similar features in the other biblical books. Therefore, with some exceptions, textual developments such as those known for the Torah in 𝔖𝔪 and the pre-Samaritan texts are not in evidence for the other biblical books.

One should always remember that it is the random preservation of evidence that determines the character of a description such as the one given here. Moreover, the textual nature of the books included in 𝔐 and 𝔊 has been determined by the selection of ancient scrolls from which these texts were composed. This selection has also come about to a great extent by chance. For example, the somewhat corrupt nature of the book of Samuel in 𝔐 (cf. p. 194) was apparently due to the copy of this book that was entered into 𝔐 and which, by chance, had become corrupted to a certain extent at an earlier stage. Accordingly, the distinctive state of Samuel does not reveal anything of the history of the book's transmission or the approach of the early copyists towards it. It only shows something of the nature of 𝔐 in this book alone. Similarly, it was only by chance that important data on the development of the book of Jeremiah were discovered in Qumran and have been preserved in 𝔊 (see pp. 325–327), and it is quite probable that other books also passed through a similar process of editing.

4

THE COPYING AND TRANSMITTING OF THE BIBLICAL TEXT

A. Demsky and M. Bar-Ilan, "Writing in Ancient Israel and Early Judaism," in: Mulder, *Mikra*, 1-38; Freedman–Mathews, *Leviticus*; Ginsburg, *Introduction*; M. Glatzer, "The Aleppo Codex—Codicological and Paleographical Aspects," *Sefunot* 4 (Jerusalem 1989) 167-276 (Heb. with Eng. summ.); Habermann, *Ketav*; M. Haran, "On the Diffusion of Literacy and Schools in Ancient Israel," *VTSup* 40 (1988) 81-95; M. Higger, *mskt swprym wnlww ʿlyh mdrš mskt swprym b'* (New York 1937; repr. Jerusalem 1970); Martin, *Scribal Character*; M.Z. Segal, "ltwldwt msyrt hmqrʾ," *mnḥh ldwd, spr hzkrwn l-d' Yellin* (Heb.; Jerusalem 1935) 1-22, 154-155; idem, *Mbwʾ hmqrʾ*, vol. IV (Jerusalem 1960) 842-892; J.P. Siegel, *The Scribes of Qumran, Studies in the Early History of Jewish Scribal Customs, with Special Reference to the Qumran Biblical Scrolls and to the Tannaitic Traditions of Massekheth Soferim*, unpubl. diss., Brandeis University, Waltham MA 1972.

Relevant major works from the study of classical **Greek** and **Latin** texts: V. Gardthausen, *Griechische Palaeographie*, vols. I-II (Leipzig 1911-1913); F.W. Hall, *A Companion to Classical Texts* (Oxford 1913; repr. Chicago 1970); L.D. Reynolds and N.G. Wilson, *Scribes and Scholars—A Guide to the Transmission of Greek and Latin Literature* (3d ed.; Oxford 1991); E.M. Thompson, *An Introduction to Greek and Latin Palaeography* (Oxford 1912).

A. Background and Chronological Framework

This chapter deals with the copying of the biblical books and their transmission from one generation to the next. The biblical text developed and changed much throughout many generations of copying and transmission, as can be seen from the many differences between the textual witnesses. The smaller differences are described in this chapter and the larger ones in chapter 7.

This chapter is devoted to the process of copying and transmission which took place during the second and last stage of the development of the biblical books. Theoretically one can divide the formation of the biblical books into two stages: a first stage in which the books were composed and a second stage during which the text was copied and transmitted. The first stage was completed with the emergence of the finished literary works, more or less similar to the biblical books now known to us. The second stage began at this point, although the process of copying was actually started even prior to the completion of the biblical books as we now know them. The biblical books underwent different stages of writing and revision and these involved a process of copying as well (chapter 3B; chapter 7A). By the same token it may be assumed that a very limited amount of literary development continued at the second stage.

The lower limit of the transmission of the text is the era of printing, for changes and corruptions were added to every biblical book until that time and in fact even beyond it, as printing errors continued to be made to a limited extent (see pp. 7–8). For the purpose of the present discussion, however, it is permissible to overlook the variants created during the era of printing and even the relatively few variants that developed during the Middle Ages. Most of the variants were created before the second century CE and it is on this period that the discussion in this chapter is concentrated. The variants that were created in a later period have been described and documented on pp. 33–35 (for the rabbinic literature; see also Table 3 there), pp. 35–36 (for the manuscripts from the Middle Ages; see also Table 4 there), and on pp. 2–8 (for differences between editions as well as printing errors).

In the past, various descriptions of the copying of the biblical books and their transmission have been made by scholars who had at their disposal such evidence as an internal comparison of parallel texts within 𝔐, manuscripts of 𝔐 and 𝔖𝔪 from the Middle Ages, the Nash papyrus (p. 118), the ancient translations, and various remarks in the rabbinic literature on the writing of the Holy Scriptures. We continue to learn much from these texts concerning the copying and history of transmission, but the discoveries of documents from the Second Temple period enriched our knowledge significantly. An examination of the texts from the Judean Desert has confirmed many details that were previously hypothetical and with the help of these scrolls we now understand other aspects of the copying and transmission of the text which were not previously known. Indeed, the corpus of the Qumran texts provides information on many aspects of the copying and transmitting of the biblical text: the writing in scrolls; the measures, content, and scope of the scrolls; the measures of columns, margins, and lines in these scrolls; scribal practices pertaining to such matters as paragraphing, ruling, correcting, word division, the use of final letters, and scribal marks; stichometric arrangement; orthographical practices; the writing in different scripts; the similarity of certain letters and the confusions caused by it; different types of errors in the text; and types of textual variation.

B. The Copying of the Biblical Text

1. *Materials, Shape, and Scope*

Extensive bibliography *apud* Eissfeldt, *Introduction,* § 114; see further:
R.T. Anderson, *Studies in Samaritan Manuscripts and Artifacts: The Chamberlain–Warren Collection* (American Schools of Oriental Research Monographs 1; Cambridge 1978); M. Bar-Ilan, *swprym wsprym bymy byt šny wbtqwpt hmšnh whtlmwd* (2d ed.; Bar Ilan University, Ramat Gan 1991); M. Beit-Arié, "Some Technical Practices Employed in Hebrew Dated Medieval Manuscripts," *Litterae textuales* (Codicologica 2, Eléments pour une codicologie comparée; Leiden 1978) 72-92; idem, *Hebrew Codicology* (Jerusalem 1981); Th. Birt, *Das Antike Buchwesen in seinem Verhältniss zur Litteratur* (Berlin 1882); L. Blau, *Studien zum althebräischen Buchwesen und zur biblischen Literaturgeschichte* (Budapest 1902 [= Strassburg 1902]); A.D. Crown, "Studies in Samaritan Scribal Practices and Manuscript History: III. Columnar Writing and the Samaritan Massorah," *BJRL* 67 (1984) 349-381; idem, *The Form and Codicology of Samaritan Biblical, Historical and Liturgical Manuscripts,* in press; M. Glatzer (see p. 199); M. Haran, "Book-Scrolls in Israel in Pre-Exilic Times," *JJS* 33 (1982) 161-173; idem, "Book-Scrolls at the Beginning of the Second Temple Period—The Transition from Papyrus to Skins," *HUCA* 54 (1983) 111-122; idem, "More Concerning Book-Scrolls in Pre-Exilic Times," *JJS* 35 (1984) 84-85; idem, "The Size of Books in the Bible and the Division of the Pentateuch and the Deuteronomistic Work," *Tarbiz* 53 (1984) 329-352 (Heb. with Eng. summ.); idem, "Bible Scrolls in Eastern and Western Jewish Communities from Qumran to the High Middle Ages," *HUCA* 56 (1985) 21-62; idem, "Book Size and the Device of Catch-Lines in the Biblical Canon," *JJS* 36 (1985) 1-11; idem, "The Codex, the *Pinax* and the Wooden Slats," *Tarbiz* 57 (1988) 151-164 (Heb. with Eng. summ.); idem, "Torah and Bible Scrolls in the First Centuries of the Christian Era," *Shnaton* 10 (1986-1989) 93-106 (Heb. with Eng. summ.); H. Hunger, "Antikes und mittelalterliches Buch- und Schriftwesen," in: H. Hunger et al., *Geschichte der Textüberlieferung der antiken und mittelalterlichen Literatur,* vol. I (Zurich 1961) 25-61; F.G. Kenyon, *Books and Readers in Ancient Greece and Rome* (Oxford 1951); *La paléographie hébraique médiévale, Colloques internationaux du Centre National* (Paris 1974); J. Poole and R. Reed, "The Preparation of Leather and Parchment by the Dead Sea Scrolls Community," *Technology and Culture* 3 (1962) 1-26; C.H. Roberts, *Manuscript, Society and Belief in Early Christian Egypt* (London 1979); E. Robertson, "Notes and Extracts from the Semitic MSS. in the John Rylands Library, III. Samaritan Pentateuch MSS. with a Description of Two Codices," *BJRL* 21 (1937) 244-272; M. Steinschneider, *Vorlesungen über die Kunde hebräischer Handschriften, deren Sammlungen und Verzeichnisse* (Leipzig 1897; 2d ed.: Jerusalem 1937); E.G. Turner, *The Typology of the Early Codex* (Philadelphia 1977); M.O. Wise, *Thunder in Gemini* (Journal for the Study of the Pseudepigrapha, Suppl. Series 15; Sheffield 1994) 103-151.

The discussion in this section principally concerns the data about the copying of the biblical text during the period of the First and Second Temple. Some details of the copying of the manuscripts of 𝔐 and 𝔖 from the Middle Ages are included, since these apparently reflect earlier practices—for an extensive discussion of transcription practices in the Middle Ages see Glatzer*.

During the First and Second Temple period, texts were written on stone, clay tablets, wood, pottery, papyrus, metal (the silver rolls from Ketef Hinnom, cf. p. 118, for early periods and the copper scroll from

a few Qumran copies of the Torah which contain two books (see Table 19 on pp. 104-105) and Mur1 probably containing Genesis, Exodus, and Numbers. Note that the Minor Prophets were regarded as one book (see MurXII and the Greek scroll from Naḥal Ḥever, 8ḤevXIIgr). On the other hand, according to opinions expressed in *b. B. Bat.* 13b, different rabbis permitted the copying of scrolls of varying scope: small scrolls containing only one book and larger scrolls encompassing all the books of the Torah, Prophets, or Writings, and even a scroll containing the entire Hebrew Scriptures. *B. Giṭ.* 60a forbids the use in the synagogue of separate scrolls of the individual books of the Torah.

The length of the scroll was determined not only by its contents as described in the previous paragraph, but also by the physical limitations of the total length of the sheets or sections of papyrus or leather that had been joined together. Very few complete scrolls have been preserved and therefore insufficient data are known about the length of the scrolls: the longest of the well-preserved Qumran scrolls are 1QIsa[a], which contains the entire 66 chapters of Isaiah (7.34 m) and the nonbiblical 11QTemple[a] (8.148 m—the reconstructed length of the complete scroll is 8.75 m). As suggested by the data in the previous paragraph, it is, however, reasonable to assume that even longer scrolls were in use at the time. For example, the reconstructed length of the Greek Minor Prophets Scroll from Naḥal Ḥever, 8ḤevXIIgr (publication: *DJD* VIII) is more than 10 meters, and that of 4QRP[b-e] (= 4Q364-367) is 22-27 meters. On the other hand, very small scrolls have also been found (see below).

Length of the sheets—among the finds from the Judean Desert, the length of the sheets of leather that were fastened together into one scroll varies from between 26 and 89 cm: 1QIsa[b] (26-45 cm), 1QIsa[a] (35-62 cm), 11QT[a] (37-61 cm), 1QH[a] (56-62 cm), MurXII (62 cm), 1QpHab (62-79 cm), 11QpaleoLev[a] (63 cm), 1QM (47-89 cm), and 11QPs[a] (72-87 cm). Papyrus scrolls have not been found.

The number of columns in the leaves and their measurements—the ruling of the empty columns (*d[e]latot*, "columns," according to Jer 36:23 and *dapim*, "pages," in Talmudic terminology) that are found at the end of several Qumran scrolls (1QpHab, 11QpaleoLev[a], 11QPs[a], 11QT[a]) shows that scribes marked out the columns on the sheets before copying. In 1QIsa[a] and 11QT[a] the leaves contain three or four columns, and in two instances 1QIsa[a] contains only two columns; 1QH[a] has 4 columns; 1QM has 3, 4, 6, and 5 columns; 11QPs[a] contains 4, 5, and 6 columns; and 1QpHab has 6 and 7 columns. The first sheet of 4QDeut[n] contains only one column. In contrast to the practice at Qumran, according to *y. Meg.*

1.71d and *Sof.* 2.10 one should not write less than three columns or more than eight, but a single column is allowed for the final sheet.

In the medieval Masoretic codices which are described by Blau*, 138-139, there were usually 2 and 3 columns.

In several Qumran texts the *length and width of the columns* was fairly consistently fixed, while in other Qumran texts the measurements varied from sheet to sheet. Most biblical scrolls contain an average of 20 lines and the width of the columns fluctuates between 6 and 20 cm (usually 10-11 cm). The measurements given in *b. Menaḥ.* 30a mentioning lines of 32 letters, including the spaces between the words, conform with the narrow scrolls from Qumran. Apart from the "Five Scrolls" (see below), the size of the book apparently did not influence the measurements of the columns. For all *external aspects* of the column structure, see Table 7 (p. 231) and plate 8a*.

It appears from the Qumran scrolls that there was a custom of writing the "Five Scrolls" in *small column blocks*: 6QCant has columns of only 7 lines, 2QRuth^{a} has 8 lines, 5QLam^{a} 7 lines, 4QLam (Qumran practice—see pp. 108–110) has 10–11 lines, 4QCant^{a} 14 lines, and 4QCant^{b} 14–15 lines. On the other hand, 4QQoh^{a} (Qumran practice) contains 20 lines.

Another scroll of *small dimensions* also written in small column blocks probably contained only the "Song of Moses" in Deuteronomy 32, viz., 4QDeut^{q} with narrow columns of 11 lines and a final column of 15 spaces. Other scrolls written in small column blocks probably did not contain the complete biblical books: 4QGen^{d} (11 lines), 4QExod^{e} (8 lines), cols. II-V of 4QDeut^{n} (12 lines), 4QDeut^{j} (14 lines), 5QDeut (15 lines), 4QEzek^{b} (11 lines) and 4QPs^{b} (16 or 18 narrow lines; see plate 7*).

Scrolls written in *longer columns*: 11QPs^{a} (25-26 lines), 1QIsa^{a} (28-32 lines), 1QIsa^{b} (35 lines), MurXII (39 lines), 11QpaleoLev^{a} (42 lines), MasPs^{b} (44 lines), XḤev/SeNum^{b} (44 lines), and 4QIsa^{b} (45 lines). Long columns are also reconstructed for the following scrolls: 4QGen^{e} (50 lines), MurGen–Num (50 lines), 4QExod^{b} (50 lines), 4QpaleoGen-Exod^{l} (55–60 lines), 4QExod-Lev^{f} (60 lines).

In the Qumran scrolls the size of the *upper margin* is usually smaller than that of the bottom margin (so also *b. Menaḥ.* 30a; *y. Meg.* 1.71d; *Sof.* 2.5).

The degree of *consistency* within each text varies from scroll to scroll. Some scrolls are written in identical columns throughout, while in others, written in the same hand, the size of the column changes slightly from one sheet to the next (e.g., 1QIsa^{a}, 4QNum^{b}, 4QCant^{b}, 4QPs^{b}, 4QLam, 8ḤevXIIgr).

2. *Writing Practices*

E.N. Adler, *An Eleventh Century Introduction to the Hebrew Bible Being a Fragment from the Sepher ha-Ittim of Rabbi Judah ben Barzilai of Barcelona, or the Similar Work of a Contemporary* (Oxford 1897); Martin, *Scribal Character*; Oesch, *Petucha*; idem, "Textgliederung im AT und in den Qumranhandschriften," *Henoch* 5 (1983) 289-321; E.J. Revell, "Biblical Punctuation and Chant in the Second Temple Period," *JSJ* 7 (1976) 181-198; G.H. Wilson, *The Editing of the Hebrew Psalter* (SBLDS 76; Chico, CA 1985) 93-138; Yeivin, *Introduction*, 36-49.

The writing practices connected with the copying of the biblical books in scrolls and codices developed over many generations. One block of writing traditions is known from Qumran, and a later one is reflected in Masoretic codices and the practices in the Talmud and collected with additions in *Massekhet Sefer Torah*, from the early post-Talmudic period, and with more details in *Massekhet Soferim*.[5] Although the latter tractate is post-Talmudic (ninth century), it is based on *Massekhet Sefer Torah* as well as on other early sources, and thus preserves earlier traditions which go back to the Talmud and the Talmudic period. *Massekhet Soferim* contains *halakhot*, "religious instructions," pertaining to such matters as writing materials, the skin and its preparation, the scribes, the measurements of the sheets, columns, lines, and margins, the correction of errors, the writing of divine names, matters of storage, and the reading of the books.

The following discussion concentrates on the early finds—principally from Qumran—of all the witnesses of the biblical text including early representatives of 𝔐. Several of the practices to be analyzed below have been discussed on pp. 49–58 in connection with 𝔐. The writing practices reflected in medieval Masoretic codices are described by Yeivin, *Introduction*; Glatzer* (see p. 199); and Steinschneider* (see p. 201).

a. Word Division

Driver, *Samuel*, xxviii-xxx; Ginsburg, *Introduction*, 158-162; A.R. Millard, "'Scriptio Continua' in Early Hebrew—Ancient Practice or Modern Surmise?" *JSS* 15 (1970) 2-15; J. Naveh, "Word Division in West Semitic Writing," *IEJ* 23 (1973) 206-208; Revell, "*Biblical Punctuation*" (see bibliography of section 2).

In most of the Qumran scrolls written in the Assyrian ("square") script as well as in the medieval codices, scribes divided the words by means

---

5 For the latter see the edition by M. Higger listed on p. xx. For the former, see idem, *Seven Minor Treatises, Sefer Torah; Mezuzah; Tefillin; Ẓiẓith; ʿAbadim; Kutim; Gerim* (New York 1930); see also the translation by A. Cohen, *The Minor Tractates of the Talmud*, vols. 1-2 (London 1965).

of spaces—a method commonly used from the beginning of the seventh century BCE for documents written in the Aramaic and Assyrian ("square") script. At an earlier stage, in the documents written in the formal style in the "early" Hebrew script, words were divided by means of very short vertical lines and at a later stage words were divided by means of dots. This system is indeed reflected in early inscriptions written in the Hebrew script. viz., the Moabite Mesha Stone, the Siloam Inscription, and the Ophel Inscription.[6] Dots were also used in almost all biblical texts from Qumran written in the paleo-Hebrew script (e.g. 4QpaleoExod^{l,m} [see plate 2*], 6QpaleoLev, 11QpaleoLev^{a}), and also in ꟿ (see plate 16*). On the basis of this evidence, it seems likely that word division of some kind was also used in ancient biblical texts (so Millard*, Naveh*).

On the other hand, many scholars claim that the first biblical texts were written without any word division in the *scriptio (scriptura) continua,* "continuous script," as already suggested by Nachmanides in his introduction to the Torah.[7] This assumption is supported both by Phoenician inscriptions, which do not contain word division, and by the following indirect evidence.

(1) Many variants in biblical manuscripts reflect differences in word division. These differences, representing different views on the content of the text, may have been created with the introduction of word division—see pp. 252–253.

(2) *Tefillin* and *mezuzot* (see p. 119 and appendix 1 to this section on pp. 230–231) were written in continuous script. However, since this writing contains letters with final forms, it apparently does not reflect an ancient custom. Moreover, these documents were written in an informal script which, like other texts written in the Aramaic script, lacks spaces between the words. It is also possible that the lack of word division was intended to save space.

However, the assumption that the first biblical texts were written in the *scriptio (scriptura) continua* is not supported by the evidence pertaining to the biblical texts written in the paleo-Hebrew or the Aramaic (Assyrian) script. At the same time, the evidence from Qumran as well as the many variations in word division (cf. pp. 252–253) show that the boundaries between words were not always indicated well.

---

6 See M. Ben Dov, "A Fragment of a Hebrew Inscription from First Temple Times Found on the Ophel," *Qadmoniot* 17 (1984) 109-111 (Heb.).

d. Stichographic Arrangement

Several of the poetic texts from the Judean Desert are arranged stichographically, and according to Oesch, *Petucha,* 335-340 these arrangements were embedded in the original writing of these sections. Three main systems are recognizable: i. One hemistich or two hemistichs (without spaces between them) per line—see plates 7* and 8*—: 4QPs^{b,d,l,w}, 4QPs^{g,h}, 11QPs^{a} (in the latter three in Psalm 119 which also in 𝔐 has a special status), 4QDeut^{b,q} and probably also 4QDeut^{c} (all: Deut 32), 4QJob^{a} and 4QpaleoJob. ii. Two (hemi)stichs per line with spaces between them in the middle of the line: 1QDeut^{b}, 4QpaleoDeut^{r} (both: Deuteronomy 32), 1QPs^{a}, 4QPs^{c}, 5QPs, 8QPs, 11QPs^{b}, 5/6ḤevPs, MasPs^{a}, 4QProv^{a}, 2QSir, and MasSir. iii. Spaces after a hemistich or a cluster of two-three words at different places in the line: MasPs^{b}, 4QProv^{b} and 4QRP^{c} (4Q365), frg. 6b in Exodus 15.

In addition, several scrolls have titles in the beginning or middle of the line, a custom not known from other ancient biblical texts, e. g. MasPs^{a} Ps 82:1 in the middle of the line: "A Psalm of Asaph."[9]

Partly different and partly similar conventions of writing in stichs became standard in the medieval writing tradition of 𝔐. As a rule, the writing system of the Masoretic manuscripts reflected the relevant statements in Talmudic sources, but this does not pertain to all Masoretic codices. See further pp. 207–208.

One method used in Masoretic manuscripts was "a half-brick, אריח, over a half-brick and a whole brick, לבנה, over a whole brick," i.e., an inscribed part above another inscribed part in the following line with an uninscribed part appearing above an uninscribed part in the following line. According to *b. Meg.* 16b, the lists of the kings of Canaan in Josh 12:9–24 and of the sons of Haman in Esth 9:6–9 are written in this way, and *Sof.* 1:11 includes Deuteronomy 32 (see plate 10*) in this arrangement. Another system of stichographic arrangement in the MT is "a half-brick over a whole brick and a whole brick over a half-brick," i.e., an inscribed part placed over an uninscribed part in the following line and vice versa (our explanation of what constitutes a half-brick and a brick follows Rashi in *b. Meg.* 16b). According to *b. Meg.* 16b (see also *b. Menaḥ.* 31b; *b. Shabb.* 103b; *y. Meg.* 3.74b; *Sof.* 1.11), this system was used for "all the Songs" contained in non-poetic books (beyond Deuteronomy 32), e.g., the Song at the Sea (Exod 15:1–18; see plate 12*) and the Song of Deborah (Judg 5:2–30; see plate 11*).

---

9 See further: 4QPs^{e} Psalm 126; 5/6ḤevPs col. VII, line 8. At the beginning of the line: 4QPs^{b} XXII, 10; 4QPs^{e} frg. 26 ii, line 3 ; 5/6ḤevPs V, line 17; VI, line 13; MasPs^{a} Ps 84.

In the Samaritan tradition of writing, certain sections are written in a fixed way with an identical arrangement of the parts of the sentence or sometimes of the stichs. In such cases, the line is divided into two or three equal parts. Apart from this, Samaritan scribes often arranged the writing block in such a way that identical letters and words were written underneath each other and the first letter(s) were separated from the continuing text by a space (see plate 16*). According to Crown* (p. 201), these Samaritan customs reflect Jewish writing traditions from the Second Temple period.

e. Scribal Marks and Procedures

Martin, *Scribal Character*, 154-189; S. Talmon, "Prolegomenon" to R. Butin, *The Ten Nequdoth of the Torah or the Meaning and Purpose of the Extraordinary Points of the Pentateuch (Massoretic Text)* (Baltimore 1906; repr. New York 1969); E. Tov, "The Textual Base of the Corrections in the Biblical Texts Found at Qumran," in: D. Dimant and U. Rappaport, eds., *Forty Years of Research in the Dead Sea Scrolls*, in press.

In the Hebrew texts from the Judean Desert—and also in the later tradition of 𝔐—various scribal marks were used which are similar to those known from Greek manuscripts from the Judean Desert and from Egypt. Not all these marks are understood, but they can nevertheless be classified as serving one of the following purposes: α. correction of errors; β. paragraphing; and γ. other markings. To these one should add δ., the signs used for or in conjunction with the tetragrammaton.

α. Correction of Errors

In ancient manuscripts, various methods were used for the correction of elements that were considered errors either by the original scribe or by a later scribe or reader. The methods used for correcting are known from the Qumran texts and from *Soferim*, chapters 3-5—methods i, v, and vi below are not mentioned in *Soferim* as legitimate practices for correction. Corrections were made in the text itself, in the margin, or between the lines. For a discussion and examples, see below and pp. 112–113 as well as Table 8 on pp. 284–285. Such correctional activity may be based on the manuscript from which the original scribe copied his text or on a different one. In the latter case, the scribe would adapt the base manuscript to another, central, manuscript, but there is little evidence for such practices. For an analysis, see p. 284.

i. *A marking of cancellation dots* above, below, or both above and below the letters, or (in the case of added words) on both sides of the word, was used to omit letters or words already written (see Martin*; Kutscher, *Language*, 531-536; Talmon*). For example,

Isa 19:5	1QIsa[a]	יחרוׄבׄ (col. XV, l. 9)
	𝔐	יחרב (= correction in 1QIsa[a])
		it will dry up
Isa 35:10	1QIsa[a]	ישיגוׄבׄהׄ (col. XXVIII, l. 28; cf. plate 3*, l. 28 in the present book)
	𝔐	ישיגו (= correction in 1QIsa[a])
		they shall attain
Isa 36:7	1QIsa[a]	לפני המזבח הזה תשתחוו בׄיׄרׄוׄשׄלׄיׄםׄ (col. XXIX, l. 10); cf. 2 Kgs 18:22 𝔐 and versions.
		at this altar you must worship, *i̊n J̊e̊r̊ů̊s̊å̊l̊e̊m̊*
	𝔐	לפני המזבח הזה תשתחוו (= correction in 1QIsa[a]; cf. 2 Chr 32:12 𝔐 and versions)
Isa 37:27	1QIsa[a]	ויׄשׄבשו (col. XXXI, l. 5)
	𝔐	ובשו (≈ correction in 1QIsa[a]: ויבשו)
		and they were ashamed

Sometimes a new word is written between the lines above the word which is replaced.

		יהוה
Isa 3:17	1QIsa[a]	·אֲ̣ד̣ו̣נ̣ ̣י̣·
	𝔐	אדני
		אדוני
Isa 3:18	1QIsa[a]	·י̣ה̣ו̣ה̣·
	𝔐	אדני (= correction in 1QIsa[a])

The practice of canceling words by means of dots has also been preserved in the *puncta extraordinaria* in 𝔐 (see pp. 55–57).

ii. *Crossing out a word with a horizontal line* (cf. *Sof.* 5.1), sometimes with the addition of the correction above the line. For example,

		יושבת
Isa 12:6	1QIsa[a]	צהלי ורני ~~בת~~ ציון
		inhabitant
		Shout and sing, O ~~daughter~~ of Zion.
	𝔐	צהלי ורני יושבת ציון (= 𝔊 𝔖 𝔗 and the correction in 1QIsa[a])
		Shout and sing, O inhabitant of Zion.
		נוראה
Isa 21:1	1QIsa[a]	ממדבר בא מארץ ~~הרחוקה~~ (*p.m.* = 𝔖; cf. p. 264)
		terrible
		It comes from the desert, from a ~~far away~~ land.

𝔐 ממדבר בא מארץ נוראה (= 𝔊 𝔗 𝔙 and the correction in 1QIsa^{a})
It comes from the desert, from a terrible land.

Dan 8:1 4QDan^{a} ~~[ד]בר נגלה~~ חזון נראה
~~A w]ord was revealed~~, a vision appeared.
𝔐 חזון נראה (= correction in 4QDan^{a})

This method is also known from some manuscripts of 𝔖𝔪.

iii. *Erasing*—the technique of erasing words with a sharp instrument is known from various texts—see 1QS and 11QpaleoLev^{a} (cf. Freedman–Mathews, *Leviticus,* 12). The erased area is sometimes left blank, and at other times letters or a word are written in or above the area. In medieval Torah scrolls this is the only accepted method.

iv. *The supralinear addition* of a single letter or letters, a word or words above an element in the text as a correcting addition—this method, recognized by *y. Meg.* 1.71d, is used frequently in 1QIsa^{a} (see many examples in Table 21 on pp. 112-113 and Table 8 on pp. 284-285 and a complete list for 1QIsa^{a} *apud* Kutscher, *Language,* 522-531, 555-558; likewise, see various examples on plates 3*, 4*, and 9*). Such additions occasionally continue into the margins and also vertically, alongside the text (1QIsa^{a}, cols. XXX, XXXII, XXXIII—see plate 4*; 4QXII^{e}, frg. 18, 4QXII^{g}, frgs. 1–4, line 18), and even below the text, in reverse writing (4QJer^{a}, col. III). For the technique of addition see also the details added in the margins of 𝔗^{N} (plate 23*). Several examples of added letters have also been preserved in 𝔐 in the form of *suspended letters*—see p. 57.

v. *Reshaping letters*—in attempting to correct a letter or letters, a scribe would sometimes change the form of a letter into another one, for example, in 1QIsa^{a} 7:11:

שאל (original *ʾaleph* of אאל changed to שאל = 𝔐); מעם (= 𝔐) probably changed from מאל.

vi. *Parenthesis Signs*—Omission of words by enclosing the elements to be omitted within scribal signs, known from the Greek scribal tradition as *sigma* and *antisigma* and from the Masoretic tradition as inverted *nunim* (see pp. 54–55). In the Qumran texts these signs occur rarely.

Many of the texts from the Judean Desert contain a relatively large number of scribal interventions such as described here, some as many as an average of one scribal intervention in every four lines of text (thus 1QIsa^{a}). On the other hand, according to Talmudic sources the sacred character of the text allows only for a minimal number of corrections.

The opinions quoted in *b. Menaḥ*. 29b mention either 2 or 3 corrections per column as the maximal number permitted, while the different opinions in *Sof.* 3.10 allow for either 1 or 3 corrections. Scrolls containing a greater number in a single column could not be used. Most of the Qumran scrolls would thus not have passed the scrutiny of the rabbis.

β. Paragraphing

Most of the horizontal lines, named παράγραφος, *paragraphos,* in Greek sources, written between the lines of the text at the beginning of the line in some twenty Qumran texts, among them 1QIsa^{a}, denote a content division of the text which was also indicated in such cases by means of spaces in the line itself, that is, the so-called closed and open sections. For an example see plate 3*, l. 20. The paragraph sign appears in various shapes, among them

in the second part of 1QIsa^{a}. The use of the *paragraphos* marker is known from both the biblical and nonbiblical Qumran texts written in the Qumran scribal practice (see pp. 108–111), from biblical texts in Greek (4QLXX-Lev^{a}, Pap. Fouad 266, 8ḤevXIIgr), and from other Aramaic and Greek texts. The *paragraphos* is already attested in Aramaic secular texts from the fifth century BCE (i.a., the Elephantine papyri).

The first lines of new sections in 4QNum^{b} and the headings in 2QPs are sometimes indicated with red ink.

γ. Other Markings

Other markings, not all of which are understood, are found almost exclusively in the margins of compositions written in the Qumran scribal practice (see pp. 108–111), especially in 1QIsa^{a} (see examples on plates 3* and 4*) and 4QCant^{b} and in several nonbiblical texts, especially 1QS, 4QpIsa^{c}, 4QDibHam^{a} (= 4Q504), and 4QShir^{b} (= 4Q511). They include paleo-Hebrew characters in 1QIsa^{a} and 4QCant^{b} and an "X" sign in 1QIsa^{a} drawing attention to issues in the text. Three scribal markings found in both 1QIsa^{a} and 1QS are not known from other texts, probably because the latter and the corrections in the former were produced by the same scribe.

δ. The Tetragrammaton

In some texts the tetragrammaton was represented by four and in one case by five dots: the corrector of 1QIsa^{a} (see plate 4*) and 4QSam^{c}, as well as ten nonbiblical texts, among which 1QS, 4QTest, 4QTanḥ (= 4Q176), 4Q382, 4Q443, and 4Q462. Note also the use of a colon before the tetragrammaton (written in the square script) in 4QRP^{b} (4Q364).

The tetragrammaton is represented in the paleo-Hebrew script in several texts written in the square ("Assyrian") script (below p. 220).

f. Breaking up of Words

Words are often broken up at the end of a line (split between lines) in inscriptions written in the "early" Hebrew and Assyrian ("square") script (see plate 1*), in Hebrew biblical scrolls written in paleo-Hebrew (see plate 2*), and *tefillin* and *mezuzot* (see plate 9*)—in the latter apparently due to considerations of space. Note the following examples of such words in 11QpaleoLev^{a}, col. III: יהו/ה, יש/ראל, ב/נ, א/ל, א/תו. This practice was not used in texts written in the Assyrian script and was forbidden by *Sof.* 2.1. See appendix 1 on pp. 230–231.

g. Spaces between Biblical Books

In scrolls containing several biblical books, spaces were left between them (cf. 4QGen-Exod^{a}, 4QExod^{b}, 4QpaleoGen-Exod^{l}, 4QRP^{c} between Leviticus and Numbers, MurXII and 8ḤevXIIgr). According to the instructions in *b. B. Bat.* 13b one has to leave four blank lines between the books of the Torah, and three lines between the books of the Minor Prophets, which were considered one unit (see also *Sof.* 3.1-3).

3. *The Script*

N. Avigad, "The Palaeography of the Dead Sea Scrolls and Related Documents," *ScrHier* 4 (1958) 56-87; M. Beit-Arié, *Specimens of Mediaeval Hebrew Scripts, vol. I, Oriental and Yemenite Scripts* (Heb. with Eng. foreword; Jerusalem 1987); S.A. Birnbaum, *The Hebrew Scripts* (Leiden 1971); F.M. Cross, Jr., "The Development of the Jewish Scripts," in: G.E. Wright, ed., *The Bible and the Ancient Near East, Essays in Honor of W.F. Albright* (Garden City, NY 1965) 133-202; D. Diringer, "Early Hebrew Script *versus* Square Script," in: D.W. Thomas, ed., *Essays and Studies Presented to S.A. Cook* (London 1950) 35-49; R.S. Hanson, "Paleo-Hebrew Scripts in the Hasmonean Age," *BASOR* 175 (1964) 26-42; idem, "Jewish Palaeography and Its Bearing on Text Critical Studies," in: F.M. Cross and W.E. Lemke, eds., *Magnalia Dei: The Mighty Acts of God. Essays . . . in Memory of G.E. Wright* (Garden City, NY 1976) 561-576; idem, "Paleography, The Script of the Leviticus Scroll," in: Freedman–Mathews, *Leviticus*, 15-23; M.M. Kasher, *The Script of the Torah and Its Characters, I, The Torah in Ivri and Ashshuri Scripts* (Torah Shelemah 29; Heb.; Jerusalem 1978); M.D. McLean, *The Use and Development of Palaeo-Hebrew in the Hellenistic and Roman Periods*, unpubl. diss., Harvard University, Cambridge, MA 1982 [University Microfilms]; J. Naveh, "The Development of the Aramaic Script," *Proceedings of the Israel Academy of Sciences and Humanities*, V,1 (Jerusalem 1970) 1-69; idem, "Hebrew Texts in the Aramaic Script in the Persian Period?" *BASOR* 203 (1971) 27-32; idem, *Early History of the Alphabet—An Introduction to West Semitic Epigraphy and Palaeography* (2d ed.; Jerusalem 1987); idem, *On Sherd and Papyrus—Aramaic and Hebrew Inscriptions from the Second Temple, Mishnaic and Talmudic Periods* (Heb.; Jerusalem 1992); J.P. Siegel, "The Employment of Paleo-Hebrew Characters for the Divine Names at Qumran in the Light of Tannaitic Sources," *HUCA* 42 (1971) 159-172; N.H. Tur-Sinai, "ktb htwrh," *Hlšwn whspr, krk hlšwn* (Jerusalem 1954) 123-164; A. Yardeni, *The Book of Hebrew Script* (Heb.; Jerusalem 1991).

a. Background

The discipline which deals with the development of writing, paleography, pertains to many aspects of the textual criticism of the Hebrew Bible, in particular to the following two.

(a) On the basis of external sources, especially dated sources, such as coins and inscriptions, it is possible to describe the development of written documents including that of the biblical texts, and to date such texts as the ones found in the Judean Desert, according to some scholars with relatively great accuracy. For example, according to Cross*, the Qumran texts written in the Assyrian ("square") script can be divided into three main periods: i. 250–150 BCE ("archaic" script); ii. 150–30 BCE (Hasmonean script); iii. 30 BCE–70 CE (Herodian script). Generally speaking carbon 14 tests (cf. p. 105) have confirmed the paleographical dates of several individual fragments.

(b) An examination of similarly shaped letters (including ligatures) makes the interchanges of similar letters such as found in all witnesses of the biblical text more understandable. These interchanges are illustrated on pp. 243–252.

b. Change of Script

Over the generations the biblical books were written in two different scripts, at first in the "early" *Hebrew* script (see plate 29*) and later in the *Assyrian* ("square") script (see plate 30*), which developed from the Aramaic script. The late books were apparently written directly in this script. These two scripts are indicated with different names in ancient sources.

(1) Originally, the biblical books were written in the "early" Hebrew script which developed from the proto-Canaanite script in the tenth or ninth centuries BCE. In Talmudic sources this script was given the name *roʿeṣ* [ר(ו)עץ], that is, "broken" or "rugged," on account of the rabbis' negative opinion towards it; see *b. Sanh.* 22a: "The Torah was originally given to Israel in this <Assyrian, "square"> script. When they sinned, it became רועץ <see above>." It is not impossible that this negative opinion also derives from the fact that the Samaritans use a form of the Hebrew script. Other names given to this script are *daʿaṣ* ("pricking" or "sticking"?), probably representing a corruption of ר(ו)עץ, rather than reflecting the original term, and *libunaʾah* ("well-balanced"?), for which see *b. Sanh.* 21b.

No early fragments of the biblical text written in the Hebrew script have been preserved,[10] but Qumran yielded various texts written in a later version of this script, now named paleo-Hebrew and evidenced in fragments from the late third or early second century BCE. Likewise, many manuscripts of 𝔪 written in a later form of the paleo-Hebrew script have been preserved. A paleographical examination of the Samaritan manuscripts revealed that they reflect the script of the second century BCE, even though they were written in medieval times.[11]

(2) The various changes occurring in the script in which the Hebrew language was written (see Naveh*, 1987, 112-124), also occurred in the writing of the Holy Scriptures. At some stage during the Second Temple period, a gradual transition occurred from the Hebrew to the Aramaic script, from which a script developed which is exclusive to the Jews and which could thus be called the "Jewish script" (thus many scholars) or the "square script" (according to the form of the letters). However, in many ancient texts (e.g., *b. Sanh.* 21b) it is called the "Assyrian script" due to the fact that its ancestor, the Aramaic script, was in use in the Assyrian Empire. According to Talmudic tradition this script was introduced by Ezra, who is called in the Bible "an expert scribe" (Ezra 7:6), while other traditions refer in more general terms to the time of Ezra.

> Mar Zuṭra or, as some say, Mar ʿUkba said: "Originally the Torah was given to Israel in Hebrew characters and in the sacred <Hebrew> language; later, in the time of Ezra, the Torah was given in the Assyrian script and the Aramaic language. <Finally,> Israel selected the Assyrian script and the Hebrew language, leaving the Hebrew characters and Aramaic language for the *hedyoṭoth* <the ordinary people>" (*b. Sanh.* 21b; cf. *b. Meg.* 9a; *t. Sanh.* 5.7; *y. Meg.* 1.71b-c); for similar statements, see Origen, Epiphanius, and Jerome (for references see Birnbaum*, 73-74).

The date attributed by tradition to the use of the square ("Assyrian") script for the writing of the biblical books appears possible but lacks external confirmation. In this context Naveh*, 1983, 234-235 speaks of a somewhat later date, viz., the third century BCE. One should note that after the introduction of the square script, the paleo-Hebrew script did not go out of use.[12] In any event, all texts written in the square script necessarily reflect a relatively late stage of writing.

---

10 Unless one wishes to consider the silver rolls from Ketef Hinnom (p. 118) as biblical texts.

11 See chapter 2, n. 58.

12 See the material collected by Naveh*, 1987, 119-124.

c. *Paleo-Hebrew Script*

At Qumran fragments of 12 biblical texts written in the paleo-Hebrew script have been found (chapter 2, n. 79; see plate 2*). These texts, rather than preceding the use of the square "Assyrian" script, were actually written at a relatively late period, as a natural continuation of the earlier tradition of writing in the "early" Hebrew script, and were concurrent with the use of the square script, as can also be proved by a paleographical examination of the paleo-Hebrew script (see Hanson*). Most scholars refer to this script as paleo-Hebrew, while Birnbaum* refers to it as Neo-Palaeo-Hebrew.

In some Qumran texts written in the square script, the tetragrammaton and some other divine names were written in paleo-Hebrew: 2QExod^{b} [a rewritten Torah text?], 4QExod^{j}, 4QLev^{g}, 11QLev^{b}, 1QPs^{b}, 4QIsa^{c}, 3QLam) and fifteen nonbiblical compositions.[13] Likewise, the scribes of several Jewish-Greek translations wrote the tetragrammaton in paleo-Hebrew characters (fragments of Aquila, 8ḤevXIIgr [see plate 21*], Pap. Oxy. 1007, Pap. Oxy. 3522) or in the square script, usually in stylized characters. This habit was mentioned by Origen in his commentary on Psalm 2 (Migne XII, 1104) and Jerome, *Prologus galeatus*.

4. *Orthography*

F.I. Andersen and A.D. Forbes, "Orthography and Text Transmission—Computer-Assisted Investigation of Textual Transmission through the Study of Orthography in the Hebrew Bible," *Text: Transactions of the Society for Textual Scholarship* 2 (1985) 25-53; F.I. Andersen and A.D. Forbes, *Spelling in the Hebrew Bible* (BibOr 41; Rome 1986); F.I. Andersen and D.N. Freedman, "Another Look at 4QSam^{b}," *RQ* 14 (1989) 7-29; L. Bardowicz, "Das allmähliche Ueberhandnehmen der matres lectionis im Bibeltexte und das rabbinische Verbot, die Defectiva plene zu schreiben," *MGWJ* 38 (1894) 117-121, 157-167; J. Barr, *The Variable Spellings of the Hebrew Bible* (The Schweich Lectures of the British Academy; Oxford 1989); F.M. Cross and D.N. Freedman, *Early Hebrew Orthography* (AOS 36; New Haven 1952); F.M. Cross and D.N. Freedman, *Studies in Ancient Yahwistic Poetry* (SBLDS 21; Missoula, MT 1975 [= 1950]); Cross, "Some Notes"; H. Donner and W. Röllig, *Kanaanäische und aramäische Inschriften*, vol. I (Wiesbaden 1966); D.N. Freedman, "The Massoretic Text and the Qumran Scrolls—A Study in Orthography," *Textus* 2 (1962) 87-102; Freedman–Mathews, *Leviticus*, 51-82; Ginsburg, *Introduction*, 137-157; D.W. Goodwin, *Text-Restoration Methods in Contemporary U.S.A. Biblical Scholarship* (Naples 1969) 27-43; A.R. Millard, "Variable Spelling in Hebrew and Other Ancient Texts," *JTS* n.s. 42 (1991) 106-115; A. Murtonen, "The Fixation in Writing of Various Parts of the Pentateuch," *VT* 3 (1953) 46-53; idem, "On the

---

13 See K. A. Mathews, "The Background of the Paleo-Hebrew Texts at Qumran," in: C. Meyers and M. O'Connor, eds., *The Word of the Lord Shall Go Forth* (Winona Lake, IN 1983) 549-568. The scribes treated the divine names with particular sanctity in order that these should not be erased (cf. *y. Meg.* 1.71d). See further: P.W. Skehan, "The Divine Name at Qumran, in the Masada Scroll, and in the Septuagint," *BIOSCS* 13 (1980) 14-44; J.P. Siegel, "The Employment of Palaeo-Hebrew Characters for the Divine Names at Qumran in the Light of Tannaitic Sources," *HUCA* 42 (1971) 159-172.

Interpretation of the Matres Lectionis in Biblical Hebrew," *AbrN* 14 (1973-4) 66-121; A. Rahlfs, "Zur Setzung der Lesemütter im AT," *Nachr. v. d. königl. Gesellsch. der Wiss. zu Gött., Phil.-hist. Kl.* (Berlin 1916) 315-347; G.B. Sarfatti, "Hebrew Inscriptions of the First Temple Period—A Survey and Some Linguistic Comments," *Maarav* 3 (1982) 55-83; Sperber, *Grammar*, 562-636; W. Weinberg, "The History of Hebrew *Plene* Spelling: From Antiquity to Haskalah," *HUCA* 46 (1975) 457-487; Z. Zevit, *Matres Lectionis in Ancient Hebrew Epigraphs* (American Schools of Oriental Research Monographs 2; Cambridge, MA 1980).

a. Background

Orthography (spelling) is the realization in writing of the spoken word and, accordingly, it is possible to represent a specific word in different spellings. In fact, many words are written in different ways within the same language, at different periods, or in concurrent dialects without any difference in meaning. For example, the following English words are spelled differently in Great Britain (fav***our***, specialis***e***) and in the United States (fav***o***r, specializ***e***) without difference in meaning. Similarly, in Hebrew, there is no difference between לא, *lʾ* and לוא, *lwʾ*, nor between שמרים, *šmrym* and שומרים, *š**w**mrym*.

When discussing orthography, most scholars do not include differences in morphology relating to words which would be pronounced differently, such as the differences between הוא of the majority tradition of the Hebrew text and הואה of some of the Qumran texts (see pp. 109–110). However, other scholars (see Cross, "Some Notes") extend the discussion of orthography to include these forms as well. The case of ⅏ is a special one because of the differences between the written form and the oral tradition of the Samaritans (see p. 81).

The orthography of the Hebrew language, in common with that of most other languages, passed through various phases, in particular, in the ever increasing use of the *matres lectionis* (the vowel letters אהו"י), which were added to the original orthography to facilitate the reading. Another such system was the addition of signs to indicate the vowels. The terms *defective* and *full* (*plene*) orthography refer to alternative forms of spelling the same word, one without one or more *matres lectionis* and the other with the addition of one or more *matres lectionis*. This terminology is, however, often not precise, since a single word can contain both types of orthography at the same time—e.g., מְנֻחוֹת, *m*^{e}*nuḥôt*, with the defective spelling in the penultimate syllable and the full spelling in the ultimate one (Ps 23:2 𝔐) and וּבִמְנוּחֹת, *ubim*^{e}*nûḥot* with the full spelling in the penultimate syllable and the defective spelling in the ultimate one (Isa 32:18 𝔐).

Although early stages of Hebrew orthography are not in evidence, Phoenician and Moabite texts, which predate Hebrew, reveal how

Hebrew texts would have been written in the First Temple period (see Cross–Freedman*). In brief, ancient Phoenician inscriptions such as Yeḥimilk from the tenth century BCE (Donner–Röllig*, 10) do not indicate the *matres lectionis* either in the middle or at the end of a word:

ושנתו (= ושנותיו, *wšnwtyw*), ז (= זה, *zh*), לפנ (= לפני, *lpny*).

Compare also the Hebrew Gezer Calender (Donner–Röllig*, 182), in which the *matres lectionis* are absent in the middle of the words and perhaps also at the end:

שערם (= שעורים, *śʿwrym*), ירח (= ירחו?).

At a later stage *matres lectionis* were added at the end of words. See, for example, the Mesha inscription (Donner–Röllig*, 181) in

בנתי (= בניתי, *bnyty*), בללה (= בלילה, *blylh*).

In the Siloam inscription (end of the eighth century; Donner–Röllig*, 189) *matres lectionis* are likewise found in final position:

וילכו, *wylkw*; זדה, *zdh*; היה, *hyh*.

At the same time, the Siloam inscription also includes forms without final vowel letters, such as

החצבם (= החצבים, *hḥṣbym*), אש (= איש, *ʾyš*).

After the introduction of vowel letters in final position, they were also introduced gradually in medial position.

b. Different Orthographical Practices in the Biblical Texts

Since no biblical texts earlier than the third century BCE have been preserved, early stages of the orthography of the biblical books are unattested—for the purposes of this discussion, the silver rolls from Ketef Hinnom (p. 118) are disregarded, since they do not contain a biblical text proper. The only orthographical practices that have been preserved derive from a later period, and they contain the biblical text itself: the proto-Masoretic texts together with 𝔐, the pre-Samaritan texts together with 𝔖, and the Qumran practice. The orthographical practices of 𝔖 and several Qumran texts have already been described on pp. 96–97 and pp. 108–110 respectively, so the discussion here is limited to the group of 𝔐. Since the orthographical practice of 𝔐 is more defective than the practices of the two other groups of texts mentioned above, in accordance with the development of the orthography of the Hebrew language as depicted in paragraph *a*, the orthography of 𝔐 must have been closer to the assumed original orthography of the biblical books.[14]

14 Freedman–Mathews* divide the evidence from Qumran into four systems of orthography: conservative, proto-Rabbinic (= proto-Masoretic), proto-Samaritan, and Hasmonean. This division is not reflected in the present discussion.

In the course of many generations, the orthography of the biblical books presumably passed through various phases, since these books or parts of them (early poems) were first written down at a stage when the orthography was still very defective. One cannot escape the assumption that with each successive transcription, the orthography of the biblical books was adapted to the system that was in practice at the time, either fully or partially. It is not clear whether it is at all possible to reconstruct the original orthography of the biblical books (see Goodwin*), since our knowledge of orthography is scant and is based primarily on a small number of inscriptions (see Donner–Röllig*), rather than on ancient literary texts. The biblical books that were composed in an early period, and in particular the ancient poetry, were probably written in a very defective orthography, but this assumption does not provide a sufficient basis for the reconstruction of that orthography. Nevertheless, some reconstructions have been made. One such attempt is reflected in Cross–Freedman*'s reconstruction of the "Song at the Sea" (Exod 15:1-18), which may well be too extreme, but there is no way of verifying any one view.

Table 1

The Presumed Original Orthography of Some Verses in Exodus 15 according to Cross–Freedman, 1975 (1950), 50*[15]

	𝔐	*reconstruction*
1	אשירה ליהוה	אשר ליהו
	כי גָאֹה גָּאָה	כ גא גא
	סוס ורכבו	סס ורכב
	רמה בים	רמ בים []
3	יהוה איש מלחמה	יהו <גבר>
	יהוה שמו	יהו שמ
4	מרכבת פרעה וחילו	מרכבת פרע וחל
	ירה בים	יר בים

c. The Orthographical Practices of the Group of 𝔐

The relatively defective orthography of the group of 𝔐, as reflected in the proto-Masoretic texts and medieval manuscripts, is discussed here somewhat *in extenso* since it is probably closer to the assumed original

15 This reconstruction, like that of other poems, is repeated with slight changes in F.M. Cross, Jr., *Canaanite Myth and Hebrew Epic—Essays in the History of Religion of Israel* (Cambridge, MA/London 1973) 127-131. This system of reconstruction was first presented by W.F. Albright, "The Oracles of Balaam," *JBL* 63 (1944) 207-233.

orthography of the biblical books than the orthographical practices reflected in the other textual witnesses. During the intervening period between the copying of the proto-Masoretic texts from Qumran written in the third and second centuries BCE (see p. 115) and that of the Masoretic codices in the Middle Ages, the orthography of these texts did not change to any great extent. It is therefore possible to discuss this group as one entity.

α. Comparison with External Evidence

Since the development of the orthography of the Hebrew language can be characterized in general terms, theoretically one could determine the place of the orthography of 𝔐 within this framework, while taking into consideration the internal differences that exist between the biblical books. Such attempts have indeed been made by Cross–Freedman*, Freedman*, Andersen–Forbes*, 1986, and Barr*. According to Andersen–Forbes*, the orthography of 𝔐 reflects practices of orthography current between 550 and 350 BCE; these scholars also suggested the possibility of relating these practices to Ezra.[16] On the other hand, Freedman*, 102, assigned the orthography of 𝔐 to the end of the third century or the beginning of the second century BCE, while Barr*, 203, thinks in more general terms of the period between 400 and 100 BCE.

For the sake of clarity, one should emphasize that the use of *matres lectionis* in 𝔐 reveals neither the absolute nor even the relative time of the composition of the biblical books, but only the time of their latest copying, since a book or section of a book composed at an early period could be represented in 𝔐 by a late copy. For example, we do not know whether the orthography of Psalm 18 bears evidence of relative lateness in comparison with the somewhat more defective orthography of the parallel psalm in 2 Samuel 22 (for a detailed analysis, see Barr*, 170-174). Nevertheless, it has been found that the biblical books written with full orthography are generally the books that were composed at a later period (see Table 3 and p. 229 below).

β. Internal Analysis

A comparison of the orthography of 𝔐 with external sources is based on a comparative analysis of the common characteristics of all of the biblical books and the external sources. At the same time one must be aware of the differences between the various books of 𝔐, described in detail by Barr*. These differences were caused by the lack of interest of scribes in

---

[16] Andersen-Forbes*, 318-321.

creating a unified orthography in any given book and by the differences in the spelling practices used over the centuries. This characteristic of 𝔐 shows that when it was decided not to insert any changes in the text of 𝔐 (see pp. 28–33), its orthographical practices, frozen in that text, were inconsistent; it also proves that afterwards no further attempt was made to unify the spelling practices.

The lack of internal consistency in 𝔐 is reflected in the following characteristics: (1) differences *between* the orthographical practice, which is relatively defective, of the majority of the biblical books and the fuller orthography of the later books (see below γ, δ) and (2) internal differences *within* the various biblical books (see Tables 4, 5, and 6).

The differences between the books are exemplified by a comparison of parallel texts (Table 2) and by data pertaining to one word (Table 3).

Table 2

The Orthography of Parallel Sections in 𝔐 Compared
(2 Samuel 23 // 1 Chronicles 11)

	2 Samuel 23		*1 Chronicles 11*
22	אלה עשה בניהו בן יהוידע	24	אלה עשה בניהו בן יהוידע
	ולו שם בשלשה הגברים		ולו שם בשל**ו**שה הגברים
23	מן השלשים נכבד	25	מן השל**ו**שים הנו נכבד הוא
	ואל השלשה לא בא		ואל השל**ו**שה לא בא
	וישמהו דוד **א**ל משמעתו		וישימהו דויד **ע**ל משמעתו
24	. . . אלחנן בן דדו בית לחם	26	. . . אלחנן בן ד**ו**דו מבית לחם
25	שמה החרדי אליקא החרדי	27	שמות ההר**ו**רי
26	. . . עירא בן עקש התקועי	28	. . . עירא בן עקש התקועי
27	אביעזר הענתתי		אביעזר הענת**ו**תי

Table 3

The Spellings דויד/דוד *in 𝔐 (according to Andersen–Forbes*, 1986, 5)*[17]

	Defect.	*Plene*	*Perc. of plene spellings*
Genesis-Judges	0	0	—
Samuel	575	0	0
Isaiah	10	0	0
Jeremiah	15	0	0
Ruth	2	0	0
Proverbs	1	0	0

17 For more detailed data, see Andersen–Forbes* (1985) 29-34. See also D.N. Freedman, "The Spelling of the Name 'David' in the Hebrew Bible," *HAR* 7 (1983) 89-104.

Ps 102:5	הוּכָּה		
Job 1:21 (see p. 255)	יצתי	*Qere*	יצאתי
Neh 13:16	דָּאג		
1 Chr 5:30	הֹלִיד		
2 Chr 2:16	הַגֵּירִים		

The inconsistency of 𝔐 is particularly striking in the combinations of *matres lectionis*: in one word the combination of two *matres lectionis* can create four different spellings, as actually found in the following examples:

הקמתי, הקמֹותי, הקימתי, (ו)הקימֹותי

(see the discussion in Elias Levita, *Massoreth Ha-Massoreth*, 166 in Ginsburg's edition; Andersen–Forbes*, 1986, 27). The plural form of נביא, *nby'*, also appears in 𝔐 in three different spellings:

נְבִיאִים (64x), נְבִאִים (32x), נְבִיאִם (3x).

The same applies to the plural form of מקום, *mqwm*:

מְקוֹמוֹת (2x), מְקֹמוֹת (11x), מְקוֹמֹת (3x).

γ. Is There a System of Orthography in 𝔐?

Upon consideration of the evidence described in the preceding paragraph, one cannot represent the orthography of 𝔐 as consistent or uniform. It is therefore unlikely that some sort of system be discovered behind this lack of consistency, although the existence of individual practices cannot be denied. Recognizing these practices, the Masoretes formulated principles of a larger system which were meant to guide the copying of the ancient and medieval manuscripts; see in particular Elias Levita, *Massoreth Ha-Massoreth* (see above). Thus, according to this treatise, nouns were usually written *plene*, whereas verbs were spelled defectively—see for example the verbal form פָּקַד in Num 3:40 as compared with the proper noun פְּקוֹד, Pekod, in Jer 50:21 (see *op. cit.*, 147). As for another example, according to Elias Levita, the pattern קְטֹלִים, *q^e^ṭolîm*, is usually written defectively with regard to the /o/ sound: גדֹלים, קרֹבים, רחֹקים, etc. Nouns of the פ״י pattern are usually written *plene*: מוֹצָא, מוֹרָא, תּוֹרָה.

Andersen–Forbes*, 1986, also discovered several features of the orthographies in 𝔐 which prove the existence of orthographical practices of some sort. First of all, the orthography of certain words such as אלהים, נאם, ירושלם, and כהן is constant.[20] Second, in many pairs of identical

20 For similar observations, see already the midrashic composition *Midrash ḥaser w^e^yater*, published by A. Berliner, *Pletath Soferim, Beiträge zur jüdischen Schriftauslegung, nebst Midrasch über die Gründe der Defectiva und Plena* (Breslau 1872) 36-45 (Heb.).

words, the scribes seem to have purposely chosen a different orthography for each word. For example,

Gen 27:22	הקל קול יעקב
Num 28:13	ועשרן עשרון
Qoh 1:6	סובב סבב

Third, scholars (e.g., Rahlfs*, 339-343 and previously Stade[21]) have recognized a phenomenon which was described in detail by Barr* (14, 25-32) as the "affix effect." That is, "when words have plural terminations or other suffixes added, this often alters the characteristic spelling away from that found in the absolute singular" (Barr*, 14). For example, in the books of the Torah, *gdwl* is usually *plene*, while the defective form *hgdl*, with the article, is more frequent than *hgdwl* (p. 30).

At the same time, the overall lack of consistency in the orthography of 𝔐 should be stressed. This characteristic derived from a lack of attention to details of orthography on the part of the scribes and from the different periods in which the biblical books were composed and subsequently copied.

δ. *Characterization of Individual Biblical Books*

On the basis of data such as those found in Tables 2 and 3, it is customary to make a distinction between the orthography of the majority of the biblical books and that of the later books. Although generally this characterization can be maintained, it tends to be an oversimplification since different words and specific patterns behave contrary to this general tendency.

Andersen–Forbes*, 1986, 312-318 claim that the Torah and Kings reflect a more conservative (defective) orthography than the rest of the biblical books and that they also contain the greatest degree of internal consistency—in the Torah this description especially applies to Exodus and Leviticus. The books with the fullest orthography are Qoheleth, Canticles, and Esther, followed by Ezra-Nehemiah and Chronicles.

5. *Scribal Schools*

M. Beit-Arié, *Hebrew Codicology* (Jerusalem 1981); A.D. Crown, "Studies in Samaritan Scribal Practices and Manuscript History: III. Columnar Writing and the Samaritan Massorah," *BJRL* 67 (1984) 349-381; E. Tov, "Hebrew Biblical Manuscripts from the Judaean Desert—Their Contribution to Textual Criticism," *JJS* 39 (1988) 5-37.

---

21 B. Stade, *Lehrbuch der hebräischen Grammatik*, vol. 1 (Leipzig 1879) 37.

Many of the Qumran scrolls reflect common characteristics in matters of orthography, morphology (see pp. 108–110), and scribal practice (see p. 111). Presumably these texts were written by a scribal school, i.e., a group of scribes who, while preserving specific individual characteristics, developed certain copying and writing practices (see Tov*).

The proto-Masoretic texts were probably also copied by a different scribal school.

The characteristics of the different scribal schools which copied the Masoretic codices and the manuscripts of 𝔖 in medieval times can be described more accurately than those of the scribal schools from antiquity, since the information about the former is more detailed (see Beit-Arié*, 1978, 1981, 1987, and Crown*). For the medieval sources, information such as described above is supplemented with detailed, "codicological," data about the manuscripts themselves.

Appendix 1

Tefillin *and* Mezuzot *from the Judean Desert*

J. Tigay, "Tpylyn," *EncBib* 8 (Jerusalem 1982) 883-895.

In many ways *tefillin* (see plate 9*) and *mezuzot* from the Second Temple period mentioned on pp. 118–119 may be considered biblical texts comparable to the texts described above. Like biblical manuscripts, they display different orthographical practices (the Qumran practice, see pp. 108-110, and an orthography similar to that of 𝔐), and they display a large variety of variants, many of which are also known from other sources. Nevertheless, their function and the way in which they were written differed from that of the biblical texts in the following ways, which makes them only partially similar to biblical manuscripts.[22]

(1) The rough surface and ragged borders of the skins on which the *tefillin* and *mezuzot* from the Judean Desert were written permitted neither the writing of even lines nor the writing in columns. Thus the writing practice does not accord with the regulations of *b. Menaḥ.* 31b and *y. Meg.* 1.71c, according to which the writing should be orderly and the text should contain a fixed number of lines of two or three words in length.

---

[22] Furthermore, in many aspects the *tefillin* and *mezuzot* found in the Judean Desert do not conform with the rules of writing as laid down in *Massekhet Tefillin*, 2 (cf. n. 5 above).

(2) For reasons of economy, the text was usually written on both sides of the leather.

(3) No spaces were left between words, even though the scribes used final forms of letters (see pp. 208–210).

(4) Words were split between lines as in inscriptions and biblical texts written in paleo-Hebrew (see pp. 218–219). For example: ח/יים, הוצ/אתיכה, לע/שותמה in 4QPhyl J.

Appendix 2

The Column Structure of a Qumran Text

Table 7 below shows the structure of a column in one of the Qumran texts (for a photograph, see plate 8a*). It presents the preserved as well as the reconstructed parts (in square brackets) of col. XXI of 4QJer^{c}, including the top and bottom margins and empty spaces in the middle or the end of a line (denoted as *vacat*). For the designation of doubtful letters, see p. xxii. The diagonals (///) denote stitches in the leather. These stitches were inserted prior to the writing, so that the leather was not inscribed in these places (see p. 206). The textual apparatus accompanying the transcription reproduces the text to be published in the official publication of this text (by the author) in *DJD*.

Table 7

A Reconstructed Column of a Qumran Scroll with Textual Apparatus:
4QJer^{c}, Col. XXI (30:17–31:4)

top margin

1	כי נדחת קראו לך [ציון היא דרש אין לה *va[cat*
2	18 כה אמר יהוה הנני ש֯[ב שבות אהלי יע]קוב ומשכנותיו
3	אר֯ח֯ם ונבנה עיר על תלה וארמ֯ון על משפטו ישב 19 ו֯י֯צ֯א
4	//////////////// *vacat* מהם תודה וקול משחקי[ם]
5	והרב֯ת֯ים [ו]ל֯א֯ ימעטו //////////////////////////
6	והכבד֯[תים] ו֯ל֯[א] יצערו 20 והיו בניו כקדם ועדותו לפני
7	[תכון ופק]דתי ע֯[ל כל לחצי]ו 21 והיו אדירו ממנו ומשלו מקרבו
8	[יצא והק]ר֯בת֯[יו ונגש]אלי כי מי הוא זה ערב את לבו
9	[לגשת אלי נאם יהו]ה 22 והייתם לי לעם ואנכי אהיה לכם
10	[לאלהים *va[cat*
11	[23 הנה סערת יהוה חמה יצאה סער מתג]ו֯רר על ר֯[אש]
12	[רשעים יחול 24 לא ישוב חרון אף יהוה]עד עשותו[ועד]
13	[הקימו מזמות לבו באחרית הימי]ם֯ תתבננו ב֯ה֯
14	[1 בעת ההיא נאם יהוה אהיה לאלה]י֯ם לכל משפ[חות]

15 [ישראל והמה יהיו לי לעם va[cat
16 [[2]כה אמר יהוה מצא חן במדבר]עֹםֹ שרידֹיֹ הֹ[ר]בֹ הלוך
17 [[3] ואהב]תֹ עולם אהבתיך [ע]לֹ כן
18 [משכתיך חסד] [4]עוד אבֹ[נך ונב]נית בתולת יֹ[שר]אֹל עוד

bottom margin

TEXTUAL NOTES

OPEN/CLOSED SECTIONS (indicated as פ or ס—cf. pp. 50–51)

l. 1 (v. 17) פ] ס $\mathfrak{M}^{L}$

l. 5 (v. 19a) פ] > $\mathfrak{M}^{L}$

l. 10 (v. 22) פ] ס $\mathfrak{M}^{L}$

l. 15 (v. 1) פ] ס $\mathfrak{M}^{L}$

VARIATIONS

l. 1 (v. 17) נדחת] נדחה 𝔐

l. 2 (v. 18) [אהלי] = 𝔐] > 𝔊*

l. 2 (v. 18) ומשכנותיו = 𝔐 MSS 19-ל מ פ] ומשכנתיו 𝔐; αἰχμαλωσίαν αὐτοῦ 𝔊*

l. 3 (v. 18) ונבנה] ונבנתה 𝔐

l. 6 (v. 19) יצערו [א]וֹלֹ [תים]והכבֹ = 𝔐] > 𝔊*

l. 6 (v. 20) ועדותו cf. καὶ τὰ μαρτύρια αὐτῶν 𝔊] וַעֲדָתוֹ 𝔐

l. 7 (v. 21) והיו = καὶ ἔσονται 𝔊, cf. 𝔗 𝔖] והיה 𝔐

ll. 9-10 (v. 22) = 𝔐] > 𝔊*

l. 11 (v. 23) רֹ[אש] = 𝔐] > 𝔊

l. 12 (v. 24) עשותֹו = 𝔐 MS ר] עשתו 𝔐

l. 13 (v. 24) תתבננו = 𝔐 MS נ] תתבוננו 𝔐

l. 13 (v. 24) בֹהֹ = 𝔐 𝔊] σ′ συνέσει (thus 𝔐 Kenn. 150 + בינה); cf. Jer 23:20

l. 14 (v. 1) כל(ל) = 𝔐] > 𝔊

l. 16 (v. 2) שרידֹיֹ = 𝔐] ὀλωλότων 𝔊 (= שדודי)

l. 16 (v. 2) הלוך = 𝔐] πορευόμενος α′ σ′ (-ον) (= ה(ו)לך),
cf. 𝔐 Kenn. 89 p.m., 19-ל הלך

l. 17 (vv. 2-3) —The reconstruction of this line according to 𝔐 would involve too long a text. Possibly part of the text was either lacking or written above the line in the text in the lacuna.

C. The Process of Textual Transmission

"The premise of the textual critic's work is that whenever a text is transmitted, variation occurs. This is because human beings are careless, fallible, and occasionally perverse." (E.J. Kennedy, "History,

Textual Criticism," *EncBrit, Macropaedia*, vol. 20 [15th ed.; Chicago 1985] 676).

S. Talmon, "Aspects of the Textual Transmission of the Bible in the Light of Qumran Manuscripts," *Textus* 4 (1964) 95-132 = Cross–Talmon, *QHBT*, 226–263.

Collections of Variants and Descriptions of Types of Readings

A. Bendavid, *Parallels in the Bible* (Jerusalem 1972); L. Cappellus, *Critica Sacra* (Paris 1650; Halle 1775–1786); S. Davidson, *A Treatise on Biblical Criticism, Exhibiting a Systematic View of That Science* (Boston 1853 = Edinburgh 1854) 294-307; idem, *The Hebrew Text of the OT, Revised from Critical Sources Being an Attempt to Present a Purer and More Correct Text Than the Received One of Van der Hooght; by the Aid of the Best Existing Materials* (London 1855); Delitzsch, *Lese- und Schreibfehler*; L. Dennefeld, "Critique textuelle de l'AT, I," *DBSup* 2 (Paris 1934) 240-256; J.G. Eichhorn, *Einleitung in das AT* (4th ed.; Göttingen 1823) I, 390ff.; J. Hempel, "Der textkritische Wert des Konsonantentextes von Kairener Genizafragmenten in Cambridge und Oxford zum Deuteronomium," NAWG I., Phil.-hist. Kl. 1959, 10, pp. 207-237; Hendel, *Genesis 1-11*; J. Kennedy, *An Aid to the Textual Amendment of the OT* (Edinburgh 1928); B. Kennicott, *The State of the Printed Hebrew Text of the OT Considered . . . Compares 1 Chron. XI with 2 Sam. V and XXIII* (Oxford 1753); H. Owen, *Critica Sacra, or a Short Introduction to Hebrew Criticism* (London 1774); Perles, *Analekten*; S. Pisano S.J.., *Additions or Omissions in the Books of Samuel—The Significant Pluses and Minuses in the Massoretic, LXX and Qumran Texts* (OBO 57; Freiburg/Göttingen 1984); L. Reinke, *Die Veränderungen des hebräischen Urtextes des AT und die Ursachen der Abweichungen der alten unmittelbaren Übersetzungen unter sich und vom masoretischen Texte nebst Berichtigung und Ergänzung beider* (Münster 1866); Sperber, *Grammar*; Tov, *TCU*, 181-228; P. Vannutelli, *Libri synoptici Veteris Testamenti*, vols. I–II (Rome 1931–1934). See further the works on the study of **classical** texts mentioned on p. 199.

1. Background

The types of minor differences between the textual witnesses of the Hebrew Bible referred to in the preceding chapters and exemplified in this section are numerous. More extensive differences are described in chapter 7. These differences came about as a result of the processes of the copying and transmission of the text, and were caused, either consciously or unconsciously, by the scribes.

The concept of readings and variants. Differences in details that were created by scribal activity are known from many manuscripts; they are described as different readings, for all details in manuscripts are considered readings (see the definition on p. 18). Since readings found in different manuscripts often differ from each other, the concept of variant readings (or variants) has been introduced. However, this term can only be used suitably if its parameters are agreed upon, for a variant has to be different from another reading which is *not* named a variant, in other words, from a central or basic reading. Thus, in the critical (diplomatic or eclectic) edition of any text (cf. p. 20), all the readings quoted in the critical apparatus differing from the text printed in the edition are considered variants. (It should, however, be remembered that some scholars use the term variants in the same neutral way as the term *readings* is implied in this book and in most text-critical discussions).[23] In all diplomatic editions, the distinction between the main reading and a variant therefore is not evaluative, and this is also the case for the textual criticism and text editions of the Hebrew Bible (see, however, p. 18, n. 15). Variants in the apparatus can thus be superior to the printed or central text, but for the sake of convenience they are presented in the apparatus as details deviating from that printed text. In the case of the biblical text, 𝔐 serves as such a central text to which all other texts are compared in the critical editions and discussions. Therefore, all the details in the textual witnesses of the Bible differing from 𝔐 are variant readings of one type or another, viz., omissions or additions of details and differences in details or in sequence. It should therefore be remembered that at the level of content, that is, at the descriptive level, all readings are equal, and no one reading is from the outset superior to another one. In the same way as the textual witnesses as a whole are theoretically of the same value (see chapter 3A), their individual readings are equal.

In this chapter the different types of readings created in the course of the transmission of the biblical text are described in detail. These types can be illustrated by comparing any two biblical texts, such as a Qumran text compared with another Qumran text, or with 𝔐, 𝔖, or 𝔊. It has, however, become customary to compare all textual evidence with 𝔐, the standard text of the Bible. This procedure is also followed in this chapter, although as stated in chapter 1, the centrality of 𝔐 in the textual procedure does not imply that we take a position in connection with its priority or quality. As far as possible, the processes of transmission are exemplified from the various strata of the biblical text:

(1) parallel texts within 𝔐 reflecting early readings;

(2) internal differences in 𝔐 between *Ketib* and *Qere* forms;

(3) differences between 𝔐 and the Qumran texts;

(4) differences between 𝔐 and the reconstructed *Vorlage* of one of the ancient versions.

In the course of copying ancient scrolls, scribes created new readings of two main types. The first type of readings was created as a result of

---

[23] For a good example of this usage in NT textual criticism, see the influential work of B.F. Westcott and F.J.A. Hort, *The NT in the Original Greek* (2d ed.; London/New York 1881), vol. II, 3: "Where there is variation, there must be error in at least all *variants* but one; and the primary work of textual criticism is merely to discriminate the erroneous *variants* from the true" (italics mine).

the textual transmission itself—such readings are inescapable in the copying of all texts, and above all, of ancient texts. The majority of them reflect various types of corruptions—at a different level of the discussion these are named genetic (cf. pp. 170, 175, 177). The readings of the second type were not a natural consequence of the processes of copying, since they were created intentionally. This group (readings intentionally created by scribes) thus forms a contrast with the former type of readings created as a result of the (often random and thoughtless) textual transmission. The classification is, however, tentative, since often one cannot be certain about the intention or lack of intention underlying the readings.

It should be emphasized that while the phenomena described below, such as haplography, dittography, and doublets, are generally accepted in textual studies, they are illustrated here by subjective examples. This subjectivity is natural, since many of the examples can often be explained with alternative explanations. Although each textual phenomenon is illustrated by examples which are hopefully sound, some of the readers may consider this or that example unconvincing. However, since most of the textual phenomena described here are also known from other texts, the textual category may be correct even if an example is considered unconvincing. The following two examples, in addition to 1 Chr 11:31 (p. 307), exemplify this subjectivity.

What looks like the omission of a consonant in 𝔐 in Gen 38:14 seemingly points to haplography (see p. 237) in accordance with the regular use of the root כס״ה in the *hithpaʿel*, reflected here in 𝔖 and in 𝔐 in Gen 24:65.

Gen 38:14	𝔐	וַתְּכַס בצעיף
		She wrapped a veil about her.
	𝔖	ות**ת**כס בצעיף
cf. 24:65	𝔐	ותקח הצעיף ות**ת**כס

However, the reflexive use of this verb in the *piʿel* in Jonah 3:6 וַיְכַס שק could be evidence against the assumption of haplography in Genesis.

Likewise, the following reading in 𝔐, which at first glance also seems to be the result of haplography, could, in light of various parallels, point to a special linguistic custom:[24]

Gen 19:33	𝔐	בלילה הוא
	𝔖	בלילה **ה**הוא

24 See Gen 30:16; 32:23; 1 Sam 19:10. In all three verses 𝔐 reads בלילה הוא, with a *Sebirin* ההוא (see p. 64). See also Gesenius–Kautzsch § 126y.

1QIsa^{a} כי בכה . . . [4]בטחו בה׳ (≈ 𝔊* 𝔖)
. . . for in You [4]*Trust* in the LORD . . .

Ezek 7:21-22 𝔐^{K} ונתתיו . . . וחללֻהָ [22]והסבותי
I will give him . . . and they shall defile *her*.
[22]I will turn . . .

𝔐^{Q} וְחִלְּלוּהוּ <masc. suffix> <preferable>

The masculine suffix is required by the context. For the feminine form, cf. v. 22 וְחִלְּלוּהָ.

γ. Homoioteleuton, Homoioarcton (Parablepsis)

The phenomena of homoioteleuton, "identical ending" (ὅμοιος, "identical," and τελευτή, "end"), and homoio*arcton*, "identical beginning" (ὅμοιος, "identical," and ἀρχή, "beginning") refer to the erroneous omission of a section influenced by the repetition of one or more words in the same context in an identical or similar way. In these cases the eye of the copyist (or translator) jumped from the first appearance of a word (or words) to its (their) second appearance, so that in the copied text (or translation) the intervening section was omitted together with one of the repeated elements. Scholars often distinguish between homoio*teleuton*, when the repeated element(s) presumably occurred at the end of the omitted section and homoio*arcton*, when the repeated element(s) presumably occurred at the beginning of the omitted section. This distinction is, however, often very complicated. Without distinguishing between the position of the omitted section, both phenomena are sometimes jointly called *parablepsis* (scribal oversight). In the examples which follow the repeated elements are printed in italics.

Josh 21:35-38 𝔐 *ואת מגרשה ערים ארבע* [36]וממטה ראובן . . . [37]את
קדמות . . . *ואת מגרשה ערים ארבע* [38]וממטה גד . . .
(≈ 𝔊 𝔗; = 𝔖)
with its pastures four towns; [36]and from the tribe of Reuben . . . [37]Kedmot . . . *with its pastures four towns;* [38]and from the tribe of Gad . . .

Because of homoioarcton, vv. 36-37were omitted in several manuscripts (among them L) and printed editions of 𝔐 as well as in manuscripts of 𝔗 and 𝔙.

1 Kgs 8:16 𝔐 לא בחרתי . . . לבנות בית *להיות שמי שם* ואבחר בדוד
להיות על עמי ישראל (= 𝔗 𝔖 𝔙; 𝔖 in Chronicles)
I have not chosen . . . for building a house *where My name might abide*, but I have chosen David to rule my people Israel.

2 Chr 6:5-6 𝔐 לא בחרתי . . . לבנות בית *להיות שמי שם* ולא בחרתי באיש להיות נגיד על עמי ישראל 6ואבחר בירושלם *להיות שמי שם* ואבחר בדויד להיות על עמי ישראל ≈ 𝔊 in Kings and 4QKings <preferable>

I have not chosen . . . for building a house *where My name might abide,* nor did I choose anyone to be the leader of My people Israel, 6but I chose Jerusalem *where My name might abide,* and I chose David to rule my people Israel.

2 Chr 6:5-6 mentions the election of Jerusalem as a city and the election of David as leader, whereas in the second part of 1 Kgs 8:16, the election of David is mentioned where the election of the city is expected. In other words, while the Chronicles text contains a negative and a positive pair, in the parallel Kings text, only the first element of the negative pair and the second element the positive pair have been preserved, the remainder having been omitted by way of parablepsis. The presumably original (longer) text of Kings has been preserved partially in 𝔊 of Kings as well as in the fragmentary text of 4QKings: ל[היות נגיד על עמ]י ישראל 6ואבחר בירושלם *להיות שמי שם* ואבחר בדוד[להיות על עמי על]ישראל

1 Kgs 8:41-42 𝔐 למען *שמך* 42כי ישמעון את *שמך* הגדול <preferable>
for *Your name's* sake, 42for they shall hear about *Your* great *name* (= 𝔗 𝔖 𝔙)

2 Chr 6:32 𝔐 למען *שמך* הגדול
for *Your* great *name's* sake

Isa 40:7-8 𝔐 7*יבש חציר נבל ציץ* כי רוח ה׳ נשבה בו אכן חציר העם 8*יבש חציר נבל ציץ* ודבר אלהינו יקום לעולם (= 𝔖 𝔙) <preferable>
7*Grass withers, flowers fade,* when the breath of the LORD blows on them; surely man is but grass. 8*Grass withers, flowers fade,* but the word of our God endures for ever.

On account of the identical words, the original copyist of 1QIsa^a omitted from vv. 7-8 the section כי . . . ציץ, "when . . . fade," thus creating a homoioarcton. A later hand (note the different handwriting in plate 4*) completed the lacking words above the line, in the remaining space at the end of the line, and in the margin.[25] The same omission was made independently by 𝔊*.

Other instances of parablepsis are to be found in 𝔐 𝔗 𝔖 𝔙 in Judg 16:13-14 (cf. 𝔊); 1 Sam 1:24 (cf. 4QSam^a^ and see chapter 2, Table 22), 10:1 (cf. 𝔊), and 14:41 (cf. 𝔊). For possible cases of homoioteleuton, see further Deut 5:29-30 (p. 345), 1 Sam 11:1 (pp. 342–344), and Isa 38:21-22 (pp. 340–341). See further Pisano*.

b. Pluses

α. Dittography

Dittography, "writing twice" (διττός, "twice," and γραφή, "writing"), is the erroneous doubling of a letter, letters, word, or words. The components which are written twice are not always identical, since at a later stage one of the two words was sometimes adapted to the context. As mentioned on p. 237, the distinction between dittography and haplography is difficult. By definition, texts in which no dittography is detected, are preferable at the level of evaluation (cf. p. 236):

Isa 30:30	𝔐	והשמיע ה׳ (= 𝔊 𝔗 𝔖 𝔙) <preferable> then the LORD shall make heard
	1QIsa^a^	השמיע *השמיע* ה׳ then the LORD shall make heard *shall make heard.*
Isa 31:6	𝔐	שובו לאשר העמיקו סרה (= 𝔊 𝔗 𝔖 𝔙) <preferable> Come back to Him whom they have deeply offended.
	1QIsa^a^	שוביו לאשר *לאשר* העמיקו סרה Come back (?) to Him *to Him* whom they have deeply offended.
Jer 51:3	𝔐^K^	אֶל *ידרך* ידרך הדרך Let the archer not (?) *draw* draw . . .
	𝔐^Q^	אֶל ידרך הדרך (≈ 𝔊 𝔗 𝔖 𝔙) Let the archer not (?) draw . . .

25 In fact the original scribe copied a text which now is v. 8, whereas the corrector made it into v. 7 by the omission of ודבר, "but the word," through use of cancellation dots (see pp. 213–214) and by the omission of אלוהינו, "of our God" (at this point he forgot to mark the omission) and by adding v. 8 above the line and in the margin (see plates 4* and 5*, l. 7). The tetragrammaton in that verse is indicated by means of four dots (cf. p. 216).

β. Doublets

S. Talmon, *Conflate Readings—A Basic Phenomenon in the Transmission of the OT Text*, unpubl. diss., Heb. University, Jerusalem 1956; idem, "Double Readings in the Massoretic Text," *Textus* 1 (1960) 144-84; idem, "Conflate Readings (OT)," *IDBSup*, 170-173; idem, "The Textual Study of the Bible—A New Outlook," in: Cross–Talmon, *QHBT*, 321-400.

A doublet (lectio duplex, double reading, conflate reading) is a particular type of redundancy created by the combination of two or three different and sometimes synonymous readings, either in juxtaposition or in close proximity. These doublets sometimes resulted from an erroneous juxtaposition of elements, but in other cases they grew out of a conscious desire to preserve alternative readings.

Some doublets were probably created when interlinear or marginal elements—possibly corrections, see pp. 215, 284—were wrongly copied as part of the running text. This could have happened in 1QIsa[a] 36:11 (col. XXIX—see plate 3*, left side), where עמנו, "to us," is written in the margin in the following way.

להשחיתה [11]ויואמרו אליו אליקים וש[ו]בנא ויואח דברנא עם עבדיך
עמנו ארמית כיא שומעים אנחנו ואל תדבר אלינו את הדברים האלה

to destroy it. [11]Then Elyakim, Shobnaʾ, and Yoaḥ said to him: "Pray, speak to your servants <*in the margin:* to us> in Aramaic, for we understand it and do not speak these words to us."

Lack of precision in the copying of this text (the marginal עמנו is written very close to the words in the text)[26] could have created a hypothetical doublet עם עבדיך עמנו, "to your servants to us." A doublet such as this is not attested, but similar instances are documented in the textual witnesses, in cases in which a presumed first stage has not been preserved, such as in 1QIsa[a] mentioned above.

In most instances the two components of the doublet were simply juxtaposed by way of harmonization (cf. p. 261). For example,

2 Kgs 19:9	𝔐	*וישב* וישלח מלאכים
		he *again* sent messengers
Isa 37:9	𝔐	*וישמע* (= 𝔖 𝔙) וישלח מלאכים
		when he heard it, he sent messengers
	1QIsa[a]	*וישמע וישוב* (= 𝔊*) וישלח מלאכים
		when he heard it, he again sent messengers <doublet>

[26] The marginal addition of עמנו, "to us," should be taken as either a correction to עם עבדיך, "to your servants," or to אלינו, "to us" later in the verse. In the latter case the marginal reading would be identical with 𝔐 in the parallel verse, 2 Kgs 18:26.

The reading which lies at the basis of 1QIsa^a and 𝔊* of the Isaiah text added a detail which is also found in the parallel text in 2 Kings.

Jer 52:34 𝔐 *דבר יום ביומו עד יום מותו כל ימי חייו* (= 𝔗 𝔖 𝔙)
an allotment for each day, to the day of his death, all the days of his life <doublet>
𝔊* ἐξ ἡμέρας εἰς ἡμέραν ἕως ἡμέρας ἧς ἀπέθανεν
= דבר יום ביומו *עד יום מותו*
an allotment for each day, *to the day of his death*
2 Kgs 25:30 𝔐 דבר יום ביומו *כל ימי חיו* (= 𝔊 𝔗 𝔖 𝔙)
an allotment for each day, *all the days of his life*

Both parts of the doublet of 𝔐 in Jeremiah ("to the day of his death / all the days of his life") are found in different places in the textual tradition of Jeremiah and Kings, and they are equally acceptable from the point of view of content.

In other cases components of the doublet were combined in the text in various ways, so that a new context was formed. Thus, in the following example from 2 Kings 11 and 2 Chronicles 23, the thematically important words הרצים, "the guards," and העם, "the people," were combined, since both of these words are referred to in the context (הרצים in 2 Kgs 11:4, 6, 11 and עם הארץ, "the people of the land," in v. 14). In 2 Kings the words were juxtaposed without any grammatical connection, but in 2 Chronicles the text was changed according to the usage of רצים in the chapter and linguistic usage in general. A similar connection was also made in 𝔊 𝔖 𝔗 𝔙 in 2 Kings.

2 Kgs 11:13 𝔐 ותשמע עתליה את קול *הרצין העם*
When Athaliah heard the noise of *the guards the people* <sic> . . . <doublet>
2 Chr 23:12 𝔐 ותשמע עתליהו את קול *העם הרצים* והמהללים את המלך
When Athaliah heard the noise of *the people running (the guards?)* and praising the king . . . <adapted doublet>

In this, as in many other instances in 𝔐, no textual evidence containing only one of the components of the doublet has been preserved. Such is also the case in the following example, in which both parts of the doublet appear in 𝔐 in adjacent verses.

1 Sam 4:21-22 𝔐 ותקרא לנער אי כבוד לאמר גלה כבוד מישראל *אל הלקח ארון האלהים* ואל חמיה ואישה [22]ותאמר גלה כבוד מישראל *כי נלקח ארון האלהים* (≈ 𝔊 𝔗 𝔖 𝔙) <doublet>

> She named the boy Ichabod, saying: "The glory has departed from Israel," *because the Ark of God has been captured* and because of <the death of> her father-in-law and her husband. [22]She said: "The glory has departed from Israel, *for the Ark of God has been captured.*"

See also the discussion of Deut 12:5 on p. 42.

Doublets are also recognizable in the combination of morphemes which seem to be mutually exclusive, usually within one word.

		doublet	*components*
Josh 7:21	𝔐	הָאָהֳלִי	הָאֹהֶל + אָהֳלִי
2 Kgs 15:16	𝔐	הֶהָרוּתיה	הֶהָרוּת + הָרוּתיה
Isa 9:12	𝔐	הַמַּכֵּהוּ (cf. 1QIsa^a ההמכהו)	הַמַּכֵּה + מַכֵּהוּ
Isa 36:19	1QIsa^a	וכיא ההצילו	ההצילו + וכי הצילו 𝔐
Isa 51:9	𝔐	הַמַּחְצֶבֶת	? הַחֹצֶבֶת + הַמֹּחֶצֶת

On the other hand, it is not impossible that these examples reflect a linguistic characteristic rather than a textual phenomenon (thus Gesenius–Kautzsch §127i).

c. Changes

The types of changes that were inserted during the copying of the biblical text, both in single letters and in complete words, are numerous. Examples of complete words that were deliberately changed by copyists are adduced in section 3 ("readings intentionally created by scribes"). This section focuses on changes in single letters.

c.i Interchange of Similar Letters

α. Graphic Similarity

Delitzsch, *Lese- und Schreibfehler*, 81ff.; R. Macuch, *Grammatik des samaritanischen Hebräisch* (Berlin 1969) 28-48; Perles, *Analekten* I, 50-61; II, 28-42; Sperber, *Grammar*, 235ff.; S. Talmon, "The Ancient Hebrew Alphabet and Biblical Text Criticism," *Mélanges D. Barthélemy* (OBO 38; Fribourg/Göttingen 1981) 497-529; idem, "The Ancient Hebrew Alphabet and Biblical Criticism," *Mélanges bibliques et orientaux en l'honneur de M. Mathias Delcor* (AOAT 215; 1985) 387-402; Tov, *TCU*, 195-205; idem, "Interchanges of Consonants between the Masoretic Text and the *Vorlage* of the Septuagint," in: M. Fishbane and E. Tov, eds., *"Shaʿarei Talmon"—Studies in the Bible, Qumran, and the Ancient Near East Presented to Shemaryahu Talmon* (Winona Lake, IN 1992) 255-266; F. Vodel, *Die konsonantischen Varianten in den doppelt überlieferten poetischen Stücken des massoretischen Textes* (Leipzig 1905).

In ancient sources many letters were interchanged because of unclear writing or roughness of the surface which caused misunderstandings in reading.[27] Most of these interchanges were created by similarities in the form of letters in the paleo-Hebrew and the Assyrian ("square") script.

An investigation of interchanges of similar letters between 𝔐 and the presumed *Vorlage* of 𝔊 (see Tov*, 1992) shows that there are generally no rules for the *direction* of the interchange. For example, for every book, a similar number of interchanges between *daleth* and *resh* is found in both directions. It appears that this relation also applies to the other textual sources.

Another conclusion pertains to the *frequency* of interchanges of similar letters which could possibly bear evidence of their changing forms over the generations. A decisive majority of the interchanges between 𝔊 and 𝔐 pertains to ד/ר and י/ו, while other interchanges are much less frequent. Thus, while in most books of 𝔊 the interchanges of *daleth* and *resh* are the most prevalent, in a few late biblical books there is a greater number of interchanges of *yod* and *waw*. This latter detail could point to the period in which these books were copied, since in the last pre-Christian centuries the similarity between these two letters was greater than previously.

(i) Graphic Similarity between Letters in the "Early" Hebrew Script

In the different manifestations of the "early" Hebrew script, in the paleo-Hebrew script, and in its Samaritan version there was an external similarity not only between certain of the letters which are also similar in the Assyrian ("square") script, such as ד/ר, but also between letters which are not similar in that script, such as א/ת, י/צ, ג/פ/נ, and to a lesser degree also מ/נ, ב/ר. See plates 16*, 29* for the shapes of the letters. Beyond the discussion below, see the examples *apud* Luzzatto in his commentary on Ezek 3:12; Talmon*, 1981, 1985; and Macuch*.

א/ת

Gen 46:16	𝔐	**אֶצְבֹּן** (= 𝔗^OJN and 𝔐𝔰 𝔖 [**א**צבעון]) *E*ṣbon
	𝔊	Θασοβαν (*et sim.*) *Thas*oban
	=	**ת**צבן

[27] This discussion does not pertain to *linguistically* close words and roots, presenting a different type of interchangeability. These instances have often been discussed by medieval Jewish grammarians, on which see especially I. Eldar, "An Ancient Genizah Treatise on Interchangeable Letters in Hebrew," *Tarbiz* 57 (1988) 483-510 (Heb. with Eng. summ.).

2 Sam 2:9	𝔐	האשורי (= 𝔗)
		the *Ash*urite
	𝔊	Θασιρι
		the *Thas*irite
	=	התשורי
Ezra 8:21,31	𝔐	אַהֲוָא (= 𝔊^MSS 𝔙)
		Ahava
	𝔊^B	Θουε
		Thoue
	=	תהוא

י/צ

Exod 14:2	𝔐	(לפני פי) הַחִירֹת (= ⅏ 𝔗^OJN 𝔖 𝔙) <preferable>
(sim. v. 9)		(before Pi-) ha*ḥi*roth
	𝔊*	(ἀπέναντι) τῆς ἐπαύλεως
		(before) the encampment
	=	הַחֲצֵרֹת (פי is probably not reflected in 𝔊)
		Haḥa*ṣ*eroth / the encampment(s)

For an additional example, see the emendation in Isa 11:15 (p. 358).

פ/נ

2 Sam 23:35	𝔐	חצרו הכרמלי פַּעֲרַי הארבי (≈ 𝔊 𝔗 𝔙)
		Heṣro the Carmelite, *Pa*ʿarai the Arbite
1 Chr 11:37	𝔐	חצרו הכרמלי נַעֲרַי בן אזבי (≈ 𝔊 𝔗 𝔙)
		Heṣro the Carmelite, *Na*ʿarai son of Ezbai

(ii) Similarity between Letters in the Assyrian ("Square") Script

Several Qumran texts show a conspicuous similarity between י/ו, ד/ר, ב/מ/כ, ה/ח, and also between other letters which are less frequently confused. Actually, in several texts such as 11QPs[a] (see plate 8*), it is very difficult to distinguish between *waw* and *yod*, especially when they are joined to other letters. See plates 29* and 30* for the shapes of the letters and see further the bibliography on pp. 233, 243.

Examples of interchanges of letters are copious. The most frequent ones are recorded below. See further ו/ר (p. 304) and י/ר (p. 361).

ד/ר

Gen 14:14	𝔐	וַיָּרֶק את חניכיו
		he *armed* (?) his followers
	⅏	וידק את חניכיו
		he *crushed* (?) his followers

Gen 22:13	𝔐	וירא והנה איל אַחַר נאחז בסבך בקרניו (= 𝔗^{O}; ≈ 𝔙) He looked up and there was *behind* <him> a ram caught by its horns in a thicket.
	ꞩ	וירא והנה איל אחד נאחז בסבך בקרניו (= 𝔐^{MSS} 𝔊 𝔗^{JN} 𝔖) <preferable> He looked up and there was *one (a)* ram caught by its horns in a thicket.
2 Sam 22:43	𝔐	כטיט חוצות אֲדִקֵּם Like the mud in the streets, *I crushed them.*
Ps 18:43	𝔐	כטיט חוצות אֲרִיקֵם Like the mud in the streets, *I emptied them.*
Isa 9:8	𝔐	וְיָדְעוּ העם כלו (= 𝔊 𝔖 𝔙) But all the people *knew.*
	1QIsa^{a}	וירעו העם כלו But all the people *shouted.*
Jer 2:20	𝔐^{K}	(ותאמרי לא) אעבד (= 𝔊 𝔖 𝔙) (and you said: "I will not) *work.*"
	𝔐^{Q}	אעבור (= 𝔗) (and you said: "I will not) *transgress.*"

Likewise, see the examples in chapter 2, Table 14, and also Gen 10:4 (p. 12); 1 Sam 10:27 (p. 343); 2 Kgs 16:6 (p. 62); Isa 33:8 (p. 354); Isa 45:2 (p. 254); Jer 41:9 (p. 304); and Jonah 1:9 (p. 257).

י/ו

Gen 36:39	𝔐	פָּעוּ Paʿ**u** (= ꞩ 𝔗^{OJN} 𝔖 𝔙)
1 Chr 1:50	𝔐	פָּעִי Paʿ***i*** (𝔗 𝔖 𝔙 reflect פָּעוּ)
Prov 17:27	𝔐^{K}	וקר רוח *and* he who has a *cool* spirit <preferable>
	𝔐^{Q}	יְקַר רוח *precious* of spirit

Likewise, see Gen 10:28 // 1 Chr 1:22 (p.13); Gen 49:7 (p. 92); 2 Sam 22:51 K/Q (p. 59); Job 17:10 (p. 26); and the examples on pp. 60–61.

At the same time, some interchanges of י/ו may reflect a phonetic phenomenon rather than an interchange of graphically similar letters:[28]

Gen 36:22	𝔐	בני לוטן חרי והֵימָם (= 𝔊 𝔗^{OJ} 𝔙 and 𝔊 in Chr; ≈ ꞩ) the sons of Lotan were Ḥori and H**ê**man
1 Chr 1:39	𝔐	ובני לוטן חרי והוֹמָם (= 𝔗 𝔖 𝔙 and 𝔖 in Gen) the sons of Lotan were Ḥori and H**o**man

28 See S. Morag, "Mešaʿ—A Study of Certain Features of Old Hebrew Dialects," *ErIsr* 5 (1958) 138-144 (Heb. with Eng. summ.).

Jer 48:21 𝔐[K] מופעת (= 𝔊)
Mopha'at
𝔐[Q] מֵיפַעַת (= 𝔗 𝔙; ≈ 𝔖)
Mêpha'at = 1 Chr 6:64, Josh 13:18 (מֵפָעַת)

ב/ד

Josh 11:2 𝔐 (בהר ובערבה) נגב (כנרות) (= 𝔗 𝔙; ≈ 𝔖)
(in the hill country, and in the Arabah) *south* of (Kinnerot)
𝔊 ἀπέναντι, "opposite." Thus also 15:3.
= נגד

Josh 15:47 𝔐[K] הגבול (see the next word וגבול)
the *boundary*
𝔐[Q] הגדול (= 𝔐[MSS] 𝔊 𝔗 𝔖 𝔙)
the *great*

Likewise, see 2 Sam 23:29 // 1 Chr 11:30 (p. 13).

ב/מ

The forms of these two letters are surprisingly close in many Qumran texts. At the same time, they are also close phonetically, so that at times it may be difficult to distinguish between textual and linguistic phenomena.

1 Kgs 12:2 𝔐 ויהי כשמע ירבעם . . . וַיֵּשֶׁב ירבעם בְּמִצְרָיִם (= 𝔊* [11:43] 𝔗 𝔖)
When Jeroboam heard this . . . Jeroboam settled *in* Egypt.

2 Chr 10:2 𝔐 ויהי כשמע ירבעם . . . וַיָּשָׁב ירבעם מִמִּצְרָיִם (= 𝔗; = 𝔊[A] 𝔙 in 1 Kings)
When Jeroboam heard this . . . Jeroboam returned *from* Egypt.[29]

2 Kgs 5:12 𝔐[K] אבנה (= 𝔊 𝔖 𝔙)
'A*b*anah
𝔐[Q] אֲמָנָה (= 𝔗)
'A*m*anah

2 Kgs 20:12 𝔐 בְּראַדַךְ בלאדן בן בלאדן מלך בבל (= 𝔗 𝔙)
*B*erodach-Bal'adan son of Bal'adan, king of Babylon

---

29 Cf. T.M. Willis, "The Text of 1 Kings 11:43–12:3," *CBQ* 53 (1991) 37-44.

Isa 39:1	𝔐	מְרֹדַךְ בלאדן בן בלאדן מלך בבל (= 𝔗 𝔙; = 𝔊 𝔖 *ad loc.* and in Kings) *M*erodach-Balʾadan son of Balʾadan, king of Babylon <preferable>

Note the large number of occurrences of the *beth* in this context.

See also Gen 25:33 (p. 120); Josh 3:16 (p. 61); Jer 29:26 (p. 256).

ב/כ

1 Kgs 22:20	𝔐	ויאמר זה בְּכֹה וזה אמר בְּכֹה (= 𝔙 *ad loc.* and of Chronicles) And one said *one thing*, and another said *another.*
2 Chr 18:19	𝔐	ויאמר זה אמר כָּכָה וזה אמר כָּכָה (= 𝔊 𝔖 of Kings and 𝔊 *ad loc.*) And one said *thus* and another said *thus.*
2 Kgs 3:24	𝔐^K	ויבו בה והכות את מואב and they *went in* (?) it, attacking the Moabites
	𝔐^Q	וַיַּכּוּ בה והכות את מואב and they *hit* it, attacking the Moabites

Likewise, see the examples in Josh 4:18 (p. 61); 1 Sam 30:30 (p. 6); and Jer 23:9 (p. 130).

כ/מ

Josh 19:2	𝔐	ומולדה (= 𝔗 𝔖 𝔙) and *M*oladah
	𝔊^B	καὶ Κωλαδαμ *et sim.*
	=	וכולדה and *K*oladah
Josh 21:38	𝔐	ואת מחנים (= 𝔖 𝔙) and *M*aḥanayim
	𝔊*	καὶ τὴν Καμιν *et sim.*
	=	ואת כחנים and *K*aḥanayim/*K*aḥanim

See also the emendation in Ezek 3:12 (p. 358).

ה/ח

2 Sam 13:37	𝔐^K	עמיחור ʿAmmi***ḥur*** (= 𝔙)
	𝔐^Q	עמיהוד ʿAmmi***hud*** (= 𝔊 𝔖)

See also Prov 20:21 (p. 62). Interchanges between *he* and *ḥeth* also have phonetic aspects (see p. 251).

(iii) Ligatures

D.M. Beegle, "Ligatures with Waw and Yodh in the Dead Sea Isaiah Scroll," *BASOR* 129 (1953) 11-14; R. Weiss, "On Ligatures in the Hebrew Bible (נו=ם)," *JBL* 82 (1963) 188-194.

In the writing of certain scribes, various letters were joined together to form one graphic entity which could easily be confused with single letters. This practice is clearly recognizable in those Qumran texts in which ע-ו, ע-ז, ע-י are joined into a shape similar in appearance to a *shin/sin* (see, for example, 11QPs[a], col. X, ll. 1, 6, on plate 8*). Likewise נ-ו were joined into a shape resembling a final *mem* (see ibid.). A phenomenon similar to that of ligatures is mentioned in *m. Shabb.* 12.5: "If one intends writing a *ḥeth*, but writes two *zayins* . . ."

Josh 5:1	$\mathfrak{M}^{K}$	עד עבר**נו** until *we* had crossed over
	$\mathfrak{M}^{Q}$	עד עבר**ם** (= $\mathfrak{M}^{MSS}$ 𝔊 𝔖 𝔙) until *they* had crossed over
2 Kgs 22:4	𝔐	וְיַתֵּ**ם** את הכסף (≈ 𝔖 𝔙) and *let him sum up* (?) the money
2 Chr 34:9	𝔐	וית**נו** את הכסף (= 𝔊 𝔗 𝔖 𝔙) and *they gave* the money
Jer 49:19	𝔐	כי ארגיעה אריצ**נו** (= 𝔙 *ad loc.* and of 50:44) for I will suddenly make *him* run away
ibid., 50:44	$\mathfrak{M}^{K}$	כי ארגעה ארוצ**ם** ($\mathfrak{M}^{Q}$ אריצ**ם**) (= 𝔊 [27:44] 𝔖 *ad loc.* and of 49:19 [30:13]) for I will suddenly make *them* run away
Ezra 2:2	𝔐	אשר באו עם זרבבל ישוע נחמיה **ש**ריה (= 𝔊 𝔖 𝔙) . . . who came with Zerubbabel, Jeshua, Nehemiah, *S*eraiah
Neh 7:7	𝔐	הבאים עם זרבבל ישוע נחמיה **עז**ריה (= 𝔊 𝔖 𝔙) . . . who came with Zerubbabel, Jeshua, Nehemiah, *Aza*riah
Neh 11:11	𝔐	**ש**ריה בן חלקיה בן משלם בן צדוק (= 𝔊 𝔙) *S*eraiah son of Ḥilkiah, son of Meshullam, son of Zadok
1 Chr 9:11	𝔐	ו**עז**ריה בן חלקיה בן משלם בן צדוק (= 𝔊 𝔗 𝔖 𝔙) *and Aza*riah son of Ḥilkiah, son of Meshullam, son of Zadok

(iv) Metathesis

H. Junker, "Konsonantenumstellung als Fehlerquelle und textkritisches Hilfsmittel im AT," *BZAW* 66 (1936) 162-174; N. Tur-Sinai, "šykwly ʾwtywt bnwsḥ hmqrʾ," *Hlšwn whspr, krk hspr* (Jerusalem 1959) 106-149.

Metathesis is the transposition of two adjacent letters. While some instances of metathesis reflect legitimate linguistic alternatives,[30] others resulted from textual error. In the following instances, the texts relate to each other as presumably original and erroneous (resulting from metathesis). In each case content analysis must determine which of the two texts resulted from metathesis. In some cases, such as the first example, there is room for more than one view.

2 Sam 22:46 𝔐 בני נכר יבלו ויחגרו ממסגרותם
aliens have lost courage, they *girded themselves* out of their chains (?)

Ps 18:46 𝔐 בני נכר יבלו ויחרגו ממסגרותיהם
aliens have lost courage, they *came out* of their chains (?)

2 Sam 23:12 𝔐 ויעש ה' תשועה גדולה (= 𝔊 𝔗 𝔖 𝔙)
Thus the LORD *wrought* a great victory.

1 Chr 11:14 𝔐 ויושע ה' תשועה גדולה
Thus the LORD *saved* <them> by a great victory.

1 Kgs 7:45 𝔐K ואת כל הכלים האהל
and all the vessels *the tent* (?)

𝔐Q ואת כל הכלים האלה (= 𝔖; ≈ 𝔊 [7:31]) <preferable>
and all *these* vessels

The following three cases of metathesis have a special status since the *ʾaleph*, *ḥeth*, and *ʿayin* were not pronounced (see below β and pp. 112–113). In such cases the two readings were pronounced almost identically (e.g., *netam* in Isa 9:8).

2 Sam 23:31 𝔐 עזמות הַבַּרְחֻמִי (≈ 𝔊 𝔙; = 𝔗)
ʿAzmaveth the Bar*ḥum*ite

1 Chr 11:33 𝔐 עזמות הַבַּחֲרוּמִי (≈ 𝔊 𝔙; = 𝔗) <preferable>
ʿAzmaveth the Ba*ḥarum*ite

בח(ו)רים, Baḥurim, was a town in Benjamin (cf. 2 Sam 3:16; 16:5; 17:18, etc.), so that the *consonantal* reading in Chronicles appears to have been original, probably to be read as הַבַּחֻרִימִי.

---

30 E.g., שמלה/שלמה and כבש/כשב. See Ibn Janaḥ, *Sepher ha-Riqmah*, § 32 (31) = pp. 352-355 in the edition of M. Wilensky (Berlin 1930).

Isa 9:18	𝔐	נֶעְתַּם ארץ
		the land is ?
	1QIsa^{a}	**נתעם** הארץ
		the land is ?
Isa 13:19	𝔐	תִּפְאֶרֶת
		glory <preferable>
	1QIsa^{a}	תפ**רא**ת
		(non-existent word)

See also n. 40; Deut 31:1 (p. 129); and the suggested emendations for Ps 22:16 (p. 360) , Ps 49:14 (ibid.), and Prov 30:17 (p. 366).

β. Phonetic Similarity

א/ה/ח/ע

Many readings were created on account of their phonetic similarity, particularly among the guttural and labial letters—the evaluation of the pair ח/ה is difficult, since they are also similar graphically (see pp. 248–249). Apart from the interchanges between 𝔐 and ɯɯ (see Table 17 on pp. 95-96), the Qumran texts (Table 21 on p. 112-113), and the Severus Scroll (Table 23 on pp. 120-121), see the following examples.

1 Sam 17:7	𝔐^{K}	ו**ח**ץ חניתו
		and the *arrow* (?) of his spear
	𝔐^{Q}	ו**ע**ץ חניתו
		and the *shaft* (?) of his spear
1 Kgs 1:18	𝔐	ו**ע**תה (אדוני המלך) (= 𝔗)
		and *now* (my lord the king)
	𝔊	(καὶ σύ)
	=	ו**א**תה (= 𝔐^{MSS} 𝔗^{MSS} 𝔖)
		and *you*
1 Kgs 12:18	𝔐	**אֲ**דֹרָם (= 𝔗)
		*A*doram
2 Chr 10:18	𝔐	**הֲ**דֹרָם (= 𝔗)
		Hadoram

For an additional example, see Deut 23:2 (p. 6).

ב/פ

Gen 31:40	𝔐	הייתי ביום אכלני חר**ב** וקרח בלילה
		Thus I was; by day *scorching heat* consumed me, and frost by night.
	ɯɯ	הייתי ביום אכלני חר**ף** וקרח בלילה

Gen 31:49	$\mathfrak{M}$	וְהַמִּצְפָּה אשר אמר יִצֶף ה׳ and *Mizpah*, for he said: "May the LORD watch . . ."
	⅏	והמצבה אשר אמר יצף ה׳ and *the pillar*, for he said: "May the LORD watch . . ."
Exod 15:10	$\mathfrak{M}$	נשפת ברוחך You made Your wind blow.
	⅏	נשבת ברוחך
2 Sam 10:16	$\mathfrak{M}$	וְשׁוֹבַךְ שר צבא הדדעזר לפניהם with Sho*b*akh the commander of the army of Hadadezer at their head
1 Chr 19:16	$\mathfrak{M}$	וְשׁוֹפַךְ שר צבא הדדעזר לפניהם with Sho*p*akh the commander of the army of Hadadezer at their head

c.ii Different Conceptions of Word Division

The examples given below present different conceptions of word division reflected in various textual witnesses of the same text. As indicated by the Qumran evidence, spaces between words were often very narrow and this situation accounts for some confusion. At the same time, as noted on p. 209, differences in word division may have been created when word division was introduced in texts which initially were written in the *scriptio (scriptura) continua*. Beyond the examples listed below, see lists 98-102 in *Okhlah we-Okhlah* (p. 74) and the examples *apud* Tov, *TCU*, 174-177.

Gen 49:19-20	$\mathfrak{M}$	והוא יגד עקב [20]מאשר שמנה לחמו (= $\mathfrak{T}^{OJN}$) but he shall raid <their> heel. [20]*Of Asher*, his food is rich
	$\mathfrak{G}$	αὐτὸς δὲ πειρατεύσει αὐτῶν κατὰ πόδας. [20]Ασηρ, πίων αὐτοῦ ὁ ἄρτος
	=	והוא יגד עקבם [20]אשר שמנה לחמו <preferable> but he shall raid *their* heel. [20]*Asher*, his food is rich
Ezek 42:9	$\mathfrak{M}^K$	ומתחתה לשכות האלה and below (?) these chambers
	$\mathfrak{M}^Q$	ומתחת הלשכות האלה <preferable> and below these chambers
Job 38:12	$\mathfrak{M}^K$	ידעתה שחר מקמו Did you ever cause dawn to know its place?

𝔐^Q ידעת **ה**שחר מקמו

Did you ever cause *the* dawn to know its place?

See also 1 Sam 10:27 (p. 343); Isa 17:6 (p. 354); Jer 29:26 (p. 256).

One word *separated* into two, and two words joined together:

Exod 2:9 𝔐 הילכי את הילד הזה (≈ ɯɯ 𝔊 𝔗^OJN 𝔙) <preferable>
Take this child <with you>.
𝔖 הא לכי טליא הנא (cf. *b. Soṭ.* 12b)
= הי ל(י)כי את הילד הזה
Lo, to you <is> this child.

Deut 33:2 𝔐^K אשדת
𝔐^Q אש דת
fire of law (?) (= ɯɯ 𝔗^OJFN 𝔙)

Isa 40:12 𝔐 מי מדד בשעלו *מים* (ושמים בזרת תכן) (= 𝔊 𝔖 𝔙)
Who measured *the waters* with the hollow of His hand (and gauged the sky with a span)?
1QIsa^a מי ים (with the duplication of the *yod*; thus also Theodotion in 24:14)
. . . *the water of the sea*

For further examples, see chapter 2, Table 23; בהבראם in Gen 2:4 as explained on p. 58; Gen 49:10 (p. 2, n. 1); Isa 17:6 (p. 354); Jer 23:33 (p. 303); 41:9 (p. 304); Amos 6:12 (emendation, p. 357); Ps 73:1 (emendation, p. 361); and *Sof.* 7.5.

c.iii Differences Involving Matres Lectionis

Delitzsch, *Lese- und Schreibfehler*, 32ff.; Driver, *Samuel*, xxvi-xxxiii; Ginsburg, *Introduction*, 137-157.

Many of the *matres lectionis* were secondarily introduced into the biblical texts, in some cases in a relatively late stage of their development (above, B4b, pp. 222-223). This process was gradual, so that the various texts reflect different orthographical practices, as may be inferred from a comparison of the orthography of 𝔐 (pp. 220–229), ɯɯ (pp. 96–97), and many of the Qumran texts (pp. 108–110).

Most variations in the use of *matres lectionis* do not bear upon the meaning of the text. At the same time, the very addition of *matres lectionis* basically reflects the understanding of the person adding the *matres lectionis*, so that one should expect some differences in perception between textual witnesses involving the employment of these vowel letters. This type of variation is demonstrated below.

1 Sam 1:24 𝔐 בפרימשלשה = בְּפָרִים שְׁלשָׁה (= 𝔗 𝔙)
(And when she had weaned him, she took him up with her,) along with *three bulls,* (an ephah of flour . . .)
𝔊 ἐν μόσχῳ τριετίζοντι
= בפרמשלש = בפר מְשֻׁלָּשׁ (= 𝔖)
along with *a three-year-old bull*
4QSam^a [בפר בן] בקר משלש
[along with (a)] *three-year-old bull*

Probably the text of 𝔐 𝔗 𝔙 on the one hand, and 𝔊 𝔖 4QSam^a on the other, derived from a common source: בפרמשלש. According to the context, it is reasonable to assume that this word cluster originally referred to a פר, "bull," in the singular,[31] i.e., "she took him up . . . along with a three-year-old bull." When word division and *matres lectionis* were added, the common source of 𝔊 𝔖 4QSam^a retained this understanding, while 𝔐 𝔗 𝔙 was corrupted.

Isa 45:2 𝔐 (אני לפניך אלך) וַהֲדוּרִים (אושר𝔐K, אֲיַשֵּׁר 𝔐Q)
(I will go before you) and ??[32] (I shall level)
1QIsa^a והררים = 𝔊 καὶ ὄρη ≈ 𝔖 <preferable>
and mountains

On the basis of contextual and linguistic considerations, the reading of 1QIsa^a 𝔊 (≈ 𝔖) appears preferable. When the word became corrupted by a *daleth/resh* interchange, a *waw* was added as a vowel letter.

See also the examples mentioned in the section on metathesis (p. 250) and in chapter 2, Tables, 1, 4, 18, 21, 24; chapter 4, Tables 2-6.

c.iv Differences Involving the Use of Final Letters

The letters מנצפ"ך (*mem, nun, ṣade, pe,* and *kaph*) were not always written in their final forms at the ends of words and sometimes they were written in their final form in non-final position. See the examples and analysis on pp. 32, 111, 119–120, 210 and see further n. 8. Since the distinction between final and non-final forms of letters was introduced at a relatively late period in the development of the biblical text, it is

31 In the following verse the bull is referred to in the singular in all the textual witnesses ("Then they slew *the bull.*").

32 The root of the word in 𝔐 is actually not known from other places, even though, *faute de mieux*, the word is often connected with הדר, "glory"(cf. 𝔙 *gloriosos terrae*) and hence explained by BDB *s.v.* as "swelling places" (cf. NEB: "swelling hills"). For a similar difference between 𝔐 and 𝔊, see Mic 2:9 הדרי—ὄρεσιν. On the other hand, C.H. Southwood, "The Problematic *h^{a}dūrîm* of Isaiah XLV 2," *VT* 25 (1975) 801-802 suggested that 𝔐 reflects an Akkadian loan word *dūru,* "city walls," which could fit the context.

permissible to replace final forms of letters with non-final forms and vice versa in the reconstruction of earlier stages of the biblical text.

c.v Vocalization

Differences in vocalization between various texts which reflect different understandings of the consonantal framework are recognizable in all witnesses of the biblical text. See especially pp. 2, n. 1 (Gen 49:10), 6, 41–43, 70–71, 246 (1 Kgs 12:2 // 2 Chr 10:2), 304 (1 Sam 1:24, 20:30), 359–360 (various emendations).

c.vi Quiescent ʾAleph

Scribes sometimes freely omitted the quiescent *ʾaleph*, i.e., an *ʾaleph* whose vowel was transferred to the preceding letter. See the discussion by Andersen–Forbes* (see p. 220) 83-88, the examples in Kutscher, *Language*, 257, 498-500, and p. 108 above. Further examples follow.

The name בֵּית שְׁאָן / בֵּית שָׁן, Beth Shean, appears six times in the Hebrew Bible with an *ʾaleph* (Josh 17:11,16; Judg 1:27; 1 Kgs 4:12, twice; 1 Chr 7:29) and three times without it, in Samuel only (1 Sam 31:10,12; 2 Sam 21:12).

Similarly, note the two different spellings of the names תגלת פל(א)סר, Tiglath-Pileser, and ש(א)לתיאל, Shealtiel, within the same context.

2 Kgs 16:7	תגלת פְּלֶסֶר
ibid., v.10	תגלת פִּלְ**אֶ**סֶר (thus also 2 Kgs 15:29)
Hag 1:12	שַׁלְתִּיאֵל (thus also 1:14; 2:2)
ibid., v. 1	שְׁ**אַ**לְתִּיאֵל (thus also 2:23; Ezra 3:2,8; 5:2; Neh 12:1; 1 Chr 3:17)

See also the following spellings in 𝔐:

Num 15:24	לְחַטָּת (= לחט**א**ת)
1 Sam 1:17	שֵׁלָתֵךְ (= ש**א**לתך)
Job 8:8	רִישׁוֹן (= ר**א**שון)
1 Chr 11:39	הַבֵּרֹתִי (= הב**א**רתי; thus the parallel in 2 Sam 23:37).

c.vii Complex Variants

Many variants display several types of differences: consonants, *matres lectionis*, final letters, word division, vocalization, etc. Apart from the examples mentioned in the other sections (c.ii, iii, iv, v, vi, viii), see:

Ps 31:3	𝔐	היה לי לצור מעוז **לבית** מצודות להושיעני Be for me a rock, *a stronghold, a shelter of fortress* to save me.
Ps 71:3	𝔐	היה לי לצור מעון **לבוא** תמיד צוית להושיעני Be for me a rock of *dwelling, to come continually you have commanded* (?) to save me.
2 Sam 23:25	𝔐	שַׁמָּה הַחֲרֹדִי Shamm*ah* the Ḥaro*d*ite
1 Chr 11:27	𝔐	שַׁמּ**וֹת** הַהֲרוֹרִי (≈ 𝔊 𝔖 𝔙; = 𝔗) Shamm***ot*** the ***H***aro*r*ite
2 Sam 23:27	𝔐	מְבֻנַּי החשתי (≈ 𝔊; = 𝔗 𝔖 𝔙) *Mebunn*ai the Ḥushathite
1 Chr 11:29	𝔐	סִבְּכַי החשתי (= 𝔊 𝔙 and 2 Sam 21:18 𝔐) *Sibbekh*ai the Ḥushathite
Jer 29:26	𝔐	(ה׳ נתנך כהן . . . להיות) פְּקִדִ**ים** בית ה׳ (The LORD has made you priest . . . to be) officer*s* <in/of> the House of the LORD.
(36:26 𝔊)	𝔊	γενέσθαι ἐπιστάτην ἐν τῷ οἴκῳ κυρίου
	=	פָּקִיד **ב**בית ה׳ (= 𝔖 𝔙; ≈ 𝔗) <preferable> *an* officer *in* the House of the LORD

These two texts reflect a different understanding of פקיד (in the singular or plural), together with an interchange ב/מ (p. 247) and a different word division (pp. 252–253).

For additional examples, see Gen 47:21 (p. 92) and Jer 41:9 (p. 304).

c.viii Abbreviations?

G.R. Driver, "Abbreviations in the Massoretic Text," *Textus* 1 (1960) 112-131; idem, "Once Again Abbreviations," *Textus* 4 (1964) 76-94; Eichhorn, *Einleitung*, II, § 90, 102; B. Kennicott, *Dissertatio generalis in Vetus Testamentum hebraicum, cum variis lectionibus ex codicibus manuscriptis et impressis* (Brunovici 1783) 49-55; M. Fishbane, "Abbreviations, Hebrew Texts," *IDBSup*, 3-4; Ginsburg, *Introduction*, 165-170; Perles, *Analekten* I, 4-35; II, 1-10.

Although the early texts provide no evidence for the existence of abbreviations (at first recognized by Kennicott*), several differences between 𝔐 and 𝔊 suggest that they were used at one time, since some elements were understood as abbreviations. Thus the existence in manuscripts of an abbreviation of the tetragrammaton as ׳ / ׳׳ is likely.

Judg 19:18	𝔐	ואת בית **יהוה** אני הלך (ואין איש מאסף אותי הביתה) (= 𝔗 𝔖 𝔙) and to *the House of the* LORD I am going (and nobody takes me into his house).

𝔊 (καὶ εἰς τὸν οἶκόν μου) ἐγὼ ἀποτρέχω ($𝔊^B$ πορεύομαι) <preferable>
= ואת ביתי אני הלך
and to *my house* I am going

Since the Levite is on his way home (cf. v. 29), the reading of 𝔊 is preferable. A probably original reading ביתי, "my house," was understood as בית י׳, "the House of the LORD," in 𝔐.

Jonah 1:9 𝔐 עברי אנכי (ואת ה׳ אלהי השמים אני ירא) (= 𝔗 𝔖 𝔙) <preferable>
I am a *Hebrew* (and I worship the LORD, the God of heaven).
𝔊 Δοῦλος κυρίου ἐγώ εἰμι
= עבד י׳ אנכי
I am a *servant of the* LORD.

A probably original עברי was understood as עבד י׳ by 𝔊 or its *Vorlage*. Jonah's answers in 𝔐 suit the various questions concerning his origin, whereas according to 𝔊 Jonah does not answer these questions. Moreover, he refers twice to the worship of God. Beyond the differences in the understanding of the *yod*, the two texts also differ in their reading of the letters ר/ד.

Jer 6:11 𝔐 ואת חמת י׳ מלאתי (= θ′ 𝔗 𝔖 𝔙) <preferable>
But I am filled with the wrath *of the* LORD.
𝔊 καὶ τὸν θυμόν μου ἔπλησα
= ואת חמתי מלאתי
But I am filled with *my own* wrath.

The following example also strongly suggests an actual abbreviation לי׳ or an understanding of לי as an abbreviation in ɯɯ 𝔊. In these two texts, ליום functions like לעת in the parallel stich (cf. also יום אידם in the third stich).

Deut 32:35 𝔐 לי נקם ושלם (= $𝔗^{OJFN}$ 𝔖 𝔙)
To be *my* vengeance and recompense . . .
ɯɯ ליום נקם ושלם ≈ 𝔊 (ἐν ἡμέρᾳ ἐκδικήσεως ἀνταποδώσω)
For the *day* of vengeance and recompense . . .

Possibly personal names were abbreviated as well. It is not likely that this also applies to pronominal and possessive suffixes as claimed by Driver*.

d. Differences in Sequence

There are many differences in sequence between textual witnesses. Larger differences are mentioned on pp. 338–340, while smaller differences are exemplified here.

Gen 30:43 𝔐 (ויהי לו צאן רבות) *ושפחות ועבדים* (וגמלים וחמרים)
(≈ 𝔐𝔐; = 𝔗^OJN 𝔙)
(He had large flocks,) maidservants and menservants, (camels and asses).
𝔊* καὶ παῖδες καὶ παιδίσκαι (= 𝔖)
= *ועבדים ושפחות*
menservants and maidservants

2 Sam 5:13 𝔐 ויולדו עוד לדוד בנים ובנות (= 𝔗)
and more sons and daughters were born to David
4QSam^a לדויד עוד = 𝔊 (τῷ Δαυιδ ἔτι) 𝔖
Cf. 1 Chr 14:3 𝔐 ויולד דויד עוד בנים ובנות (= 𝔊 𝔗)

Cf. further Gen 31:17; 42:32, all 𝔐 𝔐𝔐 𝔊.

3. Readings Intentionally Created by Scribes

Many changes of various types were inserted throughout the long period of the copying and transmission of the biblical text. The changes described in section 2 resulted from the process of transmission and most of them reflect actual mistakes. At the same time, the scribes also took the liberty, to a greater or lesser extent, of altering the *content* of the text in the broadest sense of the word. The following types of readings are recognized: (a) linguistic-stylistic changes, (b) synonymous readings, (c) harmonizations, (d) exegetical changes, (e) additions to the body of the text.

By definition, content alterations are secondary, and hence seemingly less interesting from a textual point of view. This lack of interest would be justifiable only if one could claim with certainty that a certain reading is secondary. But such certainty cannot easily be obtained, so that in a way all readings remain of equal interest. But there is more involved. Even if one would know with certainty which readings had been created secondarily, these readings actually remain of interest. For these deliberate changes illustrate the views of the ancients who took an active interest in every aspect of the Bible. This interest led the scribes to change the text here and there in accordance with their ideas as to what the Bible actually ought to have said in a given instance. Accordingly, textual critics are not merely interested in readings that were presumably contained in *the* or *an* original text; the study of ancient manuscripts also tells us the story of the history of the Hebrew language, of ancient exegesis, and of the history of ideas, how new ideas were developed and how earlier ideas were changed. This dynamic aspect of the history of the text makes the text-critical description interdisciplinary.

a. Linguistic-Stylistic Changes

Sperber, *Grammar*, 476-636.

In the process of copying, the linguistic background and views of the scribes are reflected in some changes inserted into manuscripts, as a rule consciously, but probably sometimes unconsciously as well. Such changes are spotted in 𝔐 (see chapter 2, Tables 12, 13) and in many of the Qumran texts (ibid., Table 21). This paragraph contains additional examples of other types, drawn partly from the linguistic sphere and partly from stylistic changes.

In several instances 1QIsa^a replaced rare words with more common ones, as did 𝔐 (chapter 2, Table 12) and, at an earlier stage, the Chronicler.[33] Indeed, the Chronicler may be taken as both a scribe and an author since he copied earlier literature, while rewriting many sections and adding new ones.

Isa 13:10 𝔐 כי כוכבי השמים וכסיליהם לא *יהלו* אורם
For the stars of the heaven and their constellations will not *let* their light *shine*.
1QIsa^a יאירו

The root הלל in the meaning of "to shine" appears only three more times in the Bible (Job 29:3, 31:26, 41:10) and probably for this reason the scribe replaced it with a more commonly occurring root.

Isa 47:2 𝔐 גלי צמתך חשפי *שֹׁבֶל* גלי שוק
remove your veil, strip off your *train*, uncover your leg
1QIsa^a חשופי *שוליך*

שבל is a *hapax legomenon* in the Bible and is not used in rabbinic Hebrew. On the other hand, *שולים* occurs frequently in similar contexts (Jer 13:22,26; Lam 1:9; Nah 3:5). For the phrase cf. especially Jer 13:26.

Linguistic differences are also exemplified by the following random samples.

---

33 See S. Japhet, "Interchanges of Verbal Roots in Parallel Texts in Chronicles," *Hebrew Studies* 28 (1987) 9-50; M. Fishbane* (p. 264) 56-60.

Gen 10:13		לודים		
1 Chr 1:11	𝔐K	לודיים	𝔐Q	לודים
Deut 21:7	𝔐K	ידינו לא שפכה		
	𝔐Q	שפכו (= 𝔐)		
Judg 9:8	𝔐K	מלוכה		
	𝔐Q	מְלֻכָה		
1 Kgs 7:24		שני טורים		
2 Chr 4:3		**שנים** טורים		
2 Kgs 22:19		ותב**כה**		
2 Chr 34:27		ותב**ך**		
Ps 105:11		לך אתן *את* ארץ כנען		
1 Chr 16:18		לך אתן ארץ כנען		

b. Synonymous Readings

S. Talmon, "lšˀlt ḥylwpy hgyrsh bmgylt yšˁyhw ˀ," *Spr ˀwrbk* (Jerusalem 1955) 147–156; idem, "Synonymous Readings in the Textual Traditions of the OT," *ScrHier* 8 (1961) 335-383.

Many of the variants involve words which serve a similar or identical function on the literary level although their meaning is not necessarily identical. These interchangeable words entered the manuscript tradition at all stages of the transmission, both consciously and unconsciously, and have been termed synonymous readings. For example, the basic meanings of כף, "palm of the hand," and יד, "hand," differ, yet they were interchanged on the literary level and subsequently also on the textual level as can be seen from the first example below.[34] The existence of these synonymous readings also gave rise to textual doublets (see pp. 241–243).

Note the following examples to which one should add those recorded in chapter 2, Table 16 (relating to 𝔐) and on p. 131 (Isa 36:11).

2 Sam 22:1	ביום הציל ה׳ אתו מכף כל איביו ומ**כף** שאול
	. . . after the LORD had saved him from the hand (lit. palm) of all his enemies, and from the *hand* (lit. palm) of Saul
Ps 18:1	ביום הציל ה׳ אותו מכף כל איביו ומ**יד** שאול
2 Sam 22:5	כי אפפני *משברי* מות
	For the *waves* of death encompassed me.

34 It is not impossible that some of these words were interchanged at the stage of the oral transmission of texts prior to their writing, and if that assumption could be proven, these examples need not be discussed within the present textual discussion. However, the distinction between the oral and written transmission remains vague.

Ps 18:5 אפפוני *חבלי* מות
The *snares* of death encompassed me.

Isa 39:2 𝔐 (. . . לא הראם חזקיהו בביתו ובכל) ממשלתו
(. . . which Hezekiah did not show them in his house and all) his realm
1QIsa^a ממלכתו
his kingdom

Isa 62:1 𝔐 אחשה
1QIsa^a אחריש

Alternative forms:

Gen 27:3 𝔐^K צידה
𝔐^Q ציד

Jer 42:6 𝔐^K אנו
𝔐^Q אנחנו

c. Harmonizations

Hendel, *Genesis 1-11*, 37-42, 63-80; I. Kalimi, *Die Geschichtsschreibung des Chronisten—Literarisch-historiographische Abweichungen der Chronik von ihren Paralleltexten in den Samuel-Königsbüchern*, chapter III, in press; J. Koenig, *L'herméneutique analogique du judaïsme antique d'après les témoins textuels d'Isaïe* (VTSup 33; Leiden 1982); E. Tov, "The Nature and Background of Harmonizations in Biblical Manuscripts," *JSOT* 31 (1985) 3-29.

Scribes adapted many elements in the text to other details in the same verse, in the immediate context or in a similar one, in the same book and in parallel sections elsewhere in the Bible. This phenomenon is termed harmonizing (by most scholars) or analogy (Koenig*). Examples of typical harmonizations are given above with regard to the pre-Samaritan texts and 𝔖 (pp. 85–89), in which harmonizations occur frequently, and also with regard to the medieval manuscripts of 𝔐 (chapter 2, Table 4 and p. 39). Hendel* showed that in Genesis 1-11 𝔊 contains more instances of harmonization than 𝔖. Many of these harmonizations were apparently made unconsciously (most of the instances in the medieval manuscripts), while others were made consciously (the pre-Samaritan texts and 𝔖). Additional examples beyond the ones given in chapter 2 and on pp. 241–242 are presented here.

Isa 1:15 𝔐 ידיכם דמים מלאו
Your hands are stained with crime.
1QIsa^a ידיכמה דמים מלאו אצבעותיכם בעאון
Your hands are stained with crime, *your fingers with iniquity.*

Cf. Isa 59:3	𝔪	כי כפיכם נגאלו בדם אצבעותיכם בעון For your hands are defiled with crime, *and your fingers with iniquity.*
	1QIsa^{a}	כיא כפיכמה נגאלו בדם ואצבעותיכמה בעוון

For similar additions in 1QIsa^{a}, see 34:4 (cf. Mic 1:4); 51:3 (cf. 35:10, 51:11); 51:6 (cf. 40:26); 52:12 (cf. 54:5).

Isa 60:4	𝔪	(ובנתיך על צד) תאמנה = 1QIsa^{a} (Your daughters) will be *nursed* (on <your> shoulders)
	1QIsa^{b}	(ובנתיך על צד) תנשינה (Your daughters) will be *carried* (on <your> shoulders)
Cf. Isa 66:12	𝔪	על צד תנשאו
Jer 48:45	𝔪	ולהבה *מבין* סיחון and a flame *from the midst of* Sihon . . .
	2QJer	ולהבה]מקרית[סיחון and a flame] *from the city* [*of* Sihon . . .
Cf. Num 21:28	𝔪	להבה *מקרית* סיחון

d. Exegetical Changes

Ancient scribes took the liberty of inserting various changes into the text (omissions, additions, changes in content), for at the beginning of the biblical text's transmission, intervention such as reflected in these changes must have been commonly acceptable. These changes were inserted into all texts, and therefore found their way into 𝔪, most Qumran scrolls, the Hebrew *Vorlage* of several ancient translations, and 𝔰𝔪. By means of a comparison of texts it is possible to identify deliberate changes, but the decision on what exactly comprises such a change necessarily remains subjective.

Few of these changes were pervasive and encompassing, since copyists would not change the text to any great extent. According to our understanding larger changes such as those which are also found in the textual witnesses must be ascribed to an earlier stage of the development of the biblical books. At one level of the description these larger changes can be described as changes in textual witnesses, and at another one as different stages in the literary development of the book. The latter course is chosen in the present book, and such differences are therefore described in chapter 7.

In the paragraphs which follow, examples are provided of relatively small exegetical changes inserted into the biblical text. They are subdivided (somewhat unequally) into contextual (α) and theological (β) changes. The first group pertains to the complete range of contextual changes, while the second one focuses on one area of major importance.

α. Contextual Changes

Koenig (pp. 261, 264); van der Kooij, *Textzeugen*, 81-101.

Many of the changes introduced by scribes cannot be ascribed to any external influences such as described in the other paragraphs of this section (linguistic-stylistic changes [*a*], synonymous readings [*b*], harmonizations [*c*], theological changes [β below]). They probably derived from the context itself, and they reflect the copyists' wish to adapt the text to their own understanding or to an exegetical tradition known to them (as a rule, these two possibilities cannot be separated). Some such examples have been provided, without explanation, at other places in this book: certain types of *Qere* readings (pp. 62–63), the "corrections of the scribes" (pp. 64–67), harmonizing alterations and ideological changes in 𝔐𝔐 (pp. 85–89, 94–95), contextual adaptations in certain Qumran texts, and, at a different level, the exegetical elements behind the vocalization (pp. 41–43) and accentuation (pp. 68–71). Large-scale differences, ascribed to the stage of literary development, which also involve exegesis, are mentioned in chapter 7. The analysis in this book treats the various manifestations of exegesis in different places, so that a central discussion is not needed at this point. This paragraph thus provides only a few scattered examples, while the next paragraph (theological changes) contains a fuller treatment of a major group of changes.

The examples of contextual changes in this paragraph are limited to the Qumran texts, especially 1QIsa[a].

Some of the changes derive from the copyist's *stylistic* feelings.

Isa 14:2	𝔐	ולקחום עמים (= 𝔊 𝔗 𝔖) For peoples shall take them.
	1QIsa[a]	ולקחום עמים רבים For *many* peoples shall take them. (For the addition, cf. 2:3-4; 17:12).
Isa 35:6	𝔐	כי נבקעו במדבר מים ונחלים בערבה (= 𝔊 𝔗 𝔖) For waters shall burst forth in the desert, and streams in the wilderness.

1QIsa^a כיא נבקעו במדבר מים ונחלים בערבה *ילכו*

For waters shall burst forth in the desert, and streams *shall flow* in the wilderness.

Influence from the *parallel* stich is visible in the following instances.

Isa 9:16 𝔐 על כן על בחוריו לא *ישמח* אדני ואת יתמיו ואת אלמנתיו לא ירחם

That is why my Lord will not *spare* their youths, nor show compassion to their orphans and widows.

1QIsa^a על כן על בחוריו לוא *יחמ׳ל* אדוני ואת יתומיו ואת אלמנותיו לוא ירחם

The verb was changed in 1QIsa^a in accordance with the parallel verb (cf. the parallelism of רחם and חמל in Jer 13:14; 21:7).

Isa 45:7 𝔐 עשה *שלום* ובורא רע (= 𝔊 𝔗 𝔖 𝔙)

I make *prosperity* and I create disaster.

1QIsa^a עושה *טוב* ובורה רע

I make *the good* and I create the evil.

Influence from *general usage* is visible in the following instances.

Isa 56:6 𝔐 *ולאהבה* את שם יהוה (= 𝔊 𝔗 𝔖 𝔙)

and to *love* the name of the LORD . . .

1QIsa^a *ולברך* את שם יהוה

and to *bless* the name of the LORD. . .

The reading of 1QIsa^a follows the more frequent phrase (e.g., Ps 113:2), also occurring often in the liturgy.

Isa 12:6; 21:1 The *p.m.* readings of 1QIsa^a listed on p. 214 are much more frequent than those of 𝔐 𝔊 𝔗 𝔙. For of this reason these *p.m.* readings must have found their way into 1QIsa^a, subsequently to be corrected to the reading also found in the other witnesses.

β. Theological Changes

D. Barthélemy, "Les tiqquné sopherim et la critique textuelle de l'AT," *VTSup* 9 (1963) 285-304 = *Etudes*, 91-110; J.V. Chamberlain, "The Functions of God as Messianic Titles in the Complete Isaiah Scroll," *VT* 5 (1955) 366-372; M. Fishbane, *Biblical Interpretation in Ancient Israel* (Oxford 1985) 1-88; Geiger, *Urschrift*, 259-423; J. Koenig, "L'activité herméneutique des scribes dans la transmission du texte de l'AT I, II," *RHR* 161 (1962) 141-174; 162 (1962) 1-43; C. McCarthy, *The Tiqqune Sopherim and Other Theological Corrections in the Masoretic Text of the OT* (OBO 36; Freiburg/Göttingen 1981); A. Rofé, "The Nomistic Correction in Biblical Manuscripts and Its Occurrence in *4QSam^a*," *RQ* 14 (1989) 247-254; A. Rubinstein,

"The Theological Aspect of Some Variant Readings in the Isaiah Scroll," *JJS* 6 (1955) 187-200; I.L. Seeligmann, "Researches into the Criticism of the Masoretic Text of the Bible," *Tarbiz* 25 (1956) 118-139 (Heb. with Eng. summ.)—revised version in: M. Weinfeld, ed., *A Biblical Studies Reader* 1 (Jerusalem 1979) 255-278; idem, "Indications of Editorial Alteration and Adaptation in the Massoretic Text and the Septuagint," *VT* 11 (1961) 201-221.

Many of the exegetical changes lie within the area of religion, and in modern discussions they are therefore often termed theological alterations. Although the existence of such changes is recognized for most biblical books, the same tendencies are not recognizable in all books or in all textual witnesses. Their haphazard occurrence is one of their earmarks.

Although the existence of theological changes in textual witnesses is probably accepted by most scholars, their assumed number remains a matter of dispute. From the scholarly literature one often gets the impression that ancient scribes frequently inserted theological alterations. However, the number of such changes is probably smaller than is usually assumed,[35] since most scholars provide the same examples for a phenomenon they consider to be widespread (note also that most of the examples of theological changes given by Geiger* are emendations [see chapter 8], not based on manuscript evidence). The fact that the Masorah explicitly mentions "corrections of the scribes" (see pp. 64–67), which therefore constitute a generally accepted phenomenon in the transmission of the biblical text, has influenced scholars in assuming many more such instances. This is certainly true for the detailed discussions by Geiger*, Barthélemy*, and McCarthy*, 197-243 ("An examination of certain biblical verses which illustrate with reasonable certitude that theological corrections did really take place"). The statement of the Masorah may, however, refer to an exegetical process and not to a textual phenomenon (cf. pp. 65–66), so that the basis for assuming a large number of corrections is strongly undermined. The amount of the deliberate changes inserted by scribes was probably smaller than is often believed for an additional reason as well. Many of the pervasive changes in the biblical text, pertaining to whole sentences, sections and books should not, according to our description (see pp. 313–319), be ascribed to copyists, but to earlier generations of editors who allowed themselves such massive changes in

35 Cf. G.R. Driver, "Glosses in the Hebrew Text of the OT," *L'AT et l'Orient* (Orientalia et Biblica Lovaniensia 1; Louvain 1957) 153: "Theological glosses <in our terminology: interpolations> are surprisingly few, and most are enshrined in the *tiqqûné sóp*^{e}*rim*, which are corrections of the text aimed chiefly at softening anthropomorphisms and eliminating the attribution of any sort of impropriety to God."

the formative stage of the biblical literature. Thus many of the examples that are discussed in chapter 7, such as the material from 1 Samuel 16-18, Jeremiah, and Ezekiel, should indeed be considered major changes of earlier textual forms, often in the area of what we would call religion or theology. However, since these changes preceded the textual transmission, they should not be discussed here.[36]

Although in principle the alterations discussed here are found in all the textual witnesses, they appear in a few conglomerations in certain texts. Thus good examples of such deliberate changes are recognizable in the few tendentious readings the Samaritans allowed themselves to insert into 𝔪 (see pp. 94–95); such readings reflect their ideological doctrines.[37] Other deliberate changes are more incidental and refer to

---

36 Of much interest are many types of tendentious alterations located in parallel texts in the Bible, especially in Chronicles when compared with its "sources," further in parallel psalms (see Seeligmann*, 1961, 203-204). However, most of these changes are probably to be ascribed to the compositional layer of these books, that is to the author of Chronicles or to one of the psalmists, and are therefore less relevant to the present analysis of the transmission of the biblical text. The two areas are closely connected, and the evidence shows how phenomena operative at the compositional level continued to be influential at the transmission stage, but the areas should nevertheless be separated as much as possible.

37 The only clearly recognizable readings in biblical manuscripts which exclusively reflect the views of one of the religious groups in ancient Israel, excluding those of the other groups, are Samaritan. Although many of the Qumran biblical manuscripts were presumably copied by the Essenes (see p. 102), they do not contain readings which reflect the views of the Qumran covenanters (such readings are, however, included in 1QpHab and possibly in other *pesharim* as well; cf. T. Lim, *Attitudes to Holy Scripture in the Qumran Pesharim and Pauline Letters*, unpubl. diss., Oxford University 1991). According to I.L. Seeligmann, a further exception should be made for Isa 53:11 in 1QIsa[a] and 𝔊, see "ΔΕΙΞΑΙ ΑΥΤΩΙ ΦΩΣ," *Tarbiz* 27 (1958) 127-141 (Heb. with Eng. summ.). The presence of Pharisaic, anti-Samaritan, or anti-Sadducean readings in 𝔐 was probably minimal (*pace* Geiger*, 170ff.), if at all. Thus the probability that *Ebal* in 𝔐 in Deut 27:4 is an anti-Samaritan reading (cf. p. 94) is very slight. The following reading presents an example of what constitutes, according to Geiger*, an anti-Sadducean reading.

Prov 14:32	𝔐	ברעתו ידחה רשע וחסה **במותו** צדיק (= 𝔗) The wicked man is felled by his own evil, while the righteous man finds security *in his death*.
	𝔊	ἐν κακίᾳ αὐτοῦ ἀπωσθήσεται ἀσεβής, ὁ δὲ πεποιθὼς *τῇ ἑαυτοῦ ὁσιότητι* δίκαιος (≈ 𝔖) The wicked man is felled by his own evil, but the righteous man finds security *in his piety*.

The reading of 𝔊, which clearly reflects בתומו, represents, according to Geiger*, 175, as well as many other scholars, a contextually correct and therefore original reading. On the other hand, במותו of 𝔐 would reflect an anti-Sadducean change, intended to present a point of view (reward after death) which was not acceptable to the Sadducees. In a similar fashion, according to A. Rofé, 𝔊 in 1 Sam 7:6 reflects a Sadducean reading: "The Onset of Sects in Postexilic Judaism: Neglected Evidence from the

sundry matters, although sometimes a certain trend is recognized. Many of these changes pertain to areas that were sensitive for generations of early scribes, who, as all readers of the Bible, had their own ideas about many aspects of the religion of ancient Israel. In our analysis, these changes, often named theological, are subdivided into different areas.

Several of the examples of presumed theological changes are based on the comparison of 𝔐 and 𝔊, and in these cases the changes are usually reflected in 𝔐, but some of the variants reflected in 𝔊 comprise theological alterations as well. However, since 𝔊, like all other translations, also contains theological changes by the translators,[38] possible changes recorded only in 𝔊 or another translation are not discussed in this section.

i. Anti-Polytheistic Alterations

At one stage, the theophoric element *Baʿal* must have been common in proper names, as is still visible in various layers of the biblical text. At a later stage, such theophoric elements must have become undesirable, at which point they were either removed or replaced with other elements such as the derogatory element בֹּשֶׁת, "shame,"[39]—for evidence of this change elsewhere, cf. 1 Kgs 18:19,25 𝔐 הבעל and 𝔊 τῆς αἰσχύνης, "shame," and cf. also the parallelism between בעל and בשת in Jer 11:13.[40] The phenomenon is especially evident in the comparison

---

Septuagint, Trito-Isaiah, Ben Sira, and Malachi," in: J. Neusner et al., eds., *The Social World of Formative Christianity and Judaism, Essays in Tribute to Howard Clark Kee* (Philadelphia 1988) 39-49, esp. 40-41. On the whole, possible evidence for Sadducean and anti-Sadducean changes is very slight (see further Qoh 3:21 and Ps 49:12 as discussed by Geiger).

38 See E. Tov, "Theologically Motivated Exegesis Embedded in the Septuagint," *Translation of Scripture, Proceedings of a Conference at the Annenberg Research Institute, May 15-16, 1989* (JQRSup 1990; Philadelphia 1990) 215-233.

39 Thus Geiger* and Ginsburg, *Introduction*, 399-404, and in great detail McCarthy*. For a different view, see M. Tsevat, "Ishbosheth and Congeners—The Names and Their Study," *HUCA* 46 (1975) 71-87.

40 According to Geiger*, 299ff., a similar tendency is reflected in the change of the name of the deity of the Ammonites, accepted by many of the Israelites, from מֶלֶךְ, "king," to מֹלֶךְ, *Molekh*, thus implying the pattern and vocalization of בֹּשֶׁת. Likewise, according to Geiger, in order to oust this use of "king," the scribes may have eliminated the phrase מַלְכָּם, "their king," by changing its vocalization to a non-existing deity Milkom (thus 1 Kgs 11:5,33). Again according to Geiger, 305, a similar change is evident in other situations, in such phrases as העביר בנו באש, "let his son pass the fire," and similar formulations (e.g., Deut 18:10; 2 Kgs 16:3). In this phrase, which is used in the sense of "to sacrifice," the original verb was, according to Geiger, הבעיר, "he burned," which was corrected by way of metathesis (cf. p. 250) to the less explicit העביר. According to

of Samuel—which contains most of the corrected names—and its parallel text in Chronicles.[41] Even though Chronicles was composed after Samuel, in this particular case its manuscripts often preserve earlier textual traditions. Therefore, this phenomenon pertains to the scribe(s) rather than to the author of the biblical books.

a. יְרֻבַּעַל—An alternative name for Gideon (cf. Judg 7:1) is transmitted as יְרֻבַעל, Jerubbaal, in 14 places in 𝔐 and the ancient versions (Judg 6:32; 7:1; 8:29; 9:1ff.; 1 Sam 12:11). On the other hand, in 2 Sam 11:21 the same name is transmitted in 𝔐 𝔗 𝔙 in its corrected form יְרֻבֶּשֶׁת, Jerubbesheth; in this verse the original reading "Jerubbaal" is preserved in 𝔊 Ιεροβααλ (cf. 𝔖 נדובעל). The same reading is preserved in v. 22 (in 𝔊 only). The corrected form Jerubbesheth is thus found only in one place in 𝔐 (= 𝔗 𝔙), viz., 2 Sam 11:21.

b. אֶשְׁבַּעַל—The name of Saul's fourth son, according to 1 Chr 8:33 and 9:39 (Eshbaal), was changed in 1 Sam 14:49 to יִשְׁוִי, Yishvi, representing אִישְׁיו or אִישְׁיָהוּ, Ishyahu, and further to אִישׁ בֹּשֶׁת, Ishbosheth, in all other occurrences (2 Sam 2:8ff.; 3:8ff.; 4:5ff.). The original name is thus found in Chronicles, the corrected forms in Samuel.

c. מְרִיב בַּעַל—A son of Jonathan, is called Merib-baal (1 Chr 8:34; 9:40a), מְרִי־בַעַל, Meri-baal (1 Chr 9:40b), and also in a revised form מְפִיבֹשֶׁת, Mephibosheth (all other occurrences: 2 Sam 4:4; 9:6ff.; 16:1ff.; 19:25; 21:7). The precise relation between מפי־ and מרי(ב)־ is not clear.[42]

d. אישבעֹל—It would appear that the first name in the list of David's heroes (2 Sam 23:8) is Ishbaal. This form of the name is only reflected in 𝔊[Luc] to this verse (MSS boc$_2$e$_2$: Ιεσβααλ = Vetus Latina *Iesbael*, cf. p. 139) and in manuscripts of 𝔊 elsewhere, viz., in 1 Chr 11:11. From this original form the name was changed to Ishbosheth (thus most manuscripts of 𝔊 to 2 Sam 23:8 Ιεβοσθε). In 𝔐 of the same verse, 2 Sam 23:8, the name was corrupted to יֹשֵׁב בַּשֶּׁבֶת תַּחְכְּמֹנִי and in 1 Chr 11:11 to יָשָׁבְעָם בֶּן חַכְמוֹנִי.

e. בְּעֶלְיָדָע—The second last name in the list of "those who were born" to David is *Eli*ada, אלידע, according to 2 Sam 5:16 and 1 Chr 3:8

---

that view, the original phrase has been preserved in 2 Chr 28:3 𝔐 ויבער against most other textual evidence in this verse and against the parallel 2 Kgs 16:3. The views of Geiger mentioned in this note are, however, not supported by any solid evidence.

41 For examples of similar interchanges in other names, see J. Tigay, *You Shall Have No Other Gods—Israelite Religion in the Light of Hebrew Inscriptions* (HSS 31; Atlanta, GA 1986) 8.

42 It should be remembered, however, that a form מריבעל occurs in the Samaria ostraca (Donner-Röllig [p. 220] 184,7).

(presumably the corrected form), but *Beel*iada according to the parallel list in 1 Chr 14:7, probably representing the original form.[43]

Deut 32:8 𝔐 (למספר) בני ישראל (= 𝔖𝔪 𝔗^OJFN 𝔖 𝔙)
(according to the number) of the sons of *Israel* . .
4QDeut^j בני אלהים
(according to the number) of the sons of God
𝔊^848 106c ... υἱῶν θεοῦ
𝔊^most MSS ἀγγέλων θεοῦ = Aquila

In its probably original wording, reconstructed from 4QDeut^j and 𝔊, the Song of Moses referred to an assembly of the gods (cf. Psalm 82; 1 Kgs 22:19),[44] in which "the Most High, *ʿElyon*, fixed the boundaries of peoples according to the number of the sons of the God *El*."[45] The next verse stresses that the LORD, יהוה, kept Israel for himself. Within the supposedly original context, *ʿElyon* and *El* need not be taken as epithets of the God of Israel, but as names of gods also known from the Canaanite and Ugaritic pantheon. It appears, however, that the scribe of an early text, now reflected in 𝔐 𝔖𝔪 𝔗 𝔖 𝔙, did not feel at ease with this possibly polytheistic picture and replaced "sons of *El*" with בני ישראל, "the sons of *Israel*," thus giving the text a different direction by the change of one word:

> When the Most High gave nations their homes and set the divisions of man, He fixed the boundaries of peoples according to the number of the sons of *Israel*.[46]

A similar correction may be reflected in all textual witnesses of Ps 96:7: "Ascribe to the LORD, *O families of the peoples*, ascribe to the LORD glory and strength," when compared with the presumably original (polytheistic) text of Ps 29:1: "Ascribe to the LORD, *O divine beings*, בני אלים, ascribe to the LORD glory and strength." Psalm 29, which also in other details reflects situations and phrases known from Ugaritic texts,[47] does, in this detail, provide a polytheistic picture of the assembly of gods.

---

43 The vocalization of בְּעֶלְיָדָע itself may show an effort to avoid the mentioning of Baal (*Beʿel*, not: *Baʿal*).

44 According to this view, the original reading *El* is reconstructed from the text of 4QDeut^j, בני אלהים. The evidence of 𝔊 is not specific enough. On the other hand, if the longer form of 4QDeut^j is accepted as original, the change in 𝔐 should be considered theological in a general sense (section ii below), and not anti-polytheistic.

45 Note that already 𝔗^J explained 𝔐 as referring to angels (cf. also Ibn Ezra *ad loc.*).

46 For a discussion and earlier literature, see M. Lana, "*Deuteronomio* e angelologia alla luce di una variante qumranico (*4Q Dt* 32,8)," *Henoch* 5 (1983) 179-207.

47 See F.M. Cross, Jr., "Notes on a Canaanite Psalm in the OT," *BASOR* 117 (1950) 19-21.

ii. Sundry Contextual Alterations

In the following instances, contextual (theological) problems were removed by various types of changes.

Gen 2:2 𝔐 ויכל אלהים ביום השביעי (מלאכתו אשר עשה) (= 𝔗^{OJN} 𝔙) <preferable>
On *the seventh* day God completed (the work that He had been doing).

⅏ ויכל אלהים ביום הששי (מלאכתו אשר עשה) = 𝔊 (ἐν τῇ ἡμέρᾳ τῇ ἕκτῃ . . .) 𝔖
On *the sixth* day God completed (the work that He had been doing).

According to the reading of 𝔐 𝔗^{OJN} 𝔙, God completed his work "on the seventh day," probably without implying that God actually worked on that day. However, some scribes (and possibly translators) probably found it difficult to imagine that God would have worked on the seventh day and therefore corrected the presumably original text to an easier (cf. p. 302) reading (⅏, 𝔊, 𝔖—perhaps independently).

1 Sam 2:17 𝔐 ותהי חטאת הנערים גדולה מאד את פני יהוה כי נאצו האנשים את מנחת יהוה (= 𝔗 𝔖 𝔙)
The sin of the *young men* against the LORD was very great for *the men* treated the LORD's offering impiously.

4QSam^{a} . . . נאצו את . . . = 𝔊 ὅτι ἠθέτουν τὴν . . .
they treated the . . . impiously

𝔐 𝔗 𝔖 𝔙 probably inserted האנשים, "the men," in order to mitigate the accusation against the sons of Eli (the addition suggests that also other people may have treated the offering of the LORD impiously)—contrast 1 Sam 2:22-23 discussed on p. 273. This word is lacking in 4QSam^{a} and 𝔊.

2 Sam 5:21 𝔐 ויעזבו שם את עצביהם וישאם דוד ואנשיו (= 𝔗 𝔖 *ad loc.* and in Chronicles; = 𝔙)
They <the Philistines> abandoned *their idols* there, and David and his men carried them off.

1 Chr 14:12 𝔐 ויעזבו שם את אלהיהם . . . וישָׂרפו באש (≈ 𝔊 *ad loc.* and in 2 Sam 5:21; = 𝔙)
They abandoned *their gods* there . . . and they were burned.

In the first part of 2 Sam 5:21, the original reading has apparently been preserved in 𝔊 τοὺς θεοὺς αὐτῶν and in the parallel text of Chronicles, where "their gods" refers to the idols of the Philistines. The scribe of 𝔐 in Samuel probably found cause for offense in that idols were referred to in this verse as אלהיהם, "their gods," usually employed for the God of Israel, and accordingly changed the text to עצביהם, "their idols."

iii. Euphemistic Alterations

Of the religious (theological) alterations, several resemble the euphemistic "corrections of the scribes" mentioned in the Masorah (pp. 64–67). While the "corrections of the scribes" probably represent exegetical traditions on certain readings and not actual textual variations, the examples to be mentioned below pertain to actual changes inserted in biblical manuscripts. However, the examples in this section are less certain than the examples in the other sections since textual evidence is either lacking or weak.

2 Sam 12:9 𝔐 מדוע בזית את דבר יהוה (= 𝔊 𝔗 𝔖 𝔙)
Why did you despise *the word of* the LORD?
𝔊^Luc ὅτι ἐξουδενώσας τὸν κύριον (= Theodotion)
Why did you despise the LORD?

𝔊^Luc (MSS boc_2e_2), which in this chapter may reflect the Old Greek translation (see pp. 137, 145), contains what looks like the original text (cf. v. 10 בזתני, "you have despised Me"), which has been mitigated by the addition in 𝔐 for which cf. also the next example.

2 Sam 12:14 𝔐 (אפס כי נאץ נאצת) את איבי יהוה (= 𝔊 𝔖 𝔙; ≈ 𝔗)
(However, since you have utterly scorned) *the enemies* of the LORD . . .
4QSam^a אֶ֯ת דבר יהוה
the word of the LORD

𝔐 refers to David's scorning of *the* LORD on account of his taking the wife of Uriah the Hittite (note that in v. 13 David confesses: "I have sinned against the LORD" and that v. 14 continues with the punishment "the child about to be born to you shall die"). Within this context it is likely that what looks like an addition in most textual witnesses ("*the enemies* of the LORD") reflects a euphemistic mitigation of the explicit expression of the assumed earlier text ("you have utterly scorned the LORD").[48] Furthermore, the reading of 4QSam^a makes it likely that the original text contained no mitigating word at all between the verb ("you have utterly scorned") and "the LORD," since *different* softening expressions

48 For an analysis, see Ginsburg, *Introduction*, 101; Driver, *Samuel*, 225; McCarthy*, 184-187.

were used in 𝔐 and 4QSam^a (for which cf. also the previous example). A similar euphemism, referring to David, was probably used in 1 Sam 20:16 and 25:22.

It is not impossible, however, that in this and other instances the euphemistic expression derived from the authors themselves—as suggested with supporting evidence from Egypt and Mari by Yaron and Anbar.[49] In that case these instances are *not* relevant to the textual transmission of the Bible.

Job 2:9 𝔐 ברך אלהים ומת (= 𝔗 𝔙)
Bless God and die!
𝔊 εἶπόν τι ῥῆμα εἰς κύριον
Say some word to God!

Most scholars agree that in this verse as well as in Job 1:5,11; 2:5; 1 Kgs 21:10,13 the verb "to bless" cannot be taken literally (compare Ibn Ezra's remark on Job 1:5: "a substitute term and it means the opposite"). It must be taken as a euphemism for "to curse" (thus 𝔖), inserted by early scribes, since a real blessing is contextually not appropriate. On the other hand, it is not impossible that in these six verses the original authors used a euphemism (thus McCarthy*, 191-195), and in that case, *no* scribal change was involved. The translations reflect 𝔐, exegetically explained, as in 𝔊 quoted above.

Additional examples of euphemisms in the area of sex and personal feelings include Deut 28:27, 30. These two euphemisms, mentioned on p. 63, have been incorporated by the Masorah as a *Qere*. Probably the following reading in 𝔐 reflects a euphemism as well.

Deut 25:11 𝔐 והחזיקה במבשיו (= 𝔗^{OJN} 𝔙)
. . . she seized him by his *genitals* <literally: that which excites shame>.
ɯɯ והחזיקה בבשרו
. . . she seized him by his *flesh <membrum virile>* (cf. Exod 28:42).

The reading of 𝔐 probably reflects a euphemism as compared with the more explicit text of ɯɯ.

iv. "Nomistic" Changes

The influence of the laws of the Torah upon the thinking of readers and scribes of the biblical books was increasingly felt in Second Temple times, and accordingly in various places details in the text were

49 R. Yaron, "The Coptos Decree and 2 Sam XII 14," *VT* 9 (1959) 89-91; M. Anbar, "Un euphémisme 'biblique' dans une lettre de Mari," *Orientalia* 48 (1979) 109-111.

changed to agree with these laws—see especially Rofé*. Some examples follow.

Exod 24:4 — 𝔐 — (ויבן מזבח תחת ההר ושתים עשרה) מצבה (לשנים עשר שבטי ישראל) (= 𝔗^{OJN} 𝔖)
(He <Moses> built an altar at the foot of the mountain and twelve) *pillars* (for the twelve tribes of Israel).

⅏ — אבנים = 𝔊 λίθους (stones)

Possibly an original reading מצבה, "pillar," was changed by ⅏ or its underlying text to אבנים to conform with the law according to which one is not to erect a pillar (Deut 16:22).

1 Sam 2:16 — 𝔐 — קטר יקטירון כיום החלב (≈ 𝔊 𝔖 𝔙)
Let them first burn the fat.

4QSam^{a} — יקטר הכוהן כיום ה[חלב]
Let the priest first burn the [fat].

In 𝔐 the owner of the sacrifice makes a general statement about burning the fat, while the reading in 4QSam^{a} ascribes this procedure to the priest in accordance with the law in Lev 7:31.

1 Sam 2:22-23 — 𝔐 — ושמע את כל אשר יעשון בניו לכל ישראל *ואת אשר ישכבון את הנשים הצֹבאות פתח אהל מועד* 23ויאמר להם למה תעשון כדברים האלה
When he <Eli> heard all that his sons were doing to all Israel, *and how they lay with the women who assembled (?) at the entrance of the Tent of Meeting,* 23he said to them: "Why do you do such things?" (= 𝔗; ≈ 𝔖 𝔙)

4QSam^{a} — וישמ֯ע [את] אשר [עו]שׂים בניו לבני ישראל [23ויאמר להם למה] תעשׂ֯[ן כדברים האל]ה
When he heard [that] which his sons [were d]oing to the Israelites, [23he said to them: "Why do you] do [such thin]gs?" (= 𝔊*) <preferable>

To the shorter and probably earlier text (4QSam^{a} = 𝔊) 𝔐 added a section (indicated by italics) which is based on Exod 38:8: "from the women who assemble (?) at the entrance of the Tent of Meeting," so as to increase the sin of the sons of Eli and to make "such things" in the context more explicit. Two details in the plus of 𝔐 do not accord with the context and thus disclose its secondary nature: the mention of the Tent of Meeting (cf. Josh 18:1), rather than the house of the LORD mentioned elsewhere in the context (1 Sam 1:7, 9, 24; 3:3, 15 [בית יהוה and היכל יהוה]) and the mention of women who do not appear again in the context.

v. Theological Toning Down (?)

As an *appendix* to this paragraph a few examples are mentioned of possible theological differences in *vocalization*.

Jer 7:3 𝔐 וַאֲשַׁכְּנָה אֶתְכֶם בַּמָּקוֹם הַזֶּה (= 𝔊 𝔗 𝔖)
I will *let you* dwell in this place.
α′ καὶ σκηνώσω σὺν ὑμῖν . . . = 𝔙 *et habitabo vobiscum in loco isto*
= וְאֶשְׁכְּנָה אִתְּכֶם בַּמָּקוֹם הַזֶּה
I will dwell *with you* in this place.

Jer 7:7 𝔐 וְשִׁכַּנְתִּי אֶתְכֶם בַּמָּקוֹם הַזֶּה (= 𝔊 𝔗 𝔖)
I will *let you* dwell in this place.
𝔐MSS וְשָׁכַנְתִּי אִתְּכֶם בַּמָּקוֹם הַזֶּה = 𝔙 *habitabo vobiscum in loco isto*
I will dwell *with you* in this place.

According to several scholars (see Geiger*, 320-321 and BHS) the original vocalization (reading) in Jer 7:3 has been preserved in Aquila and 𝔙. The idea of the presumably original text, according to which God would have dwelled with men, would have been repulsive to some and hence was corrected to the "easier" text of 𝔐 𝔊 𝔗 𝔖. For a possibly parallel development cf. the so-called name theology of Deuteronomy. That book often mentions the "establishing of God's name" in the chosen city (e.g., 12:5; see also Jer 7:12, in a similar context, and p. 42) rather than the dwelling of God himself, as often elsewhere in the Torah. For a reverse development see Ezek 43:7, where according to 𝔐 God dwells among the Israelites (אֶשְׁכָּן שם, "I will dwell there"; similarly v. 9), while 𝔊 reads κατασκηνώσει τὸ ὄνομά μου, "my name will dwell."

Ps 42:3 𝔐 וְאֵרָאֶה פני אלהים = 𝔊 𝔙
I will *appear* before God.
𝔐MSS וְאֶרְאֶה פני אלהים = 𝔗 𝔖
I will *see* the face of God.

The use of ראה in the *niphʿal* in connection with God occurs frequently in the Bible (e.g., Exod 23:15; 34:20,24; Deut 16:16). In all twelve verses Geiger*, 337-338, McCarthy*, 197-204 as well as other scholars (cf. BHS) accept the *qal* as the original vocalization on the basis of the assumption that the *niphʿal* form tones down the idea of the actual seeing of God expressed by the *qal*. This view was already expressed by S.D. Luzzatto on Isa 1:12 (". . . However, the punctuators, בעלי הנקוד, . . . corrected the expression out of respect."). As a rule, however, manuscript evidence is lacking for assuming this change, which in most cases amounts to an emendation of the transmitted tradition of reading as preserved in 𝔐 and translated sources (cf. chapter 8). An exception is made for the aforementioned evidence in Ps 42:3 as well as for Isa 1:12 𝔐^{MS} 𝔖. For a full discussion, see McCarthy*.

e. Additions to the Body of the Text

Delitzsch, *Lese- und Schreibfehler*, 132-143; M. Dijkstra, "The Glosses in Ezekiel Reconsidered: Aspects of Textual Transmission in Ezekiel 10," in: J. Lust, ed., *Ezekiel and his Book, Textual and Literary Criticism and Their Interrelation* (BETL 74; Leuven 1986) 55-77; G.R. Driver, "Glosses in the Hebrew Text of the OT," *L'AT et l'Orient* (Orientalia et Biblica Lovaniensia 1; Louvain 1957) 123-161; M. Elyoenay (Kantrowitz), "Explanations to Ancient Words of Difficult Meaning in the Text of the Bible," in: *Hagut Ivrit be'Eyropa* [sic] (Tel Aviv 1969) 41-48 (Heb.); M. Fishbane, *Biblical Interpretation in Ancient Israel* (Oxford 1985) 38-43, 166-170; G. Fohrer, "Die Glossen im Buche Ezechiel," *ZAW* 63 (1951) 33-53 = *BZAW* 99 (1967) 204-221; K.S. Freedy, "The Glosses in Ezekiel I–XXIV," *VT* 20 (1970) 129-152; McCarter, *Textual Criticism*, 32-36; F.W. Hall, *A Companion to Classical Texts* (Oxford 1913; repr. Chicago 1970); J. Herrmann, "Stichwortglossen im Buche Ezechiel," *OLZ* 11 (1908) 280-282; idem, "Stichwortglossen im AT," *OLZ* 14 (1911) 200-204; Klein, *Textual Criticism*, 32-36; J. Krecher, "Glossen. A. In sumerischen und akkadischen Texten," *Reallexikon der Assyriologie und vorderasiatischen Archäologie*, vol. III (Berlin/New York 1957-1971) 431–440; L.D. Reynolds and N.G. Wilson, *Scribes and Scholars—A Guide to the Transmission of Greek and Latin Literature* (3d ed.; Oxford 1991); P. Rost, "Miszellen, I. Ein Schreibgebrauch bei den Sopherim und seine Bedeutung für die alttestamentliche Textkritik," *OLZ* 6 (1903) 403-407, 443-446; 7 (1904) 390-393, 479-483; S. Talmon, "Aspects of the Textual Transmission of the Bible in the Light of Qumran Manuscripts," *Textus* 4 (1964) 95-132 = Cross–Talmon, *QHBT*, 226–263; J. Weingreen, "Rabbinic-Type Glosses in the OT," *JSS* 2 (1957) 149-162.

After the copying of individual scrolls and manuscripts was completed, different types of additions were made to the text, both by the original scribes and by later scribes and readers. Since no early sources are available (the Qumran scrolls deriving from the mid-third century BCE onwards are relatively late in the history of the transmission of the biblical text), the existence of certain scribal practices is inferred from the textual history of other texts from antiquity, from both the Sumero-Akkadian and the Greek-Latin world.

The following types of exegetical elements *may* have been added to the text upon its completion, in the margin, between the lines, or, in some scribal traditions, in the text itself, separated by a scribal sign.[50]

50 In the scribal tradition of Sumerian and Akkadian texts (see the articles quoted in n. 58) glosses were often included in the text itself, in a variety of ways. Sometimes the gloss was written in small signs next to the word it referred to; at other times it appeared between that word's different components, or was written at the edge of the tablet. At

(1) *Glosses*. Strictly speaking, these are ". . . marginal or interlinear interpretations of difficult or obsolete words,"[51] meant to remain outside the running text.

(2) *Exegetical additions*, also named *interpolations*, added to the body of the text in a physically recognizable way, or inserted directly into the running text, thus expanding the text from which the scribe copied.

Several groups of additions to the body of the text are recognized which are not in the nature of exegetical additions:

(3) *Interlinear and marginal corrections* of single letters or complete words added to the body of the text.

(4) *Remarks on the content*. The existence of remarks on the content has not been established for the Qumran scrolls. While 𝔐 𝔗 𝔖 𝔙 contain one such note in the body of the text which is not shared with 𝔊,[52] several others have been assumed without textual support.[53]

(5) *Variant readings* deriving from external sources (additional manuscripts of the same composition) and recorded in the margin or between the lines, referring to readings included in the body of the text.[54] While the Qumran scrolls contain no proven cases of interlinear or marginal variant readings, not even Isa 36:11 in 1QIsa^{a} (see p. 241), the notation of some of the *Qere* readings by the Masoretes in a later period (see pp. 58–63) probably reflects such variant readings.

(6) *Scribal remarks and marks*. The existence of scribal remarks in the margins or in the text itself has not been established for the Qumran texts. For scribal marks, see pp. 213–216.

(7) *Headings* to sections in the text.[55]

---

still other times it was separated from the preceding word by a special sign. That sign, named "Glossenkeil" by scholars, appeared in different shapes, among them a diagonal line and a double-wedge shape (on all these systems see Krecher*, 433). Neither this nor any other system of writing glosses has been preserved in ancient Hebrew texts. It has, however, been suggested that the Masoretic, and hence late, *paseq* or *pesiq* sign introduced or indicated glosses written in the body of the text—see especially H. Fuchs, *P^{e}siq, Ein Glossenzeichen* (Breslau 1907). This suggestion, which has not found many followers, is discussed by Fishbane*, 40.

51 *OCD* (2d ed.; Oxford 1970), *s.v.* "glossa" (in Latin sources).

52 Jer 51:64 "Thus far the words of Jeremiah" (the next chapter serves as an appendix to the book).

53 See A. Guilding, "Some Obscured Rubrics and Lectionary Allusions in the Psalter," *JTS* n.s. 3 (1952) 41-55.

54 In Akkadian sources such words were written in the running text itself, separated by a double-wedge mark (see n. 50).

55 See Jer 23:9 "Concerning the prophets" in all the textual witnesses (cf. p. 340).

It is not easy to distinguish between these seven groups of possible additions to the body of the text, partly because the distinctions between the types of additions are often not well defined and partly because manuscript evidence about the first stage of the addition is usually lacking. The purpose of the aforementioned groups of additions is different, and the very existence of some of them is a matter of dispute. Of these, some groups tend to be written especially in the margin, while others are written between the lines, but because of the lack of evidence on the original documents no clear statements can be made. The interlinear and marginal addition of exegetical additions (interpolations), scribal remarks, remarks on content, headings, and variant readings are rare in the known manuscripts of the Bible or not evidenced at all.

The terminology used in biblical scholarship with regard to added elements is less varied than in classical studies. While there are differences between individual scholars, most of them indiscriminately use the term *gloss* for most or all types of the added elements listed above. Especially confusing is the habit of using the term *gloss* also for interpolations.[56] A basic distinction between these two groups of additions is that an interpolation is meant to be part of the running text, while a gloss is not.

Only the first three of these categories are evidenced in ancient sources and hence are treated here in more detail. The other types of additions were probably rarely used in biblical manuscripts.

(1) *Glosses.* Explanatory short notes, explaining difficult or obsolete words, which were not meant to be integrated into the syntax of the running text, may have been added by ancient Hebrew scribes in the margin or between the lines. Direct evidence for this practice is lacking for manuscripts of the Hebrew Bible, but parallels of marginal and interlinear additions of different types in other texts make the assumed practice likely: several Sumerian and Akkadian texts,[57]among them the

56 The definition by Dijkstra*, 55, n. 2, probably reflects the consensus of scholarship in this regard: "We use a somewhat extended definition of the gloss; not only as an addition inserted between the lines or in the margin of a manuscript, but also elements of textual growth inserted in the text-base, whether intentionally or unintentionally. As we will see, it is impractical to make a distinction between glosses proper and expansions in the text-base because both are found added *prima manu* and *secunda manu.*"

57 For a very detailed description of the different types of glosses in this literature, see Krecher*.

Amarna letters,[58] a Ugaritic text,[59] many Greek and Latin texts from antiquity,[60] 𝔗[N] (see plate 23*), various manuscripts of 𝔊 and 𝔙,[61] as well as much material from the Middle Ages in many languages,[62] including Hebrew.[63] Only one such example is known from the Qumran texts.

Isa 7:25	𝔐	שמיר ושית (= 𝔊 𝔗 𝔖 𝔙) thornbush and thistle
	1QIsa[a]	ברזל שמיר ושית iron thornbush and thistle (the addition is interlinear, above שמיר).

In this case the added word in 1QIsa[a] explains a word in the text.[64]

At the same time, although pertinent evidence for glossing is usually lacking, scholars often reconstruct glosses from the available texts. That is, the recognition that the original glosses were written outside the body and syntax of the text often led to the assumption that such glosses were wrongly inserted into the running text. Strictly speaking the assumption of a misplaced gloss is an act of emendation (cf. chapter 8), but this term is not often used in this regard. Scholars regularly consider data in one of the ancient versions as real evidence which, however, is often not accepted as relevant by others.[65]

---

58 See F.M.Th. Böhl, *Die Sprache der Amarnabriefe mit besonderer Berücksichtigung der Kanaanismen* (Leipziger Semitistische Studien V,2; Leipzig 1909), esp. 80-89; P. Artzi, "The 'Glosses' in the El-Amarna Tablets," *Bar Ilan Annual* 1 (1963) 24-57 (Heb.); Krecher*. While the glosses in these sources share external features with glosses in other literatures, they contain a variety of notations, but apparently not explanatory notes of the type that is assumed for the Hebrew Bible. Many of these glosses contain translations and phonetic instructions. Furthermore, in contradistinction with the other literatures, glosses in Sumerian and Akkadian texts, often written within the text itself, were meant to be an integral part of that text, though on a secondary level. (Thanks are due to Prof. Z. Abusch for advice on the Sumerian and Akkadian texts.)

59 See S.E. Loewenstamm, "Eine lehrhafte ugaritische Trinkburleske," *UF* 1 (1969) 74.

60 For a large collection of examples, see Hall*, 193-197. See also Reynolds-Wilson*, 206.

61 See C. Morano Rodríguez, *Glosas marginales de* Vetus Latina *en las Biblias Vulgatas Españolas* (Textos y Estudios "Cardenal Cisneros" 48; Madrid 1989).

62 See B. Smalley, "Glossa ordinaria," *TRE* XIII (Berlin/New York 1984) 452–457.

63 For Ben-Sira, see W. Caspari, "Über die Textpflege, nach den hebräischen Handschriften des Sira," *ZAW* 50 (1932) 160-168; 51 (1933) 140-150.

64 In the spoken language of the Second Temple period, שמיר had a secondary meaning of "iron," to which the glossator probably referred. Relevant material was collected by S. Lieberman, "Forgotten Meanings," *Leshonenu* 32 (1967-1968) 99-102 (Heb.); E. Qimron, "Textual Remarks on 1QIs[a]," *Textus* 12 (1985) נט-ס (Heb. with Eng. summ.).

65 The evidence of the ancient versions is often adduced as support for the assumption of glosses or interpolations. Their evidence could be relevant when elements of 𝔐 are lacking in one of the versions (especially 𝔊), or reversely when elements found in one

While there are probably very few instances in the biblical text of what properly may be named glosses, some instances stand out as presenting more likely material, viz., short explanations of names added to the completed text, either during the textual transmission, or at an earlier stage.[66] For example,

Gen 14:3 — אל עמק השדים *הוא ים המלח*
. . . at the Valley of Siddim—*that is, the Dead Sea* (all textual witnesses).

Gen 36:1 — אלה תלדות עשו *הוא אדום*
This is the line of Esau—*that is, Edom* (all textual witnesses).

These remarks may have been added in the margin, or directly into the text. In the latter case the term *gloss* is used somewhat loosely. Usually textual evidence is lacking for these glosses, but it exists in the following example[67] in which the added element was inserted in a wrong place in the text, possibly from the margin.

Josh 18:13 𝔐 — ועבר משם הגבול לוזה אל כתף לוזה נגבה *היא בית אל*
From there the boundary passed on to Luz, to the flank of Luz, southward—*that is, Bethel* (all textual witnesses).

The words "that is, Bethel" refer to Luz, and not to their present position in the sentence.

Also in the following instance the explanatory note may have been added secondarily as it is missing in the parallel verse Josh 18:16.

Josh 15:8 𝔐 — אל כתף היבוסי מנגב *היא ירושלם*
along the southern flank of the Jebusites—*that is, Jerusalem* (all textual witnesses).

The examples which follow illustrate possible examples of explanations of difficult words.

---

of the versions are lacking in 𝔐. But the data in the versions are of a different nature, and probably they do not constitute relevant "evidence." When a word suspected as a gloss in one source is lacking in another textual witness, its very absence may support the assumption of a gloss, but does not prove it. After all, anything could have happened to the texts in question, including the omission or addition by the translator, without any connection with the phenomenon of glossing.

66 Cf. Driver*, 124-126; Fishbane*, 44ff.

67 For a similar instance, see the inappropriate position of Isa 7:17 את מלך אשור in the context.

Isa 51:17 𝔐 את קבעת *כוס* התרעלה (= 𝔗 𝔙)
... the bowl, *the cup* of reeling (NJPST)

Isa 51:22 𝔐 את קבעת *כוס* חמתי (= 𝔗 𝔙)
... the bowl, *the cup* of my wrath (NJPST)

קבעת is a rare word, occurring only here in the Bible, and it is claimed by some scholars that the word was glossed by the next one, being the common word for the same object.[68]

Isa 33:21 מקום *נהרים* יארים (all textual witnesses)
a region of *rivers*, of broad streams (NJPST)

According to some scholars the first word in this verse serves as a gloss, explaining the second one (Delitzsch*, 136; Driver*, 137; BHS).[69]

Gen 6:17 ואני הנני מביא את המבול *מים* על הארץ (all textual witnesses)[70]
For My part, I am about to bring the Flood—*waters* upon the earth.

BHS designates מים, "waters," which stands in a loose attributive connection to the preceding word, as a gloss, with the implication that it has to be removed from the text.

A comparable problem exists in another verse in the same context which is similarly phrased:

Gen 7:6 ונח בן שש מאות שנה והמבול היה *מים* על הארץ (all textual witnesses)
Noah was six hundred years old when the flood came, *waters* upon the earth.

---

68 BHS mentions some versional support in favor of this suggestion. However, the word is not lacking in v. 17 in 𝔊, as claimed by BHS. In that verse 𝔊 contains two different words for "cup," though in a construction differing from 𝔐. In v. 22 both 𝔊 and 𝔖 contain only one word for the two synonymous Hebrew words. However, the versional evidence does not necessarily support the claim that כוס did not appear in the *Vorlage* of the Greek and Syriac translations, for possibly the translators could not easily find two synonymous Greek or Syriac words or found it unnecessary to juxtapose two similar words in their translation. Furthermore, it is not clear why this gloss would be written twice in the same context. It may be more logical to assume that the two synonymous Hebrew words were used thus in their natural way by the original text itself. Such pairs of synonymous words are often found in the Hebrew Bible (inter alia, combinations of words in the construct and absolute state, or combinations of two construct words, as here) and likewise in the Ugaritic literature, as amply shown by Y. Avishur, *Stylistic Studies of Word-Pairs in Biblical and Ancient Semitic Literatures* (AOAT 210; Neukirchen/Vluyn 1984). This particular pair of words occurs also in parallelism in an Ugaritic text (1 Aqht 215-216; see Avishur, 375). The assumption of a gloss (Delitzsch*, 136; Driver*, 137; BHS) is therefore questionable.

69 However, the two words describe each other, in this case in apposition, and the assumption of a gloss is therefore untenable.

70 BHS mentions a Genizah fragment lacking both words ("flood" and "water").

In this verse "water(s)" is designated as a gloss by Driver*, 140, and McCarter*, 32. The latter uses this verse as an example for explaining the phenomenon of glosses added in order "to explain obscure terms."[71]

The assumption of glossing is widespread among scholars, but the discussion above shows that according to some scholars (certainly the present writer) the assumed extent of glossing is greatly exaggerated. The aforementioned examples seem to be among the strongest ones in the scholarly literature.

(2) *Interpolations* (exegetical additions), are added to the body of the text in a physically recognizable way, or inserted directly into the running text, thus expanding the source from which the scribe copied. As in the case of glosses, the Qumran texts do not contain any, or hardly any, interlinear or marginal interpolations (exegetical additions), but the following instance may present an interpolation in the realm of grammar.

Isa 44:3 𝔐 כי אצק מים על צמא ונזלים על יבשה אצק רוחי על זרעך
Even as I pour water on thirsty soil, and rain upon dry ground, <so> will I pour my spirit on your offspring.

1QIsa^{a} כיא אצק מים על צמא ונוזלים על יבשה כן אצק רוחי על זרעכה

The word "so," added in modern translations, was also added above the line in 1QIsa^{a}.

In addition to the physically recognizable interpolations, the Qumran scrolls contain several elements added by scribes into the text itself, especially in 1QIsa^{a}.

Many such added elements entered the text which is now common to all witnesses of the Bible, but as a rule it cannot be determined whether this occurred at the level of the literary growth of the book, at one of its last stages, or during the scribal transmission (for the distinction between these two levels, see pp. 170, 313–319). Most of these assumed exegetical additions, usually wrongly named glosses, are evidenced in

---

71 Whether or not *mabbul* should be considered an "obscure term" is hard to determine. It occurs a dozen times in the Bible, but it is true that the aforementioned two instances are the first ones to appear in the Bible. "Water(s)" should probably be taken as an apposition to *mabbul*. Textual support for the assumption of a gloss is lacking in 6:17 and is unclear in 7:6. In the latter case BHS and McCarter*, 33 record 𝔊 as lacking מים, but in actual fact this pertains only to MS A. The word is found in all other manuscripts, though in most of them in an inverted sequence (τοῦ ὕδατος ἐγένετο). The editions of Rahlfs (see p. 140) and Wevers (Göttingen series—see p. 140) print the text of papyrus 911 as the original text of 𝔊: ὁ κατακλυσμὸς ἐγένετο ὕδατος ἐπὶ τῆς γῆς.

all the textual witnesses, while some are lacking in a select number of sources. Some examples follow.

Gen 14:22	𝔐	ויאמר אברם אל מלך סדם הרימתי ידי אל יהוה אל עליון קנה שמים וארץ But Abram said to the king of Sodom, "I swear to *the LORD,* God Most High, creator of heaven and earth." (= 𝔗^OJN^ 𝔙)
	𝔊*	𝔖 and 1QapGen, col. XXII, l. 21 lack the italicized words.
	𝔐𝔐	reads, instead, האלהים.

The presumably original text of this verse, reflected in the shorter version of 𝔊*, 𝔖, and 1QapGen, referred to God as עליון, "Most High," a term which also occurs in Canaanite texts, in which *ʿElyon* has the function of קנה, "creator," as here.[72] 𝔐 𝔗 𝔙, however, added a single word, יהוה, "the LORD," thus identifying "Most High" with the God of Israel, as if Abram is addressing Him. The presumably original form of the text is also preserved in 𝔐 in v. 19: "Blessed be Abram of God Most High, creator of heaven and earth."

1 Kgs 8:2	𝔐	All the men of Israel gathered before king Solomon in Jerusalem in the month of Ethanim *at the Feast—that is (huʾ), the seventh month.* (= 𝔗 𝔖 𝔙).
	𝔊*	lacks the italicized words.

The minus element of 𝔊*, which may also be considered a plus of 𝔐 𝔗 𝔖 𝔙, contains the first mention of "the Feast" (of Tabernacles) in the historical books. Compare Neh 8:14, which mentions that the Israelites dwelt in booths during the feast of the seventh month. In this verse 𝔊* also differs in other details from 𝔐.

Interpolations may occur anywhere in the Hebrew Bible, but scholars often create the impression that they occur more often in certain books, especially in Ezekiel and Joshua, than in others. However, this impression is probably wrong; moreover, most of the so-called interpolations in these two books probably have to be interpreted differently. The history of the scholarly discussion of interpolations is closely linked with the book of Ezekiel, although it should be

---

72 On the background of both components, see B. Mazar, "Baʿal šamem," *ErIsr* 16 (1982) 132-134 (Heb. with Eng. summ.).

remembered that in the literature the textual phenomena under discussion are usually named glosses.[73]

Some of the plus elements of 𝔐 in Ezekiel could indeed represent individual interpolations, named glosses by most scholars. Relevant examples are provided on p. 333. Most plus elements of 𝔐 in Ezekiel, however, cannot be considered interpolations.

Because of the examples of the latter type, discussed on pp. 333–334 and in the article by Tov mentioned on p. 333, the presumed interpolations in Ezekiel (named glosses in the literature) should be taken in their totality as representative of a literary layer, added in the "edition" of 𝔐 to a shorter, earlier edition represented by 𝔊. The material of 𝔊 is taken as representing a different Hebrew text—almost always shorter than 𝔐—since that translation is relatively faithful. Accordingly 𝔐 might indeed reflect exegetical additions. However, these additions should not be viewed as individual elements, but as components of a large-scale literary layer. Examples like the ones adduced on pp. 333-334 thus do not prove that the book of Ezekiel abounds with interpolations or glosses. For one thing, it would be unnatural to assume that the book of Ezekiel was interpolated to such a great extent (see n. 73).

Many of the differences between 𝔐 and 𝔊 in Joshua are to be explained in a way similar to our explanation of the differences between 𝔐 and 𝔊 in Ezekiel and Jeremiah. The Greek text of Joshua provides now a shorter and now a longer text, often in details which have been

73 While the discussions of Delitzsch* and Driver* of interpolations (named glosses) provide many (often identical) examples from all of the biblical literature, three other discussions are limited to Ezekiel. Of great influence on scholarship was the article by Fohrer* (1951), to be followed by those of Freedy* (1970) and Dijkstra* (1986). Earlier studies, likewise on Ezekiel, less influential on scholarship in general, but of seminal importance for the analysis by Fohrer and others, had been carried out by Rost* (1903-1904) and Herrmann* (1908, 1911). All these studies were limited to Ezekiel, but they referred to a topic which was to be of general importance for biblical research, that of glosses in the biblical text. It was surmised, probably unconsciously, that the large number of presumed "glosses" in Ezekiel (364 according to Fohrer*) indicates that a similarly large number of glosses must have been inserted in other books as well. Ezekiel, however, probably presents a special situation (see below), and thus if the view about the many glosses in that book proves to be ill-founded, the views about other books need to be adjusted as well.

Many of the assumed glosses in Ezekiel were denoted "Stichwortglossen" ("caption glosses"), that is, glosses which were written in the margin, together with a catchword from the text indicating the word(s) in the text to which the gloss referred (for a possibly good example, see 2 Kgs 9:4 as described by Noth, *OT World*, 355). This understanding, suggested at first by Rost* and Herrmann*, and later by others, too, was based on suggestions made at an earlier stage with regard to Greek and Latin texts by A. Brinkmann, "Ein Schreibgebrauch und Seine Bedeutung für die Textkritik," *Rheinisches Museum für Philologie* 57 (1902) 481-497.

recognized as significant for the literary history of the book (cf. pp. 313–319). The elements of 𝔊, exemplified on pp. 328–332, comprise a separate literary layer, and not individual interpolations or glosses. Likewise, the pluses of 𝔐 vis-à-vis 𝔊 in Jeremiah are not isolated interpolations, but part of an additional literary layer (cf. pp. 319–327).

(3) *Corrections*. Several techniques of correcting are recognized in the Qumran texts. These include the canceling of letters with dots and the crossing out of elements with a horizontal line (see pp. 213–216). In fact, one might consider many, if not most, of the marginal and interlinear additions in the Qumran scrolls as corrections to the body of the text. Indeed, the great majority of these added elements in the Qumran texts agrees with 𝔐 and the ancient translations when their evidence is relevant. The combined evidence of the correcting techniques and an analysis of the content of the added elements makes it likely that the added elements in the Qumran texts are in the nature of corrections. The exact pattern of the agreements of these corrections is somewhat unclear. The agreement with 𝔐 is misleading, since the added elements usually agree also with the other textual witnesses. These corrections thus do not reflect a consistent process of revision toward 𝔐, but they probably adapted the text written by the first scribe either to the base text from which it was copied, to a text used by a later scribe, or to both (thus Tov* [p. 213]). In any event, the text to which the copied text was corrected agreed with one of the proto-Masoretic texts.

For a major correction in 1QIsa^a^, see the description of Isa 40:7-8 on p. 239. See further the following sample of corrections in 4QJer^a^, a text which contains an unusually high percentage of all types of corrections.

Table 8

*Scribal Corrections in 4QJer^a^* [74]

col. III, l. 16 (8:12) עשו (supralinear addition) = 𝔐 and other witnesses
col. IV, l. 10 (9:11) ויב׳ן (supralinear *yod*)] ויבן 𝔐 (= uncorrected text)
col. IV, l. 13 (9:14) מאכ׳לם (supralinear *yod*) = 𝔐 מאכילם
col. V.1, l. 3 (10:11) תאמרו׳ (supralinear *nun*) = 𝔐 תאמרון
col. VII.1, l. 3 (12:4) ירא<כ>ה—*kaph* possibly partly erased
col. VII.1, l. 4 (12:5) ׳בא[ר]ץ̇ (supralinear *waw*) = 𝔐 (ובארץ) 𝔊
col. VIII.1, l. 5 (13:5) או̇]תי (supralinear addition) = 𝔐 and other witnesses
col. IX,2 l. 2 (14:6) שפאִ̇ים = 𝔐 (שפים)—cancellation dots (cf. p. 213) erase the *ʾaleph*
col. XI, l. 2 (17:10) מעל׳ליו (supralinear *lamed*) = 𝔐 מעלליו

---

74 Angular brackets denote erased letters.

col. XI, l. 3 (17:11) י[עזב<נ>הו (erased *nun*, supralinear *he*)] יעזבנו 𝔐 (= *prima manu* of 4QJer^{a})

col. XI, l. 5 (17:14) תהלתי אתה (supralinear addition) = 𝔐 and other witnesses

col. XI, l. 6 (17:16) ואני לא (supralinear addition) = 𝔐 and other witnesses

col. XI, l. 7 (17:16) פניך (supralinear *nun*) = 𝔐 (פניך) and other witnesses

col. XI, l. 7 (17:17) למח[תה] (supralinear *heth*) = 𝔐 למחתה—The *prima manu* text probably represents a phonetic omission

col. XI, l. 8 (17:18) < ° °> = 𝔐—Two letters have been erased after יום.

col. XI, l. 8 (17:18) שבר<ם>ון = 𝔐 (שברון) and other witnesses—The *prima manu* text שברם was identical with the next word. The *mem* was erased and ון was added above the line.

col. XI, l. 8 (17:18) <ת>שב[רם] = 𝔐 (שברם) and other witnesses—The *tav* of the *prima manu* text תשברם was erased.

col. XI, l. 9 (17:19) ה<ו>לוך = 𝔐 הָלֹךְ—The *waw* of the *prima manu* text הולך was erased and another one was added between the *lamed* and the *kaph*.

col. XI, l. 9 (17:19) (יבוא) בו] = (יבאו) בו 𝔐 𝔊 (ἐν αὐταῖς); בו, omitted by the original scribe of 4QJer^{a} by way of haplography, was added above the line.

col. XI, l. 9 (17:19) מלכי = 𝔐 (מלכי) and other witnesses. The *prima manu* singular form מלך agrees with יבוא (see above). The correction (note final *kaph*) was made *after* the first scribe had finished writing the word, since the added *yod* was written in the space between the words.

col. XI, l. 11 (17:21) [ב]נפשותיכם (supralinear addition) = 𝔐 בנפשותיכם—The *prima manu* text read בנפשכם.

col. XI, l. 11 (17:21) תשוא (supralinear *waw*) = 𝔐 (תשאו) and other witnesses

col. XI, l. 12 (17:22) תו[ציאו (supralinear *yod*) = 𝔐 תוציאו

col. XI, l. 14 (17:24) תשמעון (supralinear *nun*) = 𝔐 תשמעון

col. XII, l. 6 (18:19) <דבֿרֿי>. The scribe who wrote this word erased it upon recognizing the mistake, and then wrote his correction next to it.

col. XIV, l. 1 (22:3) ע[שוו<ו>ק (supralinear *waw*, erased *waw*)] עשוק 𝔐 (= *prima manu* text of 4QJer^{a}).

col. XIV, l. 12 (22:12) [הג]ל<ה>ו (erased *he*, supralinear *waw*) = 𝔐 הגלו; *prima manu* of 4QJer^{a}: הגלה.

col. XIV, l. 14 (22:14) מֿ<°°[..]>[ו]חים. The text of 4QJer^{a} on the line and above the line (probably: מרוחים) equals 𝔐.

col. XIV, l. 16 (22:16) <[ו]אֿבֿוֿן> — Reading uncertain.

5

THE AIM AND PROCEDURES OF TEXTUAL CRITICISM

D. Barthélemy, "Problématique et tâches de la critique textuelle de l'AT hébraïque," in: Barthélemy, *Etudes*, 365-381; idem, *Report*; B.S. Childs, *Introduction to the OT as Scripture* (Philadelphia 1979) 84-106; F.M. Cross, "Problems of Method in the Textual Criticism of the Hebrew Bible," in: O'Flaherty* (see below) 31-54; Deist, *Text*; idem, *Witnesses*; M.H. Goshen-Gottstein, "The Textual Criticism of the OT: Rise, Decline, Rebirth," *JBL* 102 (1983) 365-399; A. Jepsen, "Von den Aufgaben der AT Textkritik," *VTSup* 9 (1962) 332-341; E.J. Kenney, "History, Textual Criticism," *EncBrit, Macropaedia*, vol. 20 (15th ed.; Chicago 1985) 676-685; R. Kittel, *Über die Notwendigkeit und Möglichkeit einer neuen Ausgabe der hebräischen Bibel* (Leipzig 1901); P. Maas, *Textual Criticism* (trans. B. Flower; Oxford 1958) = *Textkritik*, in: A. Gercke and E. Norden, *Einleitung in die Altertumswissenschaft*, I, VII (3d ed.; Leipzig 1957); M.L. Margolis, "The Scope and Methodology of Biblical Philology," *JQR* 1 (1910–1911) 5-41; Noth, *OT World*, 358-363; W.D. O'Flaherty, ed., *The Critical Study of Sacred Texts* (Berkeley Religious Studies 2; Berkeley, CA 1979); H.M. Orlinsky, "The Textual Criticism of the OT," in: G.E. Wright, ed., *The Bible and the Ancient Near East* (New York 1961) 113-132; Payne, "OT Textual Criticism"; J.P. Postgate, "Textual Criticism," *EncBrit*, vol. 14 (1929) 708-715; J.A. Thompson, "Textual Criticism, OT," *IDBSup*, 886-891; J. Thorpe, *Principles of Textual Criticism* (San Marino, CA 1972); Tov, *TCU*; N.H. Tur-Sinai, *Bʾylw drkym wbʾyzw mydh nwkl lhgyʿ lnwsḥm hmqwry šl ktby hqdš* (Proceedings of the Israel Academy of Sciences and Humanities, vol. 1; Jerusalem 1966); P. Volz, "Ein Arbeitsplan für die Textkritik des AT," *ZAW* 54 (1936) 100-113; B.K. Waltke, "Aims of OT Textual Criticism," *WTJ* 51 (1989) 93-108; Würthwein, *Text*.

A. The Aim of Textual Criticism

A discussion of the practical aspects of textual criticism (chapters 6, 8, 9) requires a prior analysis of its essence and aims. Such a discussion is now in order and could not be given at an earlier stage in the book, since it uses data provided in chapter 4, and since it is partially based on the analysis of other aspects discussed in previous chapters, especially chapter 3.

For a better understanding of the nature of the textual criticism of the Hebrew Bible, it is helpful to contrast this discipline with the textual criticism of other compositions. For example, in one of the important methodological discussions in this area Maas*, 1, writes:

> The business of textual criticism is to produce a text as close as possible to the original (*constitutio textus*)."

Postgate* (in *EncBrit*, 709) provided a more extensive definition:

> The aim of the "textual critic" may then be defined as the restoration of the text, as far as possible, to its original form, if by "original form" we understand the form intended by its author.

In a way, the article in the more recent edition of the *EncBrit* (by Kenney*, 676) goes one step back when stating at the beginning of the analysis:

> The technique of restoring texts as nearly as possible to their original form is called textual criticism.

When these definitions are applied to the Hebrew Bible, several points emerge:

(1) The three definitions mention the original form of the text rather than of the composition contained in the text. Maas* and Postgate* were thus aware that sometimes the final form of the text differed from earlier developmental stages of the composition. Therefore, the above-mentioned definitions can be applied to the Hebrew Bible in the following way: as a rule, this branch of textual criticism aims neither at the compositions written by the biblical authors, nor at previous oral stages, if such existed, but only at that stage (those stages) of the composition(s) which is (are) attested in the textual evidence. Textual analysis does not aim at oral or literary stages beyond this evidence. The very assumption of earlier stages is based merely on logical deductions (see chapter 3B) and cannot be proven.

According to the definition in chapter 3B, textual criticism aims at the "original" form(s) of the biblical books. In that discussion the view that textual criticism aims to restore the specific texts that were current in the fourth and third centuries BCE was not accepted. It would seem preferable to aim at the one text or different texts which was (were) accepted as authoritative in (an) earlier period(s).

Adherents of the oral tradition school are necessarily compelled to work with a broader definition of the goals of textual criticism. According to their view the books of the Hebrew Bible never existed in one original written form, but only in several parallel oral formulations.[1]

---

1 See H.S. Nyberg, *Studien zum Hoseabuche, Zugleich ein Beitrag zur Klärung des Problems der alttestamentarischen Textkritik* (Uppsala 1935); J. van der Ploeg, "Le rôle de la tradition orale dans la transmission du texte de l'AT," *RB* 54 (1947) 5-41; Bentzen, *Introduction*,

(2) The second problem which arises from defining the aims of textual criticism concerns the *practical aspects* of the textual analysis. The three above-mentioned scholars state that textual criticism aims at establishing a text. The implication of this statement is that textual critics aim at establishing critical or eclectic editions of texts, by selecting from the various extant texts those readings which, according to the editor, were included in the original text of a particular composition. If and when the need arises, elements of this original text are also reconstructed by means of conjectural emendation (see chapter 8).

In light of these definitions, it is evident that the textual criticism of the Hebrew Bible differs from the textual criticism of other compositions, for there have been relatively few attempts to reconstruct the original text of a biblical book,[2] for theoretical as well as practical reasons: the Hebrew *Vorlage* of the ancient translations cannot be reconstructed satisfactorily, and often it is impossible to make a decision with regard to the originality of readings. Because of these problems, most of the existing critical editions are diplomatic, that is, they reproduce a particular form of 𝔐 as base text, while recording divergent readings (or variants) from Hebrew and non-Hebrew texts in an accompanying critical apparatus. The apparatuses of BH and BHS also contain conjectural emendations (for details, see chapter 9). In these diplomatic editions the exegete should not expect to find a finished product comprising the conclusions of text-critical scholars, but rather, the raw materials which will aid him to form his own opinion based upon the available textual evidence.

The problems with which the textual critic is confronted are not characteristic of biblical research only, since other literatures such as Homer's Iliad and Odyssey[3] also developed in a similar way through complex stages of composition and editing. Likewise, the literary criticism of other compositions is also based, either partly or wholly, on translated works. Nevertheless, it seems that the textual criticism of the Hebrew Bible raises unusually difficult problems.

In light of this discussion, it is now possible to formulate the aims of the textual criticism of the Bible. The study of the biblical text involves an investigation of its development, its copying and transmission, and

---

vol. I, 92 and Appendix, p. 6; R.B. Coote, "The Application of Oral Theory to Biblical Hebrew Literature," *Semeia* 5 (1976) 60-62.

2 See chapter 9, n. 1.

3 See B.M. Metzger, *Chapters in the History of NT Textual Criticism* (Grand Rapids, MI/ Leiden 1963) 142-154.

of the processes which created readings and texts over the centuries. In the course of this procedure, textual critics collect from Hebrew and translated texts all the details in which these texts differ one from another. Some of these differences were created in the course of the textual transmission, while others derive from an earlier stage, that of the literary growth. Scholars try to isolate and evaluate the readings which were created during the textual transmission by comparing them with other textual data, especially 𝔐 (for examples, see the readings denoted in chapter 4 as "<preferable>"). This evaluation (cf. chapter 6) is limited to the readings created during the textual transmission, not including those created in earlier stages, during the literary growth of the book, even if those readings are included in textual witnesses. Most scholars believe that this evaluation involves a reconstruction of elements included in the original text(s) of the Bible, as defined in different ways by various scholars (cf. chapter 3B). With the aid of this procedure they create tools for exegesis. Textual critics are not only involved with the search for presumably original readings. Readings that developed after the formulation of the original text(s) of the biblical books (so-called secondary readings) are important sources of information for the history of the interpretation of the biblical text, the history of ideas, and the development of the biblical languages.[4]

B. The Procedures of Textual Criticism

The study of textual criticism has both descriptive and practical aspects. The descriptive aspects pertain to the copying and transmission of the biblical text throughout many generations (chapters 2, 4). The practical aspects pertain to the differences between the various texts and to the way in which these differences are approached. The textual analysis is subdivided into two areas. The first area deals with the biblical text as it is found in Hebrew manuscripts and as it is reflected in the ancient translations, while the second, conjectural criticism is concerned with the conjectural emendation of the biblical text, which is invoked when neither the Hebrew manuscripts nor the ancient versions have transmitted satisfactory evidence. The first area may be called textual criticism proper, while the second is merely supplementary to it. In the terminology of Barthélemy*, 368, the first area is named *critique*

---

4 See the analysis by A. Rofé, "The Historical Significance of Secondary Readings," in: C.A. Evans and S. Talmon, eds., *The Quest for Context and Meaning, Studies in Intertextuality in Honor of James A. Sanders* (Leiden/New York/Köln 1997) 393–402.

textuelle interne, "internal textual criticism," and the second, *critique textuelle externe,* "external textual criticism." This second area is treated in chapter 8.

Textual criticism proper is subdivided into two stages. The first stage deals with collecting and reconstructing Hebrew variants (chapters 2, 4, 7), while the second is concerned with their evaluation (chapter 6). A consideration of variant readings (in short: variants) involves all Hebrew and reconstructed details that differ from an accepted form of 𝔐, including all pluses, minuses, differences in letters, words, and in the sequence of words, and, according to some, also differences in vocalization and word division. As remarked in chapter 2, 𝔐 is taken as the point of departure for describing textual variations because it contains the *textus receptus* of the Bible, but this decision does not imply any particular preference for its contents.

As a rule, the collation of Hebrew variants from biblical manuscripts is relatively simple. Somewhat more complicated is collecting variant readings from biblical quotations in the Talmud, *midrashim,* and the Qumran writings. Likewise, the reconstruction of variant readings from the ancient translations (see pp. 129–133) is an equally complex procedure.

After collecting the variants from Hebrew and translated texts, scholars usually compare them with parallel details in 𝔐 with the implication being that reading *a* may be preferable to all other readings or that all other readings may have been derived from reading *a*. If textual corruption in the development from reading *a* to other readings is assumed, the aim of this comparison is to select the *one* reading that was presumably contained in the original form of the text as defined in chapter 3B. If more than one original form is assumed, this procedure is still followed, as long as textual corruption is involved. Some scholars allow for the selection of more than one reading as original (see chapter 3B). This comparative evaluation of variants, described in chapter 6, is necessarily subjective. The evaluation is limited to readings created during the textual transmission, excluding those created in earlier stages, during the literary growth of the book, even though they are included in textual witnesses.

6

THE EVALUATION OF READINGS

"But the worst of having no judgment is that one never misses it . . . " (A.E. Housman in the introduction to his edition of M. Manilius, *Astronomicon* [London 1903] xxxi).

G.L. Archer, *A Survey of Old Testament Introduction* (Chicago 1964) 50-53; H. Barth and O.H. Steck, *Exegese des Alten Testaments, Leitfaden der Methodik*—Ein Arbeitsbuch für Proseminare (2d ed.; Neukirchen/Vluyn 1976) 20-26; Barthélemy, *Report*; S. Davidson, *A Treatise on Biblical Criticism, Exhibiting a Systematic View of That Science* (Boston 1853 = Edinburgh 1854) 382-387; A.E. Housman, "The Application of Thought to Textual Criticism," *Proceedings of the Classical Association* 18 (1922) 67–84 = *Collected Poems and Selected Prose*, ed. C. Ricks (London 1988) 325-339; Klein, *Textual Criticism*, 69-75; Noth, *OT World*, 358-363; Payne, "OT Textual Criticism"; M. Silva, "Internal Evidence in the Text-Critical Use of the LXX," in: N. Fernández Marcos, ed., *La Septuaginta en la investigacion contemporanea* (Textos y Estudios "Cardenal Cisneros" 34; Madrid 1985) 151-167; H.P. Smith, *Samuel* (ICC; New York 1899; repr. Edinburgh 1969) 395-402; J.A. Thompson, "Textual Criticism, OT," *IDBSup*, 888-891; B. Walton, *Biblia Polyglotta, Prolegomena* (London 1657) vol. I, 36-37.

A. Background

In almost every chapter of the Bible scholars are confronted with a large number of different readings, in both major and minor details. As suggested in the preceding chapters, these readings are first collected (collated) and then compared with 𝔐. Subsequently, the readings are then evaluated, with the understanding that the comparison pertains only to readings that were created during the process of textual transmission (for examples, see below C and see the readings denoted in chapter 4 as "<preferable>"). The purpose of this procedure has been formulated in different ways. Most scholars claim that their intention is to choose the original reading from the relevant data, i.e., the one reading which, although not necessarily the best, was most likely to have been contained in the original text. Others (see n. 41) attempt to identify the reading from which all others developed, or from which their existence can be explained. The understanding behind this evaluation is that the presumably original reading belonged to that stage of development of the biblical book which was considered as determinative for textual criticism, that is, the composition that was completed from a literary point of view and which formed the basis for the known textual witnesses—see the definition in chapter 3B which considered the possibility of earlier consecutive original texts. It is possible that there existed once parallel compositions, but as these are not known, textual criticism need not take them into consideration. If they would have existed, more than one original reading may be assumed in individual instances.

Most scholars reckon with one determinative composition, or at least two consecutive original texts, as the basis for textual criticism, and accordingly try to reconstruct its or their components. Those who do not accept such an assumption are seemingly exempt from the necessity of comparing readings and reconstructing details of the original text. However, in spite of the disagreements concerning the original shape of the biblical text, there is a common denominator between all those involved in textual criticism, viz., the existence of a frequently occurring group of readings, found in all early witnesses, that is, genetic readings (see the definition on p. 170). Almost by definition these genetic readings require comparison and evaluation, especially in such instances as similar letters interchanged because of their similarity (pp. 243–251) and instances of haplography and dittography (pp. 237–240).

As a consequence, since all textual witnesses reflect readings that are genetically related to other texts, including corruptions, even those scholars who reject the assumption of one text as determinative for textual criticism admit the necessity of evaluating at least those readings which are likely to be genetically related to each other. Such evaluation is necessarily limited to readings that have been preserved. In such cases in which scholars believe that no reading has been preserved which is appropriate to the context, emendations may be suggested (see chapter 8). These emendations need not be evaluated since they are based on imagination rather than evidence.

Although most textual critics attempt to express a view on the readings which have been preserved, some are reluctant to do so on the grounds that we lack tools enabling us to form an opinion on such matters, or that such decisions are too subjective (compare the reluctance of scholars to express a view on the original shape of the biblical text [p. 168]). Those scholars who do express a view on readings do not necessarily refer to all types of readings, since it is often impossible to decide between such cases as "parallel" readings, between a long and a short text, or between two readings which are equally appropriate in the context (chapter 3B).

On the other hand, many scholars, including the present author, believe that all readings which have been created in the course of the textual transmission ought to be evaluated. This formulation thus excludes readings which were created at an earlier stage, that of the literary growth of the book—see the discussion on pp. 164–189, 287–290. Guidelines (rules) for the procedure of textual evaluation have been formulated from the seventeenth century onwards,[1] and even though such rules apply only to a small segment of the preserved readings, they are nevertheless often referred to and used by modern scholars.

In practical terms, the conclusion of the evaluating procedure is that some readings are often designated as "original" or "better" than others. It should, however, be remembered that when a reading is described by scholars as original, this does not imply that the other readings are worthless. First, it is possible that the assumption concerning the originality of the reading is incorrect, and that one of the other readings should nevertheless be considered the better one. Second, all ancient readings are valuable, since they contain important information, not only concerning the textual transmission, but also about the exegetical considerations of the early scribes and the first generations of those who read and interpreted the Bible, particularly their linguistic and intellectual milieu (see pp. 258–285).

B. Textual Guidelines

Modern biblical scholars make frequent use of textual guidelines, but it should nevertheless be investigated whether their procedures are justified. Such an investigation concerns, above all, the question whether or not this evaluation proceeds according to any fixed or objective criteria, as many scholars maintain. For example, the emphasis placed on the use of the rule of the *lectio difficilior* (see p. 302)

---

1 To the best of my knowledge, the earliest list of guidelines suggested for the comparison of readings in the Hebrew Bible is that of Walton*, 36-37 (reprinted in F. Wrangham's edition of the *Prolegomena* [Cambridge 1828] 332-336). Other rules for the *correction* ("emendation") of 𝔐 or for the detection of *errors*, were suggested by L. Cappellus, *Critica Sacra* (Paris 1650; Halle 1775–1786) VI, VIII.17-20; J. Le Clerc (Clericus), *Ars Critica* (Amsterdam 1697) xvi; C.F. Houbigant, *Notae criticae in universos VT libros* (Frankfurt 1777) cxvi-cxxiv; G.L. Bauer, *Salomonis Glassii Philologia sacra his temporibus accomodata . . . II, 1, Critica Sacra* (Leipzig 1795) 454-458. With regard to the employment of textual rules, students of the Hebrew Bible have usually followed the lead of other disciplines, especially classical and NT scholarship. For example, Cappellus, the author of the first full-scale critical analysis of the text and versions of the Hebrew Bible, quoted extensively from H. Estienne's textual treatment of Cicero: *In Marci Tulii Ciceronis quamplurimos locos castigationes* (Paris 1577) vi-xii.

as an objective criterion is questionable. The different rules are therefore critically reviewed in the following pages. Before embarking on this task, however, the reader should realize what the final conclusion is. In the next pages we develop a rather negative view on the validity of the textual rules. It is our understanding that common sense should be the main guide of the textual critic when attempting to locate the most contextually appropriate reading. At the same time, abstract rules are often also helpful.

From the seventeenth century onwards, textual guidelines have been enumerated for the textual criticism of the Hebrew Bible, for example, in the seventeenth century by Walton in the *Prolegomena* to his Polyglot,[2] in the eighteenth century by Bauer,[3] in the nineteenth century by de Rossi, Porter, Davidson, de Wette, Loisy, Kennedy, and Smith,[4] and in the twentieth century by Steuernagel, Coppens, Bentzen, Noth, Archer, Payne, Klein, Thompson, Barth-Steck, Deist, Würthwein, Barthélemy, Hayes, and several others.[5]

The present investigation is concerned only with the research of the Hebrew Bible, but the textual criteria discussed below have often been adopted from other areas of research, especially classical philology and New Testament scholarship.

Certain scholars have realized the limitations of employing textual guidelines. Davidson, for example, wrote:

> Many writers have tried to frame *general rules*, by which an accurate judgment may be formed concerning various readings. But we are satisfied that such rules as we have seen propounded are of little if any use. No one is guided by them in practice. Nor can they secure an *accurate judgment* in all cases.[6]

---

2 See n. 1, above.

3 G.L. Bauer, *Salomonis Glassii Philologia sacra his temporibus accomodata, post primum volumen Dathii opera in lucem emissum nunc continuata et in novi plane operis formam redacta, Tomus secundus, sectio prior, Critica Sacra* (Leipzig 1795) 454-458.

4 B. de Rossi, *Introduzione alla Sacra Scritture* (Parma 1817) 99-100; J.S. Porter, *Principles of Textual Criticism with their Application to Old and New Testament* (London 1848); Davidson*, 382-387; W.M.L. de Wette, *Lehrbuch der historisch-kritischen Einleitung in die kanonischen und apokryphischen Bücher des ATs* (8th ed.; Berlin 1869) 233-240; A. Loisy, *Histoire critique du texte et des versions de la Bible* (Amiens 1892) vol. 1, 239ff.; J. Kennedy, *An Aid to the Textual Amendment of the OT* (Edinburgh 1928) 189-231; Smith*.

5 Steuernagel, *Einleitung*, 72-73; J. Coppens, "La critique du texte hébreu de l'Ancien Testament," *Bib* 25 (1944) 9-49; Bentzen, *Introduction*, vol. 1, 94-98; Noth, *OT World*, 358-363; Archer*, 50-53; Payne, "OT Textual Criticism," 99-112; Klein, *Textual Criticism*, 69-75; Thompson*; Barth–Steck*, 20-26; Deist, *Text*, 243-247; Würthwein, *Text*, 130-132; Barthélemy, *Report*, v-xxxii; J.H. Hayes, *An Introduction to OT Study* (Nashville 1979) 80-81.

6 Davidson*, 383.

However, Davidson himself provided a very long list of such rules.[7] Other scholars believe that the application of intrinsically correct rules forms the key to an objective evaluation. For example, Volz stated:

> Das ein Ziel einer solchen Arbeit, einer solchen Arbeitsgemeinschaft und Arbeitsverteilung müsste sein, das ein *Regelbuch* zur Textkritik des AT geschrieben werden und jedem Mitarbeiter auf diesem Gebiet ausgehändigt werden könnte . . . Noch wichtiger als der Inhalt des Regelbuches wäre die Tatsache des Regelbuches selbst, nämlich die dadurch dokumentierte Tatsache, dass ATliche Textkritik etwas Methodisches ist und nach Regeln zu verlaufen hat.[8]

Indeed, such a *Regelbuch* has now been written (see Barthélemy, *Report*).

One further point should be noticed. Rules which are necessarily abstract can be made more acceptable by the use of tangible examples. However, the fact that these rules are usually presented without illustrations[9] seems to indicate that scholars did not wish to commit themselves with particular examples. Since most of the examples may be explained by alternative means, it is difficult to present examples which can unequivocally prove the correctness of any given rule.

Let us now turn to the criteria suggested in the literature. A distinction is often made between external and internal criteria (considerations) relating to the evaluation of readings. External criteria pertain to the document in which the reading is found, whereas internal criteria bear on the intrinsic value of the reading itself. The frequent reference to external considerations derives from NT textual criticism, where these criteria were used as textual guidelines from the seventeenth century onward.[10] The following external criteria have been brought to bear on the evaluation of readings in the textual

---

[7] Ibid., 382-387. For similar remarks, see Hayes, *op. cit.* (n. 5) 80.

[8] P. Volz, "Ein Arbeitsplan für die Textkritik des Alten Testaments," *ZAW* 54 (1936) 107.

[9] An exception should be made for Payne, "OT Textual Criticism."

[10] For details, see E.J. Epp, "The Eclectic Method in NT Textual Criticism—Solution or Symptom?" *HTR* 69 (1976) 211-256; idem, "Textual Criticism, NT," *IDBSup*, 891-895. These criteria have been summarized by Epp, "Eclectic Method," 243 as follows:

a. A variant's support by the earliest manuscripts, or by manuscripts assuredly preserving the earliest texts.

b. A variant's support by the "best quality" manuscripts <this criterion represents, in fact, both internal and external considerations as defined below>.

c. A variant's support by manuscripts with the widest geographical distribution.

d. A variant's support by one or more established groups of manuscripts of recognized antiquity, character, and perhaps location, that is, of recognized "best quality."

criticism of the Hebrew Bible.[11] The discussion of these criteria is necessarily subjective.

1. External Criteria

a. Unequal Status of Textual Sources

In Klein's words:

> A variant that occurs in the Dead Sea Scrolls, the Samaritan Pentateuch, or LXX will probably be given more attention than if it appears in a Targum or in one of the daughter translations of the LXX.[12]

By similar reasoning, readings in *certain* Qumran texts and in ɯɯ are often regarded as inferior because these texts contain many secondary readings.

All arguments based on the unequal status of texts are, however, questionable. In principle, all readings have an equal status, without any relation to the text or translation in which they are found. At the same time, special problems exist regarding the use of the ancient versions. Indeed, the reconstruction of variants from the ancient versions is precarious, but once retroverted, such variants have an equal claim to originality as Hebrew readings, if indeed the variant has been obtained by reliable methods of reconstruction. Likewise, reconstructed variants should not be differentiated according to the status of the translation in which they are found. All variants reconstructed from the ancient translations are of equal status. Thus, the fact that 𝔊—when differing from 𝔐—reflects a larger number of original (better) readings than all the other versions together does not make individual variants reconstructed from 𝔊 preferable to variants reconstructed from the other translations. Once retroverted reliably, all variants have an equal claim to originality.

By the same token, readings in ɯɯ and some Qumran texts, such as 1QIsa^{a}, should not be given less attention because these texts contain many secondary readings when compared with 𝔐 (cf. pp. 107–111, 114). Although there is certainly some statistical validity to the preference of certain textual witnesses over others, this judgment should not influence the evaluation of individual readings. Such statistical information is

---

11 The first scholar to use external criteria extensively as a separate group was probably Davidson*. However, before him some of these criteria were already used individually; see, e. g., Walton*.

12 Klein, *Textual Criticism*, 74.

irrelevant when data are evaluated. Consequently, the brief evaluations of the individual textual witnesses in each of the biblical books by McCarter, *Textual Criticism*, 87-94 are imprecise and may give rise to misunderstandings.

The view expressed here reflects a "conservative" textual approach which is not influenced by stemmatic considerations and which has been formulated as follows by P.A. de Lagarde for manuscripts of 𝔊:[13]

> ich glaube . . . dass keine hds der LXX so gut ist, dass sie nicht oft genug schlechte lesarten, keine so schlecht dass sie nicht mitunter ein gutes körnchen böte.

The main exception to this understanding concerns Hebrew medieval manuscripts, since most of their variants were created at a late stage, often as late as the Middle Ages themselves (see p. 39). Therefore, some form of prejudice must be allowed for in this case.

b. Preference for 𝔐

Many scholars make statements such as "all other things being equal, the reading of 𝔐 should be preferred"—since this formulation implies the unequal nature of textual witnesses, it presents a variation of the previous rule. For example, Würthwein:[14]

> As a general rule 𝔐 is to be preferred over all other traditions whenever it cannot be faulted either linguistically or for its material content, unless in particular instances there is good reason for favoring another tradition.[15]

It is indeed a fact that the readings of 𝔐 are, on the whole, preferable to those found in other texts, but this statistical information should not influence decisions in individual instances, because the exceptions to this situation are not predictable.[16] When judgments are involved,

---

13 P. de Lagarde, *Anmerkungen zur griechischen Übersetzung der Proverbien* (Leipzig 1863) 3, n. 1.

14 Würthwein, *Text*, 131—the translation is from the English edition of 1979 (Grand Rapids, MI) 114.

15 For a similar argumentation, see O. Thenius, *Die Bücher Samuels erklärt* (ed. M. Löhr; KeH; 3d ed.; Leipzig 1898) xci; J. Méritan, *La version grecque des livres de Samuel, précédée d'une introduction sur la critique textuelle* (Paris 1898) 58; Noth, *OT World*, 359; Thompson*, 888; M.Z. Segal, *Mbwʾ hmqrʾ*, vol. IV (Jerusalem 1960) 883; Barth–Steck*, 23.

16 Thus also J. Wellhausen, *Der Text der Bücher Samuelis* (Göttingen 1871) passim; P. Katz, "Septuagintal Studies in the Mid-Century—Their Links with the Past and Their Present Tendencies," in: W.W. Davies and D. Daube, eds., *The Background of the New Testament and Its Eschatology* (Cambridge 1956) 199; Smith*, 399, reacting against Löhr (n. 15): "Where G and H show variant readings, both being grammatically intelligible,

statistical information becomes less relevant, although it certainly influences scholars unconsciously. Furthermore, 𝔐 is not more reliable than 𝔊 or certain Qumran texts in all biblical books. This situation makes generalizations even more difficult and, at the same time, may give rise to generalizations of a different nature (such as the preference for 𝔊 or 4QSam[a] in Samuel [cf. pp. 113–114], or for 𝔊 and 4QJer[b,d] in Jeremiah [cf. pp. 325–327]), which are equally problematical.

It should be noted that criteria *a* and *b*, although seemingly reflecting external criteria, actually combine internal and external evidence. An initial preference for many elements in a given text, based on internal considerations, leads by way of induction to a general preference for that text. That preference then yields an external criterion which is used in individual instances by way of deduction.

c. Broad Attestation

It is often claimed that the better attested a reading is, the more trustworthy it is.[17] Sometimes a scholar will stress the wide geographical distribution[18] or, at other times, a narrow one, as, for example, Barthélemy and others:

> If a form of the text occurs in only one tradition, for example, the Targum, Syriac, or Vulgate, one is less inclined to regard it as original than if it occurs in more than one such tradition.[19]

The same author, however, provides an argument which undermines and, in fact, cancels the aforementioned consideration:

> In certain instances a variant form of the text may appear to have a broad base, in that it is represented in a number of different textual traditions, but a closer examination of the situation may reveal that these traditions have all followed the same interpretive tendency.[20]

---

they have *prima facie* equal claims to attention, and the decision between them must be made on the ground of internal probability."

17 The first to make this claim was probably Walton*, 37 (vol. 1, p. 334 in Wrangham's edition): "Quae lectio cum pluribus et melioris notae codicibus congruit praeferenda est ei, quae paucioribus vel non ita accuratè scriptis codicibus nititur."

18 Archer*, 52.

19 Barthélemy, *Report*, ix. However, the *Report* hastens to add: "On the other hand, in treating textual evidence, one must not count text traditions, one must weigh them."

20 Ibid., "factor 2."

Reliance on a broad attestation of textual evidence is not profitable, neither in the case of Hebrew manuscripts nor in that of the ancient versions, for it could have been created by a historical coincidence. Long ago it was recognized that *manuscripta ponderantur, non numerantur* (see p. 39, where this rule is applied to medieval Hebrew manuscripts). The same argument may be used with regard to the ancient versions. Several versions may be interdependent, as in the case of the influence of 𝔊, Symmachus, Aquila, and Theodotion on 𝔙 (cf. p. 153) and of 𝔊 on 𝔖 (p. 151). Hebrew and retroverted readings should be judged only on the basis of their intrinsic value, and consequently even minority readings are often preferable to well-attested variants. Textual criticism does not proceed according to democratic rules.

d. Age of Textual Witnesses

Older witnesses are often preferable to more recent ones,[21] because "the older one is likely to have been less exposed to textual corruption than the younger one."[22] For this reason 𝔐 is sometimes dismissed as "die jungste und schlechteste Form des Bibeltextes."[23]

Reliance on the age of documents is seemingly desirable, because the closer the document is to the time of the autograph, the more likely it is that it has preserved the wording of that autograph. In practice, however, this type of logic does not hold, since certain copyists preserved their source better than others. For example, the community which transmitted 𝔐 has left the biblical text virtually unchanged for some two thousand years, whereas the Qumran scribes modernized and changed the orthography, morphology, and content of the text already in the Second Temple period within a relatively short period of textual activity. Thus 1QIsa^a, dating from the first century BCE, is further removed from the *Urtext* of Isaiah than a Masoretic manuscript written in the tenth century CE.

Given such exceptional cases, the fallacy of dependence upon the age of witnesses was recognized long ago. In the eighteenth century, J.S. Semler[24] showed that some late manuscripts of the NT contain readings which are closer to the original text than their counterparts in older

21 Walton*, 37 (vol. 1, p. 334 in Wrangham's edition) was probably the first to make this claim: "Quae ex codicibus antiquioribus elicitur lectio, 'ceteris paribus', praeferri debet ei quae ex recentioribus colligitur."

22 Deist, *Text*, 232.

23 H.S. Nyberg, "Das textkritische Problem des Alten Testaments am Hoseabuche demonstriert," *ZAW* 52 (1934) 242.

24 J.S. Semler, *Hermeneutische Vorbereitung* (Halle 1765) 3/1, p. 88.

texts, and accordingly he reckoned with the internal and external antiquity of codices. In recent research, too, reliance on the age of documents has been attacked strongly, especially by Pasquali in a chapter titled "Recentiores non deteriores" (recent documents are not <necessarily> worse <than older ones>).[25]

In addition to the above-mentioned external criteria, the geographical provenance of readings is sometimes used as a criterion for originality,[26] but usually only in connection with other criteria.

2. *Internal Criteria*

The above discussion has shown that external criteria are usually not valid in the case of the Hebrew Bible, so that we now turn to internal criteria, that is, criteria bearing on the intrinsic value and content of the readings.[27]

The following internal criteria are recognized in the textual criticism of the Hebrew Bible.

a. Lectio Difficilior Praeferenda/Praevalet/Praestat

This rule ("the more difficult reading is to be preferred")[28] has been phrased in different ways. For example:

> When a text was particularly difficult, there was a tendency for ancient scribes and translators to simplify the text by employing contextually more fitting lexical, grammatical, and stylistic forms (these modifications are often spoken of as "facilitating").[29]

---

25 G. Pasquali, *Storia della tradizione e critica del testo* (2d ed.; Florence 1971) 41-108.

26 Especially by those scholars who adhere to a theory of local texts (recensions). See Klein, *Textual Criticism*, and above, pp. 185–187.

27 In the textual criticism of the NT, a distinction is usually made between two types of internal criteria ("probabilities"), which has recently been formulated by B.M. Metzger, *The Text of the NT* (2d ed.; Oxford 1968) 208-211 as follows: (A) "Transcriptional probabilities," such as the *lectio difficilior, lectio brevior;* (B) "Intrinsic probabilities," such as "the style and vocabulary of the author throughout the book, the immediate context, and harmony with the teaching of the author elsewhere." For the distinction, see already B.F. Westcott and F.J.A. Hort, *The NT in the Original Greek* (2d ed.; London/New York 1896) vol. II, 19-30. In the textual criticism of the Hebrew Bible, this distinction is not usually made.

28 It is not clear when this rule was introduced into the scholarship of the Hebrew Bible. In the research of the NT, it has been used since J.A. Bengel ("proclivi lectioni praestat ardua") in the *Prodromus* (1725) to his *Gnomon Novi Testamenti* (Tübingen 1742).

29 Barthélemy, *Report*, xi ("factor 4"). For similar formulations, see Bentzen, *Introduction*, vol. I, 97; Klein, *Textual Criticism*, 75; Deist, *Text*, 244-245; idem, *Witnesses*, 203.

Hence, when textual variation is encountered, one of the readings is sometimes termed the "difficult" reading, and the other(s), the "easy" reading(s), with the implication that the former has a preferable (original) status. From a theoretical point of view, this rule is logical, as some "difficult" readings were indeed replaced by scribes with simpler ones.

All examples of this rule are questionable; yet they do serve to illustrate its background. In the example from Gen 2:2 on p. 168, "on the seventh day" in 𝔐 𝔗^{OJN} 𝔙 is the more difficult reading as opposed to "on the sixth day" in 𝔖𝔪 𝔊 𝔖 and Jubilees 2:16. This also pertains to *šobel* in 𝔐 of Isa 47:2 as opposed to *šulayikh* in 1QIsa^{a} (see p. 259).

However, although the basic validity of this rule cannot be denied, many scholars have recognized that the rule is nevertheless problematic and impractical since it fails to take into consideration simple scribal errors.[30] After all, by definition, often a scribal error creates a *lectio difficilior*. If there had been a consensus with regard to the recognition of scribal errors, the rule would be more practical, but since it is often unclear whether or not a given reading reflects a scribal error, the rule of the *lectio difficilior* cannot be effectively applied.

Although scribal errors are found in all textual witnesses (see pp. 8-11 and chapter 4C), opinions differ with regard to their recognition, as demonstrated by the following two examples.

Jer 23:33	𝔐	When this people, or a prophet, or a priest asks you: "What is the burden (משא) of the LORD?," you shall answer them, "*What* burden?" (את מה משא)—cf. 𝔖.

The latter phrase is contextually difficult since the use of את is unprecedented. It reflects a *lectio difficilior* as compared with the contextually appropriate

𝔊	ὑμεῖς ἐστε τὸ λῆμμα (= 𝔙) *You* are the burden!
=	אתם המשא

Most scholars agree that the reading of 𝔐 reflects a scribal error (incorrect word division), apparently as a result of מה משא in v. 33a while 𝔊 𝔙 reflect the original reading. However, there is no unanimous

According to McCarter, *Textual Criticism*, 21 this is "the one great rule" for the evaluation of readings.

30 This claim was made by Bentzen, *Introduction*, vol. I, 97 and Steuernagel, *Einleitung*, 97.

view on this or any other reading, as can be seen from an article written in defense of 𝔐.[31]

Jer 41:9 𝔐 ביד גדליהו הוא אשר עשה המלך אסא
(The cistern into which Ishmael threw all the corpses of the men he had killed) by the hand of Gedaliah, that was the one that king Asa had constructed (on account of king Baʿasha of Israel. That was the one which Ishmael son of Nethaniah filled with corpses.) (cf. 𝔖 𝔙)
𝔊 φρέαρ μέγα τοῦτό ἐστιν ὃ ἐποίησεν ὁ βασιλεὺς Ασα
. . . that was the/a large cistern that king Asa constructed
= בור גדל הוא אשר עשה המלך אסא

In this verse, ביד גדליהו, "by the hand of Gedaliah," of 𝔐 reflects, in our view, a contextually inexplicable reading, while the presumably original reading, בור גדל הוא, is reflected in 𝔊. Here, also, a scholar has written in defense of 𝔐.[32]

If, as is likely, the aforementioned two readings in 𝔐 resulted from scribal errors, the rule of the *lectio difficilior* does not apply to them.

Moreover, in many instances this rule has been applied so subjectively, that it can hardly be called a textual rule or canon. For what appears as a linguistically or contextually difficult reading to one scholar may not necessarily be difficult to another. Furthermore, two readings may often be equally difficult, or two others, equally easy. Should we locate the more difficult or the easier reading in such cases as well? All these difficulties were recognized by Albrektson in an article dealing with this issue.[33]

The following instances show further difficulties regarding this rule:

1 Sam 1:23 𝔐 (אך יקם) יהוה את דברו (= 𝔗 𝔙)
4QSam[a]]ה יוצא מפיך (= 𝔊)

---

31 N. Walker, "The Masoretic Pointing of Jeremiah's Pun," *VT* 7 (1957) 413. For a full analysis of this verse, see W. McKane, "משא in Jeremiah 23 33-40," in: J.A. Emerton, ed., *Prophecy, Essays Presented to Georg Fohrer on His Sixty-Fifth Birthday, 6 September 1980* (BZAW 150; Berlin/New York 1980) 35-54. It is not likely that the *Vorlage* of 𝔊 should be reconstructed as the less common אתמה, as suggested by P. Wernberg-Møller, "The Pronoun אתמה and Jeremiah's Pun," *VT* 6 (1956) 315f.

32 M.J. Dahood, "Hebrew-Ugaritic Lexicography I," *Bib* 44 (1963) 302-303.

33 B. Albrektson, "Difficilior Lectio Probabilior—A Rule of Textual Criticism and Its Use in OT Studies," *OTS* 21 (1981) 5-18.

In this example, discussed and translated on p. 176, there are no convincing external or internal considerations either for or against the reading of 𝔐 𝔗 𝔙 or 4QSam^{a} 𝔊. Both readings are contextually possible.

1 Sam 1:24 𝔐 ותעלהו עמה (= 𝔗 𝔖 𝔙)
she took him up *with her*
4QSam^{a} ותעל אותו
she took *him* up
𝔊 καὶ ἀνέβη μετ᾽ αὐτοῦ
and she went up *with him*
= ותעל אִתּוֹ

4QSam^{a} and 𝔊 are both derived from אתו, which was understood as respectively *ʾotô* or *ʾittô*. Both readings, as well as 𝔐, are contextually possible.

The recognition of equally difficult readings is admittedly very subjective. For example,

1 Sam 20:30 𝔐 בֶּן נַעֲוַת הַמַּרְדּוּת
son of a perverse, rebellious woman (NRSV, NJPST)
4QSam^{b} בן נערות המרדת
= 𝔊 υἱὲ κορασίων αὐτομολούντων
son of deserting maidens

In our view, the reading of 𝔐 is as difficult as the reading of 4QSam^{b} 𝔊. The reading of 𝔐 is linguistically difficult, while that of 4QSam^{b} 𝔊 is difficult because of its contextual implications. Either of these two readings (or possibly a third one) could reflect the original text.

b. Lectio Brevior/Brevis Potior

The logic behind the rule of the *lectio brevior/brevis potior* ("the shorter reading is to be preferred")[34] is formulated well by Klein:

> Unless there is clear evidence for homoeoteleuton or some other form of haplography, a shorter text is probably better. The people who copied manuscripts expanded the text in several ways: they made subjects and objects of sentences explicit whereas they were often only implicit in the original text; they added glosses or comments to explain difficult words or ideas; and when faced with alternate readings in two or more manuscripts they were copying, they would include both of them (conflation) in a serious attempt to preserve the original. While some scribes may have abbreviated

34 I do not know when this rule was first applied to the Hebrew Bible.

> from time to time, we believe that the interpretation of a shorter reading as abbreviation should only be chosen as a last resort.[35]

This rule seems perfectly logical, yet its *raison d'être* has often been attacked. The logic behind it is that ancient scribes were more prone to add details than to omit them. Although this rule cannot be proven, it is likely that the short texts of 𝔐 in 1 Sam 1:22 (p. 114) and 2 Sam 12:9 (p. 271) preceded the longer ones. This applies also to many of the large-scale differences discussed in chapter 7B (sections 1, 2, 3, 4, 11, 12, but not 10). Note further the following examples in which it is more likely that an element was added as an explanation than dropped as superfluous.

1 Sam 1:24 𝔐 — בפרים שלשה (= 𝔗)
with three bulls
4QSam^a]בקר משלש ולחם (= 𝔊)
with a three-year-old bull *and bread*

1 Sam 2:21 𝔐 ויגדל הנער שמואל עם יהוה = 𝔊 𝔗 𝔖 𝔙 and 3:1 𝔐 𝔊 𝔖 𝔙
young Samuel grew up with the LORD
4QSam^a ויגדל שמ[ואל] לפני י[הוה]
— Sam[uel] grew up before the L[ORD]

1 Sam 2:22 𝔐 — ועלי זקן מאד (= 𝔊 𝔗 𝔖 𝔙)
And Eli was very old.
4QSam^a ועלי זקן מאד בן תשעים שנה]
And Eli was very old, *ninety years.*

However, the validity of this rule cannot be maintained in all instances. In fact, in neither the NT[36] nor the Hebrew Bible can it be decided automatically that the shorter reading is original. It would be helpful if one could identify texts which tended to add or omit details, but few such texts are known. Note, however, a distinct tendency to add details in 1QIsa^a. But even this information would not justify the automatic use of this rule. For, in addition to these difficulties, the rule does not cover scribal omissions (haplography, homoioteleuton, and homoioarcton described on pp. 238–240). Therefore, since it is often hard to distinguish between a scribal phenomenon and the addition or omission of a detail, the suggested rule is impractical, as demonstrated by the following example:

---

35 Klein, *Textual Criticism*, 75. Similarly Archer*, 52.

36 See the recent discussion by J.R. Royse, "Scribal Habits in the Transmission of NT Texts," in: O'Flaherty* (see p. 287) 139-161 (including references to the earlier studies of A.C. Clark and E.C. Colwell).

1 Chr 11:31	𝔐	מגבעת בני בנימן (= 𝔖 𝔙 and 2 Sam 23:29)	
		of Gibeah	of *the sons of* Benjamin
	𝔊	ἐκ βουνοῦ Βενιαμειν (= 𝔗)	
		of the Hill (of Gibeah) of	Benjamin
	=	מגבעת בנימן	

The shorter reading of 𝔊 𝔗 may be original (cf. 1 Sam 13:15; 14:16), whereas the reading of 𝔐 𝔖 𝔙 may have been created by dittography (cf. p. 240). Alternatively, the reading of 𝔊 𝔗 may also be secondary, created by haplography (cf. p. 257; cf. the parallel in 2 Sam 23:29 and the reading of 𝔐 𝔖 𝔙). Both explanations presuppose scribal errors involving a Hebrew manuscript. It is also possible, however, that בני was omitted or added because of contextual reasons or that an inner-translational corruption took place in 𝔊 𝔗.

The two aforementioned rules of the *lectio difficilior* and *lectio brevior* can be applied to only a small percentage of the readings which need to be evaluated. Yet, they comprise the main rules mentioned in handbooks on textual criticism and methodological discussions, and only a few additional rules have been suggested, to be illustrated below.

c. Assimilation to Parallel Passages (Harmonization)

This criterion was formulated by Barthélemy as follows:

> Some variant forms of text arose because ancient editors, scribes, or translators, assimilated the text of one passage to that of a similar or proximate passage, usually with the apparent purpose of attaining greater consistency.[37]

This criterion (cf. p. 261) can be taken as a subcategory of the *lectio difficilior*, for the assimilated reading is the "easier" one, and the other reading the more "difficult" one. Thus, when in two different texts some manuscripts of text *a* agree with text *b*, while other manuscripts of that text differ from *b*, the first mentioned group of manuscripts of *a* is suspect of having been assimilated to *b*.[38]

---

37 Barthélemy, *Report*, xi ("factor 5").

38 This phenomenon occurs frequently in "pre-Samaritan" texts, 𝔪 (see pp. 85–89), and in 𝔊^{A} (p. 138). See also my article "The Nature and Background of Harmonizations in Biblical Manuscripts," *JSOT* 31 (1985) 3-29.

d. Interpretive Modification

In Barthélemy's formulation:

> In some instances a particular form of the text may appear to be essentially interpretive. That is to say, certain ancient editors, scribes, or translators may have thought that the underlying text should be changed or amplified to conform to certain views, primarily theological. Or they may have wished the text to state explicitly a meaning which was not completely clear. Such variant forms of the text which would have arisen in later phases of textual development cannot be regarded as valid alternatives.[39]

This rule, too, can be taken as a subcategory of the *lectio difficilior*. Needless to say, its application is so subjective that it becomes very impractical as a general guideline.[40]

In short, these rules, summarized by Volz (see n. 8), in Barthélemy, *Report*, and in Payne, "OT Textual Criticism," represent the traditional approach to textual guidelines which is also reflected in other works. Summarizing, the following faults are to be found in the traditional approach.

(1) The logic underlying certain rules is questionable (*lectio difficilior, lectio brevior*).

(2) The application of abstract rules cannot make the evaluation of readings objective. The procedure remains subjective.

(3) The textual rules can be applied to only a small fraction of the readings which need to be evaluated.

(4) Textual rules are limited to internal evidence. There exist no commonly accepted or valid external rules in the textual criticism of the Hebrew Bible.

These criticisms pertain only to the *application* of textual rules. These criticisms do not imply that such rules are incorrect or should be abandoned, but rather, that they should be used sparingly and with full recognition of their subjective nature. For the evaluation of some witnesses, such as G and S, external rules can be helpful. For the Hebrew Bible, however, the employment of such rules is very limited. Furthermore, it must be realized that even if there are objective aspects to the rules, the very selection of a particular rule remains subjective. For example, a given reading can be characterized as either a *lectio difficilior*, a transcription error, or an exegetical element (see p. 303); the

39 Barthélemy, *Report*, xii ("factor 7").

40 In Barthélemy, *Report* this rule is not implemented very often.

choice of one of these options necessarily leads to different conclusions, and the subjectivity in the selection of this rule thus renders the whole procedure subjective.

This conclusion leads to some general reflections on the nature of the textual evaluation and the use of guidelines within that framework. The quintessence of textual evaluation is the selection from the different transmitted readings of the one reading (see chapter 3B) which is the most appropriate to its context. Within the process of this selection, the concept of the "context" is taken in a broad sense, as referring to the language, style, and content of both the immediate context and of the whole literary unit in which the reading is found. This procedure necessarily allows the scholar great liberty and, at the same time, burdens him with the responsibility of finding his way through a labyrinth of data and considerations. Since the context is taken in a wide sense, scholars have to refer to data and arguments bearing on different aspects of the text, hence to different disciplines: the language and vocabulary of individual literary units and of the Bible as a whole, the exegesis of individual verses, chapters, and books, and the general content and ideas of a given unit or book, including such areas as biblical history and geography. In addition to these, the scholar must be aware of the intricacies of the textual transmission, and in particular, of the types of errors made in the course of that transmission.

It has sometimes been said that one ought to regard as original that reading which, in the most natural way, explains the origin of the other readings, or the reading from which all others developed.[41] This formulation is probably acceptable, but it can hardly be considered a practical guideline for the textual critic in the manner in which it has been presented, for it is general to the point of being almost superfluous. Among other things, it refers to the choice of original readings as opposed to scribal errors, interpolations, deliberate alterations, and omissions. It also refers to unusual yet original linguistic forms as opposed to corrected ones and, conversely, to linguistically correct forms as opposed to corrupt ones.

The upshot of this analysis, then, is that to some extent textual evaluation cannot be bound by any fixed rules. It is an art in the full sense of the word, a faculty which can be developed, guided by intuition based on wide experience. It is the art of defining the problems and finding arguments for and against the originality of

41 E.g., Davidson*, 385; Steuernagel, *Einleitung*, 73; Bentzen, *Introduction*, vol. I, 97; M. Greenberg, "The Use of the Ancient Versions for Interpreting the Hebrew Text," *VTSup* 29 (1978) 148.

readings. Indeed, the quintessence of textual evaluation is the formulation and weighing of these arguments. Often it deals with arguments which cannot be compared at all, such as the style of a given literary unit, its language, the morphology of biblical Hebrew, and the logical or smooth flow of a given text. Within this subjective evaluation, there is room for more than one view. That view which presents the most convincing arguments is probably the best. Many arguments, however, have a different impact on scholars and often no decision is possible, as, for example, between synonymous readings, between long and short texts, or between two equally good readings in the context (see chapter 3B and p. 176). These difficulties, however, do not render the whole procedure of textual evaluation questionable, for such is the nature of the undertaking. Needless to say, one will often suggest solutions which differ completely from the one suggested on the previous day.

Therefore, it is the choice of the contextually most appropriate reading that is the main task of the textual critic (for examples, see the readings denoted in chapter 4 as "<preferable>"). This procedure is as subjective as subjective can be. Common sense is the main guide, although abstract rules are often also helpful. In modern times, scholars are often reluctant to admit the subjective nature of textual evaluation, so that an attempt is often made, conscious or unconscious, to create a level of artificial objectivity by the frequent application of abstract rules.

C. Preferable Readings

The practical result of the procedures described in this chapter is that readings are compared with each other, especially with 𝔐, and that an opinion is expressed on them. Scholars present their views in different ways. Some speak in terms of preferable readings, others refer to better or (more) original readings, and again others try to identify the reading from which the other ones presumably derived. The limitations of the subjective procedures used in identifying such preferable readings are described in section B. In the present section the preferences, or lack of them, expressed elsewhere in this book, are summarized.

Many readings are presented in the other chapters in a somewhat tendentious manner, that is to say, not as raw material, but rather as data presented together with our evaluation. Thus, when speaking in chapter 2 about harmonizing alterations in the pre-Samaritan texts and 𝔖 (pp. 85–89), we present the comparative data together with our view that the readings in the pre-Samaritan texts and 𝔖 are secondary when compared with 𝔐 and the other texts, since harmonizations are by definition secondary (not original). This pertains also to the following types of readings of ɯɯ presented in that chapter: linguistic corrections (pp. 89–91), ideological changes (pp. 94–95), and phonological changes (pp. 95–96), as well as to contextual adaptations recognized in some of the Qumran texts (pp. 110–111). Likewise, many of the textual phenomena described in chapter 4 presuppose an evaluation of the evidence. Thus the use of the following phenomena by definition assumes that one of the readings is original and the other one is secondary: random omissions (pp. 236–237), haplography (pp. 237–238), homoioteleuton and homoioarcton (pp. 238–240), dittography (p. 240), doublets (pp. 241–243), exegetical (contextual and theological) changes (pp. 262–275), and additions to the body of the text, especially glosses and interpolations (pp. 275–285). By definition this pertains also to the examples contained in chapter 1A2 ("mistakes, corrections, and changes in the textual witnesses, including 𝔐"; pp. 8–11).

A different type of preference is indicated in the examples of chapter 8 (conjectural emendations), since in all cases analyzed the transmitted readings are rejected in favor of a conjectural emendation suggested in that chapter.

In individual instances, a preference is expressed with regard to the examples in this chapter (chapter 6) for which the rule of the more difficult reading or the shorter reading is invoked (pp. 302–305 and 305–307). All examples are accompanied by arguments relating to the content of the readings. Arguments are also added to the contextual and theological changes in chapter 4 mentioned above. On the other hand, many of the other examples in chapter 4 denoted as "<preferable>" are not accompanied by arguments. For example, Gen 22:13 (p. 246), 1 Kgs 7:45 (p. 250), Isa 39:1 (p. 248), 1 Chr 11:33 (p. 250). This pertains also to the possible preference of a certain vocalization (see pp. 274–275), accentuation (pp. 69–70), and internal division of the text (pp. 4–5, 50–53, 210–211).

Again in other examples listed in chapter 4 (most examples on pp. 245–254), no preference is indicated because there are no compelling arguments in favor of any one reading. In other instances by definition no reading is preferred at all: orthographical differences (pp. 96–97, 108–109, 220–229) and synonymous readings (pp. 260–261). Likewise, in all the differences described in chapter 7 as having been created at the literary level, no textual preference is expressed.

7

TEXTUAL CRITICISM AND LITERARY CRITICISM

D. Barthélemy, "L'enchevêtrement de l'histoire textuelle et de l'histoire littéraire dans les relations entre la Septante et le Texte Massorétique," in: A. Pietersma and C. Cox, eds., *De Septuaginta, Studies in Honour of J.W. Wevers on His Sixty-Fifth Birthday* (Mississauga, Ont 1984) 21-40; N.C. Habel, *Literary Criticism of the OT* (Guides to Biblical Scholarship, OT Series; Philadelphia 1971); J. Lust, ed., *Ezekiel and His Book, Textual and Literary Criticism and Their Interrelation* (BETL 74; Leuven 1986); R. Stahl, *Die Überlieferungsgeschichte des hebräischen Bibel-Textes als Problem der Textkritik—Ein Beitrag zu gegenwärtig vorliegenden textgeschichtlichen Hypothesen und zur Frage nach dem Verhältnis von Text- und Literarkritik*, diss. Jena 1978 <cf. *TLZ* 105 (1980) 475-478>; H.-J. Stipp, "Das Verhältnis von Textkritik und Literarkritik in neueren alttestamentlichen Veröffentlichungen," *BZ* n.s. 1 (1990) 16-37; idem, "Textkritik–Literarkritik–Textentwicklung—Überlegungen zur exegetischen Aspektsystematik," *ETL* 66 (1990) 143-159; Tov, *TCU*, 293-306; E. Ulrich, "Double Literary Editions of Biblical Narratives and Reflections on Determining the Form to Be Translated," in: J.L. Crenshaw, ed., *Perspectives on the Hebrew Bible—Essays in Honor of Walter J. Harrelson* (Macon, GA 1988) 101-116; idem, "Pluriformity in the Biblical Text, Text Groups, and Questions of Canon," in press.

A. Background

Textual criticism is naturally involved with the study of texts and their transmission. But an investigation of these texts also leads to other areas, which principally include exegesis and literary criticism. For example, the biblical exegete learns much from exegetical elements embedded in the textual witnesses. This pertains also to the ancient translations, especially the exegetical components of the translation, provided that one is able to distinguish between these components in the translation and any Hebrew variants which may underlie that translation. Another area which builds on a study of textual witnesses is that of literary criticism, which forms the subject of the present chapter. Literary criticism is concerned with most of the essential questions pertaining to the biblical books (origin, date, structure, authorship, authenticity, and uniformity), and it thus also deals with various presumed stages in the development of the biblical books—see Habel*. From the outset it would appear that these issues are so far removed from the topics usually treated by textual critics that the relevance of textual data to literary criticism would seem to be remote. This chapter, however, demonstrates that this is not the case. As a rule, too little attention is paid to these aspects in the analysis of textual data.

Most of the data discussed in this chapter concern sizable differences between the textual witnesses, as a rule between 𝔐 (joined by 𝔗 𝔖 𝔙) on the one hand and 𝔊* (always corrected towards the Hebrew in the later manuscripts of 𝔊) or a Qumran text on the other. The underlying assumption of this chapter is that these data differ from the evidence presented elsewhere in this book. It is usually assumed that all differences between the various manuscripts and papyri derive from copyists, since they were the ones who produced these texts. Differences created by copyists—at another level named textual readings or variants—naturally belong to the area of textual criticism. This chapter, however, deals with groups of readings in manuscripts that were presumably created at an earlier stage, that of the literary growth of the books, and the assumption of the early origin of these readings is also taken into consideration in the analysis in chapter 3B of the original shape of the biblical text. The differentiation between these two types of readings is very difficult, and sometimes almost impossible. Our working hypothesis is to separate the two types of evidence with a quantitative criterion which also has qualitative aspects. It is assumed that large-scale differences displaying a certain coherence were created at the level of the literary growth of the books by persons who considered themselves actively involved in the literary process of composition. It is probably a mere semantic issue to find an appropriate term for the persons involved in this process. They were the last of the editors of the biblical books, but at the same time they also formed a transitional group to the next stage, that of the textual transmission, and hence they may also be named authors-scribes. The majority of the small differences between textual witnesses (such as described in chapter 4) which cannot be combined into a coherent pattern within a biblical book were probably created later, by the first generations of scribes, who allowed themselves the freedom of inserting these elements, and thus became small-scale partners in the creation of the biblical books. Obviously the distinction between these two groups is very difficult to determine; in particular, it is difficult to decide whether or not a difference in a small detail is part of a more extensive stratum of changes—this question is treated below, pp. 347–349.

According to our definition, the large-scale differences presented in this chapter belong to one of the stages of the literary development of the biblical books. In the past some of these elements have been described as individual cases or combined instances of scribal changes, glosses, and interpolations (see chapter 4C). However, such descriptions reflect the conditions of scribal transmission, in the course of which shorter elements were changed and added (for examples of these scribal changes of a smaller scope, see chapter 4C). The data described below are less incidental and of a wider implication. Some examples involve mere sections of biblical books, while others involve complete books.

The evidence discussed in this chapter derives from the early stages in the development of the biblical compositions, although evidenced in textual witnesses of later times. Therefore, the importance of the textual witnesses of the Bible exceeds the narrow confines of the field of textual criticism. At the same time, although these details, since they are found in textual witnesses, continue to be relevant to textual criticism, their evaluation is undertaken with the help of the tools of literary criticism. The need therefore arises to clarify more accurately the borders between these two areas.

According to the generally accepted assumption as described in chapter 3B, the biblical books passed through two main stages of development: the stage of the books' literary growth up to a form which was final in respect to their content, and the stage of the copying and textual transmission of the completed compositions (for an illustration, see the table *apud* Deist, *Text*, 23). In accordance with this description, the treatment of these subjects is divided into two areas of research, although the distinction between the two stages is largely open to doubt: literary criticism deals with the first area, the stage of the development of the biblical books, whereas textual criticism operates within the second stage, that of the books' copying and transmission.

This division determines the area covered by these two fields of scientific enquiry. Textual criticism deals with all matters pertaining to the biblical text, the nature, copying, and transmission of the biblical text, whereas literary criticism deals with various matters relating to the literary composition as a whole.

In the past the division between these two main fields was probably correct, as long as it was possible to maintain a clear distinction between the two stages. However, this is not always the case. The problem essentially stems from the fact that before the literary compositions were completed, parts of the biblical books or earlier editions of entire books preceding those reflected in 𝔐 𝔗 𝔖 𝔙 had already been set down in writing. Since most of the biblical books grew stage by stage throughout a period of several generations, even when a book seemed to have attained a completed state, it was often re-edited in a revised edition.

Similar hypotheses are posited with regard to the Homeric and Akkadian literatures, which were transmitted orally during a long period. When this approach was developed for the Hebrew Bible, it was generally agreed that such considerations must remain hypothetical since they could not be based on evidence, extant in manuscripts. In the meantime, however, the situation has been changed, for ancient texts which fit the description referred to in the preceding paragraphs have been recognized and found. Some of this new evidence has been available for a long time but was not recognized as relevant to the issue under discussion, while other data have become available in excavations, especially at Qumran. According to some scholars (see in particular Ulrich*, Stipp*, and Tov* and chapter 3B above), when the early editions of these books were completed, they were accepted as authoritative and were accordingly put into circulation, but at a later period, "revised editions" of the books, intended to replace the earlier ones, were written and again circulated. The process of substitution of consecutive editions, however, was only partial, so that the early editions did not completely go out of existence. In ancient Israel, the new edition that was later to become 𝔐—almost identical with the edition contained in 𝔗 𝔖 𝔙—replaced the earlier texts but could not replace them completely. Thus, the early editions remained in use in places that were not central from a geographical and sociological point of view, such as the Qumran repository of texts and the various manuscripts from which the Greek translation was prepared in Egypt. These early editions were thus preserved for posterity, by mere chance, in the Septuagint translation and through the discoveries in Qumran. To some extent this description is relevant to the theory of local text families, which our description partially supports (see the analysis on pp. 186–187).

Some more practical points are in order.

(1) It is the purpose of this chapter to draw attention to large-scale differences between the textual witnesses deriving from different literary strata in the composition of the biblical books up to the stage of the edition (recension, composition) contained in 𝔐. If the purpose is thus defined, literary developments subsequent to the edition of 𝔐 are excluded from the discussion. This pertains to presumed midrashic developments in the book of Kings, Esther, and Daniel reflected in 𝔊*. If in these books deviations of 𝔊* from 𝔐 𝔗 𝔖 𝔙 are indeed based on a different Hebrew or Aramaic text, as is likely, their underlying texts

differed often markedly from 𝔐 𝔗 𝔖 𝔙 (1-2 Kings)[1] or very markedly (Esther,[2] Daniel), and usually they are conceived of as subsequent to the literary compositions included in 𝔐. On the other hand, if they would have preceded the edition contained in 𝔐 𝔗 𝔖 𝔙,[3] their content is as relevant to this chapter as all other instances to be mentioned below, but we do not believe this is the case. The reasons for the exclusion from the discussion of material later than the compositions contained in 𝔐 are discussed on pp. 177–178. In our view it is the task of the textual (and literary) analysis to aim at that literary composition which has been accepted as binding (authoritative) by Jewish tradition, since these disciplines are concerned with the literary compositions contained in the traditional Hebrew Bible.

The examples given below thus pertain only to literary strata prior or parallel to the one contained in 𝔐. Only section 5 (𝔐 𝔗 𝔖 𝔙 and 𝔊 in Proverbs) pertains to presumed parallel material.

(2) This chapter contains examples of data from the textual witnesses of the Bible which are relevant to literary criticism and which, it would seem, often contain earlier formulations of the books included in 𝔐 𝔗 𝔖 𝔙. Some pertain to an entire book which was at one time circulated in an earlier edition, while others relate to a single chapter, and again others to a single section. These data point to the existence of early editions which differed slightly from the later one (𝔐 𝔗 𝔖 𝔙). However, these limited differences have far-reaching implications on our understanding of the growth of the biblical books as a whole.

---

1 Most of the differences of this type occur in the chapters which concern Solomon, Jeroboam, and Ahab. In the case of the duplicate translation of the section about Jeroboam (1 Kgs 12:24a-z), such a Hebrew *Vorlage* was reconstructed by J. Debus, *Die Sünde Jerobeams* (FRLANT 93; Göttingen 1967) and Z. Talshir, *The Duplicate Story of the Division of the Kingdom (LXX 3 Kingdoms XII 24a-z)* (Jerusalem Biblical Studies; Jerusalem 1989). For a description of the content of the differences between 𝔐 and 𝔊, see especially D.W. Gooding, "Problems of Text and Midrash in the Third Book of Reigns," *Textus* 7 (1969) 1-29 (including references to his earlier articles).

2 For a discussion of the literature on the value of the Greek versions of this book for textual and literary criticism, see Tov, *TCU*, 305-306.

3 Such a suggestion has been made for Esther in an article by Ch. Torrey, "The Older Book of Esther," *HTR* 37 (1944) 1-40. According to Torrey, both Greek versions of Esther (𝔊 and the so-called Lucianic version) derive from Aramaic originals, from which 𝔐 has been abbreviated. Also according to D.J.A. Clines, *The Esther Scroll—The Story of the Story* (JSOTSup 30; Sheffield 1984), the Greek text of Esther reflects an earlier stage of the development of that book. A similar claim has been made for the Greek text of Daniel by R. Albertz, *Der Gott des Daniel, Untersuchungen zu Daniel 4–6 in der Septuagintafassung sowie zu Komposition und Theologie des aramäischen Danielbuches* (Stuttgarter Bibelstudien 131; Stuttgart 1988).

(3) The examples adduced below add a necessarily *subjective* dimension to our analysis. Most of them are drawn from 𝔊* and the relevant texts are discussed here in their reconstructed Hebrew form retroverted from 𝔊. In all these cases it would appear that the translator had before him a different Hebrew text, a fact which is often supported by an analysis of the nature of the usually faithful translation. In addition, certain of the examples are also supported by Hebrew evidence from Qumran. It would seem that the translators did not usually introduce extensive changes such as the ones described below, not even a translator who approached his source freely, and certainly not one who represented the source literally (see pp. 123–124). It is important to remember, therefore, that the examples below pertain to units that were translated with a relative degree of faithfulness to the underlying text.

(4) Most of the examples concern data which are described here as representing a literary layer preceding 𝔐 𝔗 𝔖 𝔙. If, on the other hand, one should claim that in these examples it is rather 𝔐 𝔗 𝔖 𝔙 which contain the earlier stage, this claim would change the direction of our argumentation, since it was asserted above (1) that compositions which further developed 𝔐 are beyond the scope of textual and literary criticism. In that case the differences should simply be noted, and they remain important as textual data presenting *recensionally* different texts. Both possibilities should constantly be kept in mind. Therefore, because of the uncertainty concerning the relation between texts, the discussion should be as neutral as possible, and this neutrality is reflected in the headings of the sections below. Section heading 1 "Two Literary Strata of Jeremiah: 𝔐 𝔗 𝔖 𝔙 and 4QJer^{b,d} 𝔊*" refers to the elements discussed as two different literary strata, but it does not spell out the presumed relation between them.

(5) The examples are not intended to be exhaustive, although they obviously are more exhaustive than the material gathered in chapter 4 referring to the procedure of textual transmission. They merely exemplify the existence of different literary stages reflected in such late sources as textual witnesses. The date of these textual sources is not relevant. After all, it is mere coincidence that early evidence was preserved in such "late" textual sources, deriving from the third century BCE to the first century CE.

(6) The fact that the material is not exhaustive has repercussions on the analysis. It is important to realize that additional examples may be located for biblical books not treated. More importantly, if limited

recensional differences are recognized within a certain book, such as in 1 Samuel 16-18, the complete book, in this case Samuel, is likely to reflect such features elsewhere, including smaller details (see further below, pp. 347–349).

(7) In a way, the material gathered in this chapter resembles the differences between inner-biblical parallel texts mentioned on pp. 12–13, such as different formulations of the same psalm (Psalm 18 // 2 Samuel 22; Psalm 14 // Psalm 53), of the same genealogical list (Ezra 2 // Neh 7: 6-72), of segments of books (Jeremiah 52 // 2 Kgs 24:18–25:30; Isa 36:1–38:8 // 2 Kgs 18:13–20:11), and even of a complete book, viz., Chronicles, large sections of which run parallel to the books of Samuel and Kings. The differences between these parallel versions sometimes derive from the textual transmission and sometimes from literary development, but all this evidence is preserved without distinction in the parallel biblical texts which are contained in all the textual witnesses. With the exception of some examples on pp. 12-13 and in chapter 4C, most of the evidence from parallel segments is not dealt with in this book, because the origin of the differences (scribal *or* literary) is often not clear. In this book the discussion focuses on differences created at the scribal level. By the same token, the discussion below does not present two or more different literary versions of the same story presented in all the witnesses of the biblical text, such as the two stories of the creation, juxtaposed in the first chapters of Genesis, or the two stories of the flood, juxtaposed and interwoven into each other. That material belongs only to a literary analysis, and has no direct relevance for the textual transmission of the Hebrew Bible, since all the textual witnesses present more or less what we now consider to be inner-biblical parallel accounts. On the other hand, the material presented in this chapter is preserved in different ways in textual sources. It presents material of unusual interest for both textual and literary criticism.

B. The Evidence

*1. Two Literary Strata of Jeremiah: 𝔐 𝔗 𝔖 𝔙 and 4QJer^{b,d} 𝔊**

P.-M. Bogaert, "De Baruch à Jérémie, Les deux rédactions conservées du livre de Jérémie," in: idem, ed., *Le livre de Jérémie* (BETL 54; Leuven 1981) 168-173; idem, "Relecture et déplacement de l'oracle contre les Philistins. Pour une datation de la rédaction longue (TM) du livre de Jérémie," in: *La vie de la Parole . . . Etudes . . . offertes à Pierre Grelot* (Paris 1987) 139-150; idem, "La libération de Jérémie et le meurtre de Godolias: le texte court (LXX) et la rédaction longue (TM)," in: D. Fraenkel et al., eds., *Studien zur Septuaginta—*

Robert Hanhart zu Ehren (MSU 20; Göttingen 1990) 312-322; idem, "Les trois formes de Jérémie 52 (TM, LXX et VL)," in: G.J. Norton and S. Pisano, eds., *Tradition of the Text* (OBO 109; Freiburg/Göttingen 1991) 1-17; idem, "Le livre de Jérémie en perspective—les deux rédactions antiques selon les travaux en cours," *RB* 101 (1994) 363-406; B. Gosse, "La malédiction contre Babylone de Jérémie 51, 59-64 et les rédactions du livre de Jérémie," *ZAW* 98 (1986) 383-399; J.G. Janzen, *Studies in the Text of Jeremiah* (HSM 6; 1973); S. Soderlund, *The Greek Text of Jeremiah—A Revised Hypothesis* (JSOTSup 47; Sheffield 1985) 193-248; L. Stulman, "Some Theological and Lexical Differences between the Old Greek and the MT of the Jeremiah Prose Discourses," *Hebrew Studies* 25 (1984) 18-23; idem, *The Other Text of Jeremiah, A Reconstruction of the Hebrew Text Underlying the Greek Version of the Prose Sections of Jeremiah with English Translation* (Lanham/London 1985); E. Tov, "The Literary History of the Book of Jeremiah in the Light of Its Textual History," in: Tigay, *Models*, 211-237; R.D. Wells, "Indications of Late Reinterpretation of the Jeremianic Tradition from the LXX of Jer 21 1 — 23 8," *ZAW* 96 (1984) 405-420.

Origen, *ad Afric.* 4, mentioned the distinctive nature of 𝔊 to Jeremiah in which he found many deviations from the Hebrew text known to him. In the past two centuries this subject has also merited a great deal of scholarly attention (see the surveys by Stulman* and Bogaert* 1994). Indeed, 𝔊* to Jeremiah differs from 𝔐 𝔗 𝔖 𝔙 in two central matters: the order of the verses and chapters and the length of the text. A question which has always been asked is whether these differences were caused by the translator, or whether he actually found a different Hebrew text of the book before him. With the discovery of 4QJer[b] and 4QJer[d], which, though fragmentary, reflect the two main recensional characteristics of 𝔊*, this question has been solved, especially in studies by Janzen*[4] and Tov*. It seems very likely that 𝔊 was translated from a Hebrew text which was very close to these two Qumran texts.

The differences between 𝔐 𝔗 𝔖 𝔙 on the one hand and 𝔊* 4QJer[b,d] on the other are recognizable in two main areas, which make these texts into two *recensionally* different traditions.

1. *The Length*—𝔊* is shorter than 𝔐 𝔗 𝔖 𝔙 by one-sixth (see Table 1). It lacks words, phrases, sentences, and entire sections that are found in 𝔐 𝔗 𝔖 𝔙. This characteristic is also reflected in 4QJer[b,d] (see Table 2 on pp. 325-327).

2. *The Order of the Text*—𝔊* deviates from the order of 𝔐 𝔗 𝔖 𝔙 in several sections and chapters. For example, 𝔐 23:7-8 are found in 𝔊* after 23:40 (cf. p. 340), and the internal arrangement of 10:5–12 in 𝔊* and 4QJer[b] differs from that of 𝔐 𝔗 𝔖 𝔙 (see Table 2 on pp. 325–327).

---

4 Janzen's conclusions are only partially accepted by Soderlund*, who prefers a mediating position between the assumption of the translator's abbreviating of his *Vorlage* and that of a shorter Hebrew text. Soderlund's criticisms were, however, refuted by Janzen: "A Critique of Sven Soderlund's *The Greek Text of Jeremiah—A Revised Hypothesis*," *BIOSCS* 22 (1989) 16-47.

The most striking difference in this regard pertains to the chapters containing the prophecies against the nations, which in 𝔐 𝔗 𝔖 𝔙 are found at the end of the book in chapters 46-51, before the historical "appendix," chapter 52, whereas in 𝔊 they occur in the middle, after 25:13. This verse serves as an introduction to these prophecies: "And I will bring upon that land all that I have decreed against it, all that is recorded in this book—that which Jeremiah prophesied against all the nations."[5]

The assumption of the existence of a shorter Hebrew text underlying 𝔊* is also supported by the agreements between the short text of 𝔊*, particularly in proper nouns, with 𝔐 𝔗 𝔖 𝔙 of 2 Kings 24-25, in contrast with the longer text of the parallel chapter Jeremiah 52 in 𝔐 𝔗 𝔖 𝔙. Moreover, the translation technique reflected in Jeremiah is rather literal so that *a priori*, it is improbable that the translator would have abridged his Hebrew source.

According to Tov*, 𝔊* reflects a first, short, *edition* of Jeremiah, "edition I," which differs from the expanded edition reflected in 𝔐 𝔗 𝔖 𝔙, "edition II." In edition II changes were inserted in the order of the verses and in wording, but more frequently elements were added: sections now occurring twice (e.g., 8:10b-12 for which cf. 6:13-15; 17:3-4, cf. 15:13-14; 30:10-11, cf. 46:27-28); new verses and sections (the largest ones are 33:14-26 and 51:44b-49a); new details; brief explanations, in particular, expansions of proper nouns; expansions on the basis of the context; expansions of formulae, etc. Expansions such as these, presented in their context in chapter 27, are exemplified in Table 1. Worthy of special consideration are 27:20-22 in which the additions to 𝔐 are inappropriate to the context (anti-climactic and serving as a *vaticinium ex eventu*) and betray the post-exilic date of edition II (cf. Table 7 on p. 348; additional examples of post-exilic additions are found in edition II in 25:14; 27:7; 29:6). A reconstruction along the same lines as the one presented in Table 1, referring to chapter 27, is found *apud* Stulman* for all the prose sections in Jeremiah. The character of the added layer of edition II is discussed by Bogaert*, 1981, 1987, 1990, Wells*, Stulman*, Tov*, and Gosse*.

---

5 Our punctuation does not reflect 𝔐, but represents the presumably original intention of the text. The clause "that which Jeremiah prophesied against all the nations" is parallel to 46:1, which forms the introduction to the prophecies on the nations in 𝔐. Often the location of the prophecies against the nations in 𝔊 is taken as original, but two scholars adduced strong arguments in favor of the secondary character of that location: A. Rofé, "The Arrangement of the Book of Jeremiah," *ZAW* 101 (1989) 390–398; G. Fischer, "Jer 25 und die Fremdvölkersprüche—Unterschiede zwischen hebräischem und griechischem Text," *Bib* 72 (1991) 474–499.

Table 1

Differences between 𝔐 *and the Reconstructed* Vorlage *of Jeremiah 27*

This table presents in parallel lines 𝔐 to Jeremiah 27 (the second line, in italics) and the reconstructed Hebrew source of 𝔊* (the first line).

𝔊* 1
𝔐 *1 בראשית ממלכת יהויקם בן יאושיהו מלך יהודה היה הדבר הזה אל*

2 כה אמר ה׳ עשה (?) מוסרות ומטות ונתתם
ירמיה מאת ה׳ לאמר 2 כה אמר ה׳ אלי עשה לך מוסרות ומטות ונתתם

על צוארך 3 ושלחתם אל מלך אדום ואל מלך מואב ואל מלך בני עמון ואל
על צוארך 3 ושלחתם אל מלך אדום ואל מלך מואב ואל מלך בני עמון ואל

מלך צר ואל מלך צידון ביד מלאכים הבאים לקראתם ירושלם אל צדקיהו
מלך צר ואל מלך צידון ביד מלאכים הבאים ירושלם אל צדקיהו

מלך יהודה 4 וצוית אתם אל אדניהם לאמר כה אמר ה׳ אלהי ישראל
מלך יהודה 4 וצוית אתם אל אדניהם לאמר כה אמר ה׳ צבאות אלהי ישראל

כה תאמרו אל אדניכם 5 אנכי עשיתי את הארץ
כה תאמרו אל אדניכם 5 אנכי עשיתי את הארץ את האדם ואת הבהמה אשר

בכחי הגדול ובזרועי הנטויה ונתתיה לאשר ישר בעיני 6
על פני הארץ בכחי הגדול ובזרועי הנטויה ונתתיה לאשר ישר בעיני 6 ועתה

(?) נתתי את הארצות ביד נבוכדנאצר מלך בבל
אנכי נתתי את כל הארצות האלה ביד נבוכדנאצר מלך בבל

לעבדו וגם את חית השדה לעבדו 7
עבדי וגם את חית השדה נתתי לו לעבדו 7 ועבדו אתו כל הגוים ואת

בנו ואת בן בנו עד בא עת ארצו גם הוא ועבדו בו גוים רבים ומלכים

8 ו הגוי והממלכה אשר
גדלים 8 והיה הגוי והממלכה אשר לא יעבדו אתו את נבוכדנאצר מלך בבל ואת

לא יתן את צוארו בעל מלך בבל בחרב וברעב אפקד עליהם
אשר לא יתן את צוארו בעל מלך בבל בחרב וברעב ובדבר אפקד על הגוי ההוא

נאם ה׳ עד תמי אתם בידו 9 ואתם אל תשמעו אל נביאיכם ואל
נאם ה׳ עד תמי אתם בידו 9 ואתם אל תשמעו אל נביאיכם ואל

קסמיכם ואל חלמיכם ואל ענניכם ואל כשפיכם אשר הם אמרים
קסמיכם ואל חלמתיכם ואל ענניכם ואל כשפיכם אשר הם אמרים אליכם

לא תעבדו את מלך בבל 10 כי שקר הם נבאים לכם למען הרחיק אתכם
לאמר לא תעבדו את מלך בבל 10 כי שקר הם נבאים לכם למען הרחיק אתכם

מעל אדמתכם 11 והגוי אשר יביא את צוארו בעל
מעל אדמתכם והדחתי אתכם ואבדתם 11 והגוי אשר יביא את צוארו בעל

מלך בבל ועבדו והנחתיו על אדמתו ועבדה וישב בה 12 ואל
מלך בבל ועבדו והנחתיו על אדמתו נאם ה׳ ועבדה וישב בה 12 ואל

צדקיה מלך יהודה דברתי ככל הדברים האלה לאמר הביאו את צואריכם
צדקיה מלך יהודה דברתי ככל הדברים האלה לאמר הביאו את צואריכם

ועבדו 13
בעל מלך בבל ועבדו אתו ועמו וחיו 13 למה תמותו אתה ועמך בחרב

14
ברעב ובדבר כאשר דבר ה׳ אל הגוי אשר לא יעבד את מלך בבל 14

את מלך בבל
ואל תשמעו אל דברי הנבאים האמרים אליכם לאמר לא תעבדו את מלך בבל

כי שקר הם נבאים לכם 15 כי לא שלחתים נאם ה׳ והם נבאים בשמי לשקר
כי שקר הם נבאים לכם 15 כי לא שלחתים נאם ה׳ והם נבאים בשמי לשקר

למען הדיחי אתכם ואבדתם אתם והנבאים הנבאים לכם (ל)שקר שקר לכם
למען הדיחי אתכם ואבדתם אתם והנבאים הנבאים לכם

16 ואל כל העם הזה ואל הכהנים דברתי לאמר כה אמר ה׳ אל תשמעו אל
16 ואל הכהנים ואל כל העם הזה דברתי לאמר כה אמר ה׳ אל תשמעו אל

דברי נביאיכם הנבאים לכם לאמר הנה כלי בית ה׳ מושבים מבבלה
דברי נביאיכם הנבאים לכם לאמר הנה כלי בית ה׳ מושבים מבבלה עתה

כי שקר המה נבאים לכם 17
מהרה כי שקר המה נבאים לכם 17 אל תשמעו אליהם עבדו את מלך בבל

לא שלחתים 18 ואם נבאים הם ואם יש
וחיו למה תהיה העיר הזאת חרבה 18 ואם נבאים הם ואם יש

דבר ה׳ אתם יפגעו נא בי
דבר ה׳ אתם יפגעו נא בה׳ צבאות לבלתי באו הכלים הנותרים בבית ה׳

19 כי כה אמר ה׳
ובית מלך יהודה ובירושלם בבלה 19 כי כה אמר ה׳ צבאות אל העמדים

על (?) יתר הכלים 20 אשר לא
ועל הים ועל המכנות ועל יתר הכלים הנותרים בעיר הזאת 20 אשר לא

לקחם מלך בבל בגלותו את יכוניה
לקחם נבוכדנאצר מלך בבל בגלותו את יכוניה בן יהויקים מלך יהודה

מירושלם
מירושלם בבלה ואת כל חרי יהודה וירושלם 21 כי כה אמר ה׳ צבאות

22
אלהי ישראל על הכלים הנותרים בית ה׳ ובית מלך יהודה וירושלם 22

בבלה יובאו נאם ה׳
בבלה יובאו ושמה יהיו עד יום פקדי אתם נאם ה׳ והעליתים והשיבתים

אל המקום הזה

The main features of 𝔊* are also reflected in 4QJer[b,d] as illustrated in Table 2.

Table 2

4QJer^{b,d} and 𝔊 in Their Relation to 𝔐 in Jeremiah*

a. 4QJer^{b}: Jer 9:21—10:21[6]

1][21]דבר *כה נאם יהוה* ונפלה נבלת האדם כדמן על פני השדה וכעמיר מאחרי הקצר
ואין מאסף [22]כה אמר יהוה אל יתהלל חכם בחכ]מתו ואל̊ יתהל̊[ל]
2]הגבור בגבורתו אל יתהלל עשיר בעשרו [23]כי אם בזאת יתהלל המתהלל השכל וידע *אותי*
כי אני יהוה עשה חסד משפ]ט וצדקה בארץ כי
3]באלה חפצתי נאם יהוה [24]הנה ימים באים נאם יהוה ופקדתי על כל מול בערלה
[25]על מצרים ועל יהודה ועל אדום ועל בני עמון ועל מואב ועל כל]קצ̊ו̊צ̊י̊ פ̊א̊ה הישב[י]ם
4]במדבר כי כל הגוים ערלים וכל בית ישראל ערלי לב [1]שמעו את הדבר אשר
דבר יהוה עליכם בית ישראל [2]כה אמר יהוה]אל דרך הגוים
5]אל תלמדו ומאתות השמים אל תחתו כי יחתו *הגוים מהמה* [3]כי חקות העמים הבל
הוא כי עץ מיער כרתו מעשה ידי חרש במעצד [4]בכסף ובזה]ב ייפהו במקבות
6]ובמסמרות יחזקום ולא יפיק [5a]כתמר מקשה המה לא ידברו [9]כסף מרקע מתרשיש
יובא וזהב מאופז וידי צורף מעשה חכמים כלם?]ת̊כלת וארגמן
7]לבושם [5b]נשוא ינשוא כי לא יצעדו אל תיראו מהם כי לא ירעו וגם היטיב אין
אותם [11]כדנה תאמרון להום אלהיא די שמיא וארקא לא עבדו]יאבדו מן ארעא
8]ומן תחות שמיא אלה [12]עשה ארץ בכחו מכין תבל בחכמתו ובתבונתו נטה שמים
[13]לקול תתו המון מים בשמים ויעלה נשאים מק]צה א̊ר̊ץ ברקים
9]למטר עשה ויוצא רוח מאצרתיו [14]נבער כל אדם מדעת הביש כל צורף מפסל כי
שקר נסכו ולא רוח בם [15]הבל המה מעשה תעתעים]בעת פקדתים
10]יאבדו [16]לא כאלה חלק יעקב כי יוצר הכל הוא *וישראל שבט* נחלתו יהוה *צבאות* שמו
[17]אספי מארץ כנעתך יושבת במצור [18]כי כה אמר יהוה הנני קו]ל[ע] את ישב
11]הארץ *בפעם* הזאת והצרותי להם למען ימצאו [19]אוי לי על שברי נחלה מכתי
ואני אמרתי אך זה חלי ואשאנו [20]אהלי שדד וכל מיתרי נתקו בני יצא]נ̊י
12] 21
ד̊ר̊ש̊ו]

In this text 10:6-8, 10 are lacking as in 𝔊*. Also, it is probably impossible to reconstruct the order of the verses in 4QJer^{b} in any way other than that of 𝔊*, i.e., 3, 4, 5a, 9, 5b, 11. The

6 The reconstruction in the bracketed text, with a reasonable degree of certainty from the aspect of verse order, mainly follows 𝔊* and secondarily also 𝔐. Deviations from 𝔐 in small details are indicated by italics. For the diacritical marks see p. xxii. The lines of this Qumran fragment are very long (cf. p. 205).

section lacking in 4QJer^b and 𝔊* (vv. 6-8, 10) has a uniform character: it extols the Lord of Israel, while the remaining verses deride the idols of the heathen (see below).

b. Translation of the first eleven verses of chapter 10 according to 𝔐. Within this text, the verses lacking in 𝔊* and the reconstructed text of 4QJer^b are in italics (for the sequence of the verses in these texts, see above):

> [1]Hear the word which the LORD has spoken to you, O house of Israel. [2]Thus says the LORD: Do not learn to go the way of the nations, and do not be dismayed by portents in the sky; let the nations be dismayed by them. [3]For the laws of the nations are delusions. For one cuts down a tree in the forest, the work of a craftsman's hands, with an axe. [4]He adorns it with silver and gold; he fastens it with nails and hammer, so that it cannot totter. [5]They are like a scare-crow in a cucumber field, they cannot speak. They have to be carried, because they cannot walk. Be not afraid of them, for they cannot do evil, nor is it in them to do any good. [6]*There is none like You, O LORD. You are great, and Your name is great in might.* [7]*Who would not revere You, O king of the nations? For that is Your due. For among all the wise of the nations, and in all their kingdoms, there is none like You.* [8]*But they are altogether dull and foolish; the instruction of idols (?) is but wood!* [9]Beaten silver is brought from Tarshish, and gold from Uphaz, the work of a craftsman, and of the goldsmith's hands; violet and purple is their clothing; they are all the work of skilled men. [10]*But the LORD is the true God, he is a living God, and the everlasting king; at His wrath the earth trembles, and the nations cannot endure His rage.* [11]<in Aramaic> Thus shall you say to them: "The gods who did not make heaven and earth, shall perish from the earth and from under these heavens."

c. 4QJer^d: Jer 43:2-10

1 [אלהינו לאמר לא תבאו מצרים לגור ש]םׄ 3כׄיׄ בׄ[רוך] מׄסׄ[ית אתך בנ]וׄ [ל]מׄ[ען תת אתנו]
2 [ביד הכשדים להמית אתנו ולהגלות א]תנו בׅ[בל] 4[ו]לא [שמע י]וחנן [וכל] שרי הח[יל]םׄ וׄכל
3 [העם בקול יהוה לשבת בארץ יהודה *vac*] 5וׄיׄקׄ[ח יו]חׄנן [וכל ש]רׄי הׄ[ח]ילם את כלׄ שארית
4 [יהודה אשר שבו מכל הגוים אש]רׄ [נדחו]שׄם 6אׄת הגבריׄםׄ[ו]אׄת הנש[י]ם ואת הטף ואת בנות
5 [המלך ואת כל הנפש אשר הני]ח נבוזרדן את גדליהו בן אחיקם ואת ירמיהו הנביא
6 [ואת ברוך בן נריהו 7ויבאו א]רץ מצרים כי לא שמעו בקול יהוה [ו]יבאוׄ תחפחס
7 [8ויהי דבר יהוה אל ירמיהו] בתחפנחס לאמר 9קח בידך אבנים גדלות וטמנתם
8 [ ] אשר בפתח בתחפנחס לעיני אנׄשים יהודים *vacat*
9 [10ואמרת כה אמר יהוה צבאות אלהי ישראל הנני שלח ולקחתי את נבוכדראצר מ]ל[ך

In Jer 43:2–10, 4QJer^{d} reflects the same short text as 𝔊* (50:2-9), especially in proper nouns, as illustrated in the following comparative table. In this table the short text of 4QJer^{d} and 𝔊* is presented in the lefthand column, and the longer text of 𝔐 𝔗 𝔖 𝔙 in the righthand column. In the righthand column the minuses of 𝔊* vis-à-vis 𝔐 𝔗 𝔖 𝔙 are printed in italics.

43:4,5	4QJer^{d} 𝔊*	Johanan	𝔐 𝔗 𝔖 𝔙	Johanan *son of Kareah*
6	4QJer^{d} 𝔊*	Nebuzaradan	𝔐 𝔗 𝔖 𝔙	Nebuzaradan *the chief of the guards*
6	4QJer^{d} 𝔊*	Gedaliah son of Ahikam	𝔐 𝔗 𝔖 𝔙	Gedaliah son of Ahikam, *son of Shaphan*

2. *Two Literary Strata of Joshua: 𝔐 𝔗 𝔖 𝔙 and 𝔊**

A.G. Auld, "Textual and Literary Studies in the Book of Joshua," *ZAW* 90 (1978) 412-417; idem, "The 'Levitical Cities'—Texts and History," *ZAW* 91 (1979) 194–206; idem, "The Cities in Joshua 21—The Contribution of Textual Criticism," *Textus* 15 (1990) 141-152; M. Fishbane, "Biblical Colophons, Textual Criticism and Legal Analogies," *CBQ* 42 (1980) 438-449; M. Gaster, "The Samaritan Book of Joshua and the Septuagint," *PSBA* 31 (1909) 115-127, 149-153; L. Mazor, "The Origin and Evolution of the Curse upon the Rebuilder of Jericho—A Contribution of Textual Criticism to Biblical Historiography," *Textus* 14 (1988) 1-26; H.M. Orlinsky, "The Hebrew *Vorlage* of the Septuagint of the Book of Joshua," *VTSup* 17 (1969) 187-195; A. Rofé, "Joshua 20—Historico-Literary Criticism Illustrated," in: Tigay, *Models*, 131-147; E. Tov, "The Growth of the Book of Joshua in the Light of the Evidence of the LXX Translation," *ScrHier* 31 (1986) 321-339; E. Ulrich, "4QJoshua^{a} and Joshua's First Altar in the Promised Land," in: G. J. Brooke with F. García Martínez (eds.), *New Qumran Texts and Studies* (Studies on the Texts of the Desert of Judah 15; Leiden/New York/Köln 1994) 89-104.

The Greek translation of this book contains material of unusual interest from a literary point of view. Some of its elements are shorter than 𝔐 𝔗 𝔖 𝔙 (below, section *a*), others are longer (*b*), and again others display a different sequence (section *c*). It has been suggested by various scholars (see Auld*, Rofé*, Tov*, Mazor*) that two different literary strata are involved, with 𝔊* probably being the more ancient stratum. 4QJosh^{a} represents yet a third independent text (below section 13).

Because of the paucity of external criteria on which to base a position regarding the nature of 𝔊, one must turn to the translation itself. From the outset there is no reason to assume that the translator would have made such extensive changes as recorded here. Although the translation of Joshua is not as literal as that of Jeremiah (see above, section *1*), the degree of limited freedom in this translation does not allow us to draw the conclusion that the translator would have made these changes. This position is supported by the shorter text of Josh 8:14-18 (similar to 𝔊) in 4QJosh^{a}, frg. 18 (cf. Ulrich*).

a. The Short Text of 𝔊 versus the Long Text of 𝔐 𝔗 𝔖 𝔙*

The text of 𝔊* lacks many elements found in 𝔐 𝔗 𝔖 𝔙, altogether amounting to some 4 to 5 percent of the whole book. Most of these pertain to short elements, and they can be subdivided into small elucidations, harmonizing additions, contextual additions, theological corrections, and deuteronomistic phrases (see Tov*). While the possibility of the translator's omissions should not be ruled out, the textual evidence taken in its entirety makes it likely that 𝔐 𝔗 𝔖 𝔙 present an expanded literary stratum. Therefore, the minuses of 𝔊* should probably be presented as pluses of 𝔐 𝔗 𝔖 𝔙. In the examples which follow the elements in parentheses are lacking in 𝔊.

Josh 1:1 𝔐 ויהי אחרי מות משה (עבד יהוה) (= 𝔗 𝔖 𝔙)
𝔊* After the death of Moses (*the servant of the* LORD) . . .

For similar minuses of this formula in 𝔊*, see 1:15 (below) and 22:4. For other deuteronomistic phrases lacking in 𝔊*, see 1:11; 4:10; 24:17.

Josh 2:15 𝔐 ותורדם בחבל בעד החלון (כי ביתה בקיר החומה ובחומה היא יושבת) (= 𝔗 𝔖 𝔙)
𝔊* She let them down by a rope through the window (*for her dwelling was at the outer side of the city wall and she lived in the actual wall*).

The secondary character of the plus in 𝔐 𝔗 𝔖 𝔙 as an exegetical addition is assumed by several scholars.[7]

Some of the additions are formulated as *afterthoughts*.

Josh 1:15 𝔐 ושבתם לארץ ירשתכם (וירשתם אותה) אשר נתן לכם משה (עבד יהוה)
𝔊* Then you may return to your inherited land (*and you shall take possession of it*) which Moses (*the servant of the* LORD) gave unto you.

The first element lacking in 𝔊*, and thus actually serving as a plus in 𝔐, is a clear addition in the text, disturbing its syntax.

Josh 4:10 𝔐 והכהנים נשאי הארון עמדים בתוך הירדן עד תם כל הדבר אשר צוה יהוה את יהושע לדבר אל העם (ככל אשר צוה משה את יהושע)
𝔊* The priests who bore the Ark remained standing in the middle of the Jordan until all the instructions that the LORD had ordered

7 For a discussion, see Tov*, 333-334.

> Joshua to convey to the people had been carried out (*just as Moses had ordered Joshua*).

According to the short formulation of 𝔊*, Joshua's actions closely followed the command of God, while the plus of 𝔐, possibly deriving from v. 12, 11:15, or from Deut 3:28, stressed that the command was by Moses.

Among the shorter elements of 𝔊*, those of chapter 20 deserve special attention, since in that chapter the Greek text is much shorter than that of 𝔐 𝔗 𝔖 𝔙. In that chapter, Joshua is commanded to designate the cities of refuge subsequent to previous commands given to Moses on the same matter—see the regulations in this regard in the Priestly code (Num 35:9-34) and in Deuteronomy (19:1-13). Likewise, Deut 4:41-43 relates the designation by Moses of cities on the east side of the Jordan. Since there are two parallel sets of regulations for the cities of refuge in the Pentateuch, the question arises as to which set of regulations is reflected in Joshua 20, that of the Priestly code or that of Deuteronomy. This question is further complicated by the fact that 𝔊* and the Samaritan text of Joshua (see Gaster*) reflect a shorter text, as illustrated by Table 3.

Table 3

The Minuses of 𝔊 in Josh 20:1-6*

The text which follows presents 𝔐, in which the minuses of 𝔊*, printed in italics, are enclosed in parentheses, while the pluses of 𝔊* (for which cf. Numbers 35) are printed in smaller typeface.

> 1Then the LORD said to Joshua: 2"Speak to the Israelites, 'Designate the cities of refuge, of which I spoke to you through Moses, 3to which a manslayer who kills a person by mistake (*unintentionally*) may flee; they, the cities, shall serve you as a refuge, and the manslayer will not die from the blood avenger. (*4He shall flee to one of those cities, present himself at the entrance to the city gate, and plead his case before the elders of that city; then they shall admit him into the city, and give him a place, in which to live among them. 5And if the blood avenger pursues him, they shall not hand the manslayer over to him; because he killed the other person without intent, having had no enmity against him in the past. 6He shall live in that city*) until he can stand trial before the congregation (*until the death of the high priest who is in office at that time; thereafter the manslayer may go back to his own town and his own home, to the town from which he fled.'"*)

A comparison of the two texts shows that they are *recensionally* different, with the long text developing from the short one. 𝔐 𝔗 𝔖 𝔙 of

Joshua 20 is written in two different styles: *grosso modo* the section lacking in 𝔊 (the greater part of vv. 4-6 and the phrase בבלי דעת, "unintentionally," in v. 3) reflects the content and style of the book of Deuteronomy, whereas the rest of the chapter reflects the style and content of Numbers 35 (the Priestly code). For example, compare בשגגה, "by mistake," in v. 3 found in the priestly law (Num 35:11) with the immediately adjacent phrase בבלי דעת, "unintentionally," also found in Deut 19:4 (this phrase appears only in Deuteronomy and Josh 20:3). For a detailed discussion of the vocabulary of this passage, see Rofé* and Fishbane*.

It is suggested that the short text reflected in 𝔊* and formulated according to Numbers 35 reflects an early literary layer of this chapter. This assumption is supported by the internal tension between this layer and the layer of the additions in the long text of 𝔐 𝔗 𝔖 𝔙. The layer of additions of 𝔐 𝔗 𝔖 𝔙 in Joshua contains words and sections from Deuteronomy 19 which are meant to adapt the earlier layer to Deuteronomy—an assumption which is not surprising regarding the book of Joshua, whose present shape displays a deuteronomistic revision elsewhere in the book. The additions in chapter 20 caused an internal contradiction which further support this assumption: according to v. 4 (the long text of 𝔐 𝔗 𝔖 𝔙 and not of 𝔊*), the manslayer is received into the city of refuge as one who is recognized as having killed by mistake and who thus becomes a legally acceptable refugee. His acceptance into the city of refuge is based upon the considered opinion of the elders of the city, who heard his version of the incident (vv. 4-5). On the other hand, according to the continuation of the text in v. 6 (common to 𝔐 𝔗 𝔖 𝔙 and 𝔊*), the man-slayer has yet to be brought to trial ("until he can stand trial before the congregation"). In the short text of 𝔊*, in which v. 4 is lacking, this tension does not exist.

b. A Plus of 𝔊—The Transition between Joshua and Judges*

H.N. Rösel, "Die Überlieferungen vom Josua- ins Richterbuch," *VT* 30 (1980) 342-350, esp. 348-349; A. Rofé, "The End of the Book of Joshua according to the Septuagint," *Henoch* 4 (1982) 17-36.

It is characteristic for 𝔊* in Joshua to present a shorter text than 𝔐. It does, however, also present some significant pluses to 𝔐 which bear all the marks of originality, especially visible in their Hebraic diction. Of these, note 16:10 (cf. 1 Kgs 9:16 [5:14b 𝔊]); 19:47,48; 21:42 (cf. 19:49-50; 5:2-3); 24:30 (cf. 5:2-3); and the following case.

At the end of Josh 24:33 𝔊* adds a section which may reflect an earlier stage in the development of the Hebrew book.

> ἐν ἐκείνῃ τῇ ἡμέρᾳ λαβόντες οἱ υἱοὶ Ισραηλ τὴν κιβωτὸν τοῦ θεοῦ περιεφέροσαν ἐν ἑαυτοῖς, καὶ Φινεες ἱεράτευσεν ἀντὶ Ελεαζαρ τοῦ πατρὸς αὐτοῦ, ἕως ἀπέθανεν καὶ κατωρύγη ἐν Γαβααν τῇ ἑαυτοῦ. οἱ δὲ υἱοὶ Ισραηλ ἀπήλθοσαν ἕκαστος εἰς τὸν τόπον αὐτῶν καὶ εἰς τὴν ἑαυτῶν πόλιν. καὶ ἐσέβοντο οἱ υἱοὶ Ισραηλ τὴν Ασταρτην καὶ Ασταρωθ καὶ τοὺς θεοὺς τῶν ἐθνῶν τῶν κύκλῳ αὐτῶν. καὶ παρέδωκεν αὐτοὺς κύριος εἰς χεῖρας Εγλωμ τῷ βασιλεῖ Μωαβ, καὶ ἐκυρίευσεν αὐτῶν ἔτη δέκα ὀκτώ.
>
> On that day the children of Israel took the Ark of God and carried it about among them; and Phinees exercised the priest's office, instead of Eleazar his father till he died, and he was buried in his own place Gibeah, and the children of Israel departed every one to his place, and to his own city. And the children of Israel worshiped Astarte and Astaroth, and the gods of the nations round about them; and the LORD delivered them into the hands of Eglon king of Moab and he ruled over them eighteen years.

The Hebraic diction of this passage allows for a relatively reliable reconstruction of the Greek text into Hebrew. The asterisks indicate problematic details.

> ביום ההוא לקחו בני ישראל את ארון האלהים ויסבו/וישאו בתוכם*. ויכהן* פנחס תחת אלעזר אביו עד מותו* ויקָבר/ויקברו אתו בגבעה אשר לו. וילכו* בני ישראל איש למקומו ולעירו. ויעבדו בני ישראל את העשתרת ואת העשתרות ואת אלהי העמים אשר סביבותיהם. ויתנם ה׳ ביד עגלון מלך מואב וימשל בם שמנה עשרה שנה*

The text of 𝔐 𝔗 𝔖 𝔙 of Joshua 24 contains no parallel to this passage, but its components can be found in other places: for the first part cf. Josh 24:33 and Judg 2:9 and for the continuation cf. Judg 2:6,11-14; 3:12,14.

Rofé* demonstrated that this passage did indeed once exist in a Hebrew form in one of the early stages of the book of Joshua and that its components would have suited the original form of a combined book of Joshua and Judges. The addition is made up of elements known from other verses in Joshua and Judges, but the most remarkable aspect of this addition is that its last phrase mentions the beginning of the story of Ehud in Judg 3:12ff. It was therefore suggested that in this addition 𝔊* preserves an ancient tradition according to which the books Joshua and Judges formed one composition in the middle of which the aforementioned section would have appeared. The sequence in this earlier version of Joshua-Judges thus was (according to the verses in 𝔐):

Joshua 24, the aforementioned plus of 𝔊*, the story of Ehud in Judg 3:12ff. and the remainder of the book of Judges.

As a supporting argument for this assumption Rofé* asserted that the entire section comprising Judg 1:1—3:11 in all textual witnesses appears to be secondary. It contains (a) a collection of stories on the conquest of the land and on the failure to dispossess its inhabitants (chapter 1) which runs parallel to the book of Joshua, (b) a presumably late editorial introduction to the book of Judges as a whole (2:1—3:6), and (c) the story of the judge Othniel (3:7-11) whose character is not clearly delineated. Presumably Judg 1:1—3:11 was added in the earlier edition and at the same time, the section which is now a plus in 𝔊*, was omitted in 𝔐 𝔗 𝔖 𝔙 from the end of chapter 24, probably for ideological reasons (thus Rofé*). This view was not accepted by Rösel*, who considers the addition of 𝔊* as secondary.

c. A Significant Difference in Sequence

In chapters 8–9 𝔊* differs significantly from the sequence of 𝔐 𝔗 𝔖 𝔙. The order of the events in 𝔊* is as follows:

1. The conquest of Ai (8:1-29).
2. A summarizing notice (9:1-2): "[1]When all the kings west of the Jordan—in the hill country, in the Shephelah and along the entire coast of the Mediterranean Sea up to the vicinity of Lebanon, the <land of the> Hittites, Amorites, Canaanites, Perizzites, Hivites, and Jebusites learned of this, [2]they gathered with one accord to fight against Joshua and Israel."
3. The building of the altar (8:30-35).
4. The cunning of the Gibeonites (9:3ff.).

It is also possible to represent the differences between the two traditions in terms of a difference in the position of the section on the building of the altar (8:30-35). This section is secondary in its context for it does not have any clear connection with the surrounding verses. אז, "at that time," in 8:30 forms only an external connection, and the entire section is based on Deuteronomy 27 as well as the terminology of that book in general. It is possible, therefore, that this section was added at a later period in different places within the framework of the deuteronomistic editing of Joshua (see p. 169): in 𝔐 𝔗 𝔖 𝔙 before 9:1-2 and in 𝔊* after these verses. Although there is no basic difference between these two traditions, it seems that the position of 9:1-2 in 𝔊* is the more plausible, for here it forms a conclusion to the outcome of the preceding action according to the order of the verses (the conquest of Ai, 8:1-29). In any event, the two traditions differ recensionally (cf. section 13 below). For other differences in sequence, see below, section 8.

3. *Two Literary Strata of Ezekiel:* 𝔐 𝔗 𝔖 𝔙 *and* 𝔊*

P.-M. Bogaert, "Les deux rédactions conservées (LXX et TM) d'Ezéchiel 7," in: Lust*, *op. cit.* (p. 313) 21-47; K.S. Freedy, "The Glosses in Ezekiel i-xxiv," *VT* 20 (1970) 129-152; J. Lust, "Ezekiel 36-40 in the Oldest Greek Manuscript," *CBQ* 43 (1981) 517-533; idem, "The Use of Textual Witnesses for the Establishment of the Text—The Shorter and Longer Texts of Ezekiel, An Example: Ez 7," in: Lust* (p. 313) 7-20; E. Tov, "Recensional Differences between the MT and LXX of Ezekiel," *ETL* 62 (1986) 89-101.

The situation in Ezekiel resembles that in Joshua, since in both books 𝔊* contains a text which reflects both a slightly shorter version than 𝔐 𝔗 𝔖 𝔙 (by 4 to 5 percent) and additional recensional differences. In Ezekiel the recensional rewriting is not extensive; it is extant in chapter 7 only (cf. Table 7 on p. 348). In vv. 3–9 of that chapter the content and order of the verses in the Hebrew source of 𝔊* differ from that of 𝔐 𝔗 𝔖 𝔙.

The Greek translation of Ezekiel is relatively literal, so that it is reasonable to assume that its minuses vis-à-vis 𝔐 𝔗 𝔖 𝔙 reflect a shorter Hebrew parent text. This shorter text was slightly expanded in 𝔐 𝔗 𝔖 𝔙 by various types of elements. These may be subdivided (see Tov*) into explicative-exegetical, harmonizing, emphasis, parallel words, and new material, to be exemplified below (the words in parentheses are lacking in 𝔊*). Some of the plus elements contain deuteronomistic formulations (cf. p. 169). Most of them are explicative-exegetical, for example,

Ezek 1:22 𝔐 כעין הקרח (הנורא)
with an (*awe-inspiring*) gleam as of ice

Ezek 3:18 𝔐 להזהיר רשע מדרכו (הרשעה)
to warn the wicked man of his (*wicked*) course

Ezek 8:3 𝔐 אל פתח שער (הפנימית)
to the entrance of the (*inner*) gate[8]

Scholars often present the plus elements of 𝔐 in Ezekiel as *glosses* (*interpolations* would have been a better term)—see the views of Rost*, Herrmann*, Fohrer*, Freedy*, and Dijkstra* (p. 275) and the discussion on pp. 282–284. This view, however, is less likely because of the large number of these elements and because of the occurrence of parallel elements and synonymous words among the pluses of 𝔐 (as in the first three examples) and new material (the last two examples).[9] E.g.,

Ezek 5:14 𝔐 ואתנך לחרבה (ולחרפה) בגוים אשר סביבותיך (= 𝔗 𝔖 𝔙)
I will turn you into a ruin (*and a reproach*)
among the nations that are around you.

---

8 The addition in 𝔐 is inappropriate in the present context. "It is premature in terms of the itinerary of the divine tour as represented by this stage in the narrative" (Freedy*, 138).

9 See the discussion on pp. 283–284.

For a similar situation, see Jer 49:13 . . . כי לשמה לחרפה (לחרב), where the word in parenthesis is lacking in 𝔊.

Ezek 5:15	𝔐	בעשותי בך שפטים (באף ובחמה) ובתכחות חמה (= 𝔗 𝔖 𝔙) when I execute judgments against you (*in anger and in fury*) and by chastisements of fury.[10]
Ezek 6:6	𝔐	. . . מזבחותיכם ונשברו (ונשבתו) (= 𝔗 𝔖 𝔙) . . . your altars, and shall be ruined (*and shall be desolate*)
New material:		
Ezek 16:13	𝔐	ותיפי במאד מאד (ותצלחי למלוכה) (= 𝔗 𝔖 𝔙) You were very very beautiful (*fit to be a queen*).
Ezek 20:28	𝔐	ויראו כל גבעה רמה וכל עץ עבת ויזבחו שם את זבחיהם (ויתנו שם כעס קרבנם) (= 𝔗 𝔖 𝔙) They saw every high hill and every leafy tree, and there they made their sacrifices. (*There they placed their vexatious offerings.*)

In accordance with the discussion on pp. 282–284, the plus elements of 𝔐 should be taken in their totality as representative of a literary layer, added in the edition of 𝔐 to a shorter and earlier edition as represented by 𝔊.

*4. Two Literary Strata in 1 Samuel 16-18: 𝔐 𝔗 𝔖 𝔙 and 𝔊**

D. Barthélemy, D. Gooding, J. Lust, E. Tov, *The Story of David and Goliath, Textual and Literary Criticism* (OBO 73; Fribourg/Göttingen 1986); J. Lust, "The Story of David and Goliath in Hebrew and Greek," *ETL* 59 (1983) 5-25; S. Pisano, S.J., *Additions or Omissions in the Books of Samuel—The Significant Pluses and Minuses in the Massoretic, LXX and Qumran Texts* (OBO 57; Freiburg/Göttingen 1984); A. Rofé, "The Battle of David and Goliath—Folklore, Theology, Eschatology," in: J. Neusner et al., *Judaic Perspectives on Ancient Israel* (Philadelphia 1987) 117–151; E. Tov, "The Composition of 1 Samuel 16-18 in the Light of the Septuagint Version," in: Tigay, *Models*, 97-130; J. Trebolle, "The Story of David and Goliath (1 Sam 17-18): Textual Variants and Literary Composition," *BIOSCS* 23 (1990) 16-30.

In 1 Samuel 16-18, mainly containing the story of David and Goliath, two literary strata are visible in 𝔊* on the one hand and 𝔐 𝔗 𝔖 𝔙 on the other. This understanding may have repercussions for an analysis of the relation between those witnesses elsewhere in 1-2 Samuel (see section *10* below and pp. 113–114, 175–176).

The story of David and Goliath in 𝔊* is much shorter than that in 𝔐 𝔗 𝔖 𝔙: it lacks 39 of the 88 verses (44 percent of the entire story),

---

10 Cf. Deut 29:27 where באף ובחמה occur in a similar context.

including complete sections: 17:12-31, 41, 48b, 50, 55-58; 18:1-6a, 10-11, 12b, 17-19, 21b, 29b-30. Scholars are divided over the possible explanations for the nature of 𝔊*. While some claim that the translator omitted sections with the intention of smoothing over problems in 𝔐 𝔗 𝔖 𝔙, others are of the opinion that he found before him a short version of the story differing *recensionally* from 𝔐.

Since there is no external evidence (such as ancient Hebrew texts) which could support the assumed existence of a short Hebrew text, the nature of 𝔊* can be explained solely on the basis of an analysis of its translation character. According to Tov*, this translation unit reflects a literal method of translation, and, therefore, one cannot attribute to the translator the intention of abridging his source to such a great extent. In addition to this, the alternative explanation cannot stand in the face of criticism, since in the short version of 𝔊* there also remain problems in the text.

According to Barthélemy*, Gooding*, and Rofé*, this short Hebrew text, known to the translator and translated faithfully by him, was created at an earlier stage as an abridgement of a longer Hebrew text like 𝔐 𝔗 𝔖 𝔙.

On the other hand, according to Tov* and Lust*, 𝔊* reflects a short version of the story of the encounter between David and Goliath, which stands as a literary unit in its own right. In fact, the short version found in 𝔊* is more natural than that of 𝔐 𝔗 𝔖 𝔙 since it lacks the double accounts of the latter. This short version of the story, found both in 𝔊* and in 𝔐 𝔗 𝔖 𝔙, is called here version I. In 𝔐 𝔗 𝔖 𝔙 version II, i.e., the verses lacking in 𝔊* and constituting a separate and parallel version, have been added to this story. Both versions of the story of David and Goliath contain several parallel elements which are not linked by what we would name cross-references: David is introduced twice to Saul (17:17-23; 17:55-58), he is twice appointed as an officer in Saul's army (18:5,13), and on two occasions Saul offers the hand of one of his daughters to David in marriage (Merab, 18:17-19; Michal, 18:20-27). The two versions, however, are not completely parallel, for version I is fuller than version II. The content of both versions is presented in Table 4.

Table 4

The Two Versions of the Story of David and Goliath

	version I (𝔊 and 𝔐 𝔗 𝔖 𝔙)*	*version II (𝔐 𝔗 𝔖 𝔙 only)*
16:17-23	David is introduced to Saul as a skilful harper and he is made one of his arms-bearers.	

17:1-11	Preparations for a fight by the Philistines. Goliath suggests a duel with one of the Israelites.	
17:12-31		David is sent by his father to bring food to his brothers at the front. He hears Goliath and desires to meet him in a duel.
17:32-39	David volunteers to fight with Goliath.	
17:40-54	The duel. After Goliath's miraculous fall, the Philistines flee.	Short account of the duel (vv. 41, 48b, 50).
17: 55-58		Saul asks who David is. David is introduced to Saul by Abner.
18:1-4		David and Jonathan make a covenant.
18:5-6a		David is appointed as an officer in Saul's army.
18:6b-9	Saul's jealousy of David.	
18:10-11		Saul attempts in vain to kill David.
18:12-16	David's successes.	
18:17-19		Saul offers David his eldest daughter, Merab.
18:20-29a	Saul offers David his daughter Michal. Saul is afraid of David.	
18:29b-30		Saul's enmity for David. David's successes.

The editor of 𝔐 𝔗 𝔖 𝔙—who joined version II to version I—apparently with the intention of preserving a parallel ancient story, failed to take into consideration the contradictions that were caused by the combination of the two stories. Of these double traditions, which are apparent from an examination of Table 4, the most significant is that found in 17:55-58. In these verses Saul enquires about the identity of David, although the latter is already recorded as having been introduced to him at the end of the previous chapter (see in particular 16:21 "He <Saul> took a strong liking to him and made him one of his arms-bearers.").

5. *Two Parallel Editions of Proverbs:* 𝔐 𝔗 𝔖 𝔙 *and* 𝔊

E. Tov, "Recensional Differences between the Masoretic Text and the Septuagint of Proverbs, " in: H.W. Attridge et al., eds., *Of Scribes and Scrolls, Studies on the Hebrew Bible, Intertestamental Judaism, and Christian Origins Presented to J. Strugnell* (College Theology Society Resources in Religion 5; Lanham, MD 1990) 43–56.

Beyond the freedom of 𝔊's translation of Proverbs, one discerns in the translation editorial features recognizable in its differences in order, minuses, and pluses, all differing from 𝔐 𝔗 𝔖 𝔙. The main difference in order pertains to chapters 24–31, which appear in 𝔊 according to the following order, denoted according to the verse and chapter numbers of 𝔐.

24:1-22	
30:1-14	("The words of Agur"—part one)
24:23-34	("These are also by the Sages")
30:15-33	("The words of Agur"—part two)
31:1-9	("The words of Lemuel"—part one)
25–29	
31:10-31	("The words of Lemuel"—part two)

Many verses, such as 4:7; 8:33; 16:1,3; 20:14-19, are lacking in the translation. Likewise, many verses have been added, though only some of them are based on a different Hebrew original. For further details, see Tov*.

6. *Different Chronological Systems in* 𝔐 𝔗 𝔖 𝔙 *and* 𝔊 *in Genesis*

Hendel, *Genesis 1-11*, 49-62; R.W. Klein, "Archaic Chronologies and the Textual History of the OT," *HTR* 67 (1974) 255-263; A. Klostermann, *NKZ* 5 (1894) 208-247 = *Der Pentateuch* (2d ed.; Leipzig 1907); G. Larsson, "The Chronology of the Pentateuch—A Comparison of MT and LXX," *JBL* 102 (1983) 401-409; J. Skinner, *Genesis* (ICC; 2d ed.; Edinburgh 1930) 134, 167, 233.

In Genesis, 𝔪 and 𝔊 (albeit with differences between them) on the one hand, and 𝔐 𝔗 𝔖 𝔙 on the other hand, differ systematically in their presentation of chronological data, especially in chapters 5, 8, and 11. These discrepancies ultimately derived from differences in outlook. The data are presented in tables presented by Skinner* and Hendel* and discussed in detail by Klein*, Larsson*, and Hendel*. According to Klein*, the systems of 𝔐 , 𝔊, and 𝔪 derived from an earlier tradition, changed in all three sources. On the other hand, Larsson* defended the relative priority of 𝔐, while earlier Klostermann* had defended the priority of the system of 𝔊, which, according to him, was based on Hebrew sources.[11]

7. *Different Chronological Systems in 𝔐 𝔗 𝔖 𝔙 and 𝔊 in Kings*

C.F. Burney, *Notes on the Hebrew Text of the Books of Kings* (Oxford 1903; repr. New York 1970) xx-xxxi; R.W. Klein, "Archaic Chronologies and the Textual History of the OT," *HTR* 67 (1974) 255-263; J.D. Shenkel, *Chronology and Recensional Development in the Greek Text of Kings* (HSM 1; Cambridge, MA 1968); H. Tadmor, "Krwnwlwgyh," *EncBib* 4 (Jerusalem 1962) 245-310; E.R. Thiele, *The Mysterious Numbers of the Hebrew Kings* (Chicago 1951).

The extensive chronological differences with regard to synchronisms and the counting of the years of the divided monarchy between 𝔐 𝔗 𝔖 𝔙 and 𝔊 in Kings, listed by Burney*, were given a detailed discussion by Thiele* and Shenkel*. These differences mainly cover the periods between Omri and Joram, kings of Israel and Jehoshaphat and Ahaziah, kings of Judah. According to Shenkel and several other scholars,[12] the chronological system underlying 𝔊 has been altered to the system now reflected in 𝔐, and the differences between these systems are possibly rooted in the different understanding of the background of 2 Kings 3 (thus Shenkel*, 87ff.).[13]

Also in other details 𝔊 in 1-2 Kings (3-4 Reigns) differs recensionally from 𝔐 𝔗 𝔖 𝔙.[14]

8. *Differences in Sequence between 𝔐 𝔗 𝔖 𝔙 and 𝔊*

E. Tov, "Some Sequence Differences between the MT and LXX and Their Ramifications for the Literary Criticism of the Bible," *JNSL* 13 (1987) 151-160.

---

11 Previously E. Preuss, *Die Zeitrechnung der Septuaginta vor dem vierten Jahr Salomo's* (Berlin 1859) had ascribed these differences to the translator.

12 See J.M. Miller, "The Elisha Cycle and the Accounts of the Omride Wars," *JBL* 85 (1966) 441-454; idem, "Another Look at the Chronology of the Early Divided Monarchy," *JBL* 86 (1967) 267-288; Klein, *Textual Criticism*, 36-46; W.R. Wifall, Jr., "The Chronology of the Divided Monarchy," *ZAW* 80 (1968) 319-337; S.J. De Vries, "Chronology, OT," *IDBSup*, 161-166.

13 On the other hand, Gooding (cf. n. 1) ascribes all of these differences to midrashic tendencies in the translation.

14 See J.C. Trebolle Barrera, *Jehú y Joás. Texto y composición literaria de 2 Reyes 9-11* (Institución San Jeronimo 17; Valencia 1984); idem, "From the 'Old Latin' through the 'Old Greek' to the 'Old Hebrew' (2 Kings 10,23-25," *Textus* 11 (1984) 17-36; idem, "La primitiva confesión de fe yahvista (1 Re 18,36-37). De la crítica textual a la teología bíblica," *Salmanticensis* 31 (1984) 181-205; idem, "Old Latin, Old Greek and Old Hebrew in the Book of Kings (1 Ki. 18:27 and 2 Ki. 20:11)," *Textus* 13 (1986) 85-94; idem, "Le texte de 2 Rois 7,20—8,5 à la lumière des découvertes de Qumrân (6Q4 15)," *RQ* 13 (1988) 561-568. See further the discussion of transpositions in 1 Kings on p. 340.

Differences in sequence between 𝔐 𝔗 𝔖 𝔙 and 𝔊 are mentioned above with regard to the books of Jeremiah (section *1*), Joshua (2), Ezekiel (3), and Proverbs (5). That such differences may point to recensional differences elsewhere has been suggested by Tov*. Differences in sequence often concern sections (short as well as long ones), whose position had not yet been fixed in the various traditions because of their secondary nature. These sections were added to the text at a relatively late period, and because of uncertainty over their position, were inserted in different places in 𝔐 𝔗 𝔖 𝔙 and the Hebrew *Vorlage* of 𝔊. This uncertainty pertains to the aforementioned sections, as well as to additional ones.

α.

In 𝔊 the order of the verses in Num 10:34-36 differs from 𝔐 𝔗 𝔖 𝔙—35, 36, 34—as is apparent in the translation which follows. Unless otherwise denoted, the translation follows 𝔐 in matters of detail, but not in sequence.

35 When *the* Ark was to set out, Moses would say:
Advance, O LORD!
May Your enemies be scattered,
And *all* (𝔊) Your foes flee before You!
36 And when it halted, he would say:
Return, O LORD,
the myriads of thousands *in* (𝔊) Israel!
34 And the cloud (𝔊) kept above them by day, as they moved on from the camp.

The sequence of 𝔊*, in which v. 35, referring to *the* Ark, comes immediately after v. 33, where the Ark is also mentioned in this connection, is possibly more natural. On the other hand, in 𝔐 𝔗 𝔖 𝔙 verse 34 comes between the two. The two different sequences were created by the late addition in different places of the "Song of the Ark" (vv. 35-36), which originally was not included in its present place. According to the Masorah, this song indeed constitutes a separate unit belonging "elsewhere"—see the marking of the inverted *nunim* both before and after the song (cf. p. 55).

Other examples are mentioned in brief:

β. Chapters *20* and *21* of 1 Kings appear in 𝔊 in the reverse order. This order possibly stems from the secondary character of chapter 21 (the story of Naboth's vineyard).[15]

γ. Solomon's blessing at the dedication of the Temple (*1 Kgs 8:12-13*) appears in 𝔊* after v. 53, following Solomon's blessing in prose (vv. 14-21) and his prayer, both of which are deuteronomistic additions in the context (see p. 169).

δ. *Jer 23:7-8* appear in 𝔊* after v. 40, i.e., after the unit comprising vv. 9-40, which entirely deals with one subject, viz., prophets—note the title to the entire unit in 23:9, לנבאים, "Concerning the prophets." The position of this unit was probably not fixed.

9. Different Stages of the Development of the Parallel Accounts in 2 Kings 20 and Isaiah 38

S. Talmon, "The Textual Study of the Bible—A New Outlook," in: Cross–Talmon, *QHBT*, 328-332; Y. Zakovitch, "Assimilation in Biblical Narratives," in: Tigay, *Models*, 175-196.

1QIsa[a] *may* reflect different stages of the development of a story known from two parallel texts in the following way.

In the order of the events in 𝔐 and the other textual witnesses of 2 Kgs 20:1-11, one detects a flaw: according to vv. 1-6 Hezekiah falls ill and Isaiah passes on to him a promise from God (v. 5):

> "I am going to heal you; on the third day you shall go up to the House of the LORD."

In the continuation, however, Hezekiah asks (v. 8):

> "What is the sign that the LORD will heal me and that I shall go up to the House of the LORD on the third day?"

Thus according to v. 8 Hezekiah is not yet healed, while the preceding verse (7) reports that he has already been healed.

> "Then Isaiah said, 'Get a cake of figs.' And they got one, and they applied it to the rash, and he *recovered*."

There are also other reasons why this verse is not appropriate to the context.[16] Therefore, it would seem that v. 7 is a secondary element in

---

15 See A. Rofé, "The Vineyard of Naboth—The Origin and Message of the Story," *VT* 38 (1988) 89-104. Alternatively, it is possible that the editor of 𝔐 or the Greek translator changed the sequence of the chapters—these possibilities are discussed in detail by D.W. Gooding, "Ahab according to the Septuagint," *ZAW* 76 (1964) 269-280.

16 The description of the cure and the content of the story differ from those of other prophetic stories and the mention of the skin disease contradicts what is said at the beginning of the story about Hezekiah's being dangerously ill. See the detailed discussion *apud* Zakovitch*.

the account in Kings and was apparently added[17] in order to adapt this account to the other prophetic stories, especially those of the Elisha cycle.

While there is no counterpart to 2 Kgs 20:7 in the parallel story in Isaiah (38:1-8), the same v. 7 of Kings, together with v. 8, *are* found somewhere else in Isaiah, viz., at the end of the chapter. Therefore, the conclusion cannot be avoided that the problematic verses 7-8 were transferred from Kings to Isaiah, where they appear in a slightly different formulation at the end of the story (Isa 38:21-22). The question in v. 22 ("What is the sign that I shall go up to the House of the LORD?"), which is not followed by an answer, betrays its secondary nature. This verse ought to have appeared in Isaiah, if at all, *before* v. 7, as in its counterpart in Kings. It is not impossible that Isa 38:21-22 were placed at their present position because of the occurrence of the phrase "the House of the LORD" in v. 20 (recurring in v. 22).

Textual analysis provides background material for the content analysis of these two chapters. The fact that Isa 38:21-22 is in the nature of an addition can still be recognized by an examination of 1QIsa^{a}, in which these two verses were added in a different hand in the open space at the end of the line, and continuing on into the margin.[18] This scroll thus preserves two stages of the book's development: the base text, which includes the short original text *and* the addition made according to the parallel story in Kings, albeit in an inappropriate position, as elsewhere in the textual witnesses. If this analysis is correct, the addition in 1QIsa^{a}, apparently from Kings, made in another hand, bears evidence of the existence of different copies of the book reflecting the various stages of the growth of the book of Isaiah.[19]

On the other hand, the short text (the first hand of the scroll) could reflect an omission by way of homoioteleuton (from the first occurrence of "the House of the LORD" to the second occurrence of that phrase), in which case the concurrence of textual and literary data would be

---

17 One wonders, however, whether the story in Kings could have existed without a conclusion such as contained in v. 7 and in Isa 38:9. If v. 7 be removed from its present place, the reader would understand that the healing of the king, which is not mentioned explicitly, is implied.

18 Linguistic arguments for the lateness of this section are adduced by Kutscher, *Language*, 444-445.

19 Harmonizing interpretations of the difficulties in the text of Isaiah are mentioned by Zakovitch*.

coincidental—for another case of parablepsis in the immediate vicinity in this scroll, see Isa 40:7-8 (see p. 239).

10. Different Stages of the Story in 1 Samuel 11

A. Catastini, "4QSam[a]: II. Nahash il 'Serpente'," *Henoch* 10 (1988) 17-42; F.M. Cross, "The Ammonite Oppression of the Tribes of Gad and Reuben: Missing Verses from 1 Samuel 11 Found in 4QSamuel[a]," in: E. Tov, ed., *The Hebrew and Greek Texts of Samuel* (Jerusalem 1980) 105-120 = H. Tadmor and M. Weinfeld, eds., *History, Historiography and Interpretation* (Jerusalem 1983) 148-158; S. Pisano* (p. 334) 91-98; A. Rofé, "The Acts of Nahash according to 4QSam[a]," *IEJ* 32 (1982) 129-133.

The original, longer text of 1 Samuel 11 is probably preserved in 4QSam[a], while the text of 𝔐 𝔗 𝔖 𝔙 is based on a scribal error, the omission of an entire section. According to this view, 4QSam[a] preserves not an early stage in the growth of the book but what appears to be the original text, which was subsequently corrupted in 𝔐 𝔗 𝔖 𝔙. The plus in the Qumran text contains the prologue to the story in 𝔐, which is now more understandable (see below). After the words "and they brought him no gift" at the end of chapter 10 of 𝔐 and after an open section (cf. p. 50), 4QSam[a] adds the section presented in Table 5 as ll. 6-9 (adapted from Cross*). The words ויהי כמחריש, "but he pretended not to mind" (NJPST), of 𝔐 𝔗 𝔖 𝔙 in 10:27 appear in 4QSam[a] at the end of the section, albeit in a different form (l. 9, above the line).

Table 5

A Large Plus in 1 Samuel 11 in 4QSam[a]

6	[ונ]חש מלך בני עמון הוא לחץ את בני גד ואת בני ראובן בחזקה ונקר להם כ[ול]
7	עין ימין ונתן אי[מה ופחד] על [י]שראל ולוא נשאר איש בבני ישראל בע[בר]
8	[הירדן אש]ר ל[וא נ]קר לו נח[ש מלך] בני עמון כול עין ימין רק שבעת אלפים איש
(sup.) 9	ויהי כמו חדש ויעל נחש העמוני ויחן על יביש [גלעד]
9	[נסו מפני] בני עמון ויבאו אל [י]בש גלעד ויאמרו כול אנשי יביש אל נחש *at*[*vac*]
10	[העמוני כרת] ל[נו ברית ונעבדך ויאמר א]ל[יה]ם נחש [העמוני בזאת] אכ[רת לכם]

The translation of the plus of 4QSam[a] is printed in cursive (ll. 6-9). The other lines represent the text of 𝔐. The supralinear addition (by the same scribe) in l. 9 was made after an initial homoioteleuton (cf. p. 238) from יבש גלעד to יביש גלעד. For the notation, see n. 6 on p. 325.

6 *[And Na]hash, king of the children of Ammon, sorely oppressed the children of Gad and the children of Reuben, and he gouged out a[ll] their*

7 *right eyes and struck ter[ror and dread] in Israel. There was not left one among the children of Israel bey[ond the]*

8 *[Jordan who]se right eye was no[t go]uged out by Naha[sh king] of the children of Ammon; except seven thousand men*

9 *[fled from] the children of Ammon and entered [J]abesh-Gilead.* (**above the line**: About a month later, Nahash the Ammonite went up and besieged Jabesh-[Gilead]) and all the men of Jabesh said to Nahash

10 [the Ammonite, "Make] with [us a covenant and we shall become your subjects."] Nahash [the Ammonite said t]o [th]em, ["After this fashion will] I make [a covenant with you] . . .

According to 𝔐 𝔗 𝔖 𝔙, the condition of Nahash for making a treaty with Jabesh-Gilead is that he would gouge everyone's right eye. This gouging out of the eyes of the men of Jabesh-Gilead, mentioned in 𝔐 𝔗 𝔖 𝔙, seems to be too brutal in its present context of the conditions for a treaty, but it is understandable as the second stage after what is related in 4QSam^{a}. The text first adds a section relating how Nahash mutilated his arch-enemies of Gad and Reuben by gouging out their eyes—this punishment for arch-enemies or rebels is well known from ancient documents (see Cross*, 114). In the light of this it is understandable why Nahash would demand the same treatment for the men of Jabesh-Gilead who had earlier escaped the mutilation.

The following data bear evidence of the originality of the plus of 4QSam^{a}.

(1) The plus was known to Josephus, *Antiquities* VI, 68-71, who also transmits in other instances a text identical to that of 4QSam^{a}, usually in presumably original readings.[20]

(2) At the beginning of the plus in the Qumran text, the king is presented as "Nahash king of the children of Ammon" (ll. 6,8), and in the continuation, as "Nahash the Ammonite" (l. 9 = 11:1 in 𝔐, and also in the next verses). This method of presenting a king first with his full title and afterwards with his shortened name is customary in the Bible (see Cross*, 111).

(3) The phrase ויהי כמו חדש, "about a month later," in l. 9, above the line, which is also reflected in Josephus and in 𝔊 at 10:27 instead of the graphically similar ויהי כמחריש, "but he pretended not to mind" (NJPST), of 𝔐 𝔗 𝔖 𝔙, is appropriate to the context of 4QSam^{a}, while the reading

20 See E. Ulrich, *The Qumran Text of Samuel and Josephus* (HSM 19; Missoula, MT 1978) 165-191.

of 𝔐 is contextually difficult, though not impossible. Note the difference in word division (cf. p. 252) and the interchange of *daleth/resh* (p. 245).

(4) In general, 4QSam^a reflects a reliable text,[21] while 𝔐 of Samuel has many corruptions—however, against this statement, see the *caveat* on pp. 298–300 cautioning against resorting to generalizations.

Above all, one should notice that the additional section in 4QSam^a is not based on any other passage in the Bible, and has no defined purpose, so that its originality seems plausible. With the help of this section one can better understand that which until now has been unclear in the text of 𝔐 and other textual witnesses. The additional section in 4QSam^a was accidentally omitted at a very early stage since it is preserved in only one witness. Its omission was probably due to the fact of its being a complete content unit which in other texts began after an open section (thus l. 5 in 4QSam^a) and closed with an open section in what is now the middle of l. 9 (see p. 50). Nevertheless, the assumption of such an omission is not without problems.[22]

11. Two Literary Strata in Judges 6

J. Trebolle Barrera, "Textual Variants in 4QJudg^a and the Textual and Editorial History of the Book of Judges," *RQ* 14 (1989) 229-245.

An entire section found in 𝔐 𝔊 𝔗 𝔖 𝔙 lacks in 4QJudg^a, viz., Judg 6:7-10, as illustrated by Table 6 (see Trebolle Barrera*). If this minus did not stem from a textual accident, such as the omission of a complete paragraph, it could reflect an earlier editing of the book, in which part of the deuteronomistic framework (see p. 169), contained here in 6:7-10, had not yet been found.

In 6:7-10 a prophet appears to the Israelites telling them that God will save them, even though they have sinned in the past. This section, in deuteronomistic diction, runs parallel with vv. 11-24, in which the angel of the LORD appeared to Gideon, similarly telling him that the Israelites will be saved. On the basis of these parallel accounts various scholars have asserted in the past that Judg 6:7-10 reflects a later

---

21 See Ulrich, ibid., 193ff. At the same time, it does contain a few contextual changes, discussed by A. Rofé, "The Nomistic Correction in Biblical Manuscripts and Its Occurrence in *4QSam^a*," *RQ* 14 (1989) 247-254.

22 Rofé* explains the addition in 4QSam^a as *midrashic*, explaining unclear details in the context, and construed on the basis of themes found elsewhere in the Bible. Likewise, Catastini* considers the Qumran text as a late Jewish reinterpretation of the biblical text. See further the previous note.

addition within the deuteronomistic layer,[23] an assumption which may now be supported by the Qumran fragment, in which it is lacking.

Table 6

The Absence of Judg 6:7-10 from 4QJudg[a]

The text below represents 𝔐. The words in cursive are lacking in 4QJudg[a].

[6]Israel was reduced to utter misery by the Midianites; and the Israelites cried out to the LORD. [7]*And it came to pass, when the Israelites cried to the LORD because of Midian,* [8]*that the LORD sent a prophet to the Israelites , who said to them: "Thus says the LORD, the God of Israel, I brought you up out of Egypt, and freed you from the house of bondage.* [9]*I rescued you from the Egyptians, and from all who oppressed you, and drove them out from before you, and gave you their land.* [10]*And I said to you, I am the LORD your God; you must not worship the gods of the Amorites, in whose land you dwell; but you did not obey Me."* [11]And an angel of the LORD came, and sat under the terebinth at Ophrah, which belonged to Joash the Abiezrite, as his son Gideon was beating out wheat inside the winepress, in order to keep it safe from the Midianites.

12. Two Literary Strata in Deuteronomy 5

A. Rofé, "Deuteronomy 5:28–6:1: Composition and Text in the Light of Deuteronomic Style and Three *Tefillin* from Qumran (4Q 128, 129, 137)," *Henoch* 7 (1985) 1-14.

The text of three *tefillin*, 4QPhyl A,B,J, as reconstructed by Rofé*, lacks Deut 5:29-30 (32-33). Their shorter text, regarded as homoioteleuton by the first editor, J.T. Milik, in *DJD* VII, is explained by Rofé* as an originally short text reflecting an earlier stage of the chapter than all other textual witnesses. In this earlier text the logical continuation of 5:28 (31) is 6:1, now interrupted in vv. 29-30 (32-33) by an admonition to preserve the commandments of the LORD (cf. 11:32 in a similar context).

13. A Different Recension of Joshua Reflected in 4QJosh[a]

A. Rofé, "The Editing of the Book of Joshua in the Light of 4QJosh[a]," in: G. J. Brooke with F. García Martínez (eds.), *New Qumran Texts and Studies—Proceedings of the First Meeting of the*

---

[23] See G.F. Moore, *Judges* (ICC; Edinburgh 1895) 181; C.F. Burney, *The Book of Judges* (Oxford 1918; repr. New York 1970) 177; J. Gray, *Joshua, Judges and Ruth* (NCB; Nashville 1967) 223; J.A. Soggin, *Judges* (Philadelphia 1981) 112.

International Organization for Qumran Studies, Paris 1992 (Studies on the Texts of the Desert of Judah XV, Leiden/New York/Köln 1994) 73-80; E. Ulrich (above, p. 327).

The section which in 𝔐 narrates the building of an altar after several actions connected with the conquest (8:30-35), is located at an earlier place in the story in 4QJosh^{a}, before 5:1, immediately after the crossing of the Jordan (recorded by Ulrich* as "8:34-35;X;5:2-7"), and probably also in Josephus *Antiquities*, V:16-19. According to Ulrich* and Rofé* this sequence of events in 4QJosh^{a}, which probably reflects the original story, shows that the Qumran text constituted a third independent text of Joshua, alongside 𝔐 and 𝔊 (on which see above, section 2).

14. Rearranged and Shorter Texts (?)

P.W. Flint, "The Psalms Scrolls from the Judaean Desert: Relationships and Textual Affiliations," in: G. J. Brooke with F. García Martínez (eds.), *New Qumran Texts and Studies—Proceedings of the First Meeting of the International Organization for Qumran Studies, Paris 1992* (Studies on the Texts of the Desert of Judah XV, Leiden/New York/Köln 1994) 31-52; J. A. Sanders, *The Psalms Scroll of Qumran Cave 11 (11QPs^{a})* (DJD IV; Oxford 1965); E. Tov, "Excerpted and Abbreviated Biblical Texts from Qumran," *RQ* 16 (1995) 581–600.

Many Qumran texts arrange the biblical text differently or omit sections, especially of the Psalms. These texts have been presented by Tov* as excerpted or abbreviated texts, mainly for liturgical purposes or, in the case of 4QCant^{a,b}, as personal copies. However, several scholars present these Psalms scrolls as regular biblical texts, and if this view is correct, these scrolls, which differ distinctly from the other textual witnesses, present a significantly different picture of several books, especially the Psalter (thus Sanders* with regard to 11QPs^{a} and Flint* regarding the Psalms scrolls from cave 4). In the following scrolls, several Psalms found in 𝔐 𝔊 ℭ 𝔖 𝔙 are lacking, while others have been added, and their sequence differs, often much, especially in the last two books of the Psalter (Psalms 90-150): (1) 11QPs^{a}, whose text is also reflected in the more fragmentary 4QPs^{e} and 11QPs^{b} and probably also in 4QPs^{b}; (2) 4QPs^{a}; (3) 4QPs^{d}; (4) 4QPs^{f}; (5) 4QPs^{k}; (6) 4QPs^{n}; (7) 4QPs^{q}; (8) 4QPsAp^{a} (for details on all these, see Flint*). Other greatly different texts are 4QExod^{d}, covering Exod 13:15-16 and 15:1 and thus omitting the narrative section of 13:17-22 and all of chapter 14, 4QCant^{a} lacking Cant 4:7–6:11, and 4QCant^{b} lacking Cant 3:6-8 and Cant 4:4-7 (for details see Tov*).

15. Minor Differences

It is the purpose of this chapter to draw attention to large-scale differences between the textual witnesses deriving from different literary strata in the composition of the biblical books up to the stage of the edition (recension, composition) contained in 𝔐 (see above, pp. 313–319). It has been claimed that if such recensional differences are recognized in one section or chapter in a book, further details in that book may reflect the same recensional layer, even small details.

If this assumption is correct, the number of such small elements which may be recognized as being part of an overall recensional layer is seemingly endless, and this would again have major repercussions for our understanding of the task of textual criticism. This assumption may well be correct for those books in which overall recensional traits have been discovered. In those cases many of the differences between 𝔊 on the one hand and 𝔐 𝔗 𝔖 𝔙 on the other could have arisen prior to the textual transmission, with the exclusion of pure transmission errors, such as described in chapter 4C2. This would pertain, among other things, to the Greek translation of such books as Joshua, Samuel, Jeremiah, and Ezekiel. For example, in the wake of the shorter text of 𝔊 in 1 Samuel 16-18 (see pp. 334–336), many minuses of 𝔊* in 1-2 Samuel could similarly belong to this category, as in the following instance.

1 Sam 23:23 𝔐 וראו ודעו (מכל המחבאים אשר יתחבא שם ושבתם אלי אל
נכון) והלכתי אתכם . . . ≈ 𝔖 𝔗 𝔙
Look around and learn (*in which of all his hiding places he has been hiding, and return to me when you are certain.*) I will then go with you . . .

𝔊* καὶ ἴδετε καὶ γνῶτε καὶ πορευσόμεθα μεθ' ὑμῶν
Look around and learn and we will go with you.

The section in parentheses is lacking in 𝔊* and may have been added at a later stage in the development of the biblical text. In this section Saul gives specific instructions to find David's hiding places and to report to him.

The same type of reasoning would apply to minuses in 𝔊* in 1-2 Kings, which also elsewhere differs from 𝔐 in important details (above, sections *7*, *8*). The following verse, 1 Kgs 16:34, is lacking in $𝔊^{Luc}$ (MSS boc_2e_2; see p. 148):

> During his reign, Hiel the Bethelite fortified Jericho. He laid its foundations at the cost of Abiram his first-born, and set its gates in place at the cost of Segub his youngest, in accordance with the words that the LORD had spoken through Joshua son of Nun.

This verse, found in all textual traditions with the exception of $\mathfrak{G}^{Luc}$, is not connected to any detail in the context—note the generalized connection by means of the phrase "during his reign." Moreover, this verse disturbs the continuity: v. 34 is preceded by an account of the sins of Ahab (up to v. 33) and followed by an account of the drought (17:1), which comes as a punishment for Ahab's sins. It appears that v. 34 was added by the deuteronomistic editor of the book (see p. 169), who wished to emphasize that the curse of Joshua, presented here, in contrast with what is written in Joshua, was, as a prophecy, indeed fulfilled like many other prophecies. For an analysis, see Mazor* (p. 327).

C. Textual and Literary Evaluation of the Evidence

The evaluation of readings, described in chapter 6, is based on the assumption that these readings were created in the course of the textual transmission and that they should be evaluated according to the internal logic of that procedure. However, it appears that the data presented in this chapter were created, not in the course of textual transmission, but at an earlier stage, namely, that of the literary growth of the biblical books. Therefore, it is questionable whether textual evaluation has any application to them at all.

In our view, textual criteria should not be applied to data that were not created during the textual transmission. The details described in this chapter need mainly to be analyzed with literary criteria which differ from those used in textual criticism. Indeed, in the analysis of literary traditions one does not speak in terms of preference. Just as one does not prefer one stage in the literary development to another, so one does not prefer one of the readings described in this chapter to another. For example, if one makes a distinction between the pre-deuteronomistic stage and the deuteronomistic editing of the historical books (see p. 169), one must be satisfied with a description of the evidence and not give evaluations such as those which are customary in textual criticism.

This view pertains to all the details discussed in this chapter and also to many other examples. However, it is not easy to apply this approach to the evidence, since the data are not composed of a single block of evidence, but rather the textual complexes consist of many details often occurring at different places in the chapter or book. For example, the minuses of 𝔊 in Jeremiah, Joshua, and Ezekiel occur in different places in the books. According to the view presented here, these individual readings should not be treated separately but as one large piece of information. More specifically, these individual instances should not be evaluated at all according to textual criteria.

This, however, is not the course usually taken in scholarship. Only rarely scholars refrain from textual judgment (note, however, that the HUB and the section of 1-2 Samuel in BHS contain no evaluations). Many scholars single out individual readings from larger complexes such as described here, submitting them to textual evaluation. Thus, individual readings from the complex of typological details in the short texts of 𝔊 to Jeremiah and Ezekiel are often evaluated (and preferred to 𝔐), but in our view this procedure is irrelevant. The particular instances which for some reason have been singled out for comment in BHS (as well as in most of the commentaries on this book) are typical of the shorter text ("edition I") of Jeremiah (see section *1* above) and of the shorter text of Ezekiel (see section *3* above). One instance in Table 7, the example from Ezek 7:6-7, reflects a different layout of the chapter. In our view, in these cases one should abandon the customary textual evaluation.

Table 7

"Textual" Evaluations of Readings Which Probably Were Created during the Stage of the Literary Growth of the Biblical Books

Jer 27:19	כי כה אמר ה׳ (צבאות אל העמדים ועל הים ועל המכנות) For thus says the LORD (*of hosts concerning the columns, the sea, the stands*) . . . BHS: > 𝔊*, add cf 52,17 <cf. Table 1 above>
Jer 27:22	(ושמה יהיו עד יום פקדי אתם) (. . . *and there they shall remain, until the day when I give attention to them.*) BHS: > 𝔊*, add <cf. Table 1 above>
Jer 29:16-20	BHS: 𝔊* om 16-20, add; cf. 8[a] <cf. section 1 above>
Ezek 1:11	(ופניהם) וכנפיהם (*Such were their faces.*) As for their wings . . . BHS: > 𝔊*, dl (cf 8[c-c]) <cf. section 3 above>

Ezek 1:27	וארא כעין חשמל (כמראה אש בית לה סביב) I saw a gleam as of amber (*what looked like a fire encased in a frame*) BHS: > 𝔊*, add <cf. section 3 above>
Ezek 7:6-7	קץ בא בא הקץ(הקיץ אליך הנה באה [7]באה הצפירה) אליך יושב הארץ Doom is coming! The hour of doom is coming. (*It stirs against you, there it comes. [7]The cycle has come around)* for you (?), O inhabitant of the land. BHS: > 𝔊*, add <cf. section 3 above>

As a post-script to this section, the dangers inherent in our view should be pointed out. Although evaluation forms an obligatory part of the process of textual criticism, the difficulties described in this section cause a lack of clarity with regard to specific readings. For, with regard to many small details such as those referred to in section B15, it is not possible clearly to ascertain whether they were created in the stage of the composition of the book or in the course of textual transmission. The same uncertainty was expressed in the course of the analysis of exegetical changes, glosses, and interpolations in chapter 4 (pp. 262–275, 277–284). In this chapter the point of departure is the literary growth, while in chapter 4 it is the scribal transmission. In both cases it was realized that there is a gray area of readings found between these two realms whose allegiance is not clear. If such readings belong to the area of the literary growth, textual evaluation should be avoided, but if they were created in the course of the scribal transmission, evaluation is essential. This lack of clarity could cause scholars always to refrain from expressing an opinion on the originality of readings in general.

8

CONJECTURAL EMENDATION

> "No part of the theory of textual criticism has suffered more from misunderstanding than has conjectural emendation." (E.J. Kennedy, "History, Textual Criticism," *EncBrit, Macropaedia*, vol. 20 [15th ed.; Chicago 1985] 679).

Y. Avishur, *Stylistic Studies of Word-Pairs in Biblical and Ancient Semitic Literatures* (AOAT 210; Neukirchen/Vluyn 1984); D. Barthélemy, "Problématiques et tâches de la critique textuelle de l'AT hébraïque," in: idem, *Etudes*, 365-381; G.R. Driver, "Hebrew Scrolls," *JTS* n.s. 2 (1951) 17-30; D.N. Freedman, "Problems of Textual Criticism in the Book of Hosea," in: O'Flaherty* (p. 287) 55-76; H.L. Ginsberg, "Some Emendations in Isaiah," *JBL* 69 (1950) 51-60; P. Maas, *Textual Criticism* (trans. B. Flower; Oxford 1958) 10-21 = idem, *Textkritik*, in: A. Gercke and E. Norden, *Einleitung in die Altertumswissenschaft*, I, VII (3d ed.; Leipzig 1957); M.L. Margolis, "The Scope and Methodology of Biblical Philology," *JQR* 1 (1910–1911) 5-41; J. Reider, "The Present State of Textual Criticism of the OT," *HUCA* 7 (1930) 285-315, esp. 296-307; M. Scott, *Textual Discoveries in Proverbs, Psalms and Isaiah* (London 1927); Sperber, *Grammar*, 31-104.

A. Background

Until now, the discussion in this book has focused on the content of the textual traditions, i.e., on the many readings contained in the textual witnesses. In accordance with the analysis in chapters 3B and 5, one needs to select the best or the most appropriate readings that were supposedly contained in the original form of the biblical text, as defined in those chapters. Within the framework of this analysis the scholar compares the value of each of the known readings and expresses a preference for a specific reading, sometimes the one found in 𝔐 and sometimes one found in a Qumran scroll or 𝔊.

This procedure involves only a comparison and selection of readings and not an emendation. A common misapprehension, even among established scholars, is to see every preferred reading found outside 𝔐 as an emendation.[1] At first glance this terminology would appear to be correct since for students of the Hebrew Bible 𝔐 is the central text, with which the remaining textual witnesses are compared. This procedure, however, is a mere convention for the scholarly world. Because of its place in Judaism as the central text of the Hebrew Bible, 𝔐 also became the determinative text of the Hebrew Bible for Christianity and the scholarly world. Indeed, all printed editions of the Bible contain 𝔐. Nevertheless, 𝔐 reflects merely one textual tradition out of many that existed in the period of the First and Second Temple. Given that 𝔐 is only one among a large number of textual witnesses, one should relate to the biblical text as a large abstract entity rather than placing 𝔐 at the center of one's approach to it.

The emendation of the biblical text refers to a different process, i.e., the suggestion (invention) of new readings which are not transmitted in the witnesses of the biblical text. The logic behind this procedure can be formulated as follows: at the concluding stage of the procedure of textual criticism scholars compare all the known readings with the intention of gathering information on the changing biblical text, *inter alia*, its presumed original form, as defined in 3B. If in a particular instance a scholar does not succeed in finding among the extant textual witnesses a reading which, in his opinion, is appropriate to the context—in other words, a detail contained in the original form of the text—the scholar is likely to turn to an alternative method. The scholar may then suggest that an as yet unknown reading was contained in the original form of the text. This suggested reading stands in a special relation to the extant ones in that it is actually conjectured from the known readings. It is therefore called a conjectural (textual) emendation (the procedure as a whole is often denoted with the Latin term *divinatio*). A conjectural emendation is for the most part a new suggested reading from which all other readings, or at least one of them, presumably developed. The procedure of emending the text thus pertains to the biblical text as a

1 See, for example, the lucid description on p. xix of the introduction to NJPST: "The prophetic books contain many passages whose meaning is uncertain. Thus, in order to provide an intelligible rendering, modern scholars have resorted to emending the Hebrew text. Some of these *emendations* derive from the ancient translators, especially of the Septuagint and the Targums, who had before them a Hebrew text that sometimes differed from today's traditional text. Where these ancient versions provide no help, some scholars have made *conjectural emendations* of their own" (italics mine). The terminology used here, as often elsewhere, thus distinguishes between emendations (considered as "preferences" in this book) and conjectural emendations (named emendations in our terminology).

whole, and not solely to 𝔐, that is, one emends all the existing witnesses, and not merely 𝔐.

A proposed emendation is always a reading that is not documented in the known texts. Sometimes, however, scholars suggest a reading which, though they do not realize it, is actually found or reflected in one of the textual witnesses. This is illustrated in Table 1 below for the Qumran scrolls. When such a reading is discovered in one of the ancient sources, it ceases to be an emendation and becomes a variant reading.

Scholars are aware of the fact that conjectural emendations are hypothetical, and, therefore, sometimes alternative suggestions are made for emending the text. For some examples, see pp. 357–362. Scholars also realize that sometimes no emendation is acceptable, at which point they are likely to be content with merely stating that the text is corrupt.

Justification for conjectural emendation comes, first and foremost, from the recognition of the imperfections of the available textual evidence: Only a very small part of all the readings that were created and copied throughout the many generations of the transmission of the text are known to us. Many readings have been lost, among which were necessarily readings that were contained in the first copies. Since the evidence that has been preserved is arbitrary from a textual point of view, it is permissible to attempt to arrive at the ancient texts by way of reconstruction.

The extent to which the evidence is random can be illustrated from the Qumran discoveries. Various emendations, made in the manner described above, before these texts were discovered, have now been found actually to exist in the Qumran texts, as shown in Table 1 below. If the Qumran scrolls had not been discovered, these proposed emendations would have remained mere conjectures. The fact that they have been attested in the Qumran texts removes them from the area of conjectural emendation and confers on them the status of variant readings similar to that of all other readings. If more ancient texts like the Qumran texts are discovered, the circle of witnesses for the understanding of the biblical text will be wider and the need for suggesting new emendations will diminish. The discovery of previously unknown readings in newly discovered texts which are identical to formerly proposed emendations thus vindicates the procedure of correcting the text by way of conjecture.

Table 1

Readings in the Qumran Texts Previously Suggested as Emendations

Isa 33:8	𝔐	מָאַס עָרִים he despised *cities*
	1QIsa^a	מָאַס עדים (previously suggested as an emendation by Duhm[2]) he despised *witnesses*
Isa 43:8	𝔐	הוצִיא עַם עִוֵּר *He brought forth* the people who are blind.
	1QIsa^a	הוצִיאו עם עואר (previously suggested as an emendation by Kittel in BH[3]) *Bring forth* the people who are blind!
Isa 49:7	𝔐	לבזה נפש (difficult form)
	1QIsa^a	לבזוי נפש (previously suggested as an emendation by Duhm[4]) to one deeply despised

As stated above, there needs to be a *genetic* relation at the textual level between the proposed emendation and one or more of the existing readings which presumably were corrupted. Accordingly, when scholars suggest an emendation, they ought to take into consideration all aspects of the transmission of the biblical text; most importantly, the emendation needs to be based on textual phenomena that were likely to have occurred at the time of the text's transmission, such as the interchange of similar letters, the omission, addition, or inversion of certain details, etc. Consequently, emendations which are supported by such unlikely phenomena as the interchange of letters which are dissimilar are less plausible.

Emendations relate to a change, an omission, or an addition of an isolated letter, a complete word, or even that of an entire paragraph,[5]

2 B. Duhm, *Das Buch Jesaja* (HAT; Göttingen 1902) 211.

3 R. Kittel, who edited this section of BH, may have been the first scholar to propose this emendation.

4 Duhm (n. 2) 334.

5 Some scholars suggested that a complete section or column was sometimes erroneously omitted or transferred elsewhere. See V.A. Dearing, "A New Explanation for the Discontinuities in the Text of Isaiah 1–10," in: O'Flaherty (p. 287) 77-93; A. Rofé, "The Composition of Deuteronomy 31 in Light of a Conjecture about Inversion in the Order

including changes in the order and division of words. The assumption of a gloss or interpolation not supported by textual evidence (cf. pp. 277–284) constitutes an additional type of emendation, but this term is not often used in this regard.

Furthermore, according to many scholars, emendations also relate to details which are not represented in the written biblical text as it was transmitted in the First and Second Temple periods, but which were an inseparable accompaniment to it in the form of an exegetical (reading) tradition. This reading tradition is known to us from 𝔐 and the ancient versions (cf. pp. 40–43), but those witnesses do not always reflect the presumed original intention of the biblical authors. In such cases scholars often intervene and correct the transmitted reading tradition of 𝔐, mainly with reference to vocalization and accentuation. Emendations such as these are suggested in exactly the same way as emendations of consonants. If scholars feel that the vocalization (reading) of 𝔐 does not reflect the assumed intention of the original form of the text as defined in chapter 3B, they are likely to suggest another vocalization which is unattested, at least in Hebrew witnesses—as in the evidence referring to Ps 84:7 (p. 359). Similar emendations have been suggested in connection with the syntactic relation between words, against the evidence of the biblical accents.

There are no rules for proposing emendations, and, therefore, it is difficult to determine what the starting point of such a procedure should be. Accordingly, scholars have approached this subject in various ways. As stated above, a textual emendation must be plausible from the point of view of the procedure of textual criticism, but that does not imply that emendations are actually part of the textual procedure. In fact, usually scholars do not think in terms of proposing emendations until they have reached the stage of evaluating the combined textual evidence, as described in chapter 6. At that stage, when the biblical exegete is not satisfied with the preserved readings, scholars may resort to textual emendation. The suggested textual emendations are based on considerations outside the area of textual criticism, that is, biblical exegesis, linguistic research, literary criticism, etc. Conjectural emendation therefore derives from the combined realms of biblical exegesis in the broader sense of the word and the evaluation of readings as part of the textual procedures (thus Margolis*, 19).

---

of Columns in the Biblical Text," *Shnaton* 3 (Jerusalem 1978/1979) 59-76 (Heb. with Eng. summ.).

Emendations also are derived from the combination of linguistic analysis and textual criticism.

The procedure of emending the biblical text is one of the most subjective aspects of textual criticism in particular, and of biblical research in general. Generally speaking, in the course of the past few centuries, far too many emendations have been suggested, most of which may now be considered unnecessary. It is agreed upon by most scholars that emending the biblical text should be a last resort when solving textual problems. One should first examine whether there exists among the extant texts a reading which would suit the context and which may be considered original as defined on pp. 17, 177. Among other things, that presumably original reading should be explained with what may be considered a reasonable explanation. However, there will never be a consensus with regard to what constitutes a reasonable explanation. Difficulties arise particularly in the area of language, vocabulary, and the exact meaning of the context. As pointed out on p. 310, our judgment is guided mainly by common sense. A reasonable amount of self-criticism is also required with regard to the limits of our knowledge, especially in the area of language. Due to the fact that the available data in this area are very fragmentary, it may be that an apparently incorrect or unsuitable reading was, nevertheless, the original one. Situations like these are exemplified on pp. 361–367 below, referring to insights recently acquired in grammar and cognate languages. Similarly, it should be recognized that the biblical author may have used a word which is less suitable in the context than one which the scholar could suggest by way of emendation. In all such cases scholars should actually resist their wish to emend the biblical text.

During the seventeenth and eighteenth centuries, many conjectural emendations were proposed by such scholars as Cappellus, Clericus, Houbigant, Glassius, Michaelis,[6] and Oort.[7] Later, these emendations were included in all the critical commentaries, particularly those written in German. Selections of such emendations can be found in Perles, *Analekten*, Delitzsch, *Lese- und Schreibfehler*, and also in BH and BHS (see chapter 9). Three types of emendations are exemplified below: contextual emendations, linguistic emendations, and emendations for metrical reasons.

---

6 The works of the first three scholars are mentioned on p. 295, n. 1. See further S. Glassius, *Philologiae Sacrae* (Amsterdam 1709); J.D. Michaelis, *Deutsche Übersetzung des AT mit Anmerkungen für Ungelehrte*, vol. I (Göttingen 1772).

7 H. Oort, *Textus hebraici emendationes quibus in VT Neerlandice vertendo usi sunt A. Kuenen, I. Hooykaas, W.H. Kosters, H. Oort* (Leiden 1900).

B. Types of Emendations

1. *Contextual Emendations*[8]

The most common type of emendation derives from a specific understanding of the context. The first three of the following emendations are accepted by most scholars.

Amos 6:12a 𝔐	(הַיְרֻצוּן בסלע סוסים) אם יַחֲרוֹשׁ בַּבְּקָרִים (Can horses gallop on a rock?) Can one plough it *with oxen* (or: *in the mornings*)?
Emendation:	אם יֵחָרֵשׁ בְּבָקָר יָם Can *the sea* be ploughed *with oxen*?

The two hemistichs of v. 12a in 𝔐 are incongruous. At the same time, the first hemistich "Can horses gallop on a rock?" fits well with the context of v. 12b: "Yet you have turned justice into poison weed and the fruit of righteousness to wormwood": both sentences describe illogical situations. The exegetical problem is located, therefore, in the second hemistich of 12a, which describes an absolutely predictable activity. This issue is equally complicated if one understands בַּבְּקָרִים as the plural of בָּקָר, "oxen," which is unattested in that form (בְּקָרִים in 2 Chr 4:3 is problematic), and not of בֹּקֶר, "morning." On account of this contextual difficulty, Michaelis[9] suggested long ago to divide בבקרים into two words: בְּבָקָר, "with oxen," and יָם, "sea," and to change the vocalization of יַחֲרוֹשׁ to יֵחָרֵשׁ, with the omission of the *mater lectionis*. This emendation suits the parallelism and completes the meaning:

Can horses gallop on a rock? // Can the sea be ploughed with oxen?

The proposed emendation derives from exegetical considerations, and it also appears plausible from the aspect of the process of textual transmission (see the discussion of word division on pp. 252–254).

---

8 Almost all words for which emendations have been suggested are somehow difficult for modern scholars, and they must have been equally difficult for the ancient translators. Many of these ancient renderings reflect the translators' difficulties and are therefore not mentioned here.

9 See n. 6, loc. cit. For additional analyses and emendations of this verse, see: A. Szabó, "Textual Problems in Amos and Hosea," *VT* 25 (1975) 506-507; H.W. Wolff, *Joel and Amos* (Hermeneia; Philadelphia 1977) 284-285; M. Dahood, "Can One Plow without Oxen? (Amos 6:12): A Study of BA- and 'AL," in: G. Rendsburg, ed., *The Bible World—Essays in Honor of Cyrus H. Gordon* (New York 1980) 14, 23; A. Cooper, "The Absurdity of Amos 6:12a," *JBL* 107 (1988) 725-727; O. Loretz, "Amos VI 12," *VT* 39 (1989) 240-241.

Ezek 3:12 𝔐 — (ותשאני רוח ואשמע אחרַי קול רעש גדול) בָּרוּךְ(כבוד ה׳ ממקומו)
(Then a spirit carried me away, and behind me I heard a great roaring sound:) "*Blessed is* (the Presence of the LORD from/in His place.")

Emendation: בְּרוּם
When <the Presence of the LORD> *rose.*

It is possible that 𝔐 refers to a formula such as בָּרוּךְ כבוד ה׳ ממקומו, "*Blessed* is the Presence of the LORD from/in His place," which was recited or sung. However, here the meaning of such a formula is contextually unclear, since the text does not state who is saying these words and there is no introductory formula such as לאמר, "saying," which, incidentally, has been added in 𝔗. Similarly, it is difficult in this context to ascertain the meaning of ממקומו, "from/in His place," perhaps referring to the heaven (cf. Mic 1:3). The suggestion of Luzzatto[10] to read here בְּרוּם, "when <the Presence of the LORD> rose," is acceptable. This emendation is supported by the frequent interchange of the similar letters *kaph* and *mem* (see p. 248).[11] Cf. also the similar phrase "but when the Presence of the LORD moved from the cherubs" in Ezek 10:4 (cf. further 10:16,19).

Isa 11:15 𝔐 — (והניף ידו על הנהר) בַּעְיָם רוחו
(He will raise his hand over the Euphrates) with His ?? (NJPST: scorching) wind.

Emendation: בְּעֹצֶם רוחו
with *the might of* His wind

The meaning of בַּעְיָם in 𝔐 is not clear (Luzzatto: "a word which has no equivalent and no clear meaning in the other languages"). Nevertheless, some interpret it as "heat" according to Arabic. Various scholars suggested reading בְּעֹצֶם רוחו, "with the might of His wind," instead of 𝔐.[12] This emendation was first proposed by Gesenius[13] and Luzzatto on

10 Luzzatto (ed. A.I. Menkes, Lemberg 1876; repr. Jerusalem 1969) believes that this interchange occurred in the "early" Hebrew script and in order to prove his point he adduced examples of similar interchanges.

11 According to Geiger, *Urschrift*, 316-318, the reading of 𝔐 is tendentious, similar to the "corrections of the scribes" (see pp. 64–67) meant to avoid dishonoring God.

12 On the other hand, possibly this reading was already reflected in 𝔊 (πνεύματι βιαίῳ, "with a strong wind"), and 𝔖 (באוחדנא דרוחה, "with the force of His wind") = 𝔙 *in fortitudine spiritus sui.* If the ancient translations indeed read בְּעֹצֶם, we are faced with an early reading, and no emendation is necessary.

13 W. Gesenius, *Thesaurus philologicus criticus linguae hebraeae et chaldaeae Veteris Testamenti* (Leipzig 1829) 1017.

the basis of the similarity between *yod* and *ṣade* in the "early" Hebrew script (see p. 245).

Prov 22:20 𝔐^K	(הלא כתבתי לך) *שלשום* (במועצות ודעת)
	(Have I not written for you) *formerly* (?) (with admonition and knowledge?)
𝔐^Q	שָׁלִישִׁים or שָׁלִשִׁים
	threefold (?) or: excellent things (?)
Emendation:	שְׁלשִׁים
	thirty <precepts>

Recognizing the difficulties of 𝔐, most scholars accept an emendation based on chapter 30 of the Egyptian collection of proverbs of Amen-em-Ope (" . . . See thou these *thirty chapters*: they entertain and they instruct.").[14] This third collection of sayings in the book of Proverbs (22:17–24:22) is in other details also heavily influenced by the contents of the Egyptian collection. The emendation changes the vocalization of one of the forms of the *Qere* (cf. p. 255).

For an additional emendation for which partial evidence is available, see 1 Sam 10:27 as analyzed on pp. 343–344.

In particularly difficult verses various alternative emendations are suggested—e.g., in Judg 18:7 (below p. 367) and also in the following example recorded in BH and BHS:[15]

Hos 4:4 𝔐	וְעַמְּךָ כִּמְרִיבֵי כֹהֵן
Emendations:	וְעַמִּי כְּכָמְרוֹ בְּנֵי כְּכֹהֲנוֹ
	וְעַם כַּכֹּמֶר וְנָבִיא כַּכֹּהֵן
	(וְ)עִמְּךָ רִיבִי (הַ)כֹּהֵן
	עַמִּי כָּמוֹךָ הַכֹּהֵן
	וְעִמְּךָ אֲנִי רָב (הַ)כֹּהֵן

In other verses emendations have been suggested for almost every word, as in BH (not BHS) for Ps 84:7:

> As they go through the valley of Baca they make it a place of springs; the early rain also covers it with blessings. <Thus NRSV, except for the last word where NRSV contains an emended text, "pools," that is, בְּרֵכוֹת instead of בְּרָכוֹת in 𝔐.>

14 Translation by J.A. Wilson in: J.B. Pritchard, ed., *Ancient Near Eastern Texts Relating to the OT* (Princeton 1950) 424. For further literature on this topic, see ibid., 421 and S. Aḥiṭuv, "Mšly, spr mšly," *EncBib* 5 (1968) 559-560 (Heb.).

15 For further suggestions and an analysis, see H.W. Wolff, *Dodekapropheton 1: Hosea* (Hermeneia; 2d ed.; Philadelphia 1974) 70.

Ps 84:7 𝔐	*Emendations*	
עֹבְרֵי	עברו, יעברו	
בעמק		
הַבָּכָא	הַבְּכָאִים	(𝔐 presumably created by haplography)
מַעְיָן	מֵעַיִן	cf. also 𝔊 τόπον (probably reflecting מָעוֹן) = 𝔖
יְשִׁיתוּהוּ	יִשְׁתּוּ	(𝔐 presumably created by dittography)
גַּם	אַגְמֵי	
בְּרָכוֹת	בְּרֵכוֹת	
יַעְטֶה	עֲטֻפִים	
מוֹרֶה	רִוָּה	

Two of the above-mentioned emendations pertain only to vocalization: בְּרָכוֹת / בְּרֵכוֹת, מֵעַיִן / מַעְיָן

Many textual emendations have been proposed on the basis of the parallel hemistich in a synonymous or antithetic parallelism (see in particular the collection of examples *apud* Avishur*, 669–698).

Ps 22:16 𝔐 — (יבש כחרש) *כֹּחִי* // (ולשוני מדבק מלקוחי)
My vigor (dries up like a shard // my tongue cleaves to my palate.)
Emendation: *חִכִּי*
my palate

The assumed textual phenomenon: metathesis (p. 250). For the occurrence of חך and לשון in parallel stichs, though in reversed sequence, see Job 6:30; 20:12-13.

Ps 49:14 𝔐 — (זה דרכם כסל למו) // וְאַחֲרֵיהֶם (בפיהם ירצו)
(Such is the way of those who have foolish confidence) //*and after them* (?) (they are pleased with their own talk.)
Emendation: וְאָרְחֵיהֶם (or וְאָרְחוֹתָם)
and their paths . . .

The parallel word pair דרך, "way," and ארח, "path," appears frequently in the Bible (e.g., Gen 49:17; Ps 25:4, 27:11). The assumed textual phenomenon: metathesis (p. 250).

Ps 72:9 𝔐 — (לפניו יכרעו) צִיִּים // (ואיביו עפר ילחכו)
(Let) *desert-dwellers* (kneel before him // and his enemies lick the dust.)
Emendation: צָרִים (or: צָרָיו)
foes (or: his foes)

The parallelism אויב, "enemy" // צר, "foe" is attested frequently, both in the Bible and in Ugaritic texts (cf. Avishur*, 344-346). The assumed textual phenomenon: interchange of *yod* and *resh*, presumably interchanged because of their graphic similarity, although this interchange is not recorded on pp. 243–251.

Ps 73:1 𝔐 — (אך טוב) לְיִשְׂרָאֵל // (אלהים לברי לבב)
(Truly, <God> is good) *to Israel*, (God <is good> to those whose heart is pure.)

Emendation: (אך טוב) לַיָּשָׁר אֵל (= REB)
(Truly,) *to the upright God* (is good.)

The emendation (cf. Avishur*, 683) is based on the parallel word pairs יָשָׁר, "upright" // בר, "pure"—cf. Ps 19:9—and אֵל // אלהים (both: "God"). The emendation suits the context, since there is no national frame of reference in the psalm. The assumed textual phenomenon: different conceptions of word division (cf. pp. 252–253).

2. *Linguistic Emendations*

a. Grammar

Over the years many grammatical emendations have been proposed, usually for uncommon forms which were corrected on the basis of a formal grammatical approach. With an impressive collection of examples Sperber* rightly attacks grammatical emendations of this type, arguing that they are usually based on "school grammar." Most of the emendations mentioned by him are found in BH and in many of the commentaries, and it is worth noting that the majority of them were not repeated in BHS.

1 Sam 13:6 𝔐 — (ואיש ישראל) ראו (כי צר לו)
(The men [singular] of Israel) *saw* [plural] (that they were in trouble.)

Emendation: ראה
saw [singular]

BH adapts the predicate to the subject. With collective nouns, however, the predicate often occurs in the plural (see Sperber, *Grammar*, 91-92; Gesenius–Kautzsch §145).

1 Kgs 22:24 𝔐 — לדבר אוֹתָךְ
to speak to you

Emendation: אִתָּךְ

in connection with his unusual explanations of words in 𝔐 on the basis of Ugaritic and Phoenician.[17]

Scholars who frequently resort to Ugaritic documents from the second millennium BCE do so on the assumption that the language of the Bible was close to that of Ugarit in both time and character. In other words, the Ugaritic documents preserve several ancient idioms and linguistic phenomena that were not always correctly understood by the persons, who in a later period, vocalized the biblical text. From here it follows (in their opinion), that one must attempt to penetrate beyond the exegesis of the Masoretes into the original meaning of the biblical text by occasionally ignoring the vocalization of the Masoretes. This line of approach to the Ugaritic documents was developed particularly by Ginsberg*, and, in an extreme manner, by Dahood* in several theoretical studies and, to an even greater degree, in the application of his method to the biblical books themselves.[18] Dahood's students further developed his approach.[19]

The following examples relate to the area of *grammar*. The so-called enclitic *mem*, added as a suffix to Ugaritic words for emphasis or stylistic nuance, is one of the characteristics of Ugaritic which scholars related to 𝔐.[20] Following this Ugaritic usage, the enclitic *mem* was also detected in

---

17 See p. 71 in his study on Proverbs to be mentioned in the next note.

18 M. Dahood, "Qoheleth and Northwest Semitic Philology," *Bib* 43 (1962) 349-365; *Proverbs and Northwest Semitic Philology* (Scripta Pontificii Instituti Biblici 113; Rome 1963); *Psalms*, vols. I–III (AB; Garden City, NY 1966, 1968, 1970); "Northwest Semitic Texts and Textual Criticism of the Hebrew Bible," in: C. Brekelmans, ed., *Questions disputées d'AT* (BETL 33; Leuven 1989) 11-37. The numerous suggestions by Dahood until 1967 have been collected in an index to his work: E.R. Martinez, ed., *Hebrew-Ugaritic Index to the Writings of Mitchell J. Dahood* (Scripta Pontificii Instituti Biblici 116; Rome 1967); vol. II (Subsidia Biblica 4; Rome 1981). For further bibliography see BETL 33 (quoted above) 205-208.

19 See C.M. Blommerde, *Northwest Semitic Grammar and Job* (BibOr 22; Rome 1969); K.J. Cathcart, *Nahum in the Light of Northwest Semitic* (Rome 1973); W. Kuhnigk, *Nordwestsemitische Studien zum Hoseabuch* (BibOr 27; Rome 1974); R. Althann, *A Philological Analysis of Jeremiah 4–6 in the Light of Northwest Semitic* (BibOr 38; Rome 1983); W.L. Mitchel, *Job in the Light of Northwest Semitic* (BibOr 42; Rome 1987). For further bibliography see BETL 33 (quoted in the previous note) 205-208.

20 See H.D. Hummel, "Enclitic *Mem* in Early Northwest Semitic, Especially Hebrew," *JBL* 76 (1957) 85-107, and before him A.D. Singer, "The 'Final -m' (= mā?) in the Ugarit Tablets," *BJPES* 10 (1943) 54-62 (Heb.); M. Pope, "Ugaritic Enclitic -m," *JCS* 5 (1951) 123–128. In his *Sepher ha-Riqmah* Ibn Janaḥ already referred to the superfluous nature of this *mem*. However, he did not relate to it the same distinctive meaning as have modern scholars. See pp. 235, 360 in the edition of M. Wilensky (Jerusalem 1930). For a discussion of the scholarship on this grammatical feature, see C. Cohen, "Jewish Medieval Commentary on the Book of Genesis and Modern Biblical Philology. Part I: Gen 1-18," *JQR* 81 (1990) 1-11, esp. 7-8.

the consonantal framework of 𝔐—presumably distorted by the word division (pp. 252–253) and vocalization of the Masoretes (p. 255).

Isa 5:23 𝔐	מצדיקי רשע עקב שחד וצדקת צַדִּיקִים יסירו ממנו Who vindicate the wicked in return for a bribe and withhold vindication *of the righteous* (plural) from him
"Emendation"	צדיק + מ׳ *of the righteous* (singular)

In 𝔐 there is no agreement between the plural צַדִּיקִים and the singular pronominal suffix of ממנו, and, therefore, Ginsberg[21] suggested that צדיקים actually represented a singular form ("the righteous") with the addition of the enclitic *mem*.[22] Note also the occurrence of רשע, "the wicked," in the singular in the parallel hemistich.

Ps 29:1 𝔐	הבו לה׳ בני אלים // הבו לה׳ כבוד ועז Ascribe to the LORD, *O divine beings* (literally: O sons of gods), ascribe to the LORD, glory and strength.
"Emendation"	אל + מ׳

According to Hummel, *op. cit.* (n. 20), 101, the text refers to "the sons of *El*," sitting in the assembly of the gods, as in Ps 89:7—cf. also the variants in Deut 32:8 recorded on p. 269. According to this explanation the original text referred to *El* together with an enclitic *mem*.

Ps 29:6 𝔐	וַיַּרְקִידֵם כמו עגל He makes *them* skip like a calf.
"Emendation"	וירקד + מ׳ He makes skip.

וַיַּרְקִידֵם, "He makes *them* skip" (with the pronominal suffix), was understood by Ginsberg*, 115, as וירקד, "He makes skip." That which was understood by the Masoretes as a pronominal suffix was explained by Ginsberg as an enclitic *mem*.

Another grammatical insight pertains to the use of *lamed* as a vocative particle in Ugaritic,[23] a use which was subsequently related to several biblical texts.

---

21 H.L. Ginsberg, "Some Emendations in Isaiah," *JBL* 69 (1950) 54.

22 The fact that 𝔐MSS, 𝔊, 𝔖, and 𝔗 also reflect a singular form is not necessarily relevant, since this reading or understanding could have been secondary.

23 See A.D. Singer, "The Vocative in Ugaritic," *JCS* 2 (1948) 1–10.

3. Emendations for Metrical Reasons

Eissfeldt, *Introduction*, 57-64; D.W. Goodwin, *Text-Restoration Methods in Contemporary U.S.A. Biblical Scholarship* (Naples 1969) 137-154; R. Kittel, *Über die Notwendigkeit und Möglichkeit einer neuen Ausgabe der hebräischen Bibel* (Leipzig 1901) 67-76; J.L. Kugel, *The Idea of Biblical Poetry, Parallelism and Its History* (New Haven/London 1981); E. Sievers, *Metrische Studien I: Studien zur hebräischen Metrik* (Abh. der phil.-hist. Cl. d. Kgl. Sächs. Ges. d. Wiss. XXI, 1-2; 1901).

Several scholars developed theories on accentuation, the length and number of hemistichs, syllable count, the existence of strophes and refrains, rhythm, and meter (a fixed number of long and short vowels or stressed and unstressed syllables) in biblical poetry.[29] These theories, in their turn, served as a basis for emendations *metri causa*, "for metrical reasons," that is, emendations of details in the text which did not accord with the scholar's metrical or poetical understanding. The general argument of such emendations, the logic of which is borrowed from the study of Greek and Latin poetry, is frequently used in connection with one of the above-mentioned elements of the poetical structure, not necessarily in connection with meter alone. The various poetical systems themselves,[30] described in theoretical works and applied to various biblical books, are not discussed here, but a few emendations accompanying them are exemplified below. Most scholars regard emendations of this type as untenable.

Gen 49:2 𝔐	הקבצו *ושמעו* בני יעקב // ושמעו אל־ישראל אביכם Assemble *and listen*, O sons of Jacob // listen to Israel your father.
Emendation:	הקבצו בני יעקב // ושמעו אל־ישראל אביכם Assemble, O sons of Jacob // listen to Israel your father.

---

29 See especially the reviews of these theories *apud* Eissfeldt*; Kugel*, 287-304, and the additional literature mentioned there, p. 292, n. 17; D.N. Freedman, "Prolegomenon" to G.B. Gray, *The Forms of Hebrew Poetry* (London 1915; repr. New York 1972) xli–lii. From the more recent literature, see: M. O'Connor, *Hebrew Verse Structure* (Winona Lake, IN 1980); D.N. Freedman, *Pottery, Poetry and Prophecy, Collected Essays on Hebrew Poetry* (Winona Lake 1980); P. van der Lugt, *Strofische structuren in de bijbels-hebreeuwse poëzie* (Dissertationes neerlandicae, Series theologica; Kampen 1980); W.G.E. Watson, *Classical Hebrew Poetry—A Guide to Its Techniques* (JSOTSup 26; Sheffield 1983); A. Berlin, *The Dynamics of Biblical Parallelism* (Bloomington 1985).

30 A critical discussion of such methods can be found *apud* Gray, *op. cit.* (n. 29) 201-204 and Kugel*, 292-304.

This emendation (omission of a word, cf. pp. 236–237) by Sievers*, 367, 404, is based on the supposed appearance of an identical number of units in both hemistichs (3:3) and on the avoidance of the repetition of the word "listen." The emendation is mentioned in BH.

Gen 49:7 𝔐	ארור אפם כי עז // ועברתם כי קשתה Cursed be their anger so fierce, // and their wrath so relentless.
Emendation:	ארור אפם כי עז // וארורה עברתם כי קש[ת]ה Cursed be their anger so fierce, // *and cursed be* their wrath so relentless.

This emendation (addition) by Sievers*, 406, based on the assumption that both hemistichs should be identical (4:4), led him to repeat the word "cursed," for which cf. also Deut 28:16.

Exod 15:2 𝔐	זה אלי ואנוהו // אלהי אבי וארממנהו This is my God whom I glorify // the God of my father whom I exalt.
Reconstruction:	ז אל וארממנה // אלה אב ואנוה This is my God whom I exalt // the God of my father whom I glorify.

The reconstruction of the ancient form of the song by Cross–Freedman (cf. Table 1 on p. 223) included the inversion of ואנוהו, "whom I glorify," and וארממנהו, "whom I exalt," since these scholars were of the opinion that "as MT stands, the second colon is considerably longer than the first." The intention of the emendation was to correct the presumably unusual poetical form: "The simplest solution to this metrical imbalance is to interchange the verbs; this produces the desired symmetry" (Cross–Freedman, ibid., 55).

criticism.[1] At the same time, many of the textcritical data can be found in a more concentrated form in the *critical editions* of the Bible.

---

1 According to the sequence of the biblical books: A. Dillmann, *Die Genesis* (KeH; Leipzig 1886); G.J. Spurrell, *Notes on the Text of the Book of Genesis* (Oxford 1896); A. Dillmann, *Die Bücher Numeri, Deuteronomium und Josua* (Leipzig 1886); G.A. Cooke, *The Book of Joshua in the Revised Version with Introduction and Notes* (CB; Cambridge 1918); C.F. Burney, *The Book of Judges* (Oxford 1918; repr. New York 1970); O. Thenius, *Die Bücher Samuels erklärt* (KeH; Leipzig 1842); J. Wellhausen, *Der Text der Bücher Samuelis* (Göttingen 1871); Driver, *Samuel*; A. Fernández Truyols, *I Sam. 1–15, crítica textual* (Rome 1917); P.K. McCarter, *I Samuel, II Samuel* (AB; Garden City, NY 1980, 1984); C.F. Burney, *Notes on the Hebrew Text of the Book of Kings* (Oxford 1903; repr. New York 1970); J.A. Montgomery, *Kings* (ICC; Edinburgh 1951); A. van der Kooij, *Die alten Textzeugen des Jesajabuches* (OBO 35; Freiburg/Göttingen 1981); P. Volz, *Studien zum Text des Jeremia* (BWANT 25; Leipzig 1920); C.H. Cornill, *Das Buch des Propheten Ezechiel* (Leipzig 1886); G.A. Cooke, *Ezechiel* (ICC; Edinburgh 1936); W. Zimmerli, *Ezechiel* (BK; Neukirchen 1969); J. Taylor, *The Massoretic Text and the Ancient Versions of the Book of Micah* (London/Edinburgh 1891); J. Lachmann, *Das Buch Habakkuk. Eine textkritische Studie* (Aussig 1932); S. Zandstra, *The Witness of the Vulgate, Peshitta and Septuagint to the Text of Zephaniah* (Contributions to Oriental History and Philology IV; New York 1909); F. Wutz, *Die Psalmen, Textkritische Untersuchung* (München 1925); M. Scott, *Textual Discoveries in Proverbs, Psalms, and Isaiah* (London 1927); G. Beer, *Der Text des Buches Hiob* (Marburg 1897); M.Th. Houtsma, *Textkritische Studien zum AT, I—Das Buch Hiob* (Leiden 1925); G. Richter, *Textstudien zum Buche Hiob*(BWANT; Stuttgart 1927); E. Dhorme, *Job* (EBib; Paris 1926; repr. Nashville 1984); B. Albrektson, *Studies in the Text and Theology of the Book of Lamentations* (Lund 1963); J.A. Montgomery, *Daniel* (ICC; Edinburgh 1927); J.A. Bewer, *Der Text des Buches Ezra* 1 (FRLANT n.s. 14; Göttingen 1922); H. Gotthard, *Der Text des Buches Nehemia* (Wiesbaden 1958). For additional bibliographical references, see: E. König, *Einleitung in das AT* (Bonn 1893) 133. On all the books of the Bible see S. Davidson, *The Hebrew Text of the OT, Revised from Critical Sources; Being an Attempt to Present a Purer and More Correct Text than the Received One of Van der Hooght; by the Aid of the Best Existing Materials* (London 1855) and the three volumes of D. Barthélemy, *Critique textuelle de l'AT* (OBO 50/1,2,3; Fribourg/ Göttingen 1982, 1986, 1992).

2 Most of the modern translations included in the critical commentaries present eclectically—from the Hebrew and reconstructed readings—those readings which in the view of their editors were contained in the "original" text, even if the nature of this text has not always been well defined. See for example, the translations included in the series ICC and BK and the discussion by D. Barthélemy, *Critique textuelle de l'AT* (OBO 50/2; Fribourg/Göttingen 1986) 2*-71*. Likewise, the following studies (arranged chronologically) present a partial or complete reconstruction of (parts of) biblical books: P. Haupt, ed., *The Polychrome Bible, The Sacred Books of the Old and New Testaments: A New English Translation* (London/New York/Stuttgart 1893–1904); Cornill, *Ezechiel* (see n. 1); J. Meinhold, *Die Jesajaerzählungen Jesaja 36–39* (Göttingen 1898); R. Peters, *Beiträge zur Text- und Literarkritik sowie zur Erklärung der Bücher Samuel* (Freiburg i. Breisgau 1899) 58-62 (1 Sam. 16:1—19:18); C.H. Cornill, *Die metrischen Stücke des Buches Jeremia* (Leipzig 1901); F. Giesebrecht, *Jeremias Metrik am Texte dargestellt* (Göttingen 1905); D.H. Müller, *Komposition und Strophenbau* (Alte und Neue Beiträge, XIV Jahresbericht der Isr.-Theol. Lehranstalt in Wien; Wien 1907); P. Haupt, "Critical Notes on Esther," *OT and Semitic Studies in Memory of W.R. Harper*, II (Chicago 1908) 194-204; J. Begrich, *Der Psalm des Hiskia* (FRLANT 25; Göttingen 1926); C.C. Torrey, "The Archetype of Psalms 14 and 53," *JBL* 46 (1927) 186-192; K. Budde, "Psalm 14 und 53," *JBL* 47 (1928) 160-183; P. Ruben, *Recensio und Restitutio* (London 1936); F.X. Wutz, *Systematische Wege von der Septuaginta zum hebräischen Urtext* (Stuttgart 1937); W.F. Albright, "The Psalm of

In addition to modern reconstructions of the "original" text of books and individual chapters of the Bible,[2] there exist only two critical editions, namely, BH and BHS on the one hand, and the HUB, the edition of the Hebrew University Bible Project, on the other hand. The critical dimension of these two editions is recognizable in two areas:

1. *The text*, that is, the biblical text that was chosen as the basis for the edition. Critical editions do not choose as their base text the second Rabbinic Bible, which is represented in one form or another in most subsequent editions (see p. 78), since it is not based on a single manuscript. Such critical editions rather represent one particular manuscript which according to the editor reflects the vocalization of 𝔐 in its best possible form: L for BH/BHS and the Aleppo codex for the HUB. The editors of these works build their editions around the manuscript which, in their opinion, best represents the Tiberian vocalization according to the Ben Asher system (see p. 45). While codex A (see p. 46) indeed presents the most accurate representation of this system of vocalization, it is not complete. L (see p. 47) is the most complete source which is closest to the Ben Asher system.

2. *The critical apparatus* which contains variants and conjectural emendations. Usually, no arguments are given for the inclusion or non-inclusion of details in the apparatus, but in BH/BHS short evaluations of the important variants are given (see chapter 6). As Housman, quoted at the beginning of this chapter, rightly states, the reader of these editions has the benefit of being familiar with the editors' text-critical decisions, even though he often would like to know the arguments behind them.

In addition to the critical editions of the Hebrew Bible which, as mentioned above, are few in number, there exist a large number of critical editions disguised behind modern translations (included in most

---

Habakkuk," in: H.H. Rowley, ed., *Studies in OT Prophecy* (Edinburgh 1950) 1-18; F.M. Cross, Jr. and D.N. Freedman, *Studies in Ancient Yahwistic Poetry* (Baltimore 1950; 2d ed. Missoula, MT 1975); idem, "The Song of Miriam," *JNES* 14 (1955) 237-250; F.M. Cross, Jr., "A Royal Song of Thanksgiving II Samuel 22 = Psalm 18," *JBL* 72 (1953) 15-34; L.A.F. Le Mat, *Textual Criticism and Exegesis of Psalm XXXVI* (Studia Theol. Rheno-Traiectina 3; Utrecht 1957); M. Naor, "Exodus 1-15, A Reconstruction", in S. Abramsky (ed.), *Sefer S. Yeivin* (Jerusalem 1970) 242-282 (Heb.); P.D. Hanson, *The Dawn of Apocalyptic* (Philadelphia 1975) 46-86; B. Mazar, "hgbwrym ʾšr ldwyd," *ʿz ldwd* (Heb.; Jerusalem 1964) 248-267 = *Canaan and Israel* (Heb.; Jerusalem 1974) 183-207; A. Gelston, "Isaiah 52:13–53:12: An Eclectic Text and a Supplementary Note on the Hebrew Manuscript Kennicott 96," *JSS* 35 (1990) 187-211; P.G. Borbone, *Il libro del profeta Osea, Edizione critica del testo ebraico* (Quaderni di Henoch 2; Torino [1990]); Hendel, *Genesis 1-11*.

critical commentaries of the individual books of the Bible as well as in several separate translations).[3] On the other hand, NJPST reproduces 𝔐 as much as possible. In general, the translations in critical commentaries are more eclectic in their choice of readings than modern translations meant for the general public, but these modern translations, too, often deviate from 𝔐, sometimes with an indication of the source for the deviation, but often not. Although the background of these textual decisions has often been described[4] and discussed,[5] their legitimacy has not been sufficiently analyzed.

B. *Biblia Hebraica and Biblia Hebraica Stuttgartensia*

Deist, *Text*, 87-96; idem, *Witnesses*, 72-83; E. Levine, *Technica Biblia Hebraica (A Hebrew Guide to Biblia Hebraica)* (Heb.; Haifa 1977); H.M. Orlinsky, "The Textual Criticism of the OT," in: G.E. Wright, ed., *The Bible and the Ancient Near East* (New York 1961) 113-132; H.P. Rüger, *An English Key to the Latin Words and Abbreviations and the Symbols of Biblia Hebraica Stuttgartensia* (Stuttgart 1981); W.R. Scott, *A Simplified Guide to BHS* (Berkeley, CA 1987); Sperber, *Grammar*, 46-104; E. Tov, "*Biblia Hebraica Stuttgartensia*," *Shnaton* 4 (Heb.; 1980) 172-180; G.E. Weil, "La nouvelle édition de la Massorah (BHK IV) et l'histoire de la Massorah," *VTSup* 9 (1963) 266-284; R. Wonneberger, *Understanding BHS—A Manual for the Users of Biblia Hebraica Stuttgartensia (BHS)* (Subsidia Biblica 8; Rome 1984); idem, *Leitfaden zur Biblia Hebraica* (Göttingen 1984); Würthwein, *Text*; I. Yeivin, "The New Edition of the Biblia Hebraica—Its Text and Massorah," *Textus* 7 (1969) 114-123.

The most widely used—and at this stage the only complete—critical edition of the Bible is the Biblia Hebraica (BH)—see plate 26*—and in a later form, Biblia Hebraica Stuttgartensia (BHS)—see plate 27*. The

3 Such as RSV; NRSV; *The New American Bible* (New York/London 1970); NEB; REB; *La Sainte Bible, traduite en français sous la direction de l'Ecole biblique de Jérusalem* (Paris 1956); *Die Heilige Schrift, Altes und Neues Testament* (Bonn 1966); *Einheitsübersetzung der Heiligen Schrift* (Stuttgart 1974).

4 For some discussions see B. Ljungberg et al., *Att översätta Gamla testamentet—Texter, kommentarer, riktlinjer* (Statens offentliga utredningar 1974:33; Stockholm 1974); D.F. Payne, "OT Textual Criticism—Its Principles and Practice Apropos of Recent English Versions," *TynBul* 25 (1974) 99-112; B. Albrektson, "Textual Criticism and the Textual Basis of a Translation of the OT," *BT* 26 (1975) 314-324; idem, "The Swedish OT Translation Project—Principles and Problems," *Theory and Practice of Translation* (Bern 1978) 151-164; K.R. Crim, "Versions, English," *IDBSup*, 933-938; A. Schenker, "Was übersetzen Wir?—Fragen zur Textbasis, die Sich aus der Textkritik ergeben," in: J. Gnilka and H.P. Rüger, eds., *Die Übersetzung der Bibel—Aufgabe der Theologie* (Bielefeld 1985) 65-80, and the discussions cited in these studies.

5 See W. McKane, "Textual and Philological Notes on the Book of Proverbs with Special Reference to the New English Bible," *Transactions of the Glasgow University Oriental Society 1971-1972*, 24 (1974) 76-90; R.P. Gordon, "The Citation of the Targums in Recent English Bible Translations (RSV, JB, NEB)," *JJS* 26 (1975) 50-60; C. Locher, "Der Psalter der 'Einheitsübersetzung' und die Textkritik, I," *Bib* 58 (1977) 313-341; ibid., II, 59 (1978) 49-79; H.P. Scanlin, "The Presuppositions of HOTTP and the Translator," *BT* 43 (1992) 101–116.

editor of the former edition is R. Kittel, who also wrote a systematic introduction to the procedure of editing the text of the Bible (Kittel* [p. 371). The following editions have appeared to date.

First edition (Leipzig 1905), based on the second Rabbinic Bible, and edited by R. **K**ittel—all editions of BH up to 1951 were called BH**K** after the first editor;

Second edition (Leipzig 1913), as above;

Third edition (Stuttgart 1929–1937), based on codex L and edited by R. Kittel and P. Kahle;

Seventh edition—sometimes also called the third edition (Stuttgart 1951), based on codex L and also containing variants from several Qumran texts.

The revised edition BHS, edited by W. Rudolph and K. Elliger, was also based on L (Stuttgart 1967–1977; last printing to date: 1990). This edition includes a smaller range of variants than BH.

From the third edition of BH onwards the evidence was divided into two apparatuses; a first apparatus including "less important" evidence and a second apparatus containing "more important" data. Beginning in 1951, a third apparatus containing details from the Qumran scrolls was added. BHS, on the other hand, combines all the evidence into *one* apparatus.

A new edition, BHQ (Biblia Hebraica Quinta), is in preparation.

BH and BHS share the following features:

1. The subjective choice of variants from all the textual witnesses and a selection of emendations that have been proposed over the generations. The selection of BH is more extensive than that of BHS.

2. An evaluation of variants and conjectural emendations. These evaluations are formulated in various ways, such as *l(ege)*, "read!", *dl = delendum*, "omit!", *ins(ere)*, "insert!", and *pr(aemitte)*, "place before!" By means of this terminology the editors indicate to the reader that 𝔐 ought to be changed in a certain direction. According to the editors, these changes are meant to restore details of the presumed original text of the biblical books.

3. The biblical text presented in BH from the third edition onwards and BHS is that of L, while its arrangement in the form of poetry or prose is based on the views of the editors.

The following innovations are found in BHS:

1. The combination of the three apparatuses into one.

2. A more extensive recording of material from the *Mp* (in the margins of the text) and from the *Mm* (in a separate apparatus under the text and in an accompanying volume by Weil [see p. 76]).

3. A more elaborate listing of the evidence from the Cairo Genizah and from the Qumran scrolls, albeit without any precise indication of the sources.

4. A general indication (without details) of the differences between 𝔐 and the ancient translations in certain grammatical categories such as the differences between singular and plural, indicated as *num(erus)*. This feature was first introduced in the HUB (see below).

5. The inclusion of details from the ancient translations is usually not accompanied by reconstructions into Hebrew.

6. A greater caution with regard to conjectural emendations.

In spite of these improvements many criticisms have been voiced against this edition on account of its inappropriate selection of variants, its lack of accuracy and consistency, and the insufficient attention given to the Qumran scrolls (see Tov* and Deist*).

The system of recording in the critical apparatus of BH/BHS and the symbols used in the edition are explained in detail by Levine*, Deist*, Scott*, Würthwein*, and Wonneberger*. The main abbreviations and frequently used words are presented in Table 1.

Table 1

Abbreviations and Words Frequently Used in BH and BHS

ad	ad	to, at
add	additum, addit, addunt	add(s), an addition
al	alii, -ae, -a, etc.	others
al loc	aliis locis	in other places (in the Bible)
c	cum	with (on the basis of)
cet	ceteri	the others
c ast	cum asterisco	marked with an asterisk
cf	confer	see!, compare!
cj	conjunge, -it, etc.	connect(s), combine(s)
cod(d)	codex, codices	
conj	conjectura	conjecture (emendation)
cp	caput	chapter
crrp, corr	corruptum	corrupt
dl	dele(ndum)	delete!
dub	dubium	dubious
Ed(d)	editio(nes)	edition(s)
et		and

frt	fortasse	possibly
gl	glossa(tum), etc.	gloss, "marginal reading"
hab	habet, -ent	has, have
init	initium, -ii, etc.	begin
ins	insere, -it	insert!, inserts
interv	intervallum	interval, blank space between words or verses
ita		so, thus
l	lege(ndum)	read!
leg	legit, -unt	read(s)
mg, marg	marginalis, in margine	in the margin
m(u)lt	multi, -ae, -a, etc.	many
m(tr) c(s)	metri causa	for metrical reasons
nonn	nonnulli, etc.	some
om	omittit, -unt	omit(s)
pass	passim	in many places
p(au)c	pauci, etc.	a few
pl(ur)	plures, pluralis	many, plural
pr(aem)	praemittit, unt, -e	place(s) before, place before!
prim man	prima manu	the first hand (of a MS)
pr(o)b	probabiliter	probably
prp(on)	proponit, -unt	propose(s)
prps	propositum, -o, etc.	proposed
rel	reliqui	the remaining ones (the rest)
s (sq, seq)	sequens	the following
sec	secundum	according to
semel		once
sim(il)	similiter	similarly
s(in)g	singularis	singular
ss (sqq)	sequentes	the following ones
super		over, above
tr(an)sp	transpone(ndum), it, -unt	transpose(s), transpose!
v, vs	versus	verse(s)
v(r)b	verbum, -a, etc.	word(s)
V(e)rs	versiones	translations
vid	vide(n)tur	apparently
+		add(s)
>		lack(s)
*		reconstructed form

C. The Hebrew University Bible

Until now two volumes have been published by the Hebrew University Bible Project (HUBP), presenting the Hebrew University Bible (HUB): M.H. Goshen-Gottstein, *The Hebrew University Bible, The Book of Isaiah* (Jerusalem 1995); C. Rabin, S. Talmon, E. Tov, *The Book of Jeremiah* (Jerusalem 1997)—see plate 28*. The system of this edition had been explained previously by M.H. Goshen-Gottstein, *The Book of Isaiah, Sample Edition with Introduction* (Jerusalem 1965). The volumes of Ezekiel and the Minor Prophets are in preparation.

This edition differs in several important respects from that of BH/ BHS:

1. The HUB divides the evidence, according to the nature of the witnesses, into four separate apparatuses together with an apparatus of notes:
   a. the ancient translations;
   b. Hebrew texts from the Second Temple period: rabbinic literature and texts from the Judean Desert;
   c. a selection of medieval codices (containing consonantal differences);
   d. a selection of medieval codices (containing mainly differences in vocalization and accents).

2. The HUB does not contain conjectural emendations.

3. The HUB does not take a position on the comparative value of readings.

4. In general terms, the HUB earmarks many of the differences between 𝔐 and the ancient translations in various grammatical categories with minimal designations, such as *num(erus)* for interchanges of singular/plural, and *diath(esis)* for interchanges of active/passive, etc. The recording of these categories is confined to an indication of the phenomenon without details about the readings themselves.

5. The first apparatus does not include retroversions into Hebrew of readings included in the ancient translations. These retroversions are mentioned in the notes.

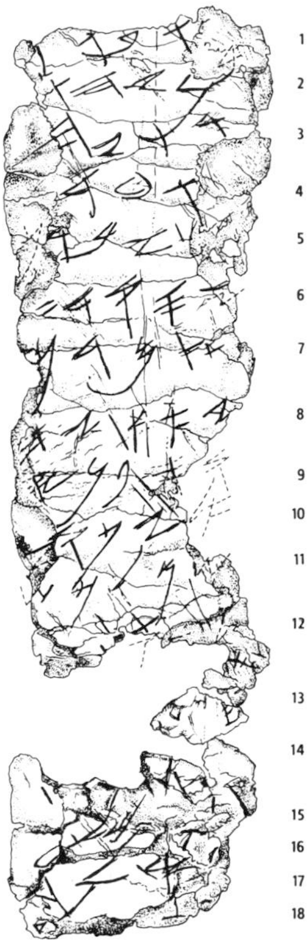

1 --הׄברׄוׄ[כ]
2 -אׄניהו-
3 -ר•יה[ו]
4 --בׄעה-
5 -שׄיברכׄ
6 יׄהוה וׄ
7 [י]שמרכ
8 יאר \| יה
9 [וה] \\ פניוׄ
10 [אל]יכ ויׄ
11 שׄמ לך ש
12 לׄוׄ[מ]--
13 -----
14 --•--
15 --כׄמׄ--
16 ------
17 -וׄרׄ-נׄ׳-
18 -----

Reconstruction of ll. 5-12

5 יְבָרֶךְ
6 יהוה וְ
7 יִשְׁמְרֶךָ
8 יָאֵר // יה
9 וה // פָּנָיו
10 אֵלֶיךָ וְיָ
11 שֵׂם לְךָ שָׁ
12 לוֹם

PLATE 1. One of the two minute silver rolls, II, found in Ketef Hinnom (Num 6:24-26). Drawing and transliteration of ll. 5-12 according to G. Barkay, "The Priestly Benediction on the Ketef Hinnom Plaques," *Cathedra* 52 (1989) 37-76 (Heb.).

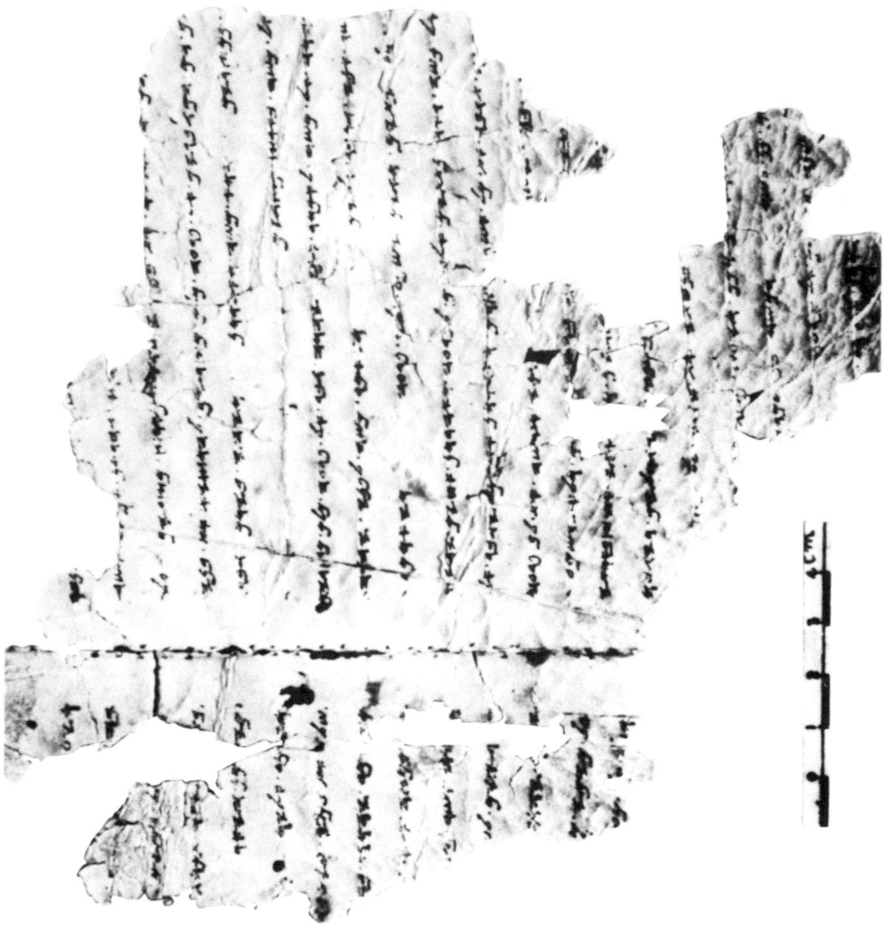

PLATE 2. A large Exodus scroll from cave 4 in Qumran in the paleo-Hebrew script, 4QpaleoExod[m], col. I (Exod 6:25–7:16).

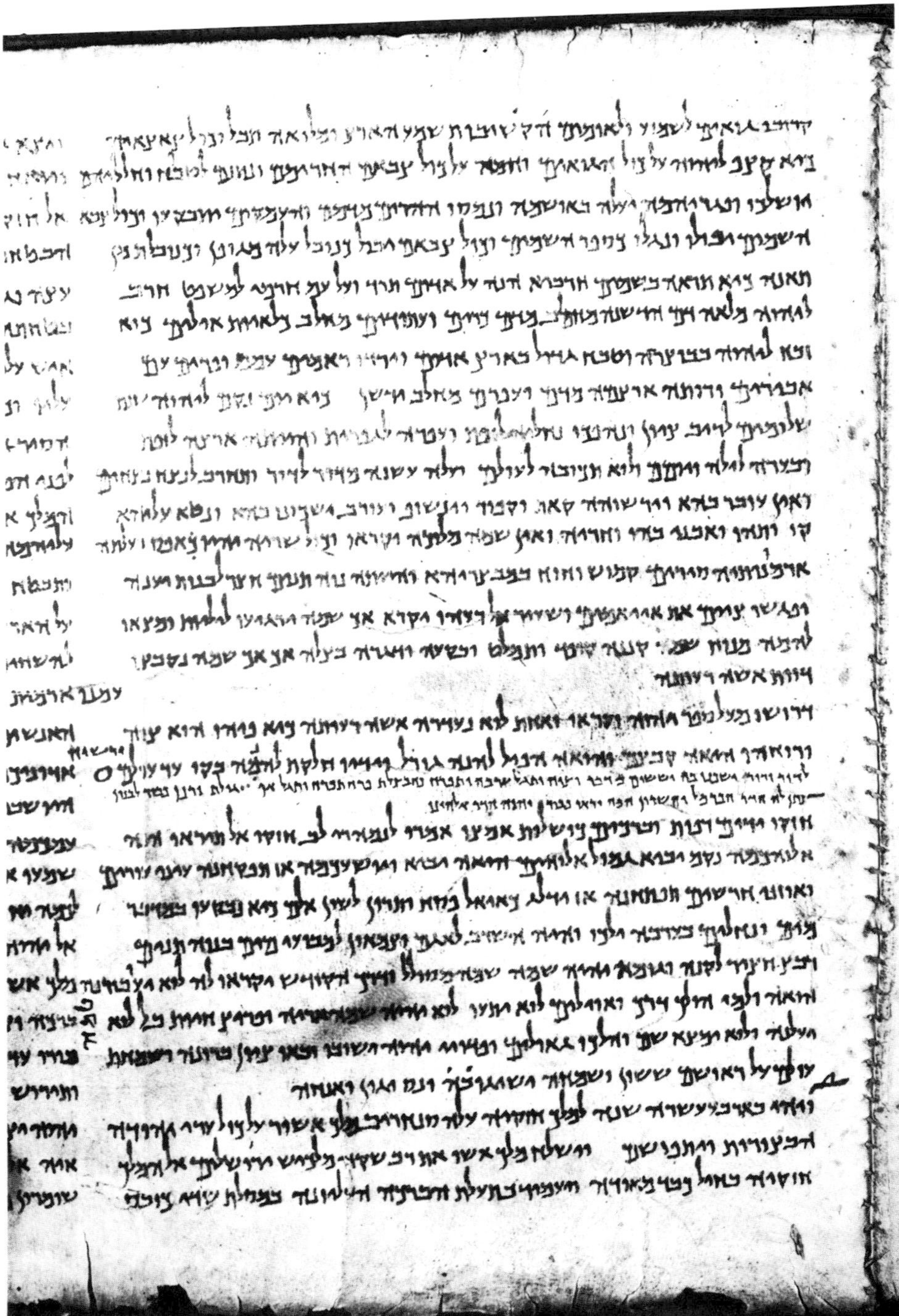

Plate 3. The large Isaiah scroll from cave 1 in Qumran, 1QIsa[a], col. XXVIII (Isa 34:1–36:2).

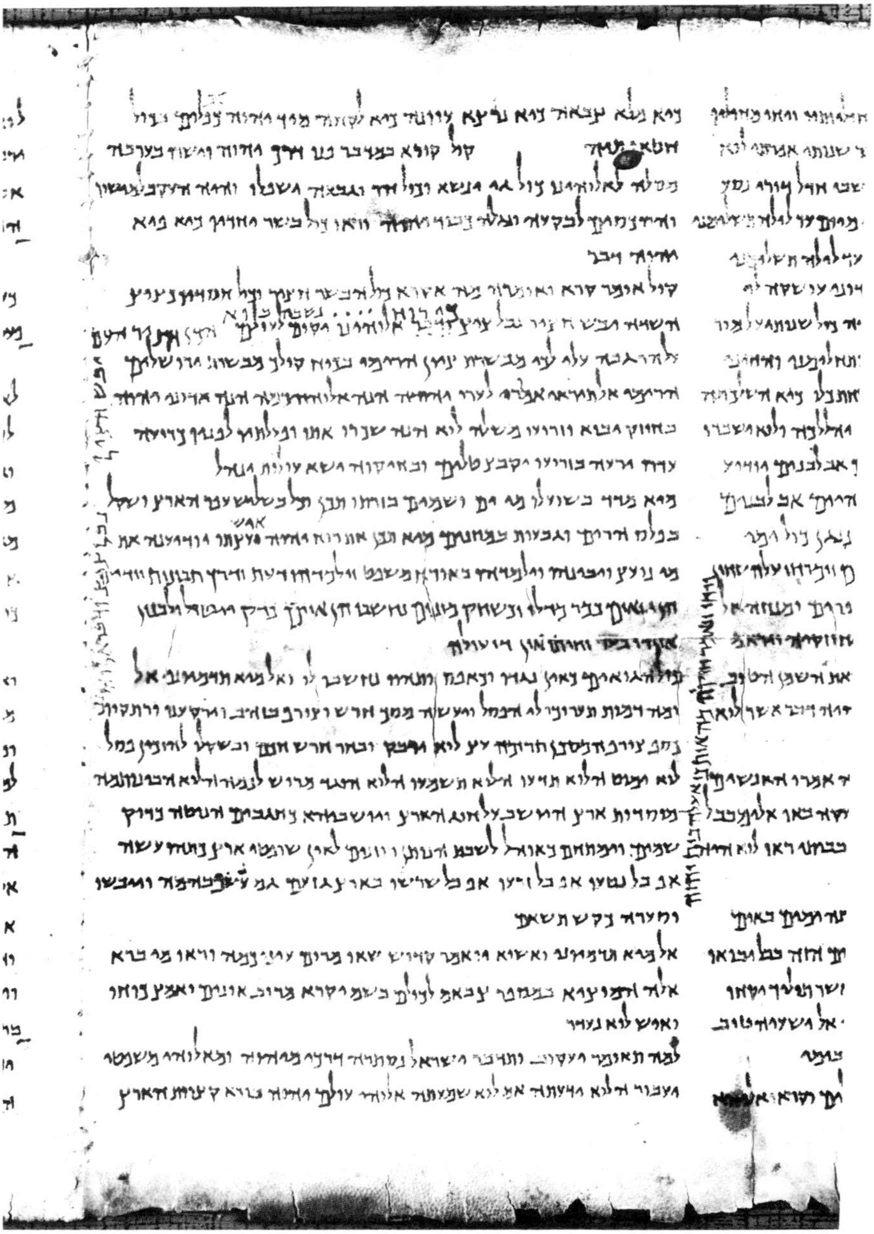

Plate 4. The large Isaiah scroll from cave 1 in Qumran, 1QIsa[a], col. XXXIII (Isa 40:2–28). Cf. plate 5.

כיא מלא צבאה כיא נרצא עוונה כיא לקחה מיד יהוה כפלים בכול
חטאותיה 3 קול קורא במדבר פנו דרך יהוה וישרו בערבה
מסלה לאלוהינו 4 כול גי ינשא וכול הר וגבעה ישפלו והיה העקב למישור
והרוכסים לבקעה 5 ונגלה כבוד יהוה וראו כול בשר יחדיו כיא פיא
יהוה דבר
6 קול אומר קרא ואומרה מה אקרא כול הבשר חציר וכול חסדיו כציץ
כי רוח .... נשבה בוא
השדה 7 יבש חציר נבל ציץ ודבר אלוהינו יקום לעולם הכן חציר העם
9 על הר גבה עלי לכי מבשרת ציון הרימי בכוח קולך מבשרת ירושלים
ו
הרימי אל תיראי אמרי לערי יהודה הנה אלוהכמה 10 הנה אדוני יהוה
בחוזק יבוא וזרועו משלה לוא הנה שכרו אתו ופעלתיו לפניו 11 כרועה
עדרו ירעה בזרועו יקבץ טלים ובחיקוה ישא עולות ינהל
12 מיא מדד בשועלו·מי ים ושמים בזרתו תכן וכל בשליש עפר הארץ ושקל
איש
בפלס הרים וגבעות במזנים 13 מיא תכן את רוח יהוה ועצתו יודיענה 14 את
מי נועץ ויבינהו וילמדהו באורח משפט וילמדהו דעת ודרך תבונות יודינו
15 הן גואים כמר מדלי וכשחק מזנים נחשבו הן איים כדק ייטול 16 ולבנון
אין די בער וחיתו אין די עולה
17 כול הגואים כאין נגדו וכאפס ותהוו נחשבו לו 18 ואל מיא תדמיוני אל
ומה דמות תערוכו לי 19 הפסל ויעשה מסך חרש וצורף בזהב וירקענו ורתקות
כסף צורף 20 המסכן תרומה עץ לוא ירבק ובחר חרש חכם ובשקלו להוכין פסל
לוא ימוט 21 הלוא תדעו הלוא תשמעו הלוא הוגד מרוש לכמה הלוא הבינותמה
מוסדות ארץ 22 היושב על חוג הארץ ויושביהא כחגבים הנוטה כדוק
שמים וימתחם כאוהל לשבת 23 הנותן רוזנים לאין שופטי ארץ כתהו עשה
ג
24 אף בל נטעו אף בל זרעו אף בל שרשו בארץ גזעם גם עשף בהמה וייבשו
וסערה כקש תשאם
25 אל מיא תדמיוני ואשוא יואמר קדוש 26 שאו מרום עיניכמה וראו מי ברא
אלה המוציא במספר צבאם לכולם בשם יקרא מרוב אונים ואמץ כוחו
ואיש לוא נעדר
27 למה תאומר יעקוב ותדבר ישראל נסתרה דרכי מיהוה ומאלוהי משפטי
יעבור 28 הלוא ידעתה אם לוא שמעתה אלוהי עולם יהוה בורא קצוות הארץ

8 יבש חציר נבל ציץ ודבר אלוהינו

Plate 5. The large Isaiah scroll from cave 1 in Qumran, 1QIsa[a], a transcription of col. XXXIII (Isa 40:2–28) from: M. Burrows, *The Dead Sea Scrolls of St. Mark's Monastery, I, The Isaiah Manuscript and the Habakkuk Commentary* (New Haven 1950). Cf. plate 4.

מח יז] כה אמר יהוה גאלך

[קדוש ישראל אני יהוה אלהיך] מ[ל]מדך להועיל מדרכיך בדרך תלך

יח-יט ולא הק[שבת למצותי ויהי כנ]הר שלמך וצדקתך כגלי הים ויהי

כחול זרעך [וצאצאי מעיך כמעת]יו לא יכרת ולא ישמד שמו מלפני

כ [צאו מבבל] ברחו מכשדים בקול רנה הגידו

השמיעו זאת הוצ[יאוה עד קצה ה]ארץ אמרו גאל יהוה עבדו יעקב

כא ולא צמאו בחרב[ות הוליכם מי]ם מצור הזיל למו ויבקע צר ויזבו מים

כב-מט א אין שלום אמר יה[וה לרשעים] שמעו איים אלי והקשיבו לאמים

ב מרחוק יהוה מבטן [קראני ממעי] אמי הזכיר שמי וישם פי כחרב חדה

ג בצל ידו החביאני וישי[מני לחץ ב]רור באשפתו הסתירני ויאמר לי עבדי

ד אתה ישראל אשר בך הת[פאר וא]ני אמרתי לריק יגעתי לתהו והבל כחי

ה כלתי אך משפטי את יהוה [ופעל]תי את אלהי וע[תה] כה אמר יהוה יוצרי

מבטן לעבד לו לשובב יעקב אליו ויש[ראל לא יאסף וא]כבד בעיני

ו יהוה ואלהי היה עזי ויאמר הנקל מה[יותך לי עבד · · · ·]ב את

שבטי יעקב ונצירי ישראל להשיב [ונתתיך לאור גוים להיות ישו]עתי

עד קצה ארץ

ז כה אמר אדני יהוה גואל ישרא[ל קדושו לבזה נפש למתעב גוי לעבד]

משלים מלכים יראו יקומו [שרים וישתחוו למען יהוה אשר נאמן]

ח קדוש ישראל ויבחרך [כה אמר יהוה בעת רצון עניתיך וביום

ישו]עה עזרתיך ואצרך ואת[נך לברית עם להקים ארץ להנחיל נחלות

ט ש]ממת לאמר לאסורים צ[או לאשר בחשך הגלו על דרכים ירעו

י ובכל שפי]ים מרעיתם ל[א ירעבו ולא יצמאו ולא יכם שרב ושמש

יא כי] מרחמם ינהגם ועל מב[ועי מים ינהלם ושמתי כל הרי לדרך ומסלתי

יב יר]מון הנה אלה מרחוק יב[או והנה אלה מצפון ומים ואלה מארץ סינים

יג רנו שמים וגילי א[רץ יפצחו הרים רנה כי נחם יהוה עמו

יד-טו ועניו י]רחם [ותאמר ציון עזבני יהוה ואדני שכחני

התשכח אשה עו]לה מ[רחם בן בטנה

מגילת ישעיה ב׳ ממערה 1 בקומראן (מג׳ ישׁ׳ב), דף 6 = לוח 8 (יש׳ מח 17 — מט 15)

PLATE 6. The short Isaiah scroll from cave 1 in Qumran, 1QIsa[b], p. 6 = plate 8 (Isa 48:17–49:15), according to the edition by E.L. Sukenik, *ʾwṣr hmgylwt hgnwzwt šbydy hʾwnybrsyṭh hʿbryt* (Jerusalem 1954).

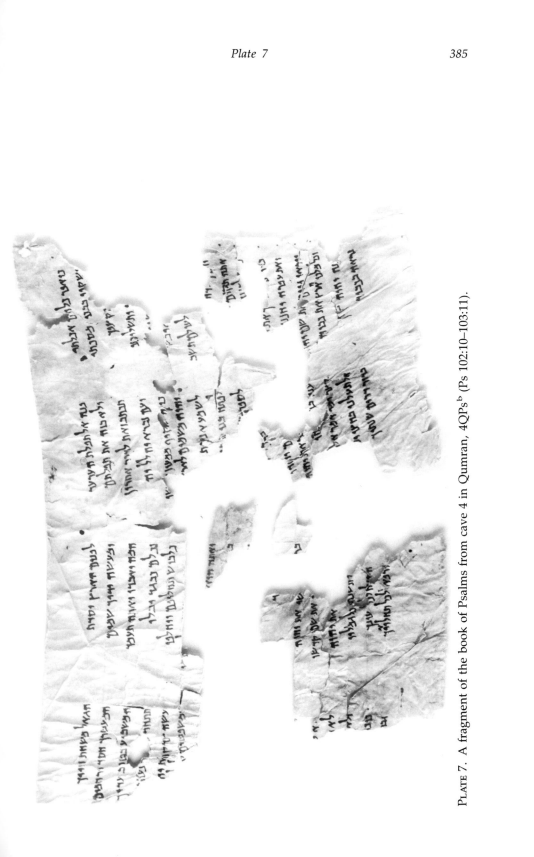

Plate 7. A fragment of the book of Psalms from cave 4 in Qumran, 4QPs^b (Ps 102:10–103:11).

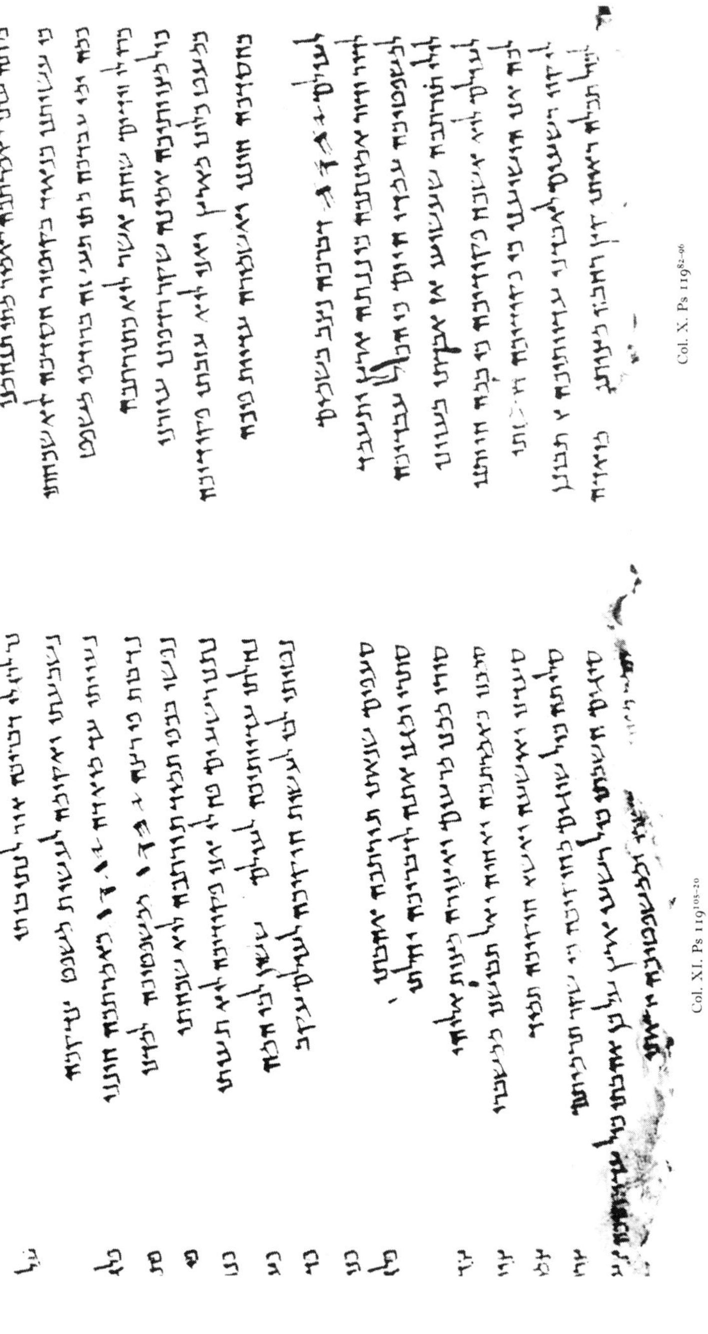

Col. X. Ps 119^{82-96}

Col. XI. Ps 119^{105-20}

PLATE 8. The so-called Psalms Scroll from cave 11 in Qumran, 11QPs^{a}, cols. X and XI (Ps 119:28–69, 105-120), from: J.A. Sanders, *The Psalms Scroll of Qumrân Cave 11* (DJD IV; Oxford 1965).

PLATE 8a. A Jeremiah text from cave 4 in Qumran, 4QJer[c], col. XXI (Jer 30:17–31:4).

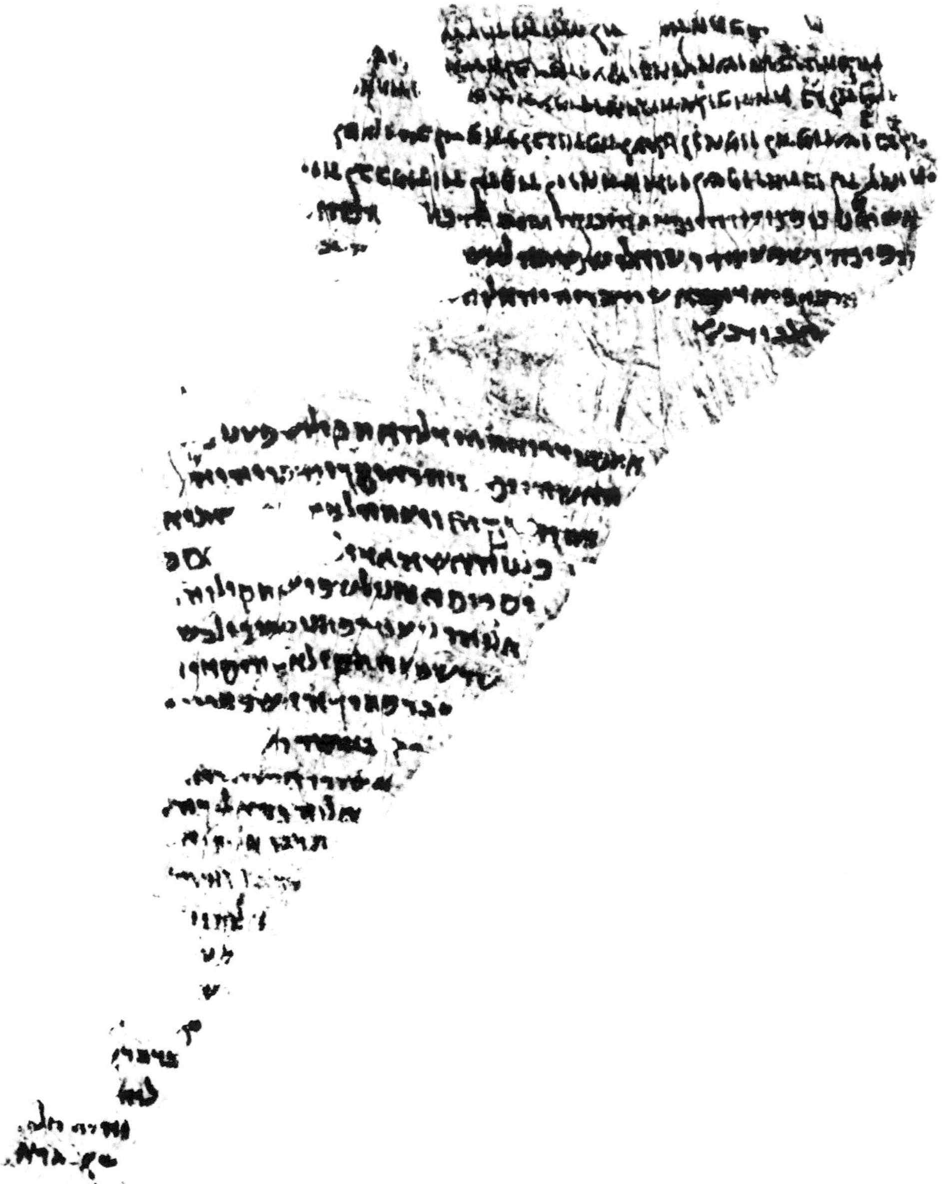

PLATE 9. *Tefillin*, 4QPhyl J verso, from Qumran (Deut 5:24–32; 6:2–3), from J.T. Milik, *Qumrân grotte 4, II* (DJD VI; Oxford 1977). Cf. plate 9′.

את כבודו ואת גודלו ואת קולו שמענו מ֯ת֯וך֯
האש היום הזה ראי{ו֯ו} כי ידבר יהוה
את ה֯אדם וחי [25]ועתה למה [נמ]ו֯ת֯ה֯ כ֯י תוא
כלנו האש הגדול[ה הזואת] א֯ם מ
וספ֯ים אנחנו לשמוע את קול יהו[ה]
אלוהינו עוד ומתנו [26]כי מי כול בש[ר א]
שר שמע את קול אלוהים חיי[ם מ]
דבר מתוך האש כמונ֯ו ו[יח]
י [27]ק[ר]ב אתה וש֯[מע את כול]
אשר יואמ֯ר֯ יהוה
אלוהינו אליכה ו[אתה]
תדבר אלינ֯ו את֯[כול אשר]
ידבר יהוה
אלוהינ֯ו [א]ל֯[יכה וש]
מענ[ו֯ ועשינו [28]וי]
שמ֯[ע יהוה את]
קו֯[ל דב]ר֯י֯כ֯[מה]
בדברכ֯[מה א]
לי וי[ואמר]
יהוה אל֯י֯
שמ֯ע֯תי א
ת֯ ק֯[ול דבר]
[י העם הזה]
[אשר דברו]
[אליכה הט]
[יבו כול א]
[שר דברו]

[[29]מי יתן ו]ה֯יה לבבמה זה להמה ליראה אותי ולשמור את כול ה֯צואתי
[כול הימים] למען יטב להמה ולבניהמה לעולם [30]לך אמור להמה שובו לכ֯ מ֯[ה]
[לאוהליכמה] [31]ואתה פ[וה ע]ומודה עמדי ואדברה אליכה את כול המצו[ה]
[החוקים והמ]שפ֯ט֯[ים] א֯שר תלמדמה ועשו בארץ אשר אנוכי נותן להמ֯[ה לרש]
[תה [32]ושמרתמה ל֯עשות כא]שר צוה יהוה אלוה[יכ]מה אתכמ֯ה֯ ל֯֯֯[ ]

אשר אנוכי מצוכ֯ה היום אתה ובנכה ובן בנכה כול [ימי ח]ייכה ול֯[מען יארכון]
ימיכה [3]ושמעתה ישראל ושמרתה לעש[ותמה אש]ר֯ יטב ל֯[כה ואשר]
תרבון מואדה כאשר דבר יהוה אלוהי֯ א֯[בותיכה לתת לכה ארץ זבת]
חלב ודבש

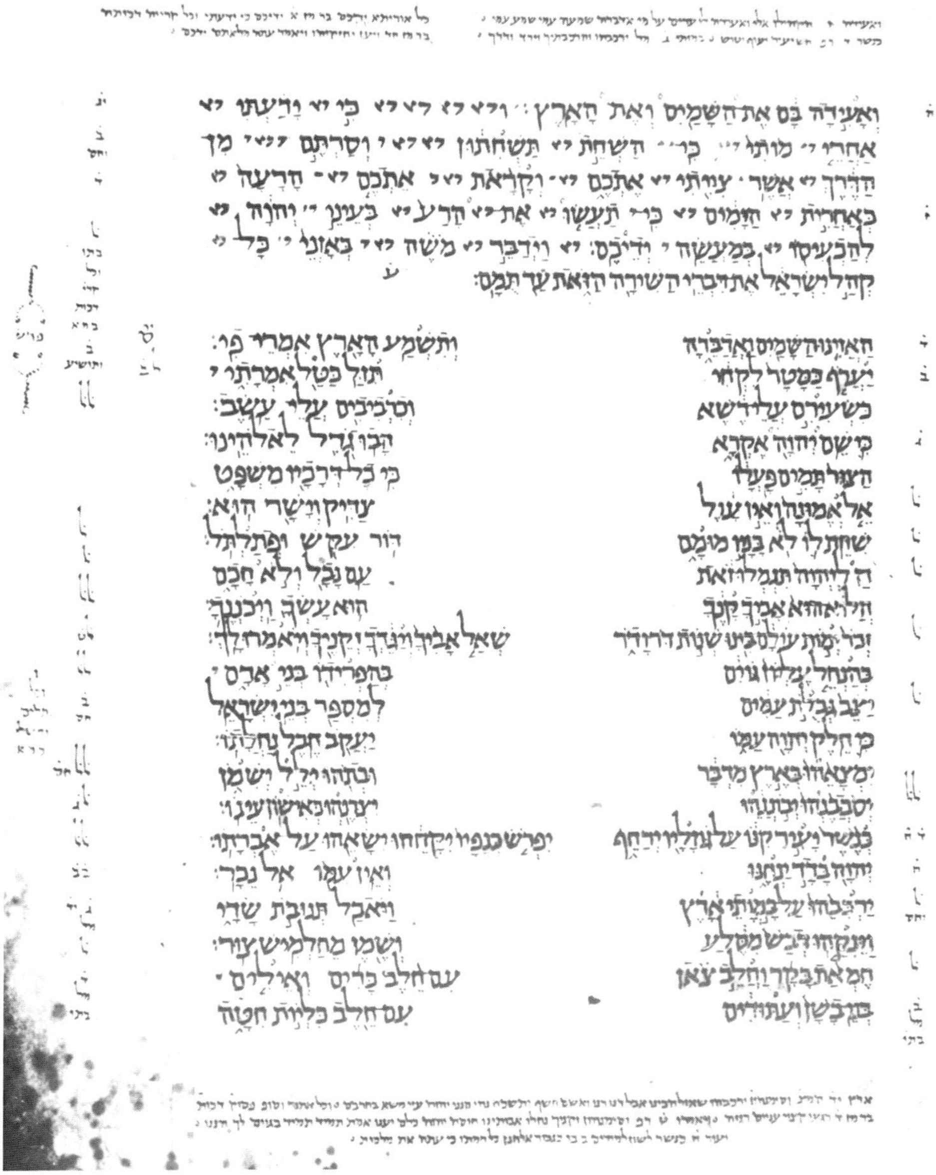

ואעידה בם את השמים ואת הארץ כי ידעתי
אחרי מותי כי השחת תשחתון וסרתם מן
הדרך אשר צויתי אתכם וקראת אתכם הרעה
באחרית הימים כי תעשו את הרע בעיני יהוה
להכעיסו במעשה ידיכם וידבר משה באזני כל
קהל ישראל את דברי השירה הזאת עד תמם

האזינו השמים ואדברה ותשמע הארץ אמרי פי
יערף כמטר לקחי תזל כטל אמרתי
כשעירם עלי דשא וכרביבים עלי עשב
כי שם יהוה אקרא הבו גדל לאלהינו
הצור תמים פעלו כי כל דרכיו משפט
אל אמונה ואין עול צדיק וישר הוא
שחת לו לא בניו מומם דור עקש ופתלתל
הליהוה תגמלו זאת עם נבל ולא חכם
הלוא הוא אביך קנך הוא עשך ויכננך
זכר ימות עולם בינו שנות דר ודר שאל אביך ויגדך זקניך ויאמרו לך
בהנחל עליון גוים בהפרידו בני אדם
יצב גבלת עמים למספר בני ישראל
כי חלק יהוה עמו יעקב חבל נחלתו
ימצאהו בארץ מדבר ובתהו ילל ישמן
יסבבנהו יבוננהו יצרנהו כאישון עינו
כנשר יעיר קנו על גוזליו ירחף יפרש כנפיו יקחהו ישאהו על אברתו
יהוה בדד ינחנו ואין עמו אל נכר
ירכבהו על במותי ארץ ויאכל תנובת שדי
וינקהו דבש מסלע ושמן מחלמיש צור
חמאת בקר וחלב צאן עם חלב כרים ואילים
בני בשן ועתודים עם חלב כליות חטה

PLATE 10. The Aleppo codex, p. 7 (Deut 31:28–32:14).

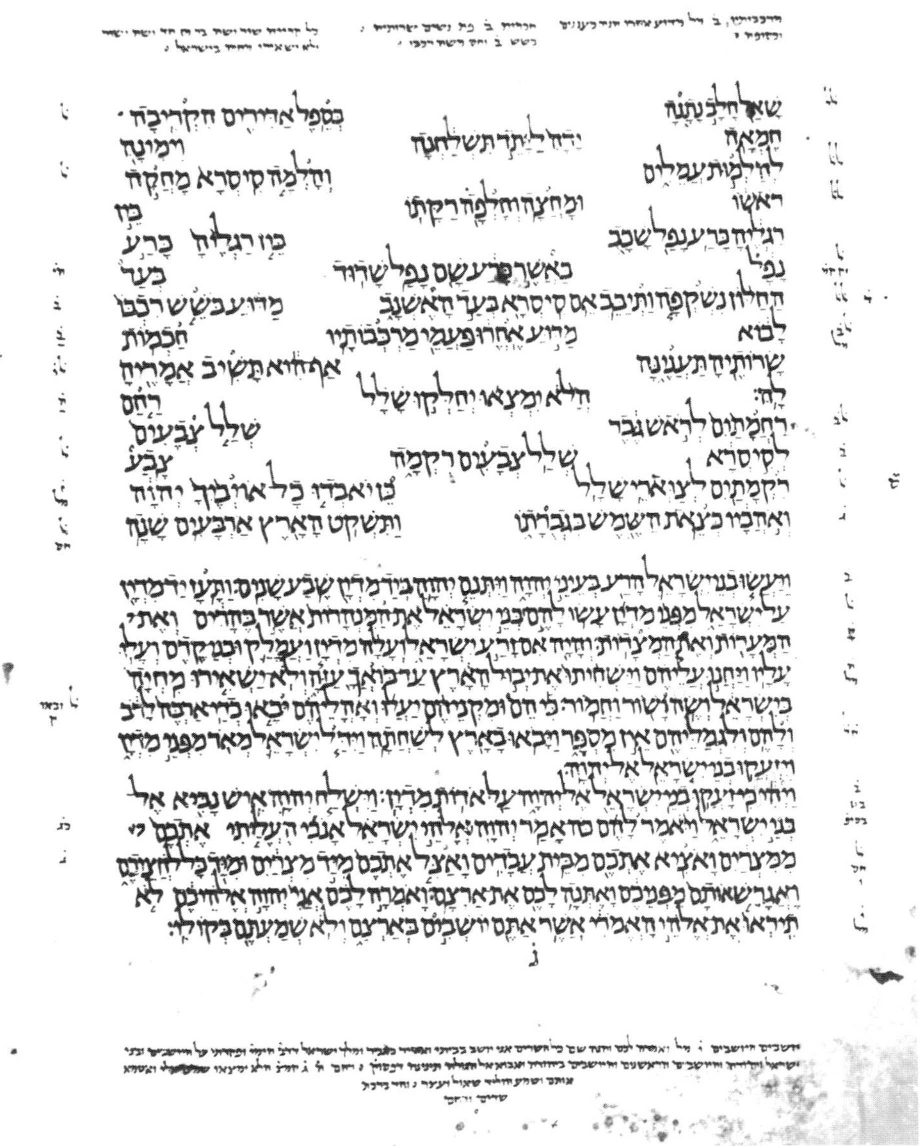

Plate 11. The Aleppo codex, p. 48 (Judg 5:25–6:10).

PLATE 12. The codex Leningrad B19[A] (Exod 14:28–15:14).

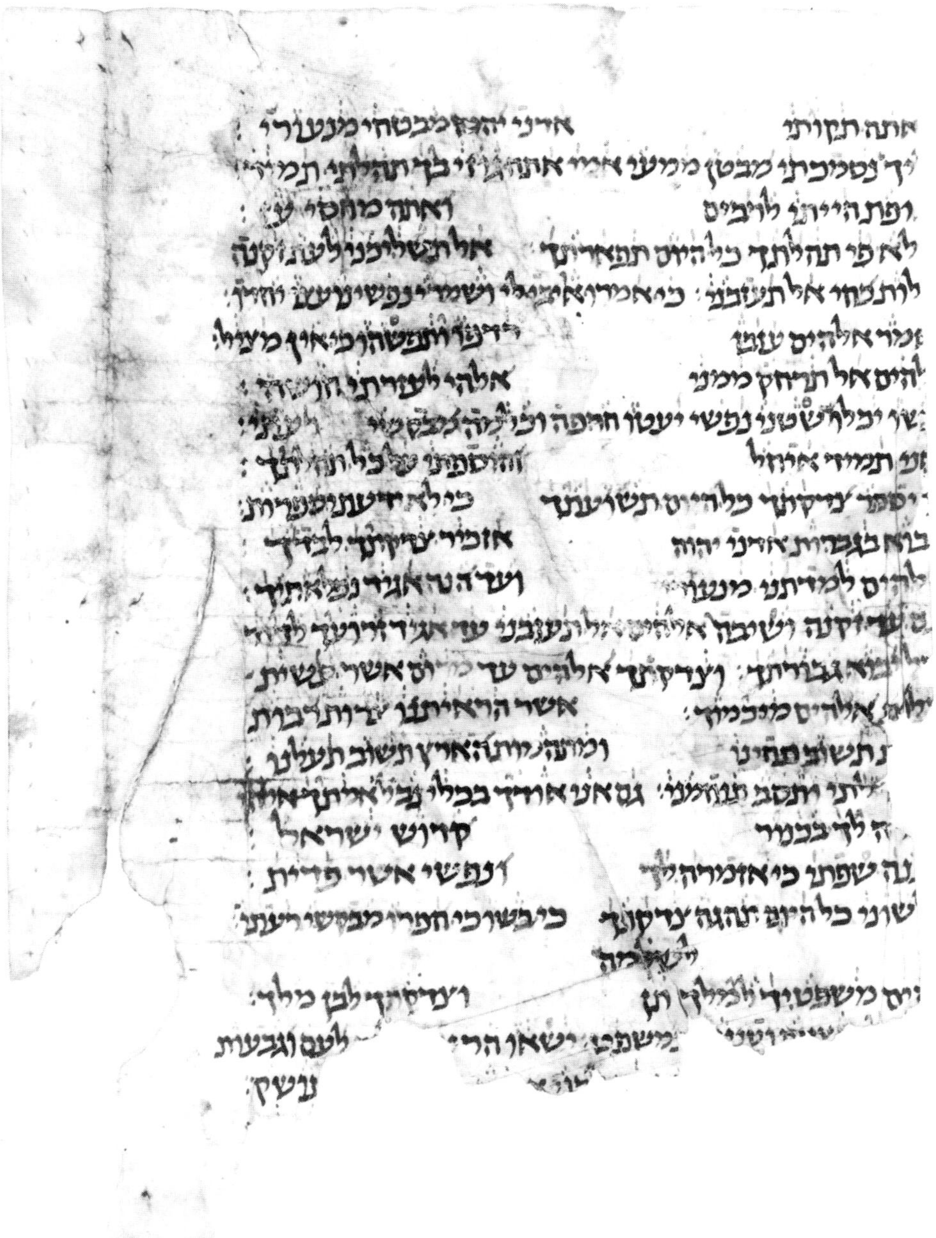

PLATE 13. A manuscript with Palestinian vocalization from the Cairo Genizah (Ps 71:5–72:4): Cambridge University Library T-S 12, 196.

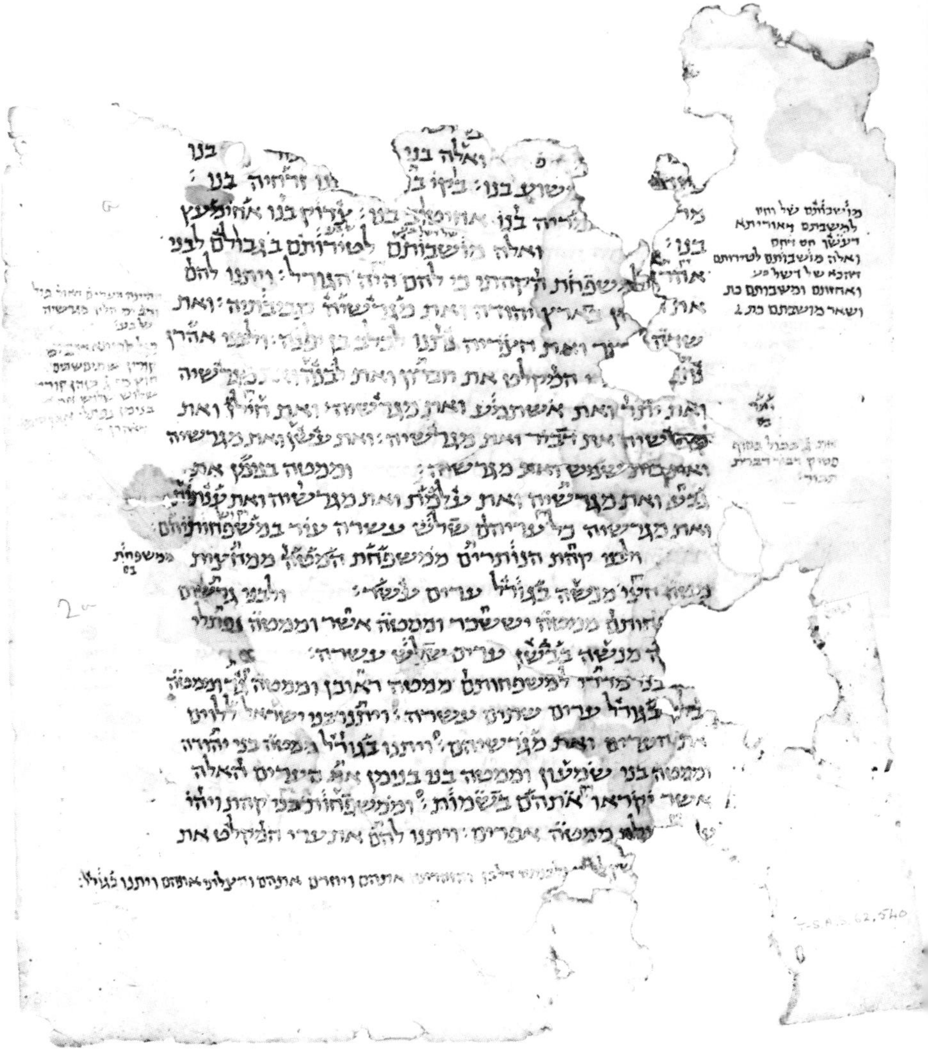

PLATE 14. A manuscript with "simple" Babylonian vocalization from the Cairo Genizah, EC 11, with notes from the *Masorah* (1 Chr 3:15–4:9): Cambridge University Library T-S Box A38,5.

TABULA ACCENTUUM

I. Accentus communes (in libris XXI)

A. Distinctivi vel domini

1. *Sillûq*, semper notat finem versus (*Sôp̄ pāsûq*), ut in . . דבר׃
2. *'Aṯnāḥ*, ut in . . . . דבר
3. *S^eḡôltā* (postpositivus), ut in דבר
4. *Šalšèleṯ*, ut in . . . . ׀דבר
5. *Zāqēp̄ parvum*, ut in . . . . דבר
6. *Zāqēp̄ magnum*, ut in . . . . דבר
7. *R^eḇî^a'*, ut in . . . . דבר
8. *Ṭip̄ḥā* (ante 'Aṯnāḥ et Sillûq), ut in . . . . דבר
9. *Zarqā* (postpositivus; ante S^eḡôltā), ut in . . . . דבר
10. *Pašṭā* (postpositivus), ut in דבר si sonus apud paenultimam , ut in . . . . מלך
11. *J^eṯiḇ* (praepositivus), nonnunquam pro Pašṭā, ut in . . מלך
12. *T^eḇîr*, ut in . . . . דבר
13. *Gèreš* vel *Ṭères*, ut in . . . . דבר
14. *Garšájim*, ut in . . . . דבר
15. *Pāzēr*, ut in . . . . דבר
16. *Pāzēr magnum* vel *Qarnê pārā* (cornua vaccae), ut in . . . . דבר
17. *T^elîšā magnum* (praepositivus), ut in . . . . דבר
18. *L^eḡarmēh* (Mûnāḥ cum Pāsēq; ante R^eḇî^a'), ut in . . . ׀דבר

B. Conjunctivi vel servi

19. *Mûnāḥ*, ut in . . . . דבר
20. *Mahpāḵ* vel *M^ehuppāḵ*, ut in דבר
21. *Mêr^eḵā*, ut in . . . . דבר
22. *Mêr^eḵā k^ep̄ûlā (M. duplex)*, ut in . . . . דבר
23. *Dargā*, ut in . . . . דבר
24. *'Azlā* (cum Gèreš: *Qaḏmā*), ut in . . . . דבר
25. *T^elîšā parvum* (postpositivus), ut in . . . . דבר
26. *Galgal* vel *Jèraḥ*, ut in . . . . דבר
27. *Máj^elā*, sed cf. I 8, ut in . . ויצא־נח

II. Accentus poëtici (in libris Psalmorum, Iob, Proverbiorum [תא״ם])

A. Distinctivi vel domini

1. *Sillûq* (cf. I 1), ut in . . . . . דבר׃
2. *'Ôlê w^ejôrēḏ* vel *Mêr^eḵā mahpaḵatum* (Mêr^eḵā cum Mahpāḵ), ut in . . . . דבר
3. *'Aṯnāḥ* (cf. I 2), ut in . . . . דבר
4. *R^eḇî^a' magnum*, ut in . . . . דבר
5. *R^eḇî^a' mugrāš* (R. cum Gèreš), ut in . . . . דבר
6. *Šalšèleṯ magnum* (cf. I 4), ut in . . . . ׀דבר
7. *Ṣinnôr* vel *Zarqā* (postpositivus), ut in . . . . דבר
8. *R^eḇî^a' parvum* (post ipsum occurrit 'Ôlê w^ejôrēḏ), ut in דבר
9. *D^eḥî* vel *Ṭip̄ḥā praepositivum* (praepositivus), ut in . . . . דבר
10. *Pāzēr* (cf. I 15), ut in . . . . דבר
11. *M^ehuppāḵ l^eḡarmēh* (M. cum Pāsēq), ut in . . . . ׀דבר
12. *'Azlā l^eḡarmēh* ('A. cum Pāsēq), ut in . . . . ׀דבר

B. Conjunctivi vel servi

13. *Mûnāḥ* (cf. I 19), ut in . . . דבר
14. *Mêr^eḵā* (cf. I 21), ut in . . . דבר
15. *'Illûj*, ut in . . . . דבר
16. *Ṭarḥā*, ut in . . . . דבר
17. *Galgal* vel *Jèraḥ* (cf. I 26), ut in . . . . דבר
18. *M^ehuppāḵ* vel *Mahpāḵ* (cf. I 20), ut in . . . . דבר
19. *'Azlā* vel *Qaḏmā* (cf. I 24), ut in . . . . דבר
20. *Šalšèleṯ parvum*, ut in . . . . דבר
21. *Ṣinnôriṯ* (ante Mêr^eḵā et Mahpāḵ in syllaba aperta), ut in . . . . . דבר (דבר)

Nota: Lineola (|), quam vocant *Pāsēq* (separator), etiam ad accentus accedit ad significandum eorum vim disjunctivam.

Württembergische Bibelanstalt Stuttgart

PLATE 15. Table of the biblical accents, from K. Elliger and W. Rudolph, *Biblia Hebraica Stuttgartensia* (Stuttgart 1967–1977).

PLATE 16. A manuscript of the Samaritan Pentateuch (Num 34:26–35:8) written by the scribe Abi-Berakhatah in the year 1215/6 (Jewish and National University Library, Jerusalem).

לוז

SAMAR.		GENES. XLIX. HEBR.	101
- - - - - - - - - - -		כי באפם הרגו איש	
- - - - - - ובֿרצונם		וברצנם עקרו שור :	
- - - - - - - - אדיר	7	ארור אפם כי עז	7
- - - - - - וחברתם		ועברתם כי קשתה	
- - - - - - - - - -		אחלקם ביעקב	
- - - - - - - - - -		ואפיצם בישראל :	
- - - - - - - - - -	8	יהודה אתה יודוך אחיך	8
- - - - - - - - ידיך		ידך בערף איביך	
- - - - - - - - - -		ישתחוו לך בני אביך :	
- - - - - - - - גור	9	גור אריה יהודה	9
- - - - - - - - - -		מטרף בני עלית	
- - - - - - - - - -		כרע רבץ כאריה	
- - - - - - - וכלביה		וכלביא מי יקימנו :	
- - - - - - - - - -	10	לא יסור שבט מיהודה	10
דגליו - - - - - - -		ומחקק מבין רגליו	
יבוא שילה - - - -		עד כי יבא שילה	
- - - - - - יקהתו - -		ולו יקהת עמים :	
עירו - - - - - - אסורי	11	אסרי לגפן עירה	11
איתנו - - - - - - - -		ולשרקה בני אתנו	
לבושו - - - - - - -		כבס ביין לבשו	
כסותו : - - - - - - -		ובדם ענבים סותה :	
- - - - - - - הכלילו	12	חכלילי עינים מיין	12
- - - - - - - - - -		ולבן שנים מחלב :	
- - - - - - - - - -	13	זבולן לחוף ימים ישכן	13
אניות - - - - - -		והוא לחוף אנית	
- - - - - - עד - - -		וירכתו על צידן :	
חמור גרים - - - - - -	14	יששכר חמר גרם	14
- - - - - - - - - -		רבץ בין המשפתים :	

SAMAR. VARIÆ LECTIONES.

7. ועברתם — וחברתם 62, 503. אחליקם — אחלקם 64 — ואחליקם 61. ביעקב — ק ‸ 66.

8 — 12. Hæc 5 commata comma feptimum fequuntur, ad imam paginam, literis minoribus, et forte ab alia manu; 127.

8. ירוך — יורך 61, 66. בערסי — בערף 197. וישתחוו 61, 62, 63, 64, 65, 66, 127. 183. 197.

9. גור 61, 64, 65. 66, 127. 197. 221, 334.

10. ומחוקק — ומחקק 62 ומחקק — 221. 183. 127, 64 וכמחקק — ומחקק 61 — ובמחקק 197. יקהתו — יקרהו 61, 63, 64, 65, 127, 183, 221, 503. 504; forte 197.

11. ולשריקה 61, 62, 183. בני — בנה 64. אתנו ~ איתנו 61.

12. הכלילו — י ‸ 127 — הכלילו 61.

13. לחוף — ה ‸ 61. על — עד 363 Houb. צידן — צרן 64 — צדון 66, 221.

14. חמור — ו ‸ 66, 127. המשפחים — מ ‸ 61.

HEBR.

כברי וזהר fup. raf. 99. כבודי 1, 6, 11, 69, 84, 89. 108. 129, 150, 173, 190, 193, 223, 226, 244, 260, 264, 298 — forte 135. איש ‸ 109. וברצינם 6, 9, 11, 17, 18, 19, 75, 89, 108, 136, 166, 186, 193, 227, 244, 249; forte 128. עקרו — הרעק 111.

7. ועברתם forte ואברתם 155.

8. יודוך — ידוך 129. ידיך his 111. אחיך ידך בערף primo; fup. raf. 6. בערף — בעירף 129, 152, 193, 244, 260; primo 67. איבך — ‸ 5 איבך 17, 80, 109, 193; primo 170. ישתחוו — וישתחוו 1, 80, 84, 152, 223, 600. בני ‸ 109. אבך primo; אביך 84 — כי fup. raf. 82.

9. בני ‸ 81. עלית — עליתה 69. רבץ primo שכב רבץ 129.

10. שבט ‸ 94. ומחקק — ומחוקק 18, 80, 84, 181, 226. עד — על 660; רגלו primo רגלת 29. רגלו מבין ‸ 314. יבוא — 152 בא — 157 ‸ יבא. כי ‸ 176. vide 2, 391.

שילה — שלח 1, 9. 18, 84, 132, 136, 158, 176, 211, 226, 300, 401, 404. 411, 448, 464, 481, 489, 562, 583. 601, 608, 611, 615, 631, 636; nunc 170 — ה fup. raf. 82, 672 C — שילו 474, 581, 651 — marg. habet ק' שילו 314. ולו — ולא 81; primo 102, 223, 423; forte 129, 155 — ו in fup. raf. 672 C — marg. habet ק' לו 227. יקהת primo יקוהת 99.

10, 11. עירה - - - - ולו fup. raf. 82.

11. עירה — י ‸ 84 — עירו 69, 80, 247, 653 — marg. habet ק' עירו 173, 178, 188, 189. ולשרקה — ולשריקה 171, 282. אתנו — אתונו 69 — אתנה 189, 227, 239. כבס — כבס 284. לבשו — לבושו 1, 4, 17, 69, 84, 108, 111, 129, 193, 226, 244, 248, 260; primo 168 — לבשה 199, 227, 239. ובדם — ו ‸ 615 — כ ‸ 158. ענבים — ענב 69. ענבים סותה fup. raf. 125. סותה — סותו 5, 9, 18, 75, 80, 109, 111, 129, 132, 136, 150, 152, 158, 168, 173, 177, 178, 181, 186, 193, 237, 244, 615 — סותו ק' 659.

12. חכלילי — ח majufc. 177, 200 — חכליל 17. עינים primo ענינים 95. שנים — שינים 1, 132, 248; primo 41 forte 155 — שניים 9.

13. זבולן — ו ‸ 81, 168, 181, 193, 216, 237 — זבולן 239 — זבלון 152. לחוף — ו ‸ 1, 9, 17, 18, 19, 75, 168, 178, 260. ישכן 9, 69, 109, 129, 170, 178, 223, 300 T. והוא לחוף אנית ‸ 109. והוא — הוא 150. לחוף — ו ‸ 1, 2, 9, 17, 18, 75, 168. אניות 1, 4, 6, 9, 11, 17, 18, 19, 69, 80, 84, 89, 101, 108, 110, 111, 132, 144, 170, 173, 176, 178, 189, 190, 193, 226, 244, 248, 249, 253, 260; primo 82; forte 139, 155 — אנית fup. raf. 129. על — עד 1, 69, 80, 125, 693 'וס; primo 84; nunc 129 — ל fup. raf. 109, 294. צידן 9, 19, 69, 80, 108, 129, 170, 181, 248, 260.

14. וזאר 1, 2, 9, 11, 17, 69, 89, 108, 109, 129, 150, 226, 244, 248, 260; primo 80, 136, 158. גרם — גרים 9. רבץ — רובץ 9, 129, 193. בין ‸ 157 — י ‸ 158.

2 C

Plate 17. The Kennicott edition of Gen 49:6–14: B. Kennicott, *Vetus Testamentum hebraicum, cum variis lectionibus*, vols. I-II (Oxford 1776–80). See p. 37.

25 וַיִּמָּלֵא שִׁבְעַת יָמִים, אַחֲרֵי הַכּוֹת יְהֹוָה אֶת
26 הַיְאֹר. וַיֹּאמֶר יְהֹוָה אֶל מֹשֶׁה, בֹּא אֶל
פַּרְעֹה וְאָמַרְתָּ אֵלָיו, כֹּה אָמַר יְהֹוָה, שַׁלַּח אֶת
27 עַמִּי וְיַעַבְדֻנִי. וְאִם מָאֵן אַתָּה לְשַׁלֵּחַ, הִנֵּה אָנֹכִי
28 נֹגֵף אֶת כָּל גְּבוּלְךָ בַּצְפַרְדְּעִים. וְשָׁרַץ הַיְאֹר צְפַרְדְּעִים,
וְעָלוּ וּבָאוּ בְּבֵיתֶךָ וּבַחֲדַר מִשְׁכָּבְךָ
וְעַל מִטָּתֶךָ וּבְבֵית עֲבָדֶיךָ וּבְעַמֶּךָ, וּבְתַנּוּרֶיךָ
29 וּבְמִשְׁאֲרוֹתֶיךָ. וּבְכָה וּבְעַמְּךָ וּבְכָל עֲבָדֶיךָ,
יַעֲלוּ הַצְפַרְדְּעִים. . . . .
. . . .
. . . .
. . . .
. . . .
. . . .
. . . .
. . . .
. . . .
. . . .
. . . .

ח

1 וַיֹּאמֶר יְהֹוָה אֶל מֹשֶׁה, אֱמֹר אֶל אַהֲרֹן,
נְטֵה אֶת יָדְךָ בְּמַטֶּךָ עַל הַנְּהָרֹת עַל הַיְאֹרִים
וְעַל הָאֲגַמִּים, וְהַעַל אֶת הַצְפַרְדְּעִים עַל אֶרֶץ
מִצְרָיִם. . . . .
. . . .
2 . . . . וַיֵּט אַהֲרֹן אֶת יָדוֹ עַל
מֵימֵי מִצְרָיִם, וַתַּעַל הַצְפַרְדֵּעַ, וַתְּכַס אֶת אֶרֶץ
3 מִצְרָיִם. וַיַּעֲשׂוּ כֵן הַחַרְטֻמִּים . . . .
בְּלָטֵיהֶם, וַיַּעֲלוּ הַצְפַרְדְּעִים עַל אֶרֶץ
4 מִצְרָיִם. וַיִּקְרָא פַרְעֹה לְמֹשֶׁה וּלְאַהֲרֹן, וַיֹּאמֶר,
הַעְתִּירוּ אֶל יְהֹוָה וְיָסֵר הַצְפַרְדְּעִים מִמֶּנִּי וּמֵעַמִּי,
5 וַאֲשַׁלְּחָה אֶת הָעָם, וְיִזְבְּחוּ לַיהֹוָה. וַיֹּאמֶר מֹשֶׁה
לְפַרְעֹה, הִתְפָּאֵר עָלַי, לְמָתַי אַעְתִּיר לְךָ וְלַעֲבָדֶיךָ
וּלְעַמְּךָ, לְהַכְרִית הַצְפַרְדְּעִים מִמְּךָ וּמִבָּתֶּיךָ,
. . . . רַק בַּיְאֹר תִּשָּׁאַרְנָה.
6 וַיֹּאמֶר לְמָחָר, וַיֹּאמֶר כִּדְבָרְךָ. לְמַעַן תֵּדַע כִּי
7 אֵין כַּיהֹוָה אֱלֹהֵינוּ. וְסָרוּ הַצְפַרְדְּעִים מִמְּךָ וּמִבָּתֶּיךָ,
8 וּמֵעֲבָדֶיךָ וּמֵעַמֶּךָ, רַק בַּיְאֹר תִּשָּׁאַרְנָה. וַיֵּצֵא
מֹשֶׁה וְאַהֲרֹן מֵעִם פַּרְעֹה, וַיִּצְעַק מֹשֶׁה אֶל יְהֹוָה
9 עַל דְּבַר הַצְפַרְדְּעִים אֲשֶׁר שָׂם לְפַרְעֹה. וַיַּעַשׂ
יְהֹוָה כִּדְבַר מֹשֶׁה, וַיָּמֻתוּ הַצְפַרְדְּעִים מִן הַבָּתִּים,
10 מִן הַחֲצֵרֹת וּמִן הַשָּׂדֹת. וַיִּצְבְּרוּ אֹתָם

וימלאו שבעת ימים, אחרי הכות יהוה את
היאר. ★ ויאמר יהוה אל משה, בא אל
פרעה ודברת אליו, כה אמר יהוה, שלח את
עמי ויעבדני. ואם מאן אתה לשלח, הנה אנכי
נגף את כל גבולך בצפרדעים. ושרץ היאר צפרדעים,
ועלו ובאו בבתיך ובחדרי משכביך
ועל מטתיך ובבתי עבדיך ובעמך, ובתנוריך
ובמשארתיך ובך ובעמך ובכל עבדיך
יעלו הצפרדעים. ★ ויבא משה
ואהרן אל פרעה וידברו אליו כה
אמר יהוה שלח את עמי ויעבדני.
ואם מאן אתה לשלח הנה אנכי
נגף את כל גבולך בצפרדעים.
ושרץ היאר צפרדעים ועלו ובאו
בבתיך ובחדרי משכביך ועל
מטתיך ובבתי עבדיך ובעמך
ובתנוריך ובמשארתיך ובך
ובעמך ובכל עבדיך יעלו
הצפרדעים ★

ויאמר יהוה אל משה, אמר אל אהרן,
נטה את ידך במטך על הנהרות ועל היארים
ועל האגמים, והעל את הצפרדעים על ארץ
מצרים. ויאמר משה אל אהרן נטה
את ידך במטך ותעל הצפרדע
על ארץ מצרים. ויט אהרן את ידו על
מימי מצרים, ותעל הצפרדע, ותכס את ארץ
מצרים. ויעשו כן חרטמי מצרים
בלהטיהם, ויעלו הצפרדעים על ארץ
מצרים. ויקרא פרעה למשה ולאהרן, ויאמר,
העתירו ליהוה ויסר הצפרדעים ממני ומעמי,
ואשלח את העם, ויזבחו ליהוה. ויאמר משה
לפרעה, התפאר עלי, למתי אעתיר לך ולעבדיך
ולעמך, להכרית הצפרדעים ממך ומבתיך,
ומעבדיך ומעמך רק ביאר תשארנה.
ויאמר למחר, ויאמר כדבריך. למען תדע כי
אין כיהוה אלהינו. וסרו הצפרדעים ממך ומבתיך,
ומעבדיך ומעמך, רק ביאר תשארנה. ויצא
משה ואהרן מעם פרעה, ויצעק משה אל יהוה
על דבר הצפרדעים אשר שם לפרעה. ויעש
יהוה כדבר משה, וימתו הצפרדעים מן הבתים,
ומן החצרות ומן השדות ויצברו אתם

Plate 18. A. and R. Sadaqa, *Jewish and Samaritan Version of the Pentateuch* (Tel Aviv 1961–1965) (Exod 7:25–8:10).

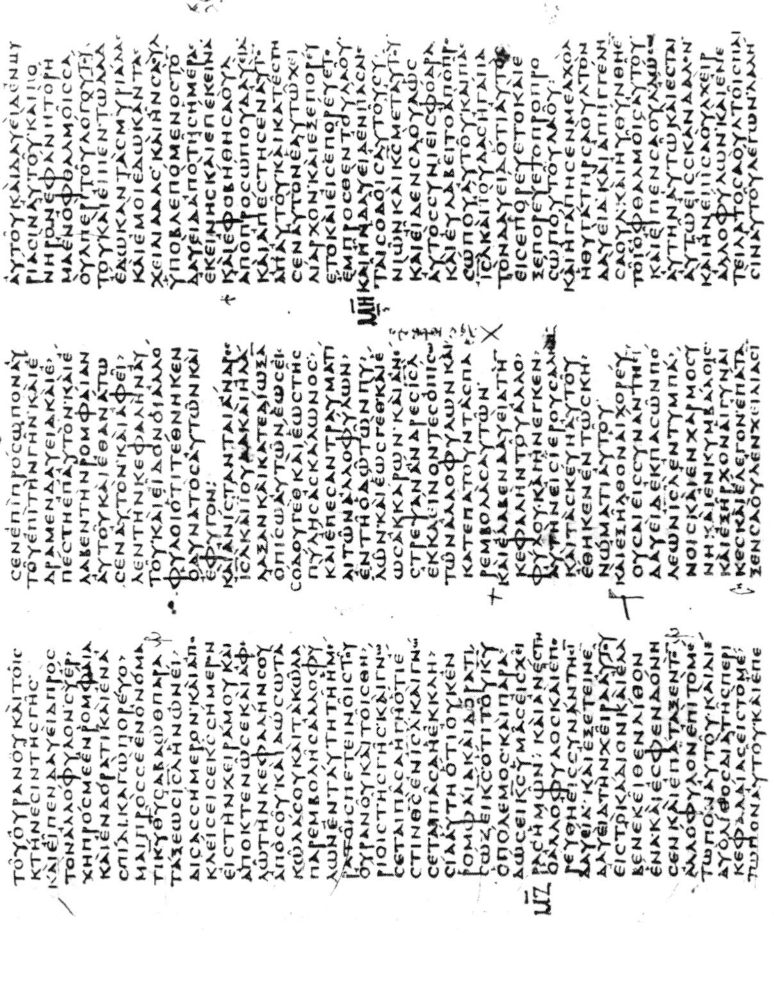

PLATE 19. Codex Vaticanus (Cod. Vat. Gr. 1209 *or* B) of the Septuagint (1 Sam 17:44–18:22) from *Bibliorum SS. graecorum codex Vaticanus 1209 (cod. B) denovo phototypice expressus iussa et cura praesidium bybliothecae Vaticanae, pars prima, Testamentum Vetus*, I (Mediolani 1905) 333.

ΙΕΡΕΜΙΑΣ

1 **1** [1]*Τὸ ῥῆμα τοῦ θεοῦ, ὃ ἐγένετο ἐπὶ Ιερεμίαν τὸν τοῦ Χελκίου ἐκ τῶν*
2 *ἱερέων, ὃς κατῴκει ἐν Αναθωθ ἐν γῇ Βενιαμιν·* [2]*ὃς ἐγενήθη λόγος τοῦ*
θεοῦ πρὸς αὐτὸν ἐν ταῖς ἡμέραις Ιωσία υἱοῦ Αμως βασιλέως Ιουδα
3 *ἔτους τρισκαιδεκάτου ἐν τῇ βασιλείᾳ αὐτοῦ.* [3]*καὶ ἐγένετο ἐν ταῖς*
ἡμέραις Ιωακιμ υἱοῦ Ιωσία βασιλέως Ιουδα ἕως ἑνδεκάτου ἔτους
τοῦ Σεδεκία υἱοῦ Ιωσία βασιλέως Ιουδα ἕως τῆς αἰχμαλωσίας Ιερου-
σαλημ ἐν τῷ πέμπτῳ μηνί.
4
5 [4]*Καὶ ἐγένετο λόγος κυρίου πρὸς αὐτόν* [5]*Πρὸ τοῦ με πλάσαι σε ἐν*

Inscriptio *Ιερεμιας* B-S-239 A-410 V-26-46-130'-233-449-544 L^{-36}-198 C'^{-764}; *ιερεμιας προφητης* Q-538; *ο προφητης ιερεμιας* 62; *ιερεμιου του προφητου* 106 Aeth; *προφητεια ιερεμιου* 36-407 613 Syh (+ *κατα την εκδοσιν των εβδομηκοντα*); *λογοι ιερεμιου υιου χελκιου* (del. *υιου χελκιου* ^{c}) et *ιερεμιας* 88

1 1 om. *Τό* Chr. VI 14 XI 439 | *τοῦ θεοῦ, ὃ ἐγένετο*] ÷ *O* | *τοῦ θεοῦ*] *κυριου* Arab Chr. XI 439; om. *τοῦ* Chr. VI 14 | *ὃ ἐγένετο*] *ο εγενηθη* Chr. XI 439; om. *ὅ* Chr. VI 14 | *ἐπὶ Ιερ.*] *επ ιηρεμιαν* A; *προς ιερ.* Chr.^{cit}; *επι τον ιερ.* 87 | *Χελκίου*] + *ος ην* PsAth. IV 289 Or.^{lat} IX 137 | *κατῴκει*] ÷ *O*; *κατοικησει* S* | *Αναθωθ*] *αθαθωθ* 198; *αναθωμ* 613; *αθωθ* 36* 87-239 130 233: cf. 11_{23} 36_{27} 39_{7} 2 *ὅς*] *ως* 22^{c}-62 534 = Sixt. | *ἐγενήθη*] *εγενετο* L'-130'-233 26 Tht. (= II 1268^{p}) | *λόγος*] pr. *ο* 534; *προς* 544 | *τοῦ θεοῦ*] *κυριου* Q-V-26-106-239-449-534-538-544 *O* Aeth Arm Eus. c. Marc. 2,4 Tht.^{cit} = 𝔐↓; om. *τοῦ* A 51-62-130' Tht. | *πρὸς αὐτόν*] *προς ιερεμιαν* Eus. Tht.^{cit}; *ad me* Aeth: cf. 4; > Bo Arm | om. *ταῖς* 26 Or. III 2 Tht.^{cit} | *Ιωσ(ε)ία* B-S-239 A]-*σιου* rel.: cf. 3 3_{6} $22_{11\ 18}$ $25_{1\ 3}$ 33_{1} 42_{1} $43_{1\ 2}$ 44_{1} 51_{31} Bar. 1_{8} et Thack. p. 162 | *υἱοῦ Αμως*] pr. *του* Or.; > 410 | *Αμως* Or.] *αμμως* 91 46; *αμων* (*αμμων* 62 544) V-544 *O* *l*-198 Arm = 𝔐: cf. 25_{3} Soph. 1_{1} Regn. IV $21_{18\ 19\ 23-25}$ Par. I 3_{14} II $33_{20-23\ 25}$ | *ἔτους τρισκαιδεκ.*] tr. 88 Arm = 𝔐 | *ἐν τῇ βασ.*] *της βασιλειας* 534 Arm 3 *Ιωσ(ε)ία*1⁰ B-S A]-*σιου* rel.: cf. 2 | *ἕως*1⁰] + *συντελειας* S *O* L'-130' Aeth Arm Or. III 2 (*της συντελειας του*) = 𝔐; pr. *και* L'-S^{ca}-130'-613; 1⁰⌒2⁰ 106 239 | *τοῦ* B] > rel.: cf. 25_{3} 26_{2} 39_{1} $43_{1\ 9}$ $46_{1\ 2}$ 51_{31} | *Σεδεκία* B-S 26]-*κιου* rel.: cf. 26_{1} 28_{59} 35_{1} $46_{1\ 2}$ $52_{1\ 5\ 10\ 11}$ et Thack. p. 162 | *Ιωσ(ε)ία*2⁰ B-S-538 V-26-46-544]-*σ(ε)ιου* rel.: cf. 2 | om. *Ιερουσαλημ* 544 | *πέμπτῳ μ.*] *μ. τω πεμπτω* *O*-233 verss.^{p} = 𝔐 4 om. *Καί* 51-449 Arm^{p} | *πρὸς αὐτόν* B-S-239-410 L'-130' Or. III 3 Tht.^{p}: cf. 2] *προς με* rel. (Eus. in Is. 44_{24}) = 𝔐: cf. 11_{13} | fin. B-S-410 407 87^{txt}-613] + *λεγων* rel. (Eus.) = 𝔐: cf. 23_{33} $33_{17\ 18}$ 46_{16} 5 *Πρὸ τοῦ*] *πριν* GregNyss. II 1184 | *με*] *εμε* GregNyss.; *σε* 46^{s} 534 | *σε*1⁰] *με* 534 | *ἐν κοιλίᾳ*] *εκ κοιλιας* A 46 534 Aeth Arab

---

1 1 *Τὸ ῥῆμα — Χελκίου*] *το εβρ' και αι λοιπαι εκδοσεις· λογοι ιερεμιου υιου χελκιου* Syh (*οι λ'*) Or. III 184 («*καὶ πάντες συνεφώνησαν*») 2 *τοῦ θεοῦ*] *ο εβρ' κυριου* Syh (mend. *κυριος*) 3 *ἕως τῆς αἰχμαλωσίας*] *α'* ⟨*εως*⟩ *μετοικεσιας* Syh Hi.^{lat} («omnes alii voce consona») 6 *Ὁ Ὢν δέσποτα κύριε*]

PLATE 20. The Göttingen edition of the Septuagint (Jer 1:1-5): J. Ziegler, *Ieremias, Baruch, Threni, Epistula Ieremiae, Septuaginta, Vetus Testamentum graecum auctoritate societatis litterarum gottingensis editum*, vol. XV (2d ed.; Göttingen 1976).

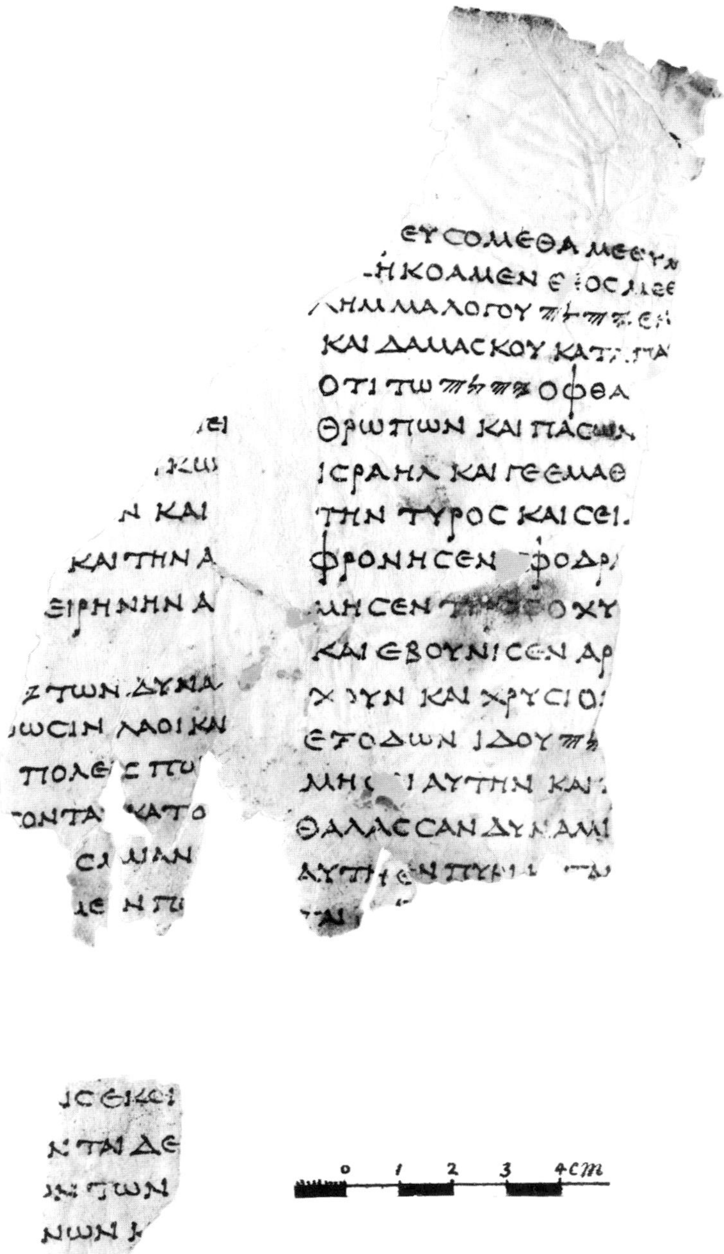

PLATE 21. The Greek Minor Prophets Scroll from Naḥal Ḥever (Zech 8:19–9:5) from E. Tov, *The Greek Minor Prophets Scroll from Naḥal Ḥever (8ḤevXIIgr) (The Seiyal Collection I)* (DJD VIII; Oxford 1990).

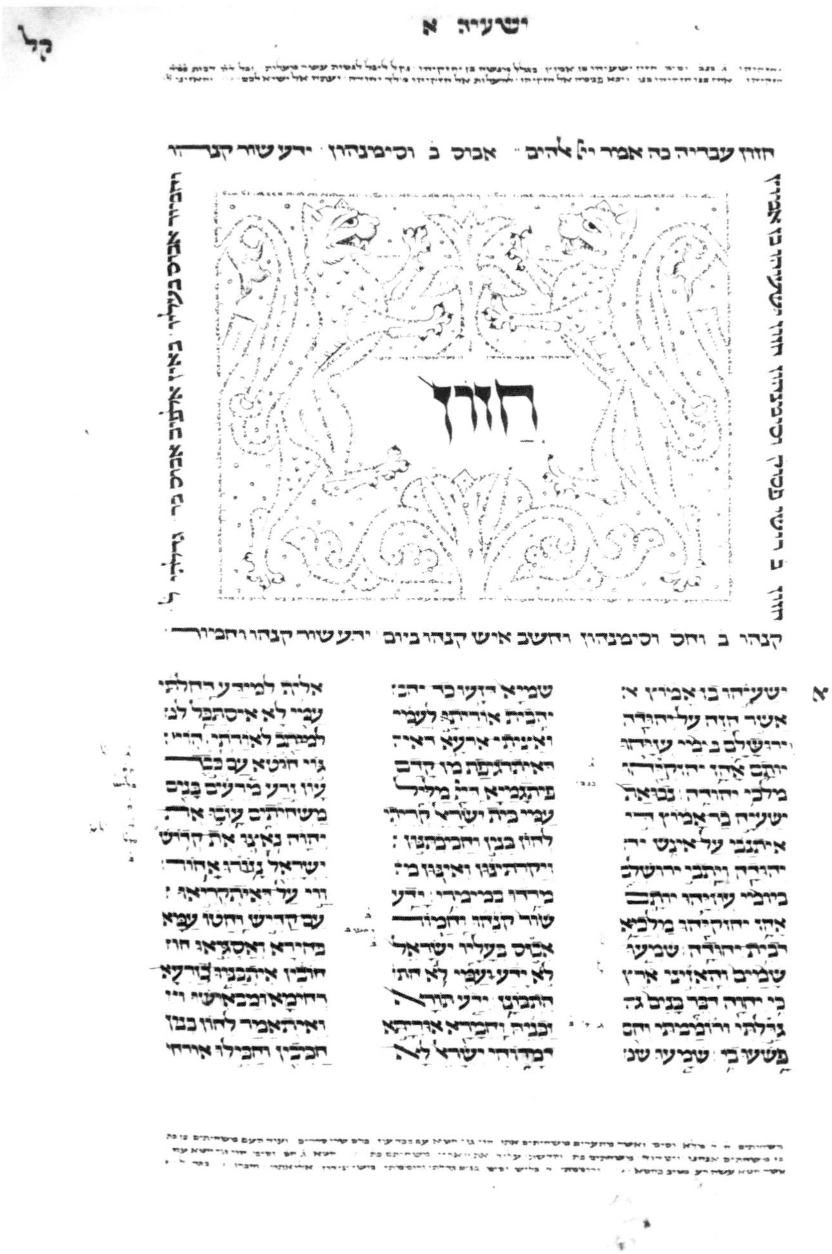

PLATE 22. Manuscript Berlin Or. Fol. 1-4 of the Prophets, number 150 in the collection of Kennicott (see plate 17) (Isa 1:1-4).

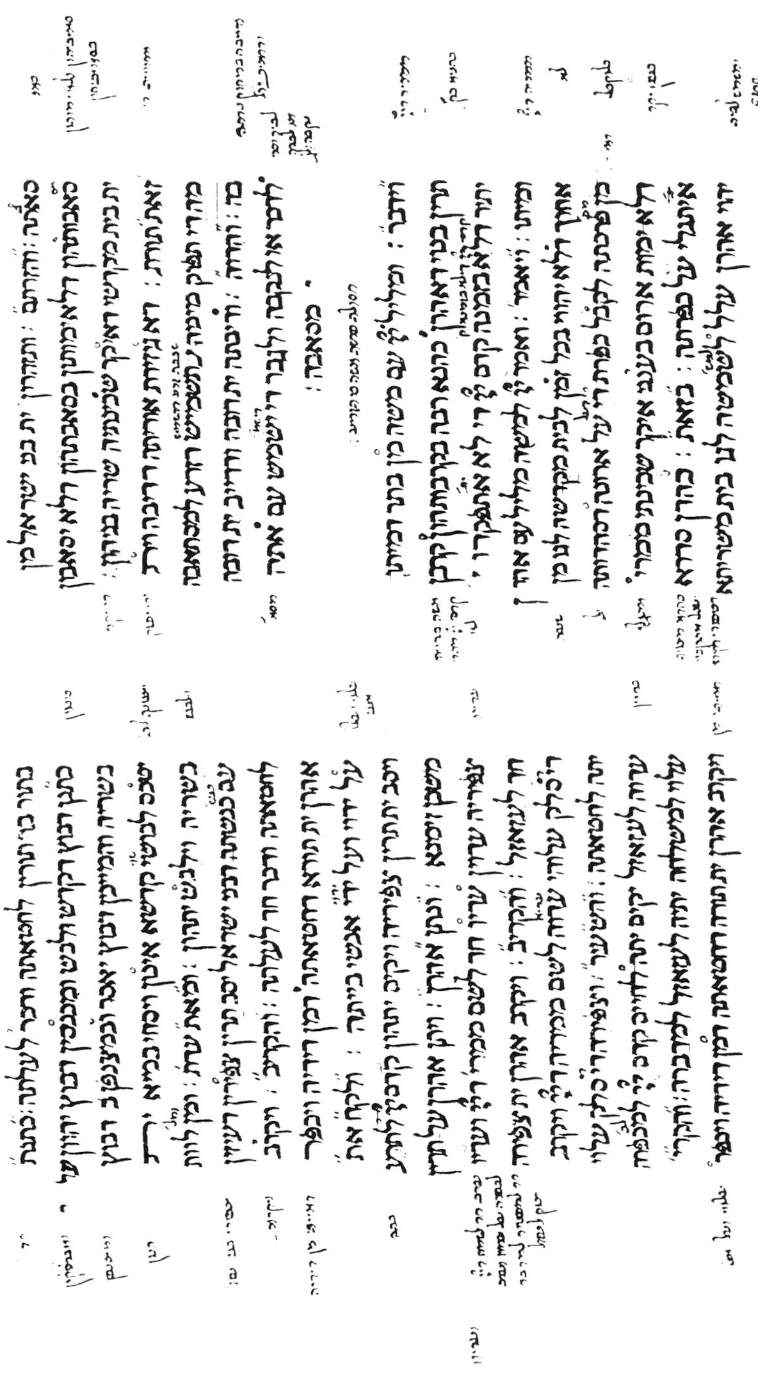

PLATE 23. Manuscript Vatican Neophyti 1 of the Palestinian Targum to the Torah (Lev 15:31–16:11), from: *The Palestinian Targum to the Pentateuch Codex Vatican (Neofiti 1)* (Jerusalem 1970).

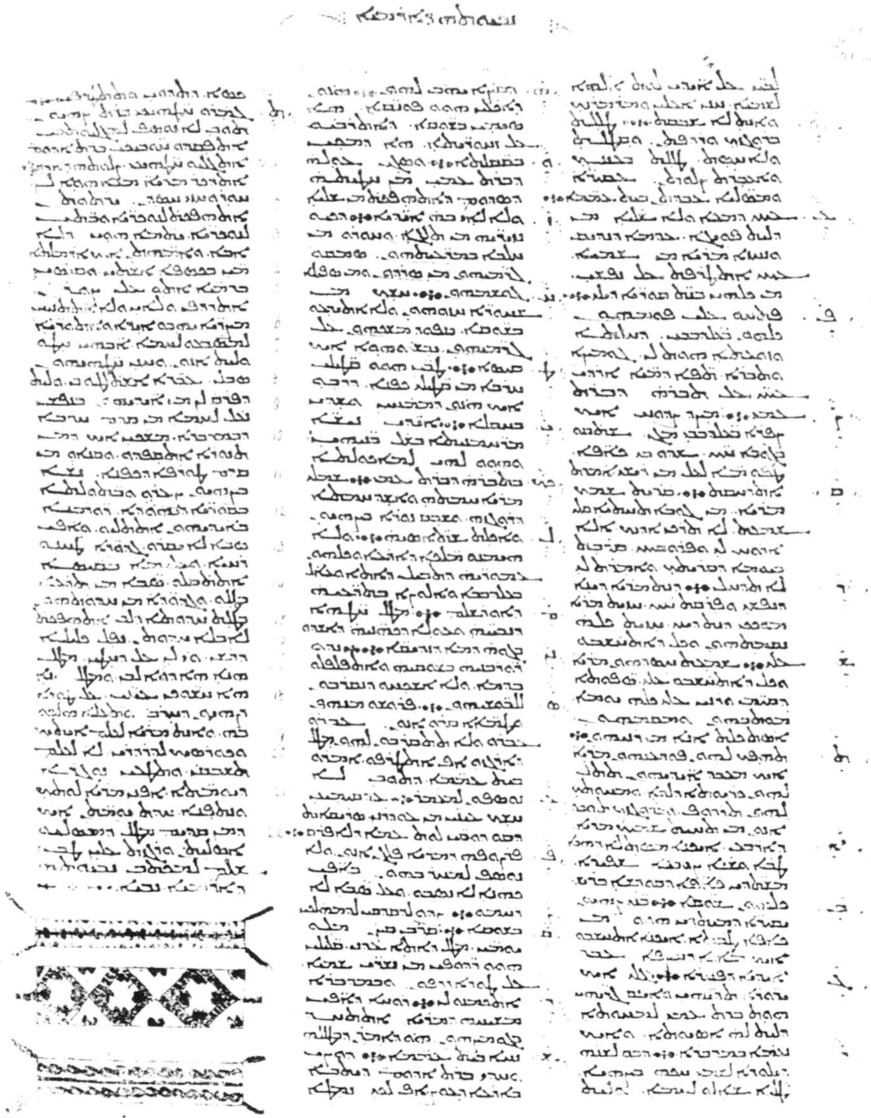

PLATE 24. Manuscript Ambrosianus (Milan, Ambrosian Library, B. 21 Inf.) of the Peshitta (Lam 3:41–5:22), from: *Translatio Syra-Pescitto, Veteris Testamenti ex codice Ambrosiano* (Milan 1876-1883).

רש״י מקץ

אבן עזרא

וישברו לנו משם ונחיה ולא נמות:
וירדו אחי יוסף עשרה לשבר בר
ממצרים: ואת בנימין אחי יוסף לא
שלח יעקב את אחיו כי אמר פן
יקראנו אסון: ויבאו בני ישראל
לשבר בתוך הבאים כי היה הרעב
בארץ כנען: ויוסף הוא השליט על
הארץ הוא המשביר לכל עם הארץ
ויבאו אחי יוסף וישתחוו לו אפים
ארצה: וירא יוסף את אחיו ויכרם
ויתנכר אליהם וידבר אתם קשות
ויאמר אלהם מאין באתם ויאמרו
מארץ כנען לשבר אכל: ויכר יוסף
את אחיו והם לא הכרהו: ויזכר
יוסף את החלמות אשר חלם להם
ויאמר אלהם מרגלים אתם לראות
את ערות הארץ באתם: ויאמרו
אליו לא אדני ועבדיך באו לשבר
אכל: כלנו בני איש אחד נחנו
כנים אנחנו לא היו עבדיך מרגלים
: ויאמר אלהם לא כי ערות הארץ
באתם לראות: ויאמרו שנים עשר
עבדיך אחים אנחנו בני איש אחד
בארץ כנען והנה הקטן את אבינו
היום והאחד איננו: ויאמר אלהם
יוסף הוא אשר דברתי אלכם לאמר
מרגלים אתם: בזאת תבחנו חי
פרעה אם תצאו מזה כי אם בבוא
אחיכם הקטן הנה: שלחו מכם אחד
ויקח את אחיכם ואתם האסרו
ויבחנו דבריכם האמת אתכם ואם
לא חי פרעה כי מרגלים אתם:
ויאסף אתם אל משמר שלשת
ימים: ויאמר אלהם יוסף ביום
השלישי זאת עשו וחיו את האלהים
אני ירא: אם כנים אתם אחיכם
אחד יאסר בבית משמרכם ואתם
לכו הביאו שבר רעבון בתיכם:
ואת אחיכם הקטן תביאו
אלי ויאמנו דבריכם ולא תמותו

PLATE 25. Second Rabbinic Bible (*Miqra'ot G^edolot*), Venice, 1524–1525 (Gen 42:3–20).

כְּכוֹכְבֵ֣י הַשָּׁמַ֔יִם וְכַח֕וֹל אֲשֶׁ֖ר עַל־שְׂפַ֣ת הַיָּ֑ם וְיִרַ֣שׁ זַרְעֲךָ֔ אֵ֖ת שַׁ֥עַר
אֹיְבָֽיו׃ 18 וְהִתְבָּרְכ֣וּ בְזַרְעֲךָ֔ כֹּ֖ל גּוֹיֵ֣י הָאָ֑רֶץ עֵ֕קֶב אֲשֶׁ֥ר שָׁמַ֖עְתָּ בְּקֹלִֽי׃
19 וַיָּ֤שָׁב אַבְרָהָם֙ אֶל־נְעָרָ֔יו וַיָּקֻ֛מוּ וַיֵּלְכ֥וּ יַחְדָּ֖ו אֶל־בְּאֵ֣ר שָׁ֑בַע וַיֵּ֥שֶׁב
אַבְרָהָ֖ם בִּבְאֵ֥ר שָֽׁבַע׃ פ
20 וַיְהִ֗י אַחֲרֵי֙ הַדְּבָרִ֣ים הָאֵ֔לֶּה וַיֻּגַּ֥ד לְאַבְרָהָ֖ם לֵאמֹ֑ר הִ֠נֵּה יָלְדָ֨ה
מִלְכָּ֥ה גַם־הִ֛וא בָּנִ֖ים לְנָח֥וֹר אָחִֽיךָ׃ 21 [a]אֶת־ע֥וּץ בְּכֹר֖וֹ וְאֶת־בּ֣וּז אָחִ֑יו
וְאֶת־קְמוּאֵ֖ל אֲבִ֥י אֲרָֽם׃[a] 22 וְאֶת־כֶּ֣שֶׂד וְאֶת־חֲז֔וֹ וְאֶת־פִּלְדָּ֖שׁ וְאֶת־
יִדְלָ֑ף וְאֵ֖ת בְּתוּאֵֽל׃ 23 [a]וּבְתוּאֵ֖ל יָלַ֣ד[a] אֶת־רִבְקָ֑ה[a] שְׁמֹנָ֣ה אֵ֗לֶּה יָלְדָ֣ה
מִלְכָּ֔ה לְנָח֖וֹר אֲחִ֥י אַבְרָהָֽם׃ 24 וּפִֽילַגְשׁ֖וֹ[a] וּשְׁמָ֣הּ רְאוּמָ֑ה וַתֵּ֣לֶד גַּם־
הִ֗וא אֶת־טֶ֙בַח֙ וְאֶת־גַּ֔חַם וְאֶת־תַּ֖חַשׁ וְאֶת־מַעֲכָֽה׃ ס
23 1 וַיִּֽהְיוּ֙[a] חַיֵּ֣י שָׂרָ֔ה מֵאָ֥ה שָׁנָ֛ה וְעֶשְׂרִ֥ים שָׁנָ֖ה וְשֶׁ֣בַע שָׁנִ֑ים [b]שְׁנֵ֖י
חַיֵּ֥י שָׂרָֽה׃[b] 2 וַתָּ֣מָת שָׂרָ֗ה בְּקִרְיַ֥ת אַרְבַּ֛ע[a] ה֥וא חֶבְר֖וֹן בְּאֶ֣רֶץ כְּנָ֑עַן
וַיָּבֹא֙ אַבְרָהָ֔ם לִסְפֹּ֥ד לְשָׂרָ֖ה וְלִבְכֹּתָֽהּ[β]׃ 3 וַיָּ֙קָם֙ אַבְרָהָ֔ם מֵעַ֖ל פְּנֵ֣י
מֵת֑וֹ וַיְדַבֵּ֥ר אֶל־בְּנֵי־חֵ֖ת לֵאמֹֽר׃ 4 גֵּר־וְתוֹשָׁ֥ב אָנֹכִ֖י עִמָּכֶ֑ם תְּנ֨וּ לִ֤י
אֲחֻזַּת־קֶ֙בֶר֙ עִמָּכֶ֔ם וְאֶקְבְּרָ֥ה [a]מֵתִ֖י מִלְּפָנָֽי׃ 5 וַיַּעֲנ֧וּ בְנֵי־חֵ֛ת אֶת־אַבְרָהָ֖ם
לֵאמֹ֥ר לֽוֹ׃ 6 שְׁמָעֵ֣נוּ ׀ אֲדֹנִ֗י נְשִׂ֨יא אֱלֹהִ֤ים אַתָּה֙ בְּתוֹכֵ֔נוּ בְּמִבְחַ֣ר
קְבָרֵ֔ינוּ[a] קְבֹ֖ר אֶת־מֵתֶ֑ךָ אִ֣ישׁ מִמֶּ֔נּוּ אֶת־קִבְר֖וֹ לֹֽא־יִכְלֶ֥ה[a] מִמְּךָ֖ מִקְּבֹ֥ר
מֵתֶֽךָ[β]׃ 7 וַיָּ֧קָם אַבְרָהָ֛ם וַיִּשְׁתַּ֥חוּ לְעַם־הָאָ֖רֶץ לִבְנֵי־חֵֽת׃ 8 וַיְדַבֵּ֥ר אִתָּ֖ם
לֵאמֹ֑ר אִם־יֵ֣שׁ אֶֽת־נַפְשְׁכֶ֗ם לִקְבֹּ֤ר אֶת־מֵתִי֙ מִלְּפָנַ֔י שְׁמָע֕וּנִי וּפִגְעוּ־
לִ֖י בְּעֶפְר֥וֹן בֶּן־צֹֽחַר[a]׃ 9 וְיִתֶּן־לִ֗י אֶת־מְעָרַ֤ת הַמַּכְפֵּלָה֙ אֲשֶׁר־ל֔וֹ אֲשֶׁ֖ר
בִּקְצֵ֣ה שָׂדֵ֑הוּ בְּכֶ֨סֶף מָלֵ֜א יִתְּנֶ֥נָּה לִּ֛י בְּתוֹכְכֶ֖ם לַאֲחֻזַּת־קָֽבֶר׃ 10 וְעֶפְר֥וֹן
יֹשֵׁ֖ב בְּת֣וֹךְ בְּנֵי־חֵ֑ת וַיַּעַן֩ עֶפְר֨וֹן הַחִתִּ֤י אֶת־אַבְרָהָם֙ בְּאָזְנֵ֣י בְנֵי־חֵ֔ת
לְכֹ֛ל[a] בָּאֵ֥י שַֽׁעַר־עִיר֖וֹ לֵאמֹֽר׃ 11 לֹֽא[a]־אֲדֹנִ֣י שְׁמָעֵ֔נִי הַשָּׂדֶה֙ נָתַ֣תִּי לָ֔ךְ
וְהַמְּעָרָ֥ה אֲשֶׁר־בּ֖וֹ לְךָ֣ נְתַתִּ֑יהָ לְעֵינֵ֧י בְנֵי־עַמִּ֛י נְתַתִּ֥יהָ לָּ֖ךְ קְבֹ֥ר מֵתֶֽךָ׃
12 וַיִּשְׁתַּ֙חוּ֙[a] אַבְרָהָ֔ם לִפְנֵ֖י עַ֥ם הָאָֽרֶץ׃ 13 וַיְדַבֵּ֨ר אֶל־עֶפְר֜וֹן בְּאָזְנֵ֤י עַם־
הָאָ֙רֶץ֙ לֵאמֹ֔ר אַ֛ךְ אִם־אַתָּ֥ה ל֖וּ[a] שְׁמָעֵ֑נִי נָתַ֜תִּי כֶּ֤סֶף הַשָּׂדֶה֙ קַ֣ח מִמֶּ֔נִּי

23 [a] ש הוליד ‖ Cp 23, 2 [a] ש + אל עמק 𝔊? + אֲשֶׁר בָּעֵמֶק ‖ [β] mlt MSS כ min ‖ 4 [a] Var^G ש𝔗^J + אֶת־ ‖ 6 [a] 32MSS קברנו ‖ [β] 𝔊 + שָׁם ‖ 8 [a] ש + הַחִתִּי.

21 [a-a] frt add ‖ 23 [a-a] frt add ‖ 24 [a] l frt וּפִילֶגֶשׁ לו ‖ Cp 23, 1 [a] ins שְׁנֵי cf 47,28 ‖ [b-b] dl c 𝔊𝔙 ‖ 5 [a]/6 l לאמֹר: לוּ שמענו (cf 13); ש𝔊 לֹא (cf 11) ‖ 6 [a] pro יִכְלָא ‖ 10 [a] l frt בְּכֹל; cf 18 [a] ‖ 11 [a] l frt c 𝔗^J לָא ‖ 12 [a] ins c 𝔗^J לו ‖ 13 [a] l frt c ש𝔊𝔗^{OJ} לִי (ἐπειδὴ πρὸς ἐμοῦ εἶ).

Plate 26. R. Kittel and P. Kahle, *Biblia Hebraica* (3d [7th] edition; Stuttgart 1951): Gen 22:18–23:13.

כִּסְדֹם הָיִינוּ לַעֲמֹרָה דָּמִינוּ׃ ס — ו[15] . ל . ל

10 שִׁמְעוּ דְבַר־יְהוָה קְצִינֵי סְדֹם
הַאֲזִינוּ תּוֹרַת אֱלֹהֵינוּ עַם עֲמֹרָה׃ — ח . ל
11 לָמָּה־לִּי רֹב־זִבְחֵיכֶם יֹאמַר יְהוָה — ו דמטע
שָׂבַעְתִּי עֹלוֹת אֵילִים וְחֵלֶב מְרִיאִים
וְדַם פָּרִים וּכְבָשִׂים[a] וְעַתּוּדִים לֹא חָפָצְתִּי׃ — ב . ה[16]
12 כִּי תָבֹאוּ לֵרָאוֹת[a] פָּנָי — ג[17]
מִי־בִקֵּשׁ זֹאת מִיֶּדְכֶם רְמֹס[b] חֲצֵרָי׃ — ב
13 לֹא תוֹסִיפוּ הָבִיא מִנְחַת־שָׁוְא קְטֹרֶת תּוֹעֵבָה הִיא לִי — ב מל[18] . ח קמ[19]
חֹדֶשׁ וְשַׁבָּת קְרֹא מִקְרָא לֹא־אוּכַל אָוֶן וַעֲצָרָה׃ — ב . ד[20]
14 חָדְשֵׁיכֶם וּמוֹעֲדֵיכֶם שָׂנְאָה נַפְשִׁי
הָיוּ עָלַי לָטֹרַח נִלְאֵיתִי נְשֹׂא׃ — ל . ג
15 וּבְפָרִשְׂכֶם כַּפֵּיכֶם אַעְלִים עֵינַי מִכֶּם — ל
גַּם כִּי־תַרְבּוּ תְפִלָּה אֵינֶנִּי שֹׁמֵעַ
יְדֵיכֶם דָּמִים מָלֵאוּ[a]׃ 16 רַחֲצוּ הִזַּכּוּ
הָסִירוּ רֹעַ מַעַלְלֵיכֶם מִנֶּגֶד עֵינָי
חִדְלוּ הָרֵעַ׃ 17 לִמְדוּ הֵיטֵב — ב . ה
דִּרְשׁוּ מִשְׁפָּט אַשְּׁרוּ חָמוֹץ[a]
שִׁפְטוּ יָתוֹם רִיבוּ אַלְמָנָה׃ ס
18 לְכוּ־נָא וְנִוָּכְחָה יֹאמַר יְהוָה — ו דמטע
אִם־יִהְיוּ חֲטָאֵיכֶם כַּשָּׁנִים[a] כַּשֶּׁלֶג יַלְבִּינוּ — ב ול בליש
אִם־יַאְדִּימוּ כַתּוֹלָע כַּצֶּמֶר יִהְיוּ׃
19 אִם־תֹּאבוּ וּשְׁמַעְתֶּם טוּב הָאָרֶץ תֹּאכֵלוּ׃ — יט בליש[21]
20 וְאִם־תְּמָאֲנוּ וּמְרִיתֶם חֶרֶב[a] תְּאֻכְּלוּ[b] — ל ר״פ בסיפ . ב
כִּי פִּי יְהוָה דִּבֵּר׃ ס — ג
21 אֵיכָה הָיְתָה לְזוֹנָה קִרְיָה נֶאֱמָנָה[a] — יו[22] . ב[23]

[15]Mm 2208. [16]Mm 2338. [17]Mm 2209. [18]Mp sub loco. [19]Mm 1092. [20]Mm 1544. [21]Mm 335. [22]Mm 1095. [23]Gn 38,15.

11 [a] > 𝔊 ‖ **12** [a] l c Ms 𝔖 לִרְ׳ ‖ [b] prp רוֹמְסֵי ‖ **15** [a] 𝔔[a] + אצבעותיכם בעאון ‖ **17** [a] l חָמוּץ ? ‖ **18** [a] l c 𝔔[a] pc Mss כשני cf 𝔊𝔖𝔙 ‖ **20** [a] 𝔔[a]𝔖𝔗 בח׳; l מֵחֶ׳ (hpgr)? ‖ [b] prp תֹּאכֵלוּ ‖ **21** [a] 𝔊 + *Σιων* cf 26/27.

Plate 27. K. Elliger and W. Rudolph, *Biblia Hebraica Stuttgartensia* (Stuttgart 1967–1977): Isa 1:10-21.

שרפות ב̇ ארצכם שממה מערמות העפר ∘ בתרייה מל ∘ לראות ג̇ בעלתך לראוה בבוא כל ישראל כי תבאו ∘

ב̇ רשעים מרחם ל ל	לא־זרו ולא חבשו ולא רככה בשמן׃ ארצכם שממה 7
ב̇ חד חס וחד חס(1)	עריכם שרפות אש אדמתכם לנגדכם זרים אכלים
ל ל	אתה ושממה כמהפכת זרים׃ ונותרה בת־ציון כסכה 8
ל̇ ל̇ ב̇ שחברה לה ל	בכרם כמלונה במקשה כעיר נצורה׃ לולי יהוה 9
ב̇ לב רשעים ל	צבאות הותיר לנו שריד כמעט כסדם היינו לעמרה
ל	דמינו׃ [פ] שמעו דבר־יהוה קציני סדם האזינו 10
ל	תורת אלהינו עם עמרה׃ למה־לי רב־זבחיכם יאמר 11
	יהוה שבעתי עלות אילים וחלב מריאים ודם פרים
ב̇ ויביאו פרים ג	וכבשים ועתודים לא חפצתי׃ כי תבאו לראות פני 12

7 וּשְׁמָמָה] 𝔊 καὶ ἠρήμωται$_{II}$(2) = 𝔙𝔗 ‖ ²זרים] 𝔊⁻ λαῶν ἀλλοτρίων(3) | 𝔙 *hostili*(4) **8** כמלונה] 𝔊𝔖 ①$_{II}$ **9** כמעט$_{\wedge}$] 𝔊𝔙𝔗𝔖 > (1) ‖ (כ)סדם] 𝔊 Σοδομα°$_{II}$ = 𝔙 ‖ לעמרה] 𝔊𝔙𝔗𝔖 ①$_{II\ III}$ | 𝔊𝔙𝔗 ptcl | 𝔊 Γομορρα°$_{II}$ = 𝔙 **10** סדם] 𝔊 Σοδομων°$_{II}$ = 𝔙 ‖ אלהינו] 𝔊⁻ > pron ‖ עמרה] 𝔊 Γομορρας°$_{II}$ = 𝔙 **11** שבעתי] 𝔊$_{var}$ 𝔙$_{\wedge}$ ‖ $_{\wedge}$וחלב מריאים...] 𝔊⁻ $_{\wedge}$ καὶ στέαρ ἀρνῶν‿° ‖ פרים—ועתודים] 𝔊 ταύρων καὶ τράγων(1) ‖ $_{\wedge}$חפצתי] 𝔊 ‿ **12** לֵרָאוֹת פני] 𝔙 *ante conspectum meum*(1) ‖ מידכם] 𝔊𝔙𝔖 num ‖ $_{\wedge}$חצרי] 𝔊 num ‿

7 ושממה] Is-a עליה (sm ? ושמימו) ושממו ‖ כמהפכת] Is-a כמפכת (sm א super?) ‖ זרים] Is-a lac ז[ ]ים **8** ונותרה] Is-a ונתרת ‖ כמלונה] Is-a וכמלונה ‖ במקשה] Is-a בּמקשה ‖ נצורה] Is-a נצוֹדה **9** כמעט$_{\wedge}$כסדם] bBer 19a *esv*; ib 60a mss; bKet 8b 1ms (sm); Yal II § 387 (omn var-herm); (cf YalMaIs); Rashi ad loc; (cf SiphDt § 322[370]) כמעט‿כסדם ‖ כסדם] Is-a כסודם ‖ לעמרה] Is-a לעומרה | bBer 19a *F*; ib 60a *MOsv*; bKet 8b *M* 1ms ולעמרה **10** Is-a pr § ‖ שמעו דבר] Is-a lac [שמ[עו ‖ סדם] Is-a סודם ‖ האזינו] Is-a ואזינו$_{III}$ ‖ תורת] Is-a תוֹרתֿ ‖ עמרה] Is-a עומרה **11** למה] Is-a לֿמהֿ ‖ רב] Is-a רוב ‖ עלות] Is-a עולוֹת **12** פני] Is-a פֿני

7 שממה] K (sol) שמה ‖ עריכם] פ; 93 96 150 (pm); KRG (mlt) ועריכם **8** כעיר] K (sol) בעיר **9** לעמרה] ר (pm); 30 93 96 150 (pm); KRG (mlt) ולעמרה **10** דבר] 96 (pm) דברי ‖ האזינו] K והאזינו **11** לי רב] K (sol) ריב לי ‖ יאמר] G (seb) אמר ‖ אילים] ר ל-18; 93; KG (mlt) אלים ‖ וכבשים ועתודים] K (sol) ~ ‖ ועתודים] K (sol) + כי **12** לֵרָאוֹת] RG לִרְאוֹת ‖ מִי] 96 supra ras

7 עָרֵיכם] פ: ועריכם; ק מ: עֲ ‖ שרפות] ל-11: שרֻפות; ל-18: שרוּפות; ר: שרופת ‖ אכלים] ל-18 ק מ: אֹ ‖ אתה] ל-20: אותה **8** ונותרה] ק מ: נוֹ ‖ כסכה] ר: כסוכה **9** כסדם] ר: כסדום ‖ לַעמרה] ר: ולעמרה; ל-18 ק מ: לֲ **10** (פ)] ל: (ס) ‖ הַאזינו] ל-18 ק מ: הֲ **11** לָמה־] ל-4 8' 18 20'? ש: לֶ ‖ רב־] מ: רֹ ‖ עלות] ל-18: עוֹלות; ר: עלת ‖ אילים] ל-18 ר: אלים ‖ מריאים] ר: מראים **12** לֵראות] ל ל-4 8 11? 18 20 ש: לֵ ‖ מִי־] ל״? ל-20 ש מ: מִ; ל-18: מֵי ‖ בִּקֵּשׁ] ל-18: קֵ; ש?: קֻ

(2) οὐκ ἔστι μάλαγμα ἐπιθεῖναι οὔτε ἔλαιον οὔτε καταδέσμους: p צֻּרִי (cf α' ἐπεδέθησαν ≈ σ' σφιγγομένη p צֹרוּ); usual order of dressing wounds **7**(1) mistake for מל; cf Ne 3_{34} (2) וְשָׁמְמָה; → reformul (3) expans (4) p צרים; cf Lam 1_7 **9**(1) hardly ‿$_{II}$ (note problem of ἄν) **11**(1) condens; cf 34_{6-7}, Dt 32_{14} **12**(1) theol; not לפניפני; cf 𝔊 ὀφθῆναι μοι; 𝔖 coniug

העברת השלילה והזרה עליה (2) אין רטייה לשים. ולא שמן ולא חבושות; א׳: ׳צֻרִי׳ (הש׳ עק: חֻבשו ≈ סמ: קשורה א׳: ׳צֹרוּ׳) לפי סדר מקובל בחבישת פצעים **7** (1) צ״ל: מל; הש׳ נחמ׳ ג 34 (2) ׳וְשָׁמְמָה׳; ← שכתוב (3) הרחבה (4) א׳: ׳צרים׳; הש׳ איכה א 7 **9** (1) ל״ס‿$_{II}$ (שים לב לבעית ἄν) **11** (1) צמצום; הש׳ לד 6-7, דב׳ לב 14 **12** (1) תאול׳; לא: ׳לפניפני׳;

[ב]

Plate 28. Hebrew University Bible (Isa 1:7-12), from: M.H. Goshen-Gottstein, *The Hebrew University Bible, The Book of Isaiah* (Jerusalem 1995).

Development of the Hebrew script: 1. Gezer Calendar; 2. Mesha stele; 3. Siloam inscription; 4. 7th-century B.C. seals; 5. Early 6th-century ostracon from Arad; 6. 2nd-century B.C. Leviticus fragment; 7. Medieval Samaritan bookhand

PLATE 29. The development of the "early" Hebrew script, from: J. Naveh, *Early History of the Alphabet—An Introduction to West Semitic Epigraphy and Palaeography* (2d ed.; Jerusalem 1987), fig. 70.

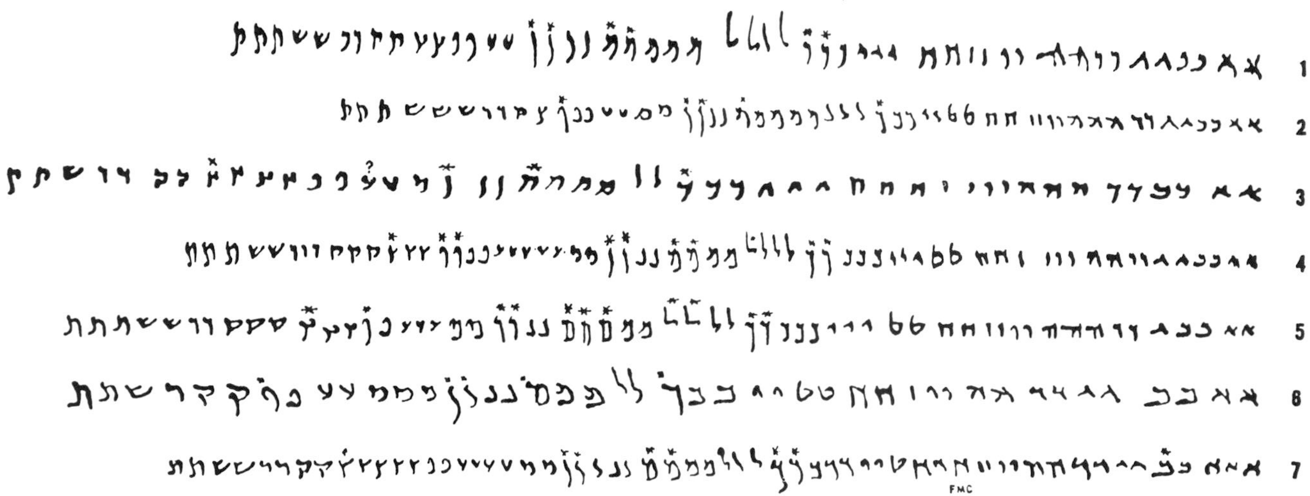

Line 1. The classical Aramaic cursive of the late Persian Empire. From Papyrus Luparensis, *CIS* (*pars secunda*) I:1, 146 A, B, Tab. XVII. *Ca.* 375–350 B.C. A script of this character was the prototype of the formal Jewish hand.

Line 2. An Aramaic vulgar cursive of the early third century B.C. from Egypt. From the Edfû Papyrus published by Sayce-Cowley, *PSBA* 29 (1907), Pls. I, II.

Line 3. An Archaic proto-Jewish hand of the mid-third century B.C. From an unpublished manuscript of Exodus from Qumrân (4QEx[f]). The script includes letter forms which ultimately evolve into the early Jewish cursive character.

Line 4. The proto-Jewish formal hand of the late third century B.C. From a manuscript of Samuel (4QSam[b]) published by the writer in *OMQ*, pp. 147–72, esp. Fig. 6 and Fig. 2, 1.2.

Line 5. The proto-Jewish formal hand of *ca.* 200–175 B.C. From an unpublished manuscript of Jeremiah from Qumrân (4QJer[a]).

Line 6. An Archaic or early Hasmonaean semiformal script of *ca.* 175–125 B.C. From a manuscript of Qohelet from Qumrân (4QQoh[a]) published by J. Muilenburg, *BASOR* 135 (Oct. 1954), pp. 20–28.

Line 7. An Archaic or early Hasmonaean semiformal script of *ca.* 175–125 B.C. From a manuscript of an unknown work from Qumrân (4Q Prières liturgiques A) to be published by J. Starcky.

Originally all scripts were traced from photographs of natural size with the exception of line 2, traced from a reduced photograph.

PLATE 30. The development of the Aramaic and Assyrian ("Jewish") script, from: Frank Moore Cross, Jr., "The Development of the Jewish Scripts," in: G.E. Wright, ed., *The Bible and the Ancient Near East, Essays in Honor of W.F. Albright* (Garden City, NY 1965) 175, figure 1.

INDEX 1

ANCIENT SOURCES

OLD TESTAMENT

MASORETIC TEXT (𝔐) AND OTHER SOURCES

BIBLICAL TEXTS FROM THE JUDEAN DESERT

Qumran

Ancient Versions

SEPTUAGINT (𝔊)

INSCRIPTIONS

VARIOUS

INDEX 2

AUTHORS

INDEX 3

SUBJECTS